Child Abuse, Child Development, and Social Policy

ADVANCES IN APPLIED DEVELOPMENTAL PSYCHOLOGY
VOLUME 8

VOLUME EDITORS:

Dante Cicchetti and Sheree L. Toth
Mt. Hope Family Center
Rochester, NY

SERIES EDITOR:

Irving E. Sigel
Educational Testing Service

ABLEX PUBLISHING CORPORATION
NORWOOD, NEW JERSEY

ISBN: 1-56750-042-0   ISSN: 0748-8572

Ablex Publishing Corporation
355 Chestnut Street
Norwood, New Jersey 07648

DEDICATION

Dante dedicates this work to his grandmother, Josephine, in appreciation of the undying support and concern, unconditional acceptance, and unwavering belief that she conveyed as she encouraged him to pursue his dreams.

> Thank you for the days
> Those endless days
> You gave me
> And though you're gone
> You're with me
> Every single day, believe me
> Days I remember all my life
> Ray Davies, 1991

Sheree dedicates this book to her family, whose support over the years has enabled her to pursue her personal and professional goals. She is especially thankful to her grandmother, Julia, her parents, Olga and Edward, and her sister, Aimee. Through words and actions, they communicated their belief in the importance of using individual talents, whatever they might be, to contribute to the welfare of society.

Contents

Contributors

Douglas Barnett
Mt. Hope Family Center
University of Rochester
187 Edinburgh Street
Rochester, NY 14608

Jennifer M. Batterman-Faunce
Department of Psychology
State University of New York at
    Buffalo
Buffalo, NY 14214

Stephen J. Ceci
Department of Human Development
    and Family Studies
Cornell University
Ithaca, NY 14853

Dante Cicchetti
Mt. Hope Family Center
University of Rochester
187 Edinburgh Street
Rochester, NY 14608

Deborah Daro
National Committee for Prevention
    of Child Abuse
332 S. Michigan Ave., Suite 950
Chicago, IL 60604

James Garbarino
Erikson Institute
25 West Chicago Ave.
Chicago, IL 60610

Gail S. Goodman
Department of Psychology
University of California at Davis
Davis, CA 95616

Jane Grady
Erikson Institute
25 West Chicago Ave.
Chicago, IL 60610

Kevin Hennessy
Mt. Hope Family Center
University of Rochester
187 Edinburgh Street
Rochester, NY 14608

Paul W. Howes
Mt. Hope Family Center
University of Rochester
187 Edinburgh Street
Rochester, NY 14608

Robert Kenney
Department of Psychology
State University of New York at
    Buffalo
Buffalo, NY 14214

Kathleen Kostelny
Erikson Institute
25 West Chicago Ave.
Chicago, IL 60610

Michelle DeSimone Leichtman
Department of Human Development
    and Family Studies
Cornell University
Ithaca, NY 14853

Jody Todd Manly
Mt. Hope Family Center
University of Rochester
187 Edinburgh Street
Rochester, NY 14608

Narina Nunez Nightingale
Department of Psychology
University of Wyoming
Laramie, WY 82070

MaryElizabeth Putnick
Department of Human Development
    and Family Studies
Cornell University
Ithaca, NY 14853

Elizabeth W. Saft
Department of Psychology
University of Virginia
Charlottesville, VA 22903

Kathleen J. Sternberg
National Institute of Child Health
    and Human Development
9190 Rockville Pike
Bethesda, MD 20814

Ross A. Thompson
Department of Psychology
University of Nebraska
Lincoln, NE 68588-0308

Sheree L. Toth
Mt. Hope Family Center
University of Rochester
187 Edinburgh Street
Rochester, NY 14608

Melvin N. Wilson
Department of Psychology
University of Virginia
Charlottesville, VA 22903

David A. Wolfe
Department of Psychology
University of Western Ontario
London, Ontario
CANADA N6A 5C2

Introduction

Irving E. Sigel

The volume you are about to read is the eighth volume in the Applied Developmental Psychology Series. The mission of the series is to provide comprehensive discussions of significant developmental issues where research and application intersect. Many social problems facing us in the later part of the twentieth century are in desperate need of a sound research base as a foundation for social action and intervention programs. The research reported in this series is an outstanding example of the Series' mission, since it is dedicated to presenting research information which can be helpful to researchers, intervention program developers, and social policymakers.

Among the myriad of pressing social problems facing us in the 1990s that requires behavioral science data is that of family violence and child abuse. The rise of the incidence of child abuse, especially in households with very young children, has risen to alarming proportions, especially during the past two decades. The social price our society pays for such deviant actions (usually perpetrated by adults) is probably immeasurable, since the costs are not only material, but also psychological. The hurt created by child abusers to themselves and their victims often affects participants psychologically, socially, and materially, not only in the immediate, but also for the long-term. The costs arising for everyone as a result of these acts are borne not only by the participants, but also by the society as a whole. Ultimately, the taxpayers bear the brunt of the financial cost brought about by the need to support the infrastructure of service personnel to work at prevention of child abuse. The professionals provide services, not only to the parties involved in the abuse situation, but also to the community by identifying and dealing with abusers and their victims.

In view of the importance of the problems of child abuse, and in view of the mission of the Applied Developmental Psychology Series, it is most appropriate to devote an issue to problems of child maltreatment in all its ramifications.

I invited Dr. Dante Cicchetti and Dr. Sheree Toth to prepare a volume on child abuse, developmental psychology, and social policy. Fortunately for the readership of this series, they accepted the offer and the edited volume is the product of their efforts. Under their leadership, a series of essays was prepared which touch on virtually every facet of the complex problems surrounding child abuse. They and their colleagues have brought the legal, social, psychological, and community issues and current research on the multifaced problem of child abuse into sharp focus.

Their interdisciplinary perspective enables us to appreciate the complexity of the problem. Their insights emerge from an integration of the relevant fields to yield a holistic perspective. The holistic view enhances our understanding of the etiology (personal and social) of child abuse in the home and in the community, the types of treatments and prevention programs, and social policy implications.

The volume is timely because there still is a need to adopt a comprehensive research-based strategy to establish effective treatment, intervention, and policy practices that will help in the struggle to come to terms with the cause and sequelae of child maltreatment.

The editors, Drs. Cicchetti and Toth, have organized the volume with a strong research focus emphasizing etiology and definition of child maltreatment, evaluation of treatment programs, assessment of children's testimony, and legal implications. In addition to attention to the child as the target, chapters in this volume provide a comprehensive approach, covering the major important fields relevant to child abuse. Attention is directed to the family or parent–child dyad, in the context of living in dangerous environments (Chapter 6), an often overlooked influence on childhood abuse and violence. This latter chapter moves the issue of violence into the community. The editors conclude the volume with a foreward-looking perspective, bringing developmental theory, social policy, and child maltreatment together in the context of the larger culture, posing the question of the future directions for child maltreatment research and policy (Chapter 13). What is unique about this edited work is its coherence with each chapter building on the other.

The questions surrounding child abuse or child maltreatment can only be done in a comprehensive way, for the pathology is not solely a function of individual dysfunction, but it is also related to a number of social and community values and practices. To isolate the individual family or the individual dyad as the key player in this problem is to isolate them from their place in the larger community and national environment (Chapter 8). The isolation tends to overlook the contributions of the broader society's role which implicitly, and at times explicitly, accepts violence as a solution for social deviance (Chapter 7). What complicates the problems surrounding child abuse is the ambiguity of the definition of what is abuse, what are the legal issues of jurisdiction—especially about the boundaries of responsibility and authority regarding child-rearing and management (Chapter 2), what are the rights of the child, what is the responsibility of the government, and what rights do parents have (Chapter 3)? The effects of abusive experiences on children are not limited to functioning at home, but also extend to the school and the community (Chapter 10). In essence, the community and the society also function as perpetrators and as the victims of child abuse.

The complexity surrounding child maltreatment requires a comprehensive approach so that eventually we come to understand the dynamics of child maltreatment and what can be done to alleviate the problems. In this way, prevention programs become possible so that victimization of the persons, the community, and the broader society can be remedied (Chapter 11).

To accomplish these goals, the editors have selected a highly competent group of investigators to present the relevant material on their specialties. The material is dynamic and forward-looking, where each of the authors not only describes the state of the art relative to the topics under discussion, but also provides suggestions as to future directions for research (Chapters 11 and 12).

These suggestions are presented in the context of a well-developed and synthetic theory incorporating the most up-to-date theoretical and empirical work in the field. The research model provides a guide by which to study child abuse in its social-cultural milieu, and to construct methods for implementation of the research, thereby yielding results which, in their collectivity, inform intervention, prevention, and social policy (Chapter 12).

The theory presented is a product of an interdisciplinary approach, taking into account the current state of knowledge of developmental, social, and family psychology, embedded in the broader context of the wider social-cultural environment.

Before one can embark on any research in this field it is necessary to define child abuse. This is no mere academic exercise but is actually crucial. When is a child abused? In the sexual area it is relatively easy to define aberrant behaviors that define abuse, but what about in the areas of physical or emotional abuse or sheer neglect? For example, our society condones the parent's rights to use corporal punishment. Is this physical abuse? How painfully does the child have to be spanked before it is abusive? Similarly, with emotional abuse such as derogating the child and attacking his or her self-esteem or neglect, when is a child neglected, or is the parent fostering independence? The terms and the attendant behaviors have to be clearly spelled out. The parent's rights and the child's rights have to be ascertained so that the child is not victimized, nor is the parent treated as the culprit. Social and cultural factors come into play in the final decision here (Chapter 7).

In this volume, four types of maltreatment are identified and discussed: physical, sexual, neglect, and emotional kinds of maltreatment. Irrespective of the type of abuse, the theory that is presented provides a framework to identify the characteristics of these various types in terms of etiology and outcome sequelae. By so doing, research can be focused and differential determination can be done. This approach does not deny the overlap of some of these types since the individual is not that compartmentalized. Nevertheless, the typing of the various forms of maltreatment provides a way to specify the salient variables and move to a treatment program. For example, differential outcomes in terms of academic success are found for children who are physically abused as compared to those who are sexually abused. I would suppose that for children whose parents or guardians engage in physical abuse, there are different underlying dynamics as compared to those who engage in sexual abuse. If this is the case, the treatment programs for parents and children will have to be appropriately differentiated.

The theoretical model flows from the definition identifying the etiology of the particular type of abuse and its subsequent treatment. Attachment theory is the overarching model explicated in some detail in the final chapter, which casts the theory into a developmental perspective, one perspective particularly important in the child maltreatment field since one of the critical requirements is to establish abuse. Aside from the importance of a socioemotional framework for understanding the dynamics and sequelae of abuse, the cognitive developmental aspects are very important. This is particularly the case when it comes to determining if abuse has, in fact, occurred. It usually requires the children's testimony to corroborate the events. This is especially critical in cases where there are physical signs of abuse, such as in beatings. In sexual abuse cases, there may be only the children's testimony as the validation of the experience. Since this is often a very private situation between the child and the abuser, there are often no witnesses. While adults are usually able to verify their claims, children are presumed to be incapable of providing valid testimony because children, especially preschoolers, are considered to be too immature to remember accurately, or they are subject to suggestions from authorities. Therefore, their testimony cannot be trusted. If that is the case, then how can abuse be investigated? This brings us to the issue of determination of children's competence to provide valid testimony. Determination of children's competence regarding valid testimony is discussed in great detail in Chapters 4 and 5. Of course, the skepticism about the child as a reliable and trustworthy witness is by no means a new issue. The research reported in this volume provides important insights into the nature of the difficulties, as well as some procedures for obtaining reliable information based on recent research and developmental theory that suggest ways of obtaining and interpreting children's testimony. This is another example of the confluence of developmental theory and research with practice.

The study of child maltreatment has as its ultimate goal to help children and families who have endured such trauma deal with the sequelae as well as prevent further abuse. This is a field of research that must strive not only to find causal connections between the familial factors that predict child abuse and domestic violence, but also come up with treatment programs for all those involved (Chapter 9). The cast of characters in this dramatic effort is large and includes not only the array of family members, but also social institutions such as courts, educational agencies, social agencies, religious institutions, police, and law enforcement officials. In the final analysis, the society itself has a stake and a responsibility to ameliorate child maltreatment in all forms (Chapter 12).

As we think of the larger societal context in which child abuse occurs, we can rightly ask: Does the maltreatment of children of any age reflect our society? Does violence beget violence? Is the violence against children a function of the acceptance of violence as part of the human condition? After all, it is expressed with such frequency in programming in our movies, our television, and our newspapers. A daily parade of a world of horror and pain at home and on the streets of our country and other parts of the world fill the content of our newspapers as well. It may be that violence of our society, and almost acceptance of violence as part of our society, are also reflected in our advocacy of punitive social policies for treatment of child molesters, along with most of the problems of crime. For example, there are those who work on child abuse problems and advocate punitive treatment of the abuser. More benign treatment approaches are often considered as "being soft" on the abuser since punitive treatment of the victimizer is perceived as a solution to the problem. Yet, as our authors point out, poverty, drug addiction, unemployment, poor housing, hopelessness, and despair are among the contributors to child maltreatment. These are social as well as personal problem areas. Perhaps one type of solution to the child abuse problem is a restructuring of our society to eliminate these various sources of pathology. Child abuse is not limited to the poor and the underprivileged; it can also be found in homes at all social class levels. More than a restructuring of the social order is called for. In other words, the discovery or the uncovering of the sources of child abuse at all social class levels accentuates the pervasiveness of the problem and defines it as a horrendous, complex, and expensive social problem (Chapter 6).

We have found little comfort in the treatment strategies offered by social science and health professionals, and we find ourselves with few constructive options. Yet, as a matter of survival as a free, safe, and democratic society, we have to move away from destructive, punitive approaches to those who are constructive in rehabilitating individuals and helping them face their reality in the context of a healing environment.

There is an urgency to support further research in all aspects of child maltreatment because of the increase in child maltreatment. The hope is that through research, such as is described in this volume, the trend toward increase in child abuse can be stopped, and healing can proceed. Unless something drastic is done, there is a frightening prospect that child abuse will continue to tear at the fabric of our families and in so doing hurt our society at large.

I am pleased to have this volume in the Applied Developmental Psychology Series since it treats a major child development problem with the scholarship, the integrity, and the constructive attitude that can only be helpful to the victims, the victimizers, and the community. Drs. Cicchetti and Toth and their colleagues have set a standard of research and practice and exposition that will move the field forward.

1

Child Maltreatment Research and Social Policy: The Neglected Nexus*

Dante Cicchetti
Sheree L. Toth

On November 20, 1989, 159 member states of the United Nations General Assembly adopted the articles emanating from the Convention on the Rights of the Child. Less than 1 year later, the treaty was ratified by more than 20 member nations and went into effect. The principles contained in the articles of the Convention convey the view of the child, not solely as a member of a family, but also as a unique individual with personal rights. Although various aspects of children's rights have been analyzed previously (Hart & Brassard, 1987; Horowitz, 1989; Melton, 1987), the Convention is unique in the integration of the political and civil rights of the child with economic, social, and cultural rights (Wilcox & Naimark, 1991). To date, only two Western nations have not ratified this treaty, one of which is the United States. The failure of one of the most powerful nations in the world to endorse a document articulating the rights and dignity of its children is cause for great concern, and it emphasizes how far we have to journey before the welfare of our children truly is a priority.

Although the Convention was initiated to improve the welfare of all children, there is little doubt that children who are at risk due to developmental impairments or adverse living conditions are the most in need of societal support. Within the range of risk, children who have been maltreated by the families entrusted with their care are especially vulnerable. It is these children, and the families who are so assaulted by an array of stressors that they are unable to provide adequately for the needs of their children, that this book addresses. The importance of meeting the needs of these children and families is emphasized in Article 19 of the Convention, which stresses the responsibility of the State to protect children from all forms of physical or mental injury or abuse, neglect, and exploitation by parents, as well as to provide preventive and treatment programs to achieve this goal.

* We thank the William T. Grant Foundation, the A. L. Mailman Family Foundation, Inc., the Smith Richardson Foundation, Inc., the Spencer Foundation, and the Spunk Fund, Inc. for their generous support of our work. We acknowledge the Monroe County Department of Social Services and the New York State Department of Special Education for their ongoing commitment to improving the quality of life for maltreating families. Finally, we thank Jennifer Boehles for typing this manuscript and for her assistance on this project.

Unfortunately, despite repeated efforts to reform the child welfare system, initiatives largely have failed to achieve their desired impact. Many factors have impeded progress in attaining the goals of protecting and helping children to realize their full potential. Some of these impediments are summarized in a report by the National Center for Children in Poverty (McGowan, 1991), including issues such as the tension between the rights of parents versus the rights of children, ambivalence regarding society's responsibility over the need to help children thrive or simply survive, an emphasis on procedural rather than substantive guarantees for children and parents, the seriousness of difficulties experienced prior to the initiation of services, and the increase in poverty among families having young children.

To this series of conditions contributing to unsuccessful welfare reforms, we add the absence of research informed policy initiatives. In fact, according to the American Public Welfare Association (1990), improvements in child welfare services have been hindered by the absence of current and consistent national data. Additionally, the report of the U. S. Advisory Board on Child Abuse and Neglect (Department of Health and Human Services, U. S. Advisory Board on Child Abuse and Neglect, 1990) states "Good policy begins with good facts. No agency or government can make informed decisions on how it should allocate resources to deal with a problem without knowing the magnitude of the problem and the trends concerning its incidence" (p. 58). While data on incidence and prevalence are necessary, we also must move beyond these epidemiological constructs to an incorporation of research findings on the effects of maltreatment on development, the consequences of failing to provide needed services to children and families, and evaluations on the effectiveness of various prevention and intervention services. It is with this goal in mind that the current volume was conceived.

Due to the integrative nature of this volume, it is important to clarify its parameters. The volume was not intended to serve as a comprehensive review on the sequelae of child maltreatment. Scholarly works in this area have been written (Cicchetti & Carlson, 1989; Starr & Wolfe, 1991). Moreover, books dedicated specifically to policy considerations and the child welfare system are available (Knudsen & Miller, 1991; Melton, 1983). Rather, *Child Abuse, Child Development, and Social Policy* seeks to consider research on child maltreatment in the context of its implications for child welfare reform and social policy. The current volume serves to elucidate the wealth of extant knowledge on maltreatment as it pertains to: definitional issues, legal considerations, community violence, cross-cultural and racial considerations, family perspectives, school functioning, and prevention and intervention efforts. In each chapter, the author(s) have drawn from a research base to inform policy considerations or recommendations that are made. It is through efforts such as this that policies in the area of maltreatment will be most likely to benefit the children and families that they are designed to serve.

An organizing theme throughout the volume is the need for increased coordination of efforts and a sharing of knowledge by professionals operating at all levels of the ecology, including the culture, the community, the family, and the individual. Interestingly, the organizational approach to studying development in families and individuals, and the transactional and ecological models of maltreatment, can serve as a template for this process.

Throughout the course of the past several decades, research conducted within the organizational perspective on development has contributed to our knowledge of how maltreatment experiences affect the course of family and individual development (Cicchetti & Carlson, 1989; Starr & Wolfe, 1991). According to theorists who adhere to the organizational approach, adaptation or competence, as opposed to maladaptation or incompetence, results from the successful resolution of the family and individual tasks most salient for a given developmental period. A hierarchical depiction of adaptation ensues, where the successful negotiation of prior stage-salient issues increases the likelihood of subsequent adaptive task resolution and competent functioning (Cicchetti & Carlson, 1989; Toth & Cicchetti, this volume).

Operating in parallel to research emanating from the organizational perspective, two different but closely related models of the etiology and sequelae of child maltreatment have been proffered (Belsky, 1980; Cicchetti & Rizley, 1981). Both of these models have had major impacts on how maltreatment is currently viewed in our society.

Cicchetti and Rizley's model addresses the causes, consequences, and mechanisms through which maltreatment is propagated. Their model advocates a transactional approach to conceptualizing the developmental process. In a transactional model, environmental forces, caregiver characteristics (including developmental history), and child characteristics (even if largely the result of maltreatment per se) all influence each other and make reciprocal contributions to the events and outcomes of child development. Cicchetti and Rizley's model focuses on the transactions among risk factors and the occurrence of maltreatment. These risk factors are divided into two broad categories: *potentiating factors*, which increase the probability of maltreatment; and *compensatory factors*, which decrease the risk for maltreatment. Furthermore, temporal distinctions are made for both categories of risk factors. For example, there are *transient* risk factors that fluctuate and may indicate a temporary "state." Conversely, there also are *enduring* factors that represent more permanent conditions or characteristics. According to this transactional model, maltreatment occurs only when potentiating factors outweigh compensatory ones.

At about the same time, Belsky (1980) proposed an *ecological* model to account for the etiology of child maltreatment. This model provides a framework for defining and understanding the "ecology" or broader environment in which child maltreatment occurs. Belsky views child maltreatment as a social-psychological phenomenon that is influenced by forces within the individual, the family, the community, and the culture in which the family and individual are embedded. His ecological model contains four levels of analysis: (a) ontogenic development, which includes factors within the individual that are associated with being a perpetrator of child maltreatment; (b) the microsystem, which includes factors within the family that contribute to the occurrence of child maltreatment; (c) the exosystem, which includes aspects of the communities in which families and individuals live that contribute to child maltreatment, and also includes elements of Bronfenbrenner's (1979) mesosystem, which is comprised of the interconnections among settings such as school, peer groups, church, and workplace; and (d) the macrosystem, which includes the beliefs and values of the culture that contribute to the perpetuation of child maltreatment. This model has been helpful in defining the broad range of influences on the etiology of child maltreatment.

Recently, Cicchetti and Lynch (1993) proposed an ecological/transactional model that discusses the pathways by which child maltreatment brings about adverse consequences for children's and families' development. In particular, with respect to the effects of child maltreatment, attitudes toward and the prevalence of violence within cultures, local communities, and families impact children's ongoing development and adaptation. The confluence of effects from culture, community, family, and previous development come together to influence developmental outcomes in children. Moreover, risk factors associated with child maltreatment are present at each level of the ecology. These factors first determine whether or not maltreatment will be present at a given level of the model.

In addition, factors within a specific level can influence outcomes in surrounding levels of the model. At higher, more distal levels of the ecology such as the macrosystem and the exosystem, potentiating factors increase the likelihood of community violence and maltreatment, whereas compensatory factors decrease their prevalence. What occurs in these environmental systems also influences what occurs in the microsystem. Within the microsystem, potentiating and compensatory factors determine the presence or absence of maltreatment within the family environment. Characteristics of the proximal environment have the most direct effects on children's development. The manner in which children handle the challenges presented by familial and community violence is seen in their own ontogenic development, which shapes their ultimate adaptation or maladaptation. An increased presence of enduring vulnerability factors and transient challengers associated with different forms of maltreatment at all ecological levels makes the successful resolution of stage salient developmental issues more problematic for children (Toth & Cicchetti, this volume). The result is an increased likelihood of negative developmental outcomes and psychopathology.

Conversely, such an ecological/transactional model of maltreatment and its effects also should help to account for resilient outcomes in some children. The presence of enduring protective factors and transient buffers at any level of the ecology may help to explain why some children display successful adaptation in the face of violence either within their communities or families. We believe that this integrative ecological/transactional model provides a framework that will help prevention and intervention efforts as well as suggest necessary directions for social policies on behalf of children and families. In particular, the ecological/transactional approach underscores that policy makers must transcend searching for simple causation and investigating effects at unitary levels of analysis. The decrying of the efficacy of linear, "main-effect" models by transactional/ecological theorists is reminiscent of Billingsley's (1968) poignant observation that "it is perhaps a peculiarly American quality to look for single causes of complex phenomena" (p. 206).

Along these lines, we have organized the chronology of chapters in this volume according to an ecological/transactional perspective. The book begins with discussions of broad-based policy issues subsumed under various sub-systems of the macrosystem, then moves into issues central to the exosystem, emphasizing the mesosystem interconnections among community settings such as the school and departments of social services with the family. Next, topics characteristic of the microsystem and of individual development are presented.

Nearly a decade ago, Aber and Cicchetti (1984) noted the importance of conducting studies on the sequelae of maltreatment and argued for the critical role that they could play in enhancing the quality of clinical, legal, and policy-making decisions for maltreated children. They stated that decisions such as whether to remove a child coercively from the home, how to develop services to meet the specific psychological needs of maltreated children, and how to evaluate these services would all benefit from a more solid and sophisticated data base on the sequelae of maltreatment. However, Aber and Cicchetti cautioned that "without rigor in design and method . . . myth will be put forward in place of knowledge as a guide to social action" (1984, pp. 196–197).

In the past decade, remarkable progress has been made in our understanding of the causes and consequences of child abuse and neglect. Additionally, knowl-edge from basic research has increasingly been used to guide and inform approaches to assessing needs and capacities, investigating consequences, and planning for children and families within the child welfare system. While answers to many important questions remain to be discovered, we know more about child maltreatment now than at any other point in history. In times of fiscal austerity, human services come under the scrutiny of budget-conscious govern-ment administrators and legislators. Increasingly, providers are being asked to document the beneficial impact of their prevention and intervention efforts. Now that stage-specific yardsticks of child and family development across multiple domains, issues, and contexts have been identified, basic research on the devel-opment of maltreated children can contribute to the development of the kind of evaluation research required to justify service dollars. Likewise, these research findings can be useful in modifying ineffective programs or policies to better address the needs of maltreated children and their families.

However, it is highly unlikely that clinicians, legal scholars, and policy decision makers will utilize knowledge gleaned from basic research without a close-knit collaboration among all parties involved. Researchers need to become increasingly cognizant of the types of data that clinicians and policy makers need to help make decisions and how they would use such data to make decisions. Clinical, legal, and policy decision makers must become more aware of the natural limits of any policy-relevant developmental study. Closer collaborations between researchers and decision makers is in the long-term interests of better research and service on behalf of maltreated children and their families.

REFERENCES

Aber, J. L., & Cicchetti, D. (1984). Socioemotional development in maltreated children: An empirical and theoretical analysis. In H. Fitzgerald, B. Lester, & M. Yogman (Eds.), *Theory and research in behavioral pediatrics* (Vol 2, pp. 147–205). New York: Plenum.

American Public Welfare Association. (1990). *A comprehensive array of services for families and children.* Washington, DC: Author.

Belsky, J. (1980). Child maltreatment: An ecological integration. *American Psychologist, 35,* 320–335.

Billingsley, A. (1968). *Black families in White America.* Englewood Cliffs, NJ: Prentice-Hall.

Bronfenbrenner, U. (1979). *The ecology of human development: Experiments by nature and design.* Cambridge, MA: Harvard University Press.

Cicchetti, D., & Carlson, V. (Eds.). (1989). *Child maltreatment: Theory and research on the causes and consequences of child abuse and neglect.* New York: Cambridge University Press.

Cicchetti, D., & Lynch, M. (1993). Toward an ecological/transactional model of community violence and child maltreatment: Consequences for children's development. *Psychiatry, 53.*

Cicchetti, D., & Rizley, R. (1981). Developmental perspectives on the etiology, intergenerational transmission, and sequelae of child maltreatment. *New Directions for Child Development, 11,* 31–55.

Department of Health and Human Services, U. S. Advisory Board on Child Abuse and Neglect. (1990). *Child abuse and neglect: Critical first steps in response to a national emergency.* Washington, DC: Author.

Hart, S., & Brassard, M. (1987). A major threat to children's mental health: Psychological maltreatment. *American Psychologist, 42,* 160–165.

Horowitz, F. D. (Ed.). (1989). Children and their development: Knowledge base, research agenda, and social policy application (Special issue). *American Psychologist, 44*(2).

Knudsen, D. D., & Miller, J. L. (Eds.). (1991). *Abused and battered.* New York: Aldine De Gruyter.

McGowan, B. G. (1991). Child welfare: The context for reform. In J. Jones (Ed.), *Child welfare reform* (pp. 21–59). New York: National Center for Children in Poverty.

Melton, G. (1983). *Child advocacy: Psychological issues and interventions.* New York: Plenum Press.

Melton, G. (1987). Children, politics, and morality: The ethics of child advocacy. *Journal of Clinical Child Psychology, 16,* 357–367.

Starr, R., & Wolfe, D. (Eds.). (1991). *The effects of child abuse and neglect: Issues and research.* New York: Guilford.

Wilcox, B. L., & Naimark, H. (1991). The rights of the child: Progress toward human dignity. *American Psychologist, 46,* 49.

2

Defining Child Maltreatment:The Interface between Policy and Research*

Douglas Barnett
Jody Todd Manly
Dante Cicchetti

Throughout the course of history as well as within contemporary times, all cultures and societies have differed with respect to their beliefs about child maltreatment and their means to eradicate it (Breiner, 1990; Korbin, 1981; Pleck, 1987; Sternberg, this volume). In both ancient and modern civilizations, examples can be found of cultures and subcultures employing widespread practices of blatant child abuse, including ritualized sadistic, sexual, and homicidal acts against children. In contrast, examples abound of past and current societies that are predominantly characterized by considerable devotion to the well-being of their children. Despite these differences, all cultures are consistent in the fact that they have implicit and explicit standards that define appropriate and inappropriate parental behavior. A review of these historical and ethnographic accounts of child abuse and neglect results in two general conclusions: First, these observations indicate that the harmful treatment of children is within the human behavioral potential. More importantly and more optimistically, these comparative accounts of child maltreatment also suggest that regulations and belief

* We would like to acknowledge the support of The William T. Grant Foundation and the Spunk Fund, Inc. Additionally, the support of The National Center on Child Abuse and Neglect Graduate Fellowship (90-CA-1477) to the first author is recognized. We also would like to thank the Monroe County Department of Social Services for facilitating our research on maltreatment definitions. We would especially like to acknowledge Diane Larter, Katherine Sosin, Carol Barnash, Kathy Lynch, Jan Reif, Kathy Renner, Dan Ross, and Carolyn Williams. Additionally we appreciate the assistance of Liz Bryden, Lauren Green, Patty Hrusa, Karen Pavlidis, Itza Morales Torres, and Martha Winter in data collection. We were grateful for Carolann Dubovsky's computer wizardry. We would like to thank Jody Ganiban for her comments on portions of an earlier draft of this manuscript. Sheree Toth's insightful commentary and critiques stimulated a great deal of constructive debate, and we are especially appreciative of her feedback.

In addition, we wish to thank those people who provided helpful feedback on the development of the maltreatment classification system, including Byron Egeland, James Garbarino, Robin McGee, David Wolfe, and our colleagues at Mt. Hope Family Center, Holly Boker, Wendy Potenza D'Alphonso, Ruth Kauffman, Michael Lynch, Barbara Mitchell, Fred Rogosch, and Sheree Toth. We also appreciate the assistance of Bridgette Abraham and Stephen Lurie, who provided consultation on legal and medical issues, respectively, that were pertinent for the system.

systems operating at all levels of social organization play important roles in deterring these inhumane practices.

In societies where children commonly receive inappropriate care, corresponding folklores and public policies that encourage these practices may be found. Ancient Grecian civilization offers one example of the manner in which such harmful treatment of children has been justified in this fashion. During the first millennium B.C., Greek states were known for their ruthless exploitation of children. Supporting these practices were mythological tales of gods who advocated such brutality. Similarly, state-sanctioned publications were available, such as the one entitled *How to recognize a newborn that is worth rearing* (Breiner, 1990). Cultural constructions such as these reinforce family practices and play an important role in precluding children's suffering from being heard, understood, and thereby prevented. In societies that refuse to acknowledge child maltreatment officially, parental actions that violate children's health occur without recognition. In such instances, maltreatment is not construed as a social problem and, in this sense, simply is considered not to exist.

Abiding by these same principles, societies that are noted for their compassionate, involved parental care also are characterized by having made the well-being of their children an explicit public agenda (Hewlett, 1991). In these instances, definitions of child abuse and neglect reflect societal beliefs and goals to insure a minimal degree of care and protection needed by children. Without these attitudes and regulations, history documents that children will be used and mistreated in every manner conceivable (Radbill, 1968). Within our own society, establishing legislated advocacy for children continues to be a slow and conflicted process. As in any other civilization, factors such as the current folklore, values, and goals of the population determine the course and outcome of the public sanctioning of family practices.

In contemporary America, theory, opinion, and research findings of social scientists and medical experts have replaced more blatant forms of superstition and mythology. We have become concerned with child maltreatment, in part, because of a growing consensus that child abuse and neglect are detrimental to children's psychosocial adaptation and lifelong productivity and, therefore, ultimately affect the collective well-being of the State (Dubowitz, 1986). Correspondingly, there has been an increasing moral conviction that the rights and protection of children supersede the rights of family privacy and autonomy in homes where children's mental and physical health are being jeopardized (Aries, 1962; Goldstein, Freud, & Solnit, 1973; Nelson, 1984).

To implement the public agenda of protecting children from harm, definitional specificity has become increasingly necessary for making systematic and relatively objective decisions about when intervention into family life is warranted. Where our society draws the line between maltreatment and nonmaltreatment has profound implications for millions of individuals, including children, parents, health care professionals, social scientists, and law enforcement and legal personnel.

To meet this challenge, theoreticians, researchers, and policy makers have come forward and have made important strides toward identifying key issues and offering resolutions to the dilemmas involved in defining child maltreatment (Aber & Zigler, 1981; Giovannoni, 1989; Giovannoni & Becerra, 1979; Zigler, 1976). However, defining child maltreatment is a continual challenge that changes with the ebb and flow of political and economic tides. In this chapter we examine the complex interaction of factors that affect working definitions of child maltreatment. By explicating the factors that influence maltreatment definitions, we contend that definitions can be developed that better meet the societal goal of ensuring the physical and emotional health of future generations.

Overview

This chapter is divided into four sections. First, we explore the cultural, political, and economic forces that have shaped definitions of maltreatment. Second, we review the impact that research and theory developed by social scientists have had on definitions of maltreatment. Third, we present work from our own laboratory that addresses the problems inherent in defining child abuse and neglect. We present this research as but one example of the type of investigations that are necessary to conduct in order to examine the assumptions of our national policies regarding what child maltreatment is and how it should be defined. Finally, we extract key issues and conclusions from the topics discussed, and delineate their implications for social policy.

What Do We Mean By Definition?

Throughout this chapter, we consider three primary components that we believe are integral to defining child maltreatment: The first element involves the conceptualization of the phenomenon, such as whether child maltreatment is best thought of as criminal behavior, psychiatric illness, or a result of environmental circumstances. Although they are frequently presented in opposition to one another, we contend that these viewpoints are not necessarily mutually exclusive. A second consideration involves the types of parental acts that are subsumed under the label child maltreatment. For example, most states recognize physical abuse, sexual abuse, and physical neglect to be incidents of child maltreatment. We describe how other parental acts, such as psychological maltreatment and inadequate supervision, are more controversial, and as a consequence are not legally well defined. The third definitional component involves the harshness of the parental acts necessary before the events are considered to be abuse or neglect. Despite the fact that clinical and legal decisions are based on implicit notions of seriousness, the continuum of severity has been poorly delineated. We present our efforts to make these dimensions more explicit so that researchers can investigate their practical implications in a more systematic fashion.

CULTURAL AND POLITICAL DETERMINANTS OF DEFINITION

A culture's position on what is and is not maltreatment reflects its attitudes about individual freedom and privacy, and its concerns about the welfare of its children. In addition, public definitions of maltreatment determine and consequently are determined by the availability and allocation of government funding. In this section, we discuss the transaction among cultural attitudes, political trends, economic forces, family well-being, and definitions of child maltreatment. The dialectic among these factors is represented in Figure 1. By examining the influence of political and economic forces on definitions of maltreatment, we can achieve an understanding of how to construct future definitions that better meet the needs of society.

Cultural Attitudes and the Call for Child Protection

Examples of child mistreatment have been chronicled in all civilizations, and no doubt predate recorded history (Breiner, 1990; Radbill, 1968; Ross, 1980). Although the mistreatment of children is not a modern invention, centralized and popularized concern over defining and counteracting child maltreatment is a

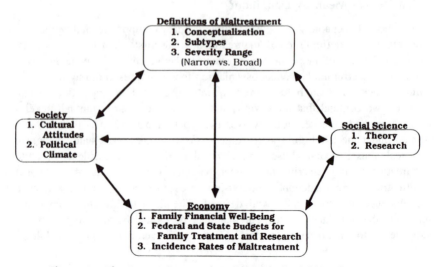

Figure 1.   The Determinants of Definitions of Child Maltreatment

relatively recent development (Zigler & Hall, 1989). Unfortunately, accounts of private matters such as public attitudes and family practices are typically not systematically documented. Therefore, it is impossible to ascertain an accurate representation of the opinions and behaviors that have changed, and the factors that affected them. However, agreement exists on several key developments, including the attitudes that promoted the child protection movement. Some of the public opinions that contributed to the rise of an organized response to child abuse and neglect included an increasing consensus that children's rights are as important as adults', a widening sympathy for the vulnerabilities of children, a questioning of the appropriateness and overall effectiveness of corporal punishment, and a growing acknowledgment that childhood experiences influence adult character.

In addition to the rise of an organized child protection movement, changes in the types of parenting practices defined to be unacceptable also are of interest. These shifts likewise reflect fluctuations in public opinions. By tracing the changes in community and state responses to child maltreatment, the types of attitudes and factors that affected these developments can be more completely understood. The following discussion is not a comprehensive history of the movement to protect maltreated children; rather, select issues and events are outlined to illustrate the forces that affect how child abuse and neglect are defined.

In America, efforts to identify and combat child abuse began in the early 17th century, during precolonial times, when representatives from the Protestant church visited pilgrim homes to insure a proper induction to church morals and values for children (Giovannoni & Becerra, 1979). The Puritan values promoted by the church included the idea that all children were in need of strong guidance and discipline. These notions manifested themselves in the justification and acceptance of severe corporal punishment. Thus, within this culture, severe corporal punishment was not considered to be child abuse. Rather, the absence of harsh guidance constituted child maltreatment. Concern over the moral character of parents, and its influence on children, has persisted as a public issue. Throughout the 19th century, state statutes advocated the severing of parental rights in cases where parents were perceived to be endangering the morals of their children (Giovannoni & Becerra, 1979). Parents who were drunkards, criminals, or prostitutes fell readily under this jurisdiction.

More controversial, by today's standards, were the "poor laws" of early America. In an effort to deter economic destitution, separation of poor children from their families was encouraged prior to the 20th century. In these cases, parents were thought to promote poverty and dependency in their children through their examples of "laziness." These ethics were slow to change. Not until the turn of the current century were distinctions made between neglecting parents and impoverished parents. In the late 19th century, poverty and parental mores were of greater concern than cases of severe corporal punishment. One hundred years later, this prioritization has been reversed in the United States.

Beginning in the 19th century, childhood began to be viewed as a particularly innocent and vulnerable time that deserves special consideration and protection (Aries, 1962; Ross, 1980). This growing perspective eventually led to public condemnation for the unjustified harsh treatment of children. In the early 1800s, situations in which parents had been exceptionally cruel to their children began to appear in public courts. Official definitions of child physical abuse were nonexistent and, therefore, set by court precedents. At that time, judges' decisions about whether or not parental actions constituted abuse were not necessarily related to the severity of a child's injuries. Rather, judges ruled against parents when evidence indicated that trauma was not inflicted as a form of punishment for a child's infraction (Solnit, 1980). Thus, if parents presented severe physical abuse as a form of discipline, then court action typically was not taken.

The year 1874 is commonly recognized as the date when child abuse become a national concern that warranted a widespread, organized response. In that year the case of Mary Ellen, a 10-year-old girl severely beaten and neglected by her stepparents, gained national newspaper coverage. Importantly, programs to provide help and protection to such children were identified to be noticeably absent. Ironically, her case was handled by the Society for the Prevention of Cruelty to Animals (SPCA), which was tellingly established 8 years prior to the Society for the Prevention of Cruelty to Children (SPCC). At the time of this now famous case, there were no formalized definitions of child abuse, and these types of parental actions could only be adjudicated in extreme cases that violated adult criminal laws. In response to the plight of Mary Ellen the SPCC was established, and she was officially deemed "case number 1" (Lazoritz, 1990).

Since the 19th century, child abuse and neglect have continued to receive increasing attention as social problems in need of remedy. Cultural attitudes have become increasingly accepting of intervention when families demonstrate little concern for their children's well-being. Nonetheless, there has been continued controversy over exactly what constitutes maltreatment, and over what the states' role should be in combating these problems. Since the early 20th century, reliance on private charities such as the SPCC to handle cases of child maltreatment has decreased. In their place, state-run agencies such as the Department of Social Services (DSS) have become the organizations primarily responsible for protecting children. Additionally, new public attitudes have promoted a greater emphasis on rehabilitating families and helping parents maintain custody of their children. With these transitions came a corresponding movement from private citizens to professionally trained mental health workers as the direct providers of service to families. Moreover, government involvement in the protection of children also reflected increasing political attention to these issues.

Political Debates Over the Definition of Child Maltreatment

In general, deciding where one person's freedoms end and another's rights begin has never been an easy task within a democracy. This task is amplified in areas of concern to families and children. Resistance to child abuse legislation has been manifested in numerous related issues, such as deciding the age at which a child should be considered a "human being." Past societies have established this age to occur relatively late in childhood. At the end of the 20th century, children's rights are considered at least as early as the beginning months of gestation, as exemplified in the arguments over abortion rights and whether mothers should be held criminally responsible for drug use during pregnancy. Other issues related to the resistance of legislated definitions of child abuse have appeared in the argument over parents' rights to raise their children free from governmental mandates. In prior centuries, the law grouped children with other parental possessions. Under this condition, public interference into parenting violated the right to manage private property.

Current opposition to governmental definitions and policies to combat child abuse and neglect continues over whether the government has the right to dictate parenting practices. Albert Solnit (1980), for example, warned that few would elect to live in a community where parental infractions were broadly defined and strictly enforced. In fact, the novelist Kurt Vonnegut (1972) has satirized one such society. In the futuristic society portrayed by Vonnegut in one of his short stories, children routinely sue their parents for what the children perceive to be their parents' shortcomings. In reality, however, no democracy represents either extreme. Striking a balance along this continuum of public jurisdiction over parenting represents a continual challenge to the modern world.

In the United States, shifts between liberal and conservative views of appropriate government involvement have impacted upon decisions and policy regarding definitions of child maltreatment. These positions stem from different interpretations of the civil rights outlined in the Declaration of Independence and protected under the Constitution. In point of fact, however, the Constitution of the United States makes no reference to parenting or family matters. These matters fall chiefly under the responsibility of the states. Theodore Roosevelt was the first president who attempted to provide guidance to the states by calling a "White House Conference on Children" in 1909. In this historic meeting, the committee declared that children should not be separated from their families solely for reasons of poverty.

Since Roosevelt, shifts in governmental concern for child welfare have fluctuated continually as the executive and legislative branches have waxed and waned through laissez-fair and "action-oriented" administrations (Nelson, 1984). As with most political issues, liberals and conservatives have had opposing perspectives on how child maltreatment should be defined. In the main, liberals have advocated broad maltreatment definitions that incorporate a wide range of parental actions. Liberals have upheld that it is the responsibility of the state to protect minors from being oppressed within their own families. People of the left wing strongly believe that government has social and moral responsibility to take action that will promote the personal well-being and equity of its people. Liberals see their administrators as kind leaders, responsible for defining maltreatment and designing and carrying out policy to combat these misdeeds. Their view of government is often referred to as the welfare state.

Conservatives, on the other hand, argue that definitions of child maltreatment must be greatly restricted. Their ideal definitions would limit maltreatment only to the severest forms of the physical and sexual abuse of children, and would not consider neglect to be worthy of State-sanctioned intervention. These right-wing convictions are driven by firm beliefs in the support for families' rights to privacy and support for patriarchal authority (Goldstein et al., 1973). Moreover, adherents to this camp believe less government is better government, and that issues such as child abuse are too narrowly defined to warrant the direct involvement of the nation's capital. Extreme supporters of the conservative position liken liberalist policy on child rearing to communist practices (Gaspar, 1980).

Nelson (1984) has described the process that allowed liberal ideals to prevail so that child maltreatment was able to move from a state to a national issue. Importantly, she described the political climate that prevented a bipartisan stalemate and permitted the adoption of a national definition of child maltreatment in 1974. Child abuse began receiving increased congressional concern in the late 1960s, in the wake of the "Camelot" administration, the "War on Poverty," the civil rights movement, and the passage of mandatory reporting laws for child abuse in all 50 states. According to Nelson, final determinants to the signing of this bicameral legislation included a long-standing liberal majority in the Senate, expansive budget proceedings in the House, proliferation of congressional special issue subcommittees, and the steadfast leadership of representatives and senators such as Walter Mondale. Their cumulative effect resulted in the passage of the Child Abuse Prevention and Treatment Act in 1974, exactly 100 years after the SPCC was founded. Included in this act of legislation was the establishment of a National Center on Child Abuse and Neglect (NCCAN) responsible for the allocation of monies for demonstration and research projects targeted at understanding and combatting maltreatment. Also sanctioned by this public law was the following broad, national definition:

> Child Abuse and Neglect means the physical or mental injury, sexual abuse, negligent treatment, or maltreatment of any child under the age of eighteen by a person responsible for the child's welfare under circumstances which indicate the child's health or welfare is harmed or threatened thereby. (Public Law 93–247, section 2)

Of greatest controversy was the inclusion of child neglect. After several reformations of the Act, this definition has remained essentially unchanged in the 1988 Child Abuse Prevention, Adoption, and Family Services Act (PL 100–284) despite prior criticism. While the spirit of this definition is worthy of praise, it has been criticized for the vagueness of terms such as mental injury, negligent treatment, maltreatment, harm, and threat (Gelles, 1975).

Economics and Family Well-Being

Although child maltreatment permeates all socioeconomic levels in our society, most maltreating parents are poor and welfare dependent. Simply stated, economic hardship and limited resources have long been linked with the occurrence of child abuse and neglect (Garbarino, 1977; Garbarino & Sherman, 1980; Gelles, 1992; Gil, 1970; Pelton, 1978). Indeed, research has supported a causal relation between economic crisis (e.g., rising unemployment rates) and increases in the incidence of child abuse and neglect (Steinberg, Catalano, & Dooley, 1981). Nonetheless, it should be noted that the majority of families living below the poverty level provide adequate care to their children. Increases in economic stress transact with parental personalities to heighten high-risk parents' propensity to maltreat their children. Consequently, during times of economic down turn, agencies have larger case loads of maltreating families.

Unfortunately, human services are typically underfunded and affected by the same financial forces that hurt families. Under economically trying conditions, programs established to help maltreating families have no choice but to direct their services to only the most severe cases (Giovannoni & Becerra, 1979). Through these mechanisms, the availability and allocation of funds for the protection of maltreated children directly alter the working definition of child abuse and neglect. It is sadly ironic that, as the number of families in crisis rises, help becomes increasing unattainable.

A nation's economy also is closely tied to its motivation to act against child abuse and neglect. For example, historically, during times of sustained economic stability, child abuse has received the most public and governmental attention. Keeping with this notion, the establishment of a large *bourgeoisie* played a key role in enabling child maltreatment to be defined as a social problem (Nelson, 1984). Unless the vast majority of the population has essential provisions such as food and shelter, issues such as child maltreatment must remain low priorities. Once a nation's families have their basic needs met, attention can be focused on the equally important task of insuring that their children receive quality parenting.

Moreover, in the past an inadvertent grouping of maltreatment and poverty has been an obstacle that has impeded budget appropriation for child maltreatment programs (Pelton, 1978). An unwillingness to set aside money for fighting child maltreatment results when legislators argue that enough attention has been devoted to the disadvantaged. In fact, strong association between child maltreatment and poverty was intentionally minimized to prevent politicians with anti-welfare attitudes from voting against the Child Abuse Prevention and Treatment Act (CAPTA). The separation of abuse and neglect from other social ills increased the public's attention to child maltreatment (Nelson, 1984).

In addition to the distinctness of a social problem, the issue's prevalence and seriousness also influence its prioritization (Mauss & Wolfe, 1977). By altering incidence rates, economic conditions and policies affect the definition of child maltreatment in counterproductive ways. Although financial crises increase the number of occurrences of child maltreatment, they also result in the employment of narrower definitions of which children should be considered maltreated (Alvy, 1975; Giovannoni, 1991). More conservative definitions of child maltreatment directly reduce epidemiological estimates (Cicchetti & Barnett, 1991). Moreover, during times of budget cutting, priorities may be manipulated by focusing on statistics that are substantially lower than more general estimates of maltreatment. For example, reporting the number of deaths resulting from abuse per year may give the illusion that child abuse is on the decline. In summary, alternating definitions result in fluctuating estimates of the incidence of abuse and neglect. This information ultimately cycles back to affect the government funding appropriated for helping maltreating families. Completing the circle, monetary allocations then influence the functional definitions of maltreatment in the fashion we have described.

Current Challenges to Future Definitions

Definitions of child abuse and neglect are not static phenomena, nor do they reflect issues that will be resolved in the decades to come. As this chapter was being written, cultural forces continued to affect future definitional changes.

During the 1980s, domestic issues pertaining to family well-being were grossly neglected. Conservative trends under the Reagan administration made reprieval of CAPTA precarious (Nelson, 1984). Moreover, while federal dollars were being diverted from programs for families and disadvantaged children, a large national debt was accumulating from other expenditures. In the 1990s, governmental spending is being further curtailed. Thus, domestic problems such as child abuse are in increased danger of being short changed.

Furthermore, we have witnessed a major redistribution of wealth in the United States during this past decade. Philips (1990) has documented the disappearance of the middle class and the burgeoning percentage of families classifiable as poor. Currently, more than one-fourth of all children under 6 years of age live below the poverty level in this country. Hewlett (1991) has described a litany of social crises currently plaguing American families across all income levels. She cogently argued that governmental policies have become unabashedly "neglectful" of issues relevant to the protection and nurturance of our nation's children. For example, increasing numbers of homeless children, rising divorce rates, growing numbers of single parents, large numbers of dual working parents, lowering of educational standards and the deregulation of children's media services, represent only a few of the challenges to the adequate provision of care to our children. She further cautioned that, unless we take steps to reverse the demise of regulations and infrastructures that support children and their parents, this escalating deterioration will have devastating consequences for the survival of the nation as a whole.

An examination of the portrayal of children and families in television shows and motion pictures in the late 1980s reveals that cultural attitudes about children may be changing. In the 1950s and 1960s, television programs typically depicted parents as self-assured, reliable, and concerned, and children as naive, vulnerable, and in need of guidance. In current drama, parents are presented that are inept, vulnerable, stressed, abandoning, and children are no longer shielded from parental stress. More significantly, children are characterized as precociously mature, and increasingly able to take care of themselves and their parents. These programs may be both reflective of and further influencing cultural attitudes. Views of children as prematurely self-sufficient will affect future definitions of maltreatment, particularly in areas such as psychological maltreatment and lack of supervision. In summary, each of the factors noted to determine definitions of maltreatment, including cultural attitudes, politics, economics, and family well-being, has been altered in recent years in a direction that is likely to be reflected in narrower, more conservative definitions of child abuse and neglect.

The dialectic among cultural attitudes, political climate, and economics is complex. Many factors and subfactors that impact upon the working definitions of child maltreatment have yet to be identified. The magnitude and complexity of these processes are overwhelming and thereby appear to be difficult to influence. However, by identifying and examining these factors, changes can be affected through more planful and comprehensive means, rather than by allowing this problem to fall to the winds of political change. We have discussed how economic crises increase the likelihood that children will be mistreated. Similarly, we have described how the proliferation of social problems alter the definitions of child abuse and neglect so that only the most serious cases receive attention.

Through these mechanisms, the current decline in family well-being and the rise of conservative political ideologies greatly jeopardize programs to help maltreated children. By understanding these forces, action can be taken to prevent definitions of child abuse and neglect from being limited in ways that are counterproductive to children's welfare. The study of these phenomena by social scientists has made increased understanding of these processes feasible. Social scientists from a wide range of disciplines also have played an important role in the development of our definitions of child maltreatment. Their contributions are described in the following section.

SOCIAL SCIENTIFIC APPROACHES TO DEFINING CHILD MALTREATMENT

The conceptualization of child maltreatment, in part, determines the way in which it is defined (Aber & Zigler, 1981; Hutchison, 1990). In turn, the theoretical definition of maltreatment dictates the type of research that is conducted, as well as the manner in which research can support or change definitional policy. In this section we examine historical changes in human service specialists' and social scientists' views of maltreatment.

The first "professional" characterization of child maltreatment can be described as the child advocacy movement. Dating back to the time of the Mary Ellen case, private charities popularized the view that parental mistreatment of children was unacceptable. They also established "cruelty to children" as the first label for this phenomenon (Knudsen, 1988). At that time child maltreatment was characterized as deviant criminal conduct. Typically, parental rights were severed. Often, parents were prosecuted and children were "protected" through removal to relatives, foster homes and institutions (Children's Defense Fund, 1979). With increasing governmental support and the leadership of social workers, this movement has continued through the 20th century.

Four more recent theoretical perspectives on defining child maltreatment have been compared and contrasted (Aber & Zigler, 1981; Gelles, 1973; Giovannoni & Becerra, 1979; Hutchison, 1990). Each approach carries its own biases as to what constitutes child maltreatment. Moreover, these conceptual definitions were derived from different theories about the etiology, sequelae, and treatment of child abuse and neglect. These theories diverge according to which characteristics should be emphasized in the definition of child maltreatment (Aber & Zigler, 1981).

The first perspective to be articulated was the medical-diagnostic definition (Kempe, Silverman, Steele, Droegemueller, & Silver, 1962). Central to this approach is the notion that child maltreatment is a symptom of a pathology, "the Battered Child Syndrome." The definitional focus was narrow and limited primarily to the severest instances of maltreatment, documented by x-rays of children that evidence injuries such as multiple fractures and subdural hematomas. Importantly, however, the emphasis was on treating a disorder that was believed to be afflicting the parent. Characterizing maltreatment as a psychiatric illness was an important step in the adoption of maltreatment as an issue worthy of public definition and increased policy attention. By grouping child abuse with other diseases of childhood, the medical community had removed society from any blame in the etiology of this disorder and had created a new optimism that this illness could be overcome through research and treatment limited to the parent (Alvy, 1975; Cicchetti, Taraldson, & Egeland, 1978).

Second, the sociological definition emerged, in part, as a reaction to and critique of the disease model of child abuse (Gelles, 1973). The sociological perspective is best exemplified by the work of Gelles (1973, 1975), Gil (1970), Giovannoni and Becerra (1979), and Zigler (1976). Central to this perspective is the belief that the definition of child maltreatment is a social judgment. Thus, maltreatment includes parental acts that are deemed to be inappropriate by cultural standards and practices. Sociological theorists stress the importance of identifying the practices and potential biases of professional gatekeepers who decide whether a parent should be labeled maltreating and be forced to receive services (Gelles, 1975). Sociologists believe that definitional decisions are best resolved through public and professional opinion surveys regarding which types of parental actions should be considered to be unacceptable. Definitional emphasis within this tradition is on the parental acts, with a key tenet being the depathologizing of maltreatment, and the examination of society's role in perpetuating maltreatment. In addition, adherents to this perspective advocate a broader definition that includes a larger class of parental actions that adversely affect children, such as failure to provide medical care, lack of supervision, and educational neglect.

Third to emerge was the legal definition, best characterized by the work of Wald and his associates on the Juvenile Justice Standards Project (JJSP, 1977). Members of this committee of the American Bar Association were concerned with establishing clear guidelines regarding which parental actions justified court action. Their goal was to provide national standards for making judicial decisions about maltreatment. According to their recommendations, making a legal definition of child maltreatment requires that parental actions caused physical or emotional harm to the child, or introduced substantial risk that the child would suffer damage. Moreover, physical harm was limited to serious injuries documented by evidence such as "disfigurement, and impairment of bodily functioning" (p. 51). Similarly, emotional harm had to be documentable and serious, including instances in which the child experienced "severe anxiety, depression, withdrawal or untoward aggressive behavior toward self or others" (p. 55). Thus, definitional emphasis in the legal sense is placed on the injuries or strong potential for injury incurred by the child. With the requirement of needing to withstand a courtroom hearing, the legal definition limits the label child maltreatment to only very severe instances.

The final perspective can be described as the *ecological definition*. This approach, developed out of Bronfenbrenner's (1979) ecological theory of child development, has been applied to the study of maltreatment primarily by Garbarino (1976) and Belsky (1980). This viewpoint places equal emphasis on the environmental and familial contributions to the occurrence of child maltreatment, and suggests a very broad definition that includes socioeconomic conditions (e.g., poverty) that are known to jeopardize children's development. In fact, according to the ecological perspective, maltreatment includes factors at all levels of the ecosystem that have been identified to promote the incidence of maltreatment. For example, maltreatment at the highest level (i.e., the macrosystem) includes a society's tolerance for and encouragement of violence and corporal punishment, as well as societal lack of policies to insure that provisions are made for all families to have equal access to food and shelter (Gil, 1975). At the level that directly impacts upon the family (i.e., the mesosystem), maltreatment criteria include factors that have been found to jeopardize parenting such as the lack of social support, and incidents of spousal conflict. Events commonly recognized as maltreatment, such as physical abuse, would be captured in ecological definitions of the microsystem, which includes parent–child interactions. This perspective is notable for the premise that society as a whole must share responsibility for the occurrence of child maltreatment within its domain.

Not surprisingly, then, each perspective places emphasis on different variables for conceptualizing maltreatment. Correspondingly, each approach advocates different criteria for defining child maltreatment (see Aber & Zigler, 1981, for an elaboration of this point) along with varied levels of intervention into the family. For the ecological approach, an emphasis is placed on the environment. Parent adjustment is the key criterion for the medical-diagnostic definition. The parental actions are central to the sociological definition. Finally, evidence of physical and emotional harm to children is necessary for making a legal determination of abuse or neglect.

The disagreement and points of conflict among these perspectives are readily apparent. However, these differences also obstruct a more general, underlying agreement shared by these four viewpoints. For example, none of the adherents to any of these perspectives would deny that each of these elements (i.e., environment, parent, act, child outcome) is only part of the entire picture of child abuse and neglect (see Figure 2). In fact, while these perspectives place emphasis on different criteria for making a judgment about maltreatment, they each also take into consideration evidence pertaining to the entire context of maltreatment,

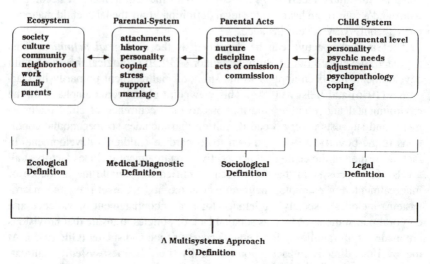

Figure 2.   Theoretical Approaches to Defining Maltreatment

including environmental conditions, the parent's emotional stability, and the consequences to the child. For example, although the medical viewpoint highlights the parent's personality as the locus of child maltreatment and the "disorder" that needs to be treated, physicians typically identify maltreatment according to its physical consequences (e.g., broken bones).

In addition, research has demonstrated that environmental factors, parent personality traits, parenting practices, and child outcomes are all interrelated in the manner predicted by the respective theories (Cicchetti & Carlson, 1989). Research also has clearly revealed that each perspective, by itself, is insufficient for accounting for the causes and effects of child maltreatment. Rather, an integration of approaches seems most warranted. Consequently, these different viewpoints should not be thought of as mutually exclusive nor should they be inappropriately or artificially pitted against one another. Each inherently contains strengths and each arose historically in the context of reaction to limitations of prior approaches. Thus, together they offer the most comprehensive outlook, strengthened by their combined insights. In the coming paragraphs, we advocate and present such an integration of approaches.

Purpose and Definition

In addition to theoretical conceptions, another factor that influences definition and is thus worth considering is the purpose of the definition (Ross & Zigler, 1980). That is, why a definition is needed and how it will be used certainly contributes to its form and content. Examples of potential uses of maltreatment definitions include aiding in decision making about legislation, child custody disputes, child protective service case management, and intervention research groupings (Aber & Zigler, 1981; Giovannoni, 1989; Hutchison, 1990). Indeed, Aber and Zigler point out that each of the theoretical approaches are guided, in part, by distinct purposes. The purpose of the medical-diagnostic definition is to identify and cure psychopathology of the child maltreater. The aim of the sociological perspective is to label and control social deviance. The goal of the legal definition strives to standardize legal decision making such as the removal of a child from the home or mandating a family to participate in therapeutic intervention (involuntary services). The rationale underlying the ecological perspective is to guide research on the multilevel processes that influence children's developmental outcomes, and to encourage higher order policies and programs to promote adaptive human development.

Although some have argued that no single definition can meet all purposes (Zigler, 1976), we believe that consensus may be reached by concentrating on the shared underlying purposes across disciplines. Common to each aim is the affirmative goal of promoting children's physical and psychological well-being through the identification and eradication of detrimental childrearing practice, and the promotion of supportive, sensitive parenting.

Toward a Unified Definition of Child Maltreatment

We believe that a unified definition of child maltreatment is not simply desirable; rather, we view it as essential. In 1991, the journal Development and Psychopathology (Cicchetti, 1991) devoted an entire issue to a professional debate over a target article that proposed a research definition of psychological maltreatment (McGee & Wolfe, 1991a). Most striking across the commentaries on this article was the backlash against fractionating definitions according to their purpose (e.g., research versus legal). Contributors argued that research findings from studies employing different definitions and perspectives would be irrelevant to those who actually would be applying the results, and in this sense disciplines would be working at cross purposes to one another (Barnett, Manly, & Cicchetti, 1991; Garbarino, 1991; Giovannoni, 1991; Haugaard, 1991; Thompson & Jacobs, 1991; Toth, 1991; Wald, 1991). This is a marked change from previous views that advocated that separate definitions of child maltreatment should be developed according to their distinct purposes.

We contend that an adversarial stance toward different definitional perspectives will not result in an integrated standardized definition of child maltreatment. Debates of this type tend to exaggerate differences among the camps and underestimate the strengths of each and the commonalities among them. Each of the definitional conceptualizations offer valid considerations, yet each, in isolation, is incomplete. Acknowledging the virtues of each perspective is an important step toward bringing about consensus. There are, however, some points of conflict among the approaches that need to be addressed.

Once source of incompatibility exists between some of the views of the sociological tradition and some of the tenets of the legal perspective. The sociological view, in part, implies that maltreatment includes those parental acts that fall outside the norms of society's accepted parenting practices. Hence, some parental acts may be detrimental to children, but because they occur so frequently, they represent the norm and are therefore not deemed maltreatment. For example, some forms of corporal punishment and failing to provide supervision for children who are home alone after school (i.e., the latchkey children) may be detrimental to children, but are not considered to be maltreatment. Conversely, some acts are considered maltreatment because they are unacceptable to the majority of the population, even though these practices may not eventuate in harm to children. The incongruity between legal and sociological requirements reminds us that public opinion about what is harmful to children is not the same as empirical evidence from clinical research. Because the legal definition states that maltreatment incidents are those parental acts that are unambiguously detrimental to children, some acts defined by the sociological definition would conflict with the legal definition.

In accord with the sociological perspective, we propose that the emphasis in defining child maltreatment should be on the parental acts that are viewed to be

unacceptable or "improper" by society, because the majority of the population
believe that they place children at risk for physical and emotional harm (cf.
Barnett et al., 1991; Giovannoni & Becerra, 1979; Haugaard, 1991). We emphasize parental actions over other variables to define child maltreatment for a
number of reasons.

First, there are an infinite number of conditions that perpetuate the occurrence
of child abuse and neglect. Although we recognize that acts of maltreatment take
place within a broad ecology of determinants, these risk factors lose their
predictive power when employed on an individual, case-by-case basis. Consequently, the utilization of etiological correlates to define maltreatment would
lead to a large number of false positive and false negative identifications of
maltreatment (Cicchetti & Aber, 1980; Cicchetti et al., 1978). Therefore, we
cannot define child maltreatment solely on the basis of parental or environmental
risk factors.

Second, not all child maltreatment leads to immediately or easily documentable harm. Consequently, basing decisions about maltreatment solely on the
demonstration of harm would prevent large numbers of children from receiving
help before they had been seriously impaired. Therefore, we cannot define child
maltreatment based exclusively on the demonstration of child injury. Although
specific theories and data about the causes and consequences of maltreatment
should inform and influence social constructions of maltreatment, they should
not be viewed as information necessary for the establishment of a definition of
maltreatment.

A Developmental Psychopathology Approach to Defining Child Maltreatment

Despite our focus on particular parental actions as integral to the definition of
child maltreatment, we conceptualize maltreatment within a wider context of
environmental and familial transactions of causes and consequences (Cicchetti &
Rizley, 1981). We place our multisystems, integrated approach to definition
within a developmental psychopathology perspective (see Figure 2). Developmental psychopathology is a broad macroparadigm whose tenets include a
recognition for the necessity of multiple perspectives, including cross-cultural
and multidisciplinary work (Achenback, 1990; Cicchetti, 1989, 1990). The
development of theories that are applicable to understanding normal and atypical
developmental phenomenon also is of central concern to developmental psychopathologists. A developmental perspective on child maltreatment provides a
broad umbrella under which multiple perspectives and viewpoints can be understood and integrated.

Consummate to understanding the multifaceted nature of the causes and
consequence of maltreatment is the recognition of the developmental aspects of

child abuse and neglect. Each of the components involved in child maltreatment, the environment, the parent, and the child, are transacting over time (Cicchetti & Rizley, 1981). Because more is known about child development than about adult and environmental development, ontological factors influencing maltreatment become most readily apparent when considering the child's contribution. For example, we know that children's needs change as they mature. The need for autonomy expresses itself differently for a toddler than for a school-aged child or for an adolescent. The same is true of other child needs such as those for attachment, acceptance, and positive regard. As these developmental child needs change, so must parental supports. Caregivers must be able to adapt to the growth of their children. And in this sense, the parental acts that are judged to be unacceptable by society change as a function of the child's age. Moreover, the types of parental acts that can enhance development, or that can result in psychological harm to children, also change over the course of development. Thus, acts that might be maltreatment for a toddler would not be for an adolescent, and acts that are maltreatment for an adolescent might not be for a preschooler (Garbarino, Guttman, & Seeley, 1986). For example, leaving a child unattended for several hours would be considered maltreatment for an infant but not for an adolescent. Consequently, parental acts must be viewed within the context of particular concerns at specific developmental stages (Cicchetti, 1989; Cicchetti & Rizley, 1981).

In addition, the consequences of child maltreatment manifest themselves differently according to the child's developmental level. Consequently, the criteria for documenting psychological harm will necessarily vary with the age of the child. Aber and Zigler (1981) note that special attention needs to be paid to the fact that emotional problems such as aggression and depression manifest themselves differently at each developmental stage. Moreover, Cicchetti (1989) has posited that the sequelae of maltreatment are best assessed by focussing on developmental issues that are most salient at the time of assessment. For example, attachment in infancy, self- and language development in toddlerhood, and peer relations in middle childhood represent the central emotional and social tasks that children must master during the developmental course. Child abuse and neglect have been shown to undermine the negotiation of these stage salient issues (Cicchetti, 1989; Toth & Cicchetti, this volume).

In addition to the child component, each of the elements in the systemic picture of maltreatment is constantly in flux. We have already noted that parental acts have to change in accord with the child's growth. In addition, parents are developing cognitively, socially, and emotionally (Newberger & Cook, 1983). Moreover, the family system is constantly in transition as new siblings are born, and as parental relationships and supports change (Cicchetti & Howes, 1991; Howes & Cicchetti, this volume). Finally, the extrafamilial environment also should not be viewed as static, since neighborhoods and economies also go through transformations (Bronfenbrenner, 1979).

RESEARCH ON THE DEFINITION OF CHILD MALTREATMENT

Research concerning the definition of child abuse and neglect has traditionally examined the opinions of professionals and the lay population about the types of acts that constitute maltreatment. Investigators primarily have explored these issues by either administering surveys of hypothetical instances of maltreatment, or by examining professional decision making about actual reports of child abuse and neglect. The empirical literature on the results of surveys, as well as the reporting and substantiation process of Child Protective Service investigations, is far ranging. Although a comprehensive review of these studies is beyond the scope of this chapter, a summary of the two largest studies addressing these topics is presented as a representation of the findings and implications of the research in this area.

Giovannoni and Becerra (1979) conducted the most comprehensive study, examining the views of professional (i.e., lawyers, pediatricians, social workers, and police), and lay members of various ethnic groups (i.e., White, Black, and Hispanic individuals) (see Wilson & Saft, this volume). The findings of their surveys indicated a number of consistencies across the various lay and professional samples. All groups agreed that maltreatment is not a single entity, and a number of acts were consistently grouped together in related categories (e.g., emotional maltreatment, lack of supervision, failure to provide). Moreover, all groupings agreed that acts of maltreatment are not all equally serious in their impact on children. There were between- and within-group differences in the overall level of severity that acts of maltreatment were assigned. However, Giovannoni and Becerra (1979) also found that, "there was amazing similarity in the judgments of the relative seriousness of different kinds of mistreatment both among the professionals and among the lay respondents" (p. 240).

In other words, although the overall ratings of severity differed among groups, there was agreement in the order in which the maltreatment acts were ranked. Based on the consistency of their findings, they concluded that better operationalized, more precise definitions could be developed by researchers and practitioners than previously had been employed. In our own efforts to develop more clearly operationalized definitions, we have drawn heavily from the extensive research and experience of Giovannoni and Becerra.

Knudsen (1988) examined the reports and investigations of a Child Protective Service unit in a Indiana county made from 1965 through 1984. He examined the substantiation process of child maltreatment reports for "physical abuse, sexual abuse, verbal and emotional maltreatment, and neglect." Consistent with Giovannoni and Becerra (1979), he found that the vast majority of child maltreatment reports come from private citizens. Thus, it is primarily nonprofessionals who identify, and thereby define, what events constitute child maltreatment. In addition, Knudsen and others note that approximately one-third to one-half of all reports are considered founded reports of maltreatment.

Knudsen focused his investigation on the factors and processes that contribute to the outcomes of maltreatment investigations. Across the various subtypes of maltreatment, the most consistent finding was the absence of clear criteria for defining maltreatment and systematizing the investigation and substantiation process. Consequently, cases frequently were decided upon in an idiosyncratic fashion guided primarily by the beliefs and practices of the individual case workers. Based on his investigation, Knudsen deduced three principles that influence the substantiation of child abuse and neglect reports: First was the "rule of optimism," that a child was not considered maltreated until all other alternative explanations were eliminated. A second, key criteria for substantiation was the Child Protective worker's decision about the severity of injury or level of danger to the child. Higher degrees of judged seriousness were more likely to be considered founded cases of maltreatment. The third factor that related to the substantiation of the report was the length of time that elapsed between the maltreatment referral and the investigation, pointing to the need for immediate action in making decisions about maltreatment.

Studies also have examined factors related to decision-making processes about maltreatment such as gender, ethnic background, and experience of the investigator. Other investigators have examined the factors that affect court decisions on the severing of parental custody rights following instances of child maltreatment (e.g., Bishop, Murphy, Jellinek, Quinn, & Poitrast, in press; Murphy, Jellinek, Quinn, Smith, Poitrast, & Gosho, 1991). Consistent across all investigations into the decision-making process about defining child maltreatment is the glaring absence of clear definitional or decision-making guidelines or criteria. Clearly, there is a tremendous need to develop precise definitional criteria. Research could then begin to focus on the effectiveness and utility of the definitions, in addition to professional and nonprofessional opinions about maltreatment, and random variables that affect the definitional process. Next, we examine the type of research required to examine the effectiveness and utility of maltreatment definitions.

Can Research on the Developmental Consequences of Maltreatment Inform Definitional Policy?

An additional type of research on the definition of maltreatment involves examining the impact of various parental acts on children's well-being. This strategy can implicate certain types of parental acts that typically result in harm to children; therefore, these acts should be considered in the definition of maltreatment (Giovannoni, 1989; McGee & Wolfe, 1991b). This research strategy has the potential to provide objective data that can be utilized to assist in the development and evaluation of maltreatment definitions. However, the assumptions behind this research approach warrant careful consideration.

The key assumption of the research perspective is that a parental act becomes abusive when the act is found to be statistically associated with adverse outcomes for children's psychological well-being (Barnett et al., 1991). In the past, psychological research was focused primarily on examining whether child maltreatment has negative psychological consequences, what those consequences are, and through what mechanisms maltreatment results in a given effect. As a result, research on the sequelae of child maltreatment has clearly demonstrated that children labelled as maltreated by protective service units typically evidence deviant adjustment (see Cicchetti, 1989; Wolfe, 1987, for reviews).

However, it may be beyond the capacity of research to provide empirical evidence that can be employed for making systematic decisions about whether specific parental actions should be labeled maltreatment. Information for this purpose would require the accumulation of studies conducted with a range of populations. Moreover, because parental acts of maltreatment cannot be experimentally manipulated, extremely large sample sizes would be necessary to obtain sufficient subgroups of particular types of maltreatment under comparable conditions. These acts also would need to be reliably and validly documented and assessed a priori in prospective longitudinal investigations to provide the database necessary to inform definitional decisions. Unfortunately, the societal forces and zeitgeists that influence the availability of funding for research on child maltreatment increase the difficulties of accumulating systematic information of this nature.

Research can play an important role in challenging common and uncontested notions about the nature of maltreatment. For example, decades of research on the etiology of maltreatment have demonstrated that single variable cause-and-effect models designed to explain the occurrence of maltreatment are too simplistic (Belsky, 1980; Cicchetti & Rizley, 1981; Wolfe, 1985). Furthermore, years of research on the sequelae of maltreatment clearly indicate that maltreatment is not synonymous with the effects of poverty (Cicchetti, 1989). However, just as research on the etiology of maltreatment has moved away from simple cause-and-effect models, so has the research on the consequences of maltreatment. We now know that all maltreated children do not evidence the same psychological and behavioral profile, and that biological factors such as children's temperament play a role in how maltreated children cope with these stressful events (Barnett, Ganiban, & Cicchetti, 1992; Cicchetti, Ganiban, & Barnett, 1991). The investigations conducted over the past three decades on child maltreatment are a testament to the idea that research has helped the public become more informed and realistic in their thinking about the types of acts that constitute maltreatment. Moreover, our theories and research on the causes, consequences, and treatment of maltreatment are significantly more sophisticated now then ever before. Therefore, it is safe to assume that knowledge on how maltreatment should be defined will most likely continue to become more complex (Aber & Zigler, 1981).

Another important function research has played is that of helping maltreatment to remain an issue of focus for so long. Nelson (1984) notes the importance of media attention as an essential vehicle in the maintenance of public agendas (see also Cicchetti et al., 1978; Gerbner, Ross, & Zigler, 1980). More than almost any other public issue, child maltreatment has been able to maintain constant media attention. Moreover, news stories about maltreatment have moved from sensationalistic coverage by the tabloids to a more persistent visibility in the nation's most respected periodicals. The growing body of scientific information that was accumulating about the phenomenon contributed to the longevity and growing respectability of maltreatment as a subject worthy of attention (Nelson, 1984). Of relevance to the question of definition, continued scientific examination resulted in the proliferation of topics from a focus on the physical battering of children to a host of related issues such as spousal violence, physical neglect, sexual abuse, psychological maltreatment, and parental drug and alcohol use. Thus, research has resulted in differentiation of the categories of maltreatment. The expansion of research, consequently, contributed to the increased media coverage. Newspaper, magazine, and television reporting of research findings has resulted in a widening public condemnation of these related parental practices, which ultimately has led to changes in the state and national definition of maltreatment.

Research can never answer moral questions such as whether the state should condemn particular parenting practices. Questions of this type can only be answered through public opinion. However, when policies are developed based on particular assumptions such as whether or not the state should intervene when children are placed in situations that jeopardize their future mental health, research can help to examine whether particular parenting experiences tend to be associated with particular outcomes under particular conditions. The empirical study of child maltreatment may eventually lead to a clearer understanding of the implications of narrow as opposed to broad definitions of maltreatment. Progress achieved in this vital area may eventuate in a better understanding of the differential effects of various subtypes of maltreatment. Perhaps more importantly, research can be used to inform and evaluate the means through which interventions and preventions can be effective (see Cicchetti, Toth, & Hennessy; Daro; Toth & Cicchetti; and Wolfe, all this volume).

A System for Classifying Maltreatment Records

Because extensive research information is required if it is to be useful in making policy decisions, researchers must be able to communicate their findings and compare their results across laboratories and across samples. Without such comparability, meaningful integrations of individual studies are impossible. Currently, generalizability across studies is seriously compromised by differences in sampling and operational definitions of maltreatment. Since the field is moving toward more complex models of the precursors and consequences of maltreatment, greater sophistication in the measurement of the maltreating acts themselves is imperative. Some researchers have dealt with the heterogeneity within maltreatment by restricting their sample to only the most severe or clear examples of certain subtypes (especially physical abuse). While studies using narrow definitions may be helpful in examining specific, differential effects of unique subtypes of maltreatment, in reality, pure subtypes are not typically found in the maltreating population, and results from such atypical samples may not be generalizable to the majority of maltreated children (Aber & Cicchetti, 1984; Cicchetti & Rizley, 1981); thus, research that is limited to such rare, circumscribed samples can only produce restricted information about the broader phenomenon. At some point, researchers must incorporate the difficult populations that are typically seen by clinicians, Child Protective caseworkers, and family court judges.

Although grappling with ambiguous cases is more controversial, and it is often difficult to distinguish between subtypes of maltreatment or between maltreatment and poor parenting, these delineations are critical for formulating policy relevant to the population that is typically served by state and local agencies. Therefore, a systematic, comprehensive method must be implemented that articulates operational definitions for different subtypes of maltreatment, that delineates the exclusion and inclusion criteria for these subtypes and for differentiating maltreatment from poor parenting, and that can be communicated across laboratories and disciplines. Such a system also should include multiple dimensions of maltreatment experiences so that the important elements within the phenomenon can be identified and investigated.

Because no such system had been developed as we began conducting research within our laboratory (although other researchers began tackling the problem of classification concurrently), we felt it necessary to devise a way to measure several key dimensions of our subjects' experiences, including definitional criteria for subtypes of maltreatment. This process of developing a classification system for maltreatment has illustrated many of the problems that arise in trying to impose a structure on the diverse experiences that occur within the chaotic and dysfunctional families that comprise our maltreatment sample. We present our system in this context to draw attention to the aspects that we feel have not received adequate empirical study and that may ultimately play a role in shaping policy decisions. We focus on dimensions that may influence the impact that maltreatment has on children and families, and therefore, that will affect provision of the most appropriate intervention and treatment methods. The goal for our classification system was to quantify dimensions of maltreatment so that they could be examined systematically, in order to explore empirically the relationships of these variables to etiology, sequelae, and treatment methods.

Use of Child Protective Records

The methods for classifying maltreatment information must be understood within the context of the measurement strategy. We chose to use records from Child Protective Services as our primary means of obtaining maltreatment data. Through negotiation with the Department of Social Services, these records were made available to us, and we wanted to make use of this rich and varied source of information. Child Protective records provide several advantages as an assessment strategy. These reports include dates of maltreatment incidents, the names of those who were involved, a narrative account of the event with statements from the parent, the child, and the source of the report. An investigation is conducted by a trained professional who integrates information from multiple sources, including hospitals, schools, police officers, neighbors, and family members. A determination is made regarding whether enough evidence is present to substantiate the claim according to legal statutes. These determinations are made independent from the research project by workers with no knowledge of the family's research participation or of the research hypotheses. Additionally, research personnel have no knowledge of the subjects' maltreatment record, thus preventing biases related to the family's maltreatment status.

Another advantage to the use of Child Protective records is that the maltreating families who do participate in research projects are often suspicious of outsiders (Cicchetti & Manly, 1990). If the maltreatment information were collected directly within the research project, many families may be alienated and refuse to participate. Having maltreatment issues addressed by an outside authority not affiliated with the research facilitates participation by these mistrustful families.

Additionally, since 49 out of 50 states have state registries for recording maltreatment reports (U. S. Department of Health and Human Services, 1988), a classification system using such records could be implemented nationwide. Our system was developed in New York State, but we believe that, with minor modifications, it could be adapted for use in other states as well.

We recognize that use of Child Protective records also has disadvantages. For example, many incidents of maltreatment may not come to the attention of authorities, either because the events were not observed outside the family or because they were not reported. The cases that are reported may be the most severe or occur in the lowest functioning families. Certain types of maltreatment, such as emotional maltreatment, are often difficult to document and have been recognized only recently as a serious form of maltreatment (McGee & Wolfe, 1991a). As has been discussed with regard to the implications of economic factors on definition, budget cuts and decreased availability of resources may lead to definitions of maltreatment that are increasingly narrow. If this occurs, then only the most extreme and easily documentable cases will receive services and will be present in Child Protective records.

Although the families identified by Child Protective Services are only a subset of the maltreating families in the general population, they are typical of the families who are receiving services and for whom intervention is targeted (Cicchetti & Barnett, 1991). Laws mandating professionals who work with children to report any suspicions of maltreatment help to insure that maltreatment is reported when it occurs.

Another disadvantage of Child Protective reports is that Child Protective workers vary in the amount of detail they provide in their reports and the amount of evidence that is necessary to substantiate a report. The narrative format of the reports is often difficult to quantify. The variability of the reports provided the impetus for systemically classifying the records according to careful decision-making criteria. In our classification system, we decided not to use Child Protective labels for the maltreating acts, but instead to gather information from the narratives and then classify them according to our criteria. Our eventual goal is that a systematic approach that provides increased clarity and consistency in classifying maltreatment could be incorporated into assessments made by Child Protective workers to improve systematization at the level of the original investigation.

Using the Child Protective records provides one strategy for surmounting some of the problems associated with alternative methods of obtaining information. Self-report by the parents is often unreliable and/or incomplete. For example, many of the parents in our research report no maltreatment history during initial screenings of prospective comparison (nonmaltreating) families; however, when Child Protective records are checked, evidence of maltreatment emerges, and the family cannot be considered a comparison family. Additionally, parents often are not reliable reporters of the details of the report, such as dates, medical reports, etc. Self-report by the child victim may be problematic because of research evidence that many children tend to minimize their maltreatment experiences (McGee, Wolfe, Yuen, & Carnochan, 1991). Asking children about their maltreatment experiences also may alienate the families and result in parental withdrawal of permission for their children to participate in research.

Another possible strategy for collecting maltreatment information is direct observation of the family. This approach can be very useful for assessing family dynamics and interactional patterns. However, an observational strategy may miss acute episodes of child maltreatment, and certain subtypes, such as sexual abuse, occur most often in private. Although some incidents of rough handling of children or neglect of children's emotional needs has occurred with researchers present in the home, most families are unlikely to maltreat their children in front of a professional who is legally mandated to report any maltreatment to Child Protective Services. Consequently, a complete maltreatment history cannot be obtained with observational data. We do advocate using multiple assessment strategies for collecting maltreatment information, such as interviews with the family's social worker, self-report from family members, and observations of family interactions during home visits and in laboratory assessments (Cicchetti & Barnett, 1991; McGee & Wolfe, 1991b; McGee et al., 1991). Child Protective records provide an invaluable component to a comprehensive assessment package.

In summary, we have chosen to collect information from Child Protective records, which we classify according to systematic criteria. We make use of information related to several dimensions that we believe are important facets of maltreatment that previously have received little attention in the literature. We use these dimensions to highlight features within the broad rubric of maltreatment that may play a role in how maltreatment is defined, what impact the maltreatment has on the child, and what decisions are made regarding intervention for a maltreated child. These dimensions include subtypes of maltreatment, the severity of the incidents within each of the subtypes, the frequency and chronicity of maltreatment reports and Child Protective involvement, the developmental period during which the maltreatment occurred for each child, the type and number of placements that occurred outside the home, and the perpetrator of the incident. These dimensions are presented in Figure 3, and they will be described in turn, with information regarding why the dimension was chosen for focus, and some of the relationships that are emerging as we begin to apply our system to other data on family environments and child outcomes.

1. Subtypes. Of the multiple dimensions that are assessed in our classification system, the one that has been the most widely recognized and the most frequently researched involves subtypes of maltreatment (Aber & Cicchetti, 1984). Some subtypes have received more empirical attention than others. For example, many samples of maltreated children have been restricted to those who have experienced Physical Abuse. Another subtype that has been researched independently from other types of maltreatment is Sexual Abuse, in part because of the unique aspects of sexual exploitation. Physical Neglect has received somewhat less attention, particularly with regard to Lack of Supervision, which is one of the most prevalent forms of maltreatment (Starr, Dubowitz, & Bush, 1990; Wolock & Horowitz, 1984).

Preliminary studies have examined factors that discriminate among the various subtypes of maltreatment. The next step for social scientists is to explore thoroughly similarities and dissimilarities in the etiological factors, the childhood outcome variables, the family environment, and the treatment response patterns associated with each subtype (Cicchetti & Rizley, 1981). Researchers, interventionists, and policy makers must also consider the co-occurrence of different combinations of child abuse and neglect within many maltreating families.

The frequency with which maltreatment subtypes overlap has been a critical difficulty in investigating these factors. Assessing the patterns associated with particular subtypes becomes extremely complex because of the rarity of pure subtypes (Cicchetti & Rizley, 1981). Consequently, sampling groups of families who, for example, are characterized by Physical Abuse without Physical Ne-

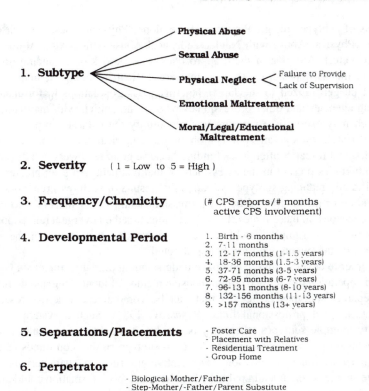

Figure 3.   Maltreatment Classification System

glect, Sexual Abuse, or Emotional Maltreatment is quite problematic. The heterogeneity of maltreatment samples frequently is not acknowledged in published studies, and this omission contributes to the perception that multiple subtypes of maltreatment either do not exist or are infrequent. In fact, in our research with nearly 200 maltreating families, we have found that three-quarters of the families had more than one subtype of maltreatment in the Child Protective records. The most common pattern was a combination of Physical Abuse, Physical Neglect, and Emotional Maltreatment.

Researchers faced with such high rates of co-morbidity have several alternatives for conducting research on subtypes. One approach would be to categorize families according to the predominant subtype and overlook the existence of additional subtypes in the family history. Another possibility would be to include only those families who were characterized by a single subtype. A third method would be to statistically control for the potential confound of multiple subtype occurrence. Alternately, one could create multiple groupings of different combinations of subtypes (e. g., Physical Abuse alone, Physical Abuse with Sexual Abuse, Physical Abuse with Neglect, Physical Abuse with Sexual Abuse and Neglect, etc.). Any one of these approaches runs the risk of producing results that are inconsistent across studies, that are difficult to interpret, and/or that cannot be generalized to the larger heterogeneous population. Unfortunately, funding agencies and other professionals who are unfamiliar with maltreatment research may exert some pressure to oversimplify the natural complexities of such research without an appreciation of the empirical risks. Consequently, maltreatment research often loses funding because grant reviewers do not accept the ambiguities present in the assessment of maltreatment. An even greater risk of artificially reducing subtype overlap is that results of such research would be misleading or misinterpreted by the professionals and policy makers who must make decisions on these issues. Policy decisions based on overgeneralizations of unrepresentative samples could result in intervention that is not in the best interests of the clients who are being affected.

In order to develop a more complete understanding of maltreatment subtypes, a clear, operationally defined comprehensive method of identifying and delineating separate subtypes is needed that can be communicated across research laboratories and professional lines (Besharov, 1981). Such a system should identify multiple subtypes when they occur, but it should also carefully define the inclusion and exclusion criteria for each subtype so that confounds can be minimized as much as possible. Descriptive information characterizing the sample should be included in published studies, and this information could aid in interpretation of the results. The use of such detailed data in large longitudinal studies would allow researchers to explore the contributions of each of the different subtypes and combinations of subtypes to etiology, sequelae, and treatment responses.

In pursuit of this goal, our system provides clear, semantic definitions, inclusion and exclusion criteria, and exemplars for each subtype. The subtypes that are included in our taxonomy are Physical Neglect (which is composed of Failure to Provide and Lack of Supervision), Physical Abuse, Sexual Abuse, Emotional Maltreatment, and Moral/Legal/Educational Maltreatment. These subtypes were derived from distinctions within the maltreatment literature, and they are widely recognized as separate phenomena. We drew especially from the seminal work of Giovannoni and Becerra (1979) in the development of the subtype definitions. However, we collapsed some of the categories that were present in Giovannoni and Becerra's work in order to be parsimonious and to facilitate data analysis. For example, our *Failure to Provide* category includes failure to meet the child's nutritional, medical, or cleanliness needs. Giovannoni and Becerra (1979) had laymen and professionals rate the three areas separately; they found that the areas tended to be treated similarly by raters, and therefore clustered together in analyses. That is, failure to provide for these basic physical needs seemed to be conceptually similar and were grouped together. Thus, our

Failure to Provide subtype encompasses parental neglect of the child's need for food, clothing, shelter, medical care, and adequate hygiene.

An alternate form of Physical Neglect, the *Lack of Supervision* subtype, was viewed as particularly important because of its frequent occurrence in Child Protective records and because of the paucity of research on the subtype. Because inadequate supervision is qualitatively different from failing to meet the child's physical needs (Zuravin, 1991), and it was viewed as conceptually distinct by the professionals in Giovannoni and Becerra's studies, Lack of Supervision was defined as a separate subcategory of Physical Neglect. Lack of Supervision includes either leaving a child unattended or in the care of an inadequate caregiver, such as someone with a known history of violent acts toward children. The category has been difficult to develop because few standards exist regarding the age at which it is appropriate to leave a child alone, and the culturally approved strictures seem to be changing as "latch-key children" are becoming more and more common. Additionally, Lack of Supervision is one type of maltreatment in which endangering the child is at issue rather than actual harm that a child has sustained. In fact, some have argued that Lack of Supervision should not be considered maltreatment, because no injury is sustained (see JJSP, 1977, discussed earlier).

In our definition of Lack of Supervision, we have included factors that pose a risk to the child, whether or not physical injury resulted. These risk factors include the length of time the child is unattended, the hazards present in the environment, and the individual needs of the child, such as a history of dangerous or destructive actions suggesting a need for more intensive supervision. The child's developmental period is also an important consideration, and we have included consideration of the child's developmental needs in the criteria for some severity levels within Lack of Supervision. In addition, developmental period is assessed separately, as will be discussed in a section that follows.

The subtype that is most easily documented and the most frequently studied is *Physical Abuse*. This subtype is scored whenever a caregiver inflicts a physical injury to the child by other than accidental means. Whereas extreme forms of physical abuse are generally regarded as maltreatment, the lower boundaries of the category are more controversial because of the acceptance of corporal punishment in this country (Giovannoni & Becerra, 1979). Typically, Child Protective reports of excessive corporal punishment are not substantiated unless an injury to the child has been sustained.

Another subtype that has a fairly sizable literature associated with it is *Sexual Abuse*. Sexual Abuse has been seen as a qualitatively different form of maltreatment, because sexual relationships between adults and children are viewed as being socially taboo, and a wide consensus exists that identifies this type of maltreatment as socially deviant (Garbarino, 1991; Giovannoni & Becerra, 1979). Although this subtype has received empirical attention, sexual abuse is rarely studied in conjunction with other subtypes.

By far the most problematic and difficult subtype to define is that of *Emotional Maltreatment*. As previously mentioned, the special issue of *Development and Psychopathology* highlights the struggle that is underway in the field to operationalize and quantify the many ways in which psychological interactions between parents and children can negatively impact children's social and emotional development (McGee & Wolfe, 1991a, b). In our system, Emotional Maltreatment was conceptualized as those acts that were judged by Child Protective Services to be instances of maltreatment that involved thwarting of children's basic emotional needs. These needs included needs for psychological safety and security in the environment, for acceptance and positive regard, and for age-appropriate autonomy, with sufficient opportunities to explore the environment and extrafamilial relationships. We did not separate subtypes within Emotional Maltreatment, but we included the dimensions that have been identified by Garbarino et al. (1986) and Hart and Brassard (1987). Additionally, we recognize that, because our classification system uses Child Protective records, there are likely to be family dynamics that constitute Emotional Maltreatment that are unavailable in the records. Nevertheless, we felt it was critical to document and analyze the psychological elements that were contained in the reports. We restricted the category to exclude other subtypes of maltreatment. While we agree with others (Brassard, Germain, & Hart, 1987; Garbarino et al., 1986; Hart & Brassard, 1991) that all forms of maltreatment contain an emotional component, for research purposes we and others (e. g., McGee & Wolfe, 1991a) have felt it necessary to restrict the amount of confounding among subtypes as much as possible.

The *Moral/Legal/Educational Maltreatment* subtype subsumes Giovannoni and Becerra's (1979) Moral/Legal, School, and Drugs, Alcohol categories. These were all felt to be areas that undermine the child's adequate socialization to society and that may foster delinquency. This subtype includes a child's being exposed to illegal activities through the participation of household members, and involvement in illegal activities as a result of lack of adult intervention or because of encouragement or coercion by the adult. Additionally, the failure of the caregiver to provide for the child's adequate education also is included in this category. Failing to send a child to school also was considered to be a means of missocializing the child and hampering the child's integration into the expectations of society. Educational neglect can be identified independently or combined with Moral/Legal maltreatment. In our research to date, we have combined the groups because infrequent occurrence of these subtypes has resulted in samples that are too small to be analyzed separately.

Based on definitional criteria for each of these subtypes, parental acts of maltreatment are scored for each subtype present in our taxonomy. This approach permits the recording of overlapping categories directly. Each report of maltreatment was transcribed from the narrative description of the incident plus the determination made by the Child Protective investigator following the investigation of the report. Each report was evaluated for the presence of every subtype. A single report could contain elements of many different subtypes. For example, a child may have been beaten during an episode of molestation, in which case both Physical and Sexual Abuse would be scored. By identifying each type of maltreatment that occurred for the families in our research, we can explore the heterogeneity inherent in the sample and examine the various combinations of subtypes empirically.

The results of several studies conducted in our laboratory suggest that different subtypes of maltreatment are associated with different developmental patterns. For example, Kaufman and Cicchetti (1989) found that physically abused children were rated as more aggressive with peers than were non-physically-abused maltreated children or nonmaltreated children. Furthermore, in a study of vulnerability to childhood depression among children with multiple subtypes of maltreatment, Toth, Manly, and Cicchetti (1992) found that children from physically abusive families differed significantly from children from either neglectful or nonmaltreating families. Those children who lived in abusive homes evidenced significantly more depressive symptomatology than either children in the neglect group or in the comparison group. A significantly greater percentage of children in the physical abuse group exhibited depression scores high enough to reach criteria for clinical depression than in either of the other two groups. Additionally, children from physically abusive homes evidenced significantly lower self-esteem than nonmaltreated children. Thus, evidence is accumulating that the subtype of maltreatment that children experience may differentially affect their development (see also, for example, the findings of Egeland, Sroufe, & Erickson, 1983; Erickson, Egeland, & Pianta, 1989; Hoffman-Plotkin & Twentyman, 1984; Kaufman, 1991; Kent, 1976; and Reidy, 1977).

Other researchers have found that the subtype of maltreatment was related to familial interactional patterns. For example, Burgess and Conger (1978) found that abusive and neglectful families had different family patterns in areas such as the frequency of positive and negative interactions with the children and the roles of mothers and fathers in the family. Abusive parents were noted for their infrequent verbal and physical interactions with their children, whereas neglecting parents were especially negative and had very few positive interactions with their children. Additionally, Crittenden (1988) found that abusing mothers were more controlling with their children, whereas neglecting mothers were more unresponsive. She found differences in the patterns of attachment, and in the behavior of abused versus neglect children.

Familial interactions that accompany different maltreatment subtypes may mediate the developmental outcome of maltreated children. Our research is beginning to explore not only the direct impact of maltreatment subtypes on child development, but also the process by which maltreatment exerts its negative effects. Therefore, we are examining the relations of maltreatment subtypes to child outcome, to familial interaction patterns, and to the interaction of family and child variables.

Clinical experience and research findings with maltreating families have suggested that specific acts of maltreatment happen within a variety of familial contexts. For example, Physical Abuse may occur within a family environment characterized by rigidity and by a strong emphasis on structure and strict discipline. It also may take place in homes in which disordered, chaotic, and undisciplined patterns are more prevalent. The preliminary results of our research indicate that the context within which the maltreatment occurs is as important as the act of maltreatment for understanding the impact that maltreatment subtypes have on children's developmental outcomes (Barnett, Manly, & Cicchetti, 1992). Consequently, maltreatment research must continue to move in the direction of investigating the reciprocal interactions and transactional processes within the family system (Cicchetti & Howes, 1991). The subtype of maltreatment that children experience may affect their future adaptation directly, or there may be indirect effects associated with the interactional patterns present in the family. Empirical investigations must address parental and child individual behaviors as well as the family dynamics, including discrete episodes of maltreatment and enduring familial styles. Clear definitions of maltreatment subtypes are essential for understanding the interface among family environment, parental acts of maltreatment, and the effects of child outcome.

2. Severity. As previously discussed, many of the clinical decisions in maltreatment cases are based on the assumption that more severe instances of maltreatment are worse for the child victims and lead to more deleterious consequences. However, research on the relationship between severity of maltreatment and child outcome is virtually nonexistent. Such research is necessary for informing policy decisions because legal intervention may be affected by the seriousness of the maltreating act.

One major obstacle to the investigation of differential sequelae by severity is the difficulty in quantifying the seriousness of an event with regard to its potential psychological impact. It is obvious that a minor bruise is less severe than a fatal injury, but evaluating finer grain distinctions in the middle of the continuum is a much more difficult task. Additionally, quantifying the level of severity is especially complex for subtypes in which endangerment is involved rather than documented harm. With regard to emotional maltreatment, little agreement exists over the definition of the subtype, and research is only in an early phase. In some cases the distinctions in levels of severity are difficult to establish because there are no standards of appropriate behavior. The Lack of Supervision subtype is particularly problematic because few guidelines exist for determining the age at which a child may be left unsupervised, or the age at which a child may supervise younger children. In the few maltreatment studies that have included an assessment of severity, researchers have taken different approaches to rating the seriousness of an incident. Severity has been determined by child outcome (Claussen & Crittenden, 1991; Kazdin, Moser, Colbus, & Bell, 1985), or by checklists or scales (Giovannoni & Becerra, 1979; Kaufman, 1991; McGee & Wolfe, 1989). In our system, we have established an ordinal scale of severity for each subtype of maltreatment that is based primarily on the parental act. Several authors have noted the importance of separately identifying the definition of maltreatment and the psychological sequelae in order to avoid a tautology (McGee & Wolfe, 1991a; Zuravin, 1991).

While we were careful to assess maltreatment and child psychological outcome independently, the child's physical condition was included in the severity scales of our system in the cases of Physical Abuse and Failure to Provide. Thus, if the parent inflicted a third-degree burn to the child, that act would be rated as more severe than causing minor bruising. The physical condition of the child is one indication of the force with which a child was physically attacked and/or the extent of physical deprivation the child experienced. We are interested in studying the resulting impact on the child's socioemotional development, which is assessed separately from the child's maltreatment history or physical health.

At each point on the continuum of severity, we have provided descriptors as well as examples that illustrate what was meant at each level. Because every possible act of maltreatment could not be included in the scale, the descriptors are intended to be viewed as anchors of the level of harshness needed for coding at each level; coders can then make decisions about where on the scale a particular event is best suited. The examples were drawn from the case records of the families in our original sample and provide guidelines for events that are found more commonly in the records. Each report of maltreatment is evaluated for severity within each subtype, and then summary variables of the average and most severe ratings for each subtype are calculated for each child and family. (See the Appendix for a description of the maltreatment definitions and severity ratings of our Maltreatment Classification System.)

In our research, a wide range of severity has been found for each subtype. With the exception of the most severe Physical Abuse ratings, we have families in our samples representing each point of the continuum of severity within each subtype. The most severe forms of Physical Abuse are not present because fatal or permanently disabling injuries would preclude the longitudinal assessments of child outcome that are conducted separately.

Preliminary results of our research have indicated that there are some relations between severity of maltreatment and family environment (Barnett et al., 1992). More severe Physical Abuse is associated with increased parental emphasis on achievement, control, and morality within the family. Severity of Physical Neglect was related to the degree of family disorganization. However, we have not found direct relations between severity of maltreatment and child outcome. Within the maltreated group, those who had experienced less severe maltreatment were impacted equally adversely to those who had experienced more severe forms of maltreatment. This pattern was true for children who had been physically abused, physically neglected, and who had been both abused and neglected. Nonetheless, there were significant differences in child outcome between children who had been maltreated as opposed to low-income comparison children who had not been maltreated. It is possible that as our research proceeds, we will uncover differences according to severity of maltreatment, using multidomain assessments of stage-salient developmental issues. It also is possible, given our initial results, that mild forms of maltreatment exert a powerful effect on children's adjustment.

A failure to find significant differences within the dimension of severity may be equally relevant to social policy decisions. As budget cuts impinge on available resources, it is likely that services will be curtailed for all but the most severe cases of maltreatment. This strategy could lead to an unfortunate omission of intervention if, indeed, relatively minor forms of maltreatment have enduring deleterious consequences but services become increasingly unavailable. A narrowing of the definition of maltreatment to include only the severe end of the continuum may be overlooking a substantial number of maltreated children who also suffer deleterious psychological developmental consequences (Claussen & Crittenden, 1991; McGee & Wolfe, 1989).

3. Frequency/chronicity. Another dimension that is assessed within our system involves the amount of time that a family has been experiencing maltreatment concerns. The maltreatment experience may range from a single isolated event to a chronic pattern with repeated instances of dysfunction across decades within the family. The time period of the maltreatment also may interact with the severity such that a single, very serious incident may be considered maltreatment, but a less severe act can be considered maltreating only if it occurs repeatedly or in a chronic pattern (Zuravin, 1991). In our system, the time dimension is assessed in two ways, by documenting the frequency and chronicity of the maltreatment. The *Frequency* is measured using the number of indicated Child Protective reports that are made regarding a family. In our research, maltreating families have received between 1 and 27 separate reports of maltreating acts, suggesting that there is considerable variability along this dimension.

The *Chronicity* of the maltreatment is assessed by the amount of time the family has been actively monitored by Child Protective Services. Our samples have included families with anywhere from 1 month to 23 years of active Child Protective involvement. An initial examination of the data on maltreating families has revealed that families with prolonged Child Protective involvement were more disengaged, more disorganized, less interested in morality, and had more family conflict than families with acute CPS involvement (Barnett et al., 1992). We also have found significant differences between chronic and acutely maltreating families in their level of stress and perceptions of support, factors that may have important potentiating or buffering effects in the etiology of maltreatment (Cicchetti & Barnett, 1991; Cicchetti & Rizley, 1981).

Our experience has suggested that the amount of time that a family is active with Child Protective services may be impacted by funding considerations as well. Often Child Protective services will end with cases when caseloads become too great, with the less severe or more resistant cases being the first to be terminated. In many cases that we have been following clinically, Child Protective monitoring ends when a referral is made to another agency, even though the children's welfare continues to be a significant concern. Thus, fiscal realities may impinge on adequate coverage of maltreating families, resulting in premature termination for some needy families.

4. Developmental period. A fourth dimension within our classification system is the developmental period of the child. The child's developmental period is critical for several reasons. For one, decisions concerning whether or not an act constitutes maltreatment may be affected by the child's developmental stage. As previously mentioned, an act that is maltreating for an infant may not be considered maltreatment for an adolescent, and vice versa. Zuravin (1991) points out that this is especially true for failing to provide adequate supervision. The amount of supervision that is necessary depends on the child's age and developmental capabilities. Additionally, certain forms of emotional maltreatment are affected by the child's developmental needs (Garbarino et al., 1986). For example, isolating an adolescent from peer experiences is detrimental given the stage-salient importance of forming relationships outside of the family. In contrast, preventing an infant from interacting with peers could not be considered emotional maltreatment. For other subtypes of maltreatment, age is not as critical for determining whether an event can be considered maltreatment. Physical abuse is recognized as maltreatment across developmental periods. It should be recognized, however, that the consequences of the physical abuse could be different for children of different ages.

Much of the developmental research that has been conducted with maltreated children has examined the impact of maltreatment on early developmental issues, particularly in infancy and early childhood (Cicchetti, 1989; Erickson et al., 1989). A body of research has been growing within the field of attachment that examines the impact of maltreatment on attachment relationships and related constructs (Crittenden & Ainsworth, 1989). The results that are emerging from prospective longitudinal studies of maltreatment suggest that the consequences of maltreatment manifest themselves differently as a function of age and context (Cicchetti, 1989; Erickson et al., 1989). Thus it is crucial to assess stage-salient developmental issues using measures that are developmentally sensitive. Assessing the ways in which the sequelae of maltreatment are manifest at different developmental stages is critical to understanding the phenomenon.

A separate but related question pertains to whether maltreatment has a differential impact depending on the child's developmental stage at the time of the incident. The same act of maltreatment could affect children differently, at least in part because of the way the act would be interpreted and understood by the child. These different perceptions would be influenced by the child's developmental stage. The way the maltreatment is viewed by society also changes in relation to the child's age. Physical abuse of an adolescent is perceived differently than the same type of abuse perpetrated against a younger child (Garbarino, 1989). Very little research has been conducted on the consequences of maltreatment with regard to when the maltreatment occurred developmentally. One complicating factor is that, in cases of chronic family dysfunction, it becomes difficult to tease apart the impact of developmental issues from the chronicity of the maltreatment. Maltreatment that occurs over several developmental stages may be more deleterious, but the impact may be greater, not because it impacts multiple developmental stages, but because of longer duration or more frequent acts of maltreatment. In other words, it may be that the cumulative or multiplicative effects of chronic maltreatment result in more harm, regardless of the timing of the acts.

Another impediment for conducting developmental research on maltreatment is the heterogeneity of the phenomenon, which makes it difficult to find large enough samples of certain types of maltreatment that occur at specific developmental periods. Despite the difficulties in conducting developmental research, it is imperative that developmental issues be examined more systematically.

In our research, we have addressed developmental issues in two ways. In our classification system, we have carefully recorded the age at which each report of maltreatment occurred for each child. We have tracked the developmental periods for each subtype of maltreatment. Additionally, we have assessed many stage-salient issues, including aspects of socioemotional development that are relevant as they emerge in development as well as through the life span. These have included attachment relationships, emotional regulation, perceptions of the self, cognitive organization, friendship and peer relationships, language development, moral reasoning, and symptoms of psychopathology (see Cicchetti & Manly, 1990, for an elaboration of our measurement domains and constructs). By measuring both the ages at which the children were maltreated and their mastery of developmental issues, we will be able to begin to explore the relationships between when the maltreatment occurred and its impact on the emergence of stage-salient aspects of development.

5. **Separations/placements.** A fifth dimension that is assessed in our classification system is the history of separations that the children have experienced from their primary caregivers. Court intervention in maltreating families often results in foster care or other out-of-home placements, such as placing the child in a relative's custody or in a residential treatment facility. Difficult decisions are required in such circumstances regarding whether removal is the best solution. Although removal from the home may temporarily ensure the child's safety, such separations from primary caregivers also may have a deleterious impact on the child's functioning and the mastery of developmental tasks, such as the formation of a secure attachment relationship (Goldstein et al., 1973). It is likely that

much of the research that is conducted with maltreated children consists of at least some percentage of children who have experienced such separations; however, this information is rarely reported or examined empirically. Systematic recording of information related to out-of-home placements is included in our system as a means of exploring the issues related to such separations. It is difficult to conduct controlled research involving foster care placements because of the ethical constraints that prevent empirical experimentation (Wald, Carlsmith, & Leiderman, 1988). Often research on placements is confounded with severity of maltreatment and other factors; however, empirical investigations are essential for determining the best means of intervening and for improving the efficacy of placements when they occur. The information that is collected in our system includes the number of placements that have occurred, the number of months of separation, and the type of placement. Additionally, the developmental period of the child at the time of placement is assessed in order to examine the impact of the separation on attachment relationships and other stage-salient developmental tasks. In our longitudinal research, approximately one-third of the maltreating families have had at least one child placed in foster care.

6. Perpetrator. The identity of the perpetrator affects the definition of maltreatment as well as the impact that the act has on the child's development. Whether a narrow or broad definition of perpetrator is adopted influences the inclusion criteria for maltreating acts. Under a narrow definition, only acts committed by the primary caretaker would be considered maltreatment, whereas a broad definition could include alternate adults in the home, such as babysitters, as well as adults in other settings, such as school personnel, or group home staff members. Additionally, the identity of the perpetrator, particularly the relationship between the perpetrator and the child, could influence the meaning that the maltreating act has for the child. For example, if the maltreatment were committed by a known and trusted primary caregiver, it could be perceived differently than if it were committed by a stranger or less familiar babysitter. The identity of the perpetrator may interact with the subtype of maltreatment, as well. Zuravin (1991) recommends adopting a broad definition for certain subtypes (Physical Abuse) and a narrow definition for others (Physical Neglect). She asserts that anyone who physically abuses a child is endangering his or her welfare, although the psychological sequelae may vary according to the identity of the perpetrator; however, because it is the parents' responsibility to provide for the care of their children, and because the parents are responsible for insuring that alternate substitute care is provided when they are not directly caring for their child, in most cases, the parents should be considered the perpetrator(s) if the child's physical needs are not met.

It also is possible for someone outside the family to perpetrate the abuse (e.g., to molest a child), but also for the primary caregiver to be implicated for allowing the child to have contact with the perpetrator, especially if the perpetrator had a known history of violent or sexual acts toward children. Our system includes identifying the perpetrator(s) of each report of maltreatment. New York State Child Protective reports are limited by a narrow definition of perpetrator because individuals who commit maltreating acts who are not primary or substitute caregivers are prosecuted through criminal court, and unless the primary caregiver is also implicated, the report may be investigated through the police department rather than through Child Protective Services. Nevertheless, information regarding the perpetrator is an important component of the maltreatment incident that requires additional empirical attention.

SUMMARY AND POLICY IMPLICATIONS

In this chapter we have examined political, social, economic, and scientific factors that shape definitions of child maltreatment. We have presented a history of changing conceptions of child abuse and neglect by describing how definitions have been influenced by these processes. We then presented our work on developing clearly delineated definitions of several forms of child maltreatment and the applications of a classification system to the study of the etiology and sequelae of child abuse and neglect.

An implicit theme that runs through this chapter is that maltreatment definitions are not static. There will never be a final definition of maltreatment that will be satisfying to professionals and families, and that will remain relevant to future generations. This statement, however, applies principally to the "grey area" that lies between insensitive parenting and outright abuse and neglect. Relative agreement has been achieved concerning many grossly deleterious acts that are considered child maltreatment by the majority of past and present societies. These commonalities should not be trivialized. Rather, they should be systematically delineated, and then act as guidelines from which debate may extend out to more controversial areas. Our working definitions represent an effort to reach these goals.

Our presentation also points to a mounting paradox. That is, scientists have been successful in increasing our knowledge of child maltreatment, but our nation has been comparatively unsuccessful in benefitting from this progress. While there are many essential questions research must address, we now know more than any other generation about the prevalence of child maltreatment, its many manifestations, its causes, and its consequences. Yet despite this knowledge, we are still subject to the same political and economic tides that constrain our ability to act on our knowledge. As this chapter was being written, the combination of the current economic slump and the defeat of the incumbent county executive resulted in the elimination of the local child abuse reporting hotline. In addition, our clinical experiences have demonstrated that parental acts that would have been considered to be maltreatment by Child Protective Services (CPS) in the late 1980s are now being viewed to be too minor to warrant the time and money required for investigation. These events are simple yet powerful examples of how economic and political winds can paralyze and turn back progress that has been achieved in the fields of social science and public health.

A desired goal of this chapter is that efforts could be made to uncouple the coercive effects of economics on efforts to help maltreating and at risk families. As we move toward the 21st century, American demographics concerning family structure, income level, parental availability, and education are all rapidly shifting in a direction proven to be associated with increased susceptibility to child maltreatment. Unless national investments in children are made an explicit financial priority, incidents of child maltreatment and its insidious correlates of school drop-out, substance abuse, criminal activity and psychopathology will continue to increase in epidemic proportions. While protecting our children and promoting their optimal development is clearly a humane endeavor, it also is an essential investment in our nation's economic future. Preventive and protective efforts in childhood will translate directly into dollars saved through decreased psychopathology and increased productivity when these children reach adulthood (see, for example, Daro, this volume; Dubowitz, 1986; Hewlett, 1991; Institute of Medicine, 1989; and Schorr, 1988). Consequently, legislators and private sector entrepreneurs who espouse more of a "survival of the fittest" philosophy should consider investing in children to be more crucial to our nation's competitiveness than short-term monetary outlays in, for example, tobacco industry subsidies and junk bonds. Key to securing monies for research and intervention for child maltreatment will be the establishment of lobbyist groups for children with the same degree of representation, organization, and power as groups such as the National Rifle Association, and the American Association of Retired Persons.

One step toward severing the negative impact of the economy on the protection of children would be to establish very detailed, well-operationalized definitions of child abuse and neglect, as well as systematized efforts to investigate, document, and eradicate its presence. By establishing clear maltreatment definitions, we could guard the grey area around the less severe end of maltreatment that is typically disregarded during economic crunches and cutbacks. As preliminary research described in this chapter suggests, children who have been subjected to comparatively less severe forms of maltreatment nonetheless may exhibit higher rates of behavior problems than nonmaltreated children. Consequently, decisions concerning whether or not families receive services must not be based simply on the severity of the maltreatment incident (e.g., bruises versus broken bones). Rather, our initial findings suggest that protective service workers also should consider the overall parenting context within which the maltreatment occurs. Additionally, systematized definitional criteria may facilitate increased funding for maltreatment research by improving the scientific rigor necessary to satisfy funding agencies.

Once systematized, clearly worded, operationalized definitions have been established, they should be used by CPS investigators as well as by researchers. From this common ground and language, research and CPS investigations can precede with systematic feedback from these efforts being utilized to update and amend definitions in a manner that is based on objective data. The effects of variables such as unemployment rates, budget cuts, and political debates on our definitions of maltreatment should be minimized. Progress toward more useful definitions should proceed in a more planful, linear fashion. A model in which feedback from research and practical application can be employed to update definitions is presented in Figure 4. Our initial definitions are based on areas of agreement, of which there are many. Our next step is to begin to work toward wider use of these standardized definitions by researchers and practitioners. From this more unified perspective, we can begin to tackle more ambiguous issues such as those pertaining to less severe forms of abuse and neglect, as well as more controversial forms of maltreatment such as lack of supervision, psychological maltreatment, and prenatal drug use.

Particularly difficult and essential will be incorporating developmental considerations into definitions of child maltreatment. Clearly, much debate and research is needed in this area. Issues such as how long a child can be left unattended safely at various ages are simple, common examples of the kind of developmental concerns that have received scant empirical and legal attention. Part of the reason developmental questions largely have been unaddressed in the definitional literature is due to the complexity inherent in introducing a developmental dimension. However, developmental issues can no longer be ignored.

Standardizing and unifying our definitions of child maltreatment reflect fundamental steps toward improving our research and hence our knowledge base about abuse and neglect. Systematized definitions also represent an essential aspect of ensuring consistent services to children in need. Indispensable to meeting these and other goals outlined in this chapter is the establishment of increased and consistent funding for programmatic research and treatment. We can no longer allow resources directed toward the amelioration of child abuse and neglect to be disrupted by trendy decisions about funding priorities. We have

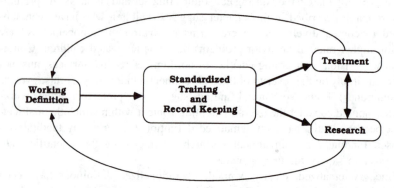

Figure 4. Model System for Revising Definitions of Child Maltreatment

made excellent progress toward understanding maltreatment and thereby combating it. Continued progress requires a sustained commitment by our society.

REFERENCES

Aber, J. L., & Cicchetti, D. (1984). Socioemotional development in maltreated children: An empirical and theoretical analysis. In H. Fitzgerald, B. Lester, & M. Yogman (Eds.), *Theory and research in behavioral pediatrics* (Vol. 2. pp. 147–205). New York: Plenum Press.

Aber, J. L., & Zigler, E. (1981). Developmental considerations in defining child maltreatment. In R. Rizley & D. Cicchetti (Eds.), *Developmental perspectives in child maltreatment: New Directions for child development* (pp. 1–29). San Francisco: Jossey-Bass.

Achenback, T. M. (1990). Conceptualization of developmental psychopathology. In M. Lewis & S. M. Miller (Eds.), *Handbook of developmental psychopathology* (pp. 3–14). New York: Plenum Press.

Alvy, K. T. (1975). Preventing child abuse. *American Psychologist, 30,* 921–928.

Aries, P. (1962). *Centuries of childhood.* New York: Vintage Books.

Barnett, D., Ganiban, J., & Cicchetti, D. (1992, May). *Emotional reactivity, regulation, and attachment organization in children with Type D attachments: A longitudinal analysis across 12-, 18-, and 24-months of age.* Paper presented at the 8th biennial meeting of the International Conference on Infant Studies, Miami, FL.

Barnett, D., Manly, J. T., & Cicchetti, D. (1991). Continuing toward an operational definition of psychological maltreatment. *Development and Psychopathology, 3,* 19–29.

Barnett, D., Manly, J. T., & Cicchetti, D. (1992). *Operational definitions of child maltreatment: An empirical analysis.* Manuscript in preparation.

Belsky, J. (1980). Child maltreatment: An ecological integration. *American Psychologist, 35,* 320–335.

Besharov, D. (1981). Toward better research on child abuse and neglect: Making definitional issues an explicit methodological concern. *Child Abuse and Neglect, 5,* 383–389.

Bishop, S. J., Murphy, J. M., Jellinek, M. S., Quinn, D., & Poitrast, F. G. (in press). Protecting seriously mistreated children: Time delays in a court sample. *Child Abuse & Neglect.*

Brassard, M. R., Germain, R., & Hart, S. N. (Eds.). (1987). *Psychological maltreatment of children and youth.* New York: Pergamon Press.

Breiner, S. J. (1990). *Slaughter of the innocents: Child abuse through the ages and today.* New York: Plenum Press.

Bronfenbrenner, U. (1979). *The ecology of human development: Experiments by nature and design.* Cambridge, MA: Harvard University Press.

Burgess, R. L., & Conger, R. D. (1978). Family interaction in abusive, neglectful, and normal families. *Child Development, 49,* 1163–1173.

Children's Defense Fund. (1979). *Children without homes: An examination of public responsibility to children in out-of-home care.* Washington, DC: Children's Defense Fund.

Cicchetti, D. (1989). How research on child maltreatment has informed the study of child development: Perspectives from developmental psychopathology. In D. Cicchetti & V. Carlson (Eds.), *Child maltreatment: Theory and research on the causes and consequences of child abuse and neglect* (pp. 377–431). New York: Cambridge University Press.

Cicchetti, D. (1990). A historical perspective on the discipline of developmental psychopathology. In J. Rolf, A. S. Masten, D. Cicchetti, K. H. Nuechterlein, & S. Weintraub (Eds.), *Risk and protective factors in the development of psychopathology* (pp. 2–28). New York: Cambridge University Press.

Cicchetti, D. (Ed.). (1991). Special issue: Defining psychological maltreatment. *Development and Psychopathology, 3*(1).

Cicchetti, D., & Aber, J. L. (1980). Abused children-abusive parents: An overstated case? *Harvard Educational Review, 50*, 244–255.

Cicchetti, D., & Barnett, D. (1991). Toward the development of a scientific nosology of child maltreatment. In W. Grove & D. Cicchetti (Eds.), *Thinking clearly about psychology: Essays in honor or Paul E. Meehl, Volume 2: Personality and psychopathology* (pp. 346–377). Minneapolis: University of Minnesota Press.

Cicchetti, D., & Carlson, V. (Eds.). (1989). *Child maltreatment: Theory and research on the causes and consequences of child abuse and neglect.* New York: Cambridge University Press.

Cicchetti, D., Ganiban, J., & Barnett, D. (1991). Contributions to the study of high-risk populations to understanding the development of emotion regulation. In J. Garber & K. Dodge (Eds.), *The development of emotion regulation and dysregulation* (pp. 15–48). New York: Cambridge University Press.

Cicchetti, D., & Howes, P. (1991). Developmental psychopathology in the context of the family: Illustrations from the study of child maltreatment. *Canadian Journal of Behavioural Science, 23*, 257–281.

Cicchetti, D., & Manly, J. T. (1990). A personal perspective on conducting research on maltreating families: Problems and solutions. In G. H. Brody & I. E. Sigel (Eds.), *Methods of family research: Biographies of research projects, Volume 2: Clinical populations* (pp. 87–133). Hillsdale, NJ: Erlbaum.

Cicchetti, D., & Rizley, R. (1981). Developmental perspectives on the etiology, intergenerational transmission, and sequelae of child maltreatment. In R. Rizley & D. Cicchetti (Eds.), *Developmental perspectives in child maltreatment: New Directions for child development,* (Vol. II, pp. 31–55). San Francisco: Jossey-Bass.

Cicchetti, D., Taraldson, B., & Egeland, B. (1978). Perspectives in the treatment and understanding of child abuse. In A. Goldstein (Ed.), *Prescriptions for child mental health and education* (pp. 301–391). New York: Pergamon Press.

Claussen, A. H., & Crittenden, P. M. (1991). Physical and psychological maltreatment: Relations among types of maltreatment. *Child Abuse and Neglect, 15*, 5–18.

Crittenden, P. M. (1988). Relationships at risk. In J. Belsky & T. Nezworski (Eds.), *Clinical implications of attachment* (pp. 136–174). Hillsdale, NJ: Erlbaum.

Crittenden, P. M., & Ainsworth, M. D. S. (1989). Child maltreatment and attachment theory. In D. Cicchetti & V. Carlson (Eds.), *Child maltreatment: Theory and research on the causes and consequences of child abuse and neglect* (pp. 432–463). New York: Cambridge University Press.

Dubowitz, H. (1986). *Child maltreatment in the United States: Etiology, impact, and prevention.* Background paper prepared for the Congress of the United States, Office of Technology Assessment.

Egeland, B., Sroufe, L. A., & Erickson, M. (1983). The developmental consequence of different patterns of maltreatment. *Child Abuse & Neglect, 7*, 459–469.

Erickson, M. F., Egeland, B., & Pianta, R. (1989). The effects of maltreatment on the development of young children. In D. Cicchetti & V. Carlson (Eds.), *Child maltreatment: Theory and research on the causes and consequences of child abuse and neglect* (pp. 647–684). New York: Cambridge University Press.

Garbarino, J. (1976). A preliminary study of some ecological correlates of child abuse: The impact of socioeconomic stress on mothers. *Child Development, 47*, 178–185.

Garbarino, J. (1977). The human ecology of child maltreatment: A conceptual model for research. *Journal of Marriage and the Family, 39*, 721–735.

Garbarino, J. (1989). Troubled youth, troubled families: The dynamics of adolescent maltreatment. In D. Cicchetti & V. Carlson (Eds.), *Child maltreatment: Theory and research on the causes and consequences of child abuse and neglect* (pp. 685–706). New York: Cambridge University Press.

Garbarino, J. (1991). Not all bad developmental outcomes are the result of child abuse. *Development and Psychopathology, 3,* 45–50.

Garbarino, J., Guttman, E., & Seeley, J. W. (1986). *The psychologically battered child: Strategies for identification, assessment, and intervention.* San Francisco: Jossey-Bass.

Garbarino, J., & Sherman, D. (1980). High-risk neighborhoods and high-risk families: The human ecology of child maltreatment. *Child Development, 51,* 188–198.

Gaspar, J. (1980). Beating up on the family. *Conservative Digest, 6,* 36–41.

Gelles, R. J. (1973). Child abuse as psychopathology: A sociological critique and reformulation. *American Journal of Orthopsychiatry, 43,* 611–621.

Gelles, R. J. (1975). The social construction of child abuse. *American Journal of Orthopsychiatry, 45,* 363–371.

Gelles, R. J. (1992). Poverty and violence toward children. *American Behavioral Scientist, 35,* 258–274.

Gerbner, G., Ross, C. J., & Zigler, E. (Eds.). (1980). *Child abuse: An agenda for action.* New York: Oxford University Press.

Gil, D. (1970). *Violence against children: Physical child abuse in the United States.* Cambridge, MA: Harvard University Press.

Gil, D. G. (1975). Unraveling child abuse. *American Journal of Orthopsychiatry, 45,* 346–356.

Giovannoni, J. (1989). Definitional issues in child maltreatment. In D. Cicchetti & V. Carlson (Eds.), *Child maltreatment: Theory and research on the causes and consequences of child abuse and neglect* (pp. 3–37). New York: Cambridge University Press.

Giovannoni, J. (1991). Social policy considerations in defining psychological maltreatment. *Development and Psychopathology, 3,* 51–60.

Giovannoni, J. M., & Becerra, R. M. (1979). *Defining child abuse.* New York: The Free Press.

Goldstein, J., Freud, A., & Solnit, A. (1973). *Beyond the best interests of the child.* New York: The Free Press.

Hart, S. N., & Brassard, M. R. (1987). A major threat to children's mental health: Psychological maltreatment. *American Psychologist, 42,* 160–165.

Hart, S., & Brassard, M. (1991). Psychological maltreatment: Progress achieved. *Development and Psychopathology, 3,* 61–70.

Haugaard, J. J. (1991). Defining psychological maltreatment: A prelude to research or an outcome of research? *Development and Psychopathology, 3,* 71–78.

Hewlett, S. A. (1991). *When the bough breaks: The cost of neglecting our children.* New York: Basic Books.

Hoffman-Plotkin, D., & Twentyman, C. (1984). A multimodal assessment of behavioral and cognitive deficits in abused and neglected preschoolers. *Child Development, 55,* 794–802.

Hutchison, E. D. (1990). Child maltreatment: Can it be defined? *Social Service Review, 64,* 60–78.

Institute of Medicine. (1989). *Research on children and adolescents with mental, behavioral, and developmental disorders.* Washington, DC: National Academy Press.

Juvenile Justice Standards Project. (1977). *Standards relating to child abuse and neglect.* Cambridge, MA: Ballinger.

Kaufman, J. (1991). Depressive disorders in maltreated children. *American Journal of Child and Adolescent Psychiatry, 30,* 257–265.

Kaufman, J., & Cicchetti, D. (1989). The effects of maltreatment on school-aged children's socioemotional development: Assessments in a day camp setting. *Developmental Psychology, 25,* 516–524.

Kazdin, A. E., Moser, J., Colbus, D., & Bell, R. (1985). Depressive symptoms among physically abused and psychiatrically disturbed children. *Journal of Abnormal Psychology, 94,* 298–307.

Kempe, C. H., Silverman, F. N., Steele, B. B., Droegemueller, W., & Silver, H. K. (1962). The battered child syndrome. *Journal of the American Medical Association, 181,* 17–24.

Kent, J. (1976). A follow-up study of abused children. *Journal of Pediatric Psychology, 1*, 25–31.

Knudsen, D. D. (1988). *Child Protective Services: Discretion, decisions, dilemmas.* Springfield, IL: Charles C. Thomas Publisher.

Korbin, J. E. (Ed.). (1981). *Child abuse and neglect: Cross-cultural perspectives.* Berkeley, CA: University of California Press.

Lazoritz, S. (1990). Whatever happened to Mary Ellen? *Child Abuse and Neglect, 14,* 143–149.

Mauss, A. L., & Wolfe, J. C. (Eds.). (1977). *This land of promises: The rise and fall of social problems in America.* New York: J. B. Lippincott.

McGee, R. A., & Wolfe, D. A. (1989, April). *Psychological maltreatment: Conceptual and empirical definitions.* Paper presented at the biennial meeting of the Society for Research in Child Development, Kansas City.

McGee, R. A., & Wolfe, D. A. (1991a). Psychological maltreatment: Toward an operational definition. *Development and Psychopathology, 3,* 3–18.

McGee, R. A., & Wolfe, D. A. (1991b). Between a rock and a hard place: Where do we go from here in defining psychological maltreatment? *Development and Psychopathology, 3,* 119–124.

McGee, R. A., Wolfe, D. A., Yuen, S., & Carnochan, J. (1991, April). *The measurement of child maltreatment: A comparison of approaches.* Paper presented at the 1991 biennial meeting of the Society for Research in Child Development, Seattle.

Murphy, J. M., Jellinek, M., Quinn, D., Smith, G., Poitrast, F. G., & Gosho, M. (1991). Substance abuse and serious child mistreatment: Prevalence, risk, and outcome in a court sample. *Child Abuse & Neglect, 15,* 197–211.

Nelson, B. (1984). *Making an issue of child abuse: Political agenda setting for social problems.* Chicago: University of Chicago Press.

Newberger, C. M., & Cook, E. H. (1983). Parental awareness and child abuse: A cognitive developmental analysis of urban and rural samples. *American Journal of Orthopsychiatry, 53,* 512–524.

Pelton, L. (1978). Child abuse and neglect: The myth of classlessness. *American Journal of Orthopsychiatry, 48,* 608–617.

Philips, K. (1990). *The politics of rich and poor: Wealth in the American electorate in the Reagan aftermath.* New York: Harper Collins.

Pleck, E. (1987). *Domestic tyranny: The making of American social policy against family violence from colonial times to the present.* New York: Oxford University Press.

Radbill, S. X. (1968). A history of child abuse and infanticide. In R. E. Helfer & C. H. Kempe (Eds.), *The battered child* (pp. 3–20). Chicago: University of Chicago Press.

Reidy, T. J. (1977). The aggressive characteristics of abused and neglected children. *Journal of Clinical Psychology, 33,* 1140–1145.

Ross, C. J. (1980). The lessons of the past: Defining and controlling child abuse in the United States. In G. Gerbner, C. Ross, & E. Zigler (Eds.), *Child abuse: an agenda for action* (pp. 63–81). New York: Oxford University Press.

Ross, C. J., & Zigler, E. (1980). An agenda for action. In G. Gerbner, C. Ross, & E. Zigler (Eds.), *Child abuse: an agenda for action* (pp. 293–302). New York: Oxford University Press.

Schorr, L. B. (1988). *Within our reach: Breaking the cycle of disadvantage.* New York: Anchor Press.

Solnit, A. (1980). Too much reporting, too little service: Roots in prevention of child abuse. In G. Gerbner, C. Ross, & E. Zigler (Eds.), *Child abuse: An agenda for action* (pp. 135–146). New York: Oxford University Press.

Starr, R. H., Dubowitz, H., & Bush, B. A. (1990). The epidemiology of child maltreatment. In R. T. Ammerman & M. Hersen (Eds.), *Children at risk: An evaluation of factors contributing to child abuse and neglect* (pp. 23–53). New York: Plenum Press.

Steinberg, L. D., Catalano, R., & Dooley, D. (1981). Economic antecedents of child abuse and neglect. *Child Development, 52,* 975–985.

Thompson, R. A., & Jacobs, J. E. (1991). Defining psychological maltreatment: Research and policy perspectives. *Development and Psychopathology, 3,* 93–102.

Toth, S. L. (1991). Psychological maltreatment: Can an integration of research, policy, and intervention efforts be achieved? *Development and Psychopathology, 3,* 103–109.

Toth, S. L., Manly, J. T., & Cicchetti, D. (1992). Child maltreatment and vulnerability to depression. *Development and Psychopathology, 4,* 97–112.

United States Department of Health and Human Services. (1988). *Study findings: Study of national incidence and prevalence of child abuse and neglect* (DHHS Publication, No. (OHDS) 20-01099). Washington, DC: U. S. Government Printing Office.

Vonnegut, K. (1972). The big space fuck. In H. Ellison (Ed.), *Again, dangerous visions* (pp. 246–250). Garden City, NY: Doubleday & Company.

Wald, M. S. (1991). Defining psychological maltreatment: The relationship between questions and answers. *Development and Psychopathology, 3,* 111–118.

Wald, M. S., Carlsmith, J., & Leiderman, P. H. (1988). *Protecting abused/neglected children: A comparison of home and foster placement.* Palo Alto, CA: Stanford University Press.

Wolfe, D. A. (1985). Child-abusive parents: An empirical review and analysis. *Psychological Bulletin, 97,* 462–482.

Wolfe, D. A. (1987). *Child abuse: Implications for child development and psychopathology.* Newbury Park, CA: Sage.

Wolock, I., & Horowitz, B. (1984). Child maltreatment as a social problem: The neglect of neglect. *American Journal of Orthopsychiatry, 54,* 530–543.

Zigler, E. (1976). Controlling child abuse in America: An effort doomed to failure? In W. A. Collins (Ed.), *Newsletter of the Division on Developmental Psychology, American Psychological Association* (pp. 17–30). Washington, DC: American Psychological Association.

Zigler, E., & Hall, N. W. (1989). Physical child abuse in America: Past, present, and future. In D. Cicchetti & V. Carlson, (Eds.), *Child maltreatment: Theory and research on the causes and consequences of child abuse and neglect* (pp. 38–75). New York: Cambridge University Press.

Zuravin, S. J. (1991). Research definitions of child physical abuse and neglect: Current problems. In R. H. Starr & D. A. Wolfe (Eds.), *The effects of child abuse and neglect* (pp. 100–128). New York: Guilford Press.

APPENDIX
MALTREATMENT SUBTYPE DEFINITIONS AND SEVERITY RATINGS

Overview. In this appendix, we present our research definitions and severity ratings for six subtypes of maltreatment. The additional aspects of the Maltreatment Classification System (frequency/chronicity, developmental period, separations/placement, and perpetrator) are described in the accompanying chapter and presented in Figure 3. Additional information about these dimensions also may be obtained by contacting the authors. Within this appendix, the following subtypes of maltreatment are presented: Physical Abuse, Sexual Abuse, Physical Neglect - Failure to Provide, Physical Neglect - Lack of Supervision, Emotional Maltreatment, and Moral/Legal/Educational Maltreatment. Each subtype consists of a semantic definition with inclusion and exclusion criteria. These criteria specify (a) the general class of acts encompassed within each subtype, (b) the points that distinguish one subtype from another, and (c) the most common conditions under which two or more subtypes co-occur. For each of the six subtypes, we also included several examples to provide greater clarification of each domain.

The subtypes are not intended to be mutually exclusive. Every narrative report of an incident of maltreatment is evaluated for the presence of each subtype. A single report could contain characteristics of multiple subtypes. For example, an infant could be diagnosed with nonorganic failure-to-thrive as a result of the caregiver's failure to provide adequate nourishment to the child. Additionally, evidence of a shaken infant syndrome could be present. In this case both Physical Neglect - Failure to Provide and Physical Abuse would be scored. Descriptions are included of common points of overlap among subtypes to enable coders to determine when multiple subtypes should be scored and when the acts are best captured under a single subtype.

Each subtype contains five levels of severity. In our system, severity refers to the relative seriousness of the act with regard to the potential negative psychological impact that a caregiver's act may have on the child's socioemotional development. We acknowledge that on a case-by-case basis, individual instances will have idiosyncratic significance to particular children. At the same time, we wanted to provide guidelines that would allow for standardized estimation of the level of potential psychological impact. Empirical research will explore the relationships between the severity ratings and multiple domains of child development in order to assess the validity of the scale.

We have included descriptions and exemplars at each point along the continuum of severity for each subtype. This degree of operationalization assists coders in the difficult task of making more objective decisions regarding the level of severity. Consequently, they contribute to increasing consistency and interrater reliability.

The scales were designed to be used for categorizing case records from Child Protective Services (CPS), and they were intended to be flexible. Because it is impossible to catalogue all potential incidents of maltreatment, the scales were constructed to be both as specific as possible to promote consistent ''objective'' classifications and ratings, and general enough to provide coders with guidelines and leeway for evaluating unusual instances of maltreatment. Applying the scales to actual CPS records requires coders to have a thorough understanding of the system and to be able to apply the definitional criteria flexibly. Consequently, coding requires training to establish valid and reliable use of the scales. We are fully cognizant of the limitations of CPS records, in that at times they may contain relatively sparse details about an instance of maltreatment, making coding difficult. We have written the scales so that under these less than optimal conditions raters can still handle reports in a systematic manner. Similarly, the wording of the scales was written to be as clear as possible. However, some level of ambiguity will always remain given the criteria that the scales must be adaptable enough to handle unusual maltreatment phenomena as well as CPS records that may be unclear.

Purpose. The scales grew out of a well-established need for a standardized method of quantifying children's maltreatment experiences (Besharov, 1981; Cicchetti & Rizley, 1981). These needs are elaborated within our accompanying chapter. Thus, these operational definitions and severity scales were developed to record, quantify, and analyze systematically families' Child Protective Service records for developmental psychopathology research. These scales were developed for use with cases that CPS workers had already investigated and considered to be substantiated instances of child maltreatment.

It should be noted that the definitions were *not* developed for the purpose of making clinical or legal decisions pertaining to whether an act does or does not constitute maltreatment. How applicable these scales are for CPS investigations and decision making is an unanswered question, but one we believe is worth pursuing. To our knowledge, no clearly operationalized criteria exist to assist CPS workers. Consequently, CPS investigations are subject to inconsistencies and subjectivity in the decision-making process and in the documentation of child maltreatment. The utility and appropriateness of these scales for standardizing CPS investigations and record keeping requires careful assessment. Although we do not endorse their application to nonresearch functions, we do advocate that their utility for standardizing record keeping be evaluated. We believe that if the scales were used at the initial phase of the CPS investigation, they would contribute to the simplification and standardization of CPS documentation. A note of caution applies to the use of these scales for decision-making purposes because of the potential for misuse of the scales. For example, making a determination not to substantiate a report because it received a low ranking of severity would be a grave error. We believe that less severe acts may carry deleterious consequences for a child, and families engaging in acts of maltreatment across the range of severity may be in need of intervention.

"Developmental history" of the scales. A brief statement regarding the process of designing and writing the definitions and severity scales of maltreatment is in order. This brief review provides readers with a broader context within which to evaluate the operational definitions. We began developing the scales in 1987, and it was 5 years before we considered them to be publishable. In a true sense, the scales evolved through a series of many revisions driven by four primary sources of input and feedback: (a) their practical application to actual CPS records, (b) a careful study of the literature on defining child maltreatment, (c) a survey completed by professionals with expertise in child maltreatment of severity rankings for vignettes typical of examples in the records, and (d) a series of critiques by researchers and clinicians who specialize in work with maltreated children and families. Although we knew that this work was going to be difficult, we encountered subtle and pervasive intricacies in establishing operational definitions that we never anticipated. We often were amazed that CPS and legal services had never established standardized, nonambiguous guidelines for subtypes such as Lack of Supervision. Over time, we began to appreciate why few clearly operationalized definitions of maltreatment with sufficient detain existed in research or clinical practice. It is a Herculean task! However, we felt that the importance of the task justified facing the challenges involved. We have certainly learned a great deal along the way, and we plan to continue the task of capturing additional dimensions of family dynamics of maltreatment that are not present in CPS files. We would strongly encourage those interested in assessing and quantifying child maltreatment to expend equal effort in measuring the overall parenting context within which maltreatment occurs, including sensitive, supportive parenting that may be present within maltreating families.

Requests for materials. As with any paradigm used to assess complex constructs, additional revisions may be incorporated into the classification system as validation and reliability studies are completed. The goal of the system is to provide greater standardization of the assessment and quantification of maltreatment across research laboratories. Therefore, we request that individuals interested in using the definitions and scales contact one of the authors to arrange to receive training materials and consultation. Formalized training will facilitate communication and improve reliability across research laboratories. It also will provide the authors with a means for receiving feedback from professionals employing the system. Additionally, contacting the authors will ensure that the most current versions of the classification system are made available.

SYSTEM FOR QUANTIFYING CHILD PROTECTIVE SERVICE RECORDS SUBTYPE DEFINITIONS AND SEVERITY SCALES

Subtypes

1. Physical Abuse (PA)
2. Sexual Abuse (SA)
3. Failure to Provide (FTP, Physical Neglect)
4. Lack of Supervision (LOS, Physical Neglect)
5. Emotional Maltreatment (EM)
6. Moral/Legal/Educational Maltreatment (MLE)

Please note: Throughout the scales, 1 = least severe, 5 = most severe.

Physical Abuse

Physical Abuse is coded when a caregiver or responsible adult inflicts a physical injury upon a child by other than accidental means. Injury does not include culturally sanctioned physical alterations such as circumcision and ear piercing.

There are some situations in which the distinction between Physical Abuse and other subtypes becomes ambiguous. The following criteria are provided as guidelines to assist coders in making these distinctions. Physical restraint is typically scored under Emotional Maltreatment. However, in cases in which a child incurs physical injuries when the parent is attempting to restrain the child (e.g., rope burns), then the injury would be scored as Physical Abuse, and the restraint would also be scored under Emotional Maltreatment. If the caregiver threatens the child but there is no physical contact with the child, Emotional Maltreatment would be scored rather than Physical Abuse. Please see the Emotional Maltreatment scale for further elaboration of these points.

Physical injuries that occur as a direct result of sexual interaction (e.g., vaginal or rectal tears) are coded solely under Sexual Abuse. Other injuries that may accompany sexual acts in an effort to force a child to engage in sexual relations (e.g., beatings, burning) are scored under both Physical Abuse and Sexual Abuse.

Severity Rating

1 = The caregiver inflicted *minor marks* on the child's body during a spanking; there were no marks to the neck or head.

Reports indicated that the caregiver had *beaten* the child; no other information was given.

The child received *injuries* that were documented to have occurred by *nonaccidental means*. The details of the report were not specific enough to warrant a higher rating.

The caregiver was reported to have spanked the child with an open hand or an *object likely to inflict only minor marks* in most cases (e.g., a switch, a soft belt, a ruler, a paddle), with the child sustaining marks on or below the shoulders.

Examples:
- The child received a bruise on the arm after being hit with an open hand.
- Minor bruises on the child's bottom were reported following a spanking with a belt.

2 = The caregiver inflicted *numerous* or *nonminor marks* to the child's body from any incident.

The caregiver spanked the child with an *object likely to leave a nonminor mark* (e.g., a hair brush, a belt buckle, an electrical cord), or kicked or punched the child with a fist, leaving marks on the child's body below the neck.

Examples:
- The child sustained welts on the back after being beaten with a hair brush.
- The child was beaten with an electrical cord, resulting in numerous marks.

3 = The caregiver inflicted *marks on the child's head, face, or neck* (e.g., a black eye).

The caregiver's rough handling of the child resulted in *serious bruises or minor lacerations* (e.g., required stitches or minor medical attention).

The caregiver inflicted *minor burns* (e.g., minor cigarette burns) to the child's body.

Examples:

- The child received a hand print on the neck after the parent grabbed him.
- The child had a black eye resulting from being punched in the face.
- Small circular burns on the child's hands were identified as cigarette burns.

4 = The caregiver hit the child with an *object* (e.g., a baseball bat, a telephone) *likely to result in serious injury* (e.g., nonminor lacerations, second-degree burns, fracture, or concussion), or threw the child against the wall, but injuries that were sustained did not require hospitalization, according to available medical information.

The caregiver attempted to *choke or smother* the child, but no emergency medical care was required.

The caregiver inflicted *serious burns* (second degree) to the child's body, but the injury did not require hospitalization.

The caregiver inflicted an injury that required some *hospital care,* such as treatment in the Emergency Room, but did not require hospitalization for more than 24 hours (e.g., stitches, fractures, nonminor sprain).

Examples:

- The child was beaten with a board that had nails in it. The child received bruises and cuts.
- The child was thrown down the stairs, and fractured one arm.
- The child was severely burned by the parent and was treated in the Emergency Room.

5 = The caregiver inflicted an injury to the child that required *hospitalization* (e.g., severe/multiple burns, internal injuries), and/or that was permanently physically damaging, or disfiguring (e.g., resulting in brain damage, severe scarring, crippling). The caregiver inflicted a *fatal injury*.

Examples:

- The child was set on fire, resulting in severe burns that were permanently disfiguring.

- The child was hospitalized for one week for internal injuries and evidence of a shaken infant syndrome.

Sexual Abuse

Sexual abuse is coded when any sexual contact or attempt at sexual contact occurs between a caregiver or other responsible adult and a child, for purposes of the caregiver's sexual gratification or financial benefit. In cases of sexual abuse, caregiver or responsible adult refers to any family member or friend who has a relationship with the child, or is in a position of authority over the child (e.g., babysitter). Because this system assesses Child Protective records only, there are instances of sexual abuse that are not available in the Child Protective records. For example, sexual abuse that occurs outside of the home perpetrated by nonfamily members typically is investigated solely by criminal courts, and consequently, may not be accessible. Any relevant information in the records related to sexual abuse should be scored. Researchers should be aware of this issue, and we encourage investigators to use additional methods for exploring extrafamilial maltreatment that may not be available through Child Protective records.

Please note that caregivers may use physical or psychological coercion in their attempts to engage a child in sexual relations. In cases where the caregiver verbally threatens a child in an effort to have sexual relations, then Emotional Maltreatment and Sexual Abuse would both be scored. As noted under Physical Abuse, physical injuries that occur as a direct result of sexual interaction (e.g., vaginal or rectal tears) are coded solely under Sexual Abuse. Other injuries that may accompany sexual acts in an effort to force a child to engage in sexual relations (e.g., beatings, burning) are scored under both Physical Abuse and Sexual Abuse.

Severity Rating

1 = The caregiver *exposes the child to explicit sexual stimuli* or activities, although the child is not directly involved.
   Examples:
   - The caregiver exposes the child to pornographic materials.
   - The caregiver makes no attempt to prevent the child from being exposed to sexual activity.
   - The caregiver discusses sex explicitly in front of the child in a non-educational fashion. Non-educational discussion of sex includes graphic depiction of parents' sexual activity or fantasies to the child. These discussions are held without any attempt to prevent the child from exposure to such descriptions.

2 = The caregiver makes direct *requests for sexual contact* with the child.
The caregiver *exposes his or her genitals* to the child for the purposes of adult sexual gratification or in an attempt to sexually stimulate the child.

Examples:
- The caregiver asks the child to engage in sexual relations, but no physical contact is involved.
- The caregiver invites the child to watch him masturbate.

3 = The caregiver engages the child in mutual *sexual touching,* or has the child touch the caregiver for sexual gratification.
The caregiver touches the child for sexual gratification.

Examples:
- The caregiver fondles the child for sexual gratification.
- The caregiver engages in mutual masturbation with the child.

4 = The caregiver physically *attempts to penetrate the child* or actually penetrates the child sexually. This includes coitus, oral sex, anal sex, or any other form of sodomy.

Examples:
- The caregiver molests the child.
- The caregiver engages or attempts intercourse with the child.
- The child has venereal disease. No information regarding the sexual contact is known.
- A mother has oral sex with her son.

5 = The caregiver has *forced intercourse* or other forms of sexual penetration. Force includes the use of manual or mechanical restraint, for the purpose of engaging the child in sexual relations. Force also includes use of weapons, physical brutality, and physically overpowering the child, specifically for engaging in sexual relations. Note that Physical Abuse may be scored in addition to Sexual Abuse in cases in which the child is injured as a result of physical force, and the injury is not a direct result of the sexual penetration.
The caregiver *prostitutes the child*. This includes using the child for pornography, allowing, encouraging or forcing the child to have sex with other adults.

Examples:
- The caregiver ties the child to the bed and rapes the child. (Note that Emotional Maltreatment would also be scored.)
- The caregiver sodomizes the child at gunpoint.

- The caregiver forces the child to participate in the filming of pornographic movies.
- The caregiver invites one or more other partners to have sexual relations with the child.

Physical Neglect, Failure to Provide (FTP)

Physical Neglect, Failure to Provide, is coded when a caregiver or responsible adult fails to exercise a minimum degree of care in meeting the child's physical needs. When families are below the poverty level, physical neglect is scored if children's physical needs are not met because the parents fail to access available community resources for the well-being of their children. For example, parents are unable to provide food for their children; however, they have not taken the necessary steps to apply for food stamps or to seek alternate sources of emergency sustenance.

Failure to provide includes not meeting children's physical needs in any of the following domains:

a. supplying the child with adequate *food*,
b. ensuring that the child has *clothing* that is sanitary, appropriate for the weather and permits the child freedom of movement,
c. providing adequate *shelter*,
d. ensuring adequate *medical, dental, and mental health care*,
e. ensuring the child's adequate *hygiene*.

As with each of the severity scales, the 5-point range for Failure to Provide is meant to be a helpful guideline in making judgments about the seriousness of the impact of the incident on the child's development. However, as with each subtype of maltreatment, there will be occurrences in which the specific nature of the incident dictates to the coder that an event requires a higher rating than indicated by the guidelines of the system. For example, parental failure to follow through with treatment for a low to moderate elevation in the child's blood lead level would typically be given a code of 3. However, if the child has extremely high lead levels that remain untreated through parental negligence, a 4 or a 5 could be scored, depending on the severity of the impairment to the child. In general, when in doubt, coders should stay within the guidelines of the system. Only when a situation clearly goes beyond the nature of the example, should a coder adjust the level of severity.

1 = The caregiver does not ensure that food is available for *regular meals*. The child (less than age 10) often has had to fix his or her own supper and/or occasionally misses meals because of parental negligence.

The caregiver fails to provide *clothing* for the child that is adequately clean and that allows *freedom of movement* (e.g., the clothing is so small that its restricts movement or so large the child often trips or has difficulty keeping the clothing on).

The caregiver does not attempt to *clean the house*. Garbage has not been removed, dirty dishes are encrusted with food, and floors and other surfaces are very dirty. An unpleasant odor from garbage and debris permeates living quarters.

The caregiver has missed several of the child's *medical or dental appointments,* and often fails to take the child to the doctor or dentist for "checkups" or "well baby" appointments. The caregiver does not ensure that the child is taken to the doctor or health clinic for adequate immunizations, and medical personnel have expressed concern.

The caregiver does not attend to a *mild behavior problem* about which professionals or paraprofessionals have commented (e.g., the child exhibits some symptomatology, but displays relatively mild impairment in social or school functioning).

The caregiver does not attempt to keep the child clean. The caretaker *bathes* the child and/or washes the child's hair very infrequently. The child brushes teeth only infrequently or not at all, and signs of tooth decay or discoloration are evident.

Examples:
- A 9-year-old child fixes dinner several times per week because the caregivers are sleeping.
- The child always wears clothing that is so small it restricts movement.
- The caregiver has failed to sign papers for evaluation of a behavior problem that has been reported at school.
- The child is dirty and frequently scratches matted hair.
- Clothing is dirty and smells of urine.

2 = The caregiver does not ensure that any *food is available*. The house is without food often, and two or more consecutive meals are missed 2-3 times per week. The caregiver does not feed the child for 24 hours.

The caregiver does not dress the child in *clothing* that is *appropriate for the weather* (e.g., lightweight clothing during the winter).

The caregiver is aware that the *house is infested* with roaches or other vermin and has not attempted to improve the conditions.

The caregiver does not ensure adequate *sleeping arrangements* for the child (e.g., there are no beds or mattresses, or the mattresses are filthy and sodden with urine or other substances likely to promote the growth of mold or mildew).

The caregiver seeks medical attention but does not follow-through consistently with *medical recommendations* for a minor illness or infection (e.g., prescribed medicine is not administered for mild infection, chronic head lice is not treated).

The caregiver does not change the infant's diaper frequently, often leaving *soiled diapers unchanged* for several hours, resulting in diaper rash.

Examples:

- A child has walked to school several consecutive days wearing only a thin jacket without hat or gloves. The temperature has averaged 25 degrees Fahrenheit.
- A social worker has visited the home several times when no food has been available. The children report that they do not have lunch or dinner two or three times per week.
- The child has been diagnosed with an ear infection, but the parent does not follow through with administration of the prescribed antibiotic.

3 = The caregiver does not provide meals on a regular basis, thereby perpetuating a pattern of *frequently missed meals;* as many as four or more periods of at least two consecutive meals per week are unavailable to the child.

The caregiver fails to make *adequate provisions for shelter* for the family. For example, the caregiver does not acquire or maintain public assistance, resulting in a loss of residence or loss of financial assistance for seven days or more.

The caregiver does not seek or follow through with *medical treatment for moderately severe medical problems* (e.g., the caregiver does not follow preventive measures for a chronic heart condition, or moderately elevated blood lead levels are left untreated), or the caregiver administers medical treatment that is inappropriate without consulting a doctor (e.g., caregiver gives child mild sedatives to control child, without a doctor's consultation).

The caregiver does not follow through on *treatment* or treatment program for a diagnosed *psychological or behavioral disorder.* This disorder is interfering with the child's ability to engage in developmentally appropriate peer relationships or school functioning.

The caregiver maintains a *somewhat unsanitary living situation,* where spoiled food or garbage are frequently present and/or where rat or vermin infestation is extreme and untreated.

The expectant mother jeopardizes the health of her unborn child by using *alcohol or drugs during pregnancy,* but no fetal alcohol or drug symptoms are evident.

Examples:

- The children are not fed frequently. They have missed two consecutive meals an average of four times a week for the last several months.
- The family has been evicted because the parent did not take appropriate actions to maintain public assistance and made no other arrangements for making rent payments. The family had no stable living arrangements for 2 weeks.
- The parent has been drunk several times during pregnancy.
- The child has come to school with an infected cut. Despite notes from the school nurse recommending medical attention, the cut continues to be untreated.
- A social worker has visited the home several times, and each time the house has been a mess. Dirty dishes and spoiled food were all over the kitchen table, counters, and sink. Rats were seen in the open garbage bins by the front door.
- The child is emotionally disturbed and is in a treatment program. The caregiver has not sent the child to the program for 6 weeks.

4 = The caregiver has made *no arrangements for adequate shelter* (e.g., the caregiver has not sought heat during the winter; the family is living in a car because alternative housing was not sought). The condition continues for prolonged periods.

The caregiver maintains the home environment such that *living conditions are extremely unhealthy* (e.g., feces and urine are present in the living areas).

The caregiver does not seek or comply with *medical treatment for potentially life-threatening illness or injury* (e.g., the child is not taken to the Emergency Room for severe bleeding, third-degree burn, fractured skull).

The caregiver has provided such poor nourishment that the child *fails to gain weight or grow at the rate expected* for their development. The failure to grow as expected is not due to any identifiable organic factors.

Examples:

- The children live in an unheated home because the parents have failed to ensure that heating was available. During the winter, the children came to school with frostbite.
- The child was hit by a car, receiving a fracture and severe cuts and bruises. The child came to school complaining of pain and stated that the parents would not take him to the hospital.

5 = The caregiver has provided such *poor nourishment or care* to the child that physical consequences have ensued such as weight loss in an infant, severe malnutrition, or severe nonorganic failure-to-thrive.

The caregiver has abused alcohol or drugs during pregnancy to the extent that the infant is born with Fetal Alcohol Syndrome or a *congenital drug addiction*.

The caregiver provided such *gross inattention to the child's medical needs* that the child died or was permanently disabled as a result of lack of medical treatment (e.g., severe starvation or dehydration).

The caregiver does not seek professional help for the child's *life threatening emotional problems* (e.g., suicidal or homicidal attempts).

Examples:
- At birth, the child is addicted to heroin.
- The child is diagnosed as being severely malnourished.
- The caregiver was informed that the child had expressed suicidal ideation, but the caregiver did nothing to ensure the child's safety.

Physical Neglect, Lack of Supervision (LOS)

Presently, Lack of Supervision is one of the most frequently reported subtypes of maltreatment; however, it is a particularly ambiguous subtype, in part because no clear criteria or standards exist regarding what constitutes age-appropriate supervision. Within this system, Lack of Supervision is coded when a caregiver or responsible adult does not take adequate precautions to ensure a child's safety in and out of the home, given the child's particular emotional and developmental needs. The parent's failure to insure the child's safety may include both permitting the child to be exposed to dangerous situations (e.g., allowing the child to play in an unsafe area, permitting the child to accompany someone with a known history of violent acts) as well as failing to take adequate precautions to evaluate the conditions pertaining to the child's safety (e.g., neglecting to screen the background or competency of alternate caregivers, failing to ascertain the child's whereabouts). There are four broad elements that caregivers may violate to jeopardize children's physical safety:

1. *Supervision*—failing to take steps to ensure that the child is engaging in safe activities. According to this dimension, as the number of hours that the child is unsupervised increases, so does the potential for harm. Therefore, severity scores for Lack of Supervision are augmented with

more prolonged periods of inadequate supervision. To assist coders in making distinctions about the relative seriousness of particular instances of Lack of Supervision, we have provided approximate durations of inadequate supervision that are intended to serve as guidelines rather than as firm criteria. We recognize that these cutoff points are somewhat arbitrary and that exact times are frequently unavailable in the records; however, we felt that establishing ranges of time was necessary to clarify coding decisions and, thus, to increase reliability among coders.

2. *Environment*—failing to ensure that the child is playing in a safe area. This dimension is distinguished from lack of hygiene or medically unhealthy conditions of the living environment covered under Failure to Provide. In the case of Lack of Supervision, environment refers to immediate physical dangers inside or outside the home such as broken glass, unguarded electrical fixtures, toxic chemicals, and firearms.

3. *Substitute Care*—failing to provide for adequate substitute care in the caregiver's absence, or mental or physical incapacity. In this respect, lack of substitute care includes situations when auxiliary supervision is not obtained, when parents do not ensure that substitute caregivers are able to adequately supervise the child, when caregivers are unable to adequately monitor the child's safety because the caregivers are intoxicated with alcohol or drugs, or when caregivers have a severe psychiatric condition that makes appropriate supervision of children highly unlikely (e.g., caregiver has delusions or hallucinations).

4. *Development Needs*—failing to recognize the developmental needs of the child in providing adequate supervision to ensure the child's safety. Because, in general, the consequences of failing to supervise younger children are potentially more serious, the influence of the child's developmental level should be considered when making decisions about the severity of parental failure to provide adequate supervision.

Additionally, children who have a history of dangerous, impulsive, or immature behavior require more intensive supervision, and may be given a higher severity rating if they are unsupervised. For example, an adolescent who is known to exhibit poor judgment and to engage in impulsive and destructive behavior would require more supervision than most children of the same age. It is difficult to quantify the amount of supervision that is required at each developmental level. The examples provided give some guidelines of relative severity, but the information available for each case must be considered with regard to the age and particular developmental needs of each child.

In summary, when making individual decisions about severity, the coder should take into account the length of time the child was left unsupervised, the amount of danger present in the physical environment, the adequacy of potential substitute caregivers, and the developmental needs of the child.

Severity Rating

1 = The caregiver fails to provide adequate supervision or arrange for alternate adequate supervision for *short periods of time* (i.e., less than 3 hours) with *no immediate source of danger* in the environment.

Examples:
- An 8-year-old is *left alone* during the day for a few hours.
- Preschoolers play outside unsupervised or are left in the care of an 8-year-old supervisor for the afternoon. (In this case, the preschoolers who are unsupervised in an environment with a few hazards reported would receive a code of 1. Similarly, supervision of preschoolers by a slightly older child would represent mildly inadequate alternate supervision, which would also be coded 1. The 8-year-old is unsupervised, receiving a code of 1 for the short duration. The presence of Emotional Maltreatment should also be evaluated in cases in which the 8-year-old is expected to assume inappropriate responsibility.)
- Children are left in the care of *questionably suitable babysitters* (e.g., preadolescent, mildly impaired elderly person).

2 = The caregiver fails to provide supervision or arrange for alternate adequate supervision, or provides poor supervision for *several hours* (approximately three to eight hours), with *no immediate source of danger in the environment.*

The caregiver fails to provide supervision for *short periods of time* (less than 3 hours) when the children are in an *unsafe* play *area.*

Children receive *inadequate supervision despite a history of problematic behavior* (e.g., impulsive behavior, hyperactivity).

Examples:
- The child is left alone frequently during the day *without a responsible caregiver* available.
- An infant is left in the care of an 8-year-old for several hours (In this case the infant is given a code of 2. The 8-year-old would be given a code of 1, similar to the example under level 1).
- The child is allowed to play in an unsafe play area (e.g., broken glass present, old basement or garage cluttered with toxic chemicals, power tools, or old refrigerator) unsupervised.

• Children get into trouble with neighbors because of lack of supervision.

3 = The caregiver fails to provide adequate supervision for *extended periods of time* (e.g., approximately 8 to 10 hours).
The caregiver allows the child to play in an *unsafe play area* for *several hours* (approximately 3 to 8 hours):
Examples:
   • The child is left *alone at night* (e.g., for 8 to 10 hours).
   • A 6-year-old is locked out of the home alone, and the caregiver does not return until evening.
   • The child is left in the care of an unreliable caregiver (e.g., one who is known to drink, or is extremely inattentive, or the parent makes no attempt to ensure that the caregiver was reliable) for several hours.

4 = The caregiver does not provide supervision for *extensive periods* of time (e.g., overnight, or approximately 10 to 12 hours).
The caregiver allows the child to play in an area that is *very dangerous* (i.e., high probability that the child will be hit by a car or fall out of a window, get burned, or drown).
A child with a known *history of destructive or dangerous acts* (e.g., fire-setting, suicidal ideation) is left unsupervised.
Examples:
   • A grade-school-aged child is *left alone overnight.*
   • The child is allowed to play by highway, or on the roof of a condemned building.
   • The child is *allowed to go with a caregiver* who has a known history of violence and/or sexual acts against children or who has a restraining order prohibiting contact with the child.

5 = The caregiver fails to provide adequate supervision for *more than 12 hours.*
The caregiver places the child in a *life-threatening situation*, or does not take steps to prevent the child from being in a life-threatening situation.
Examples:
   • A preschool child is *left alone for 24 hours.*
   • The child is *kicked out* of the home with no alternative living arrangements.
   • The caregivers keeps *loaded firearms* in a location that is accessible to the child.

- A toddler plays near a swimming pool unsupervised. (Note that, for a toddler, being unsupervised near water is considered life threatening because of the high frequency of deaths by drowning to this age child.)

Emotional Maltreatment (EM)

There is a growing consensus that virtually all acts of abuse and neglect carry negative emotional/psychological messages to their victims. Consequently, it may be argued that every act of maltreatment constitutes Emotional Maltreatment. We have differentiated acts of Emotional Maltreatment from other forms of maltreatment for the purposes of maintaining the individual conceptual integrity of each of the subtypes defined within our system. The majority of incidents falling into Emotional Maltreatment involve persistent or extreme thwarting of children's basic emotional needs. This category also includes parental acts that are harmful because they are insensitive to the child's developmental level. These needs include, but are not limited to, the following:

1. *Psychological safety & security*: the need for a family environment free of excessive hostility and violence, and the need for an available and stable attachment figure. Note that this category refers to the interpersonal climate of the home, whereas Lack of Supervision (LOS) refers to cases in which the physical environment is unsafe. (See below for additional distinctions among subtypes.)
2. *Acceptance & self-esteem*: the need for positive regard and the absence of excessively negative or unrealistic evaluation, given the child's particular developmental level.
3. *Age appropriate autonomy*: the need to explore the environment and extrafamilial relationships, to individuate within the bounds of parental acceptance, structure, and limit setting, without developmentally inappropriate responsibility or constraints placed on the child.

There are acts of maltreatment that may be scored solely as Emotional Maltreatment or that may be scored in conjunction with other subtypes of maltreatment. To clarify potentially confusing areas, we specify the following inclusion/exclusion criteria:

1. One area of interface between Emotional Maltreatment and incidents of Physical Abuse concerns physical restraint or confinement of a child. Because restraint or confinement jeopardizes the child's need for autonomy, we consider these acts to be Emotional Maltreatment. However, if the acts result in physical injuries (e.g., rope burns), these acts would be scored as both Emotional Maltreatment and Physical Abuse.

A second area of overlap surrounds incidents of homicidal threats. In situations in which parents attempt to terrorize children by threatening them or making gestures of harm, Emotional Maltreatment is scored. However, if during the act, the parents actually inflict injury to the children, the act is considered Physical Abuse.

2. In instances in which there is evidence that threats or psychological coercion is employed in an effort to engage the child in sexual relations, then both Sexual Abuse and Emotional Maltreatment would be scored. (Please see Sexual Abuse for an elaboration of this point.)

3. An important distinction between Emotional Maltreatment and Physical Neglect is necessary in instances of abandonment. In cases in which a parent abandons a child but ensures that the child is adequately supervised and that the child's physical needs are met (e.g., leaves the child with relatives with no information about the parent's whereabouts), we consider this to be Emotional Maltreatment. If the child is left completely alone with no provisions for supervision or physical needs, then Lack of Supervision, Failure to Provide, and Emotional Maltreatment may each be scored.

4. In situations in which a young child is forced to accept primary responsibility for the care of another individual and in which criteria for Lack of Supervision are met (as a result of either child's need for more intensive supervision), then both Emotional Maltreatment (for the supervising child) and Lack of Supervision (for one or both children) would be scored.

Severity Ratings

1 = The caregiver regularly expects or requires the child to assume an *inappropriate level of responsibility* (e.g., school-aged child assuming primary responsibility for caretaking younger children; the report must include an explicit statement that the child is responsible for the caretaking role).

The caregiver *undermines the child's relationships* with other people significant to the child (e.g., makes frequent derogatory comments about other parent).

The caregiver often *belittles or ridicules the child* (e.g., calls the child "stupid," "loser," "wimp").

The caregiver *ignores or refuses to acknowledge* the child's bids for attention (e.g., the caregiver generally does not respond to infant cries or older child's attempts to initiate interaction).

The caregiver *uses fear or intimidation* as a method of disciplining.

Examples:
- The caregiver expects her 10-year-old to take responsibility for the care of an infant.
- The caregiver talks on the phone and leaves the baby to cry for extended periods in the crib.
- The caregiver shows no interest in the child's achievements.

2 = The caregiver does not permit *age-appropriate socialization* (e.g. school-aged child not permitted to play with friends).

The caregiver places the child in a *role-reversal* (e.g., child is expected to take care of the caregiver).

The caregiver consistently thwarts the child's developing sense of maturity and responsibility (e.g., *infantilizes* the child).

The caregiver *rejects or is inattentive* to or unaware of the child's needs for affection and positive regard (e.g., the caregiver does not engage in positive or affectionate interactions with the child; this lack of attention is a chronic pattern).

The caregiver allows the child to be exposed to the caregiver's extreme but *nonviolent marital conflict.*

Examples:
- The caregiver is extremely passive and unable to meet the children's needs for attention. Any interactions that do occur are harsh and critical.
- The caregiver does not want the child to go out of the house after school because the caregiver is lonely and wants company.
- The caregiver frequently yells, screams, and insults the spouse in front of the child.
- The caregiver encourages a 4-year-old to continue to wear diapers despite the child's physical and psychological ability to use the toilet appropriately.

3 = The caregiver *blames the children for marital or family problems* (e.g., tells the children that they are the reason for the spouses divorce).

The caregiver sets-up the child to fail or to feel inadequate by having *inappropriate or excessive expectations* for the child.

The caregiver makes a serious and convincing *threat to injure* the child.

The caregiver calls the child *derogatory names* (e.g., "slut," "whore," "worthless").

The caregiver *binds* the child's hands and feet for moderate periods of time (e.g., approximately 2 to 5 hours), the child is not unattended.

The caregiver exposes child to *extreme, unpredictable, and/or inappropriate behavior* (e.g., violence toward other family members, psychotic or paranoid ideation that results in violent outbursts that terrorize the child).

The caregiver demonstrates a pattern of *negativity or hostility* toward the child (e.g., the caregiver screams at the children that they can never do anything right).

Examples:

- The caregiver constantly screams and curses at the children and calls them names.
- The caregiver chronically rejects the children.
- The caregiver threatened to throw the child out of the window.

4 = The caregiver *threatens suicide or abandonment* in front of the child.

The caregiver allows the child to be exposed to *extreme marital violence* in which serious injuries occur to the caregiver.

The caregiver *blames* the child for the *suicide or death* of another family member.

The caregiver *confines and isolates the child* (e.g., locks the child in his or her room), and the confinement is between five and eight hours.

The caregiver uses *restrictive methods to bind* a child or places the child in close confinement (e.g., the child is tied to a chair, or locked in a box) for less than two hours. (Close confinement is scored in situations in which the child's movement is extremely restricted, or the temperature, ventilation, or lighting is severely limited or is maintained in a detrimental range.).

Examples:

- The children witnessed a fight between the parents in which the mother had to be hospitalized after being assaulted by the father.
- The caregiver locked the child in a room for ten hours for misbehavior.
- The caregiver tells the children that they are going to be put up for adoption because they are so bad.

5 = The caregiver makes a *suicidal attempt* in the presence of the child.

The caregiver makes a *homicidal attempt or realistic homicidal threat* against the child without actual physical harm to the child.

The primary caregiver *abandons the child* for 24 hours or longer without any indication of when or if he or she will return and where he or she can be located (Note: Lack of Supervision and/or Failure to Provide may also be scored unless provisions are made for the child's physical well-being and need for supervision to be addressed. See description above for an elaboration of the interface among Emotional Maltreatment, Lack of Supervision, and Failure to Provide in instances of abandonment.)

The caregiver uses *extremely restrictive methods to bind* a child or places the child in close confinement for two or more hours (e.g, the child is tightly tied to a chair, or locked in a trunk).

The caregiver *confines the child to an enclosed space* (e.g., locks the child in a closet or small space) for extended periods (e.g., more than 8 hours)..

Examples:
- The caregiver chains the child to the wall of the apartment with a dog collar for two days.
- The mother left the children with their grandmother for 2 weeks without any indication of where she was and when (or if) she would be returning.
- The caregiver chased the child with the car in an effort to terrorize the child. The child was not physically injured.
- The caregiver took an overdose of sleeping pills in the children's presence. The caregiver told the children that life with them was intolerable.

Moral-Legal/Educational Maltreatment

Moral-Legal/Educational Maltreatment is coded when any behaviors on the part of the caregiver or responsible adult occur that fail to demonstrate a minimum degree of care in assisting the child to integrate with the expectations of society, which includes insuring the child's adequate education. The caregiver either exposes or involves the child in illegal activity or other activities that may foster delinquency or antisocial behavior in the child. Alternately, the caregiver does not ensure that the child is properly socialized by regularly attending school.

1 = M-L: The caregiver permits the child to be present for adult activities for which the child is under age.

ED: The caregiver often lets the child stay home from school, and the absences are not the result of illness or family emergency (e.g., a death in the family). The absences occur for less than 15% of the reported period.

Examples:
- M-L: The caregiver takes the child to drunken parties and adult bars that are clearly not family situations.
- ED: The caregiver allows the child to miss 25 days of school in a school year without explanation.

2 = M-L: The caregiver participates in illegal behavior with the child's knowledge (e.g., shoplifting, selling stolen merchandise).

     ED: The caregiver allows the child to miss school as much as 15%–25% of the reported period, not due to illness.

Examples:

- M-L   The child was present when the caregiver was selling drugs.
- ED: The caregiver did not send the child to school so that the child could baby-sit for younger siblings. The child missed 9 out of 45 days.

3 = M-L: The caregiver knows that the child is involved in illegal activities, but does not attempt to intervene (e.g., permits vandalism, shoplifting, drinking).

     ED: The caregiver keeps the child out of school or knows that the child is truant for extended periods (26%–50% of year, or as may as 16 schools days in a row) without caregiver's intervention.

Examples:

- M-L: The caregiver has been informed that the child has been shoplifting, but the caregiver has done nothing.
- ED: The child has missed 3 consecutive weeks of school, not due to illness.

4 = M-L: The caregiver involves the child in misdemeanors (e.g., child is encouraged to shoplift, child is given drugs). Adults encourage or force participation in illegal activities.

     ED: The caregiver frequently keeps the child out of school for significant amounts of time (more than 50% of the reported period, or 16+ days in a row), but the child maintains school enrollment.

Examples:

- M-L: The caregiver encourages the child to steal food from the grocery store.
- ED: The family has moved several times, and each time, the child has missed significant periods of school. The child is enrolled, but has missed more than half of the school year.

5 = M-L: The caregiver involves the child in felonies (e.g., the child participates in armed robbery, kidnapping).

     ED: The caregiver encourages a child (less than 16 years old) to drop out of school or does not send the child to school at all.

Examples:

- M-L: The child has lived in a drug house run by the caregivers. The child has been involved in selling drugs and has participated in armed conflicts with other drug dealers.
- ED: The caregiver has not enrolled the child in school, and the child is receiving no educational instruction.

3

Developmental Research and Legal Policy: Toward a Two-Way Street*

Ross A. Thompson

With distressing frequency, children are arriving at hospital emergency rooms with lacerations, deep bruises, head trauma, burns, and internal injuries sustained at the hands of their caregivers. They are discovered alone in inner-city apartments suffering from malnutrition, underweight for age, and inadequately clothed in garments reeking from urine and feces. They are born showing signs of acute drug withdrawal and may experience enduring behavioral problems owing to an intrauterine environment that was marked by maternal ingestion of crack cocaine, heroin, or other drugs. They grow up in environments in which they are terrorized by gang warfare, domestic violence, and/or the economy of drug trafficking. They report experiencing traumatizing episodes of sexual abuse. They are kept from receiving a normal education in school, are persistently belittled, threatened, and rejected by caregivers, and are sometimes denied much-needed medical treatment. With alarming regularity, these are the conditions that children in America experience as they are growing up.

Is it any surprise that those who are concerned about children, including developmental researchers, are strongly motivated to contribute to interventions on their behalf? According to a report released recently by the U.S. Advisory Board on Child Abuse and Neglect (1990), the number of reports of child maltreatment reached 2.4 million in 1989, compared to about 60,000 cases reported in 1974. Of these, more than 900,000 cases in 1989 were officially substantiated as maltreatment, which likely underestimates the actual frequency of child abuse and neglect. Perhaps more disturbing was their conclusion that maltreatment is becoming a more complex phenomenon, tied to increased poverty, changing family and child-care patterns, heightened substance abuse in new subpopulations, neighborhood dysfunction, and the growing incidence of sexual maltreatment. Even more concerning was their conclusion that current circumstances represent "a national emergency" because the child protection system that was designed to respond to child abuse and neglect is broken and failing.

* I am very grateful for the helpful comments on an earlier draft of this chapter provided by Dante Cicchetti, Mary Fran Flood, Patricia Hashima, Gary Melton, Sheree Toth, and Michael Wald—none of whom share responsibility for features of this discussion with which they disagree!

Why is it failing? The Advisory Board cited the dramatic rise in reports of child maltreatment coupled with declining revenue and resources during the 1980s as a major contributor (see also Select Committee on Children, Youth, and Families, 1987; Thompson, 1993). As a consequence, most child protective systems must focus primarily—and often inadequately—on investigating and substantiating abuse reports and consequently can devote fewer resources toward devising helpful interventions or monitoring their efficacy. High turnover, low morale, and poor training of social service caseworkers is both an outcome of, and a contributor to, this broken system. Moreover, realistic interventions are becoming constrained by the inherent difficulties of some cases (involving maltreatment in the context of substance abuse, mental illness, neighborhood dysfunction, or poverty), obstacles to the effective prosecution of alleged offenders (especially in sex abuse cases), and significant problems in the foster care system, which at times perpetuates rather than prevents the maltreatment of children. Moreover, when abuse is intrafamilial—which is the focus of this chapter—detection is more difficult, interventions involve a more challenging calculus of benefits and costs, and evaluating progress is more problematic.

Problems in the child protection system are also revealed in the extraordinarily difficult questions a caseworker must consider in deciding whether, and how, to intervene in situations of reported child maltreatment. For example, what factors should determine whether an initial report warrants immediate investigation, based on the potential of serious harm to the child? How should children be treated during this initial investigative phase (e.g., under what conditions is removal from the home warranted)? What factors in the family, offender, and/or child best predict the *recurrence* of maltreatment? How do these factors differ for different kinds of maltreatment, children of different ages, or different offenders? How well can one predict likely maltreatment based on the parent's current status (e.g., spouse abuse, substance abuse, emotional or mental disorders, etc.), even without evidence of immediate harm to the child? If maltreatment is substantiated, for which children is out-of-home placement preferable, and for which children is remaining in the home (with the provision of social services to the family) the best option? For what kinds of offenders are different intervention options best? How are children affected by their experience with the social service and legal systems if abuse allegations are criminally prosecuted?

Other questions mingle knowledge and experience with value judgments. How strongly should family reunification goals influence casework decision-making? How important is permanency planning in out-of-home placements? What are its consequences for children, their families, foster families, and the child protection system? If treatment and counseling of parents is provided, by what criteria of change or improvement in family and/or parental conditions should the child be allowed subsequently to return home? Is preventive parental screening likely to be an effective means of reducing future child maltreatment?

How helpful is current developmental research in resolving these thorny legal policymaking questions? Unfortunately, it is not usually very helpful. One reason is that many of these dilemmas depend, not on pertinent research findings, but on value judgments, made proximally by the caseworker but also by society at large. Decisions concerning the kinds of parental behavior that fall outside an "acceptable" range and warrant legal intervention, for example, or the extent to which family privacy and integrity should be safeguarded, or the importance of remedial versus criminal interventions when abuse is substantiated all rely on broader social values concerning children, families, and the state. These values evolve and are frequently the focus of intense debate as they change in response to changing social conditions. Nevertheless, they provide an important and legitimate foundation for sociolegal policymaking concerning child maltreatment as the core consensual assumptions upon which relations between individuals and the state are based. I shall argue that researchers can advance this debate about underlying values as their research contributions modify public perceptions of children's and family's needs, but that these contributions primarily help to alter the consensual values applied to such policy problems rather than providing direct research-based solutions in themselves.

A second reason for the limited assistance of developmental research is that many of these policymaking questions cannot easily be addressed using current research methodologies. Even a cursory effort to plan a well-designed study that would address any one of the questions outlined above reveals the significant ethical and technical obstacles a developmental researcher would encounter. Access to relevant subject populations of satisfactory size, random assignment to different experimental and control conditions, the design and selection of valid outcome measures, and addressing pertinent ethical issues (e.g., privacy violations, compliance with mandatory child abuse reporting laws) are significant ingredients to valid and generalizable—and thus useful—research findings. But these factors also constitute formidable (if not insurmountable) obstacles to successfully conducting the research at all. This puts the researcher in the difficult position of determining whether the results of research using significantly compromised design features will ultimately advance knowledge of policymaking relevance, or prove more misleading in the end. This difficult issue will also be discussed later in this chapter.

The third reason why developmental research often does not provide substantive assistance to policymakers is that it is usually not formulated to do so. Indeed, policy-relevant research applications—or "usable knowledge" (Lindblom & Cohen, 1979)—is unlikely to emerge unless researchers design their studies and apply their findings with a thorough knowledge of the policymaking process and its implementations. As the assortment of decision-making dilemmas outlined above may suggest, policy-relevant questions are forged in the practical contexts of trying to fashion and implement effective child protection, and developmental investigators whose theories and research concern children in more typical rearing conditions are unlikely to be familiar with these concerns. One of the most important reasons that current research does not provide many helpful solutions to policymakers, therefore, is that it is usually not designed or conceived to do so, and one of the reasons that the policy recommendations of researchers are not embraced by policymakers is that they are often irrelevant to the dilemmas that policymakers truly face. In other words, for developmental research to provide "usable knowledge," there must exist a two-way process of knowledge dissemination between the research and policymaking communities. This does not exist at present, and this chapter is devoted to strengthening this linkage.

This is not to say that developmental research has few useful applications to the problem of child maltreatment. As the chapters in this volume abundantly reveal, current developmental research and studies devoted specifically to problems of child abuse and neglect have important applications to clinical intervention (Cicchetti & Toth, this volume), educational policy (Toth & Cicchetti, this volume), and program evaluation (Daro, this volume). This is due, in part, to the close collegial ties between researchers and educators, clinicians, and members of related professional communities, and to their shared questions and perspectives. In some specific domains of policy relevance, moreover, there exist well-developed research literatures, such as studies concerning children's eyewitness accounts and influences on their testimony (see Ceci, Nightingale, DeSimone, & Putnicle, this volume; Goodman, this volume). In addition, the study of child maltreatment yields profound insights into developmental processes in normal as well as atypical populations, consistent with the claims of students of developmental psychopathology (e.g., Cicchetti, 1990; Cicchetti & Howes, this volume). Developmental research on child maltreatment has thus yielded considerable usable knowledge for a variety of professional applications as well as advancing basic knowledge about human development.

But with respect to legal policy, the contributions of developmental research have been more limited. This chapter is devoted to examining the useful applications that exist as well as to exploring why they are so difficult to enumerate. To describe the policymaking process and the tensions inherent in generating "usable knowledge," I will first examine how policies concerning children and families are developed at two levels of analysis. One level concerns the broad and overarching values guiding child and family policy in America (what I call "fundamental values"), and the other level concerns how these values are implemented at the practical level of local case-by-case decisionmaking (what I call "the trenches"). In a sense, these two levels of policy analysis can be regarded as the Constitutional "blueprint" of fundamental values that is the basis for legislative and courtroom policymaking, on the one hand, and how that blueprint is applied by child protection caseworkers, social service personnel, lawyers, judges, and program administrators in local jurisdictions, on the other. Understanding each level is essential to understanding the tensions that exist in policymaking concerning child maltreatment and in policy applications of developmental research. A discussion of current policy proposals concerning the psychological maltreatment of children exemplifies these tensions.

Following this, I will also consider the diverse ways that research can inform the policymaking process. This is important because researchers often have an impoverished view of the relevance of research, regarding it primarily in terms of its direct problem-solving applications and neglecting its more general and indirect influences. Considering the diverse uses of research knowledge can also assist researchers in determining the ways their research is (and is not) applicable to specific policymaking problems: Does it help to identify and/or describe a problem? provide tools for its assessment? conceptualize solutions? test specific remedies? By understanding the tensions inherent in policymaking and the diverse kinds of research applications to policy, developmental scientists can, I argue, strengthen their contributions to the policymaking community. In the final section, I will suggest specific directions in which such contributions can proceed.

FUNDAMENTAL VALUES

Although our concern about maltreated children reflects a fundamental interest in protecting children from harm, other interests are also entailed in policy considerations. When a child protection caseworker appears at the home, perhaps in response to an anonymous complaint of suspected child abuse, parents and children have a legitimate concern that children are not removed without just cause and that parents have a chance to defend themselves against abuse allegations. When a father or mother is accused by a spouse of sexual maltreatment, perhaps in the context of divorce and a child custody dispute, they have a legitimate interest in insuring that unproven allegations do not unjustly prejudice their efforts to maintain contact with offspring. When an alleged offender is tried in court, he or she is legitimately concerned that the use of videotaped child testimony or clinical evidence using unvalidated assessment techniques does not unduly bias the jury toward assuming that abuse allegations are true. In short, there is a tension in child protection between the efforts of the state to protect its young citizens, and other protections that all citizens legitimately expect (see Melton & Thompson, 1987).

In the legal system, these fundamental values and interests are institutionalized in judicial deference to the rights explicitly or implicitly identified in the Constitution, especially the Bill of Rights and the 14th Amendment (the latter concerning "equal protection" under the law and "due process" guarantees). The Supreme Court has long recognized these rights as *fundamental*, which means that the State's intrusion into these rights is strictly limited. More specifically, the state must demonstrate that any regulation intruding on these rights is

(a) motivated by a compelling state interest, (b) involves regulation that is closely related to this compelling interest, and (c) the regulation is the least intrusive means of insuring the state's interest. In short, any action by the state that intrudes on fundamental Constitutional guarantees to citizens is strictly scrutinized by the courts.

What fundamental rights or interests apply to child protection? The Supreme Court has long recognized that parents have a fundamental right to the custody, care, and nurturance of offspring (e.g., *Meyer v. Nebraska*, 1923; *Pierce v. Society of Seven Sisters*, 1925; *Prince v. Massachusetts*, 1944; *Wisconsin v. Yoder*, 1972; *Santosky v. Kramer*, 1982). There are several reasons for this (McCarthy, 1988). Parental autonomy has been defended by the presumption that parents are usually most knowledgeable and motivated to advance the interests of offspring, and that children are likely to benefit when parents are protected from interference in their individualized childrearing decisions by authorities who are less knowledgeable or committed to the particular child's needs. Moreover, parental autonomy is a guarantee of desirable pluralism in childrearing goals and philosophy, consistent with democratic principles and ensuring heterogeneous views in a democratic society. Parental autonomy preserves ethnic and cultural heritages, for example, from intrusion by the majority culture. Finally, parental autonomy is important because of the disutility of state-governed childrearing practices or discretionary interventions by authorities into family life: quite simply, the state is likely to do more harm than good by trying to closely regulate childrearing practices. To this list contemporary developmental psychologists would probably add the importance to children of maintaining strong, consistent attachments to caregivers that are not easily threatened by the intrusion of authorities into family life (e.g., Goldstein, Freud, & Solnit, 1979).

It is important to note that, even though these justifications for parental autonomy rely heavily on children's interests, a judicial finding of child maltreatment does not eliminate this fundamental parental right. In *Santosky v. Kramer* (1982), the Court affirmed that a high standard of proof was still necessary to terminate parental rights even when parents had been found neglectful. The Court argued, in essence, that parents do not automatically lose their responsibilities and rights even when they have failed. Although this decision was based on a fundamental rights analysis, it is supported also by a recognition in the psychological literature that children often maintain strong emotional attachments to caregivers who have maltreated them, and that severing their relational ties sometimes poses greater potential harm than benefit to offspring.

However, the state has a compelling interest in preventing harm to its minor citizens. In stating that the family is not beyond state regulation, the Court has affirmed that, although parents may become martyrs if they wish, parents are not "free . . . to make martyrs of their children" (*Prince v. Massachusetts*, 1944, p. 170). In legal doctrine, the state's power to intervene into families to protect children is based on its *parens patriae* power, a 17th-century doctrine enjoining the sovereign to prevent the exploitation of children by third parties (Areen, 1975), and which has expanded in recent years with the recognition that minors enjoy many of the Constitutional guarantees of mature citizens (*In re Gault*, 1967). At a minimum, therefore, the state is empowered to intervene into family life in circumstances that warrant significant concern for a child's safety, health, and well-being. It can do so punitively (by criminalizing parental misconduct as a strong statement of social values concerning appropriate parental behavior), and/or it can do so preventively (by acting to minimize the incidence or recurrence of abuse through either in-home interventions or out-of-home placements when children have been maltreated).

One of the tensions in child protection, therefore, is the intrusion on a fundamental value (parental autonomy in childrearing) by a compelling state interest (prosecuting and preventing harm to its minor citizens). As earlier noted, Constitutional analysis requires that state action in such circumstances is closely related to its compelling interest and provides the least intrusive means of accomplishing its interest. With respect to child protection, this means several things. First, the state must be explicit in its criteria for intervention into family life (see, for example, *Alsager v. District Court of Polk County, Iowa*, 1975, with respect to interventions leading to removal of children from the home). Vague, highly discretionary, and/or broad, general criteria are Constitutionally impermissible because they do not clearly define the parental conduct that warrants state intervention, and they permit the arbitrary exercise of judicial discretion. When ill-defined criteria are used, in other words, parents are not forewarned about the conditions warranting the intervention of legal authorities, and similar cases may be treated differently depending on the personal opinions and viewpoints of the judges, lawyers, and caseworkers involved in each case. These are significant violations of distributive justice principles. This means that the criteria defining child maltreatment must be clear, explicit, and operational.

Second, the individual(s) accused of maltreatment must be provided certain other due process guarantees, such as the right to a hearing, representation by counsel, confrontation with witnesses, appellate review, and other provisions. This has important implications for the adjudication of child maltreatment, including evidentiary issues (e.g., direct contact with child witness in criminal proceedings) as well as practical problems concerning the duration of adjudication and its costs as well as benefits to children. One of the most difficult problems in the criminal prosecution of alleged child abusers, for example, is that doing so can involve prolonged adjudication that provides no immediate solutions for the child and may, in fact, involve long-term stresses.

Third, the state's efforts to punish and prevent child maltreatment must be closely related to its compelling interest in protecting children, and the procedures it uses must not be unnecessarily broad or expansive. For example, proposals to prevent maltreatment by conditioning welfare (AFDC) benefits on parent training, or requiring mandatory parent education for all teenagers, or by "licensing" parents (e.g., Mangel, 1988; McIntire, 1973) would likely be deemed Constitutionally impermissible because the proposals involve unduly sweeping interventions into fundamental rights, and are not narrowly tied to the state's specific interests in abuse prevention (e.g., Sandmire & Wald, 1990). From a Constitutional standpoint, it is one thing to treat or prosecute abusive parents to prevent the recurrence of abuse; it is another thing to regulate all parenting behavior in order to reduce the incidence of abuse, because the latter remedy is a broad infringement on the rights of parents without just cause or clear evidence that it advances the state's interest in abuse prevention.

It should be apparent that, from the standpoint of fundamental values, child and family policy involves a delicate balancing of state interests in child protection and Constitutional guarantees of family integrity and parental autonomy. This balancing derives from the importance of the family as the foundational unit of social organization and the arena for child development, and from the fact that the state is ill-equipped to assume its functions. Consequently, great care must be taken to avoid erroneous or unnecessary intrusions into the family, even in the interests of child protection. Policy proposals offered by researchers to remedy child maltreatment must take this delicate balancing of interests and concerns into account.

Not surprisingly, the manner in which this balancing of compelling state interests and Constitutional protections is achieved evokes considerable debate. Some child advocates argue that an emphasis on parental autonomy and family privacy undermines legitimate state interests in child protection, and specifically undermines child welfare by hiding parental misconduct from detection and intervention (Feshbach & Feshbach, 1976, 1978; Garbarino, 1977; Garbarino, Gaboury, Long, Grandjean, & Asp, 1982; Garbarino & Stocking, 1980). They would risk infringing on parental rights and the possibility of unwarranted interventions into family life in order to maximize the state's capacity to detect and combat child maltreatment. Other advocates also question current safeguards of parental autonomy and family privacy from the standpoint of child empowerment: They argue that children should be enabled to exercise independent decision making concerning their own needs and interests, and that the parental autonomy tradition undermines children's autonomy and privacy (Melton, 1982, 1983). On the other hand, some current child advocates would strengthen rather than reduce protections of parental autonomy against state intervention in suspected child maltreatment (Goldstein, Freud, & Solnit, 1973, 1979). Their argument derives from observations that state interventions to remedy child abuse—especially those in which children are removed from the home—are often more psychologically traumatizing to children than the experience of abuse, and sever attachments to caregivers who remain important to children.

These alternative views underscore that the current balance of state interests and Constitutional protections is neither static nor resolved, and that the tensions between fundamental values remain significant catalysts within policy analysis.

However, any effort to contribute to this policy debate must recognize seriously and encompass these tensions in order to provide a useful contribution.

THE TRENCHES

Fundamental values are applied in the statutory guidelines, regulations, and procedures that underlie the child protection system in local jurisdictions. Because of the exceedingly complex and case-specific decision making of child protection caseworkers, lawyers, judges, social service personnel, program administrators, and other professionals at the local level, however, it is arguable that true reform in the child protection system will derive, not from broader statutory reform, but instead from changes in procedures, resources, and training in local casework activity.

The child protection system itself has changed significantly in recent decades (Wald, 1988). The system has been beset by a rapidly escalating series of demands as public consciousness of child maltreatment and the apparent incidence of child abuse has grown significantly. Moreover, the nature of child maltreatment has become both more diverse and more complex. Public concern that was initially galvanized by the discovery of the "battered child syndrome" (Kempe, Silverman, Steele, Droegemueller, & Silver, 1962) in the early 1960s has now widened to include concerns over the prevalence of neglect and its links to family poverty in the late 1960s, the "discovery" of sexual abuse in the late 1970s and early 1980s, and the contemporary concern with drug-exposed babies and the effects of poverty on children. In addition, the range of intervention options has also been subjected to recent scrutiny. In the mid-1970s, for example, a number of commentators voiced great concern over the experience of children in the foster care system, in which children could remain in a series of changing "temporary" foster care placements interminably with little hope for a permanent, stable placement, and in which the possibility of further abuse was distressingly high (e.g., Mnookin, 1973). These concerns remain current, together with worries about the diminishing availability of suitable foster care placements. A continuing decline in funding and other resources for child protection systems during the last decade has exacerbated these dilemmas over what beneficial interventions the state is capable of providing to the children it identifies as maltreated.

What happens when a report of possible child maltreatment is received by local authorities? Although specific procedures vary (sometimes substantially) by local jurisdiction, some common characteristics are usually evident (Cunningham & Horowitz, 1989; U.S. Advisory Board on Abuse and Neglect, 1990; Wald, 1988). With the advent of mandatory child abuse reporting laws in all states (especially since the federal 1974 Child Abuse Prevention and Treatment

Act), this initial report may come from an identified or anonymous informant, from a professional specialist (such as a physician, teacher, day-care worker, or researcher) or a nonprofessional source, from someone who has directly observed maltreatment or suspects abuse without certainty, or from someone who is either intimately or distally connected with the family. The report may go to a child protection office, an emergency 24-hour hotline, the police, or another agency.

Once the report is received, most state reporting laws require an immediate investigation, although resource restrictions in many jurisdictions require that cases are prioritized according to the threat of immediate danger to the child (Giovannoni, 1991; Rosenberg, 1987). In light of the variety of reports that may be received and the quality of available information, making this determination can be extraordinarily difficult. Once an investigation is initiated, however, interviews with parents, other caregivers, the child, siblings, and (in most cases) the informant ensue, together with a direct physical and/or mental health examination of the child and an inspection of the home. Existing records (e.g., school, medical) may also be examined. Needless to say, this initial investigation is disruptive to the child and family, and can be highly coercive if parents are uncooperative. This investigation is usually conducted by social service personnel, although the police may also be involved. Throughout this investigation, caseworkers are striving to answer several questions. First, did child maltreatment take place—and if so, by whom and under what circumstances? Second, do these conditions entail a continuing danger or threat of danger to the child? Third, in light of the foregoing, can the child safely remain in the home, or should he or she be removed? Fourth, if maltreatment is substantiated, what initial plans for proceeding with this case should be considered (e.g., services to the family, criminal prosecution, etc.)?

A high proportion of abuse reports fail to be substantiated, and although this does not necessarily mean that maltreatment did not occur, the case is likely to be closed. Substantiating abuse allegations after an initial investigation can be difficult because evidence of maltreatment is often elusive, inconsistent, and nondeterminative. Substantiating abuse thus depends very much on the investigative skills and experience of the caseworker, although more objective child abuse potential inventories are being used in an increasing number of jurisdictions to systematize and organize how caseworkers gather and evaluate pertinent information (Wald & Woolverton, 1990). Often these inventories yield a summary score or categorization of the seriousness of the circumstances related to maltreatment, and they guide the caseworker's evaluation of the current situation as well as consideration of possible interventions. In general, however, caseworkers do not have many resources when investigating abuse allegations.

If maltreatment is deemed substantiated, the caseworker must decide whether immediate removal of the child from the home is warranted, based on the seriousness of existing or potential harm to the child. If removal is deemed necessary, the caseworker (sometimes with police assistance) often has authority to temporarily remove the child at the time of the initial investigation. This must be followed soon afterward, however, by a court order authorizing removal (in some states, the order must precede removal) and a hearing at which parents may be present. The child, meanwhile, may be placed with friends, relatives, or in a temporary foster home that will be the child's residence for an indeterminate period, and supervised visitation with the parent(s) may be arranged, especially when eventual reunification is expected.

The caseworker must also decide on a case plan. Most commonly this involves an agreement with the family involving the enlistment of supportive social services such as counseling, parent education classes, detoxification and/ or substance abuse rehabilitation programs, the enlistment of welfare benefits, vocational counseling, child care services, and similar provisions. Parent participation is mandatory but no further legal action is usually expected. These services are typically organized and evaluated by a different caseworker than the one who conducted the initial investigation, and who assumes responsibility for monitoring parental compliance and progress toward case closure.

Alternatively, legal action may be recommended, at which time the case involves legal authorities who proceed with investigation and prosecution, in collaboration with the caseworker. This can involve civil charges that may lead to the state assuming greater control over the child's welfare (including custody of the child), and/or criminal charges that may lead to incarceration of the parent. In civil action (usually in juvenile or family court) the focus is on the child's welfare; in criminal action (in criminal court) the focus is on punishing the alleged offender. Thus the purposes and goals underlying legal action vary. In some civil cases, for example, the capacity of the family to obtain needed social services depends on a judicial finding of child abuse or neglect, and a case plan involving these social services is presented as a proposed treatment for the family with the child remaining at home. Thus the family is adjudicated as a means of obtaining services to benefit the child, in the form of a case plan that is approved by the court. This case plan can be modified from time to time as the case proceeds and the family's circumstances change. In other civil cases, circumstances are sufficiently serious that a temporary removal of the child from the home is necessary, and circumstances may warrant an eventual adjudicated termination of parental rights and the adoption of the child by a new family. In still other cases legal action is based on criminal prosecution, in which the parent(s) may be incarcerated because of abusive behavior.

These alternative actions involve different court systems, procedural rules, and actors and agencies. In each case, however, a series of hearings occurs at which parents and their legal representatives, representatives of various state agencies, and a legal representative for the child are present. The evaluations of psychological experts as well as medical and social data concerning the child and the family may assume an influential role in the adjudication. So also do concerns about the admission and weighing of pertinent evidence related to child maltreatment, which may include the parent's prior behavior, medical testimony, circumstantial evidence, second-hand reports of the child's behavior or utterances on earlier occasions, the child's responses to anatomically correct dolls used during the investigatory interviews, and the extent to which the alleged abuser fits the profile of an abusing parent or the child a profile of the "battered child syndrome" (Kempe et al., 1962) or the "sexual abuse accommodation syndrome" (Summit, 1983).

There are also important evidentiary issues concerning child testimony, especially when there is little evidence of abuse other than the child's allegations, and these issues may concern the child's emotional distress or trauma at having to testify in the presence of the alleged abuser, the age of the child and the reliability of the testimony, the child's fears of parental retribution or of what will happen to the parent and the family, and the child's subsequent recanting of initial abuse allegations. These issues are sometimes addressed by enlisting expert witnesses to clarify the meaning of the child's statements or behavior. At times, there are efforts to introduce procedural reforms that protect children from some of these potential harms, such as videotaped testimony or testifying on closed-circuit television or behind one-way mirrors, special admission of forms of hearsay evidence, and similar procedures. There is considerable variation between different states about how these issues can be resolved in court, as legislatures and state courts struggle with the relative calculus of child protection concerns and due process guarantees to defendants (see, e.g., *Coy v. Iowa*, 1988).

If the child is temporarily or permanently removed from the home, further legal action on the child's behalf ensues. Since the passage of the 1980 federal Adoption Assistance and Child Welfare Act, a child's out-of-home placement must be reviewed by the court every 6 months, and, although these reviews can be extremely cursory events, they underscore the importance of child protection agencies seeking permanent, stable homes for children who are wards of the state, consistent with a policy emphasis on "permanency planning." In addition, the long-standing policy goal that guides casework decision making is the eventual return of the child to the original home. This means that child protection systems must also make "reasonable efforts" to foster the child's return home. Importantly, whatever the child's placement (in home, with a relative, family friend, or foster family), children very rarely receive treatment, counseling, or other mental health or special educational services related to their experience of abuse (U.S. Advisory Board on Child Abuse and Neglect, 1990).

This scenario is a "bare bones" outline of what happens in the trenches, and it can be complicated by a number of factors in particular cases: criminal prosecution of parents for substance abuse, the enlistment or denial of welfare benefits to the family, inconsistent action by juvenile and criminal courts, inadequate communication between various agency representatives involved with the case or representatives of different jurisdictions, turnover in child protection caseworkers, and many other factors. This outline also indicates mandated procedures in case investigation and management, and in jurisdictions with very heavy caseloads social service personnel may be unable to complete all the important facets of an investigation or to follow the case appropriately to its closure. Indeed, this may be true in most jurisdictions. It is worth noting, however, that the large majority of substantiated cases of child maltreatment do not result in criminal prosecution of the alleged offender. Instead, case plans are usually negotiated between families and child protection caseworkers, with court action largely entailed in ratifying and monitoring this agreement. Moreover, it is important to note that the majority of abuse reports concern child neglect, which poses a different set of intervention challenges than do physical or sexual abuse (Select Committee on Children, Youth, and Families, 1987).

Implications

Despite these caveats, however, this outline of what happens in "the trenches" reveals several important features of the child protection system. First, there is a great amount of discretionary decision making by caseworkers, police, social service administrators, prosecutors, judges, and others who are directly involved with children and families. These decision makers differ significantly in the training, background, institutional commitments, interests, resources, and perspectives they bring to each case of alleged child maltreatment—and in these characteristics they also differ significantly from those who usually propose and design policy reforms. Consequently, it is incumbent on those who offer proposals for policy reform to appreciate that new policies are likely to be implemented by individuals who vary significantly in their underlying assumptions and interpretations of policy, and that policy proposals may thus not extend as far as they were initially intended, or may be applied in unexpected or potentially inappropriate ways, because of the diverse and discretionary decision making incorporated throughout the system.

This underscores the need for clear and explicit definitions of child maltreatment, and emphasizes that policy reformers should become acquainted with the variations in viewpoint, resources, and backgrounds of social service personnel in their efforts to alter current practices. What are the assumptions about children and their needs that guide the specific decisions of these local policymakers? On what do they base their underlying views about the nature of family functioning and how it can be changed when families become dysfunctional? With what assumptions do they make judgments concerning the likelihood of future abuse? In what ways do existing resources guide casework decisionmaking (e.g., availability of temporary foster care placements) or program eligibility requirements shape the portrayal of a child's problems? By posing questions such as these, research scientists who hope to influence the policy process can become better acquainted with their intended targets of reform, and can also begin considering how proposals for policy reform are likely to be implemented by local jurisdictional decision makers.

Second, evaluations of current procedures within the child protection system, and proposals for procedural reform, must start from a utilitarian balancing of the benefits and risks of alternative policies. These benefits and risks must take into consideration existing resource constraints and limitations of social service and legal agencies, as well as the nature of the social conditions related to child maltreatment. Procedural or institutional reforms may remedy certain problems at a cost to other aspects of the child protection system. For example, if current efforts to provide assistance to dysfunctional families are undermined by the overwhelming demands of investigating escalating numbers of child abuse allegations, what happens to the system if statutory definitions of maltreatment are broadened to include new kinds of abuse? Will this require greater emphasis on prioritizing incoming case reports according to suspected severity? Should mandatory abuse-reporting laws instead be tightened to reduce the frequency of unsubstantiated abuse reports and thus reduce demands on investigators (Besharov, 1988; Meriwether, 1988; Repucci & Aber, 1992)? If so, how likely is this to result in serious amounts of undetected maltreatment?

Utilitarian cost–benefit analysis is also relevant to the weighing of alternative intervention options. For example, given the problems of the foster care system and severe limitations in the counseling, mental health, and other support services typically available to the victims of child maltreatment, under what conditions does state intervention provide a significant benefit to children? What sorts of services are needed to provide meaningful assistance to maltreated children? How do we weigh existing benefits of state intervention against the costs of service delivery to children, especially when intervention involves family disruption, privacy violations, and coercive case plans in which the child is the locus of family conflict and state remediation efforts? When children suffer from neglect owing to poverty, which kinds of state interventions benefit children and which do not? Does prosecuting substantiated abusers aid children, and in what circumstances?

It is partly due to these kinds of utilitarian considerations that recent commentators have recommended that the "best interests of the child" standard for state intervention into families be replaced by a standard of "least detrimental alternative" to remedy a specific harm to the child when maltreatment is concerned, given the limitations in the state's capacity to benefit the children it takes into its care (e.g., Goldstein, Freud, & Solnit, 1979; Lloyd, 1990). Others argue that the focus of limited public resources should be on intervening less frequently into families but doing so more effectively, rather than on intervening more but doing it poorly (Besharov, 1988; Wald, 1975, 1980). Such utilitarian considerations must prevail until there are realistic, optimistic indications that the child protection system will benefit immediately from dramatic increases in resources and training of personnel.

Third, this summary of child protection in the trenches also reveals the number of important and (for the most part) researchable questions that merit attention from developmental scientists. More systematic study of the etiology of various forms of child maltreatment (e.g., physical abuse, sexual abuse, drug-exposed babies, educational neglect, emotional maltreatment, etc.) might yield proposals for different intervention options that are well suited for particular kinds of maltreatment. A comprehensive examination of the outcomes of children who experience different intervention alternatives (e.g., placement with relatives, foster-care placement, remaining at home with services to the family, etc.) might yield useful information about which children and families benefit from which kinds of placements. Systematic study of the factors that contribute to the reincidence of abuse after contact with local authorities would contribute to the development of more valid and reliable child abuse prediction inventories for use by child protection caseworkers. The development of well-designed and operational outcome measures concerning parental and child behavior might assist caseworkers who must determine when a child is ready to return to the home, or when a case is ready to be closed. In short, a careful examination of how casework occurs at the level of local jurisdictions reveals a number of important questions for which useful answers do not currently exist, and about which developmental scientists can assist practitioners.

In the end, an acquaintance with policymaking in the trenches is as important as an understanding of policymaking involving fundamental values because each reveals the tensions inherent in formulating and implementing effective interventions on behalf of maltreated children. Although the impulse to act effectively to assist these children is as strong in developmental scientists as it is in others who are concerned about child abuse and neglect, this impulse does not lead to "usable knowledge" or useful policy recommendations unless it entails due consideration of these inherent tensions in child and family policy.

PSYCHOLOGICAL MALTREATMENT AS AN ILLUSTRATION

These tensions in formulating public policy concerning child maltreatment—from both fundamental values and the trenches—and the enlistment of developmental researchers in this process are usefully illustrated in current debates concerning the definition and assessment of psychological maltreatment.

In recent years, a number of developmental investigators have strongly urged that definitions of *child abuse and neglect* be expanded to include the psychological maltreatment of children (sometimes called "emotional abuse or neglect," "psychological harm," or "mental injury"). The parental behaviors that constitute psychological maltreatment are varied: they can include "rejecting," "degrading," "isolating," or "exploiting" the child (Hart, Germain, & Brassard, 1987), "psychologically unavailable caregiving" (Egeland & Erickson, 1987), "ignoring," "corrupting," or "terrorizing" children (Garbarino, Guttman, & Seeley, 1986), or "any communication pattern" that may potentially damage the child psychologically, especially by undermining the child's resolution of important developmental tasks (McGee & Wolfe, 1991). According to some commentators, psychological maltreatment is also involved in prejudice and racism, living in dangerous environments, families with substance abuse problems, and the child's exposure to "negative and limiting models" (Telzrow, 1987) in certain social environments (see contributors to Brassard, Germain, & Hart, 1987). From this perspective, psychological maltreatment is not only extensively involved in other forms of child abuse, but it is also the most prevalent and destructive form of child maltreatment (Hart & Brassard, 1987; McGee & Wolfe, 1991).

It is reasonable for developmental scientists to be concerned about the psychological maltreatment of children. Their awareness of the potentially deleterious effects of parental behavior has been enhanced by a generation of research examining the psychological effects of parenting practices on offspring, the most recent of which include longitudinal studies of the effects of secure or insecure attachments in infancy (see, e.g., Lamb, Thompson, Gardner, & Charnov, 1985; Maccoby & Martin, 1983, for reviews). A considerable research literature now attests to the fact that children who consistently experience insensitive, unresponsive, and unhelpful parental care often show long-term consequences, including impaired peer relations, diminished self-esteem, and behavioral problems at home and school. When these studies are considered together with research on the etiology of childhood psychological disorders, as well as the literature on the causes and consequences of child maltreatment, there is rather convincing evidence that the quality of parental care that children receive has important consequences for their mental health and psychological well-being (Cicchetti, 1990).

On the basis of this conclusion, efforts to increase public awareness of the origins and outcomes of psychological maltreatment can have a number of beneficial effects. In clinical interventions, for example, therapists are alerted to the psychological consequences of abusive parental behavior that can be included in a treatment plan. In the design of preventive and educational programs targeted for at-risk populations, an awareness of the origins and consequences of psychological maltreatment can inform program design and implementation. When maltreated children are placed in foster homes or provided in-home services, knowledge about psychological maltreatment can sensitize caseworkers to significant dimensions of children's needs. More generally, the results of developmental research and advocacy efforts concerning the psychological maltreatment of children can promote changes in social values concerning the parameters of "appropriate" parenting practices. In this sense, the debate concerning psychological maltreatment advances public discourse about the range of parental behaviors that are deemed "acceptable."

When concepts of psychological maltreatment are proposed as the basis for reforms in legal policy, on the other hand, additional issues must also be considered (Melton & Thompson, 1987; Thompson & Jacobs, 1991). As we have seen, these pertain to fundamental values guiding the state's intrusion into family life, and practical problems in the implementation of policy in local jurisdictions.

With respect to fundamental values, the concept of psychological maltreatment poses significant challenges to the need for clear, explicit criteria governing intrusions on parental autonomy and family privacy. At present, researchers have provided few explicit guidelines for how psychological maltreatment can be operationalized and assessed in the home by social service caseworkers. Is a parent who is overwhelmed with marital problems or struggling to juggle domestic and employment responsibilities likely to be accused of being "psychologically unavailable" to offspring? Are a farm couple who require children to assist with chores guilty of "exploiting" their children? Is a parent who conditions praise on the child's compliance with toilet training, self-care, or other maturity demands imposing "communication patterns" that might be psychologically damaging? These are disturbing questions if current conceptualizations of psychological maltreatment are proposed as the basis for policy reform, and the uncertainty of the answers makes it likely that any current proposal would, if adopted, be deemed unconstitutional because of vagueness in the standards for state intervention into family life.

Moreover, it is arguable that such broad, vague portrayals of psychological maltreatment are impermissible also because they are not narrowly tailored to the state's compelling interest in preventing specific forms of child abuse or neglect. Our society has reached consensus that broken bones and sexual trauma warrant state intervention into family life, but there is less consensus about insecure attachment or diminished self-esteem, which are also affected by many influences besides parenting practices. Until researchers provide clear evidence to convince a skeptical public that specific forms of parental behavior are reliably linked to specific harms to children that are sufficiently severe to warrant state concern, current portrayals of psychological maltreatment seem unduly expansive to be a basis for policy reform.

In the trenches, current conceptualizations of psychological maltreatment are problematic for other reasons. Although terms like *missocializing, exploiting,* or *isolating* offspring may enjoy shared, intuitive meaning among the developmental research community, it is likely that their intuitive meaning is much different to the social service personnel, child protection caseworkers, lawyers, judges, program administrators, and others who must implement these criteria on a case-by-case basis. As a consequence, the applications of these terms may extend much farther than they were originally intended, or not far enough, and this can result in many unwarranted or inappropriate interventions into family life. Families are likely to feel unfairly treated by a system that deems certain behavior maltreating—by one caseworker's, police officer's, prosecutor's, or judge's viewpoint—whereas the same behavior may be deemed nonmaltreating by other personnel or in another jurisdiction. Cultural or socioeconomic bias in the definition of psychological maltreatment becomes likely. Such violations of distributive justice principles are inevitable when vague and broadly worded definitions of maltreatment are used for policymaking.

Furthermore, the expansion of the concept of maltreatment to include psychological maltreatment is likely to have other consequences for policymaking within the trenches. Given the extraordinary and escalating demands upon social service agencies in the context of diminishing resources, it seems likely that statutory provisions concerning psychological maltreatment would either divert attention and resources from other, potentially more serious, forms of child abuse, or be functionally ignored as incoming cases are prioritized according to suspected severity (Giovannoni, 1991). In either case, children do not benefit from such an expanded definition of maltreatment. Although an emphasis on psychological maltreatment could also be justified as a preventative approach to more severe forms of maltreatment—that is, identifying and helping dysfunctional families early before abuse becomes more serious—the experience of other sociolegal systems suggests that this strategy is unlikely to prove successful. Programs in the juvenile justice system, for example, have sometimes used more expansive definitions of target populations to identify "youth at risk" or "predelinquents" in an effort to identify problem children early. This phenomenon (described as "widening-the-nets," [Austin & Krisberg, 1981]) has meant, however, that the system has also labeled children and intervened in the lives of many families who did not, in fact, require services, and has also placed greater strain on limited program resources as additional numbers of youth have been served (Osgood & Jacobs, 1985). The same consequences are likely within a more expansive statutory definition of psychological maltreatment: Many children would be targeted who probably do not warrant state concern, and the system's overstrapped resources would be further depleted.

These utilitarian cost–benefit considerations extend also to questions of how best to intervene in the lives of children who have been identified as psychologically maltreated. Given that state intervention—whether it involves the provision of in-home services to the child, out-of-home treatment for the abusing parent, or placement of the child with a relative or foster family—is necessarily psychologically invasive and distressing to children, to what extent do these interventions provide more benefit than harm to children who have been psychologically maltreated by a parent? When children experience psychological maltreatment that is unaccompanied by other forms of abuse (which is rather rare; see Daro, 1988), this question becomes an issue of how well the state can assist children in emotional need without doing them emotional harm in the process. When children experience psychological maltreatment that is accompanied by physical abuse, marked neglect, sexual abuse, or other forms of maltreatment, on the other hand, the concept of psychological maltreatment is probably redundant as an intervention tool, and may be useful only as a means of defining new dimensions of concern for children who have already been identified by social service agencies for potentially more severe forms of abuse. In short, including the concept of psychological maltreatment in policy reform may not help social agencies identify and assist a distinct new population of children needing state protection—and when it does, the state may have few guarantees of effective intervention. If considerable debate currently exists concerning whether protective interventions into the family to address manifest physical or sexual abuse prove more damaging than helpful to children, then it is wise to be cautious about extending the basis for intervention to include cases of psychological maltreatment alone.

These tensions in policymaking, therefore, create tensions for researchers who seek to contribute meaningfully and helpfully to the policy debate concerning child maltreatment. What should developmental scientists do? As suggested earlier, there is considerable potential value to the concept of psychological maltreatment as a catalyst for clinical efforts, prevention and educational program design, and the organization of services for maltreated children. Basic research on the causes and consequences of different kinds of parental practices can advance these efforts. Furthermore, researchers have a legitimate role to play in advancing the public debate on the parameters of acceptable parenting behavior in our society (Garbarino, 1991). They can do so by offering research findings that demonstrate the consequences of improper parenting practices on offspring, although ultimately this debate is a question of social values and priorities for which research findings can be informative and influential, but nondeterminative (Giovannoni, 1991; Thompson & Jacobs, 1991). Finally, there is a considerable amount of policy-relevant research that remains to be done if scientists are truly interested in advancing the concept of psychological maltreatment for purposes of policy reform. Developing clear and operational definitions of the various dimensions of psychological maltreatment (and their associations with other forms of maltreatment), establishing causal links between specific forms of inappropriate parenting behavior and specific consequences for offspring, and demonstrating the efficacy (and cost-effectiveness) of interventions that are within the state's capacity to provide would be a good start to such a research agenda.

When the discussion turns to policy reform, however, developmental scientists have an ethical responsibility to be cautious in their recommendations based on current evidence, for several reasons. First, if researchers do not have a serious understanding of the tensions involved in policymaking, they are likely to offer well-meaning but naive policy proposals that understate the possible costs and emphasize the potential benefits of policy reform. As a consequence, their recommendations will foster greater confidence in policy reform than is perhaps warranted. It is one thing, for example, to advance portrayals of psychological maltreatment that are useful in therapeutic or research contexts where the costs of inappropriate application are minimal and errors can be fairly easily detected. It is quite another to offer the same portrayals in proposals for legal policy reform when these safeguards cannot as easily be guaranteed, and when the costs of misapplication are very high.

Caution is also required because the application of developmental research findings to policy problems usually assume value judgments that are not scientifically determined. Is the state's interest in children who are psychologically maltreated a "compelling" interest, as it is with other forms of maltreatment? Does sufficient social concensus exist concerning the acceptable parameters of the psychological treatment of offspring to warrant state intervention? Are the deleterious outcomes of psychological maltreatment sufficiently severe to warrant the state's concern? These are not scientific questions but value judgments, and policy recommendations based on developmental research usually presume answers to these questions, even though research cannot provide the answers.

Finally, caution is warranted in proposing policy reform because it is easy to inadvertently overstate the scientific basis for policy recommendations. When exploring a phenomenon as complex as child maltreatment, researchers rely on subject populations that are sometimes different from those to whom findings are generalized, recruit samples that are often rather small, depend on theory to affirm links between cause and effect, and conduct their research using ecological settings and methods that are sometimes much different from the settings in which children live. Their intervention recommendations are usually based on assumptions concerning behavioral remediation that have not been tested and evaluated in a programmatic manner in field settings. These problems are especially apparent in the research literatures pertaining to the psychological maltreatment of children. Given the caution and critical skepticism that attends theory development in the behavioral sciences, developmental researchers must extend that healthy self-criticism to their presentation of research and policy recommendations in applied forums, and be cautious in offering proposals for policy reform based on current research evidence.

At times, an understanding of the tensions in policymaking can highlight rather than obscure the policy implications of developmental research, and this is also true concerning the psychological maltreatment of children. Although Melton and Thompson (1987) criticized the concept of psychological maltreatment as it is applied to the regulation of family functioning, for example, they noted that the same concept might have useful applications for the regulation of institutions affecting children, such as state hospitals and schools. They argued this from a fundamental values perspective, noting that state interests conflict with fundamental values when intervention into families is concerned, but fundamental values *require* the regulation of institutions on behalf of the children who reside there. They also advanced this argument from a trenches viewpoint, noting that the risks to children of unwarranted interventions into institutions are significantly less than the risks of inappropriate intrusions into family life. In short, an understanding of the policymaking process significantly complicates efforts to apply research findings to legal policies concerning child maltreatment, but in ways that may reveal as well as curtail avenues for policy reform, hopefully to the benefit of the children we hope to assist.

MODES OF RESEARCH APPLICATION

Thus far, the discussion has focused on errors to avoid in efforts to enlist developmental research in the generation of legal policies benefitting maltreated children. But it is also worth recognizing that research *does*, in fact, affect the policymaking process in diverse ways. Recognizing the various modes of research application to policymaking can help developmental researchers appreciate the multiple and complex ways their studies influence the policymaking process, and can make their contributions more precise. Research that is useful to the description or conceptualization of maltreatment may not, for example, contribute directly to problem solving, and thus research should be applied and disseminated in a manner that is appropriate to its specific policymaking contributions. Moreover, these alternative modes of research application influence the policymaking process in different ways. Research that contributes to problem solving becomes enlisted in fashioning alternative policy proposals, but research that describes or conceptualizes the problem influences the core assumptions by which policymakers in local jurisdictions (e.g., caseworkers, police, lawyers, judges, etc.) interpret and implement policy guidelines, and lastly, the technological contributions of research are instrumentally employed locally by various actors in the child protection system. Thus an appreciation of the diverse modes of research application highlights the different actors, applications, and dissemination modes that are relevant to the enlistment of developmental research in policymaking concerning child maltreatment. These are the issues of this section.

Research as Problem Solving

As Weiss (1978, 1987) and other students of research-policy applications have noted, researchers most commonly and intuitively think of their studies in terms of their direct problem-solving applications: How can research be enlisted to resolve an important social problem like maltreatment? We have already noted that this involves a giant leap between research findings and policy reform because (a) research is ill-equipped to address the thorny problems of defining and balancing fundamental social values, (b) many policy problems are difficult to study given existing research technology and ethical constraints, and (c) research is often limited by sampling problems and measurement difficulties that constrain direct applications to policy problems. This means that designing and conducting problem-solving research not only encounters formidable conceptual obstacles, but also requires considerable funding resources in an environment of declining research support from federal and private agencies.

Nevertheless, a number of recent investigations illustrate the uses of developmental research for problem-solving policy applications concerning child maltreatment. One is an ambitious longitudinal study conducted by Wald, Carlsmith, and Leiderman (1988) that sought to examine whether maltreated children were best served by foster care placements or in-home services. Wald and his colleagues took advantage of a unique historical opportunity: In 1977 the California legislature created an experimental project in two counties in which many maltreated children who would otherwise have been removed from their homes were instead provided intensive services while maintaining at home. In these jurisdictions, in other words, foster care was reserved for only the most serious cases of abuse or neglect. The purpose of this legislation was to determine whether children would show better developmental outcomes in the context of in-home rather than foster-care placements—consistent with ongoing controversies concerning the efficacy of foster care as a remediation regime for child maltreatment—and the targeted counties were provided supplementary funding to provide special in-home services for these children.

This research group thus embarked on a 2-year longitudinal study examining the developmental progress of a sample of 5- to 10-year-old maltreated children maintained in their homes in one of the targeted counties with a matched group of children in foster care placements in nearby counties. The nature of child maltreatment was comparable between the samples, and the children in the targeted county were those who, according to caseworkers, would have been placed in foster care prior to the legislative change. Both of these maltreated groups were also compared with a sample of nonabused children of similar social class. Children were followed for 2 years following their identification by the state as maltreated, and outcome measures concerning the academic, socioemotional, cognitive, and physical functioning of the children were derived from the children themselves, their teachers, caregivers, and social workers involved in their cases. The children were observed and interviewed at 6-month intervals, their caregivers every 3 months, and other data sources were periodically sampled over the 2-year period.

The results provided a very depressing portrayal of these placements and their efficacy in remediating the consequences of maltreatment. Children who remained at home were reabused in the majority of cases, and even with the additional services provided by the targeted counties many families received no services at all, and in no case did services last longer than 6 months by legislative mandate. Children in foster care were frequently moved from one home to another, and most experienced a drastic decline in contact with their original parents that distressed them. Although children in foster care fared somewhat better on several developmental measures, children in both groups continued at substantial risk. As Wald and his colleagues concluded, "we must ask who were worse off—the foster children who longed to return to their original homes, or the home children who longed for a loving relationship, free of pain, fear, and insecurity" (p. 144).

The findings of this study have some limited policy implications. They suggest that the extremity of concern about the detrimental consequences of foster care for children of this age may be softened somewhat, at least in comparison to the outcomes for children who are instead maintained at home. They suggest that funding for intensive services that will enable maltreated children to remain at home will not always reach the targeted families, and in any case are likely to be ineffective if they are maintained for only a few months. Wald and his colleagues also recommended that permanency planning in out-of-home placements should be emphasized more than current policies do, and that services to children—whether in home or foster care placements—should be strengthened.

But these implications were offered cautiously, in light of the difficulties Wald and his colleagues encountered in completing this research. Their overall sample size was small—consisting of only 19 children at home and 13 children in foster care—because of sample attrition, changes in placements during the study, and ethnic and minority group confounds. As the authors recognized, this is hardly a sufficient sample size to instill confidence in the reliability of the findings emerging from this project. Moreover, the in-home and foster-care samples also differed initially on several developmental measures in ways that made later outcome differences harder to interpret. Indeed, the volume emerging from this research is a unique study of the problems and challenges inherent in conducting good problem-solving policy-analytic research, which are discussed honestly and insightfully by the authors. But in illustrating these difficulties and the cautions they require in the interpretation of results, this research also contributes to a useful model of the kinds of future studies that are needed in this field.

Other problem-solving research concerning maltreatment consists of field tests of intervention programs that can provide the basis for planning state interventions for maltreated children. One example is the Elmira Prenatal/Early Infancy Project, designed by Olds and his colleagues (e.g., Olds & Henderson, 1989) to examine whether home visitation beginning prenatally could reduce the incidence of child maltreatment in a high-risk sample. A large sample of first-time mothers (which included mothers who were predominantly young, poor single parents) was divided into four treatment groups using stratified random assignment: one group received only periodic infant assessments during the child's first 2 years of life; another group also received free transportation to regular prenatal and well-child visits during this period; and a third group, in addition to these services, also received biweekly visits from a registered nurse during the mother's pregnancy. The fourth group received the most intensive services of all: in addition to the foregoing, the nurse continued to visit weekly after the child was born, eventually tapering off to visits every 4 to 6 weeks by the time of the child's second birthday. Home visits (averaging more than an hour each) focused on parent education and childrearing practices, enhancing the mother's personal growth, strengthening informal supports to the family, and consolidating ties with formal health and social service agencies in the community. Each of the four comparison groups numbered 90–116 mothers at the beginning of the study, although the proportion of high-risk mothers was less than half of each group.

The intensive, long-term interventions provided the fourth treatment group had a small but important effect: these mothers were less likely than mothers without nurse visits to be identified by local social service agencies for child maltreatment, although the difference was statistically marginally significant. Mothers who had received only prenatal nurse visits also showed lower abuse rates than mothers without this service, although the difference was not as large. The mothers receiving intensive services also showed more positive reactions to their infants: during home observations they were less likely to punish or restrict the child, were more likely to provide appropriate play materials, and they generally reported more positive temperamental characteristics in offspring than did mothers without nurse visitation.

These results are both encouraging and discouraging in their policy implications. Given the limited success of many child abuse prevention programs, evidence of demonstrated efficacy from an intensive program of home visitation is hopeful (see contributors to Willis, Holden, & Rosenberg, 1992). Moreover, the apparent success of a home visitation program suggests that one way to insure that families benefit from available social services (a problem noted by Wald and colleagues) is to provide services at home, rather than elsewhere. Families may be more responsive to home-based services, and their efficacy does not depend as much on the parent's willingness to make personal effort to attend and participate. However, it is important to note that the effects of these intensive services were fairly minimal in relation to the overall costs of the program (which included the intensive services of well-trained nurse visitors over a 2-year period), and may have been specific to the population of young, poor, single mothers. Although this is precisely the population at greatest risk for child abuse, this study raises difficult questions concerning the cost-effectiveness of universally providing such an intensive, long-term program for this population to reduce the incidence of child maltreatment. Systematic follow-up studies to determine more precisely which elements of the intervention strategy were effective are also needed.

The potential importance of sample-specific intervention efficacy is further underscored by a third example of problem-solving policy-relevant research reported by Daro (1988), which will be described more briefly here (see Daro, this volume). This study was initiated and funded by the National Center on

Child Abuse and Neglect (NCCAN), a federal agency of the Department of Health and Human Services created by Congress in 1974 to foster research, service delivery, and policy development concerning child maltreatment. In 1978, NCCAN provided funds for 19 existing social service agencies throughout the country to develop or enhance child maltreatment intervention programs in order to explore the efficacy of distinct treatment and prevention programs on different maltreatment subpopulations. These subpopulations included families in which either physical abuse, physical neglect, emotional maltreatment, or sexual abuse was predominant. The major goals of the evaluation component of this project were to identify the distinguishing etiological characteristics of each maltreatment subpopulation and the extent to which each subpopulation required distinct investigatory, treatment and preventive interventions. Outcome measures of the 986 families involved in this project primarily emphasized clinical judgments of likely abuse reincidence and the quality of child and family functioning. Comparisons of the treatment regimes characteristic of each site—which ranged widely from parent-centered individual therapy to broadly based multisystemic approaches for the family—were also systematically conducted.

In general, the results of this project confirmed that different forms of child maltreatment are characterized by different etiological features, with different treatment and prevention implications. Not surprisingly, for example, financial difficulties were almost uniform in families characterized by physical neglect, while emotionally maltreating parents showed greater rates of substance abuse, social isolation, and mental illness, and sexually abusive families exhibited greater interspousal conflict. More importantly, group differences were also apparent in treatment and reincidence. With respect to sexual abuse, for example, clinical judgments of the family's progress and of reincidence were most optimistic, especially when the parent recognized that a problem existed and complied with remediation efforts, often in the context of individual therapy. By contrast, the prognosis was much less optimistic with respect to physical neglect, partly due to the multiple problems faced by these families at intake, and family counseling together with broad community service referrals and education and skill development classes proved most helpful. In all instances, outcome judgments were positively influenced by the duration of treatment, the length of the prior history of abuse, and parental compliance with the treatment regimen.

This research underscores that the term *maltreatment* embraces a heterogeneous variety of family conditions and parental behavior, and that policies addressing this problem should tailor different intervention and prevention strategies to different maltreatment subpopulations. It makes little sense, for example, to remove children from a physically neglectful home or incarcerate the parents if the provision of much-needed social services can remediate these conditions at much less cost to the state and less trauma to children. Understanding the efficacy of in-home services versus out-of-home placements is also enhanced by considering what kind of maltreatment is to be prevented: physical abuse, emotional maltreatment, and sexual abuse are differentially affected by different placement alternatives. However, this investigation is also distressing in its reliance on clinical judgments (provided by individuals who had been intimately involved in the delivery of services to these families), the absence of control groups for comparison purposes, and impoverished statistical analysis of large-sample data. Moreover, outcome measures did not include the actual reincidence of abuse, only clinical judgments of likely reabuse. However, this research illustrates the strong need for systematic and comprehensive monitoring of the kinds of services provided maltreated children and their families by local child protection agencies, and their effects on the targeted families. Only in this manner can researchers and policymakers have useful information concerning the kinds of interventions and services that are normatively available, and their efficacy, for different maltreatment subpopulations.

Challenges to problem-solving applications. It is no surprise that the three examples of problem-solving policy-relevant research discussed in this section are each large-scale, expensive, longitudinal projects. The kind of research that is likely to contribute directly to addressing the dilemmas of policymakers (at both national and local levels) is commonly difficult, time-consuming, and expensive. But like most of the goals underlying ambitious and difficult research projects, efforts to provide "usable knowledge" concerning the prevention and treatment of child maltreatment justifies such efforts.

The challenges in conducting problem-solving policy-relevant research raise a formidable problem, however. Given the need for effective interventions to address a growing and disconcerting number of child maltreatment reports and the lack of a large problem-solving policy-relevant research literature, to what extent should researchers offer informed judgments based on more limited, compromised, and/or incomplete studies (such as those using unvalidated measures, or limited subject samples, or which may not easily generalize to child maltreatment issues)? Do responsible research applications derive only from well-designed, comprehensive studies of the kinds described above (despite their limitations), or are researchers ethically responsible for taking *whatever* pertinent research exists—however limited—to provide empirically based recommendations to the policymaking community?

It seems clear that developmental scientists should contribute to the policy-making debate even when they lack comprehensive studies that provide direct problem-solving applications. The information they provide even from limited research can contribute usefully to a more complete picture of the considerations necessary for responsible policymaking. But a heavy responsibility accompanies this contribution, because it is easy for researchers to inadvertently misrepresent the strength of their research or its policy relevance. This is, therefore, another reason why the cross-fertilization of ideas and concerns between research and policymaking communities is essential. It is likely that researchers will offer more informative (and less misleading) recommendations from limited or compromised data when their knowledge of the policymaking process can guide their appreciation of whether—and how—the research is germane to the policy problems under consideration.

When policymakers are making utilitarian judgments, for example, of the consequences of alternative policy options based on erroneous assumptions about child development (e.g., that children necessarily benefit from removal from an emotionally abusive family), research findings can be enlisted to question these assumptions even when they do not offer specific intervention alternatives. Indeed, developmental research might be especially useful for challenging prevailing assumptions within the policymaking community even though it may be more difficult to specify what new assumptions should replace them (cf. Gardner, Scherer, & Tester, 1989). Similarly, researchers can provide information that highlights dimensions of concern about policy alternatives (e.g., the importance of a child's sense of time and permanency in placement alternatives at various developmental periods) that might not otherwise be included in the calculus of policy considerations. In the end, limited data allow limited and cautious applications to policy problems, with due consideration of both what is known and what is *not* known about policy-relevant developmental issues. Although this sometimes undermines researchers' authority and expertise in the minds of policymakers, it is consistent with the scientific mandate to inform rather than mislead policymakers about the state of existing knowledge.

These tensions in research applications to policy are especially important to acknowledge because of the strong desire to *do something* about the problem of child maltreatment. As a consequence, it is easy to assume that a stronger research foundation exists for policy proposals than is actually true. In the area of child sexual abuse, for example, heightened public concern has resulted in a proliferation of policy initiatives, ranging from support for sex abuse prevention programs in public schools to the enlistment of anatomically correct dolls in the initial interviewing of children (Levy, 1989). Yet despite these efforts, we still know remarkably little about the origins, detection, treatment, and prevention of child sexual abuse. In two recent authoritative reviews of the child sexual abuse prevention literature (Finkelhor & Strapko, 1992; Melton, 1992), for example, both reviewers concluded that we still do not know whether prevention programs actually reduce the incidence of child sexual abuse, and the potentially negative effects of these programs (e.g., heightening fear and anxiety in children) cannot be ruled out. These are, of course, the central concerns to policymakers in evaluating child sexual abuse prevention programs, and thus claims concerning the state of our knowledge about child sexual abuse prevention should be duly cautious and constrained. When developmental scientists remain cognizant of the limitations of existing research concerning important policy-relevant dimensions of child maltreatment such as these, they can inform rather than mislead policymakers concerning the state of knowledge, and can advance new research initiatives with useful problem-solving applications.

Research as Conceptualization

Although a small proportion of developmental research studies have direct problem-solving applications to policy problems, a much larger literature contributes to policymaking through the manner in which social problems are conceptualized by legal and social authorities. The importance of research as conceptualization should not be underestimated: Weiss (1987), Caplan (1979), and other students of research utilization have emphasized the "knowledge creep" by which social science findings become absorbed within the policy-making community through the mass media, presentation by advocacy groups, reports by expert commissions, and other sources. Concepts, ideas, and theories from developmental research become part of the background framework of assumptions and values by which policymakers weigh, evaluate, and organize the specific considerations involved in alternative policy proposals and their implementations. This occurs despite the fact that the research that constitutes the basis for problem conceptualization may be only distally relevant to the problem itself.

A good example of the use of research as conceptualization to the field of child maltreatment is the application of "psychological parenting" theory in general—and attachment theory in particular—to how policy alternatives in this area are conceptualized. As a consequence of the now widespread realization that children develop attachments to significant caregivers that are central to psychological health and well-being—and that these attachments are not specific to biological kin—some of the policy options concerning maltreatment are now framed differently. In particular, policymakers are more concerned with the effects on children of removal from the home, and of the detrimental consequences of severing emotional attachments to caregivers who may also be abusing them. Policymakers are also concerned about the attachments children are likely to develop to foster families with whom they have temporary placements. Indeed, the emphasis on "permanency planning" in the federal 1980 Adoption Assistance and Child Welfare Act derives in fundamental ways from how problems of child protection have been reconceptualized owing to an increased recognition of the importance of attachments and "psychological parenting" in a child's experience.

Importantly, these conceptualizations do not in themselves lead directly to new policy alternatives or even to strong recommendations for reform (i.e., to problem solving); more commonly, they complicate rather than resolve existing policy dilemmas. But in doing so, they help to reorient prevailing ideas concerning maltreatment interventions in ways that hopefully better reflect children's interests and needs. Moreover, research-as-conceptualization contributes to the evolution of public perceptions of the characteristics and needs of children, the nature of family functioning, and the potential benefits of various kinds of interventions into family life. In so doing, research contributes to gradual changes in the concensual values by which alternative policy proposals are developed and evaluated.

Research as Description

At times, the most important use of developmental research in policymaking is as a potent description of children's conditions. Indeed, the modern awareness of child maltreatment was inaugurated with the compelling description of the "battered child syndrome" by Kempe and his colleagues (Kempe et al., 1962), which alerted medical authorities to a constellation of symptoms revealing physical abuse and highlighted the likely prevalence of this problem. This research report subsequently became the basis for advocacy efforts (spearheaded by Kempe himself) within the policymaking community that contributed to the early genesis of mandatory reporting laws, changes within the child protection system, and the enlistment of other federal efforts on behalf of maltreated children. More recently, descriptive data have been the basis for the discovery of the prevalence of child neglect, child sexual abuse, and prenatal drug exposure, and descriptive data have also been helpful in elucidating the social conditions surrounding these forms of child maltreatment.

The influence of research-as-description on policymaking concerning maltreatment includes, among other things, the uses of social indicators that reveal the conditions in which children in America are currently growing up (Zill, 1991; Zill & Rogers, 1988; Zill, Sigal, & Brim, 1983), the presentation of statistical data concerning the incidence and prevalence of various forms of maltreatment (now typically gathered by the National Center on Child Abuse and Neglect and the American Association for Protecting Children), and gathering social service data concerning the availability of services for maltreated children and their families. But research as description can also include smaller scale studies of children and families that focus on the conditions surrounding child maltreatment and the efficacy of intervention alternatives (cf. Wald et al., 1988). In this respect, intensive descriptive small-sample and case studies can be as potentially informative as social indicators data.

As noted throughout this discussion, the availability of descriptive data of this kind not only can inform policymaking decisions, but can also become (like Kempe's seminal study more than 25 years ago) the basis for advocacy efforts on children's behalf. As policymakers and the public at large become aware of the prevalence of child abuse and neglect, concern about children becomes galvanized into funding for new policy initiatives. However, it is important to keep in mind that research-as-description is not the same thing as research-as-problem-solving. Understanding the conditions associated with child maltreatment does not lead directly to intervention strategies, because interventions require a variety of additional considerations, such as the availability of social resources, priorities among the various goals underlying intervention strategies, and the relative costs and benefits of alternative intervention options. Thus while the availability of descriptive data concerning child maltreatment can contribute significantly to well-informed and clearly conceived policy options, descriptive research should not be portrayed as providing intervention solutions.

Research as Technology

At times, the most useful contributions of researchers to policymaking are not the research findings they provide, but the assessment tools they develop that can be applied in field settings. As we have noted, many of the utilitarian deliberations related to child maltreatment policies concern the extent to which various forms of child abuse and neglect can be reliably detected by child protection case-workers, how the consequences of maltreatment to children can be validly appraised, and how the efficacy of various intervention alternatives on children and their families can be assessed. To the extent to which considerable doubt exists about the ability to validly detect maltreatment or to measure the effective-ness of treatment, policymakers tend to narrow the range and scope of interventions on behalf of maltreated children. One important manner in which developmental scientists can contribute to policymaking is in the development of sensitive, reliable, and valid assessment tools to assist in the practical implementation of social interventions to assist targeted children and their families.

This is a more formidable challenge than may at first appear. Developing effective and useful assessment tools requires identifying the child outcomes of greatest concern to the child protection system and to society in general, and this is a question of values as well as of social utility. When evaluating the results of treatment interventions, for example, should the state be concerned solely with reabuse rates? the child's physical well being? the child's happiness or self-esteem? the nature of parent–child interaction? the adult's knowledge of child development? all of these? Beyond these conceptual hurdles, many assessment tools used by developmental researchers are ill suited to field settings, either because they require laboratory-based assessments, extensive interviews, observational procedures, or highly skilled assessors. Moreover, they are likely to be used by caseworkers, social service personnel, and perhaps also police who do not share the conceptual orientations, backgrounds, and prevailing assumptions of the research community, and this enhances the challenges of adapting existing assessment tools to field applications, or developing new assessment methods altogether. Finally, a considerable amount of additional research is needed to develop some of the assessment procedures that would be most useful to policymakers in the area of child maltreatment. Procedures for predicting the likely recurrence of abuse based on child, family, and situational conditions, for example, requires extensive knowledge about the conditions associated with abuse recidivism following the intervention of legal authorities—and there currently exists little information concerning these conditions.

Because of the strong public impetus to develop new and effective interventions, however, a number of assessment tools have already been developed and used extensively in field settings. An important technological contribution of developmental scientists, therefore, is to study the validity and reliability of these instruments in order to better define their uses and limitations and, at times, correct erroneous assumptions about their utility. In the area of child sexual abuse, for example, the need for useful interviewing devices led quickly to the widespread use of anatomically correct dolls that were presumed to facilitate the interviewing process, especially with young children whose lack of knowledge or understanding of the abusive experience, or reticence to disclose, could undermine effective reporting. It is only recently that serious questions have been raised concerning the interpretation of children's behavior with these dolls, and the ways that interviewing may be misdirected rather than facilitated when anatomically correct dolls are incorporated into the interview protocol. At the same time, developmental scientists are beginning to examine how nonabused children respond to such dolls to provide a baseline of normative data with which the responses of sexually abuse children can be compared (e.g., Goodman & Aman, 1991).

This means that some of the more important contributions of research-as-technology is defining the strengths and limitations of existing assessment instruments, as well as developing better tools, based on scientific knowledge of test construction and validation. In an increasing number of jurisdictions, for example, child protection caseworkers use one of a variety of risk assessment instruments to provide a more objective basis for gathering and weighing pertinent information concerning the family. The summary judgments derived from such instruments can, as noted earlier, influence immediate decisions concerning the severity of the family conditions and the likelihood of reabuse of children, as well as longer term considerations pertaining to case planning. Given the interpretive and dispositional burden these instruments assume, it is important to note a number of methodological and conceptual problems inherent in their construction and implementation (see Sandmire & Wald, 1990, and Wald & Woolverton, 1990, for summaries). First, there is very limited research knowledge concerning the factors predictive of abuse recidivism after a family has been involved with the child protection system, so necessarily such instruments are based on quasi-clinical estimations of the most powerful predictive factors. Second, given that the overall base rates of reabuse are rather low and the predictive factors are only moderately discriminating, it is likely that there will be a rather high proportion of false positives yielded by such assessment instruments—that is, families identified as potentially reabusive who will not, in fact, maltreat their children again. High rates of false positives have important public policy implications, because they permit the continuing intervention of the legal system in families when other circumstances may not warrant it. Third, when risk assessment instruments also use scores derived from their inventories to identify families in "high," "moderate," and "low" risk groups, there are further assumptions concerning the extremity of the factors predictive of differing risk levels that have no substantive empirical basis, and defining the meaning of risk levels in absolute rather then relative terms is also problematic (e.g., does *high* risk mean that families will reabuse offspring 70% of the time? 50%? 20%? 5%?). In sum, it is important for developmental scientists to remind users of risk assessment instruments of the very limited research foundation for their design and implementation, and thus that the decisions derived from reliance on such assessment tools are not scientifically well-founded and may be invalid. Moreover, to the extent to which they are used by caseworkers with differing perspectives, training, and prior experience, their implementation is potentially unreliable as well.

These examples suggest that researchers have both a deconstructive and a constructive role to assume in the development of assessment tools for the investigation and treatment of child abuse and neglect. On the one hand, their most important contributions may be, at times, to cast a critical light on assessment instruments that have been quickly developed and implemented in the rush to intervene effectively in child maltreatment cases. They must indicate the limitations of these tools, necessary cautions in their interpretation, and the steps necessary to improve their validity and reliability. On the other hand, caseworkers, clinical evaluators, and family lawyers will experience justified frustration if developmental researchers do not assume their positive responsibility for assisting in the development of better instruments to replace those they criticize. In these dual tasks of deconstruction and reconstruction, research-as-technology can assume an important role in improving how the child protection system addresses the problem of child maltreatment.

Researchers as Child Advocates

The research community has at least two resources to offer the child protection system: the research findings it generates, and the perspectives of researchers themselves. It is important not to neglect the latter. As the result of professional careers devoted to understanding child development and its challenges, developmental scientists are likely to be sensitive to dimensions of child protection that might be neglected from other perspectives. They can pose important questions about the experience of children within the social service system, for example, that are useful catalysts for the development of more child-oriented procedures. They can define dimensions of child functioning as the basis for outcome assessments (and aid in the development of assessment tools) that will help caseworkers consider the experience of children in the evaluation of treatment plans. They can raise concerns about how children are affected by dispositional alternatives that may currently be framed according to the interests of other family members, and propose child-centered options that may not have yet been considered. In short, as a result of their professional training, developmental scientists may provide a uniquely child's-eye-view of the child protection system that can be an important contribution to policy reform, especially when it is combined with the advocacy efforts that developmental scientists are also capable of contributing.

For these contributions to be most useful, however, developmental scientists must know enough about the child protection system to offer pertinent critique and constructive alternatives. Otherwise their recommendations are either irrelevant, inapplicable, or uselessly general. Thus whether their contributions are in the form of research evidence or advancing values, researchers must engage in the two-day dialogue with policymakers at various levels of the system to discover how their contributions can be most useful and valuable.

TOWARD A CHILD-ORIENTED CHILD PROTECTION SYSTEM

These diverse potential contributions of developmental scientists are urgently needed. In portraying current circumstances as a "national emergency," the U.S. Advisory Board on Child Abuse and Neglect (1990) urged the development of a new child protection system that is both neighborhood-based and child-oriented. A neighborhood-based system, according to the Advisory Board, requires building on the resources of local communities and integrating prevention and intervention efforts with community initiatives and supports. A child-oriented system, in turn, addresses the treatment, remediation, and support needs of children as a paramount priority in child protection efforts.

The Advisory Board has specified a general blueprint for child protection reform, but most aspects of this plan remain to be developed. What would a child-oriented child protection system look like, for example (Thompson, 1993)? One feature of such an ideal system is that its effectiveness would be measured in terms of the child's developmental achievements during the period immediately following intervention owing to maltreatment. There would be a focus on remedial and treatment efforts that restore the child's functioning to age-appropriate norms, in other words, and alleviate the consequences of earlier abuse or neglect. Currently, child protection efforts are primarily concerned with abuse recidivism, which is arguably the most important policy goal for intervention efforts. After all, we do not want children to be victimized again. However, such a goal orients the system toward the remedial and treatment needs of the perpetrator, with children receiving little therapeutic, educational, or other supportive assistance in a system of limited resources (Select Committee on Children, Youth, and Families, 1987; U.S. Advisory Board on Child Abuse and

Neglect, 1990). In a child-oriented child protection system, intervention efforts would be deemed unsuccessful, not only if the minimalist goal of preventing reabuse was not achieved, but also if intervention occurred at a cost to the child's developmental achievements, or if the child was not provided living conditions that supported age-appropriate functioning and mental health, or if the psychological consequences of earlier maltreatment were unremediated. In a sense, the needs of the victim of abuse as well as of the perpetrator would be primary in such a system.

This has important implications for how the child protection system would be designed. For example, systematic, periodic, long-term follow-up data concerning children taken into its care would be required to evaluate the effectiveness of child protection interventions. Designing practical, age-appropriate assessment tools that could be used for such purposes thus becomes an important research task. In addition, systemic changes in service delivery and funding provisions would be required to insure that children receive the therapeutic, educational, and other assistance required by their developmental needs and prior experience of maltreatment. Currently, service delivery for maltreated children is encumbered by the idiosyncratic eligibility requirements and agency jurisdictions of different programs such that children's needs are fitted into program requirements rather than programs accommodating to children's needs. In a child-oriented system, services would be coordinated around an individualized treatment plan that takes into account the child's age and developmental level, the type of maltreatment, the nature of the family and its circumstances, other challenges or disabilities the child faces, and specific factors in the child's background that are relevant to treatment and intervention. Developmental, community, and clinical researchers could fruitfully explore how such individualized service delivery models would be realized.

Another feature of a child-oriented child protection system would be respect for the child's family, recognizing the importance of the emotional ties that bind children to family members, even when they are abusive. Current child protection policies recognize this in their emphasis on family preservation and reunification, but there would be more substance to this concept in a child-oriented system. For example, parents would commonly be enfranchised in case planning and treatment decision making concerning the child, whether the child receives services at home or is placed out-of-home (except when there is little home of family reunification). In out-of-home placements, parents might become involved in aiding the child's transition to the foster placement (e.g., accompanying the child during the initial visit to the foster family, helping to select toys and other security/transitional objects, etc.), visiting regularly and assisting with the child's care in that placement, and eventually participating actively in planning the child's transition home. Members of the extended family would be sought as support agents on the child's behalf. In such a system, interventions in cases of child neglect (which constitute the majority of abuse allegations) would focus on providing needed social services to enable the family to remain intact while also remediating problems of inadequate care or supervision, rather than removing children from the home. And the system would seek alternative avenues to enlisting children as informants concerning their own maltreatment within the family, recognizing the psychological risks to children of the resentment and recrimination of family members that may result. Each of these elements of a child-oriented system defines a research agenda to better understand the strengths that can be enlisted even in abusive families, the kinds of intrafamilial and extrafamilial supports that maltreated children might be able to draw upon, and how these and other elements of a system that respected a child's family ties could be tested and evaluated.

A third aspect of a child-oriented child protection system is that it would provide supportive assistance to children throughout the various phases of investigation, prosecution, treatment, and remediation. In current child protection efforts, children are sometimes victimized by the system that has been designed to protect them because the system itself is not "child friendly:" the agencies that assist them are not primarily concerned with children, few actors within the system have substantive background in child development, and other agendae (e.g., procedural due process, resource constraints, etc.) compete with a primary concern with maltreated children. In a child-oriented system, by contrast, tangible efforts to provide support to children who have been abused or neglected would be incorporated throughout the design of the system. For example, individuals in a child's extended family or neighborhood who have prior acquaintance with the child would be formally enlisted as special advocates to accompany the child throughout the various phases of case planning and disposition, informing the child of decisions that have been made and their implications, helping the child anticipate future events, soliciting the child's own preferences and opinions concerning case planning, and communicating the child's views to social service and legal personnel. A special investigative unit within the police or county attorney's office would include well-trained personnel who specialize in investigating child abuse allegations and who would also assist in interviewing children with sensitivity to the child's experience and developmental needs. These and other aspects of a "child friendly" child protection system would need to be carefully crafted in relation to children of different ages, and this is also an important task for developmental researchers.

Finally, a child-oriented child protection system would recognize that maltreated children are often multiproblem children who each possess a rather unique constellation of vulnerabilities and resiliency owing to their developmental level, intrinsic capabilities, and experiential history (cf. Maccoby, 1983; Thompson, 1990). They come to child protection agencies, not only with a history of abuse or neglect, but also often with mental illness, learning disabilities, attention deficit hyperactivity disorder, behavioral problems, and other challenges. Moreover, the resources and supports within the family and neighborhood ecology that children can draw upon are also likely to be unique. An individualized treatment, educational, and remediation plan recognizes this, but incorporating this awareness of individualized needs and resources throughout the system is perhaps the greatest challenge of reforming current child protection efforts.

There is a considerable research agenda incorporated into this sketchy outline of what a child-oriented child protection system would look like, and further development of a detailed portrayal of such a system is required. Moreover, other elements of a research agenda await the attention of developmental researchers. We must know more about what happens to children when they enter the child protection system—what are the decision-making processes by which their life experience is guided and directed, and what are the alternative pathways by which they are directed through the system. We require more systematic testing of the efficacy of alternative in-home intervention efforts, especially with respect to identifying the most significant features of the programs that work and identifying the essential requisites of effective intervention strategies. Similarly, we need to know much more about abuse prevention, especially strategies that enlist informants besides children, and that are systematically tested so their efficacy can be demonstrated. In short, a considerable amount of important, developmentally oriented research is needed for progress toward a child-oriented child protection system.

CONCLUSION

By describing the tensions inherent in policymaking concerning child maltreatment, and outlining various modes of research applications to policy, the purpose of this chapter has been to underscore the importance of an ongoing, mutual dialogue between developmental scientists and policymakers. Without an intimate knowledge of policymakers' concerns, developmental scientists are more likely to propose solutions that are irrelevant, unrealistic, or excessively broad in the eyes of the policymaking community. Moreover, their research will continue to neglect many of the significant—and challenging—questions for which answers are desperately needed. In turn, without an awareness of the conceptual and scientific contributions that the developmental research community can potentially offer, policymakers are more likely to devise interventions that neglect children's needs, based on conceptualizations of family functioning, descriptive information and assessment instruments that are potentially misleading. Policymakers can additionally benefit from the overall framework of knowledge about child development that researchers can provide with which to evaluate policy alternatives and prioritize values in child protection (cf. Monahan & Walker, 1986, 1988). In a sense, each community needs the other to devise the most effective remedies to this national problem.

It is appropriate that these concerns about research and policymaking are being raised at this time, shortly after the 30th anniversary of the founding of Head Start. For developmental researchers, Head Start was the most important of the Great Society initiatives affecting children, and its continuing legacy has been a source of pride to policymakers and researchers alike. For present purposes, Head Start has also been an influential model of the kind of dialogue that can occur between researchers and policymakers, with researchers generating basic insights into developmental processes to whom policymakers could turn for advice and assistance in addressing social needs. The current generation of interest in the social policy applications of developmental research derives, in part, from the experience of earlier developmental scientists who found that their basic studies of cognitive and intellectual processes in early childhood assumed an authoritative role in the development of a major, federally funded intervention on behalf of disadvantaged children.

But the Head Start model of the role of research in policymaking is fundamentally misleading if it contributes to the view that developmental scientists may remain disinterested but authoritative academics to whom the policymaking world turns for answers. The complexity of the problems of child maltreatment, the diversity of the social service systems that assume a role in intervention and treatment, the intractability of many of the social conditions contributing to child abuse and neglect, and the challenges of most of the fundamental policy questions in this area require that developmental scientists themselves must become immersed in the system they hope to improve. The policymaking world will not turn to developmental scientists for answers they cannot provide. If the developmental research community is concerned about the problem of child maltreatment, and seeks to address this problem as part of its ethical mandate to improve the conditions of people (American Psychological Association, 1990), it requires a radical change in how developmental scientists regard their roles vis-à-vis policymakers, and in the approaches they take to designing research, conceptualizing problems, and applying knowledge to practice (Thompson, 1991).

The kind of two-way street envisioned here has broader implications for the professional research community. With respect to the dissemination of knowledge, for example, it suggests that the publication of research and empirical reviews exclusively in academic journals is an inappropriate means of influencing the policymaking process. The journals, periodicals, and books that are influential with different policymaking groups are unfamiliar to most developmental scientists, but they should not be: thoughtful reviews of research findings pertinent to policy questions can be part of academic psychology's contributions to these forums. With respect to professional affiliations, moreover, it is essential that developmental scientists not only read but talk to the individuals who formulate policies concerning maltreated children to discover what their concerns and interests are. These individuals are not hard to find, and they are important contributors to policy reform.

When the U.S. Advisory Board on Child Abuse and Neglect (1990) declared that current protections of maltreated children constitute a "national emergency," it also declared the need for generating, diffusing, and responsibly applying knowledge concerning child abuse and neglect. It did so with the confidence that knowledge is one of the most important foundations for developing more effective interventions on behalf of children and their families. It thus presented an important challenge to the developmental research community.

REFERENCES

Alsager v. District Court of Polk County, Iowa, 406 F. Supp. 10 (S.D. Iowa 1975).

American Psychological Association. (1990). Ethical principles of psychologists. *American Psychologist, 45*, 390–395.

Areen, J. (1975). Intervention between parent and child: A reappraisal of the state's role in child neglect and abuse cases. *The Georgetown Law Journal, 63*, 887–937.

Austin, J., & Krisberg, B. (1981). Wider, stronger, different nets: The dialectics of criminal justice reform. *Journal of Research in Crime and Delinquency, 18*, 165–196.

Besharov, D. J. (1988). The need to narrow the grounds for state intervention. In D. J. Besharov (Ed.), *Protecting children from abuse and neglect: Policy and practice* (pp. 47–90). Springfield, IL: Charles C. Thomas.

Brassard, M. T., Germain, R., & Hart, S. N. (1987). *Psychological maltreatment of children and youth.* New York: Pergamon.

Caplan, N. (1979). The two-communities theory and knowledge utilization. *American Behavioral Scientist, 22*, 459–470.

Cicchetti, D. (1990). The organization and coherence of socioemotional, cognitive, and representational development: Illustrations through a developmental psychopathology perspective on Down syndrome and child maltreatment. In R. A. Thompson (Ed.), *Socioemotional development.* Nebraska Symposium on Motivation (Vol. 36, pp. 259–366). Lincoln, NE: University of Nebraska Press.

Coy v. Iowa, 108 U.S. 2798 (1988).

Cunningham, C., & Horowitz, R. (1989). *Child abuse and neglect: Cases, text and problems.* Washington, DC: American Bar Association.

Daro, D. (1988). *Confronting child abuse.* New York: Free Press.

Egeland, B., & Erickson, M. F. (1987). Psychologically unavailable caregiving. In M. R. Brassard, R. Germain, & S. N. Hart (Eds.), *Psychological maltreatment of children and youth* (pp. 110–120). New York: Pergamon.

Feshbach, N. D., & Feshbach, S. (1976). Punishment: Parent rites versus children's rights. In G. P. Koocher (Ed.), *Children's rights and the mental health professions* (pp. 149–170). New York: Wiley.

Feshbach, S., & Feshbach, N. D. (1978). Child advocacy and family privacy. *Journal of Social Issues, 34*, 114–121.

Finkelhor, D., & Strapko, N. (1992). Sexual abuse prevention education: A review of evaluation studies. In D. J. Willis, E. W. Holden, & M. Rosenberg (Eds.), *Child abuse prevention.* New York: Wiley, in press.

Garbarino, J. (1977). The price of privacy in the social dynamics of child abuse. *Child Welfare, 56*, 565–575.

Garbarino, J. (1991). "Not all bad developmental outcomes are the result of child abuse." *Development and Psychopathology, 3*, 45–50.

Garbarino, J., Gaboury, M. T., Long, F., Gradjean, P., & Asp, E. (1982). Who owns the children? An ecological perspective on public policy affecting children. In G. B. Melton (Ed.), *Legal reforms affecting child and youth services* (pp. 43–63). New York: Haworth.

Garbarino, J., Guttman, E., & Seeley, J. W. (1986). *The psychologically battered child.* San Francisco: Jossey-Bass.

Garbarino, J., & Stocking, S. H. (Eds.). (1980). *Protecting children from abuse and neglect.* San Francisco: Jossey-Bass.

Gardner, W., Scherer, D., & Tester, M. (1989). Asserting scientific authority: Cognitive development and adolescent legal rights. *American Psychologist, 44*, 895–902.

Giovannoni, J. (1991). Social policy considerations in defining psychological maltreatment. *Development and Psychopathology, 3*, 51–59.

Goldstein, J., Freud, A., & Solnit, A. J. (1973). *Beyond the best interests of the child.* New York: Free Press.

Goldstein, J., Freud, A., & Solnit, A. J. (1979). *Before the best interests of the child.* New York: Free Press.

Goodman, G. S., & Aman, C. (1990). Children's use of anatomically detailed dolls to recount an event. *Child Development, 61*, 1859–1871.

Hart, S. N., & Brassard, M. R. (1987). A major threat to children's mental health: Psychological maltreatment. *American Psychologist, 42*, 160–165.

Hart, S. N., Germain, R. B., & Brassard, M. R. (1987). The challenge: To better understand and combat psychological maltreatment of children and youth. In M. R. Brassard, R. Germain, & S. N. Hart (Eds.), *Psychological maltreatment of children and youth* (pp. 3–24). New York: Pergamon.

In re Gault, 387 U.S. 1 (1967).

Kempe, C. H., Silverman, F. N., Steele, B. F., Droegemueller, W., & Silver, H. K. (1962). The battered child syndrome. *Journal of the American Medical Association, 181*, 17–24.

Lamb, M. E., Thompson, R. A., Gardner, W., & Charnov, E. L. (1985). *Infant-parent attachment.* Hillsdale, NJ: Erlbaum.

Levy, R. L. (1989). Using "scientific" testimony to prove child sexual abuse. *Family Law Quarterly, 23*, 383–409.

Lindblom, C. E., & Cohen, D. K. (1979). *Usable knowledge: Social science and social problem solving.* New Haven, CT: Yale University Press.

Lloyd, D. (1990, September). *Models for an effective child protection system: Legal perspectives.* Paper presented at the Fifth Summer Institute on Mental Health Law, "Developing and Implementing Integrated Mental Health Policy: Juvenile Justice and Child Maltreatment," University of Nebraska, Lincoln, NE.

Maccoby, E. E. (1983). Social-emotional development and response to stressors. In N. Garmezy & M. Rutter (Eds.), *Stress, coping, and development in children* (pp. 217–234). New York: McGraw-Hill.

Maccoby, E. E., & Martin, J. A. (1983). Socialization in the context of the family: Parent–child interaction. In P. H. Mussen (Ed.), *Handbook of child psychology, Vol. IV. Socialization, personality, and social development* (E. M. Hetherington, Vol. Ed.) (pp. 1–101). New York: Wiley.

Mangel, C. (1988). Licensing parents: How feasible? *Family Law Quarterly, 22*, 17–39.

McCarthy, F. B. (1988). The confused Constitutional status and meaning of parental rights. *Georgia Law Review, 4*, 975–1033.

McGee, R. A., & Wolfe, D. A. (1991). Psychological maltreatment: Toward an operational definition. *Development and Psychopathology, 3*, 3–18.

McIntire, R. W. (1973). Parenthood training or mandatory birth control: Take your choice. *Psychology Today, 34*, 34–143.

Melton, G. B. (1982). Children's rights: Where are the children? *American Journal of Orthopsychiatry, 52*, 530–538.

Melton, G. B. (1983). Toward "parenthood" for adolescents: Autonomy and privacy as values in public policy. *American Psychologist, 38*, 99–103.

Melton, G. B. (1992). The improbability of prevention of sexual abuse. In D. J. Willis, E. W. Holden, & M. Rosenberg (Eds.), *Child abuse prevention.* New York: Wiley.

Melton, G. B., & Thompson, R. A. (1987). Legislative approaches to psychological maltreatment: A social policy analysis. In M. R. Brassard, R. Germain, & S. N. Hart (Eds.), *Psychological maltreatment of children and youth* (pp. 203–216). New York: Pergamon.

Meriwether, M. H. (1988). Child abuse reporting laws: Time for a change. In D. J. Besharov (Ed.), *Protecting children from abuse and neglect: Policy and practice* (pp. 9–45). Springfield, IL: Charles C. Thomas.

Meyer v. Nebraska, 262 U.S. 390 (1923).

Mnookin, R. H. (1973). Foster care: In whose best interest? *Harvard Educational Review, 43*, 599–638.

Mnookin, R. H. (1975). Child-custody adjudication: Judicial functions in the face of indeterminacy. *Law and Contemporary Problems, 39*, 226–293.

Monahan, J., & Walker, L. (1986). Social authority: Obtaining, evaluating, and establishing social science in law. *University of Pennsylvania Law Review, 134*, 477–517.

Monahan, J., & Walker, L. (1988). Social science research in law: A new paradigm. *American Psychologist, 43*, 465–472.

Olds, D. L., & Henderson, C. R., Jr. (1989). The prevention of maltreatment. In D. Cicchetti & V. Carlson (Eds.), *Child maltreatment* (pp. 722–763). Cambridge, UK: Cambridge University Press.

Osgood, D. W., & Jacobs, J. E. (1985). Programs for juvenile offenders: What have we learned? In J. Boulet, S. A. Ray, & A. M. DeBritto (Eds.), *Understanding the economic crisis: The impact of poverty and unemployment on children and families* (pp. 155–164). Ann Arbor, MI: Bush Program in Child Development and Social Policy.

Pierce v.Society of Seven Sisters, 268 U.S. 510 (1925).

Prince v. Massachusetts, 321 U.S. 158 (1944).

Reppucci, N. D., & Aber, M. S. (1992). Child abuse prevention and the legal system. In D. J. Willis, E. W. Holden, & M. Rosenberg (Eds.), *Child abuse prevention.* New York: Wiley.

Rosenberg, M. S. (1987). New directions for research on the psychological maltreatment of children. *American Psychologist, 42*, 166–171.

Sandmire, M. J., & Wald, M. S. (1990). Licensing parents—A response to Claudia Mangel's proposal. *Family Law Quarterly, 24*, 53–76.

Santosky v. Kramer, 455 U.S. 745 (1982).

Select Committee on Children, Youth, and Families. (1987). *Abused children in America: Victims of official neglect.* Washington, DC: U.S. Government Printing Office.

Summit, R. C. (1983). The child sexual abuse accommodation syndrome. *Child Abuse and Neglect, 7*, 177–193.

Telzrow, C. F. (1987). Influence by negative and limiting models. In M. R. Brassard, R. Germain, & S. N. Hart (Eds.), *Psychological maltreatment of children and youth* (pp. 121–136). New York: Pergamon.

Thompson, R. A. (1990). Vulnerability in research: A developmental perspective on research risk. *Child Development, 61*, 1–16.

Thompson, R. A. (1991, Fall). Developmental research and social policymaking: Creating usable knowledge. *Society for Research in Child Development Newsletter*, pp. 3–10.

Thompson, R. A. (1993). Toward a child-oriented child protection system. In G. B. Melton (Ed.), *Toward a child-centered, neighborhood-based child protection system.* Lincoln, NE: University of Nebraska Press.

Thompson, R. A., & Jacobs, J. E. (1991). Defining psychological maltreatment: Research and policy perspectives. *Development and Psychopathology, 3*, 93–102.

U. S. Advisory Board on Child Abuse and Neglect. (1990). *Child abuse and neglect: Critical first steps in response to a national emergency.* Washington, DC: U.S. Government Printing Office.

Wald, M. (1975). State intervention on behalf of "neglected" children: A search for realistic standards. *Stanford Law Review, 27,* 985–1040.

Wald, M. S. (1980). Thinking about public policy toward abuse and neglect of children: A review of "Before the Best Interests of the Child." *Michigan Law Review, 78,* 645–693.

Wald, M. S. (1988). Family preservation: Are we moving too fast? *Public Welfare, 46,* 33–46.

Wald, M. S., Carlsmith, M., & Leiderman, P. H. (1988). *Protecting abused and neglected children.* Palo Alto, CA: Stanford University Press.

Wald, M. S., & Woolverton, M. (1990). Risk assessment: The Emperor's new clothes? *Child Welfare, 69,* 483–511.

Weiss, C. H. (1978). Improving the linkage between social research and public policy. In L. E. Lynn, Jr. (Ed.), *Knowledge and policy: The uncertain connection* (pp. 23–81). Washington, DC: National Academy of Sciences.

Weiss, C. H. (1987). The diffusion of social science research to policymakers: An overview. In G. B. Melton (Ed.), *Reforming the law: Impact of child development research* (pp. 63–85). New York: Guilford.

Willis, D. J., Holden, E. W., & Rosenberg, M. (1992). *Child abuse prevention.* New York: Wiley.

Wisconsin v. Yoder, 406 U.S. 205 (1972).

Zill, N. (1991, Winter). U.S. Children and their families: Current conditions and recent trends. *Newsletter of the Society for Research in Child Development,* pp. 1–3.

Zill, N., & Rogers, C. C. (1988). Recent trends in the well-being of children in the United States and their implications for public policy. In A. Cherlin (Ed.), *The changing American family and public policy* (pp. 31–115). Washington, DC: The Urban Institute Press.

Zill, N., Sigal, H., & Brim, O. G., Jr. (1983). Development of childhood social indicators. In E. F. Zigler, S. L. Kagan, & E. Klugman (Eds.), *Children, families, and government* (pp. 188–222). Cambridge, UK: Cambridge University Press.

4

The Suggestibility of Children's Recollections

Stephen J. Ceci
Michelle DeSimone Leichtman
MaryElizabeth Putnick
Narina Nunez Nightingale

Between June 16 and September 20, 1691, a group of children known as the "circle girls" testified in the witchcraft trials of over 20 residents of Salem Village and Salem Farms, Massachusetts. The girls claimed to have seen the defendants flying on broom sticks and to have observed celestial apparitions in the form of speaking animals. This was the first recorded instance of child witnesses testifying without corroboration about their own victimization, as some of the circle girls claimed that the defendants had cast spells on them and instructed insects to fly into their mouths and deposit bent nails and pins into their stomachs. (They subsequently vomited nails and pins during their testimony, and went into apoplectic fits at the sight of the defendants.) In fact, although the Salem Trials are always described as witchcraft proceedings, the fact is these trials represent the first child abuse trials in America: Dr. Brown, an expert witness from Scandinavia, testified that the children were to be believed when they described the events they claimed to have witnessed.

Although bizarre by today's standards, the testimony of the circle girls was often the only "eyewitness" evidence brought to bear against those who were found guilty of practicing witchcraft—and subsequently executed. Today, researchers are feverishly studying factors that influence the accuracy of children's testimony, for clues to the veracity of their statements made in the context of child abuse proceedings, especially child sexual abuse proceedings (see Ceci & Bruck, in press). In towns across the U.S. one sees case after case in which children in juvenile and criminal justice proceedings offer details about their alleged victimization that sound as though they were taken directly from the transcripts of the Salem trials. For example, in the Old Cutler Presbyterian Church case in Miami, FL, this year, preschoolers testified that the defendant, a 13-year-old boy, had in the course of sexually abusing them, forced them to eat the flesh of a dismembered baby. Numerous cases across the country raise the spectre of witchcraft and sorcery, with a few making claims of even more outrageous forms of abuse involving human and animal sacrifice.

Ever since the time of Salem, society has been ambivalent about the credibility of child witnesses. For nearly 200 years following those harrowing days when the circle girls gave patently false testimony, society has been reluctant to accept the uncorroborated statements of children in courts of law. Elsewhere, we have reviewed the social science and legal opinions relating to the credibility and suggestibility of children's recollections (e.g., Ceci & Bruck, in press; Ceci, Ross, & Toglia, 1987; Ceci, Ross, Stern, & Dunning, 1990), and we shall not rehash that evidence here. Suffice to say that, throughout history, there have been pronounced differences of opinion as to the suggestibility of young children, and, because of this, their reliability as witnesses.

It has only been in the past decade that many states have dropped corroboration rules that required children's testimony to be supported by the testimony of another. This was due to the increasing awareness of sexual abuse, a crime that is by its nature private, and therefore usually without corroborating witnesses. As just one example of the trend that led states to abandon their corroboration requirement for child sexual abuse victims, the state of New York provides a "telling" example: In 1982, the last year before New York changed its corroboration rule to allow alleged child sex abuse victims to testify without corroboration, there were approximately 1,100 reports to the New York State Maltreatment and Abuse Register in Albany. Of these, 180 reports were deemed to be "founded" or "indicated." (Most of the remaining 920 cases were not classified as founded because they lacked "hard" evidence needed to prosecute, and not because of a lack of basis in fact.) Of the 180 founded cases, just 11 were prosecuted in court, and of these, only 5 resulted in convictions. The majority of cases never came to court because the victim was the sole witness. (It should be mentioned, however, that some cases are not litigated, not because of any lack of corroborating testimony, but rather because social services personnel make a determination that litigation is not in the best interests of the child. In these cases they allow defendants to agree to counselling, supervised visitation, plea bargains to noncriminal offenses, etc., as alternatives to litigation. Hence, the real prosecutorial effectiveness is underestimated by looking at only the few cases that terminate in convictions.)

In light of the vast number of cases of sexual abuse that began coming to light a decade ago, and the failure of law enforcement officials to effectively prosecute the vast majority of these cases, researchers revisited the older, and often flawed paradigms of earlier investigations that had led to the claim that children were untrustworthy witnesses. During the past decade, more research has been conducted on this topic than in all of the prior years combined (Ceci, Ross, et al., 1990). In general, this new research is methodologically superior to the older work. In addition, it aims for greater realism by moving away from sanitized laboratory studies of children's reports to the examination of children's reports of naturally occurring stressful events.

Disagreement over the suggestibility of child eyewitnesses, however, has hardly been resolved by the advent of modern psychological science. While cognitive, social, and developmental psychologists have attempted to provide insight into the intricacies of children's memories, the literature remains riddled with what appear on the surface to be contradictory findings. Elsewhere it has been suggested that much of this lack of consensus is due to the use of different methodologies, stimuli, and procedures (Baxter, 1990; Ceci et al., 1987; Toglia, 1991). Researchers have failed to reach a consensus on several major issues, and as a result of this failure one can find a diversity of pronouncements in newspapers, magazines, and journals—much to the confusion of researchers, policy-makers, and advocacy groups. Depending on which modern expert one reads, the child witness is described as rarely lying, resistant to suggestion about actions involving his or her own body, and every bit as reliable as adult witnesses (e.g., Goodman, Rudy, Bottoms, & Aman, 1990), or as frequently useless, due to difficulties distinguishing reality from fantasy, and easily coached by powerful authority figures (Underwager & Wakefield, 1989; Wakefield & Underwager, 1988). In this chapter we hope to provide a resolution of this contradictory state of affairs. We will argue that the modern research, although superior to the older work that depicted child witnesses as wholly unreliable, suffers from two serious scientific problems, (a) an absence of ecological validity, and (b) a lack of effort on the part of investigators to disconfirm their own hypotheses—in part because of their strong advocacy positions. Science is best conceptualized as "proof by disproof" (Ceci & Bronfenbrenner, 1991), meaning that scientists have a responsibility to attempt to disprove alternative hypotheses rather than exclusively amass data consistent with their own pet theories. The latter tendency has, unfortunately, been the modus operandi in this politically charged arena in which scientific findings have a way of turning up in newspapers and congressional hearings with great rapidity.

In addition to the failure to seriously tackle alternative hypotheses, another problem with research in the area of child witnesses has been its failure to achieve a sufficient level of ecological validity to permit generalization from the research contexts to the real-world analogs (i.e., the manner in which children's memories are pursued by investigators in the aftermath of a sexual abuse report). While much research on children's recollections is currently carried out in naturalistic contexts (e.g., testing preschoolers' recollections of a genital exam in a doctor's office, or testing their memories of a stressful dental procedure in a dentist's office), this does not make it generalizable to a particular court case unless the research context closely mirrors the precise factors (e.g., stress level, motivations or inducements to lie) bearing on that particular court case. In doing research that is intended to generalize to a sex abuse case, factors that should be considered include the level of victimization that the subject perceives, the level of arousal, the degree of personal embarrassment and loss of control, the cognitive factors known to influence the integrity of a memory trace (e.g., length of retention interval, degree of leading questions, level of original trace strength), and, most importantly, motivations and threats to withhold or disclose information (Ceci, 1991). While many researchers have examined cognitive mechanisms that affect the accuracy of recall (e.g., the length of the retention interval, the type of leading question, the trace strength of the original and misleading events), very few researchers have considered how emotional and motivational factors interact with the operation of these cognitive mechanisms.

One reason for the dearth of motivational research is that it is difficult to do such research in an ethically permissable manner. Thus it is important when reviewing the work described below to keep in mind the types of threats, motives, inducements, and suggestions that may affect the way in which a child perceives and constructs an abusive situation. It is our contention that any of these motivational forces is capable of reversing the findings that will be reported. Unfortunately, none of the studies to date that have alleged that children are resistant to postevent suggestions have included strong motivational manipulations; thus they are unable to provide insights into the recollections made in the aftermath of actual abusive incidents where such motivations abound. On the other hand, none of the studies that have claimed that children are inherently unreliable have bothered to assess motives that would foster resistance to suggestion. In short, the available research is lopsided in its aim to amass confirmatory evidence without a serious attempt to disprove alternative hypotheses.

In order to evaluate the synthesis we provide in the final section of this chapter, a closer examination of recent empirical work is necessary. We will argue that some of the empirical work is not generalizable to real world circumstances, due to the absence of motivational manipulations and/or to lack of ecological validity. Further, we will argue that many of the conflicting results that are currently found in the literature can be explained by the disparate methods that researchers employ to answer their questions. Thus, a closer examination of recent empirical findings is in order.

The question of whether children's recollections are open to the distorting influences of pre- and postevent suggestions seems simple enough, yet it has divided respectable researchers into separate camps; those that view children as nonsuggestible and those that view children as suggestible. In order to make an evaluation, we need to examine the empirical evidence provided by researchers in both camps, keeping in mind the concerns that were raised about ecological validity and serious efforts to disprove one's pet hypothesis.

Children as nonsuggestible. Perhaps no other researcher has done more to redress the imbalance in favor of child witnesses than has Gail Goodman. After almost a century of research that has criticized and belittled the accuracy and suggestibility of child witnesses, Goodman has presented a picture that is far more optimistic. Her work has been motivated by a desire to know whether nonabused children will make false claims of abuse in response to erroneous suggestions by adults. In order to examine this question, Goodman's strategy has been to interview nonabused children about sexual as well as nonsexual experiences. In one study, 18 pairs of same-age, same-sex 4- and 7-year-old children were left in a trailer with a strange adult. One child played a game with the adult that involved being dressed in a costume, lifted into the air and photographed, while the other child was encouraged to carefully observe the interchange between the other child and the adult. About 10 days later, both children were asked general and specific questions about the event by a different adult. During this interview, straightforward questions about the event were asked, as well as misleading questions which suggested the stranger had committed acts that he had not. Goodman showed that, under these circumstances, child participants and child bystanders are equally accurate in resisting the interviewer's erroneous suggestions about abusive actions. In fact, these children demonstrated surprise in response to the misleading questions. As expected, older children gave more elaborate and more accurate responses than did the younger children, but neither group showed a significant level of suggestibility.

A study by Goodman and Aman (1990) concerns the suggestibility of children interviewed with anatomical dolls to facilitate reports of the details of sexual abuse. In this study, 60 3- and 5-year-olds were questioned 1 week after playing alone with a male confederate. During the interviews, children were questioned under one of three conditions: (a) using anatomical dolls, (b) using regular dolls, or (c) using no dolls. As in the previous study, children were first asked to provide general information about their recollection of the event, and were then asked straightforward as well as misleading questions, some of which related to sexual abuse. There were no significant differences in either age group among doll conditions. However, there were differences between the age groups in the number of commission errors made in response to suggestive abuse questions. Three-year-olds made more such errors than 5-year-olds, and younger 3-year-olds made more than older 3-year-olds. Upon further probing, Goodman and Aman found that the younger subjects misunderstood the term *private parts* which was used in the interviews. The researchers attributed the increased rate of commission error in younger subjects to this misunderstanding.

In order to address the possibility that some commission errors were made because children felt intimidated by the interviewer, Goodman et al. (1990) manipulated this variable in another study. After an inoculation at a clinic, half of a group of 72 3- to 7-year-olds were interviewed by a "nice" interviewer" and half by a "neutral" interviewer. The 3- to 4-year-olds made twice as many errors in response to abuse questions in the neutral condition. On the other hand, interviewer condition had no effect on the older children.

A final study by Goodman and her colleagues deserves note (Saywitz, Goodman, Nicholas, & Moan, 1989). In this study, the researchers examined children's vulnerability to suggestion in a more ambiguous and, arguably, realistic situation. Children were questioned following a genital and anal examination by a doctor, during a routine visit for a check-up. One week or 1 month later children were asked to recall the exam, demonstrate the event with anatomical dolls, and answer several misleading questions. The results indicate that children resisted the misleading suggestions, whether tested 1 week or 1 month later. Children did not generally disclose genital contact without specific, probing questions. Although other researchers have found that leading questions often produce false reports, in this study such questions produced false reports only 1% of the time.

In the studies that have been reviewed, there is no motivation for children to lie. In fact, if any motivation exists, it is to tell the truth. Adults who conducted the studies provided no reason for children to withhold or distort what they experienced, and certainly there are implicit motives for the children to actually correctly report what they saw because to do otherwise would bring embarrassment on them. For example, why ought one expect errors of commission (claiming the doctor took her clothes off and kissed them while they were naked)? To do so would only bring embarrassment to them, as such behavior is "naughty." Unlike the real world of sexual abuse, there are no motives at work in these studies that could prompt children to commit errors, that is, no inducements, bribes, threats, or worries. What then do these studies tell us about children's suggestibility? It seems that the message is a clear and potentially important one: Children may be resistant to misleading questions when there is no motivation to distort the truth, and when the truth is less threatening than a distortion. Thus, children are capable of distinguishing truth from fantasy and are capable of resisting the influence of misleading questions under certain circumstances. This is a nontrivial finding, but not one that translates to the context of sexual abuse.

Children as suggestible. As suggested earlier, not all researchers have found children's eyewitness memory to be as impervious to outside influences as Goodman and her colleagues' work suggests. As noted in the introduction, the historical consensus has been exactly the opposite. Most of the older studies, however, arrived at this conclusion on the basis of experiments that bear little relevance to the types of testimonial situations that children are likely to find themselves in, thus rendering their conclusions tentative. For example, many of these older studies that concluded there were reliable age differences in suggestibility employed verbal learning paradigms (recalling word lists) or used brief encounters with stories or pictures that were unrelated to the theme of sexual abuse, hence providing little insight into the manner in which children may process and recall more salient events.

A study conducted by Clarke-Stewart, Thompson, and Lepore (1989) has provided some evidence that young children might be suggestible even in contexts that are relevant to some forms of sexual abuse. These researchers focused on the way in which children interpret events which might be construed as either sexually abusive or innocent. Eighty-eight 5- and 6-year-olds interacted individually with a confederate posing as a janitor. The confederate followed one of two scripts, both of which involved the handling of several toys in the research room. In both scripts, the confederate cleaned the room, and then he began either cleaning the toys, including a doll, or handling the doll roughly and suggestively. The dialogue undertaken by the confederate complemented his activities in both cases, reinforcing either the idea that he was cleaning the doll, or playing with it in a rough manner. In both cases, the child was invited to join in the activities of the confederate.

An hour after the child's interaction with the "janitor," another confederate entered the room and interviewed the child about the janitor's activities. The interview was either (a) neutral and nonsuggestive in tone, (b) accusatory in tone (suggesting that the janitor had been inappropriately playing with the toys instead of working), or (c) exculpatory in tone (suggesting that the janitor was just cleaning the toys and not playing). In the two latter types of interview, the questions ranged from mildly to strongly suggestive as the interview progressed. At the end of the interview, all children were asked an open-ended free-recall question about what they had witnessed the janitor doing, and 17 straightforward factual questions regarding the janitor's activities. Finally, they were asked six interpretive questions about the event. Following the first interview, each child was interrogated by another confederate, and this second interview either reinforced or contradicted the first. After this second interview, children were asked by their parents to recount what the janitor had done.

The results of this study indicate that, when children were given no misleading suggestions, their accounts of what they had witnessed were both factually correct and in line with the script delivered to them by the confederate. However, when the first interviewer contradicted the script, children changed their stories to confirm the suggestions of the interviewer. Specifically, by the end of the first interview two-thirds of the group for whom the interviewer contradicted the script answered in line with the interviewer's suggestions. Others reported that a combination of the actual events and the interviewer's suggestions had occurred. At least four of the six interpretive questions at the end of the first interview were answered by 90% of these children in agreement with the interviewer, as opposed to what actually happened in the script. When the second interview contradicted the script in the same manner as the first, the children answered virtually all of the interpretive questions at the end of the second interview in line with the interviewer's suggestions. When this interview contradicted the first, the majority of children also fit their stories to the suggestions of the second interviewer. Moreover, children's reports to their parents were consistent with the suggestions of the interviewers. Strikingly, while children's answers to the interpretive questions were thus easily manipulated by the suggestions of the interviewers, their answers to the factual questions remained accurate and stable over time. The question of whether sexual abuse has occurred is often a matter of interpretation of an event within a context, as opposed to factual memory for that event.

Another aspect of this study pertains to individual differences found among children. Clarke-Stewart et al.'s (1989) analysis suggests that the children who were the most suggestible, converting most rapidly to the interviewer's viewpoint, shared other characteristics as well. The profiles of these children revealed them to be more suggestible in many contexts, less knowledgeable about telling lies, more likely to have parents who placed less value on self-direction, and to have parents who were less strict about lying than other parents. As a group, the more suggestible children also showed superior verbal memory.

The results of the work conducted by Clark-Stewart et al. (1989) seem to directly contradict the work of Goodman; however, we argue that the results are actually congruent. Children in both groups of studies were accurate in response to factual questions. However, the children's suggestibility in the interpretations of the factual events was different. There are several noticeable differences that might explain the disparate results. The children in the Clark-Stewart et al. study were not the "victims," while the children in Goodman's study were. It might be tempting to attribute the contradictory results to this difference were it not for other studies that have yielded results similar to Clark-Stewart and her colleagues when the children *were* the "victims." For example, in one study (Ceci, DeSimone, et al., 1990), children are kissed while they are bathed and later questioned in a highly leading manner. In contrast to the claim that children never distort information about actions involving their own bodies, these children did get it wrong, as will be seen.

In another study, conducted by Peters (1991), a stranger visits a nursery school and vigorously rubs some children's heads while taking their pulse. Later, these "victims" perform as one would expect from Clarke-Stewart et al.'s findings. However, when the children were later asked whether they had been touched by the stranger, aside from his taking their pulse, children who were rubbed on the head frequently denied having been rubbed. Those children who were not touched by the stranger were significantly more accurate in their recall. Children's understanding of the questions was tested, and the investigators found that their errors were not due to a misunderstanding of the terms *touching* or *rubbing*. The results of this study contradict Goodman's findings in two ways; they indicate that, at least under some conditions, stress may impair preschoolers' recognition memory, and they provide evidence for distortion of children's reports of physical contact with a strange adult, at least some of the time.

While the contradictory results may seem confusing, they are congruent with what we have stated earlier. That is, in Goodman's study there were no motivations to distort the truth, while in Peters's study the children may have been motivated not to reveal having been touched due to a fear of embarrassment.

The work reviewed thus far suggests that whether children accurately remember and interpret an event is more complex than originally thought. Perhaps we should not ask whether children's recollections are reliable, but rather under what conditions they are reliable. In other words, we need to clarify the ecological and motivational variables that might affect the accuracy of a child's testimony. While the number of factors that might potentially affect a child's memory is limitless, there are some that are particularly salient to our discussion and will be reviewed briefly here.

The role of stress in children's recollection. The manipulation of emotional as well as cognitive variables has been shown to affect children's reports in a series of studies by Douglas Peters. In addressing the effects of arousal on children's memory performance, Peters (1991) has concluded that high levels of arousal (stress) experienced at encoding will sometimes impair childrens' subsequent memories. His studies indicate that this is true both when the event experienced by the child is personally meaningful, such as when it involves the child's body, and when it is not as significant to the child.

Peters and his colleagues have conducted studies of children's recollections of various stressful events, utilizing naturally stressful contexts (e.g. a child's dental visit, and an innoculation clinic). In all of his studies, anxiety ratings (e.g., pulse, blood pressure, observational) were made for the control and experimental children. These studies demonstrate that anxiety consistently undermines accuracy of recall.

Another study by Peters employed a contrived stressful event. The study used a fire alarm to manipulate anxiety, and in addition looked at the effects of misleading information on eyewitness performance. Children had their blood pressure, pulse, and weight measured while performing a card-sorting task and answering simple questions. Either a fire alarm was sounded for a radio volume was turned up to approximately the same decibel level during the test. Ten seconds after the test began, a confederate entered the room, stayed for 1 minute, and left. The noise was turned off 10 seconds after the confederate left. After completing a buffer task, the children's memories for the event were tested using free recall and probed recall, with five of the probe questions being misleading for half of the children. Following another buffer task, the children were asked questions to determine the influence of the misleading suggestions.

Measures of blood pressure and pulse rate taken before and after the onset of the noise (alarm or radio) showed a significant elevation for only the fire alarm group. While no significant memory differences were found between the two groups in the free recall narrative, on the 10 objective questions the control (i.e., radio) group's responses were significantly more correct than those of the alarm group. A significant interaction was observed between the type of question asked (misleading vs. neutral) and the event-stress condition (alarm vs. no alarm). Recall was distorted by misleading questions in both the alarm and control conditions, but the difference was significantly greater in the alarm condition. Thus, the stress of the alarm condition coupled with exposure to misleading questions greatly reduced the accuracy of these children's recall.

The children in Peters's studies are questioned about the events they witnessed at intervals ranging between 1 and 30 days. He has not found that the length of the retention interval has any influence on children's report accuracy, at least within the range he has employed. In all of his studies, children are given tests of voice and face recognition for the adults in the scripts (e.g., the dentists, nurses, strangers). He usually manipulates the line-ups that children are presented, with half of them containing the actual adult perpetrator and the other half "blank." Like others who work in this field, Peters always finds that children are far less accurate identifying adults in the blank line-ups than in the line-ups that actually contain the perpetrators. However, even in the perpetrator-present line-ups, children exposed to high levels of stress commit a greater number of identification errors (false identifications) than do children who are not stressed. Stress, it appears, does have a deleterious effect on young children's performance, despite cautions that the perpetrator may not be in the line-up.

A final study by Peters manipulated both stress at encoding and stress at the time of identification, utilizing a scenario involving a simulated theft. Six- to 8-year-olds were assigned to one of eight conditions, in a design that involved two levels of event stress, two types of lineup (live vs. photo), and two lineup conditions (target-present vs. target absent). All subjects were left alone in a room containing a box of money. Half were advised that the money would be picked up by a man, and this occurred. The other half were not warned of this, and while they were in the room a stranger came in, distracted them, and then stole the moneybox in an obvious way. For all subjects, soon after the stranger left the room with the money box, the researcher and a parent entered the room and asked who had taken the moneybox. Subjects in the theft condition were then asked to identify the thief in the live or photo condition, while subjects in the control condition played a "game" to see whether they could identify the person who had stopped by for the box. Anxiety ratings were made independently by a parent and a researcher for each child at the time that the stranger was in the room with the child, and later at the time of line-up identification. As expected, there was significantly more stress observed in children who were exposed to the simulated theft than to their peers in the nontheft condition. There was also more stress observed in children who were exposed to the live line-up compared to those exposed to the photo identification procedure. The highest level of correct identifications was made by subjects in the nontheft, target-present photo lineup condition. The fewest correct identifications were made by the group in the theft condition that viewed a live target-present line-up. The results reveal a significant interaction between theft vs. no theft condition and live vs. photo line-up condition, leading to the conclusion that the presence of a live line-up at the time of identification impairs memory especially when the initial event provokes significant anxiety.

Adding variables to the study of child witnesses. Recently, Lindberg (1991) has pointed out that, to date, no adequate theoretical framework has been developed to explain the discrepancies in the literature regarding the effects of different variables on memory. He asserts that such a framework is impossible to develop at present because research has been more concerned with the isolation of single variables than with the interaction between variables. In order to establish a model that predicts when children are and are not especially susceptible to suggestion, the interactions between variables must be better understood. Like Peters and Goodman, Lindberg has studied the interaction of variables. The three variables of interest to him are the locus of memory process (i.e., encoding, storage, or retrieval), the focus of study (e.g., episodic vs. semantic, central vs. peripheral details), and the subjects' characteristics (e.g., age, gender).

In one study, Lindberg (1991) had subjects from grades 3, 6, and college watch a film of students taking an exam. "The accuracy of memory was manipulated by: (a) suggesting at the time of encoding that there were cheaters in the class, (b) supplying a leading question at the time of retrieval that suggested cheating had occurred, (c) both of the above, or (d) neither of the above. Subjects were asked questions that accessed different types of information about the film (i.e., they required differences in focus). Some of the questions concerned the gist of the film, others concerned the specific details; some concerned peripheral aspects, and others concerned central information.

Lindberg found significant relationships between these variables. For example, recall of the gist was more affected by biased information at the time of encoding than by biased information received at the time of retrieval. In contrast, recall of information about the details of the film was more suggestible during retrieval. Younger children's memory for the gist was more vulnerable to suggestion if they were misled at both times, whereas older children and college students were equally effected whether they received misleading information once or twice. Younger children remembered peripheral information better than older people, but their memory for details was poor in comparison to that of older individuals. However, even when they had a strong memory trace, as in the case of peripheral details, younger children were more influenced by a retrieval manipulation than were older individuals. Testimony requiring inferences, as opposed to factual recall, was more affected by a retrieval manipulation than by an encoding manipulation, especially for younger children. From these findings, which demonstrate the complexity of the suggestibility issue, Lindberg concluded that "any single manipulation is meaningless in itself."

Incorporating lies into the equation. Most of the research on children's eyewitness testimony has addressed *cognitive* characteristics that affect children's competence as witnesses, and this trend is readily apparent in the above synopsis, all of which focused on "trace alteration" as a function of erroneous postevent suggestions (e.g., the role of storage and retrieval factors in suggestibility, the differential role of the length of the retention interval, the impact of stress on encoding). However, a separate and equally important consideration in evaluating children as eyewitnesses has not been given adequate treatment in the research. This is the question of the conditions under which children consciously and deliberately distort the truth. In general, psycholegal research has not made a clear distinction between distortion that results from unconscious mnemonic processes and that which is due to socially induced factors that are fully conscious.

In our past research we, too, have studied unconscious trace alteration and have shown that the contents of one's memory trace is susceptible to erroneous suggestions even when the individual is unaware of this happening, and that this type of distortion is more prevalent among very young children than among older ones (Ceci et al., 1987). Although there is some disagreement as to the exact age when children reach adult levels of resistance to distortion, in our work this has occurred at a fairly young age (around 7). Our current program of research addresses what we regard to be the missing link in this earlier work, namely, children's conscious distortion of truth in their reports to adults. We are particularly interested in exploring the situations under which children will be motivated to present such distortions. Since the conscious distortion of truth is commonly referred to as *lying*, we use this term for ease of reference in discussing our work. However, we should make note of the fact that, in using the term, we do not assume any malintent on the part of the *liar* that the term sometimes connotes. We use it to refer to the deliberate, conscious, production of a response that the child knows to be incorrect for the purpose of achieving a goal. In some of the work we have done, there is also another component that we have observed: children who lie exhibit a recursive awareness of the cognitive state of the person to whom they are lying. That is, they demonstrate an appreciation that another's perception of their own truthfulness must be taken into account. This will become clearer later when we give an actual example.

The motivations to lie that we have delineated in our work thus far are *personal aggrandizement, protecting a loved one, avoiding embarrassment, sustaining a game, and conforming to a stereotype.* In order to look at lying behavior in the presence of these motivations we conducted an experiment in two phases. The first phase was an intensive case study of 10 3- to 4-year-old children. Each of five researchers spent over 20 hours developing a close relationship with 2 of the 10 children. The researchers spent time with children in their own homes, and also took them on outings such as picnics, movies, the circus, and playgrounds. At the end of the 20 hours, the researchers were quite well known to the children and, according to parental reports, were considered loved ones by the children, who frequently asked when the researchers were to return to play with them. After close relationships were established, the experimenters brought the children in pairs to a specially designed laboratory with the appearance of a playroom. The room was equipped with a one-way mirror, through which we filmed the events. The study was designed in two parts, a play period during which several manipulations were carried out, and two subsequent interrogations, one by a confederate playing the role of a nursery school teacher, and the other by the loved experimenter. The interrogations were conducted individually for each child.

Our first manipulation was directed at the motivation to protect a loved one. Soon after the children's arrival with the loved one, a confederate who assumed the role of a nursery school teacher entered the room and after a brief introduction informed the children that the toys in the room were hers. She then instructed the children and their loved one not to play with a particularly attractive mechanical toy. After she left the room, the loved one pretended to break the forbidden toy, drawing attention to herself in the process by exclaiming, "Gee, I didn't mean to break it. I hope I don't get into trouble!" During the later interrogations, each child was asked whether she knew who had broken the toy. Later, the loved one asked the children whether they had told the teacher who had broken the toy.

The second manipulation was primarily concerned with lying for personal aggrandizement. The children played with blocks, and then were asked by the loved one to pick them up, as she left the room for a moment. Before the children could pick up the blocks, however, a confederate unknown to the children entered the room and quickly picked up the blocks himself. As he left the room, he "accidentally" kicked over a dollhouse, pointing out to the children that he had done so. In the interrogation that followed the teacher's return, the children were informed that the teacher was very pleased with whomever had picked up the blocks and was prepared to offer that individual a gift (a sheet of stickers or a plastic necklace) that she displayed. Each child was asked if he or she was the one who had cleaned up the blocks. The children were also asked if they knew who had kicked over the toy house.

With the next manipulation we looked at whether children could be induced to lie in the context of a game. While the loved one and the children were alone in the room, the loved one pretended to find a watch left behind by the teacher. After showing the children the watch and admiring it, the loved one told the children that they were going to make a game of hiding the watch from the teacher. The children were told that the game was a secret, and that they should not tell anyone about it, even if asked. During the interrogation, the children were asked if they knew who had taken the watch. Afterwards, they were asked by the loved one if they had given away the secret of the game. The purpose of this manipulation was twofold: first, to simulate as closely as possible a common sexual abuse context in which the abuse is presented to the child as a secret game, with implied retribution if the child reveals the secret; and second, to replicate the work of Warren-Leubecker and Tate (1990), who used a similar paradigm, with different stimuli and a different set of instructions. These investigators found that only 15% of the youngsters went along with deception to sustain a secret game.

With some of the children, we were able to include a scenario more closely approximating one of the conditions of actual sexual abuse. The evening before they were brought to the laboratory playroom, these children were kissed by a parent while they were being bathed and dressed. During the interrogation, these children were first told that it was very bad to let someone kiss them when they didn't have their clothes on. They were then asked whether anyone had ever kissed them in such a situation ("No one ever kissed you when you didn't have any clothes on, did they? . . . Did anyone kiss you last night when you were in the bathtub?"). Immediately following the children's reply, they were told that it was not bad to be kissed by a parent or close relative. This was excerpted from a "good-touching/bad touching" curriculum. Later, they were reasked by a parent whether they had been kissed while being bathed.

The second phase of this study was conducted in an actual nursery school with a larger group of children, whom the researchers had visited and interacted with many times. In this phase of the experiment, we endeavored to test the phenomena that were observed in the above-described case study, but in a larger sample of 3- and 4-year-olds. Again, we looked at personal aggrandizement and lying to protect a loved one. The children played two games, *musical chairs* and *hot potato*, each of which had a clear winner. Before beginning these games, one of the researchers, who had developed an affectionate bond with most of the children, pretended to break the tape recorder that was required to play the games.

When the group games were finished, the children were interrogated. They were brought individually to a small room containing a large, shiny gumball machine. Each child was asked three questions. First, the researcher told the child that he or she could have a penny for the gumball machine only if he or she was the winner of the *hot potato* game. He or she was then asked directly if he or she had won the game. If the child answered that he or she had not won the game, the child was not given a gumball. Next, the child was given another opportunity to receive a gumball. He or she was asked if he or she had won the *musical chairs* game. The third and final question looked at the children's protection of the researcher who had broken the tape recorder. The children were asked if they knew who had broken the tape recorder, and were pressed by the interviewer with more specific questions about the incident.

Another facet of this study considered whether children would distort facts in response to a stereotype. During three separate visits by some of the researchers to the nursery school, a character named "Harry" was described to the children. Harry was portrayed as a bumbling, thoughtless friend of the researchers who was actually "nice," but who had a disturbing tendency to touch things that were not his, and to break or otherwise destroy things. By way of introducing the character of Harry, for example, the researchers read to the children during their story time. As soon as the researcher had gained their undivided attention, the children were shown a story book that had been partially ripped up and scribbled in. The researcher explained to the children that this had been her favorite book, but that her friend Harry had ruined it during one of his visits to her house. After some discussion of this, the researcher proceeded to read the story to the children, commenting on the pages with scribble marks. After three visits and accompanying descriptions of Harry's destructiveness, the children had clearly adopted the desired stereotype of Harry. They spontaneously yelled that Harry was naughty and should not be allowed to touch anything, and they would beat him up if he came to their house. One day the children were informed that Harry was planning to visit their classroom to meet them. They were assured that he was nice and that, whenever he broke anything, he replaced it. On the day that "Harry" visited the nursery school, he was present when a tape recorder was broken by the loved one, and he was also seen playing with a large coin bank. Later, the children were individually interrogated about three items. They were asked who had broken the tape recorder, who had broken a toy dog that they had not seen Harry touch, and who had taken money from the bank that they had seen Harry playing with (but not removing money from). If preschoolers are strongly influenced by stereotypes, they would be expected to attribute to Harry all of the negative events that occurred on the day of his visit (e.g., breaking the tape recorder, stealing money from the bank, breaking the toy dog).

The results of this two-part study indicate that children will indeed consciously and willingly distort the truth, given the proper motivations. But not all motivations produced lying. In particular, we found these children to be quite resistant to conforming to the Harry stereotype, and we are following up this result at present. Strikingly, we have found that material and psychological motivations do not need to be of a large magnitude to be extremely effective. Certainly, none of our manipulations were even remotely reminiscent of the powerful emotional and material pressures often placed on children who testify in court proceedings. Such pressures, which might include threats to a child's loved ones, lifestyle, conscience, self-esteem, and, in some cases, life itself, render our manipulations hardly significant (e.g., obtaining a gumball or to protect a favorite babysitter in the context of a broken game). Still, over 50% of the nursery school children did lie to obtain the gumball.

It was clear from the performance of control subjects who were not offered any gumball, that children knew exactly who had won the games, so simple memory failure can be ruled as an explanation of their erroneous claims. Interestingly, we discovered that children rarely lied to sustain a game (only 10%), replicating Warren-Leubecker and Tate's finding that only about 15% of their children lied in response to this motive. The most serious example of lying, as far as sexual abuse goes, concerns the children who were kissed while being bathed. As will be recalled, these children were told at the start of interview that it was very naughty for an adult to kiss them while they were naked (later, they were assured that it was not naughty if done by a parent or sitter). In this context, children first replied that they had not been kissed. Later, when one of their parents interviewed them, and they were again asked if they had been kissed the evening before while being bathed, they affirmed that they had, offering specific and accurate details (e.g., "Yes, I think mommy kissed me three times"). Interestingly, the children quickly added a codicil: "But it's OK, because I know her.'' This codicil was nearly a verbatim restatement of the interviewer's assurance that it was OK to be kissed by a parent or a sitter, after they initially had denied having been kissed.

The results of our work strongly suggest that children may not only be succeptible to misleading questions, but under the right circumstances may knowingly distort or withhold the truth. We have outlined a few circumstances in which lying may occur, some of which are salient in real world situations (e.g., lying to protect a loved one). Before we move on to the next section, however, it is important to note that we are not saying that child witnesses have nothing of value to offer counts. We make no such claims. Our research simply calls into question the rather simplistic advocacy claims from some quarters that have attempted to depict child witnesses as invulnerable to bribes, threats, and inducements. They are not invulnerable; they are human.

A SYNTHESIS

We believe that the results of our lying research, taken together with that of our memory distortion research, lead to the following three conclusions. First, children often will lie when the motivational structure is tilted toward lying. In this sense they are probably no different than most adults. The data from our own study are not developmental, so we can not make age comparisons in willingness to lie in response to the motives we used, though in studies that contrasted age groups on a measure of lying the developmental picture is unclear. Our study was done to test the extreme statements that some have proferred in the media (e.g., ''Children never lie when the event concerns their own body'' vs. ''Children are incapable of getting it right because they cannot distinguish reality and fantasy''). That they were found to lie ought not surprise anyone, save the rather extreme advocates who have made such claims. Children are, after all, members of the human race, and as such should be susceptible to the same influences that other members are. Extreme statements on either side are not supported by the present research, nor by the older, more laboratory-like studies that psychologists reported during the earlier part of this century. Sometimes children will lie, but certainly not all of the time and not in response to all motives. Finally, when young children do lie, they appear to be more ''leaky'' in their facial expressions than adults, a finding twice observed now (see Peters, in press). They tend to avoid eye contact, to become upset, and to cease answering questions. These are not diagnostic attributes, however, because occasionally they will occur during truth telling.

Second, very young children appear to be disproportionately more vulnerable to erroneous postevent suggestion than are older individuals. This conclusion follows from the synopsis of past and current research. The exact mechanisms that are involved in producing memory distortion are still being hotly debated by researchers. Some believe that their findings are best seen as evidence that young children's faulty reports are the result of an "erasure" mechanism in which erroneous postevent suggestions overwrite the original memory trace, rendering it forever inaccessible (Ceci et al., 1987; Ceci, Toglia, & Ross, 1988). Others believe that their findings are best seen as the result of social (not cognitive) processes that distort children's reports (Zaragozza, 1991), rendering it only temporarily inaccessible. But *all* of these researchers agree that young children's reports are more likely to be distorted by erroneous postevent suggestions than older children's reports, the only issue being the mechanism responsible for it.

Third, notwithstanding the aforesaid, it is clear that children—even preschoolers—are capable of providing much that is forensically relevant, if adults who have had prolonged access to them have not tried to distort their testimony through various outright threats, inducements, etc. That their memories are more vulnerable to postevent distortion than older persons' memories is not meant to imply that they are incapable of providing accurate testimony. In fact, as has been demonstrated in most of the studies that have been reported during the past decade, young children are able to accurately recollect the majority of the information that they observe. They may be more likely to succomb to erroneous suggestions than older children and adults, but their vulnerability is a matter of degree only. Even adults are suggestible (Ceci & Bruck, in press), so the question ought not be "Are children suggestible?" but rather "Is their level of suggestibility so much greater than an adult's as to render their testimony worthless?" We feel the answer to this question is a qualified "no."

What then are we to make of the sometimes heated arguments that spring up among both researchers and service providers? There are those that continue to hold to radical positions with regard to child witnesses (e.g., Children never lie and are not influenced by misleading questions *vs.* Children cannot distinguish fact from fantasy, and their testimony is therefore worthless). As repeatedly asserted throughout this chapter, such extreme statements are inconsistent with the bulk of the scientific literature. Certainly, based on what we know, we can "rig" experiments to support our pet theories about children, but this approach does little to further our understanding of actual child witnesses. What it suggests instead is that the biases of researchers rather than the credibility of children should be investigated. Scientists have a moral responsibility to take cognizance of what other scientists have done, and give their pet hypotheses a real chance of being disproved.

IMPLICATIONS AND PRESCRIPTIONS

Finally, it is interesting to step back from the debate over children's credibility and ask about the implications of this research for those charged with investigating child abuse and/or testifying as expert witnesses. What lessons are to be found in this research for Child Protective Service workers, police, attorneys, parents, and psychologists who testify as expert witnesses?

Based on the best research, there are a handful of generalizations that ought to guide the interviews of child victim-witnesses. First, minimize the number of times a child is being interviewed and the amount of leading and suggestive questioning used by those conducting these interviews. Nearly all officials who have responsibility for eliciting the testimony of children appear to be aware of this first generalization. Second, conduct interviews as early as possible following disclosure. Many times this is impossible, as the report may not come to the attention of investigators for months or even years following an abusive incident. Procedures need to be streamlined so that children are permitted to tell their stories as soon as possible following disclosure, to as few people as is legally permissible, with minimal input from those attempting deliberately to confuse or mislead the child. Third, children's errors are affected by the attitude and demeanor of the interviewer vis-à-vis the child (Ceci & Bruck, in press). While this would seem to argue that the interviewers need to be nurturant and engaging, other research suggests that it is unwise to merge the goal of a therapeutic interview (i.e., to evoke emotionally meaningful material) with the goal of a forensic interview (to obtain as clear and unguided a picture of exactly what occurred). Finally, interviewers' questions should be framed in such a way as to not embarrass the child or otherwise encourage him or her to distort or withhold information. In this vein, interviewers should be aware that outside influences can motivate children to distort testimony in two directions: They may either elaborate on actual events or withhold information. Interviewers should be sensitive to the possibility that motivational forces are already at work before the child enters the interview, and minimize additional impetus to distort information, while attempting to "problem-solve" the possibility that others who have had access to the child have exerted motivational leverage on the child outside of the interview.

Another useful fact that emerges from research in this area has to do with claims of tests or schemes that can distinguish truthtelling from lying. Simply stated, there are no "Pinnochio Tests." No test or indicia can reliably differentiate truthful reports based on anything we have read in the scientific literature. There are some promising techniques for interviewing children that are still in the exploratory stage (e.g., Statement Validity Analysis, Suggestibility Questionnaires), but much work remains to be done before they are validated (e.g., see Warren, Hulse-Trotter, & Tubbs, 1991, for evidence that young children's suggestibility can be minimized through simple cautions at the beginning of an interview). Until such time, it is important to avoid as much as possible the use of suggestive questions, and to avoid conveying to the child a desired statement. Children, we have seen, are adept at inferring an interviewer's wishes and may at times attempt to alter their testimony to conform to their impression of these wishes. To judge from some of the sex abuse cases that have attained national prominence, expert witnesses sometimes operate as if they possessed extraordinary acumen into human nature that defies the empirical findings and goes well beyond what those of us involved in research are willing to claim. (For a particularly pathetic example of this, see Kirschbaum's, 1990, description of the contradictory yet unequivocal conclusions reached by several of the expert witnesses in the Morgan-Foretich case involving the alleged abuse of their daughter Hilary.)

The issues of modifying children's in-court testimony is a controversial one that we need not wade into deeply here. At its heart, the issue is confused by the competing goals of the prosecution and the defense in child sexual abuse cases. In our experience it is unfortunately the case that attorneys on both sides of the case, while espousing their desire to see justice carried out, actually are motivated by a somewhat different desire, namely to win at all costs. In Sandra Craig vs. State of Maryland, the U.S. Supreme Court is currently hearing arguments as to whether its former ruling (Stinsor vs. Kentucky) should be amended. At issue is whether young children can provide testimony via one-way television, silvered mirrors, and so on, if there is reason to believe that their testimonial reliability will suffer in the absence of such devices. The use of indirect methods of testimony that spare children from the ordeal of face-to-face confrontation with their alleged abusers is resisted by attorneys and expert witnesses for the defense on the grounds that it denies the defendant's sixth amendment right to confront one's accusers. Several amici briefs were filed in this latest Supreme Court case, and, not surprisingly, they are at variance on some of the central issues (cf. American Psychological Association, 1990; Institute for Psychological Therapies, 1990). It is safe to say the critical research is yet to be done to demonstrate what most of us believe to be true, namely, that confrontational stress is detrimental to the quality of children's testimony, not to mention their emotional well-being.

To clarify our position, we would like to point out that the issue of whether confrontational stress impairs children's testimony is independent of the legal question of whether children should be exempted from the rules governing adult testimony. The testimony of adult rape victims may also be impaired by the stress of confronting their alleged abusers, yet the law requires them to do so. The framers of the Constitution insisted on the right of the accused to confront their alleged victims, because they believed an accuser would be less likely to lie in the presence of the accused and also that a jury could usefully study the emotional expressions on the faces of witnesses when they testified in the presence of defendants. Whether or not our forefathers' insights were correct, we lack evidence that the current method of eliciting testimony is so stressful to young children that it causes them to distort or deny out of fear, but the evidence that Peters has begun to provide is an important step in that direction.

Finally, what are the questions that need to be asked in the future? Although several researchers have explored the effects of stress on children's testimony (Peters, 1991; Lindberg, 1991), many aspects of this relationship have yet to be delineated. In particular, high stress and arousal and high personal relevance, which co-occur in child abuse situations, have potentially conflicting effects on children's construal of their experiences and accuracy of their reports. The effect of this combination of factors has not yet been elucidated. Because stress is often a concomitant of personal relevance, it is vital that they be studied together.

Another pressing issue facing those concerned with the prosecution of child sexual abuse is the degree to which children assimilate interviewers' or parents' wishes and subsequently actually believe that they have experienced what has been suggested to them by these adults. We have many indications that children will incorporate the suggestions of others into their memories of minor events, but so far no one has provided evidence that this occurs when the events are of great significance to the child and others. Future studies should consider factors that may motivate children to assimilate adult suggestions, either into memory, or simply into their testimony.

Finally, there is some highly preliminary evidence that individual differences among children can be identified and linked to their eyewitness accuracy. For example, the work of Clarke-Stewart et al. (1989), although still exploratory, is highly promising, because courts demand to know, not just group averages, but individual level data (i.e., whether this particular child in this particular situation was likely to get it right). Recent efforts to innoculate children against suggestibility (Warren et al., 1991) show that the large suggestibility effects that are seen with preschoolers can be diminished greatly through interviewer cautions. Measures of individual differences in suggestibility, such as that developed in the United Kingdom by Gudjonsson (1989), may be the crucible that courts are looking for. But much, much, more research is needed before such instruments can be adapted for use in child witness situations. Until then, we are stuck with an adversarial system of justice in which one side demands any and all modifications that may tilt the odds in favor of maximizing convictions (e.g., the admission into testimony of hearsay and the child's own excited utterances, the use of Federal Rules of Evidence that drop competency requirements, the use of video and other techniques to avoid face-to-face confrontation), while the other side insists that the desire to gain maximum convictions is inconsistent with our legal philosophy and therefore opposes any and all efforts that can lead to changes that favor the prosecution. It is unlikely that social science research will settle such philosophical disputes.

REFERENCES

American Psychological Association (Levine, M., Goodman, G., Melton, G., Saks, M., & Bulkey, J.). (1990, April). Motion for leave to file brief amicus curiae to the Supreme Court in Sandra Craig *vs.* State of Maryland (Ogden & Block, Attorneys for Amicus).

Baxter, J. (1990). Children's suggestibility. *Applied Cognitive Psychology*, *3*, 1–15.

Ceci, S. J. (1991). Some overarching issues in the child suggestibility debate. In J. L. Doris (Ed.), *The suggestibility of children's recollections* (pp. 1–9). Washington, DC: American Psychological Association.

Ceci, S. J., & Bronfenbrenner, V. (1991). On the demise of everyday memory: Rumors of my death are greatly exaggerated. *American Psychologist*, *46*, 27–31.

Ceci, S. J., & Bruck, M. (in press). The suggestibility of the child witness: A historical review and synthesis. *Psychological Bulletin*.

Ceci, S. J., DeSimone, M., Putnick, M. B., Toglia, M., & Lee, J. M. (1990, March 15). *Children's lies: A motivational analysis*. Paper presented at the Biennial Meeting of the American Psychology and Law Society, Williamsburg, VA.

Ceci, S. J., Ross, D., & Toglia, M. (1987). Age differences in suggestibility: Psycholegal implications. *Journal of Experimental Psychology: General*, *117*, 250–262.

Ceci, S. J., Toglia, M., & Ross, D. (1988). On remembering . . . more or less. *Journal of Experimental Psychology: General*, *118*, 250–262.

Ceci, S. J., Ross, D., Stern, L., & Dunning, D. (1990). *The suggestibility of child witnesses: A synthesis*. Unpublished manuscript, Department of HDFS, Cornell University, Ithaca, NY.

Clarke-Stewart, A., Thompson, W., & Lepore, S. (1989, May). *Manipulating children's interpretations through interrogation*. Paper presented at the Biennial Meeting of the Society for Research on Child Development, Kansas City.

Goodman, G. S., & Aman, C. (1990). Children's use of anatomically detailed dolls to recount an event. *Child Development*, *61*, 1859–1871.

Goodman, G. S., & Clarke-Stewart, A. (1991). Suggestibility in children's testimony. In J. L. Doris (Ed.), *The suggestibility of children's recollections* (pp. 92–105). Washington, DC: American Psychological Association.

Goodman, G. S., Rudy, L., Bottoms, B., & Aman, C. (1990). Children's memory and concerns: Ecological issues in the study of children's testimony. In R. Fivush & J. Hudson (Eds.), *What children remember and why*. New York: Cambridge University Press.

Gudjonsson, G. H. (1989). Compliance in an interrogative situation: A new scale. *Personality and Individual Differences*, *10*, 535–540.

Institute for Psychological Therapies (Underwager, R. & Wakefield, H.). (1990, May). Motion for leave to file brief amicus curiae to the Supreme Court in Sandra Craig *vs.* State of Maryland (Louis Keifer, Counsel of Record).

Kirschbaum, J. (1990, June). The tormenting of Hillary. *Vanity Fair*, pp. 119–204.

Lindberg, M. (1991). A three factor framework for evaluating children's suggestibility. In J. L. Doris (Ed.), *The suggestibility of children's recollections* (pp. 47–55). Washington, DC: American Psychological Association.

Maryland *v.* Craig (1990). 110 S. Ct. 3157, 3169.

Peters, D. P. (1991). Confrontational stress and children's testimony. In J. L. Doris (Ed.), *The suggestibility of children's recollections* (pp. 60–76). Washington, DC: American Psychological Association.

Saywitz, K., Goodman, G., Nicholas, G., & Moan, S. (1989, May). children's memory for a genital exam: Implications for child sexual abuse. In G. Goodman (Chair), *Can children provide accurate eyewitness reports?* Symposium presented at the biennial meeting of the Society for Research in Child Development, Kansás City.

Toglia, M. P. (1991). The misinformation effect: Its more prevalent than you think. In J. L. Doris (Ed.), *The suggestibility of children's recollections* (pp. 40–46). Washington, DC: American Psychological Association.

Underwager, R., & Wakefield, H. (1989). *The real world of child interrogations*. Springfield, IL: C. C. Thomas.

Wakefield, H., & Underwager, R. (1988). *Accusations of child sexual abuse*. Springfield, IL: C. C. Thomas.

Warren, A., Hulse-Trotter, K., & Tubbs, E. (1991). Inducing resistance to suggestion. *Law & Human Behavior*, *15*, 273–285.

Warren-Leubecker, A., & Tate, C. S. (1990, March 15). *Can young children lie convincingly if coached by adults?* Paper presented at the Biennial Meeting of the American Psychology and Law Society, Williamsburg, VA.

Zaragoza, M. (1991). In J. L. Doris (Ed.), *The suggestibility of children's recollections* (pp. 27–39). Washington, DC: American Psychological Association.

5

Optimizing Children's Testimony: Research and Social Policy Issues Concerning Allegations of Child Sexual Abuse*

Gail S. Goodman
Jennifer M. Batterman-Faunce
Robert Kenney

Only a short time ago, we didn't have to worry much about children's testimony in sexual abuse cases. As a society, we "knew" that children's testimony could not be trusted. It was only to be considered even potentially credible if it could be corroborated by physical evidence or an adult eyewitness report, which happened relatively infrequently. We knew from Freud and his followers that children readily fantasize sexual incidents, and we knew from experimental psychologists that children are highly suggestible. Besides, sexual abuse and incest were rare occurrences anyway.

However, most of these claims have now been challenged. Kempe and his colleagues (Kempe, Silverman, Steele, Droegmuller, & Silver, 1962) brought worldwide attention to the plight of physically abused children. Focus on other types of child abuse, including sexual abuse, naturally followed. Moreover, spearheaded by the women's movement (e.g., Brownmiller, 1975), exposure of callous treatment of rape victims led to greater awareness of sexual victimization, including the sexual victimization of children (Rush, 1980).

This increase in societal consciousness was accompanied by research indicating that, rather than being a rare event, child sexual abuse was much more prevalent than formerly believed (Finkelhor, 1984; Russell, 1983). The public's eyes began to open. But, with eyes open, it then became incumbent on society to protect children from sexual exploitation. As a result, laws began to change to accommodate children's testimony about sexual abuse. Corroboration laws were largely dropped. Hearsay exceptions became more liberally applied. Innovative techniques to protect children in court became more accepted (Bulkley, 1981).

Nevertheless, society remains split about the validity of children's reports of sexual abuse. We now know why it is necessary to listen to children, but how and when to listen to them is still a matter of considerable debate. Many have

---

* The research reported in this chapter was supported by grants to Gail S. Goodman from the National Center on Child Abuse and Neglect, Department of Health and Human Services, and from the Baldy Center for Law and Social Policy at the State University of New York at Buffalo.

accepted that child sexual abuse represents an all-too-prevalent social ill, but it can be another matter whether to believe a specific child's report in a specific case. Such doubts result in part from concerns about the validity of children's reports.

In this chapter, we discuss a number of issues related to the accuracy of children's testimony, with a special focus on techniques to optimize children's abilities as witnesses. We pay particular attention to the role of context and how context can interact with children's competencies to enhance children's performance in forensic interviews and courtroom settings. We address the important issue of laypersons' and professionals' assessments of children's reports. Finally, we discuss the social policy implications of research on child witnesses.

Developmental Theory and Context Effects

Children's testimony, like their abilities more generally, is best understood if conceptualized as resulting from age X task X context interactions (Donaldson, 1979; Fischer, 1980; Melton & Thompson, 1987). That is, in relation to a child's age, if the task is complex and the context unsupportive or unfamiliar, children's performance may falter. If, instead, the task is simplified and the context is more supportive and understandable, children's performance is optimized. Thus, the accuracy of children's testimony is not solely a function of developmental level or age. Rather it varies along a continuum determined in part by task and contextual demands.

Cognitive/developmental level may, however, place important upper limits on a child witness's performance. According to developmental theory, cognitive level may affect the number of concepts and the degree of abstraction of those concepts that a child can mentally coordinate (Case, 1986; Fischer, 1980; Piaget, 1963). Such limitations may affect a child's performance as a witness. For example, if asked the question, "To your knowledge, and to the best of your ability, please indicate about how long ago it was that you last interacted with this man?" even an older child may have difficulty holding in mind and mentally coordinating the multiple concepts and relations involved. Under a state of intense emotion (e.g., the anxiety and fear associated with courtroom questioning or the despair of remembering a highly traumatic event), the cognitive resources needed to answer such questions might further diminish. Young children may be more subject to false suggestion when they cannot hold the truth of what occurred in mind while at the same time considering the multiple relations and possible misinformation contained in a question. Children perform best when questions asked are simplified and tasks match their cognitive capabilities.

Nevertheless, even very young children have the ability to recount accurate memories of personally meaningful experiences, including traumatic events, be they novel or repeated (Fivush, Gray, & Fromhoff, 1987; Nelson, 1986; Price &

Goodman, 1990; Terr, 1988). Much of the information required of a witness does not involve the reporting of complex, abstract relations. After all, the courts want "just the facts," that is, a concrete and accurate description of what occurred, without elaboration based on abstract inferences.

Although research on memory development indicates that children can provide accurate reports of real-life events (e.g., Nelson, 1986), it is also well known that children's free recall (i.e., response to open-ended questions such as "What happened?") is often skeletal. Children typically remember more than they can verbally express in decontextualized forensic settings. Their memories may be reflected in their play, sparked by a reminder in their home, or shared only with loved ones. The lack of "retrieval control" young children sometimes show has been a basis for the admission of hearsay evidence in child sexual abuse cases; a child may recount information to parents or therapists when least expected and yet be unable or unwilling to do so in a court of law. Nevertheless, the legal system has a strong preference for children, like adults, to testify live in court.

How can we maximize obtaining accurate and complete reports from children? In addition to simplifying the task involved, providing children with contexts that maximize their performance is essential. The term *context* typically implies what we will call *environmental context*, that is, the physical setting in which an event occurs or a report is made. However, some of the contexts that also affect child testimony concern the socioemotional setting (e.g., the intimidation associated with facing the defendant in court), linguistic context (e.g., framing of questions in "legalese"), and the broader context surrounding an event (e.g., expectations about the legal system). As described next, all four of these contexts are important for optimizing or undermining a child's report.

Holding the truth in mind and being able to express that truth are key components of accurate testimony. Reminders of an event provided by the environmental context in which a child is questioned can help children bring memories to mind and exert conscious, verbal control over them. For example, children can recount more about an event when tested back in the context in which the event occurred (Price & Goodman, 1990; Wilkinson, 1987). The rich external retrieval cues provided by the original context may make up, at least in part, for a deficit in internal retrieval cues. Other external cues, such as props representing features of an event, can also permit children to act out what happened so that children do not have to rely solely on verbal skills. The cues provided by adults in their questioning of children are also important and can support greater or lesser accuracy; adult questioning may provide retrieval paths and strategies that children lack on their own and that may eventually help form children's internalized memory systems.

The socioemotional context in which a child is questioned can affect, not only children's ability to report an event, but also their willingness to do so. When a child is overcome with emotion or feels intimidated, embarrassed, or scared, children may have greater difficulty accessing their memories or may simply be unwilling to disclose what happened (Saywitz, Goodman, Nicholas, & Moan, 1991). Emotion can limit the cognitive resources a child brings to a task, such as dealing effectively with questioning. Alternatively, the presence of a support person, such as a loved one or friend, can foster children's accuracy (Goodman et al., in press; Moston, 1987). Thus, socioemotional context can affect children's eyewitness performance.

The linguistic context provided by an interviewer refers to such factors as the syntactic complexity of the questions asked and the difficulty of the words used in relation to the child's cognitive and linguistic skills. Children can become easily confused and demoralized if the linguistic context is developmentally inappropriate. Even when environmental and emotional context are optimal, if the child is asked age-inappropriate questions, the child's performance will suffer (Carter, 1992).

The broader context in which a child is interviewed can also influence the child's performance. The contexts of particular interest to eyewitness testimony researchers are the forensic interview and the courtroom context. When questioned by a police officer or social service worker, a child's response may depend upon her or his understanding of the purpose and implications of the interview. For example, if a child believes that the police officer might arrest the child's parent, or that a social worker might take the child from the home, the child may be understandably hesitant to disclose abuse. If a child believes that a police officer would question the child only if something bad happened, the child's testimony might be swayed toward implication of guilt. Similarly, in the courtroom context, the belief that a judge might send a child witness to jail might adversely affect the child's testimony.

In sum, children's performance as witnesses depends on an intricate interaction of developmental level, task complexity, and contextual supports. Child witness researchers are spending considerable effort in an attempt to understand these interactions, especially as they relate to children's performance in the context of a forensic interview or courtroom questioning.

The Context of the Forensic Interview

When abuse is suspected, children may be interviewed by parents, teachers, hospital staff, police, social workers, clinicians, or attorneys. Typically, the main topic of questioning concerns actions of a sexual nature, such as whether the child's or perpetrators' clothes were removed, where and how the child was touched, if the child was penetrated, and if there was oral-genital contact. Across a number of studies, we have found that children show surprising accuracy when asked questions regarding such abuse-related matters (Rudy & Goodman, 1991; Saywitz et al., 1991). This is not to say that children never get it wrong. In fact, important age differences exist, with young preschool children on average showing higher error rates to abuse-related questions than older children (Goodman & Aman, 1990). However, individual differences can be strong at young ages, with many young children being highly resistant to abuse-related suggestions.

An important caveat regarding these studies is that the questioning was not couched in a realistic forensic context. Because context can affect children's accuracy, it is important to examine children's responses to abuse-related questions when children are led by a police officer to believe that something bad might have happened.

To begin to examine the effects of forensic context on children's testimony in relation to allegations of sexual abuse, Tobey and Goodman (1992) asked 4-year-old children, who did not know they were in a study, to interact individually with a "babysitter" who supposedly watched the child while the child's parent completed a set of forms. Nine to 13 days later, half of the children individually met with a police officer who told the children that he was concerned that the babysitter might have done some "bad things" and that the officer needed to find out what happened.

The children were then interviewed by the police officer's "partner," a female laboratory assistant. She asked the child to recall what happened and to answer a set of leading and misleading questions. Included among the questions were abuse-related questions such as "Did he kiss you?", "Did the man take any of his own clothes off?" and "He took your clothes off, didn't he?" The other half of the children were interviewed in an identical fashion except that they did not meet with the accusatory police officer, were not told that the babysitter might have done something bad, and were not told that the interviewer was a police officer's partner.

The results of the study were consistent with those of our earlier research concerning children's answers to abuse-related questions. The children's answers to these leading and misleading questions were nearly perfect. All of the children denied having their clothes removed or that the babysitter removed his own clothes. All of the children denied having been hit. Only one error was made: A boy who talked to the police officer said "yes" when asked if the babysitter kissed him.

However, the children did make other errors. Two children in particular who talked to the accusatory police officer provided several inaccurate statements in free recall or spontaneous comments. The worst was a child who spontaneously said to her mother, "I think the babysitter had a gun and was going to kill me," and later to the interviewer, "That man he might try to do something bad to me . . . really bad, yes siree." However, most of the children (80%) in the police condition did not make errors of this kind despite the police officer's accusatory statements. Instead, the children were more likely to make comments such as "Nothing bad happened to me" and "We were playing and had lots of fun."

This study confirms children's substantial resistance to suggestion when asked abuse-related questions, even when such questions are posed in an accusatory forensic context. Also, the study confirms our previous findings of notable individual differences in young children's memory accuracy and suggestibility, with most of the young children being quite accurate but with a few of them being highly suggestible to misleading implications. Finally, the study reveals how the context in which children are questioned can affect their performance; although the context did not affect the children's responses to abuse-related questions, it did affect children's accuracy to other questions, and it even affected a few children's spontaneous comments.

There are, however, contexts in which children's answers to abuse-related questions can be adversely affected. Goodman, Bottoms, Schwartz-Kenney, and Rudy (1991) found that more commission errors to abuse-related questions are made by young children when they are interviewed in a cold and intimidating context. Perhaps if the police officer or interviewer in the Tobey and Goodman study had been more intimidating or insistent, errors to the abuse-related questions might have resulted. Given that errors can occur, it is important to consider contextual and other influences on the types of errors children have made in our studies, especially in regard to abuse-related suggestions.

Sources of Error

Despite children's now well-documented resistance to abuse-related suggestions, it is important to understand the sources from which errors can arise. In our studies, when children have made commission errors to abuse questions or spontaneously offered statements that might sound incriminating or bizarre (both of which have mainly occurred with children 3 or 4 years of age), the sources of the errors can be grouped into the following categories.

Contacting the wrong event. Mental reinstatement of the context in which an event occurred can provide powerful retrieval cues for memory. However, what if the interviewer's question inadvertently reinstates the wrong context in the child's mind? Some of the worst inaccuracies we have seen result from the interviewer and the child talking about two different events. Our impression is that when a child makes an error, especially a series of consistent, coherent errors, it is often because the interviewer has not contacted the right event in the child's mind. At times the source of the error can be corroborated by parent report. The types of errors that can result are best illustrated by a series of examples from our studies.

When asked about playing an arm game, a 3-year-old boy in a study conducted by Goodman and Reed (1986) told the interviewer about an event that had frightened him. He described how all the lights had gone out in his house during a storm and how the family had to use candles. The problem was that he failed to tell the interviewer that he was describing a different event than the one the interviewer was asking about. To the interviewer, it might well have appeared that the boy was having flights of fantasy.

A young, previously abused preschooler in a study by Goodman, Rudy, Port, England, Bottoms, and Renouf (1989) was asked what happened when he played games with the study's confederate. The boy proceeded to tell the interviewer that his mother was nice to him, that she took him to the dentist, and that his father was in jail. Even though the interviewer continued to question him about the confederate's activities, the boy for some time answered the questions in relation to his mother. Fortunately, the boy's errors were obvious, since he kept insisting that he never played our games with his mother. Still, possible confusion could have resulted in an actual investigation.

As a final example, one boy in the Rudy and Goodman (1991) study claimed that he had seen bones and blood in our research trailer. Fortunately his mother clarified that the boy was talking about a trip he had just taken that day to an anatomy museum. At the museum there were plastic models of the human body, toy skeletons, and the like. If the mother had not been there to clarify, the child's comments would have seemed like bizarre and macabre fantasy, perhaps connoting images of ritualistic abuse.

When a young child intrudes such events into his or her report, it is often an event that has special, personal significance to the child, frequently because it was novel or scary. For example, the boy who talked about the lights in his house going out and the boy who talked about blood or bones were both describing what were probably novel and somewhat scary events for them. For the abused boy we questioned, our interview apparently reminded him of an anxiety-provoking social service investigation, and even at his young age, he wanted to defend and protect his mother. In any case, our research suggests that professionals who interview child witnesses should be careful to insure they reinstate the intended event in the child's mind.

Weak memory. As appears to be the case for adults (Loftus, 1979), children's resistance to suggestion is strengthened when their memory is strong. As a result, children are more suggestible about information that is nonsalient to begin with (e.g., whether a rug is red or brown, the color of someone's eyes) than about salient, central information. Also, children's suggestibility increases as their memory fades (Goodman, Bottoms, et al., 1991). Research indicates that the memory support provided by environmental context cues, in the form of more specific questions or returning to the site of an event, can be particularly important when a child's memory is weak (Fivush & Hudson, 1987).

However, we have noticed that, even after long delays, children's errors more often involve falsely agreeing with plausible suggestions than with unlikely ones concerning socially taboo acts, such as those associated with sexual abuse. Even after delays as long as 1 to 4 years, children resisted the false suggestion that they had been hit or that their clothes had been removed by a stranger (Goodman, Bottoms, et al., 1991; Goodman, Wilson, Hazan, & Reed, 1989). However, as described below, after a 4-year delay, we found that a few children who had merely played a game with a man said "yes" when asked if the man had taken their picture in the bathtub, and one child falsely agreed that the man had given her a bath.

Linguistic and communicative factors. As mentioned earlier, the linguistic context of an interview is an important influence on children's accuracy. If an interviewer uses difficult sentence construction or language that a child does not understand, problems can result (Brennan & Brennan, 1988). For example, in a study of 5- to 7-year-old children's memory for medical examinations, Saywitz et al. (1991) asked, "Did the doctor ever touch you before that day?" Several of the children erred by answering "yes" to this question. However, note that the question uses a difficult sentence construction, requiring the child to mentally manipulate the concepts "that day," "before that day," "ever," and "touch." As discussed above, cognitive developmental theory would predict children's difficulty in mentally manipulating numerous concepts simultaneously (e.g., Fischer, 1980).

Attorneys are notorious for using language foreign to adults; the same language may be incomprehensible to children. How do children respond to such questions? In a recent study, Carter (1992) investigated the effects of asking children questions in legalese. Specifically, she varied the complexity of the sentences asked, so that half of them were modeled after complex ones used by attorneys while cross-examining child witnesses and the other half were simplified versions of the same questions. When abuse-related questions were asked in legalese (i.e., age-inappropriate, complex language), a significantly higher rate of commission errors occurred.

Even if sentence construction is not too difficult, use of an unfamiliar word within a sentence can lead to misunderstandings. When Goodman and Aman (1990) asked children whether a man had touched their "private parts," some 3-year-olds said "yes" when in fact the man had not. However, upon further exploration, it was found that the children did not know what the interviewer meant by *private parts*. Thus, the interviewer was employing a term that the children did not understand. If this term had been inappropriately used in an actual case, a misleading conclusion might have been drawn.

Sometimes an interviewer uses a word that a child knows in general but misinterprets in context. For example, in one of our studies (Goodman, Bottoms, et al., 1991) in which children received inoculations from a female nurse, we asked, "Did she hit you?" Whereas we had previously obtained a 100% accuracy rate on this question, we now found a number of children who made errors. These children's errors resulted at least in part from children's interpretation of the word *hit* as including being poked with a needle. Several of the children pointed to the area on their arms where they had received their shots and said, "Yes, well, she gave me the shot right here."

We have noticed that the word *touch* can be problematic. Specifically, children often fail to report touching when asked questions such as "Did he touch you?" or "The man didn't touch you, did he?" (see also Peters, 1991). It is possible that many children do not understand the word *touch* or easily forget that they were touched, but we doubt it. It seems more likely that in the context of our other abuse-related questions, the children weren't sure exactly what we meant by touch (e.g., Did we mean "good touch" or "bad touch"?). When we asked about being touched, some children specifically told us that there was no "bad touch" with the confederate. Steward and Steward (1990) report that painful touch is more likely to be reported by children than nonpainful touch. The touch in our studies has been relatively innocuous, which might also have contributed to the children's omissions.

Even if the interviewer uses the most age-appropriate language possible, she or he may have to struggle to understand some of the answers children give. Although young children's communication is not necessarily egocentric, at times it can be. Children may fail to tell an interviewer details that the interviewer needs to know in order to understand what the children are trying to say (Flavell, 1985). There is thus the risk that the interviewer will misinterpret the child's statement. For example, a 4-year-old boy in the Rudy and Goodman (1991) study talked about a blue dog being on his hand. Since dogs are not normally blue and do not fit on the hands of 4-year-olds, this little boy's statement might well have been interpreted as fantasy in an actual forensic investigation. In fact, he was referring to a blue dog puppet.

Social influence and approval. The socioemotional context in which a child is interviewed can influence the extent to which a child will conform to social influence and be desirous of social approval. Many researchers and expert witnesses focus on social influence as an important source of children's suggestibility, and it certainly can be one source of error. For example, in some studies of children's testimony a small number of children, when queried about their inaccurate responses, explained that they responded inaccurately because they wanted to go along with what they thought the interviewer wanted to hear (e.g., King & Yuille, 1987). Effects of intimidation and authority may also fall under this heading. However, when the socioemotional context in which a child is interviewed is warm and accepting, and the child feels comfortable to counter false suggestions, children can show greater resistance to suggestion (Goodman, Bottoms, et al., 1991).

Fantasy. On rare occasions we have seen errors that seem to result mainly from children's fantasies. At least in the context of our questioning, these errors tend to be made most often by young (3 to 4 years old) boys, and to have aggressive or adventurous rather than sexual themes. For example, a boy in one of our studies claimed to have played cowboys and Indians with our confederate and to have been tied up, when in fact he had only played games such as Simon Says and puppets (Goodman & Aman, 1990). Another child, who had gone to an inoculation clinic but had not received any shots, seemed to be more concerned with bravado than with answering questions seriously. When asked our first question—an open-ended question about what happened—he laughingly claimed that he had beaten up the nurse, cut her throat open, and had gone to jail. Although his demeanor defied belief, his words were frightening. We later learned that his inaccuracy may have been influenced by the fact that his mother had gone to jail for assaulting a woman, and that the child had visited her while she was confined in jail (Goodman, Hirschman, Hepps, & Rudy, 1991). As another example, the same little boy who spontaneously described blood and bones being in the research trailer in the Rudy and Goodman (1991) study, also described during the course of more specific questioning that the confederate had put a hot dog in another boy's mouth and had used a magic wand to make the other boy disappear, neither of which was true.

The emotional context of an interview, particularly a context that is stressful, may exacerbate some children's use of fantasy as a coping mechanism. One hyperactive 8-year-old boy in a recent study of ours appeared sufficiently embarrassed by our questioning regarding genital contact that he expressed wild sexually oriented fantasies about what occurred during a medical examination. We know of sexual abuse cases in which during a deposition, a child was so stressed that he reported impossible acts (e.g., that there were car steering wheels that popped out of the walls of the preschool during an imagined storming of the preschool building by the police). Thus the socioemotional context under which a child is interviewed, if too stressful, can lead children to resort to fantasy.

Lying. Another source of possible error is when a child intentionally lies about an event. Everyone knows that children, like adults, sometimes lie. Thus, the simplistic question "Do children lie?" is really a nonissue (see Berliner, 1991; Conte, 1991). Of more concern is the question of whether children lie about sexual abuse, or more specifically, how often and under what circumstances children might lie about sexual abuse.

Recently, several studies have investigated children's lying and secret keeping (e.g., Bussey, 1990; Warren & Tate, 1990). In most of these studies, the lies children told were primarily false denials rather than false accusations. Child abuse professionals have long emphasized that children, like adults, will conceal information to protect a loved one (e.g., Goodwin, Sahd, & Rada, 1979). We demonstrated such concealment in a recent experimental study. Bottoms, Goodman, Schwartz-Kenney, Sachsenmaier, and Thomas (1990) asked mothers of 3- and 5-year-olds to engage their children in a set of forbidden activities (e.g., playing with toys the researcher said were for someone else). The mothers then told their children not to tell. The children were immediately interviewed about whether or not they and their mothers played with the toys. Older children were more likely than younger children to conceal the transgression. A number of the older children lied by denying that they and their mothers touched the toys, but they did not make false allegations against others.

Although studies of children's lying are of interest, the lying studies to date, including our own and those of others (see Ceci, this volume), do not concern lying about sexual matters. Thus they do not directly answer the question of whether children lie about sexual abuse and in that sense are not ecologically valid. Nevertheless, intentional lying is one possible source of children's errors in responding to abuse-related questions.

Summary. Although we have occasionally seen children make these errors and such errors could be of importance in actual investigations, they have been surprisingly infrequent. Most of the children we have tested have been highly accurate about the main actions that occurred and especially about abuse-related actions (see also Davies, Tarrant, & Flin, 1989; Leippe, Romanczyk, & Manion, 1991). Nevertheless, because of the possible ramifications of children's errors in legal settings, understanding the sources of such errors is important. Hopefully, such knowledge can reduce miscommunication when children report events to authorities or testify in court.

Improving Children's Reports in the Forensic Context

What can be done to reduce children's errors and optimize their testimony? Efforts are currently underway to develop techniques to bolster children's accuracy of report in the forensic context. Such efforts are of considerable importance. If we can devise the appropriate tasks and contexts to support the most complete and accurate testimony from children, we can hopefully enhance children's credibility, reduce misunderstanding, and best serve the interests of justice.

As discussed above, children, especially young children, tend to have more difficulty than adults generating their own internal retrieval strategies for recalling events. Children's memories can, in effect, become locked inside their minds. One possible key to unlocking their memories is to ask specific or even leading questions; however, in the legal context, one then risks damaging the child's credibility and possibly obtaining inaccuracies in the child's statements. One set of techniques currently being explored by researchers concentrates on providing children with retrieval strategies and cues while at the same time avoiding leading questioning. The ''cognitive interview'' is one such technique. Developed originally by Geiselman and his colleagues to be used with adult witnesses, Geiselman, Saywitz, and Bornstein (1990) have adapted the cognitive interview for use with older children (7- to 11-year-olds). The cognitive interview begins with building rapport with the child and giving the child general instructions (e.g., to say ''don't know'' if the child doesn't remember an answer, not to change an answer just because the interviewer asks the same question twice). The interviewer then asks the child to describe the environmental and personal context in which the event took place. Once that context has been described by the child, she or he is instructed to describe what happened from beginning to end, being as complete as possible (e.g., ''Sometimes people leave out little things because they think little things are not important. Tell me everything that happened''). Following the narrative, the interviewer asks specific questions to clarify what the child reported. Then the child is asked to recall the event in backwards order, from the end to the beginning. Finally the child is asked to "Put yourself in the body of _____, and tell me what that person said?" that is, to take the perspective of another person involved in the event. Geiselman et al. (1990) report that, compared to a regular interview, the cognitive interview increased the number of correct facts recalled by 26% without increasing error rates.

Although quite promising, the cognitive interview has yet to be adapted for use with young children. Moreover, further research is needed to insure the technique is usefulness in optimizing children's reports of highly stressful events or events about which children feel conflicted to report.

Context reinstatement is another potentially useful technique for improving children's reports. Experimental as well as clinical studies indicate that taking a child back to the scene of an event helps to reinstate the child's memory (Price & Goodman, 1990; Pynoos & Nader, 1988; Wilkinson, 1987). For example, in a study by Wilkinson (1987), 3- to 4-year-old children went for a walk with an experimenter. At various points along the way, specific activities were performed (e.g., finding a ball, going to a shop to buy something). The next day, half of the children were questioned while taking the walk again. The other children were questioned in a quiet room at their preschool. Children tested back in the context of the event recalled significantly more about what happened than children tested in the preschool. Similar context effects have been found for children as young as 2.5 years (Price & Goodman, 1990). Although context does not eliminate developmental differences in children's performance, it can considerably increase the amount of information children report.

However, if a child experienced a traumatic criminal event, returning the child to the scene of a crime could have negative emotional effects and should be attempted with caution. Nevertheless, under the guidance of a skillful clinician, such reexposure could be therapeutic. Pynoos and Nader (1988), for example, worked with children who had witnessed a sniper attack at their school, an attack during which one child and a passerby were killed and 13 children were injured. As part of a semistructured interview, Pynoos later walked with each child around the school yard as the child recounted what happened. Pynoos believes that children need to explore their traumas in an assisted interview to recover from a traumatic event (Pynoos & Eth, 1986).

Techniques have also been explored to improve children's ability to identify briefly seen strangers from photo line-ups. There is increasing evidence that, in standard studies of children's testimony, children produce more false identification errors of briefly seen strangers than do adults (Parker & Carranza, 1989). Can children's tendency to make false identifications be reduced? Goodman, Bottoms, Schwartz-Kenney, and Rudy (1991) provided children with training trials on which children were presented with practice target-present and target-absent line-ups. For example, the children viewed a line-up that did not include their mother and were asked if their mother was shown in the photographs (target-absent line-up). Children were also shown a line-up that included a bear and asked if a bear was in the line-up (target-present line-up). Errors were corrected. Such training was found to reduce significantly the number of false identifications made by 5- to 7-year-olds to a target-absent line-up concerning a person with whom the children had experienced a relatively brief but stressful interaction. However, the training did not significantly improve the performance of younger children (i.e., 3- to 4-year-olds), who may have needed more training trials.

These studies indicate that researchers have much to offer the legal and social service systems in tackling the challenges posed when interviewing child witnesses. However, the development of techniques to better the testimony of young children (e.g., preschoolers) may be particularly difficult and thus is an especially pressing issue at present.

The Courtroom Context

Although many more children are interviewed by authorities than ever testify in court, children do take the stand in court proceedings, including at trial. Seeing a small child testify in a serious legal proceeding seems strange and incongruous. One can't help wondering how well a child can withstand the formality and intimidation of a system designed to be stressful even for adults. How can a child who may barely understand court proceedings (e.g., Saywitz, 1989) match wits with a sophisticated attorney trained to befuddle even mature, assertive adults? Is such a context the best way to facilitate the accuracy and completeness of a child's testimony?

The validity of children's testimony in actual legal proceedings is difficult to assess because the truth is generally unknown. However, researchers have studied the emotional effects on children of criminal court testimony and have observed children testify in court. For at least a subset of children, legal involvement and testifying for the prosecution is associated with continuation of pretestimony behavior disturbance (e.g., Goodman et al., 1992; Runyan, Everson, Edelsohn, Hunter & Coulter, 1988). Goodman et al. (1992) found that, when child victim/witnesses were observed in court, children who evidenced fear of the defendant had a more difficult time answering the prosecutor's questions. Moreover, defense attorneys were less emotionally supportive than prosecutors in their questioning of children and used more age inappropriate language. Children often expressed nervousness before testifying; while some children were relieved afterwards, others continued to view it as a highly stressful and negative experience (e.g., children who were cross examined by a violent defendant who was representing himself; children who felt the defense attorney tried to twist their words). Given what we know of the contexts that support accurate child testimony, it would appear that, for at least some children, the standard adversarial system does not provide the ideal setting for optimizing children's testimony.

Improving Children's Testimony within the Courtroom Context

To the extent that the adversarial system does not provide the best setting for interviewing children, we see two choices: (a) help children optimize their testimony while operating within the current legal system, or (b) change the adversarial system when children testify. Scientific and legal advances have been made on both grounds.

Preparing children to testify. Researchers are exploring ways to prepare children to withstand the stress of courtroom questioning and perform to their best ability in the courtroom context. Such preparation efforts have mainly taken one of two forms: (a) training children in techniques to improve their courtroom testimony, and (b) working with children to lessen the intimidation and emotional distress associated with the courtroom context.

Saywitz and Snyder (1993) have developed several promising training techniques to increase the accuracy of children's in-court testimony. They hypothesized that children may be unaware of the types of information or level of detail required in a courtroom setting. In an attempt to partially remedy this problem, Saywitz and Snyder successfully trained 7- to 11-year-old children to report greater detail in free recall by using a set of schematic cards to prompt children to describe the setting of the event, the participants, the conversation and affective states of the participants, the actions, and the consequences. In conjunction with Susan Moan (as cited in Saywitz & Snyder, 1993), they were also able to develop techniques to reduce children's suggestibility in response misleading questions. These techniques included practice with feedback in answering misleading questions and explanations of the consequences of incorrectly "going along" with false suggestions.

Researchers are also working on how to prepare children emotionally for testifying. Sas (1991) and her colleagues developed an elaborate preparation program for 5- to 17-year-old children who were likely to be called as victim/witnesses in child sexual abuse cases. Preparation classes included an educational component (e.g., familiarizing children with legal terms, procedures, and concepts; role playing being a witness; explanation of the adversarial nature of the criminal justice system) and a stress-reduction component (e.g., therapeutic support, relaxation exercises, and for highly fearful children, systematic desensitization).

Evaluation of the preparation classes indicated that, compared to children who did not experience the program, "prepared" children had fewer fears. Also, prosecutors thought that the prepared children did better overall and had a better orientation to court than nonprepared children. Moreover, guilty verdicts were more likely in cases involving children who went through the preparation program.

Research by Saywitz and Snyder, as well as by Sas, indicates that much can be done while working within the current legal system to make children more accurate and less stressed witnesses. However, efforts to protect child witnesses from adverse effects of testifying and efforts to provide a context to support accurate child testimony have also led to more radical reforms of the legal system.

Protective measures in the courtroom. Concern about the emotional effects on children of courtroom intimidation has led to legislative and court action to protect children from system-induced stress while at the same time maintaining the integrity of trial proceedings. Of the various innovative techniques employed, use of closed-circuit testimony has received the most attention, probably because it is considered to be one of the most dramatic departures from standard courtroom practice. In America, the Sixth Amendment of the Constitution specifies that the accused has the right to confront witnesses against him or her in a face-to-face encounter in court. Yet facing the accused is a fear often expressed by child witnesses. Laboratory research and field work in the courts both indicate that fear of the defendant results in less complete testimony by child witnesses (e.g., Bussey, Lee, & Grimbeek, 1993; Goodman et al., 1992). Courts in several countries have recently approved use of closed-circuit television as a means of shielding children from a literal face-to-face encounter with the defendant. When such technology is used, children testify in a more supportive context than the courtroom (e.g., from a room adjoining the court), and their testimony is broadcast into the court for the jury, defendant, and judge to see and hear.

In England, the courts have experimented with closed-circuit television, wisely asking research psychologists to evaluate its effects; Davies and Noon (1991) were chosen to evaluate the use of closed-circuit television when children testify. They studied 100 prosecutions, mostly involving sex crimes, concerning 154 child victim/witnesses (100 girls and 54 boys) ranging in age from 4 to 13 years old. (Most of the children, however, were 8 years or older.) Compared to a sample of children who testified in open-court in Scotland, children who testified via closed-circuit television in England were rated not only as happier but also as more consistent, fluent, confident, and audible. Interestingly, the researchers found nothing in their data to suggest that closed-circuit testimony affected the outcome (guilty vs. not guilty) of the criminal case, which may help alleviate concerns that closed-circuit testimony biases a trial by implying that the defendant must be guilty if the child has to be shielded. According to judges and attorneys involved the cases, one of the main advantages of use of closed-circuit television was the protection it offered to children from the emotional distress of facing the accused and testifying in front of an audience; one of the main disadvantages was that the child's testimony had less emotional impact on jurors. Based on these findings, the researchers concluded that closed-circuit television had positive and facilitating effects on the children's courtroom testimony, and that its use had widespread acceptance among legal professionals.

In America, the U.S. Supreme Court ruled in Maryland v. Craig (1990) that, if, in a criminal trial for child sexual abuse, a child would be so traumatized by facing the defendant in court that the child's testimony would be adversely affected, the child could testify via closed-circuit television. Nevertheless, closed-circuit television has been relatively rarely used in criminal cases, making evaluation difficult. Even if it were widely used, however, one question that cannot be answered based on studies of real trials concerns how closed-circuit television affects the accuracy of children's testimony and jurors' abilities to reach the truth. In real trials, the truth is a matter of debate; if the truth were fully known, a trial would not be necessary. Therefore, to examine how closed-circuit television might affect accuracy, researchers must resort to laboratory studies.

We recently completed a large-scale study concerning the effects of closed-circuit television on children's and jurors' accuracy (Goodman et al., 1992). Eight-year-old children individually made a movie with a man who either videotaped the children exposing parts of their bodies (i.e., their toes, upper arm, or belly buttons) or videotaped them with these same body parts unexposed. Then, in a realistic mock trial, children testified about what happened either in a regular courtroom or via one-way closed-circuit television. Mock jurors watched each child testify under direct and cross examination, and then made judgments about the children's accuracy and whether the defendant was guilty of the mock crime of videotaping a child exposing body parts.

Analyses to date indicate little effect of testimony condition on 8-year-old children's accuracy. For example, there were no significant differences in the children's correct answers or commission errors to specific, misleading, or correctly leading questions. In addition, jurors rated the defendant just as guilty in the closed-circuit as in the regular trial. However, jurors rated the children as more believable when children testified live in court than when they testified via closed-circuit television. This latter finding is consistent with prosecutors' views that victims are more credible when they testify live in court and is also consistent with the views expressed by legal professionals surveyed by Davies and Noon (1991) that use of closed-circuit television may lessen the impact of the child's testimony on jurors. Again, these results may help alleviate defense attorneys' fears that closed-circuit television biases a jury against the defendant. However, they may place prosecutors somewhat in a moral bind given a desire to protect children who must testify while still needing to enhance the impact of witness testimony on jurors. Fortunately, the results of laboratory and field studies to date indicate that use of closed-circuit television has little effect on final verdicts (Davies & Noon, 1991; Swim, Borgida, & McCoy, 1991).

In summary, research is exploring ways to work within the current court system to optimize children's accuracy (e.g., by preparing children for their day in court) and also to change the legal system to create a context in which children can perform at a more optimal level (e.g., by implementation of innovative measures such as use of closed-circuit television). So far the results are encouraging.

Improving the Ability to Accurately Assess Children's Testimony

To date, researchers interested in children's testimony have concentrated largely on children's memory and suggestibility. However, as Wigmore (1909) noted long ago, and as Melton and Thompson (1987) wisely remind us, an even more crucial question, legally speaking, is whether adults in factfinder roles can reach the truth based on children's statements. Even if children's testimony is partly inaccurate, as long as fact finders can reach the right verdict, justice is served.

Studies of mock jurors' reactions to child witnesses have mainly tapped biases concerning children's abilities. Generally, the studies indicate that mock jurors (typically college students) have a negative bias about the believability of young children's testimony when the main issue is witness accuracy. In contrast, when the main issue in a trial is the honesty or naivete of a witness, as it might be in many sexual abuse cases, children tend to have a credibility advantage over adult victim/witnesses (e.g., Bottoms & Goodman, 1989; Duggan et al., 1989).

Although studies of adults' biases are of considerable interest, they do not answer the question of how well factfinders can assess the accuracy of children's testimony, as might be required of jurors in a trial or of police and social service workers in determining whether to pursue a case. Few studies have investigated adults' abilities to accurately evaluate children's testimony; most that do exist concentrate on mock jurors' rather than professionals' assessments of children's accuracy. Moreover, most studies address the ability to assess only one level of accuracy, specifically, the accuracy of children's statements; legally the more crucial question, at least for jurors, is the ability to reach the correct verdict; for social service workers and police, the ability to reach the correct decision (e.g., whether the case is "founded" or "unfounded") is critical.

In studies of adults' abilities to assess the accuracy of children's testimony, researchers typically expose children to real-life or videotaped events and then obtain the children's testimony about what happened. A videotape of the children's testimony is then shown to mock jurors. It is the mock jurors' job to determine whether or not the children are accurate.

Goodman, Bottoms, Herscovici, and Shaver (1989) found that, when young children (4- to 7-year-olds) were subjected to direct and cross examination about a real-life event (i.e., receiving an inoculation) one year after they experienced it, mock jurors were unable to discern the accuracy of the children's reports. Mock jurors rated the older and more confident children as the most correct, when in fact the relation between accuracy and age was just the opposite and no appreciable relation existed between accuracy and confidence. These findings are consistent with those from several written-scenario studies indicating that adults judge older children and adults to be more credible witnesses than younger children when memory is the main issue (e.g., Goodman, Golding, Helgeson, Haith, & Michelli, 1987; Leippe & Romanczyk, 1987).

Perhaps adults have difficulty assessing the accuracy only of young children's reports. Would the same result hold for older children? In a study by Wells,

Turtle, and Luus (1989), 8-year-olds, 12-year-olds, and adults testified about a staged abduction presented on videotape. The witnesses were then placed under direct and cross-examination, and videotapes of their responses were shown to mock jurors. Wells et al. (1989) found that mock jurors were better able to assess the accuracy of 12-year-olds' and adults' testimony then that of 8-year-olds, who provided fewer correct responses to suggestive questions than mock jurors realized.

Leippe and his colleagues (Leippe, Manion, & Romanczyk, 1992), who have conducted some of the most sophisticated studies on this issue, present data that bridge Goodman et al.'s and Wells et al.'s findings. Five- to 6-year-olds, 9- to 10-year-olds, and adults engaged in a "touching experience" with a man who played the role of the "toucher." Shortly after being touched, each witness was interviewed. Videotapes of the "victim/witnesses" were then shown to undergraduate students serving as mock jurors. Leippe et al. found that highly accurate 5- to 6-year-olds received lower believability ratings than adults, even if the adults were less accurate than the children. Presumably, a negative bias about children's testimony could not be overcome even when the young children were quite accurate. As witness age increased, however, fact finders were better able to discern the witnesses' accuracy.

In the above studies of fact finders' ability to discern children's testimony, the children were trying to tell the truth. How well can fact finders discern children's intentional lying? Westcott, Davies, and Clifford (in press) examined this question by having 7- to 8-year-olds and 10- to 11-year-olds testify about a trip to the British Museum, a trip that only half of the children actually experienced. The other half simply watched a videotape of the visit. Adults then viewed videotapes of the children testifying about the trip and rated the children's honesty. The adults were significantly better than chance at detecting honest children versus deceivers, especially when the children were young. These findings fit well with those reported by other researchers who find that young children's lies are particularly easy to detect, whereas with age, deception becomes less recognizable (see DePaulo & Jordan, 1982, for a review). Thus it appears that although mock jurors are better able to assess the accuracy of older compared to younger children when children are trying to tell the truth, just the opposite relation holds when children are intentionally lying. Then mock jurors have more difficulty assessing the accuracy of older compared to younger children.

Although these studies do not address several factors that may have a significant influence on jurors in actual sexual assault cases (e.g., the victim's emotionality while testifying), the studies are of considerable interest regarding jurors' abilities to reach the truth based on children's testimony. However, it should be noted that these studies did not explicitly concern sexual contact and did not concern adults' abilities to reach a proper verdict.

Moreover, although studies of adults' assessments of children's testimony have typically tried to mimic direct- and cross-examination at trial, in fact most child sexual assault cases never reach the trial stage. Of more frequent importance is the ability of investigative factfinders, such as police officers and child protective service workers, to infer accurately the validity of children's statements at pretrial stages. Do fact finders err by overinterpreting errors made by nonabused children so as to misjudge them to be actual abuse victims?

In a preliminary examination of this question, Goodman, Batterman, Kenney, and Wilson (1990; see also Batterman-Faunce, 1991) asked undergraduates and child protective service workers to watch videotapes of one of eight children supposedly being interviewed in a child sexual abuse investigation. In fact, each of the children viewed had been a participant in our research. Specifically, the children had played an arm game for 5 minutes with a man 4 years earlier when the children were either 3 or 6 years old (see Goodman & Reed, 1986). When we interviewed the children 4 years later, the now 7- and 10-year-olds could not remember much, if anything, about the brief, innocuous event. Given our interest in creating a false memory, the children's lack of recollection was not problematic. We were still able to question the children to determine whether we could produce false reports of abuse.

As in our previous work, we interviewed the children as if they were participating in a child abuse investigation. The children were asked a variety of questions, including whether they had been hugged and kissed or had their clothes removed, whether the man had taken the children's picture in the bathroom, and whether the man had touched the child in any way that the child didn't like. To add to the realism of the questioning, the interviewer made comments such as "Are you afraid to tell or do you just not remember?" and "It's OK to tell. Don't be afraid."

None of the children made straightforward false claims of abuse. Some of the children did, however, answer our questions in ways that might cause concern. For example, a few children said "yes" to our questions about their picture having been taken in the bathroom, about being hugged and kissed, and about whether the man did anything to make them feel uncomfortable. However, all of the children affirmed that their clothes had remained on, that they had not been hit, and that they had not been threatened. Given that some ambiguous responses occurred, we wondered whether the errors would lead factfinders to believe the children had been abused.

The 32 undergraduates (16 females and 16 males) who participated ranged in age from 17 to 24 years, with a mean of 18.6 years. None of the students reported any experience related to child abuse investigations or interviews. The 24 child protective workers (16 females and 8 males) ranged in age from 29 to 51 years, with a mean age of 37 years. On average, they had 8.58 years (range = 2 to 25 years) of experience as professionals and an average of 6.6 years (range = 2 to 22 years) of experience working on child abuse cases. Twenty-one percent had masters degrees and 75% had bachelors degrees. (Four percent declined to indicate education level.) Over the course of their careers, they had interviewed an average of 1,046 children (range = 30 to 5,000).

Before the factfinders saw the videotape, they were provided with a brief description of a child sexual abuse investigation at a child care center, one that we made up for purposes of the study that was believable given the nature of our questioning. Subjects were led to believe, and indicated later that they did believe, that the tapes were from an actual investigation. After viewing the tape, the factfinders made judgments about the child's accuracy, the probability that the child had been abused, the believability of the child, and the typicality of the child's responses.

The results indicated that on average college students and social workers did not judge the child they viewed to be an abuse victim. However, child protective workers were less likely than undergraduates to judge the children as abuse victims when a *founded* versus *nonfounded* rating was required. *Founded* was defined as the existence of some credible evidence of child abuse. Of interest, a number of child protective workers commented that although some of the other children in the case might be abuse victims, the child they saw interviewed acted more like a nonabused child than an abused child. A few child protective service workers did, however, judge the children to be possible abuse victims. These respondents indicated that further investigation was warranted.

We were also interested in the attributions participants made concerning the children's responses. When each respondent's yes–no score was considered concerning whether she or he thought the child forgot the event, on average, 31% of the undergraduates and 25% of the social workers thought the child had forgotten what happened, a difference that was not statistically significant. Undergraduates and social workers did differ, however, in their responses to the question about whether they thought the child was too afraid to tell. Thirty-eight percent of the undergraduates and 17% of the social workers endorsed that view. Twenty-eight percent of the undergraduates and 54% of the social workers indicated that they thought the child was accurate; there was thus a tendency for social workers to be more likely to view the children as accurate (e.g., in generally denying that abuse took place) than did the undergraduates. Finally, 3% of the undergraduates and 8% of the social workers indicated that they thought the child was inaccurate.

These results indicate that child protective service workers were better able than undergraduates to accurately assess whether or not the case should be founded and that the children were generally accurate denying that abuse took place. Undergraduates tended to err in thinking that the children were too afraid to tell when the truth was that the children had not been abused.

Interestingly, the amount of experience the child protective service worker had on the job with children was predictive of their performance. The social worker's judgments of the typicality of the child's responses were inversely related to the number of children the social worker has interviewed, $r = -.42, n = 23, p < .05$, meaning that social workers who had interviewed many children were less likely to view the child's responses on the videotape as typical of child abuse victims. Also, social workers who had interviewed more children were more likely to characterize the child viewed on the videotape as having forgotten what happened, $r = .41$, $n = 24$, $p < .05$, which was generally true.

These results are encouraging in several ways. Child protective service workers, as well as undergraduates, did not, on average, tend to think the children were abused, despite some errors in the children's testimony. Child protective workers, particularly those with more experience, were better able than undergraduates to assess the accuracy of the children's statements.

These findings have at least one implication for improving factfinders' abilities to reach the truth. Specifically, they imply that experience interviewing children in actual child abuse cases is associated with greater accuracy in assessing children's reports of abuse. Although most jurors would not have such experience, most child protective service workers would. Unfortunately, our study does not address the question of how well fact finders can detect accuracy when actual abuse victims are interviewed. A study similar to ours adding videotapes of actual abuse victims would be of interest in answering that question.

SOCIAL POLICY

Society faces a difficult moral issue in dealing with children's testimony in child sexual abuse cases. There is currently little consensus on how best to protect children from sexual exploitation while at the same time protect innocent defendants from false reports of abuse. If we do not ask children directly about abuse experiences, children are not likely to tell us and we will then fail to protect the most vulnerable members of our society from an all-too-prevalent form of abuse, one that places children at risk for later psychological disturbance (Brown & Finkelhor, 1986). If we ask incorrectly, we may obtain a false report and run the risk of sending an innocent person to jail, unnecessarily removing a child from home, or restricting a parent's access to his or her child.

Social Policy and Research on Children's Testimony

Wittingly or not, researchers who study children's testimony take part in the societal dilemma concerning child witnesses and also influence social policy for such children. Even if a disclaimer is added to the end of a paper, by couching a study in the context of children's testimony, one has entered the child witness debate. Although researchers must maintain as their major goals the advancement of science and the discovery of scientific truths, they should also be aware of the social policy implications of their research. Such awareness may affect the type of research conducted, the comparison groups included in a study, and what is viewed as the most important questions to ask.

However, for better or for worse, what is viewed as the most important questions to investigate can be colored by researchers' sympathies and points of view. A survey study by Kassin, Ellsworth, and Smith (1989) found that experimental psychologists who testify about eyewitness testimony in criminal court do so primarily for the defense. For example, experimental psychologists who were surveyed indicated that they agreed to testify for the defense in 755 cases and for the prosecution in only 44 cases. Although the psychologists were asked to testify for the prosecution much less often than for the defense, this is likely to reflect the fact that the psychologists were known as "defense experts."

It seems unlikely that this situation was created solely by the knowledge base in psychology. In our view, it is more likely to do with the following factors: The study of eyewitness testimony grew up in a historical period (the 1960s and 1970s) when there were great concerns about the power of the State. Antiwar protestors were being hauled into court, racism was more blatant, and concerns about false accusations were high. Moreover, initial studies of eyewitness memory malleability and effects of misleading questioning (e.g., Loftus, 1979), while landmarks in their time, tend to be quite unrealistic by current standards, especially in regard to the testimony of victim/witnesses. In retrospect, these studies seem bound to make eyewitness performance look bad. Subsequent studies by many eyewitness testimony researchers have most often concentrated on the negative consequences of leading questioning without considering possible positive effects. Thus the questions primarily asked by researchers, while of substantial theoretical interest, may have reflected a certain social policy slant.

In any case, social pressure for eyewitness testimony researchers conform to this "politically correct" view has been strong (e.g., DiAngelis, 1989; Doris, 1991). Taking a defense perspective, one would obviously want to highlight research demonstrating children's suggestibility and tendency to lie (e.g., Ceci, this volume; Loftus, 1979; Raskin & Esplin, 1991). Although these are legitimate concerns, should all research on child witnesses in relation to sexual abuse cases be based on the premise that children are highly suggestible liars? We think not. Although it is impossible to know for certain, existing evidence indicates that most reports of child sexual abuse reflect valid concerns (Jones & McGraw, 1987), and that the false report rate in child sexual abuse cases is not higher than in many other kinds of cases (Finkelhor, 1990; Spencer & Flin, 1990).

An unbalanced perspective rather than a more balanced view omits an important ingredient—a concern for the victim. However, the situation is actually more complex than a simple advocacy contest might suggest. As Loftus (1979) has pointed out, for every defendant falsely accused, the real perpetrator goes free. Moreover, if a child has not been abused but is led to believe that abuse occurred, the child may suffer psychological damage (Conte, 1991). If children are led to make false reports, their credibility is harmed generally and protection of actual abuse victims becomes more difficult. Balancing all of these concerns is a difficult task. To the extent that research affects how children are interviewed and how court cases are argued, researchers need to conduct their studies in the most informed way possible, sensitive to all sides of the issues. Although in the laboratory we cannot mimic the emotion stirred in custody proceedings involving allegations of child abuse, and we would be hard pressed to create the secrecy and fear that may influence a child victim's willingness to disclose abuse, scientists can conduct research that is as ecologically valid as possible and that focuses in a balanced way on issues related to children's testimony in abuse cases. In this way, both social policy and science would be best served.

Social Policy Implications of Child Witness Research

The research we have discussed in the present chapter has important social policy implications. The research suggests that we as a society must provide the most supportive contexts possible for interviewing children, whether in forensic interviews or in the courtroom. The contexts should be supportive of accurate memory retrieval and positive emotional growth. In that way we can improve children's performance and lives, and hopefully optimize the performance of factfinders in assessing the truth.

Specifically, we offer the following suggestions. First, society must devote sufficient funds for researchers to develop and field test techniques to optimize children's testimony. Important research has begun but further investigation is sorely needed. For example, there is still virtually no published research on children's suggestibility about repeated, stressful events involving familiar persons, yet most child sexual abuse involves events that fall in that category. Development of techniques to elicit more accurate and complete reports from young children, such as preschoolers, should also be a priority. Finally, studies of how best to communicate with children as a function of their developmental level, cultural background, and social class—that is, studies of the language of interviews—are needed. In conducting their studies, researchers interested in children's testimony would profit from exposure to interviewing children in actual cases.

Second, more intense training is needed of professionals who provide front line work in child sexual abuse cases. The training should include techniques to optimize children's reports, with exposure to multiple points of view on how best to accomplish that task. Geiselman et al. (1990) provide valuable suggestions for interviewing children, based on their research. Jones and McQuiston (1985), Boat and Everson (1986), Sgroi (1982), and Yuille, Hunter, Joffe, and Zaparniuk (1993) also provide varying but well-founded formats for conducting child witness interviews. However, given the need for further research, opinion on how to interview children still outweighs scientific evidence. Opinion varies from conservative approaches of asking children only the most general, open-ended questions to liberal approaches of asking a substantial number of leading questions in a forceful way. Until the research base matures, it would be premature for us to recommend one interview format over another; rather, considerable flexibility and professional judgment are needed to deal with the complexities of a specific case.

Training is also needed in the ability to assess children's reports. Although factfinders may at times have difficulty assessing the precise accuracy of children's statements, it is as yet unclear how often they form the right versus the wrong "bottom-line" decision about whether a child has been victimized. Knowledge about children's testimony may play an important role in educating factfinders about children's ability to describe events accurately, children's suggestibility as well as their resistance to suggestion, and the ways in which disclosures of abuse unfold. Hopefully, such research, in addition to experience in actual cases, will help factfinders fine tune their decision-making abilities.

Third, courts should offer appropriate preparation programs for children who testify. The programs should satisfy high standards of effectiveness, as demonstrated by evaluation studies. Moreover, the programs should meet with the approval of defense and prosecution bars.

Fourth, the courts should experiment with contexts that foster the most complete and accurate testimony by child witnesses. Use of closed-circuit technology in child sexual abuse cases is a start. However, we see no reason why frightened children who testify about other traumatic events, such as murder, should not be given the same protections as child sexual assault victims. Moreover, experimentation should be conducted to determine if children's courtrooms, in which children are interviewed by a neutral party who has established rapport with the child, offer even more emotionally and cognitively supportive contexts than provided by closed-circuit technology.

Conclusion

In previous times, such social policy issues were less pressing. Sexual abuse of children was not a salient social issue. Most people would not have guessed that, as surveys now reveal, about 15% to 38% of adult women and about 6% to 10% of adult men in America have suffered some form of sexual victimization before the age of 18 years (Finkelhor, 1984; Russell, 1983). Times have changed. More than ever before, we need to know how to optimize children's testimony.

REFERENCES

Batterman-Faunce, J. M. (1991). *Perceptions of child witnesses interviewed after a four-year delay.* Unpublished paper, State University of New York at Buffalo.

Berliner, L. (1991). The question of belief. *Journal of Interpersonal Violence, 6,* 240.

Boat, B. W., & Everson, M. D. (1986). *Using anatomical dolls: Guidelines for interviewing young children in sexual abuse investigations.* Unpublished manuscript, University of North Carolina School of Medicine, Chapel Hill, North Carolina.

Bottoms, B. L., & Goodman, G. S. (1989, April). *The credibility of child victims of sexual assault.* Paper presented to the Eastern Psychological Association, Boston, MA.

Bottoms, B. L., Goodman, G. S., Schwartz-Kenney, B., Sachsenmaier, T., & Thomas, S. (1990, March). *Keeping secrets: Implications for children's testimony.* Paper presented to the American Psychology and Law Meetings, Williamsburg, VA.

Brennan, M., & Brennan, R. (1988). *Strange language.* Wagga Wagga, Australia: Riverina Murray Institute of Higher Education.

Brown, A., & Finkelhor, D. (1986). Impact of child sexual abuse: A review of the research. *Psychological Bulletin, 99,* 66–77.

Brownmiller, S. (1975). *Against our will: Men, women and rape.* New York: Simon and Schuster.

Bulkley, J. (Ed.). (1981). *Innovations in the prosecution of child sexual abuse cases.* Washington, DC: American Bar Association.

Bussey, K. (1990, March). Adult influences on children's eyewitness testimony. In S. J. Ceci (Chair), *Do children lie?* American Psychology and Law Meeting, Williamsburg, VA.

Bussey, K., Lee, K., & Grimbeek, E. J. (1993). Lies and secrets: Implications for children's reporting of sexual abuse. In G. S. Goodman & B. L. Bottoms (Eds.), *Child victims, child witnesses: Understanding and improving children's testimony* (pp. 147–168). New York: Guilford Publications.

Carter, C. (1992). *The effects of linguistic complexity and social support on children's reports.* Dissertation submitted to the State University of New York at Buffalo.

Case, R. (1986). *Intellectual development.* New York: Academic Press.

Ceci, S. (1991, April). Discussant comments. In M. Simone & M. Toglia (Chairs), *Lying and truthfulness among young children: Implications for their participation in legal proceedings.* Paper presented at the Society for Research in Child Development Meetings, Seattle, WA.

Conte, J. (1991). Believe the client: Slogans as miscommunication. *Journal of Interpersonal Violence, 6,* 243–245.

Davies, G., & Noon, E. (1991). *An evaluation of the live link for child witnesses.* London: Home Office.

Davies, G., Tarrant, A., & Flin, R. (1989). Close encounters of the witness kind: Children's memory for a simulated health inspection. *British Journal of Psychology, 80,* 415–429.

DePaulo, B., & Jordan, A. (1982). Age changes in deceiving and detecting deceit. In R. Feldman (Ed.), *Development of nonverbal behavior in children.* New York: Springer.

DiAngelis, T. (1989). Controversy marks child witness meeting. *The APA Monitor, 20,* 1, 8–9.

Donaldson, M. (1979). *Children's minds.* New York: Norton.

Doris, J. (Ed.). (1991). *The suggestibility of children's recollections.* Washington, DC: American Psychological Association.

Duggan, L. M., III, Aubrey, M., Doherty, E., Isquith, P., Levine, M., & Scheiner, J. (1989). The credibility of children as witnesses in a simulated child sex abuse trial. In S. Ceci, D. Ross, & M. Toglia (Eds.), *Perspectives on children's testimony* (pp. 71–99). New York: Springer-Verlag.

Finkelhor, D. (1984). *Child sexual abuse: New theory and research.* New York: Free Press.

Finkelhor, D. (1990). Is child abuse overreported? *Public Welfare, 48,* 23–47.

Fischer, K. W. (1980). A theory of cognitive development: The control and construction of hierarchies of skills. *Psychological Review, 87,* 477–531.

Fivush, R., Gray, J., & Fromhoff, F. A. (1987). Two-year-olds talk about the past. *Cognitive Development, 2,* 393–409.

Fivush, R., & Hudson, J. (1987). *As time goes by: Sixth graders remember a kindergarten experience* (Emory Cognition Project, Rep. #13). Emory University, Atlanta, GA.

Flavell, J. H. (1985). *Cognitive development.* Englewood Cliffs, NJ: Prentice-Hall.

Geiselman, R. E., Saywitz, K. J., & Bornstein, G. K. (1990). *Cognitive questioning techniques for child victims and witnesses of crime* (Final Report to the State Justice Institute). Los Angeles: University of California at Los Angeles.

Goodman, G. S., & Aman, G. S. (1991). Children's use of anatomically detailed dolls to recount an event. *Child Development, 61,* 1859–1871.

Goodman, G. S., Batterman, J. M., Kenney, R., & Wilson, M. B. (1991, August). Media effects and children's testimony. In D. Singer (Chair), *The Impact of the media on the judicial system.* Invited symposium. American Psychological Association, Boston.

Goodman, G. S., Bottoms, B., Herscovici, B. B., & Shaver, P. (1989). Determinants of the child victim's perceived credibility. In S. Ceci, D. Ross, & M. Toglia (Eds.), *Perspectives on children's testimony* (1–22). New York: Springer-Verlag.

Goodman, G. S., Bottoms, B. L., Schwartz-Kenney, B., & Rudy, L. (1991). Children's memory for a stressful event: Improving children's reports. *Journal of Narrative and Life History, 1,* 69–99.

Goodman, G. S., Golding, J., Helgeson, V., Haith, M. M., & Michelli, J. (1987). When a child takes the stand: Jurors' perceptions of children's eyewitness testimony. *Law and Human Behavior, 11,* 27–40.

Goodman, G. S., Hirschman, J., Hepps, D., & Rudy, L. (1991). Children's memory for stressful events. *Merrill-Palmer Quarterly, 37,* 109–158.

Goodman, G. S., & Reed, R. S. (1986). Age differences in eyewitness testimony. *Law and Human Behavior, 10,* 317–332.

Goodman, G. S., Rudy, L., Port, L. K., England, P., Bottoms, B. L., & Renouf, A. (1989, August). Do past abuse experiences intrude into children's reports? In G. S. Goodman (Chair), *Child sexual abuse: Understanding and improving children's testimony.* American Psychological Association Meetings, New Orleans.

Goodman, G. S., Sachsenmaier, T., Batterman-Faunce, J., Tobey, A., Thomas, S., Orcutt, H., & Schwartz-Kenney, B. (1992, August). *Impact of innovative court procedures on children's testimony.* In B. L. Bottoms & M. Levine (Chairs), *Children's eyewitness testimony.* Symposium presented at the American Psychological Association Convention, Washington, DC.

Goodman, G., Taub, E., Jones, D., England, P., Port, L., Rudy, L., & Prado, L. (1992). Testifying in criminal court: Emotional effects on child sexual assault victims. *Monographs of the Society for Research in Child Development. 157,* (5, Serial No. 229).

Goodman, G. S., Wilson, M. E., Hazan, C., & Reed, R. S. (1989, April). *Children's testimony nearly four years after an event.* Paper presented to the Eastern Psychological Association, Boston, MA.

Goodwin, J., Sahd, C., & Rada, R. (1979). Incest hoax: False accusations, false denials. *Bulletin of the American Academy of Psychiatry and Law, 6,* 269–276.

Jones, D. P. H., & McGraw, J. M. (1987). Reliable and fictitious accounts of sexual abuse to children. *Journal of Interpersonal Violence, 2,* 27–45.

Jones, D. P. H., & McQuistin, M. (1985). *Interviewing the sexually abused child.* Denver, CO: Kempe Center.

Kassin, S. M., Ellsworth, P., & Smith, V. (1989). The "general acceptance" of psychological research on eyewitness testimony. *American Psychologist, 8,* 1089–1098.

Kempe, H., Silverman, F., Steele, B., Droegemueller, W., & Silver, H. K. (1962). The battered child syndrome. *Journal of the American Medical Association, 181,* 17–22.

King, M., & Yuille, J. C. (1987). Suggestibility and the child witness. In S. J. Ceci, D. F. Ross, & M. P. Toglia (Eds.), *Children's eyewitness memory* (pp. 24–35). New York: Springer-Verlag.

Leippe, M., & Romanczyk, A. (1987). Children on the witness stand: A communication/persuasion analysis of jurors' reactions to child witnesses. In S. J. Ceci, M. P. Toglia, & D. F. Ross (Eds.), *Children's eyewitness memory* (pp. 155–177). New York: Springer-Verlag.

Leippe, M., Romanczyk, A., & Manion, A. (1991). Eyewitness memory for a touching experience: Accuracy differences between child and adult witnesses. *Journal of Applied Psychology, 76,* 367–379.

Leippe, M., Manion, A., & Romanczyk, A. (1992). Eyewitness persuasion: How and how well do factfinders judge the accuracy of adults' and children's memory reports? *Journal of Personality and Social Psychology, 163,* 181–187.

Loftus, E. F. (1979). *Eyewitness testimony.* Cambridge, MA: Harvard University Press.

Maryland v. Craig (1990). 110 S. Ct. 3157.

Melton, G. B., & Thompson, R. A. (1987). Getting out of a rut: Detours to less traveled paths in child-witness research. In S. J. Ceci, M. P. Toglia, & D. F. Ross (Eds.), *Children's eyewitness memory* (pp. 209–229). New York: Springer-Verlag.

Moston, S. (1987, September). *The effects of the provisions of social support in child interviews.* Paper presented at the British Psychological Association Conference, York, England.

Nelson, K. (1986). *Event knowledge: Structure and function in development.* Hillsdale, NJ: Erlbaum.

Parker, J. F., & Carranza, L. E. (1989). Eyewitness testimony of children in target-present and target-absent lineups. *Law and Human Behavior, 13,* 133–150.

Peters, D. (1991). The influence of arousal and stress on the child witness. In J. Doris (Ed.), *The suggestibility of children's recollections* (pp. 60–76). Washington, DC: American Psychological Association.

Piaget, J. (1963). *The origins of intelligence in children* (M. C. Cook, Trans.) New York: Norton.

Price, D. W. W., & Goodman, G. S. (1990). Visiting the wizard: Children's memory of a recurring event. *Child Development, 61,* 664–680.

Pynoos, R., & Nader, K. (1988). Children's memory and proximity to violence. *Journal of the American Academy of Child and Adolescent Psychiatry, 28,* 236–241.

Pynoos, R., & Eth, S. (1986). Witness to violence: The child interview. *Journal of the American Academy of Child Psychiatry, 25,* 306–319.

Raskin, D., & Esplin, P. (1991). Assessment of children's statements of sexual abuse. In J. Doris (Ed.), *The suggestibility of children's recollections* (pp. 153–164). Washington, DC: American Psychological Association.

Rudy, L., & Goodman, G. S. (1991). Effects of participation on children's reports: Implications for children's testimony. *Developmental Psychology, 27,* 527–538.

Rush, F. (1980). *The best kept secret: Sexual abuse of children.* Englewood Cliffs, NJ: Prentice-Hall.

Russell, D. (1983). The incidence and prevalence of intrafamilial sexual abuse of female children. *Child Abuse and Neglect, 7,* 133–146.

Sas, L. (1991). *Reducing the system-induced trauma for child sexual abuse victims through court preparation, assessment and follow-up.* London, Ontario: London Family Court.

Saywitz, K. (1989). Children's conceptions of the legal system: "Court is a place to play basketball." In S. J. Ceci, D. F. Ross, & M. P. Toglia (Eds.), *Perspectives on the child witness* (pp. 131–157). New York: Springer-Verlag.

Saywitz, K., Goodman, G. S., Nicholas, E., & Moan, S. (1991). Children's memories of physical examinations involving genital touch: Implications for reports of child sexual abuse. *Journal of Consulting and Clinical Psychology, 59,* 682–691.

Saywitz, K., & Snyder, L. (1993). Improving children's testimony with preparation. In G. S. Goodman & B. L. Bottoms (Eds.), *Child victims, child witnesses: Understanding and improving children's testimony* (pp. 117–146). New York: Guilford Publications.

Sgroi, S. (1982). *Handbook of clinical intervention in child sexual abuse.* Lexington, MA: Lexington Books.

Spencer, J. R., & Flin, R. (1990). *The evidence of children: The law and the psychology.* London: Blackstone Press.

Steward, M., & Steward, D. (1990). *The development of a model interview for young child victims of sexual abuse: Comparing the effectiveness of anatomical dolls, drawings, and video graphics.* (Final report submitted to the National Center on Child Abuse and Neglect, Washington, DC). Davis, CA: University of California at Davis.

Swim, J., Borgida, E., & McCoy, K. (1991, August). Children's videotaped testimony and jury decision making. In A. Brown (Chair), *Child witnesses and children's testimony*. Annual meeting of the American Psychological Association, San Francisco, CA.

Terr, L. C. (1988). What happens to early memory of trauma? A study of twenty children under age five at the time of documented traumatic experiences. *Journal of the American Academy of Child and Adolescent Psychiatry, 27*, 96–104.

Tobey, A., & Goodman, G. S. (1992). Children's eyewitness memory: Effects of participation and forensic context. *Child Abuse and Neglect, 16*, 779–796.

Warren, A., & Tate, C. S. (1990, March). *Can young children lie convincingly if coached by adults?* Paper presented at the American Psychology and Law Society Convention, Williamsburg, VA.

Wells, G. L., Turtle, J. W., & Luus, C. A. E. (1989). The perceived credibility of child eyewitnesses: What happens when they use their own words? In S. J. Ceci, D. F. Ross, & M. P. Toglia (Eds.), *Perspectives on the child witness* (pp. 23–36). New York: Springer-Verlag.

Westcott, H., Davies, G. M., & Clifford, B. R. (in press). Adults' perceptions of children's videotaped truthful and deceptive statements. *Children and Society*.

Wigmore, J. H. (1909). Professor Munsterberg and the psychology of evidence. *Illinois Law Review, 3*, 399–445.

Wilkinson, J. (1987, August). *Context effects in children's event memory*. Paper presented at the P.A.M. Conference, Swansea University, Swansea, England.

Yuille, J. C., Hunter, R., Joffe, R., & Zaparniuk, J. (1993). Interviewing children in sexual abuse cases. In G. S. Goodman & B. L. Bottoms (Eds.), *Child victims, child witnesses: Understanding and improving children's testimony* (pp. 95–116). New York: Guilford Publications.

6

Children in Dangerous Environments: Child Maltreatment in the Context of Community Violence

James Garbarino
Kathleen Kostelny
Jane Grady

INTRODUCTION

In the short space of little more than a decade, public awareness of child maltreatment as a major social issue has increased dramatically—from an estimated 10% of the adult population defining it as a major problem in the mid-1970s to a documented 90% doing so now (NCPCA, 1988). Creating this public awareness, creating a professional infrastructure of protective services, and initiating efforts aimed at prevention have been major accomplishments, but now the hardest work begins.

This difficult task involves developing effective strategies for ameliorating child abuse and neglect among the populations at highest risk—what Wilson (1987) calls the *underclass*, where poverty and violence are pervasive and conventional human service models are often inappropriate and ineffective (Schorr & Schorr, 1988). In this chapter we examine some of the special issues faced by efforts to understand and deal with child maltreatment in the context of life in dangerous inner-city environments. We seek to address the unique demands and obstacles an extremely violent environment creates for those providing helping services.

CHILD MALTREATMENT IN SOCIAL CONTEXT

Child maltreatment takes place in a social as well as a psychological and cultural context. Prevention, treatment, and research should incorporate this contextual orientation (Garbarino, Stocking, & Associates, 1980). For many purposes, this means examining high-risk neighborhoods as well as high-risk families as the context for child maltreatment (Garbarino & Gilliam, 1980).

Our previous research has sought to explore and validate the concept of "social impoverishment" as a characteristic of high-risk family environments, and as a factor in evaluating support and prevention programs aimed at child maltreatment. The starting point was identifying the environmental correlates of child maltreatment (Garbarino, 1976; Garbarino & Crouter, 1978). This provided an empirical basis for "screening" neighborhoods to identify high- and low-risk areas. The foundation for this approach is the well-documented link between low income and child maltreatment (Garbarino, 1985; NCCAN, 1981; Pelton, 1981). Poverty is associated with a significantly elevated risk of child maltreatment.

TWO MEANINGS OF HIGH RISK

The statistical technique of multiple regression analysis was used to illuminate two meanings of high risk (Garbarino & Crouter, 1978). The first, of course, refers to areas with a high absolute rate of child maltreatment (based on cases per unit of population). In this sense, concentrations of socioeconomically distressed families are most likely to be at high risk for child maltreatment. In the first city we studied (Omaha, NE), socioeconomic status accounted for about 40% of the variation across neighborhoods in reported rates of child maltreatment.

We should note that the magnitude of this correlation may reflect a social policy effect. We have hypothesized that, in a society in which low income is *not* correlated with access to basic human services (e.g., maternal infant health care), this correlation would be smaller. In a society totally devoid of policies to ameliorate the impact of family-level differences in social class, it might be even larger.

This hypothesis merits empirical exploration, but is consistent with the observation that socioeconomic status is a more potent predictor of child development in the United States than in some European societies (Bronfenbrenner, 1979). This is evident in low infant mortality rates in some poor European countries— for example, Ireland and Spain (Miller, 1987).

It is a second meaning of *high risk* that is of greatest relevance here, however. *High risk* can also be taken to mean that an area has a higher rate of child maltreatment *than would be predicted knowing its socioeconomic character*. Thus, two areas with similar socioeconomic profiles may have very different rates of child maltreatment. In this sense, one is *high risk* while the other is *low risk*, although both may have higher rates of child maltreatment than other, more affluent areas. Figure 1 illustrates this.

In Figure 1, areas A and B have high actual observed rates of child maltreatment (36 per 1000 and 34 per 1,000, respectively). Areas C and D have lower actual rates (16 per 1,000 and 14 per 1,000). However, areas A and C have higher actual observed rates *than would be predicted* (10 per 1,000 predicted for

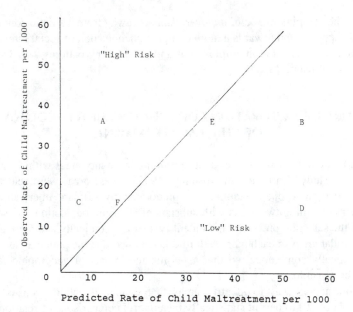

Figure 1. Two Meanings of "Risk" in Assessing Community Areas

A, 7 per 1,000 for C), while areas B and D have lower actual observed *than predicted rates* (55 per 1,000 for B, and 54 per 1,000 for D). In this sense, A and C are both high risk, while B and D are both low risk. Areas E and F evidence a close approximation between predicted and actual rates. As we shall see, this classification system can provide the basis for identifying contrasting social environments.

THE HUMAN SIGNIFICANCE OF "COMMUNITY RISK"

What do low- and high-risk social environments look like? Addressing this question involves examining a pair of real neighborhoods with the same predicted but different observed rates of child maltreatment (i.e., one high risk and the other low risk for child maltreatment). This permits a test of the hypothesis that two such neighborhoods present contrasting environments for child rearing.

An earlier study provided support for this hypothesis: relative to the low-risk area, and even though it was socioeconomically equivalent, the high-risk neighborhood was found to represent a socially impoverished human ecology (Garbarino & Sherman, 1980). It was less well socially integrated, had less positive neighboring, and represented more stressful day-to-day interactions for families. Subsequent studies have reaffirmed the general outlines of this analysis while refining the meaning of *social impoverishment*—away from a simple concept of "social support" and towards a more complex phenomenon of social integration (particularly as reflected in employment and neighboring patterns—cf. Deccio, Horner, & Wilson, 1991).

FURTHER EXPLORATIONS OF THE COMMUNITY ECOLOGY OF CHILD MALTREATMENT

To build on our prior work, we identified four community areas within Chicago for further study (Garbarino & Kostelny, 1991). These areas were selected to result in two pairs, one containing two predominantly African American areas, the other containing two areas with substantial Hispanic populations. A second goal of the selection process was to identify socioeconomically and demographically similar areas in each pair. A third criterion was that the paired areas not be geographically contiguous, so that assessing the impact of geographic factors would be feasible.

A fourth goal was to identify areas that contained enough census tracts (minimum of 20) to permit statistically meaningful comparisons of relationships between factors, within each community area. A fifth criterion was that some common prevention and family support programs operated across the areas selected. Finally, the selection process began with the fact that the Department of Children and Family Services (DCFS) was committed to funding a special project to enhance child abuse prevention activities in one of the areas. This necessitated selecting the "North" area as one of the targets for the study, so as to provide an "experimental condition."

With these selection criteria in mind, we reviewed the Chicago community areas seeking a match for the predominantly African-American "North" area (27 census tracts). The eventual choice was the predominantly African-American "South" community area (20 census tracts). Both have received extensive professional and public attention as "social hot spots."

The process of selecting a pair of heavily Hispanic community areas proved very difficult for reasons having to do with demographics and geography. Our eventual resolution was to selected the "West" area (57% Hispanic) as one member of the second pair (36 census tracts). Selecting a single second member proved impossible. No one area met all our selection criteria.

We resolved the problem by treating two adjoining areas as if they were one (and thus were able to meet the criterion of sufficient census tracts to permit statistical analysis of subunits within the community area). This combined "East" area served as our second Hispanic target area (75% Hispanic). Together these areas contain 35 census tracts.

In order to conduct the desired analyses, it was necessary to individually code more than 60,000 cases of child maltreatment and plot their location. DCFS data files were made available for this purpose. The result was a mapping of reported child maltreatment cases for three time periods between 1980 and 1986.

IDENTIFYING HIGH-RISK NEIGHBORHOODS

Our initial analysis sought to replicate the earlier research documenting the role of socioeconomic and demographic factors in differentiating among neighborhoods. The results approximate the earlier studies (e.g., Garbarino & Crouter, 1978). Much of the variation among community rates of child maltreatment is linked to variations in nine socioeconomic and demographic variables (percentage living in poverty, percentage African American, percentage Hispanic, percentage female headed households, unemployment rate, percentage affluent, median education, percentage overcrowded housing, and percentage resident less than 5 years). The multiple correlation was .89, thus accounting for 79% of the variation.

We also conducted this analysis for 113 census tracts contained *within* our four target community areas. There are 118 tracts among the four areas, but five are empty and thus not included in the analysis. In this analysis, multiple correlation was R = .52, and the proportion of variance accounted for was 27%.

The discrepancy between the magnitude of the correlation for community areas and census tracts derives from several factors related to the statistical procedures employed and to some systematic differences among the four community areas in the direction and magnitude of some correlations. The higher proportion of variance accounted for in the results from the analysis of community areas reflects the larger units of analysis used in community areas and the apparently idiosyncratic nature of the four target areas as social environments. Since community areas encompass a greater number of individuals than the census tract analysis, the estimates of the predictors (e.g., poverty, unemployment, female headed households, etc.) *and* measures of the rate of child maltreatment are more numerically stable (and thus reliable in a statistical sense) and, thus, more likely to produce a higher correlation.

In our previous research (Garbarino & Crouter, 1978) we observed a similar result. In that study of Omaha, Nebraska, the multiple correlation for 20 ''community subareas'' was $R = .90$ (accounting for 81% of the variance) while for the 94 census tracts it was $R = .69$ (accounting for 48% of the variance). In addition, the variation or range of socioeconomic, demographic, and child maltreatment measures is much greater when contrasting all 77 community areas than when comparing the 113 census tracts within the four target areas—all of which have major difficulties. For example, within the two predominantly African American areas, the census tract with the *lowest* poverty rate still has 27% living in poverty—in contrast to the full range of 77 community areas, in which 33 have poverty rates of less than 10% and seven have more than 40%.

We charted child maltreatment rates for the four community areas for the years 1980, 1983, and 1986 to observe trends over time. As Figure 2 indicates, there is wide variation in these four areas. In "East," child maltreatment rates have been consistently below the city average (6.9 in 1980, 7.8 in 1983, and 10.6 in 1986) during these three years, while "West" has been close to the city average. In contrast, in "North" and "South," rates of child maltreatment have been consistently above the city average.

Of particular interest to us were the different trends observed for "North" in contrast to "West." In 1980 these two areas had similar actual maltreatment rates. However, "North's" actual rate of 9.1 was below its predicted rate of 11.1 making it a low-risk area (in relation to its socioeconomic profile). "West's" actual rate of 8.4 was slightly above its predicted rate of 7.8, making it a somewhat high-risk area.

However, by 1986, the two areas had changed dramatically in relation to each other: "North's" actual maltreatment rate had soared to 21.8 (with a predicted rate of 14.7 for 1986), while "West's" actual rate had increased only slightly to 10.9, but fell below its predicted rate of 12.4 for 1986. In terms of the ratio of actual to predicted rates, "North" had become a very high-risk area, while "West" had become a low-risk area.

We also analyzed maltreatment rates by census tracts within each community area and found that wide variations exist at this level as well. In "North," for

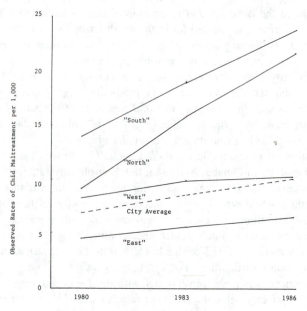

Figure 2.   Child Maltreatment Rates in Four Community Areas

example, while indicated rates of child maltreatment increased at the community level, analysis at the census-tract level revealed that rates had actually reached a plateau or decreased in 54% of the tracts. Thus, the escalation in rates was due to a large increase in the remaining 46% of the tracts (some of which had rates as high as 34.5, compared to a city average of 10.6).

Additionally, multiple regression analyses were conducted for each of the 3 years. While 13 out of "North's" 24 census tracts fell within the predicted range for maltreatment for at least 2 out of the 3 years, the remaining 11 tracts had rates which fell outside the predicted range—6 tracts had rates that were consistently lower, while 5 tracts had rates that were consistently higher than predicted based upon their socioeconomic and demographic profile.

THE VIEW FROM THE TRENCHES

We also undertook a small set of interviews to illuminate the important but elusive variable of "community climate." To shed some light on this factor, we interviewed community leaders in "North" as a "higher than predicted abuse rate" community and "West" as a "lower than predicted abuse rate" community. We used a 16-item questionnaire based on prior research (Garbarino & Sherman, 1980).

Our hypothesis was that, in the high-abuse community, we expected social service agencies would mirror the high social deterioration characteristic of the families and the community, while conversely, that the low-abuse community would have a strong, informal support network among the social service agencies. The results of the interviews supported this hypothesis, suggesting that there is a clear difference in the climate of these two communities.

The strength of this difference is perhaps best illustrated as follows: Jobs were mentioned as being of primary importance in both communities. However, they were talked about very differently. In "North," respondents reported that it was important to remember that their community had only an 18% employment rate; in contrast, the majority of the "West" respondents described their area as a community of the working poor.

The consequences of these differences in employment are profound. Indeed, Deccio et al. (1991) reported that it was precisely such a measure of employment that differentiated the low- from the high-risk neighborhoods in their study. Employment, even at low wages, is a social indicator of prosocial orientation and of functionality—apart from the income implications of being employed.

The general tone of the "North" respondents was somewhat depressed; people had a hard time thinking of anything good to say about the situation. The physical spaces of the programs themselves seemed dark and depressed, and to a casual visitor the criminal activity was easily spotted. In "West," people were eager to talk about their community. While they listed serious problems, most of them felt that their communities were poor but decent places to live. ''Poor but not hopeless'' was the way one respondent described it. While ''West'' respondents also reported drug and crime problems, they were not apparent to the casual visitor.

In ''North,'' the subjects knew less about what other community services and agencies were available, and demonstrated little evidence of a network or support system, either formal or informal. In ''West,'' there were more services available, agencies knew more about what was available, and there were very strong formal and informal social support networks. The respondents in ''West'' also reported strong political leadership from the local state senator. The ''North'' subjects did not report positive feelings about their political leaders.

At least in terms of this study, it seems fair to say that the social service agencies in a community mirror the problems facing the community. In ''North,'' the leaders interviewed described a situation in which their agencies mirrored the isolation and depression of their community. In ''West,'' the agencies mirrored the strong informal support networks that existed between families in their community. They seemed hopeful because many of their families were hopeful.

The interviews with professionals complement our statistical analyses, and provide further indication of the serious difficulties facing ''North'' as a social system. The extremity of the negative features of the environment—poverty, violence, poor housing—seem to be matched by negative community climate—lack of community identity, fragmented formal support system networks.

The final piece of evidence available to us in our analysis concerns child deaths due to maltreatment. Such child deaths are a particularly telling indicator of the bottom line in a community. There were 19 child maltreatment deaths reported for the four community areas we studied during the period 1984–1987. Eight of these deaths occurred in ''North,'' a rate twice that of ''West.'' The fact that deaths due to child maltreatment were twice as likely in ''North'' seems consistent with the overall findings of our statistical analyses and interviews. This is an environment in which there is truly an ecological conspiracy against children (Garbarino, 1989).

COMMUNITY VIOLENCE AND DOMESTIC VIOLENCE

Our studies highlight both the general impact of poverty on the conditions of life for children and the fact that there exist community climate variables at work that are not isomorphic with low income. The existence of these forces is a fact of life for those who would pursue child abuse prevention and deliver child protective services. But while the role of poverty is often considered in protective service decision making and in child abuse and neglect program design, and the impact of community violence and social deterioration are often noted as social problems, rarely are these factors considered in relation to the stresses it places on those providing services, especially in the context of pervasive violence.

Human service workers increasingly find themselves serving children and families who live in community environments that are chronically violent. These include some large public housing developments and socially deteriorated, low-income neighborhoods in cities across the nation (Marciniak, 1986; Merry, 1981).

In Chicago, over 100,000 children live in public housing. An analysis of Chicago's police data (Reardon, 1988) revealed that the officially reported rate of violent crime victimization for residents in the housing projects was 50% higher than for the city as a whole (34 per 1,000 vs. 23 per 1,000). This means that children in public housing projects are twice as likely to be exposed than are other children (since the overall 23 per 1,000 victimization rate includes the housing projects, which inflates the overall figure substantially).

In addition to exposure to crime, children living in these areas are more likely to be a victim of child abuse and neglect. We have found that for census tracts having high crime rates, child maltreatment rates were up to four times higher than the city average (Garbarino & Kostelny, 1992). These incidents of domestic violence interact dynamically with the incidents of "community" violence: Some of the incidents outside the homes are in fact related to domestic conflicts; children and parents are exposed to violence in other families indirectly (as part of their life experience as neighbors and friends).

IMPLICATIONS FOR SOCIAL SERVICES TO FAMILIES

The fact that high-risk families live in high-risk neighborhoods is not the whole or only story with which we must be concerned in considering the social policy issues faced by efforts to deal with child maltreatment where it happens most. We have more than a conspiracy on the "demand" side of the equation. We must also confront the fact that the people who provide services to families in high-risk communities are also at risk for crime victimization in the course of their day-to-day work. Thus there is an effect on the "supply" side of the human service equation as well. For example, one of the regional directors of the Department of Children and Family Services reported that, at any given time, at least 2 of his 40 caseworkers are unable to work because of injuries sustained while going to and coming from the homes of the families they serve. Many more are fearful when asked to investigate cases in high-risk communities.

Clarifying the stresses these workers face, and illuminating the support they need, will be an important addition of efforts to improve and inform services.

To date the interventions proposed by research have been confined to intra-personal, interpersonal, and managerial efforts to alleviate stress felt by human service providers while performing their job. However, there has been little research conducted on the effects of immediate and long-term consequences of exposure to environmental violence on service providers. Our work points to some additional challenges. For example:

- Although gun play is an activity that most children engage in, teachers report that they can distinguish between fantasy play and reenactment of violent events in the community. If an actual shooting occurs in the community, they observe that children's play takes on a more realistic quality, reenacting the events they witnessed. But teachers don't know how to respond.

- One of the social service staff who conducts home visits with parents of Head Start children described how she, while walking across a playground, had to take cover to avoid being hit by random bullets from two rival gang factions. She stated, "I was caught in the cross fire." She witnessed the shooting of one young man before the gunfire stopped. When it stopped, she ran back to the children's center and reported the event to a co-worker, who listened sympathetically. The coworker responded that "then it was over." The next day, the same social worker had to resume her responsibilities. There was no intervention.

- When a teacher at one center heard gunshots outside the classroom window recently, she and all 20 of the children got down on the floor. But, although this teacher knew how to protect children in a crisis situation, she was unable to deal with the long-term consequences of the event, for example, both her and the children's fear that this event could reoccur at any moment.

- At an after-school program, as some of the children were entering the building, shooting by gang members started nearby. One girl described crawling on her hands and knees to get to the center. However, once the children were in the building, the staff were confused about whether to talk about the event or ignore it and go about planned activities. Such discussion often leads eventually to reports of domestic violence. Staff must often come to terms with domestic violence before they can respond to community violence.

- Professionals who deal with these children of violence are often at a loss in how to respond to the child. For example, in six training sessions involving Head Start staff from four major Chicago public housing complexes, the majority of the 60 staff participating expressed their feelings of inadequacy at being unable to help their students deal with the violence they encounter in their daily lives. How does this relate to prevention and protective services?

Successful child abuse prevention and child protective services must address the issues of powerlessness, traumatization, and immobilizing fear that impede effective family life and social development for a significant and growing proportion of children in Chicago and other areas with underclass populations. Part and parcel of this is understanding the needs of professionals who work in these environments.

These professionals themselves often feel powerless, traumatized, and afraid. How do they make sense of prevention and protection missions in neighborhoods so violent they fear for their personal safety? How are they to bring messages of family safety? Does everyone concerned accept lower standards for child protection in such environments? Do they fall silent when confronted with harsh, even violent childrearing?

Halpern (1990) has identified such "domains of silence" as a significant impediment to the delivery of effective family services, most especially among paraprofessionals recruited from high-risk populations. The significance and seriousness of this impediment will become clear as we examine the social policy considerations that arise from understanding the impact on children of living in dangerous environments and this experience as a context for understanding child maltreatment. To accomplish this we must start with a developmental perspective on danger and trauma.

A DEVELOPMENTAL PERSPECTIVE ON THE MEANING OF DANGER AND TRAUMA

The combination of living in high-risk families set within high-risk communities creates a situation of special danger for children. How do we understand danger in the lives of children and youth? How do we understand the origins, mechanisms, and coping processes employed by children and youth in dealing with danger? In short, how can we understand danger developmentally?

What happens when a child or youth is hurt? The consequences can range from minor injury to death, with the outcome reflecting a host of organismic and situational factors. Physical disability has certain objective realities, of course, but the consequences of greatest concern are psychological and moral.

We know that intense danger can be traumatic in the clinical sense. The emergent field of traumatic stress studies is increasingly recognizing the importance of understanding the phenomenon of Post-Traumatic Stress Disorder as a response to childhood trauma (Eth & Pynoos, 1985). We know that exposure to danger and psychic trauma may engender self-destructive behavior, as is evident in childhood suicide (cf. Orbach, 1988).

The same physical consequences can have very different life-course effects, as a function of cultural, social, and psychological influences. Thus, for example, it matters developmentally whether a child's leg is broken by a parental assault or through play, whether in the course of running away from a fight or in the course of standing up for a friend, whether there are compensatory psychological forces at work in the child's life—to remediate the effects of negative family relations in the outside community or to remediate the effects of a hostile neighborhood environment through a warm and supportive family. Our central concern, of course, is when the child faces serious threat both within and outside the family, in the intersection of domestic and community violence.

The preliminary clues for the needed framework are there to be found in existing studies. For example, clinical researchers studying the impact of extra-familial trauma report that one of the mediators of PTSD in children so exposed is the preexposure quality of the child's family relationships (cf. Pynoos & Nader, 1988; Terr, 1990). This leads naturally to the hypothesis that children who have been maltreated at home are particularly vulnerable to the traumatic effects of community violence (Cicchetti & Lynch, in press).

One element of this foundation is the distinction between acute danger (e.g., when a deranged individual enters a normally safe school and opens fire with a rifle, or in which a child is subjected to a single incident of assault) and chronic danger (e.g., when gangs regularly attack students and teachers in or around the school as a means of asserting their control over disputed neighborhood turf, or when a child is subjected to ongoing child abuse).

ACUTE AND CHRONIC DANGER IN THE LIVES OF CHILDREN AND PARENTS

Acute danger requires a process of adjustment, through some measure of objective change in the conditions of life and/or subjective alteration of one's stance toward life events. Acute incidents of danger often simply require *situational* adjustment by normal children leading normal lives—assimilation of the traumatic event into the child's understanding of his or her situation. The therapy of choice is reassurance: "You are safe again; things are back to normal."

This is not to deny that children and youth exposed to acute danger may require processing over time (Pynoos & Nader, 1988). And, if the traumatic stress is intense enough, it may leave permanent "psychic scars," particularly for children made vulnerable because of disruptions in their primary relationships (most notably with parents). These effects include excessive sensitivity to stimuli associated with the trauma and diminished expectations for the future (Terr, 1988).

But chronic danger imposes a requirement for *developmental* adjustment—accommodations which are likely to include persistent Post Traumatic Stress Disorder, alterations of personality, and major changes in patterns of behavior or articulation of ideological interpretations of the world that provide a framework for making sense of ongoing danger—particularly when that danger comes from the violent overthrow of day-to-day social reality as is the case in war, communal violence, or chronic violent crime (Garbarino, Kostelny, & Dubrow, 1991a).

The therapy of choice in situations of chronic danger is one that builds upon the child's primary relationships to create a new positive reality for the child that can stand up to the "natural" conclusions a severely traumatized child is likely to draw otherwise about self-worth, about the reliability of adults and their institutions, and about the safe approaches to adopt toward the world (see Toth & Cicchetti, this volume).

HOME AND NEIGHBORHOOD AS WAR ZONES

There is a growing body of research and clinical observation based upon a concern that children and youth caught up in war and other forms of social crisis will adapt in ways that produce developmental impairment, physical damage, and emotional trauma, and will be mis-socialized into a model of fear, violence, and hatred as a result (Garbarino, Kostelny, & Dubrow, 1991b; Goleman, 1986; Rosenblatt, 1983).

Children who experience warm, strong, and supportive relationships with parents are most likely to avoid this pattern; positive family relationships buffer the effects of community violence as they do all forms of environmental threat (cf. Sameroff & Fiese, 1990; Werner, 1990). Conversely, children who have been victims of child maltreatment are particularly at risk (Cicchetti & Lynch, in press).

Just as wars have increasingly resulted in civilian (as opposed to military) casualties (cf. UNICEF, 1986) so some observers have noted a similar trend in the case of the high crime neighborhoods of American cities—that is, increasing victimization of women and children. However, epidemiological data continue to portray young males (i.e., the "soldiers") as the predominant casualties of neighborhoods saturated by crime, particularly gang- and drug-related crime. Nonetheless, children are still victimized by this exposure to violence— particularly if it resonates with violence and neglect in the home. Children are still "innocent bystanders" or "in training" for the front lines of violent conflict. Even these roles can be traumatic.

ALTERNATIVE DEVELOPMENTAL PATHS FOR CHILDREN IN DANGER

But the recognition that danger leads to developmental impairment is clearly not the whole story. A second theme in studies of children in danger emphasizes the role of social crisis in stimulating moral development. Coles (1986) noted this in his study of the political life of children: Under conditions of violent political crisis, *some* children develop a precocious and precious moral sensibility.

What are the mediators between danger and trauma, on the one hand, and between danger and moral development on the other? Why do some children survive such danger and even overcome its challenges in ways that enhance development? Anna Freud's reports on children exposed to trauma during World War II presents this latter view (at least in the short run): children in the care of their own mothers or a familiar mother substitute were not psychologically devastated by wartime experiences, principally because parents could maintain day-to-day care routines *and* project high morale (Freud & Burlingham, 1943).

A similar theme emerged from a recent study of safety issues for children in a public housing project in Chicago that is saturated with violence (Dubrow & Garbarino, 1989). Mothers in the project identified "shooting" as the major safety concern for their children, but identified a variety of coping mechanisms to protect their children from immediate harm.

The more effective the parent in devising and communicating positive strategies for coping, the more likely the children are to appear resilient and robust. This parallels Scheinfeld's (1983) finding that parents who develop a sense of positive competence in their children produce children much better equipped to triumph over the threats of inner city life and take advantage of whatever educational and vocational opportunities are present in the environment.

This is not to say that children with positive family relationships escape unscathed, however. A recent in-depth study of children growing up in Chicago's war zone points to the insidious effects of the urban war zone as much as it does to the buffering effects of positive family relationships (Kotlowitz, 1991). If the environment is terrible enough, it can overwhelm even children who come from intact and functioning families, particularly if we take a long-term view.

Follow-up studies of severely war-traumatized children cared for by Anna Freud and her colleagues revealed a significant proportion who evidenced chronic and profound problems despite receiving compensatory care. Recent longitudinal analyses of the impact of divorce on children suggest a similar "sleeper effect," with life-adjustment problems emerging 10 or more years after family dissolution (Wallerstein & Blakeslee, 1989).

Being a child in a highly stressful environment can lead to long-term mental health concerns, even when the child has access to parental protection in the short term. This is evident in economically stressful situations, even if they do not include acute danger. For example, Elder and Rockwell (1978) found that the effects of having been a child during the Great Depression of the 1930s in the United States were often seen decades later in the life course of adults, particularly for males (Masten, Best, & Garmezy, 1990).

Convergent findings from several studies of life course responses to stressful early experience suggest a series of ameliorating factors, factors that lead to prosocial and healthy adaptability (Lösel, & Bliesener, 1990):

- actively trying to cope with stress (rather than just reacting)
- cognitive competence (at least an average level of intelligence)

- experiences of self-efficacy and a corresponding self-confidence and positive self-esteem
- temperamental characteristics that favor active coping attempts and positive relationships with others (e.g., activity, goal orientation, sociability) rather than passive withdrawal
- a stable emotional relationship with at least one parent or other reference person
- an open, supportive educational climate and parental model of behavior that encourages constructive coping with problems
- social support from persons outside the family

These factors have been identified as important when the stresses involved are in the "normal" range found in the mainstream of modern industrial societies— for example, poverty, family conflict, childhood physical disability, and parental involvement in substance abuse. Nonetheless, they may provide a starting point for efforts to understand the special character of coping in the stressful circumstances of prolonged violence (war, communal conflict, and pervasive violent crime), where the risk of socially maladaptive coping is high.

SOCIALLY MALADAPTIVE METHODS OF COPING WITH DANGER

Children forced to cope with chronic danger may adapt in ways that are dysfunctional. The psychopathological dimensions of such adaptation are now widely recognized—most notably PTSD. The social dimensions are equally worthy of attention, however.

Children (and parents) may cope with danger by adopting a world view or persona that may be dysfunctional in any "normal" situations in which they are expected to participate—for example, in school. For example, their adaptive behavior in the abnormal situation of chronic crisis may be maladaptive to school success if they defend themselves by becoming hyperaggressive (which stimulates rejection at school).

What is more, some adaptations to chronic danger, such as emotional withdrawal, may be socially adaptive in the short run, but become a danger to the next generation, when the individual becomes a parent. This phenomenon has been observed in studies of families of Holocaust survivors (Danieli, 1985).

Even in the absence of this intergenerational process, however, the same links between danger and trauma observed in children may operate directly among parents. Their adaptations to dangerous environments may produce child rearing strategies that impede normal development, as in the case of a mother who doesn't allow her child to play on the floor because there is poison on the floor to kill the rats that infest the apartment, but who, in doing so, may deprive the child of important opportunities for exploratory play. Likewise, the parent who prohibits the child from playing outside for fear of shooting incidents may be denying the child a chance to engage in social and athletic play, as an undesirable side effect of protecting the child from assault (Garbarino & Kostelny, 1993).

Similarly, the fear felt by parents of children in high-crime environments may be manifest as a very restrictive and punitive style of discipline (including physical assault) in an effort to protect the child from falling under the influence of negative forces in the neighborhood (e.g., gangs). Unfortunately, this approach is likely to have the result of heightening aggression on the child's part, with one consequence being a difficulty in succeeding in contexts that provide alternatives to the gang culture, and endorsing an acceptance of violence as the modus operandi for social control. Holding the child back from negative forces through punitive restrictiveness is generally much less successful as a strategy than promoting positive alternatives to the negative subculture feared by the parent (Scheinfeld, 1983).

In all three of these examples, the adaptation is well intentioned and may appear to be practically sensible, but its side effects may be detrimental in the long run. The onus here, of course, is on the social forces that create and sustain danger in the family's environment, thus forcing the parent to choose between the lesser of two evils.

In addition, early adaptation may lead to a process of "identification with the aggressor" in which children model themselves and their behavior on those powerful aggressive individuals and groups in their environment that cause the danger in the first place (e.g., gangs in the public housing project or enemy soldiers under conditions of occupation).

Children exposed to the stress of extreme violence (as was the case in Cambodia) may reveal mental health disturbances years after the immediate experience is over (Goleman, 1986). For example, a follow-up study of Cambodian children who experienced the moral and psychological devastation of the Pol Pot regime in the period 1974–1979 revealed that, 4 years after leaving Cambodia, 50% developed Post Traumatic Stress Disorder. Of particular interest for our concerns is the fact that those children who did not reside with a family member were most likely to show this and other psychiatric symptoms (Kinzie, Sack, Angell, Manson, & Rath, 1986).

THE ROOTS OF EFFECTIVE MEDIATION OF DANGER

Children in danger need relationships with adults, "teaching" relationships, to help them process their experiences in a way that prevents developmental harm. Vygotsky (1986) referred to this process of operating in the developmental space between what the child can do alone and what the child can do with the help of a teacher as the *zone of proximal development*.

Developmentalists have come to recognize that it is the dynamic relationship between the child's competence alone and the child's competence in the company of a guiding teacher that leads to forward movement. Children who experience child maltreatment are generally denied that processing within the family. These children also receive just the opposite of what they need as residents of dangerous environments outside the home, and are thus double victims. This is one reason why the problem of child maltreatment in the urban war zone must have the highest priority as a matter of social policy; these are the children who can least tolerate maltreatment (as conversely, victims of maltreatment are least able to tolerate community violence).

The critical function of mediation and processing seems particularly important in the case of moral development. The key here is a process of "optimal discrepancy," in which the child's moral teachers (be they adults or peers) lead the child towards higher order thinking by presenting positions that are one stage above the child's characteristic mode of responding to social events as moral issues.

When all this happens in the context of a nurturant affective system—a warm family, for example—the result is ever-advancing moral development, the development of a principled ethic of caring (Gilligan, 1982). What is more, even if the parents create a rigid, noninteractive "authoritarian" family context (and thus block moral development) the larger community may compensate: "the child of authoritarian parents may function in a larger more democratic society whose varied patterns provide the requisite experiences for conceptualizing an egalitarian model of distributive justice" (Fields, 1987, p. 5).

VIOLENCE AND TERROR

If school teachers and other adult representatives of the community are disinclined to model higher order moral reasoning or are intimidated if they try to do so, then the process of moral truncation that is "natural" to situations of violent conflict will proceed unimpeded. This appears to have happened in Northern Ireland, for example, as both Protestant and Catholic teachers learned that if they tried to engage their students in dialogue that could promote higher order moral reasoning, they would be silenced by extremist elements (Conroy, 1987). This may well be happening in many urban school systems in which teachers are demoralized and students apathetic. The result is to permit the "natural" socialization of the urban war zone to proceed, with its ethic of revenge, aggression, and exploitation.

Situations of chronic danger *can* stimulate the process of moral development *if* they are matched by an interactive climate created by adults (and endorsed—or at least not stifled—by the larger culture through its political, educational, and religious institutions) and if the child is free of debilitating psychopathology (e.g., PTSD). Victims of child abuse who live in chronically dangerous environments represent a kind of "worst case scenario" in this respect.

Families can provide the emotional context for the necessary "processing" to make positive moral sense of danger (and even trauma itself). But to do so they must be functioning well to start with. This is hardly the case where there is child abuse present. Thus, in cases of child maltreatment occurring in the context of dangerous environments, communities usually must carry things the next step—that is, stimulating higher order moral development.

They do this by presenting a democratic milieu—for example, in schools. However, when danger derives from political conflict in an anti-democratic social context *and* occurs in an authoritarian social climate as manifest within the family, the result is likely to be the "truncated" moral reasoning observed by Fields, particularly among boys, who are more vulnerable to this consequence of living "at risk" as they are to most other risks (Werner, 1989).

PROSPECTS FOR CHILDREN IN THE LONG RUN

Children will continue to cope with difficult environments and maintain reservoirs of resilience so long as parents are not pushed beyond their "stress absorption capacity." Once that point is exceeded, however, the development of young children deteriorates rapidly and markedly. Reservoirs of resilience become depleted. Infant mortality rates soar. Day-to-day care breaks down, and rates of exploitation and victimization increase. And moral development itself may be compromised.

What should we look for in defining the minimum standard of care for young children? Our first hypothesis is that the well-being of *young* children in a society depends upon how well that society is doing in sustaining the basic infrastructure of family life. And what are the critical elements of this infrastructure? We can identify three: parent–child attachment, parental self-esteem and identity, and stability of routine caregiving arrangements (cf. Bronfenbrenner, 1986). All three are threatened by the processes and factors that give rise to child maltreatment and urban violence.

When we look at infant mortality rates, at rates of abandonment and exploitation of young children, and at the overall level of stress-related behavioral and developmental problems in children, we begin to see a common picture around the world. If parents (particularly mothers in most cases) can sustain a strong attachment to their children, can maintain a positive sense of self, and can have access to rudimentary shelter, food, and medical care, then children will manage (although it may be at great cost to the psychic and physical welfare of those parents).

We have seen this in our visits to war zones around the world (Garbarino, Kostelny, & Dubrow, 1991). We knew communities were working when children were cared for by their mothers who themselves had access to food and fuel, water and basic medicines. In a functional community the children appeared normal. This was true even in the midst of what was from a societal point of view a period of crisis, disorganization, and trauma. From a child's point of view, there was a semblance of normality in day-to-day life, even in the midst of national crisis.

This is different from situations of "acute disaster," in which there is a dramatic and overwhelming destruction of the infrastructure of daily life. Erikson's (1976) study of an Appalachian community devastated by flood speaks to the latter point. In this case young children were confronted with vivid and concrete evidence of their vulnerability. Their homes were destroyed and their parents were demoralized and (apparently) socially powerless: "The major problem, for adults and children alike, is that the fears haunting them are prompted not only by the memory of past terrors but by a wholly realistic assessment of present dangers" (p. 238).

Once again, child maltreatment serves as a special risk factor for children in situations of community catastrophe. Such children have access to neither the buffering of parents through the context of their positive attachments nor to the ameliorating and compensating influences of the community beyond the family. The quality of life for young children—and their reservoirs of resilience—thus become a "social indicator" of the balance of social supports for parents and parental capacity to buffer social stress in the lives of children (Garbarino & Associates, 1992).

After reviewing a large body of research dealing with violence and aggression, Goldstein concluded that "aggressive behavior used to achieve a personal goal, such as wealth and power, and that may be perceived by the actor as justified (or even as non-aggressive) is a primary cause of the aggressive and criminal behavior of others" (Goldstein, 1986, p. ix).

This places child abuse squarely in the center as a threat to socialization. As a "personal" use of violence it is a prime stimulator of aggression, aggression that resonates and conspires with the extrafamilial experiences of the child living in a dangerous environment. At present we know little about how this conspiracy works against the child's development, and against child protection and child abuse prevention efforts. That it should become the focus of research and policy initiatives is clear.

CONCLUSION

The U.S. Advisory Board on Child Abuse and Neglect has concluded that our nation faces a child maltreatment "emergency." Rates of child maltreatment continue to increase in many areas, and public agencies are pushed beyond their capacity to respond. The link between poverty and child maltreatment continues as a powerful feature of the problem (Garbarino, 1992). Poverty for families has been increasing. And in urban areas, poverty is becoming ever more concentrated in geographically segregated neighborhoods (Garbarino & Kostelny, 1992). That being the case, it is little wonder that the problem of child maltreatment is worsening in urban areas of concentrated poverty.

We call attention to an important reality about neighborhood life: Social momentum is a powerful force. When things are going badly, the tendency is for all the social systems to be pulled down together. It takes extraordinary energy and effort to resist such negative social momentum (e.g., a political leader of special talent, commitment, and resources; a powerful social program that creates its own positive momentum in the neighborhood).

Child maltreatment is a symptom of not just individual or family trouble, but neighborhood and community trouble as well. It also may well conspire with those negative community forces to jeopardize still further the development of children. We know that many children can absorb and overcome an experience with one or two risk factors. But when the risk factors add up, they may well precipitate developmental crisis and impairment (Sameroff & Fiese, 1990). This, we believe, is the situation faced by abused and neglected children living in the urban war zone.

The challenge is to deal with the conspiracy of negative social indicators. But as social indicators, they can be responsive to social change (e.g., the energizing effect of community mobilization). As we plan and implement "child abuse prevention" initiatives, we must recognize that the task is not easy.

Indeed, if we hope to have a significant effect when addressing neighborhoods of concentrated poverty and social disorganization, we must introduce powerful efforts to reverse negative social momentum. And we must do so with an appreciation for the compounding of problems engendered by the problem of community violence in the lives of victimized children.

This is the difficult course we must follow. Translating this broad conclusion into specific policy and programming is a challenge. One appealing approach is to identify "prevention zones" that can become the target for comprehensive, sustained intervention by a wide range of public and private agencies. For example, one Chicago community received intensive child abuse prevention programs through the schools, health care services, and various community organizations in an effort to reduce child maltreatment. Only in this way, it would seem, can we hope to reverse the destructive pressure of negative social momentum observed in this study in some poor neighborhoods, and replace it with the positive momentum observed in others.

Leadership here means a willingness to go beyond cosmetic public relations to the inspired investment of major resources to make a better community for children. We have reason to hope that less child maltreatment will be one result.

REFERENCES

Bronfenbrenner, U. (1979). *The ecology of human development: Experiments by nature and design.* Cambridge, MA: Harvard University Press.

Bronfenbrenner, U. (1986). Ecology of family as a context for human development. *Developmental Psychology, 22,* 723–742.

Cicchetti, D., & Lynch, M. (in press). Toward an ecological/transactional model of community violence and child maltreatment: Consequences for children's development. *Psychiatry.*

Coles, R. (1986). *The political life of children.* Boston: Houghton Mifflin.

Conroy, J. (1987). *Belfast diary.* Boston: Beacon Press.

Danieli, Y. (1985). The treatment and prevention of long-term effects and intergenerational transmission of victimization: A lesson from Holocaust survivors and their children. In C. R. Figley (Ed.), *Trauma and its wake.* New York: Brunner/Mazel.

Deccio, G., Horner, B., & Wilson, D. (1991). *High-risk neighborhoods and high-risk families: Replication of research related to the human ecology of child maltreatment.* Cheney, WA: Eastern Washington University.

Dubrow, N., & Garbarino, J. (1989). Living in the war zone: Mothers and children in a public housing project. *Child Welfare, 63,* 3–20.

Elder, G., & Rockwell, R. (1978). Economic depression and postwar opportunity in men's lives: A study of life patterns and health. In R. Simmons (Ed.), *Research in community and mental health* (pp. 240–303). Greenwich, CT: JAI Press.

Erikson, K. (1976). *Everything in its path: The destruction of community in the Buffalo Creek flood.* New York: Simon and Schuster.

Eth, S., & Pynoos, R. (1985). Developmental perspective on psychic trauma in childhood. In C. Figley (Ed.), *Trauma and its wake* (Vol. 1, 36–52). New York: Brunner Mazel.

Fields, R. (1987, October 25). *Terrorized into terrorist: Sequelae of PTSD in young victims.* Paper presented at the meeting of the Society for Traumatic Stress Studies, New York.

Freud, A., & Burlingham, D. (1943). *War and children.* New York: Ernest Willard.

Garbarino, J. (1976). A preliminary study of some ecological correlates of child abuse: The impact of socioeconomic stress on mothers. *Child Development, 47,* 178–185.

Garbarino, J. (1988). *The future as if it really mattered.* Longmont, CO: Bookmakers' Guild.

Garbarino, J. (1989). Preventing childhood injury: Developmental and mental health issues. *American Journal of Orthopsychiatry, 58,* 25–45.

Garbarino, J. (1985). *Adolescent Development: An Ecological Perspective.* Columbus, OH: Merrill.

Garbarino, J. (1992). The meaning of poverty in the world of children. *American Behavioral Scientist, 35* (3).

Garbarino, J., and Associates. (1992). *Children and families in the social environment* (2nd ed.). New York: Aldine.

Garbarino, J., & Crouter, A. (1978). Defining the community context of parent-child relations. *Child Development, 49,* 604–616.

Garbarino, J., & Gilliam, G. (1980). *Understanding abusive families.* Lexington, MA: Lexington Books.

Garbarino, J., Guttman, E., & Seeley, J. (1986). *The psychologically battered child.* San Francisco: Jossey-Bass.

Garbarino, J., Dubrow, N., Kostelny, K. & Pardo, C. (1992). *Children in danger; Coping With the Consequences of Community Violence.* San Francisco, CA: Jossey-Bass.

Garbarino, J., & Kostelny, K. (1992). Child maltreatment as a community problem. *Child Abuse and Neglect, 16,* 455–464.

Garbarino, J., & Kostelny, K. (1993). Neighborhood and community influences on parenting. In

T. Luster & L. Okagaki (Eds.), *Parenting: An ecological perspective*. Hillsdale, NJ: Erlbaum.

Garbarino, J., Kostelny, K., & Dubrow, N. (1991a). What children can tell us about living in danger. *American Psychologist*, 46(4), 376–383.

Garbarino, J., Kostelny, K., & Dubrow, N. (1991b). *No place to be a child: Growing up in a war zone*. New York: Lexington Books.

Garbarino, J., & Sherman, D. (1980). High risk neighborhoods and high risk families: The human ecology of child maltreatment. *Child Development, 51*, 188–198.

Garbarino, J., Stocking, S., & Associates. (1980). *Protecting children from abuse and neglect: Developing and maintaining effective support systems for families*. San Francisco: Jossey-Bass.

Gilligan, C. (1982). *In a different voice*. Cambridge, MA: Harvard University Press.

Goldstein, J. (1986). *Aggression and crimes of violence*. New York: Oxford University Press.

Goleman, D. (1986, September 2). Terror's children: Mending mental wounds. *The New York Times*, p. B15.

Goodwin, J. (1988). Post-traumatic symptoms in abused children. *Journal of Traumatic Stress, 1*, 475–488.

Halpern, R. (1990). Community-based early intervention. In S. J. Meisels & J. P. Shonkoff (Eds.), *Handbook of early childhood intervention* (pp. 469–498). Cambridge, England: Cambridge University Press.

Janis, I. (1951). *Air war and emotional stress*. New York: McGraw-Hill.

Kinzie, J., Sack, W., Angell, R., Manson, S., & Rath, B. (1986). The psychiatric effects of massive trauma on Cambodian children. *Journal of the American Academy of Child Psychiatry, 25*, 370–376.

Kotlowitz, A. (1991). *There are no children here*. New York: Doubleday.

Lösel, F., & Bliesener, T. (1990). Resilience in adolescence: A study on the generalizability of protective factors. In K. Hurrelmann & F. Lösel (Eds.), *Health hazards in adolescence* (pp. 299–320). New York: Walter de Gruyter.

Marciniak, E. (1986). *Reclaiming the inner city*. Washington, DC: National Center for Urban Public Affairs.

Masten, A., Best, K., & Garmezy, N. (1990). Resilience and development: Contributions from the study of children who overcome adversity. *Development and Psychopathology, 2*, 425–444.

Merry, S. (1981). *Urban danger, life in a neighborhood of strangers*. Philadelphia, PA: Temple University Press.

Miller, A. (1987). *Maternal health and infant survival*. Washington, DC: National Center for Clinical Infant Programs.

National Committee for Prevention of Child Abuse (NCPCA). (1987). *Public attitudes and actions regarding child abuse and its prevention: The results of a Louis Harris public opinion poll*. Chicago: Author.

National Center on Child Abuse and Neglect (NCCAN). (1981). *The national incidence study of child abuse and neglect: Report of findings*. Washington, DC: Author.

Orbach, I. (1988). *Children who don't want to live*. San Francisco: Jossey Bass.

Pelton, L. (Ed.). (1981). *The social context of child abuse and neglect*. New York: Human Sciences Press.

Pynoos, R. S., & Nader, K. (1988). Psychological first aid and treatment approach to children exposed to community violence: Research implications. *Journal of Traumatic Stress, 1*, 445–473.

Reardon, P. (1988, June 22). CHA Violent crime up 9% for year. *Chicago Tribune*, sec. 1, p. 1.

Rosenblatt, R. (1983). *Children of war*. New York: Doubleday.

Sameroff, A., & Fiese, B. (1990). Transactional regulation and early intervention. In S. J. Meisels & J. P. Shonkoff (Eds.), *Handbook of early childhood intervention* (pp. 119–149). Cambridge, England: Cambridge University Press.

Scheinfeld, D. (1983). Family relationships and school achievement among boys of lower-income urban black families. *American Journal of Orthopsychiatry*, *53*(1), 127–143.

Scheper-Hughes, N. (1987). Culture, society, and maternal thinking: mother love and child death in northeast Brazil. In N. Hughes (Ed.), *Child survival* (pp. 187–210). Boston: D. Reidel.

Schorr, L., & Schorr, D. (1988). *Within our reach: breaking the cycle of disadvantage.* New York: Anchor Press.

Terr, L. (1988). Treating psychic trauma in children: A preliminary discussion. *Journal of Traumatic Stress*, *2*, 3–20.

Terr, L. (1990). *Too scared to cry.* New York: Harper Collins.

United Nations Children's Fund, Executive Board (UNICEF). (1986, March 10). *Children in situations of armed conflict.* New York: UNICEF.

van der Ploeg, H., & Kleijn, W. (1989). Being held hostage in the Netherlands: A study of long-term aftereffects. *Journal of Traumatic Stress*, *2*, 153–169.

Vygotsky, L. S. (1986). *Thought and language.* Cambridge, MA: MIT Press.

Wallerstein, J., & Blakeslee, S. (1989). *Second chances: Men, women, and children a decade after divorce.* San Francisco: Ticknor & Fields.

Werner, E. (1989, April). Children of the garden island. *Scientific American*, pp. 106–111.

Werner, E. (1990). Protective factors and individual resilience. In R. Meisells & J. Shonkoff (Eds.), *Handbook of early intervention.* Cambridge, UK: Cambridge University Press.

Wilson, W. J. (1987). *The truly disadvantaged.* Chicago: University of Chicago Press.

7
Child Maltreatment: Implications For Policy From Cross-Cultural Research

Kathleen J. Sternberg

Since the "discovery" of child abuse as a social problem in the 1960s (Pfohl, 1977), the topic of child maltreatment has gained extensive attention in the popular and professional literature. Professionals and laypersons alike were initially shocked when they were forced to reckon with the existence of child maltreatment as a social phenomenon, and most research efforts were initially focused on the search for the cause of child maltreatment. How was it that a parent could bring himself or herself to physically harm a child?

The first model for explaining child abuse, coined the *medical* or *psychiatric model*, focused on the psychopathology of abusers and served an important purpose for the community, distancing abusers from "good parents." The psychiatric model (Parke & Collmer, 1975) was subsequently abandoned, because it simply did not fit the data and sociological models focusing on society's role in precipitating child maltreatment began to emerge.

Sociological models stressed factors like unemployment, crowded living conditions, societal endorsement of violence, and poverty (Gil, 1973; Straus, 1980). Some sociologists and anthropologists suggested that child maltreatment was associated with industrialization and the fast pace of modern life which allowed less contact within the extended family and other social support networks (Garbarino & Gilliam, 1980; Korbin, 1991). This thesis stimulated an interest in the examination of parent–child interactions in non-Western cultures. Gradually, as anthropologists and developmental psychologists began to examine these cultures, it became clear that child maltreatment existed in a variety of cultures around the world (Korbin, 1981, 1987). In spite of the fact that cross-cultural research failed to provide "the explanation" for child maltreatment, an examination of parenting practices, both normative and abusive, within and between cultures, yielded information helpful in understanding the etiology and effects of child maltreatment, as well as insights into intervention strategies for abusive families and children. Whereas most research on child maltreatment initially involved samples from the United States and Canada, there has recently been a substantial increase in the number of studies conducted outside North America. These studies vary in purpose and scope but together provide us with some understanding of how child maltreatment is viewed in a variety of cultures throughout the world.

The purpose of this chapter is to review the various ways cross-cultural research on child maltreatment can enhance our understanding of the prevalance, etiology, and effects of maltreatment on children, and aid in the development of sensitive policies designed to facilitate prevention and treatment. A thorough review of the cross-cultural literature on child maltreatment is beyond the scope of this chapter. Instead we attempt to highlight some of the ways in which cross-cultural research can be used to better understand the phenomenon of child maltreatment, particularly issues related to social policy and intervention.

We proceed by presenting a series of questions posed by researchers and practitioners and attempting to illustrate how cross-cultural research can help address these questions. First we discuss the professional and cultural biases that influence the disposition of child maltreatment cases in the United States and illustrate how they have negative implications for children and families affected by these decisions. We present evidence from the developmental literature suggesting that an understanding of cultural context is necessary in order to accurately interpret the meaning of behavior and to evaluate its potential outcome. Second, research in the United States has been confounded by a variety of social and demographic characteristics which make it difficult to untangle the factors fostering abuse from those fostering other social problems and to examine the effects of domestic violence independent of drug abuse, single parenting, poverty, etc. Cultures which differ socially and demographically from the United States provide us with natural laboratories for examining the prevalence, etiology, and the effects of domestic violence in ways precluded by demographics and administrative constraints of the social welfare system in the United States. Finally, in spite of increased professional and public awareness of child maltreatment, there is a lack of consensus about how prevention and intervention efforts should be designed and implemented. Examination of policies related to child maltreatment in other cultures may provide us with new ideas related to the effectiveness and evaluation of prevention and intervention programs. Perhaps we can benefit from the experience of other cultures in learning about the implementation of novel programs as well as the conditions under which they should be avoided.

HOW DO CULTURAL BIASES AFFECT THE IDENTIFICATION AND TREATMENT OF CHILD MALTREATMENT?

Extensive attention has been devoted to the definition of child abuse and exploration of the extent to which definitions influence the labeling and diagnosis of abusive interactions between parents and children. In this section, we attempt to demonstrate how cultural biases of professionals empowered to label child abuse can have a profound impact on children and their families. In the second part of this section, we examine studies focused on normative as well as deviant patterns of behavior among cultures within North America and abroad, and demonstrate their potential for familiarizing us with a wider range of childrearing practices than our own subculture (whatever that may be!) can. Without this broader perspective, our efforts to diagnose and understand the effects of child maltreatment, and to prevent and intervene, will be handicapped by a variety of personal and cultural biases resulting in less than optimal decisions about the child's wellbeing.

A review of statutory laws across jurisdictions in the United States reveals marked variations and a lack of consensus about which actions should be deemed abusive. Although professionals often assume they agree about which parental behaviors constitute child maltreatment, a number of researchers have suggested that there is substantial variability within and among different professions about which behaviors should be defined as abusive and about the relative severity of different types of abuse (Gelles, 1982, 1987; Giovannoni, 1989; Giovannoni & Becerra, 1979). Because child abuse is not an objective phenomenon but one that refers to the labeling of an interaction between a parent and a child, it is extremely difficult to establish an operational definition of the phenomenon (Barnett, Manly, & Cicchetti, this volume). The process by which actions are labeled as abusive is far from uniform. Some rules focus on the intent of actions, while others focus on whether or not the action was harmful to the child. Both *intent* and *harm* are terms that are subject to interpretation. Intent can never be observed from someone's actions, it can only be inferred. Harm is also an amorphous term, because in order to evaluate whether an action is harmful, one must know the meaning and context in which the interaction took place. Only in rare cases is empirical information available about the extent of harm attributable to specific childrearing practices resulting in professional reliance on personal opinions about which actions are harmful. In summarizing the difficulties involved in objectively defining child abuse, Gelles has written:

> Officially recognized cases of child abuse are products of social labeling and social processes by which behavior of caretakers is labeled as abusive or their children are recognized as being abused. Once the label "abuse" has been attached, the labeler must be able to make the label "stick". Thus, what is perceived as being child abuse will vary from individual to individual and professional group to professional group; and the process used to affix the label "child abuse" means that certain children and families are tagged as abused and abusers while others are insulated from the label despite engaging in the same behavior as those labeled child abusers. (Gelles, 1982, pp. 1–2)

Part of the problem stems from the fact that society has given child protective workers an ambiguous and complicated mission. On the one hand, they are charged with protecting children from potentially dangerous circumstances and looking out for the "best interests of the child" while on the other hand they must be careful to protect individuals' (parents') rights to privacy and intervene only when children are "really in danger." Drawing the line between these two extremes is not easy. An attempt to strictly defend either one of these positions can lead caseworkers to misdiagnose the presence or absence of abusive behaviors.

The problem of diagnosis is further complicated by the fact that ethnic identity and socioeconomic status influence the probability of being diagnosed as abusive. Although child maltreatment occurs at all social and economic levels, the social welfare system in the United States is organized such that children from less economically advantaged families are more likely to be deemed *abused* than children from more economically advantaged families (Gelles, 1989; Gil, 1973; Giovannoni & Becerra, 1979; Parke & Collmer, 1975; Pelton, 1978; Pfohl, 1977; Schepher-Hughes, 1989). Unfortunately, those members of society who enact legislation and diagnose maltreatment often come from different social, cultural, and economic circumstances than those whose behavior is most likely to be labeled *abusive*. All too often they are unfamiliar with parenting practices in subcultures other than their own and reach conclusions about the presence or absence of abuse based on personal biases instead of empirical information about the potential effect of specific parental behaviors. As Giovannoni and Becerra summarized:

> At the heart of the controversies over what should and should not be considered mistreatment warranting state instrusion into family life is concern that such intrusion may simply constitute the imposition of the values of one segment of the community on other segments with different values. Professionals are seen as imposing their views on the populace at large, or at best upholding the values of only middle-class whites, those most like themselves, but not those of lower socioeconomic and other ethnic statuses. (Giovannoni & Becerra, 1979, p.158)

Handelman (1987) argues that the process of identifying and diagnosing child abuse cases within social welfare agencies needs to be restructured to enable more thorough evaluation of the decision-making process. He claims that, because much of the process of diagnosing the abuse takes place "within the head of the caseworker," it is impossible to objectively monitor the process. Assumptions about the alleged perpetrator's behavior quickly become "facts," and a full-fledged investigation is launched by protective service workers.

The investigation of instances marked by uncertainty is pervaded by psychologistic thinking in which emphasis is laid less on how parents behave toward their children, but more on their presumed intentions and motivations, and on the psychopathologies that underlie these. Investigators rely on their perceptions of the minds and psyches of the possible perpetrators in order to establish what happened, why it happened, and what may happen in the future (Handelman, 1987).

When the cultural background of those labeling behaviors is very different from those who are being labeled, the potential for misinterpretations of behavior are exaccerbated. Anthropologists like Korbin and Kranzler have offered us numerous examples of how professionals in decision-making capacities interpret interactions between parents and children in accordance with their own value systems and label them abusive, even in the absence of empirical information about the effects of the particular practices (see Wilson & Saft, this volume). Krantzler (1987) devoted an entire chapter to describing how a social service agency brought charges against a Samoan family on the grounds of medical neglect for refusing treatment. An adolescent woman who was diagnosed with juvenile diabetes was trapped between the advice offered by a Western physician and the treatment prescribed by her father, a traditional faith healer. A brief excerpt from the physician's report illustrates the lack of understanding between the family and the medical staff and illustrates how the frustration of the physician escalated until neglect charges were leveled against the young woman's family.

> Her diabetes appeared to be very much out of control at that time but I was having a very difficult time with the patient and her father. I showed them how to do the Chem-strip method, which they seemed to be apathetic about. I consented to the father's wishes to have him supplement the insulin with some potion of his that he had prepared especially to control her sugar. Our agreement was to see her again in 2 days. At that time, if her sugar was still high, we would definitely admit her to the hospital. I kept the insulin doses as stated and then (2 days later) I saw them again. This time the father claimed that he had been giving Mary an herbal potion which he claimed would help control her sugar. He had been giving it to her on the morning of this visit and was convinced that her blood sugar would be down. Well, her blood sugar was 878 with a Chem-strip showing 400–800 and acetone of 60. I commented to the father that the diabetes was out of control and there was some danger of her going into diabetic ketoacidosis, but at that time he became very angry with me and claimed that he would take her from my service and take care of her on his own. He did not believe that there was such an illness which would require daily injections for the rest of one's life and thanked me for my efforts but claimed that he would like to have total control of his daughter's illness at this time. He refused to bring her into the hospital. He did not believe any of the chronicity that I tried to point out with this illness, that all of the manifestations now present . . . were related to the diabetes. (Kranzler, 1987, p. 329)

Given popular biases that members of ethnic minorities, particularly those in poor economic circumstances, are more tolerant of abusive behavior, professionals are unofficially mandated to err on the side of invading upon the privacy of poor minority families under the guise of "protecting their children" (see Wilson & Saft, this volume). In a chapter entitled "When Cultural Rights Conflict With the Best Interests of the Child," Hughes (1987) describes his own experiences as a clinical social worker and the difficulty he had in distancing himself from his own Western value orientation. He describes three cases of child abuse in which the proposed interventions involved taking what his supervisors considered to be risks while recognizing the children's need to maintain contact with their families and communities. In summarizing the tendency of child protective service (CPS) workers to ignore the importance of children's cultural identity in their diagnosis and treatment of abuse, a process he considers institutional abuse, Hughes wrote:

> The "child saver" ethos is strongly inculcated in CPS workers through the moralistic and often class-biased tone of the traditional social work philosophy and education. Ironically, this education allows one to be somewhat more suspect of negative stereotypes toward non-white clients than of negative stereotypes toward poor, white clients who are, in fact, closer to the cultural backgrounds of many social workers. The "child saver" mentality must be recognized as a potent psychological force in sustaining the artificial conflict between a child's "best interests" and his or her "cultural" (and class) interests. (Hughes, 1987, p. 383)

When professionals, in the course of their routine work, make decisions about potential cases of child maltreatment, many factors influence their judgments. Several studies have been conducted suggesting that ethnic background, professional training, education, and social class all influence the way behaviors come to be labeled *abusive*. Thus any conclusion that a specific interaction between a parent and a child constitutes child abuse depends to some extent on the personal and professional background of the professional asked to make this decision.

Giovannoni and Becerra (1979) explored the relationship between ethnic background (African American, Caucasian, Hispanic) and social class on non-professionals' ratings of vignettes describing interactions between parents and children which were potentially abusive. There was little agreement among the three ethnic groups with respect to the severity of the different categories of maltreatment. Overall, African Americans and Hispanics rated the vignettes more seriously than Caucasian respondents did. Furthermore African-American respondents consistently rated vignettes involving nutrition, medical care, supervision, cleanliness, education, clothing, and housing more seriously than Hispanic respondents, while Hispanic respondents rated vignettes involving sexual abuse, physical injury, and substance abuse as more serious than their African-American counterparts did.

The fact that the definition and diagnosis of child maltreatment is heavily influenced by individual, professional, and ethnic biases often has powerful implications for individual children and their families. Researchers, clinicians, and policy makers need to constantly review and scrutinize their definitional criteria to reduce reliance on personal biases and maximize the use of empirical information in formulating definitions and professional opinions.

Two lines of research focusing on development and culture underscore the importance of understanding behavior in context. From anthropological studies describing patterns of parent–child relationships, we can learn a great deal about the range of childrearing conditions considered acceptable by different cultures. Although some of these behaviors and attitudes may appear bizarre to us, examining them from the perspective of the culture in which they occur (emic) underscores the fact that "appropriate/normal behavior" is not an absolute but a relative notion. In addition, they may foster a more critical examination of practices considered normative (i.e., circumcision at birth) by some members of the dominant culture but which may be painful for children and considered harmful for children in other cultures. In focusing our attention on the contribution of anthropological research on childrearing, Korbin (1987b) wrote:

> All cultures have continua for acceptable parenting. The most indulgent of cultures, in which children are rarely subjected to any sanctions, and the most punitive of cultures, in which children may be severely beaten for misbehavior, have concepts of child maltreatment. Polynesia is a culture noted for its indulgence of children. In one Polynesian society, children could be pinched lightly on the mouth for misbehavior. More severe punishments were prohibited. In administering this punishment, one man left a scratch on the lips of his grandchild. From the etic perspective of United States child protection workers, this would hardly be cause for alarm. However, this deviation from culturally accepted practices resulted in the grandfather being soundly berated by his cultural peers for the abuse by emic standards. At the other end of the spectrum stand the Ik of East Africa. Relocated from their traditional lands to an area that provided only marginal sustinance, the Ik considered it foolhardy to share food or shelter with their children past the age of three. A mother who behaved in a contrary fashion, sheltering her daughter, was considered neglectful in that the child would not learn to fend for herself. And indeed, when her mother could no longer care for her, the girl perished, "proof" of the error of the mother's ways. (p. 32)

A second body of research that is useful in highlighting the importance of evaluating caretaking practices within their cultural context are developmental studies that have found that specific caretaking practices affect children differently depending on the cultural and social niche in which they live. In her study of parenting styles, Baumrind (1972) found that *authoritative parenting* (fostering independence and encouraging a child to comply with parental rules by explaining the purpose and meaning of the rule) promoted social competence among white middle-class children, whereas an authoritarian parenting style (emphasizing compliance as a virtue and the use of punishment to obtain compliance with parental standards) fostered social competence in African-American middle-class girls. In another study Smilansky (1992) found that a teaching style encouraging children's exploration, independence, and creativity in the kindergarten classroom fostered competence amoung Israeli kindergartners from European and American backgrounds while causing confusion and acting out among Israeli children from North African backgrounds. According to Smilansky, the style used by the teachers was compatible with the values and socialization practices of the parents from European backgrounds but contradicted the North African parents' expectations that children should be quiet and comply strictly with adult requests. These examples illustrate how a given style of interacting with children can be positive or problematic depending on the niche in which the children spend the rest of their time (Baldwin, Baldwin, & Cole, 1990). Another example illustrating the danger of proscribing an "American pattern" of socialization for children who live in a different subcultures is provided by Erikson (1970). Erikson described how "well-intended" dorm counselors who encouraged American Indian adolescents to use makeup and perfume caused substantial identity problems and confusion for these young women when they visited with their families. Grooming norms considered appropriate for young Caucasian girls were considered totally unacceptable by Indian parents, who considered their daughters' behavior to be promiscuous.

Summary

In this section, we reviewed the sorts of biases affecting the way professionals label parent–child interactions as *abusive* or *normative* and how these biases may influence interventions. Examples are given to illustrate the process by which parents from cultural minority groups are more exposed to the social welfare system in the United States and are thus more likely to be categorized as abusive than parents from white middle-class families. Results from several developmental studies support the importance of considering how caretaking behaviors can differentially influence children depending on their cultural background. Attention now shifts from the impact of culture on diagnosis and intervention to the variations in social and demographic circumstances that provide interesting contexts for examining the etiology and effects of maltreatment on children's development.

HOW CAN RESEARCHERS USE OTHER CULTURES AS "NATURAL LABORATORIES" TO STUDY CHILD MALTREATMENT?

Because most of the research on domestic violence has been conducted in the United States, our understanding of the prevalence, etiology, and effects of domestic violence are limited by the characteristics of the United States population in general and the welfare population in particular. Examination of child maltreatment in societies with cultural, economic, and demographic circumstances different than those in North America may provide natural laboratories for studying and understanding the etiology and effects of child maltreatment.

In North America, the occurrence of child maltreatment is associated with a variety of social and demographic characteristics. Domestic violence is likely to be higher in areas characterized by high crime rates and tolerance for ownership of weapons (Garbarino, this volume; Garbarino, Kostelny, & Dubrow, 1991). Furthermore, the occurrence of child maltreatment is associated with a variety of social and economic exigencies. Investigators have consistently reported that the incidence of child maltreatment is higher among single-parent families, families with unemployed fathers, substance abusers, nonbiological parents, and families characterized by poverty and poor housing conditions (Gelles, 1989; Gil, 1970; Straus, Gelles, & Steinmetz, 1980). Given the potentially negative impact of any one of these factors—unemployment, poverty, drug use—it is difficult to ascertain how exposure to family violence interacts with these other stressful circumstances to explain the prevalence of abuse and the effects of abuse on children. In this section, a sociological survey and two developmental studies will be used to illustrate how research conducted outside the United States can enhance our understanding of domestic violence by "altering" some of the conditions correlated with domestic violence in the United States.

Incidence and Etiology of Domestic Violence

In comparison with other societies, the United States is characterized by extremely high rates of interpersonal violence (Cicchetti & Lynch, in press). Contrary to popular belief, the family is one of the most violent institutions in American society. In attempting to understand why this is the case, Straus and Gelles (1988) explored a variety of attitudinal and demographic factors which may explain the violent nature of the American family. The following passage illustrates how standards for violence appear to differ within and outside the family:

> It can be noted that there was violence between the spouses in only 16% of the couples, that is, 84% were not violent. Moreover, most of those violent incidents were minor, such as slapping or throwing things. Suppose however that we had studied universities rather than families. It seems unlikely that the findings would be dismissed by saying that 84% of the faculty did not hit a student in 1987 and, in any case, most of those episodes involved slapping the student or faculty member, rather than punching or beating up. (Straus & Gelles, 1988, p. 153)

Straus and Gelles then point out the broad consensus among American parents with respect to the use of physical punishment toward children. A survey conducted in 1983 suggested that most American parents with children over the age of 3 endorsed physical punishment, a form of violence in itself (Straus & Gelles, 1983).

Although the empirical association between physical punishment and child abuse is somewhat unclear, social learning theorists suggest that the rates of violence toward children are influenced by a society's overall tolerance for violence, conveying the message that aggression is an acceptable form of conflict resolution, particularly toward people you love. Often, children are explicitly told "I'm spanking you because I care about you," and light spankings are often referred to as "love taps." Straus and Gelles (1988, p.156) bemoan the facts that (a) love and aggression are inappropriately associated; (b) hitting is often used to reinforce moral behavior; and (c) parents discipline by hitting after their frustration and anger have escalated, thereby teaching children to use violence in similar situations.

Other research confirms that Americans are more tolerant of violence in the family than outside the family, and that violent incidents committed within the family are more likely to be excused than the same incidents committed against nonfamily members. Grumet (1970) reported that assault committed within the family carries a shorter sentence than the same offense committed outside the family.

Why is it that Americans are willing to excuse assault within the family but less lenient on similar incidents which occur outside the family context? Is it uniquely American to condone violence within the family, or is this the nature of families in general? Do attitudes about violence in different societies influence the prevalence and incidents of domestic violence and the willingness to intervene in cases of suspected abuse? In order to begin examining these questions, it is valuable to examine the association between violence within and outside the family across cultures.

In an attempt to understand how demographics and social values affect the incidence of domestic violence, Gelles and Edfeldt (1986) conducted research in Sweden, a country with a very different demographic profile. In particular, Sweden differs from the United States in a number of ways that made it an interesting site to test hypotheses about the association between abuse and stressful life circumstances. In Sweden, generous health and social welfare policies make it possible to obtain adequate housing, daycare, and health benefits for adults and children. This drastically reduces the types of stresses associated with inflated rates of domestic violence in the United States. Unemployment in Sweden is two to three times lower than in the United States, and the social benefits provided to the unemployed are far more generous and comprehensive. In addition, social attitudes toward violence in Sweden have led to legislation and policies that differ drastically from those in the United States. Corporal punishment in the schools has been prohibited since 1979, the ownership of weapons is severely limited, there are severe restrictions on the portrayal of aggression and violence in the media, and replicas of 20th-century weapons cannot be sold even as toys (Nilsson, 1991).

By comparing survey data from Sweden and the United States, Gelles and Edfeldt (1986) were able to explore how variations in social attitudes and economic conditions influenced parents' reports of the use of violence toward their children. It was possible to ascertain whether certain demographic factors like single parenting were associated with an increase in the incidence of abuse, as is the case in the United States where most single mothers are also very young and poor (Gelles, 1989).

Gelles and Edfeldt (1986) compared the responses of approximately 1,100 respondents in Sweden and the United States using the Conflict Tactics Scales.

On these scales, respondents are asked to indicate which tactics they have used in the last year to resolve conflicts with their children. Items range in severity from calmly discussing the area of disagreement to using a knife or gun. Although Swedish parents reported using less violence than parents in the United States, there were no statistically significant differences between Swedes and Americans with respect to the use of abusive or severely violent techniques. Swedes were less likely than Americans to use spanking and slapping to resolve problems with their children. Younger parents in both countries were more likely than older parents to use violent techniques with their children. In Sweden, education was unrelated to violence, whereas in the United States those parents with the most and least formal education were more likely to use violent techniques toward their children. Interestingly, violence was no more common in single-parent families than in two-parent families. This finding suggests that the economic stress characteristic of single-parent homes in the United States may account for more variation in violence toward children than single-parenthood as an independent factor.

Findings like these may offer important implications for policy. In interpreting their results, Gelles and Edfeldt (1987) take into consideration a variety of factors which might influence the differences in the reported behavior of Swedish and American parents, emphasizing how cautious one must be when comparing data from different cultures and how important it is to entertain a variety of possible explanations.

The Effects of Child Maltreatment

Although international awareness of the topic of child maltreatment has increased over the past 20 years (Gelles & Cornell, 1985; Korbin, 1987a), few systematic studies have been conducted outside North America. As with studies focused on the prevalence and etiology of child maltreatment, research on the sequelae of maltreatment has largely been limited to North America. Whereas some of the major surveys have included respondents from all social and economic groups in the United States, most research evaluating the effects of domestic violence on children's development has been conducted with samples recruited from social service agencies. The nature of the families in these samples is such that the children have experienced a variety of stressful life events in addition to being victims and/or witnesses of domestic violence. Factors like single parenthood, divorce, poverty, substance abuse, moving to a shelter, and/ or being institutionalized, which are characteristic of samples in studies of domestic violence, have been implicated as conditions that increase children's vulnerability to negative developmental outcomes. In attempting to assess the impact of abuse, there are some who question whether domestic violence per se, rather than factors associated with it, are responsible for the negative outcomes that have been empirically linked to abuse (Elmer, 1977; Emery, 1989). Although Elmer's study had some important methodological limitations (Aber & Cicchetti, 1984) it was very influential in drawing attention to the fact that abuse is often confounded with other negative life events, making it difficult to assess the independent contribution of abuse (Toro, 1982). Similar concerns have been raised by other researchers about the co-occurrence of abuse and other harmful factors like single parenting, substance abuse, and stepparenting (Gelles, 1989; Malkin & Lamb, in press; Wilson & Daly, 1987); these problems also pertain to research on children who experience psychological maltreatment and witness spousal violence (Hart & Brassard, 1987; Jaffe, Wolfe, & Wilson, 1990). Studies examining the effects of witnessing violence on children have almost exclusively involved mothers and children in battered women's shelters (Jaffe et al., 1990). Although these studies suggest that children who witness violence may be at risk for a variety of developmental problems, the conclusiveness of these findings is limited by the fact that these children have experienced other stressful life events, like separation from their fathers and familiar neighborhoods, as well as transitions to the often chaotic lifestyle of the shelters.

Currently the public policy trends in Israel are such that social workers are encouraged to keep families together in cases of physical and sexual abuse unless circumstances suggest that the child's life is in danger. This approach was summarized in a recent publication by the Ministry of Labour and Social Affairs (1991):

> The principle set by the Director-General is that the raising of the child within his own natural family ensures his normal development, and so every effort should be made to develop the tools and services in the community in order to help the family raise its children. In any case, a permanant home should be available for every child. Among the services to which the child is entitled within his family is counselling and guidance for violent parents. For parents who have difficulty in raising their children, placement in day-care centres is made available, as well as day-time foster care, therapeutic clubs, tutors to help with school work. There are also centres for single parent families, programmes to help parents of children with special needs, diagnostic services to detect developmental difficulties in very young children and direct material assistance, such as dental care, household equipment, medical insurance in special cases, etc. (1991, p.7)

The structure of Israeli society in general, and that of the social welfare system in particular, provided us with an opportunity to explore the effects of maltreatment independent of other life events known to have negative effects on children's development (i.e., single parenting, substance abuse, foster/shelter placement and stepparenting).

The purpose of our study was to explore how different forms of domestic violence (being a victim of physical child abuse, observing spouse abuse, and being both a victim and observer of physical abuse) affect behavior and development. The ideological preference for family preservation in Israel facilitated the identification of a sample of children living at home with both their biological parents and thus examine the effects of domestic violence independent of the confounding effects of single parenthood and foster/shelter placement characteristic of research on abusive populations in the United States. By conducting the study in Israel, we were also able to contrast the effects of the different types of domestic violence which often co-occur in the samples recruited for study in the United States. This study was also unique in that we obtained information about the target child's adjustment from multiple informants—the child's mother, father, teacher, peers, and the child himself or herself. Because the percentage of single mothers is substantially lower in Israel than in the United States, it was possible to obtain a representative sample of children living with their biological parents. And because recruitment of families was conducted with the assistance of senior social workers, it was possible to obtain extensive information about the histories of the children in the study and to recruit a well-matched comparison group of children who had not experienced domestic violence.

In this study, we examined children's behavior problems, depressive symptomatology, and perceptions of their abusive and nonabusive parents. The results of this study suggested that reports of children's problem behaviors differed depending on the informant (Sternberg et al., 1993). According to their mothers, children had high levels of problematic behavior when spouse abuse had occurred, whereas children reported higher levels of problematic behavior when they themselves had been abused. Abused children also reported higher levels of depressive symptomatology than children in the comparison group did (Sternberg et al., 1993). With respect to parental perceptions, abused children more frequently reported negative perceptions of their perpetrating parents, although children in the four groups did not differ with respect to the number of positive attributes assigned to their parents (Sternberg et al., 1992).

Overall, the results of the study demonstrated that domestic violence had broad effects on child development that varied in nature depending on the type of domestic violence and the source of information about the child's adjustment. Importantly, these effects were evident even after the effects of poverty and marital discord had been taken into account. Information from teachers and peers is currently being analyzed, and we are planning a follow-up study of the children in this study. Because of the relatively low rates of geographic mobility in Israel, it was possible to locate most of the families from the original sample. Our plan is to follow these children through the completion of their military service at age 21. Because of the difficulties in conducting longitudinal research in the United States, little is known about the long-term effects on children's development. If we are able to follow the children in our sample through early adulthood, this would provide a valuable contribution to the field.

Evaluation of Children's Reports of Physical and Sexual Abuse

As with other areas of research on child maltreatment, research on the accuracy and competency of children's reports of maltreatment has been constrained by social and legal policies characteristic of the United States. Because child abuse allegations are handled so differently in Israel and in the United States, Israel has again provided a natural laboratory for us to examine some of the issues facing professionals in the United States.

Children's eyewitness testimony has been the focus of heated professional and popular debates in the United States. The recent increase in the number of allegations of child abuse has led to a series of dilemmas related to children's presence in the courtroom (Perry & Wrightsman, 1991). Questions about children's memory capacities, suggestibility, the trauma of testifying in court, and juxtaposition of children's and defendants' rights are among the major issues debated by psychologists, legal scholars, child advocates, and judges concerned with children who are alleged to have been victims of abuse (Lamb, Sternberg, & Esplin, 1992). Unfortunately, the empirical investigation of the relevant issues is very complicated, and the scientific evidence has lagged behind the adversarial legal debates, most of which occur in the context of the courtrooms where the well-being of children and adults is at stake (see Thompson, this volume; Goodman, Batterman, & Kenney, this volume).

Because laws vary across jurisdictions in the United States, there is a lack of uniformity with respect to the investigation of allegations. Reports of physical and sexual abuse are handled by a variety of professionals, including policemen, child protection workers, therapists, and psychologists. Children are routinely interviewed by multiple interviewers with different responsibilities and agendas and the information obtained is not coordinated or centralized. Because the legal system in the United States is such that children are often required to testify in court, studies focusing on the validity of children's allegations of abuse are often complicated by factors like the time lapse between the incident and the provision of testimony during the trial. In addition, confrontation with defense attorneys in pretrial depositions and courtroom hearings complicates the examination of children's reports of abuse.

In Israel, by contrast, uniform and strict procedures regulate the interviews of minors (under age 15) who are alleged victims, witnesses, and perpetrators of abuse. Specially trained child investigators are the *only* individuals who are allowed by law to interview children, and they are required to interview the child within 72 hours of receiving a report or referral. Children are routinely interviewed once, with an occasional supplementary interview if additional information is needed. These investigators are given extensive power and have the sole authority to decide whether or not the child victim should testify in court, attempt to identify alleged perpetrators, and participate in procedures designed to reconstruct the event (Harnon, 1989). When they believe that it would be harmful for children to testify, youth investigators testify in lieu of the child (Harnon, 1989).

The youth investigator plays multiple roles—he or she is responsible for collecting evidence from the child, representing the child in court, and providing an expert opinion about the veracity of the child's statement. The Israeli system is considered by some to protect children's rights while jeopardizing the rights of alleged offenders, and would certainly be unacceptable in the United States where the constitution guarantees defendants the right to "confront" their accusors. Nevertheless, the implementation of this law, with its provisions for uniform and centralized data collection, can provide researchers unique opportunities for examining different aspects of children's testimony in cases of alleged sexual and physical abuse.

We are currently in the process of collecting a nationally representative sample of audiorecorded interviews with Israeli children who have reported incidents of physical or sexual abuse. Because the sample includes all interviews conducted in Israel is a 12-month span, sufficient numbers of cases will make it possible to examine variations in the quality and style of children's reports across a range of ages, types of incidents, socioeconomic status, and religious and ethnic groups. We plan to compare the information provided by children in the interviews with independent information obtained from police and medical files. Because children are required to "tell their story only once" and all interviews must be recorded, it is possible to examine the validity of children's allegations while reducing some of the variation characteristic of samples in the United States.

Although the Israeli system has many limitations and contains elements that would be unacceptable in the United States, our study emphasizes how researchers can take advantage of differences in cultural and political milieux when studying aspects of child maltreatment. The Israeli system makes it possible to examine the validity and usefulness of children's testimony in ways that would not be possible in the United States.

Summary

In this section we have described several studies that illustrate how researchers can take advantage of differing cultural and political contexts to examine important questions related to child maltreatment. In Sweden and Israel, it was possible to examine the etiology and effects of child maltreatment independent of the social and economic conditions which commonly co-occur with abuse in the United States. In addition, it was possible to take advantage of the centralized system for investigating child abuse allegations in Israel to examine issues related to the validity and quality of children's reports. Because geographic mobility is limited in both Israel and Sweden, these countries promise interesting sites for longitudinal research on child maltreatment which is difficult to conduct in the United States.

Our illustrations are limited to Israel and Sweden because those are the countries in which we have conducted most of our own research, of course. Undoubtedly, researchers familiar with different cultures could describe other equally interesting contexts for conducting research. All would underscore the unique value of cross-national research on child maltreatment.

HOW CAN POLICIES AND PRACTICES IN OTHER CULTURES INFORM PRACTICE IN THE UNITED STATES?

As noted above, cross-cultural research can assist scholars by clarifying the importance of cultural, professional, and subcultural influences on the definition, diagnosis, and treatment of child maltreatment. It can also permit researchers to distinguish the effects of domestic violence from the effects of other stressful or traumatic life events with which domestic violence is often associated. In this section, we discuss a third way in which a cross-cultural perspective can be helpful: providing examples of innovative or alternative policies and practices.

Because of ideological preference for family preservation and the limited capacity and quality of traditional foster care in Israel, a number of innovative programs have been developed for abused children and their families. These programs involve varying degrees of intervention by social service agencies and take into account the age of the child, the severity of abuse, and the parenting capacities of the child's parents. The goal of these programs is to provide abused children and their families with the amount of support and surveillance necessary while maintaining the integrity of the family wherever possible. These programs focus both on reducing the probability of recurrent abusive interactions by providing support to parents (though home child guidance programs, parenting classes, access to free public laundry facilities, organized outings for parents, free or subsidized daycare) and by providing services directly to abused children (homework assistance programs, counseling services, and after-school programs). For abused children deemed in need of closer supervision and care, there are a variety of residential programs. Some children are offered placements in "afternoon clubs"—they are bussed from school to the club at 1:00 where they are served a hot lunch, provided an opportunity to rest or nap, assisted in the preparation of their homework, provided with structured and free play time, and served dinner before they are collected by their parents in the evening (Novak & Yotkovsky, 1988). This program reduces stress on parents by reducing the amount of time children spend in the home and eliminating potentially stressful situations like mealtimes and homework preparations. Likewise, children are provided with an array of activities which foster their development and enhance their functioning in school. Because the "club" staff has daily contact with the abused child and at least one of their parents, it is possible to monitor the child's well-being and if necessary activate more serious means of intervention. This program makes it possible for children to continue living with their abusive parents even when the parents are incapable of providing optimal full-time care. A unique feature of this program is the way the services are "marketed" to parents. Caseworkers present the program to parents as an after-school enrichment program and thus in many cases can avoid evoking a more authoritarian and coercive approach, which tends to alienate parents from social services. Services are offered to the family in a fashion which avoids "blaming" the parents for their abusive behavior and reduced competence while adequately monitoring the child's well-being.

In cases where the abuse is more serious or the abilities of the parents to care for their children are more limited, the Jerusalem Municipality has organized a number of "family homes." Twelve children live in a large home with "surrogate parents" who are assisted by a day counselor. They attend a neighborhood school and thus are integrated in the education system. Children are placed close to their parents' neighborhoods, and parents are encouraged to visit the children in the family homes. In addition, children spend two weekends a month and holidays with their parents or other family members. Although these family homes provide parents with less autonomy and contact with their children than the "afternoon clubs," they protect children deemed to be at greater risk while allowing them some contact with their parents. Some parents are offered counseling designed to facilitate family reunification when this is deemed to be a realistic therapeutic goal.

In sum, the programs described in Israel illustrate an array of interventions for abused children. These programs differ in their degree of intrusiveness to the family unit and are designed to meet the needs of children and families with different risks and capacities. It is important to point out that, although these programs provide adequate protection for most abused children while enabling them to continue contact with their biological parents, they do not eliminate the need to remove children from their homes in more serious cases.

Evaluations of these programs are currently in progress. Their cost effectiveness in relation to rates of recidivism of abuse and children's psychosocial adjustment will be helpful in deciding which elements of these programs might be suitable for intervention with maltreated children in the United States.

Turning our attention to the United States, it is valuable to examine the treatment of sexual abuse offenders in the Native American community of Warm Springs, Oregon. Warm Springs is a prosperous community with a population of 3,000 inhabitants from three different Indian tribes—the Wascon, Warm Springs, and Piauate. Drawing heavily on tribal values, a comprehensive social welfare system has been developed by the Native Americans who govern the area. Because Warm Springs is not governed by Oregon law, and because federal courts prosecute only one out of every 100 reported cases of child sexual abuse, sexual abuse offenders in Warm Springs are treated quite differently than in other parts of the United States. Tribal courts cannot impose sentences of more than 6 months or fines of more than $5,000 (compared to 10–30-year sentences for comparable offenses in other parts of the United States), and thus local leaders and mental health professionals have been "forced" to rely heavily on treatment programs instead of punitive sanctions. The emphasis on treatment rather than punishment is also fostered by tribal values such as "everyone makes mistakes," "the community has a responsibility to assist in healing," "family unity is important," and "individuals are capable of change." Treatment is provided by individuals who are familiar with tribal values and can blend traditional folk values with conventional psychotherapeutic practices to provide services which are both culturally appropriate and effective. Thus members of the local population are hired for mental health positions whenever possible, and so within the Division of Human Services, approximately 60% of the staff are Native Americans. Because many of the staff are paraprofessionals, furthermore, frequent "in-service" workshops, using curricula developed by child welfare experts at the Northwest Indian Child Welfare Association, are organized, and generous undergraduate and graduate scholarships are used to encourage young adults to pursue advanced training in the mental health professions. In addition, extensive efforts are made to familiarize non-Native American mental health professionals with tribal values and practices in order to maximize the quality of services provided. Further details about these programs are provided by Cross and his colleagues (Cross, 1984, 1987; Cross, Bazron, Dennis, & Isaacs, 1989).

In sum, intervention programs in Israel and the United States both illustrate how cultural values influence the development and implementation of policies related to child maltreatment. These illustrations reveal how culture shapes the development of intervention programs and demonstrate some of the ways practitioners can adapt their prevention and intervention techniques to better suit the needs of specific ethnic communities.

CONCLUSION

The purpose of this chapter was to show how cross-cultural research can enhance our understanding of child maltreatment and to review how policies and experiences in other cultures can be used to evaluate and improve our own prevention and treatment policies. We began by examining the ways in which professional and personal biases influence the definition and diagnosis of *child maltreatment* and suggested that a more pluralistic approach may improve the appropriateness and quality of services provided to abused children and their families. This suggestion was supported using examples of developmental and cross-cultural studies illustrating how childrearing practices have differing effects on children depending on the cultural niche in which they live. We then showed how variations in the social, demographic, and legal structures of Sweden and Israel provide "natural laboratories" for studying important questions related to child maltreatment. Finally, we examined several intervention programs currently being developed in other cultures and discussed the features of these programs that might be considered for implementation in the United States.

This chapter was not designed to provide an exhaustive review of research on maltreatment in other cultures but rather to illustrate the ways in which cross-cultural research can be used to advance our understanding of this difficult problem. Several large scale studies of child maltreatment that are currently underway have not been discussed. Bouchard and his colleagues at the University of Quebec in Montreal (Bouchard, Tessier, Fraser, & Laganiere, 1992) are currently conducting a province-wide survey of the incidence of family violence using a French-Canadian translation of the popular Conflict Tactics Scale (Straus, 1979). Likewise, the staff of the Family Advocacy Program of the United States Air Force (Mollerstrom, 1993) have translated the Child Abuse Potential Inventory (Milner, 1986) into a variety of languages including Korean, Japanese, and Filipino and are studying the antecedents and incidence of child abuse in a number of cultures. Studies such as these promise to add further to our understanding of child maltreatment, the treatment of its victims, and the rehabilitation of its perpetrators.

REFERENCES

Aber, J. L., & Cicchetti, D. (1984). The social-emotional development of maltreated children: An empirical and theoretical analysis. In H. Fitzgerald, B. Lester, & M. Yogman (Eds.), *Theory and research in behavioral pediatrics* (pp. 147–205). New York: Plenum.

Baldwin, A. L., Baldwin, C., & Cole, R. E. (1990). Stress-resistant families and stress-resistant children. In J. Rolf, A. Masten, D. Cicchetti, K. Nuechterlein, & S. Weintraub (Eds.), *Risk and protective factors in the development of psychopathology* (pp. 257–280). New York: Cambridge University Press.

Baumrind, D. (1972). An exploratory study of socialization effects on black children: Some black-white comparisons. *Child Development, 43*, 261–267.

Bouchard, C., Tessier, R., Fraser, A., and Laganiere, J. (1992, March). *La violence familiale envers les enfants: Prevalence dans la Basse-Ville et etude de validite de la mesure*. Paper presented to Le Symposium Quebecois sur L'Enfance et la Famille, Quebec, Canada.

Cicchetti, D., & Lynch, M. (in press). Toward an ecological/transactional model of community violence and child maltreatment: Consequences for children's development. *Psychiatry*.

Cross, T. L. (1984). *Module II: Protective services for Indian children*. Portland, OR: Northwest Indian Child Welfare Association.

Cross, T. L. (1987). *Cross cultural skills in Indian child welfare: A guide for the non-Indian*. Portland, OR: Northwest Indian Child Welfare Association.

Cross, T. L., Bazron, B. J., Dennis, K. W., & Isaacs, M. R. (1989). *Toward a culturally competent system of care*. Washington, DC: Georgetown University Press.

Elmer, E. (1977). *Fragile families, troubled children*. Pittsburgh: University of Pittsburgh Press.

Emery, R. (1989). Family violence. *American Psychologist, 44*, 321–328.

Erikson, E. H. (1970). *Childhood and society*. Middlesex, UK: Penguin.

Garbarino, J., & Gilliam, G. (1980). *Understanding abusive families*. Lexington, MA: Heath.

Garbarino, J., Kostelny, K., & Dubrow, N. (1991). *No place to be a child: Growing up in a war zone*. Lexington, MA: Lexington Books.

Gelles, R. J. (1982). Problems in defining and labeling child abuse. In R. H. Starr (Ed.), *Child abuse prediction: Policy implications*. Cambridge, MA: Ballinger.

Gelles, R. J. (1987). The family and its role in the abuse of children. *Psychiatric Annals, 17*, 4.

Gelles, R. J. (1989). Child abuse and violence in single parent families: A test of the parent-abuse and economic deprivation hypotheses. *American Journal of Orthopsychiatry, 59*, 492–501.

Gelles, R. J., & Cornell, C. P. (1985). *Intimate violence in families*. Beverly Hills, CA: Sage.

Gelles, R. J., & Edfeldt, A. W. (1986). Violence towards children in the United States and Sweden. *Child Abuse and Neglect, 10*, 501–510.

Gelles, R. J., & Straus, M. A. (1979). Violence in the American family. *Journal of Social Issues, 35*, 15–39.

Gil, D. G. (1973). *Violence against children: Physical Child Abuse in the United States*. Cambridge, MA: Harvard University Press.

Giovannoni, J. (1989). Definitional issues in child maltreatment. In D. Cicchetti & V. Carlson (Eds.), *Child maltreatment: Theory and research on the causes and consequences of child abuse and neglect* (pp. 3–37). New York: Cambridge University Press.

Giovannoni, J., & Becerra, R. M. (1979). *Defining child abuse*. New York: Free Press.

Grumet, B. R. (1970). The plaintive plaintiffs: Victims of the battered child syndrome. *Family Law Quarterly, 4*, 296–317.

Handelman, D. (1987). Bureaucracy and the maltreatment of the child: Interpretive and structural implications. In N. Scheper-Hughes (Ed.), *Child survival* (pp. 359–376). Dordrecht: Reidel.

Harnon, E. (1989). Children's evidence in the Israeli criminal justice system with special emphasis on sexual offenses. In J. R. Spencer, G. Nicholson, R. Flin, & R. Bull (Eds.), *Children's Revidence in legal proceedings* (pp. 81–97). London: Blackstone.

Hart, S. N., & Brassard, M. R. (1987). A major threat to children's mental health: Psychological maltreatment. *American Psychologist, 42*, 160–165.

Hughes, D. M. (1987). When cultural rights conflict with the "best interests of the child": A view from inside the child welfare system. In N. Scheper-Hughes (Ed.), *Child survival* (pp. 377–388). Dordrecht: Reidel.

Jaffe, P. G., Wolfe, D. A., & Wilson, S. K. (1990). *Children of battered women*. Newbury Park, CA: Sage.

Korbin, J. E. (1977). Anthropological contributions to the study of child abuse and neglect. *Child abuse and neglect: The international journal, 1*, 7–24.

Korbin, J. E. (1987a). Child abuse and neglect: The cultural context, In R. E. Helfer & R. S. Kempe (Eds.), *The battered child* (4th ed., pp. 3–41). Chicago: University of Chicago Press.

Korbin, J. E. (1987b). Child maltreatment in cross-cultural perspective: Vulnerable children and circumstances. In R. E. Gelles & J. B. Lancaster (Eds.), *Child abuse and neglect: Biosocial dimensions* (pp. 31–56). New York: Aldine De Gruyter.

Korbin, J. E. (1991). Cross-cultural perspectives and research directions for the 21st century. *Child Abuse and Neglect, 15*, 67–77.

Krantzler, N. J. (1987). Traditional medicine as 'medical neglect': Dilemmas in the case management of a Samoan teenager with diabetes. In N. Scheper-Hughes (Ed.), *Child survival*. Dordrect: Reidel.

Lamb, M. E., Sternberg, K. J., & Esplin, P. W. (in press). *Interviewing young victims of sexual maltreatment*.

Malkin, C. M., & Lamb, M. E. (in press). Child maltreatment: a test of sociobiological theory. *Journal of Comparative Family Studies*.

Milner, J. (1986). *The child abuse potential inventory: (Manual 2nd ed.)* Webster, NC: Psytec Corporation.

Ministry of Labour and Social Affairs, Department of International Relations, State of Israel. (1991). *Selected Israeli laws concerning children and youth*. Jerusalem: Author.

Mollerstrom, W. (1993, July). *Language and subcultural issues in assessing, treating and evaluating maltreating families*. Paper presented at the International Society for Behavioral Development, Recife, Brazil.

Nilsson, N. (1991). Children and commercial exploitation of violence in Sweden. *Current Sweden 384* (Serial No. 384).

Novak, R., & Yotkovsky, R. (1988). *Therapeutic centers ("afternoon clubs")*. Jerusalem Municipality, unpublished manuscript.

Parke, R. D., & Collmer, C. W. (1975). Child abuse: An interdisciplinary analysis. In E. M. Hetherington (Ed.), *Review of child development research* (Vol. 5, pp. 1–102). Chicago: University of Chicago Press.

Pelton, L. (1978). Child abuse and neglect: The myth of classlessness. *American Journal of Orthopsychiatry, 48*, 608–617.

Perry, N. W., & Wrightsman, L. S. (1991). *The child witness: Legal issues and dilemmas*. Newbury Park, CA: Sage.

Pfohl, S. J. (1977). The discovery of child abuse. *Social Problems, 24*, 310–323.

Scheper-Hughes, N. (1989). Introduction: The cultural politics of child survival. In N. Schepher-Hughes (Ed.), *Child Survival* (pp. 1–29). Dordrect: Reidel.

Sternberg, K. J., Lamb, M. E., Greenbaum, C., Cicchetti, D., Dawud, S., Cortes, R. M., Krispin, O., & Lorey, F. (1993). The effects of domestic violence on children's behavior problems and depression. *Developmental Psychology. 29*, 44–52.

Sternberg, K. J., Lamb, M. E., Greenbaum, C., Dawud, S., Cortes, R. M., & Lorey, F. (1992). *The effects of domestic violence on children's perceptions of their perpetrating and nonperpetrating parents*. Unpublished manuscript, NICHD, Bethesda, MD.

Straus, M. A. (1979). Measuring intrafamily conflict and violence: The conflict tactics (CT) scales. *Journal of Marriage and the Family, 41*, 75–88.

Straus, M. A. (1980). A sociological perspective on family violence. In M. Green (Ed.), *Violence and the family* (pp. 7–31). Boulder, CO: Westview Press.

Straus, M. A., & Gelles, R. J. (1988). Violence in American families: How much is there and why does it occur? In C. M. Chilman, F. M. Cox, & E. Nunnally (Eds.), *Troubled relationships* (pp. 141–162). Newbury Park, CA: Sage.

Straus, M. A., Gelles, R. J., & Steinmetz, S. (1980). *Behind closed doors: Violence in the American family*. Garden City, NY: Anchor Press/Doubleday.

Toro, P. A. (1982). Developmental effects of child abuse: A review. *Child Abuse and Neglect, 6*, 423–431.

Wilson, M., & Daly, M. (1987). Risk of maltreatment of children living with step-parents. In R. J. Gelles & J. B. Lancaster (Eds.), *Child abuse and neglect: Biosocial dimensions* (pp. 215–232). New York: Aldine De Gruyter.

8

Child Maltreatment in the African-American Community

Melvin N. Wilson and Elizabeth W. Saft

For most of us, families stand as a simple, unavoidable, and necessary fact of life. The continued existence of the family in modern life attests to its fundamental importance to both the individual and society. In fact, the family is the primary link between the two, serving as crucible of the former and microcosm of the latter (van den Berghe, 1988). Families offer opportunities for crucial affective and instrumental support for their members, providing the context for physical maintenance, affection, and social control. Lee (1977) reports that although the universal presence of family does not imply a universal structure, the family often includes an association of adults of both sexes and dependent children. Indeed, central to the development of family is bearing, rearing, and caring for children. Moreover, parents often maintain a lifelong benevolent interest in their offspring's welfare (Daly & Wilson, 1978).

As a small part of a larger social organization, a family is influenced and facilitated by the opportunities and constraints of the social context of its existence (Bronfenbrenner, 1977; Myers, 1982; Wicker, 1979; Wilson, 1986). In order to insure its own continued existence, a family adapts and commits available family resources to normal and nonnormal transitional and crisis events (Barbarin, 1983; Carter & McGoldrick, 1988; Duvall, 1971; Wilson, 1989). Family resources involve the ability of family members to contribute tangible help such as material support, income, childcare and household maintenance, and nontangible aid such as expressive interaction, emotional support, instruction, and social training and regulation. Marriage, fecundity, and death exemplify normal familial events, whereas hospitalization and unemployment are nonnormal events (Carter & McGoldrick, 1980; Duvall, 1971). In a family, then, stress is mitigated by defining and addressing stressful situations as group as well as individual concerns (Barbarin, 1983).

Although child maltreatment in the context of the family has existed universally throughout human history, it is antithetical to basic familial beliefs, values, and ideals. Beyond sentimental aversions to the emotional and physical injury of children, when children are maltreated, their development of self-esteem and social competence, and their capacity for intimacy and healthy interpersonal relationships, are jeopardized (Garbarino, Guttman, & Seeley, 1986; Aber, Allen, Carlson, & Cicchetti, 1989). The destruction of the child's spirit is magnified through a reduced ability to participate as part of the family, and thus, as part of the larger social world. Energy normally given to exploration and mastery is diverted into self-protection and self-nurturance.

Child maltreatment is a broad concept covering all forms of abuse and neglect, including physical, emotional, and/or sexual abuse, and physical and/or emotional neglect. Whereas child maltreatment is defined either as an act of commission resulting in harm to a child, or as an act of omission resulting in the neglect of the child's well-being (Giovannoni, 1971), this dichotomy can obscure the multifaceted nature of child maltreatment. For example, psychological maltreatment can be described in ways which either link the aversive behaviors to a withdrawal of attention or to an increase in verbal assault (Garbarino et al., 1986). In addition to definitional issues, Cicchetti and Rizley (1981) contend that understanding child maltreatment is further complicated by a wide range of etiologies and variations in response to treatment interventions among maltreating families. According to Cicchetti and Rizley (1981), "child maltreatment is a heterogeneous problem which is influenced by difficulties in defining and categorizing its expressions, in identifying its etiologies, and in predicting its responses to interventions" (p. 35).

Moreover, the incidence of child maltreatment is particularly affected by whether a legal, clinical, or research orientation is taken (Aber & Zigler, 1981; Barnett, Manly, & Cicchetti, this volume). Whereas these different approaches do overlap sometimes, often the different approaches lead to differences in maltreatment incidence. The legal approach, which focuses on provable conditions, is concerned with determining responsibility for maltreatment, while the clinical approach, which is concerned with observable consequences, focuses on assessment for treatment purposes. Additionally, the research approach, which broadly is focused on emotional as well as physical harm, prevention, and context, is concerned with accuracy and consistency in incident reports (Aber & Zigler, 1981; MacPhee & Rattenborg, 1991). Cicchetti and Barnett (1991) argued that better definitions of child maltreatment are needed in order to progress in understanding the causes, consequences, and treatment of child maltreatment. Definitions of child maltreatment that are specifiable in terms of case comparability, reliable incident accountability, and taxonomic delineation are necessary not only for increased empirical understanding but also for improved clinical and legal applications (Besharov, 1981).

Indeed, MacPhee and Rattenborg (1991) found that the inconsistent and ambiguous definitions were unrelated to abuse rates. Moreover they also revealed that the various aspects of statutory definitions were not related to reported or substantiated rates of child abuse, although some indices of social well-being were. MacPhee and Rattenborg were interested in determining the influence of definitional inconsistencies on abuse rates. They noted that prevalence differences in the Russell (1983) and the Wyatt and Peters (1986) studies diminished when equivalent criteria were used. Like Aber and Zigler (1981),

MacPhee and Rattenborg (1991) argue for a decision-making model that is organized around functions served by a definition of maltreatment, that is, identifying, validating, and disposing of child maltreatment cases.

The confusion surrounding the definition of child maltreatment is exacerbated by the fact that child maltreatment does not have a standard set of predictors, any more than it has a standard definition. Although much is known about factors contributing to child maltreatment, demonstrated consistency in specific patterns of child and parent characteristics, and/or societal and environmental stressors, does not exist or has not been corroborated by research (Pianta, 1984). Instead, a wide variety of disparate and sometimes contradictory traits and situations have been shown to form various constellations of factors that place the family at risk for child maltreatment. Cicchetti and his colleagues (1989; Cicchetti, Carlson, Braunwald, & Aber, 1987; Cicchetti & Manly, 1990; Cicchetti & Rizley, 1981) have been especially critical of child maltreatment research, citing a plethora of studies dependent upon retrospective analyses, case studies, and clinical observations. All of these methods have theoretical and methodological flaws that make their findings suspect. Because such studies have largely been theoretically inadequate, definitionally imprecise and confounded, and methodologically imperfect, erroneous conclusions have typically resulted. Cicchetti and his associates have called for carefully matched comparison-group studies as a partial solution to this problem.

A universal definition of child maltreatment does not eschew the issue of cultural relativity. The clarification of what does and does not constitute maltreatment is highly dependent upon the cultural context in which the behavior occurs (Garbarino & Ebata, 1983; Gelles, 1987). Even if universal markers could be found for each type of maltreatment, the discrepant social and symbolic significance of maltreatment within different cultures would not diminish, because behaviors have diverse meanings and consequences in different cultural contexts (Alfaro, 1981; Fabrega, 1989; Sternberg, this volume). Cultural differences in socialization and childrearing techniques, especially nurturance and discipline practices, influence the subsequent determination of child maltreatment (Berelson & Steiner, 1984; Garbarino & Ebata, 1983; Gelles, 1987). The importance of understanding child maltreatment from a cultural context is demonstrated by the overrepresentation of reported cases of maltreatment among the less educated, the poor, and ethnic minorities (Alfaro, 1981; Gil, 1970). On the other hand, White American children are underrepresented in the reported cases of maltreatment (Altemeier, O'Connor, Sherrod, Tucker, & Vietze, 1986; American Humane Association, 1987). Given the fact that incidence reports are grossly confounded by social class (Garbarino & Ebata, 1983), such disproportionate prevalence leads to the conclusion that those in social and economic power are judging those who are relatively powerless (Ogbu, 1981; M. N. Wilson, 1987). Failure to assess cultural context can lead to inadequate methods of prevention and treatment, unreliable incidence reports, and institutional racism (Korbin, 1979; Ogbu, 1981; Wilkinson, 1987). In order to reduce the incidence of child maltreatment, then, it is necessary to understand both the universal and culturally specific factors (Garbarino & Ebata, 1983).

Korbin (1987a) suggests that cross-cultural comparisons can be made, not between divergent childcare practices, but between those behavioral occurrences that fall outside the realm of what is considered acceptable behavior within each culture. Korbin notes that different cultures diverge from each other with respect to certain aspects of childrearing and parental discipline. In addition, she suggests that similar childrearing practices that arise between different cultures are the results of convergent evolution; as such, the antecedents and consequences for these similar practices may differ markedly between those societies. Also, the parents' volitional and motivational intent behind a given behavior must be considered before an assessment of child maltreatment can be made. Finally, Korbin's model suggests that the children's perceptions of parental discipline must be taken into account, and that the interactions that take place between the child's developmental stages with his or her cultural, social, and economic environment must also be recognized (Korbin, 1979). Korbin's approach is consistent with that of others (Dubanoski, 1981; Dubanoski & Snyder, 1980; Giovannoni & Becerra, 1979; Perlmunn, 1988; White, Benedict, Wulff, & Kelley, 1987; Zuravin & Starr, 1991) who have researched ethnicity and child maltreatment.

The relationship between the child and the parent is a critical factor in the healthy development of the child. In addition to the general requirement of availability and functional interactions, the parenting role involves specific activities and behaviors typically subsumed under the general role of caring for and nurturing the child. The most frequent childrearing activities in which parents engage are: *nurturance*, which refers to parental support, affection, and/or encouragement; *demand*, which refers to parental action involving supporting achievement-oriented behavior or skill acquisition; *control*, which refers to parental action involving reinforcing, setting, and enforcing limits on socially appropriate behavior; and *punishment*, which refers to parental punitive actions such as the withdrawal of affection and/or privileges (Baumrind, 1971, 1972; Becker, 1964; Belsky, Robins, & Gamble, 1984; Emmerich, 1977; Maccoby, 1980; Maccoby & Jacklin, 1980). Corporal and physical punishments can either be considered one of the important aspects of appropriate parenting behaviors or, when the degree of severity and the intent to inflict physical injury surpasses social standards, a critical marker of child and family abuse (Lassiter, 1987; Steinmetz, 1987). As the most frequent form of family violence, child maltreatment continues to require serious definitional efforts (Cicchetti, 1991; Gelles, 1978; Giovannoni, & Becerra, 1979; Light, 1973).

However, the issues of definitional inconsistencies are exaggerated by efforts that strive to implement universal interventions for child maltreatment (Cicchetti, 1989; Steinmetz, 1987). According to Wright and Wright (1976), indicators of social class, ethnicity, and geographic location account for almost equivalent amounts of variance in child maltreatment. Moreover, recent research has highlighted the difficulty of definition and identified important demographic, epidemiologic, and dynamic factors related to child maltreatment (Crnic, Greenberg, Ragonzin, Robinson, & Basham, 1983; Culp, Richardson, & Heide, 1987; Giovannoni & Becerra, 1979; White et al., 1987).

The present chapter is limited to understanding child maltreatment in the African-American community and suggesting the implications of that understanding for public policy. It is important to discuss first the context of African-American family life, including those socioeconomic, familial, and racial factors that make the African-American family vulnerable to child maltreatment, and only then to attempt to understand the incidence and forms of child maltreatment in that community, which may inform and determine policy implications.

Although there has been an ever-increasing volume of research, numerous articles, and at least two entire journals committed to the subject of child maltreatment in the United States, investigations into the particular dimensions of child maltreatment have heretofore largely been confined to white American children and families. Research on child maltreatment in the African-American community is sparse, and its conclusions contradictory and often equivocal. In some cases, the demographics have not been stated or appropriately analyzed.

THE AFRICAN-AMERICAN FAMILY AND FACTORS OF CHILD MALTREATMENT

The African-American family differs from the white American family in a number of ways. Whereas the white American family structure historically has implied opposite-sex parents living with their children in one household, the African-American family structure is more often extended, and not limited to membership involving nuclear family, one household, or blood relatives. If we take as the critical ingredients of family life the availability, proximity, frequency and functionality of kin contact, then the African-American family reflects the best manifestation of a traditional extended, cooperative, and collective familial structure. Whereas the white American family model emphasizes the nuclear structure and composition, the structure and composition of the African American family can vary according to the presence or absence of persons who are parents, children, and/or other adult or child family members (Hill & Schackleford, 1972; Martin & Martin, 1978; Reid, 1982; Soldo & Lauriat, 1976; Wilson, 1986). Thus, the African American family represents significant associations and influences that extend beyond mother, father, and children to include parental, sibling, and cousin links of mates and offspring (Foster, 1983; Shimkin, Shimkin, & Frate, 1978; Stack, 1974; Tinsley & Parke, 1984).

Put another way, if we are to understand the African-American family in a relevant cultural context, then we must expect a sundry assortment of familial living arrangements that goes beyond marriage, parentage, and children to include other adult and child shared-resident situations. For example, Billingsley (1968) described 27 different combinations of family composition and structure, while Kellam and his associates (Kellam, Ensminger, & Turner, 1982) found 81 different organizations of extended households. With an estimated incidence of extended families in the African-American community ranging between 25% (Tienda & Angel, 1982) and 53% (Langston, 1980), the extended family is a significant proportion of the African American community.

From an African-American child's perspective, there is nearly an equal likelihood that the child will live in a single-parent family (41% of African-American children) as in a dual-parent family (40% of African-American children). The remaining percentage of African-American children live with a parent and another relative (19% of African-American children; U.S. Bureau of the Census, 1991). Moreover, the most common composition of extended households involves a single-parent family structure that includes a mother and her children, and the single mother's mother (Reid, 1982; Soldo & Lauriat, 1976; Sweet, 1977). The presence of other adult family members implies that each family role can serve as a potential resource to the child.

Single mothers, including those who are divorced, separated, widowed or never married, account for 94% of African-American single parents (Reid, 1982). When comparing single mothers on age, number of children, and income, mothers who are older, have larger numbers of children, higher incomes, or are migrant workers are more likely to live as a single parent (Reid, 1983; Sweet, 1977). On the other hand, a younger, never-married mother is less likely to live as an only adult in a household and more likely to share residence with her mother (Reid, 1982; Soldo & Lauriat, 1976; Sweet, 1977). The age of the child and the educational level of the mother also affect the nature of the single mother's living arrangements. Mothers with younger children and less education are less likely to live as an only adult in a household (Sweet, 1977). Therefore, a single-parent family unit involving a young mother of limited education having a few children and low income will likely share a residence with extended family members (Beck & Beck, 1984, 1989; Reid, 1982; Soldo & Lauriat, 1976; Sweet, 1977).

As Langston (1980) reported, 85% of her African-American elderly sample shared their residence with someone who was either a spouse, an adult child, or a grandchild. Nationally, research indicates that 51% of the African-American elderly population shares a residence with a relative, as compared to 40% of the white American elderly population (Beck & Beck, 1984, 1989; Sweet, 1977). In fact, about 10% of African-American children below the age of 18 live with their grandparents (Beck & Beck, 1984, 1989). Three times as many African-American children under age 18 live with a grandparent as white American children, while the proportion of African-American and white American young adults living with parents is about equal (Soldo & Lauriat, 1976).

This structure is not only attitudinal and value-driven, but also a response to economic and social necessity. Wilson (1986, 1989) asserts that the preponderance of nonnormal stresses affecting African Americans is a primary reason for the formation of extended family support networks. A common stressful situation in the African-American community is the lack of adequate adult resources in single-parent family units. The extended family formation occurs when one family unit absorbs another, thus pooling and expanding limited resources and buying power. Once formed, the extended family tends to persist throughout the life span of its members. In general, most African Americans report that the perceived reciprocal obligations that exist in the kin network are more often affectional than task assistance, and when task assistance, more indirect that direct (Slaughter & Dilworth-Anderson, 1988; Tinsley & Parke, 1984; Wilson, 1989).

Overall, these structural and living arrangement percentages suggest several things about African-American families. First, African-American children are more likely than white American children to be living in a single-parent household or with grandparents. Second, elderly African Americans are more likely to be living with grandchildren than are their white American counterparts. Moreover, African-American elderly persons are more likely to share a residence with an unrelated person than are white American elderly persons. Finally, young, low income, and single mothers are more likely to be sharing residence with other family members than are older middle-income single mothers. The implication is clear: each family role can serve as a potential resource to the African-American child.

Like any family organization, the African-American family promotes the welfare of dependent family members in dealing with normal and nonnormal life events, and provides leadership by giving its members a sense of security, identity and direction (Martin & Martin, 1978). In the African-American family this takes on added meaning because of the large percentage of African-American children living in single-parent homes. African-American mothers who are rearing children alone exist within an extended family context (Ladner, 1972; Martin & Martin, 1978; McAdoo, 1980; Stack, 1974; Wilson, 1984). Detrimental effects of rearing children in single-parent homes are reportedly minimized by the support from the extended family, which offsets the absence of the father (Heiss, 1977; Peters & deFord, 1978; Rubin, 1979; Savage, Adair, & Friedman, 1978).

The African-American extended family is characterized by a familial interaction network involving relatives, friends, and neighbors who provide emotional and economic support (Cazenave & Straus, 1979; Martin & Martin, 1978; McAdoo, 1977a, b; Slaughter & Dilworth-Anderson, 1988). This system serves as a buffer against negative ecological forces and provides a pattern of response for coping with external stress. This "kin-help survival insurance policy" (McAdoo, 1977b) is an alternative structure of support that supplements the necessities of nuclear family units and protects the integrity of the African-

American family (Guttman, 1976; Martin & Martin, 1978; McAdoo, 1977b; Stack, 1974). For example, nurturance, material assistance, and mutual aid are provided by a network of kin and friends to dependent loved ones (Martin & Martin, 1978).

Consistent findings in the research on social networks are the frequent socializing among African-American family members (Aoyagi, 1978; Hale, 1982; McLanahan, Wedemeyer, & Adelberg, 1981), a high degree of residential propensity among related households (Aschenbrenner, 1978; Martin & Martin, 1978; Stack, 1974; Wilson, 1984), and emphasis on participation in family occasions, especially funerals, holiday celebrations, and birthdays (Aschenbrenner, 1978; Martin & Martin, 1978; McAdoo, 1978; Stack, 1974). For example, African-American women often list relatives as friendship contacts (Hale, 1982; Martin & Martin, 1978; Stack, 1974). Moreover, the nature of familial interactional influence expands the extended family relationship beyond the family into the greater African-American community (Aschenbrenner, 1978). Such a system of familial support and community integration could serve as a protective factor against the occurrence of child maltreatment.

Giving advice and guidance to adults occurs frequently in African-American families (Martin & Martin, 1978; McAdoo, 1977b; Stack, 1974). Family members often turn to their elders for counsel on job choices, major purchases, and decisions concerning children (Martin & Martin, 1978; McAdoo, 1978; Stack, 1974). This represents a significant difference from the modal way decisions are made in white American families. That is, the African-American adult will involve both conjugal and extended family sources, while the white American adult will rely heavily on conjugal sources (Landry & Jendrek, 1978).

Whereas accumulated evidence suggests that one-parent families are more involved in extended family networks than are two-parent families, the presence of additional adults in one-parent families affects childrearing activity by: (a) providing alternative sources of intimacy and emotional support to the mother and children, (b) providing assistance in childrearing to the mother, and (c) assisting the mother in setting and enforcing limits on children (Colletta, 1979, 1983, 1983; Field, Widmayer, Stringer, & Ignatoff, 1980; Kellam, Adams, Brown, & Ensminger, 1982; Wilson, 1984; Wilson, Tolson, Hinton, & Kiernan, 1990; Wilson et al., 1990). Behaviorally, this means that extended family members, particularly grandparents and adult siblings of single mothers, often serve critical support roles in caring for, nurturing, and rearing children.

In many instances, the presence of a second adult is essential to the family's well being. For instance, the perception of family climate and observed adult–child interactions are significantly affected by the number of adults present in the home (Tolson & Wilson, 1990; Wilson, 1989; Wilson & Tolson, 1986). In homes where there were two or more adults present, the respondents, including adults and children, perceived more of a familial moral-religious emphasis and less organization than did the respondents when there was only one adult present. In addition, mothers in single parent homes demonstrated a greater conversational preference toward interaction with others adults than interactions with children (Wilson & Tolson, 1986; Wilson, Hinton et al., 1990).

In general, most empirical research (Field et al., 1980; Stevens, 1984) on the extended family examines the effect of a grandmother's presence on childrearing. The presence of a responsive, sensitive grandmother seems to buffer the infant against the deleterious influence of an insensitive mother (Crockenberg, 1981). For example, 12-month-old infants who were first classified as avoidant and anxiously attached and 6 months later as securely attached were more likely to be observed living in three-generational households composed of their mothers, grandmothers, and mothers' siblings (Egeland, Jacobvitz, & Papatola, 1987). Other researchers have suggested that there are indirect as well as direct effects of grandmother's presence for children of single mothers (Field et al., 1980; Martin & Martin, 1978; McAdoo, 1978). Dornbush and his colleagues (1985) found that, when grandmothers were present in one-parent families, mothers exercised more parental control, and adolescents had less autonomy in family decision making and participated in fewer deviant activities, than in family situations involving one-adult households.

In summary, it appears that childrearing in the African-American community is most often and best accomplished as a cooperative venture involving adequate adult resources. Moreover, research evidence suggests that adequate adult resources involve the availability of at least two adults.

Familial Instability

Family changes and disruptions increase the risk of child maltreatment both directly and indirectly. They expose the child to increased levels of family tension and stress, parental and/or familial conflict, or diminished parental efficacy and attention in the caregiving role (Emery, 1982). African-American families experience more changes and disruptions than do white American or other ethnic minority groups. For example, 62% of African-American parents are divorced, separated, widowed, or never married; 55% of African-American births are to single mothers; and 10% of African-American children under 18 years live with a nonparent relative (Glick, 1976, 1981; Reid, 1982; Sweet, 1977; U.S. Bureau of the Census, 1991). Several researchers (Furstenberg, 1980; Slesinger, 1980; Smith, 1980; Stack, 1974) have indicated that African-American low-income, extended, and one-parent families are more likely to make frequent changes in their living arrangements than their white American counterparts. For example, lives of African-American adolescent mothers (Furstenberg, 1980; Furstenberg, Brooks-Gunn, & Morgan, 1987; Furstenberg & Crawford, 1978) and single-adult mothers (Slesinger, 1980; Smith, 1980; Stack, 1974) include frequent moves among situations involving independent living, cohabitation, and/or marital living arrangements, and their families of origin. Some data suggest that maltreating parents move frequently, thus creating residential instability that affects the ability to maintain familial ties (Martin & Martin, 1978) and establish social ties (Gil, 1970; Seagull, 1987). Moreover, Bolton and MacEachron (1986) have observed that recently divorced parents are vulnerable to maltreating their children because they report a sense of being alone, out of control, and overwhelmed by their changed status in life. Their research suggests that parent–child interaction in maltreating families is marked with less parental responsiveness to the child, higher levels of disapproval and reduced amounts of verbal interaction. Bolton and MacEachron indicate that as the level of social and familial support to aid in coping with stresses decreases, the risk of parent–child relational failures increases.

Socioeconomic factors. Poverty is often considered a major cause of chronic stress (Gephart & Pearson, 1988). Belle, Longfellow, and Makosky (1982), for example, found that African American single mothers who experienced high frequencies of nonnormal changes and events in their lives more often blamed their depressions on low income and chronic money problems than on any other stressful nonnormal events. The chronic effects of low income present major difficulties for African American families. Although most are not poor, a significant proportion of African American families has always lived below poverty levels (Duncan, 1968; Reid, 1982). In 1990, the average rate of poverty for African-American families was 32%, a figure three time higher than the proportion of white American families living below poverty levels (U.S. Bureau of Census, 1991). Among one-parent families, poverty is particularly evident: 61.9% of single-parent African-American families, and 34% of single-parent white American families, were classified as poor.

Poor socioeconomic factors adversely affect individual well-being and family functioning, since women who rear children with inadequate incomes are vulnerable to impairment in their parenting role (Belle, Longfellow, & Makosky, 1982; Parcoe & Eurp, 1984; Pearlin & Johnson, 1977). In particular, it has been shown repeatedly that the prevalence and severity of child maltreatment is strongly associated with poverty, and the related factors of unemployment, overcrowded housing, and money worries (Hampton & Gelles, 1991; Spearly & Lauderdale, 1982; Steinberg, Catalano, & Dooley, 1981; Wortman, 1981). These socioeconomic factors provide a chronically stressful context within which maltreatment is potentially more likely to occur. Pelton (1978, 1981) has argued that this strong association is not an artifact of reporting bias but the real result of the many stresses of poverty. In contrast, Newberger and his colleagues (1983; Daniel, Hampton, & E. Newberger, 1983) assert that belonging to a low SES group itself puts a family at risk of being reported to protective services. In addition, in the case of child neglect, Pelton (1978) found that mothers from the lower SES level more often have little choice when it comes to leaving their children unattended. These mothers cannot easily obtain or afford childcare each time they must leave their homes on errands or other necessary business (Daniel, Hampton, & E. Newberger, 1987; Dubowitz, Hampton, Bithony, & Newberger,

1987). Thus, the stress of poverty is compounded by lack of childcare options, and potentially by a reporting bias on the part of protective service workers.

Garbarino and Sherman (1980a,b) proposed that families living in communities with high maltreatment rates must compete for scarce sources of social support. Families in these areas used whatever social resources were available in their communities less frequently than did families in the low-risk communities. Moreover, families in these high-risk areas rated their neighborhoods more unfavorably and exhibited more hostility towards their neighbors, thus lessening the likelihood of extrafamilial support. In contrast, families in low-risk areas rated their communities more positively and exhibited more affiliative attitudes and behaviors towards their neighbors.

Because African Americans are exposed to more stress factors than any other demographic group in the United States (Fuchs, 1990; Hacker, 1991; van den Berghe, 1987), stress factors involving socioeconomic and demographic factors are intimately tied to the etiology of child maltreatment in African American families (McAdoo, 1988). As Daniel and her associates (1983) noted, at-risk families tend to suffer from the accompanying consequences of low-SES status: residential transiency, poverty, unemployment, isolation, and other stressful living conditions. Moreover, these families are often forced to cope with stress without the mitigating effects of supportive social networks found in higher income neighborhoods (Cazenave & Straus, 1979). In addition, Garmezy, Masten, and Tellegen (1984) noted the importance of critical life events that may spark abusive or neglectful behavior. For example, potentially exacerbating factors include the presence of an incapacitated member among families from the low-SES level that may tax already limited familial coping resources.

Stress by itself, however, cannot account for why some parents develop abusive behavior while other parents do not. Moreover, the mere presence of stress does not explain why relatively well-off families develop maltreatment-related syndromes while families from the low SES undergoing greater adversity manage to survive without resorting to child abuse or neglect (Sattin & Miller, 1971; Stewart, Senger, Kallen, & Scheurer, 1987). Garbarino, Sebes, and Schellenbach (1984) have proposed that each family has its particular level of tolerance to environmental stress; the level of tolerance varies from family to family according to its situation and coping resources. Thus, families that exhibit a high level of tolerance will be better able to cope with more environmental stressors than will a family that possesses only a low level of tolerance. Garbarino and his collaborators speculate on the basis of this model that, at the outset of maltreatment, maltreating parents either have low thresholds of tolerance, or a normal or even higher-than-average level of tolerance which they nevertheless quickly exceed.

The effect of racial status on child maltreatment. In many aspects of family life, racial status has been a significant demographic predictor. For instance, race-specific effects have been determined at every socioeconomic level

(Cutright, 1971; Lieberson, 1980; Lieberson & Carter, 1979). African-American families consistently have had a lower income relative to white Americans (Cutright, 1971; Duncan, 1968; Lieberson, 1980; Lieberson & Carter, 1979; Reid, 1982). The consumable income (family income per family member) of African-American working and middle-SES level families has typically been affected by the greater likelihood of additional child and adult household members (Cutright, 1971; Glick & Norton, 1979; Reid, 1982). Moreover, it appears that the ability of African-American children of middle-class parents to maintain a comparable socioeconomic level as adults is less than that of their white American counterparts (Duncan, 1968; Lieberson, 19880; Lieberson & Carter, 1979; McAdoo, 1978; Reid, 1982).

With regard to child maltreatment, however, ethnic comparisons reveal that race does not exert a consistent demographic effect. For example, the 1980 *National Study of the Incidence and Severity of Child Abuse and Neglect* (NIS-1; U.S. Department of Health and Human Services, 1981), which was repeated in 1986 and referred to as NIS-2 (U.S. Department of Health and Human Services, 1988), conservatively estimated the annual incidence of founded child maltreatment cases to involve about 1.2 million children. African-American children, who compose 15% of the national population, were underrepresented in all categories of maltreatment except educational neglect. When categories of maltreatment were summed into one, the incidence for African-American children was about the same as the general population (16%). Thus, racial differences were uncovered in the types, although not incidence, of child maltreatment. NIS-1 concluded that, since African-American children are overrepresented in the low-income groups, and incidence of various types of maltreatment ranged from two to three times more prevalent in the low-income (under $7,000 annual income) group, the incidence rates for African-American children must be lower than those for white American children. These findings are in contrast to those of other researchers, and certainly to expectations, considering the various stresses impinging upon the families.

In contrast to the NIS-1 report, NIS-2, a 6-year replication, found no racial differences in any of the areas of child maltreatment. Although income emerged again as a powerful correlate, with families whose annual income was under $15,000 being five times more likely to have a maltreated child than families whose annual income was over $15,000, when income and other demographic variables were controlled, no racial or ethnic differences were found. Thus, two of the broadest and best-known studies on the incidence of child maltreatment emerged with contradictory findings about racial differences. It is unlikely that African-American families maltreated their children more frequently in 1986 than six years earlier, yet one reasonable explanation for these discrepancies has been offered by Cicchetti and Barnett (1991). They suggest that the definitional emphasis was changed between the first and second NIS reports. By shifting from the legal documentation of maltreatment to a sociological criteria, the counted incidence of maltreatment was dramatically altered.

Although racial status has not proven to be a consistent main effect in the national studies of child maltreatment, other regional studies have uncovered interesting race-specific differences in particular types of maltreatment.

In Georgia, Jason and Andereck (1983) observed that the overall rates of fatal child abuse were higher for African-American children compared with white American children. However, when considering economic and geographic statuses, the highest fatal child abuse rates were found in poor, rural, white American families and, next, in poor, urban, African-American families. Adolescent childbearing and socioeconomic stress appeared to be the most common links in fatal child abuse cases (Jason & Andereck, 1983; Weisheit, 1986).

Lindholm and Willey (1986) examined ethnic differences (i.e., African American, Hispanic, and White American) among 4,132 physical and sexual abuse cases reported to the Los Angeles County Sheriff's Department. They found that the most significant differences were between African American and non-African American groups. Specifically, African-American families were overreported compared to non-African-American families. Moreover, there were sex differences in maltreated children, with girls and boys equally likely to be maltreated in African-American families and girls more likely than boys in non-African-American families. In addition, African-American abusers inflicted different types of physical abuse; African-American children were less likely to be sexually abused than non-African-American children. Finally, the types of sexual abuse perpetrated against African-American children differed from those against non-African-American children.

Pierce and Pierce (1984) compared a sample of 56 African-American victims of child sexual abuse to 149 white American victims of substantiated child sexual abuse garnered from 4 years of two Illinois counties' Child Abuse Hotline case records. In comparison to white American abuse victims, African-American victims were younger, had younger parents, were less often abused by their biological fathers, were less likely to be removed from their homes, had fewer previous incidents, were more often turned over to protective services, were reported more quickly, and were less fearful of reporting the abuse and more frequently believed by their mothers when they did disclose abuse.

Wyatt (1985) provided partial support of Pierce and Pierce's (1984) findings in a retrospective analysis of childhood (before age 18) sexual abuse of 126 African-American and 122 white American women between the ages of 18 and 36. Wyatt's definition of sexual abuse included noncontact abuse, that is, exposure, solicitations for sex, and unwanted kissing and fondling. This definition is broad and varies from definitions used by other researchers that are often either undefined in the maltreating incidents or slightly different themselves, thus hampering metaanalytic techniques (Wyatt, 1988). Whereas African-American women related slightly less sexual abuse than white American women, the African-American women reported a higher overall prevalence rate than has been indicated in other studies. Thus, some of Wyatt's data accords with other research, while some is in conflict.

Among women who suffered contact abuse, Wyatt found that African-American women tended to be maltreated more often between the ages of 9 and 12, while white American women reported more abuse between the ages of 6 and 8. If her sample findings are accurate and generalize to the population, the fact that, in Wyatt's sample, African-American women tended to be maltreated by African-American men and white American women by white American men, could indicate differences in perpetrator motivation, as well as childrearing differences. Perhaps African-American girls are supervised more closely until a later age than are white American girls and, therefore, do not provide as many opportunities for abuse until later.

Several researchers have noted that the profile of the maltreating parent is consistent on certain demographic and socioeconomic correlates (Bloom, White, & Asher, 1979; Bolton, 1978; Bolton & Laner, 1986; Brandewein, Brown, & Fox, 1974; Finkelhor & Baron, 1986). Lauderdale, Valiunas, and Anderson (1980) looked for a relationship between ethnicity and the number of child maltreatment cases in Texas. They found that ethnicity predicted maltreatment rates, with African Americans accounting for the majority of all maltreatment cases, followed by Mexican Americans. The lowest frequency of all maltreatment cases was found among white Americans. When physical abuse within each group was analyzed, however, an interesting trend surfaced: the lowest frequencies of physical abuse were found among African-American families, followed by Mexican Americans, while white Americans exhibited the highest abuse frequencies. The low abuse rates found among the African-American families as opposed to white American families suggest the involvement of definitional issues. However, given the degree to which socioeconomic factors confounded the reporting of child maltreatment, Garbarino and Ebata (1983) have noted that, where ethnic groups are socioeconomically marginalized, SES-relevant factors will confound child maltreatment assessments. Thus, what could be the result of environmental stressors associated with a low socioeconomic status will undoubtedly be confounded with race and ethnicity (Bolton & Mac-Eachron, 1986; Garbarino & Ebata, 1983; Lauderdale et al., 1980).

Other researchers who controlled for SES found that different ethnic groups did not significantly differ in child maltreatment rates (Hampton, 1987a,b; Lassiter, 1987). Daniel and her associates (1983) found in their comparative study of accident and child abuse rates among African-American and white American families that the two ethnic groups did not differ significantly on these two measures once SES was controlled. Moreover, research findings consistently reveal that single parenthood is associated with at-risk status for later development of abusive or neglectful behavior (Bloom et al., 1979; Bolton, 1978; Bolton & MacEachron, 1986; Brandwein et al., 1974; Burgess, Anderson, Schellenbach & Couger, 1981; Daniel et al., 1983; Hetherington, 1979; Hetherington, Cox, & Cox, 1977; Longfellow, 1979). Due to these findings, most researchers conclude that child maltreatment can be traced to the environmental stressors commonly found among lower income families (Bronfenbrenner & Crouter, 1983; Garbarino & Sherman, 1980b; Steinberg et al., 1981; Stewart et al., 1987).

Additional evidence of the importance of SES and demographics comes from Garbarino and Crouter's (1978) analysis of the community context of child maltreatment. Their data indicated that racial, ethnic, and cultural differences could not account for the differences of maltreatment rates that were seen between economically depressed areas and economically stable regions. Moreover, Garbarino and Crouter found that female-headed households were particularly at risk for child maltreatment.

In spite of the overall preponderance of SES and demographically related variables in child maltreatment vis-á-vis racial, ethnic, or cultural considerations, genuine cross-cultural differences in child maltreatment patterns do occur (Dubanoski, 1981; Dubanoski & Snyder, 1980; Korbin, 1979, 1987a,b; Perlmunn, 1988). Interestingly, many of these differences are biased in favor of African Americans when compared to white Americans. For example, some surveys show that African-American children are less often victims of child maltreatment than are white American children.

Moreover, Garbarino and Ebata (1983) have found race–income interactions in reported child maltreatment cases: poor African-American families show lower frequencies of maltreatment compared to white American families from the same socioeconomic background. Garbarino and Ebata suggest that group-specific patterns of maltreatment may reflect different social and environmental conditions or group-specific differences in the perception and evaluation of child maltreatment (Garbarino & Ebata, 1983). In a similar fashion, Ogbu (1981, 1988) proposed that minority children be assessed and evaluated in a cultural–ecological framework in which goal and process of acquiring adult appropriate behaviors are considered within the context of the child's specific cultural background.

For examples, Jones (1979) examined the relationship between the personality patterns of Black Americans and Black Jamaicans to determine whether there was a similarity that might stem from a common cultural heritage. He found that the two national groups of Black people were more similar to each other than were Black Americans similar to white Americans. This study suggests that Black Americans ought to be considered as representative of another culture when being compared to other Americans. Other researchers have reached similar conclusions regarding the similarity of Black Americans to Black West Indians (Arnold, 1982; DeChesnay, 1986).

Effect of maltreatment on the child. In general, studies assessing the individual characteristics of child maltreatment victims have shown that they exhibit important qualitative differences from their nonabused peers on cognitive, behavioral, affective, and social measures (Browne & Saqi, 1988; Burgess et al., 1981; Burgess & Garbarino, 1983). Maltreated children lag behind their peers on intelligence tests. Moreover, maltreated children confidentially report scores lower than their peers' on self-esteem and other self-concept measures. These findings hold true across racial and ethnic groups once confounding factors such as SES and demographics are held constant (Martin & Walters, 1982; Toth & Cicchetti, this volume).

However, there is a dearth of studies that have examined the effects of maltreatment on African-American children. The existing information comes from studies on white American families or from studies that did not include breakdowns of participants' ethnic or racial background. For example, we know that the sequelae of maltreatment include insecure attachment relationships (Carlson, Cicchetti, Barnett, & Braunwald, 1989; Crittenden, 1988; a,b; Schneider-Rosen, Braunwald, Carlson, & Cicchetti, 1985; Toth & Cicchetti, this volume), communicative problems (Coster, Gersten, Beeghly, & Cicchetti, 1989), poor-quality peer relations (Cicchetti, Toth, Hennessy, this volume; Kaufman & Cicchetti, 1989; Toth & Cicchetti, this volume), and behavior problems and psychopathology (Kasdin, Moser, Colbus, & Bell, 1985; Toth, Manly, & Cicchetti, 1992). Cicchetti and Barnett (1991) estimate that the effects of child maltreatment may last a lifetime.

Cicchetti and Rizley (1981) suggest that maltreatment also leads to more subtle effects on the child's socioemotional development. The difficulties inherent in identifying such developmental effects of maltreatment are due to the heterogeneous problems in labeling maltreatment, its etiology, and its treatment outcomes. One consistent sequelae for adult victims of child maltreatment are reports of personality and interpersonal difficulties including low self-esteem, negativity, loneliness and isolation, and frequent life stresses (Altemeier et al., 1986; Dean, Malik, Richards, & Stringer, 1986; Russell, Schurman, & Trocki, 1988; Wyatt, 1990). Olweus (1980) found that victims of abuse at home are often perpetrators at school. In addition, Sroufe and Fleeson's (1986) study of the consequences of insecure attachment showed that children who were maltreated at home played both the victim and perpetrator in their peer relations. Securely attached children were not found in either of these (victim or perpetrator) roles.

Slade and his associates (Slade, Steward, Morrison, & Abramowitz, 1984) found that physically abused children tend to attribute their failures to external causes more often than do their nonabused peers. On the other hand, abused children were just as likely as their nonabused peers to attribute their successes internally (Galambos & Dixon, 1984).

Nevertheless, these general patterns across ethnic groups should not be used to obscure the distinctions that exist among the different ethnic groups. Although researchers have not addressed those distinctions, variations may arise between groups. The evidence still shows that the processes by which child maltreatment arises is similar across groups, particularly with regard to the effects of social class, demographic factors, and effects upon individual children.

Social isolation. Whereas the presence of poverty and family disruption increase the risk of child maltreatment, and those social ills have greater likelihood in the African-American community, poverty and familial disruption alone do not put African-American children at greater risk than other children (Bell, 1991; Giovannoni & Becerra, 1979; Lindholm & Willey, 1986; Pittman & Adams, 1988). In fact, research indicates that SES and familial disruption do not necessarily have the strong predictive and invariant relationship to child maltreatment that one might expect (Hampton, 1987a; Hampton, Gelles, & Harrop, 1991; Leventhal, 1988; Spanier, 1989; Starr, 1988; Steinberg et al., 1981). The critical presence of social isolation, in combination with low income and family disruption, considerably increases the risk of maltreatment in the African-American community (Alfaro, 1981; Dembo, Dertke, LaVoie, Borders, Washburn, & Schmeidler, 1987; Johnson & Sowers, 1985; Seagull, 1987; Spearly & Lauderdale, 1982; Taylor & Newberger, 1979; Wortman, 1981). Whether by individual design, cultural difference, or socioeconomic and racial segregation, social isolation appears to greatly exaggerate the overall effect of poverty and family disruption. For example, Trickett and Susman (1988) suggest that the subtle difference between maltreating and nonmaltreating families indicates an increasing disengagement from the larger community and family group in maltreating families. Daniel and her colleagues (1983) found that African-American mothers indicated more neglectful behaviors when they felt a lack of social support and felt that others did not have an interest in their problems. Their findings also indicate that maltreating families experience greater social isolation than their matched controls, more geographic mobility, a maternal child history of corporal punishment through adolescence, and current high levels of stress. Polansky and his colleagues (1985; Gaudin & Polansky, 1986) found an association among child maltreatment, single mothers' loneliness, and family social isolation. In separate reports involving robust correlations between social isolation and child maltreatment, Polansky and associates have indicated that the most lonesome people were urban, single, African-American mothers.

Zuravin and Starr (1991) found that African-American maltreating mothers compared with African-American control mothers reported more isolation during their growing-up years, negative perceptions of attachments to parents, more foster care placements, greater isolation from their immediate family members during adulthood, more worry about relationships with men, severe depression and greater likelihood of substance abuse. Giovannoni and Billingsley (1970) found that, although neglectful African-American mothers perceived a higher degree of emotional attachment to familial networks than do white American mothers, African-American mothers participated in mutual-aid and social support activities to a lower degree than did their African-American control group.

Polansky (1985) suggests that maltreating parents are less likely to reciprocate social gestures; their neighbors as a whole rated them as less reliable and less neighborly. Because reciprocity is important in social exchange, maltreating parents' particular interactions with the outside social structure may elicit negative reactions from their neighbors and hence perpetuate the social isolation and loneliness that these parents experience. Therefore, the isolation and loneliness of maltreating parents is due to the parents' maladaptive behaviors, which elicit a negative response from potential supportive members of their community (Polansky, Ammons, & Gaudin, 1985). The individual characteristics of the maltreating parent determine that parent's behavior which, in turn, shapes that parent's environment, including his or her social environment.

Gaudin and Polansky (1986) observed that nonmaltreating persons tend to distance themselves from maltreating families, perceiving deviations from existing community standards within the maltreating parents. Gaudin and Polansky found no significant differences between African Americans and white Americans on the likelihood of social distancing. Instead, they found that working-class subjects were less tolerant of maltreatment than were middle-class subjects.

The work of other researchers had revealed additional character differences between maltreating parents and nonmaltreating parents. In their study of physically abusive and neglectful mothers, Culp and associates (Culp, Culp, Soulis, & Letts, 1989; Culp et al., 1987) found that subjects' self-reports indicated significantly higher levels of depression than a comparison group of nonmaltreating mothers. In addition, abusive mothers scored lower on self-esteem measures than did mothers in the neglectful and normal comparison groups. Interestingly, Culp and his colleagues did not find significant differences between neglectful mothers and nonmaltreating mothers on reported self-esteem ratings.

Newberger and Cook (1983) propose that the parental awareness of maltreating adults is underdeveloped as opposed to nonmaltreating parents. Maltreating parents were less likely to consider the perspective and feelings of their children compared to their nonmaltreating counterparts. Moreover, maltreating parents showed less maturity in selecting the appropriate conflict resolution strategy when dealing with their children compared to nonmaltreating parents.

Interestingly, parental immaturity appeared to be associated with situations involving adolescent childbearing (Jason & Andereck, 1983; Miller, 1984; Schilling, Schinkle, Blythe, & Barth, 1982).

Understanding the effects of the social environment has special implications for the African-American family. This is especially true for female-headed households, which depend on extensive social networks in the form of the extended family structure to mitigate deleterious environmental effects (McAdoo, 1987). Moreover, these findings suggest strategies for facilitating the extended kin network in order to utilize it as an instrument in child maltreatment prevention.

Not surprisingly, the rates of child maltreatment are dependent upon the definition of child maltreatment. When broad definitions are applied, the rate of child maltreatment in the African-American community is greater than that of the white American community. However, using legal definitions, the rates in the

African-American community are lower than in other communities. Such fluctu-ations point to the serious definitional issues confronting those researchers who want to understand child maltreatment in the African-American community.

According to Pierce and Pierce (1991), child welfare agencies are forced to focus on identifying legal occurrences and risk assessment of child maltreatment rather than treating cases of child maltreatment. The priority activities are focused on assessing the safety of the child victim, identifying and isolating the offender, determining the degree to which the nonoffending caretaker is capable of protecting the victim, accurately diagnosing the effect of maltreatment, determining the type and level of necessary treatment, orchestrating collateral support systems, and initiating any indicated court actions. Thus, child welfare agencies must use current criteria and definitions that are universal. However, when working within the African-American community, it is important that child welfare agencies implement services that are flexible, open, warm, and empa-thic, and which, thereby, signal an attitude and atmosphere of tolerance and acceptance of cultural differences. Because of the tendency to normalize or minimize judgment of pathology (Adebimpe, 1981), cultural factors are often not considered by social welfare agencies (Bell, 1991).

Many have suggested that a cultural approach must sanction cultural knowl-edge in policy formulation and service delivery (see Sternberg, this volume). This approach can begin by using the family as the preferred point of interven-tion. Clients, who are viewed within the context of their own group, then would be referred to services that developed out of the specific needs of that population.

POLICY IMPLICATIONS FOR THE AFRICAN-AMERICAN COMMUNITY

Research Implications

Several important policy implications can be drawn from this brief review. First, the study of child maltreatment along racial lines in the United States has so far presented a conundrum. Those factors that research has shown generally to be correlates of child maltreatment exist in the African-American community. However, given the inconsistency of race as a main and interactive effect, poverty, familial disruption, and social isolation seem to differ little from the factors which place any child at risk. Despite, this, if any differences exist, child maltreatment rates in the African-American community are lower than or, at the worst, equal to the rates found in the larger white American community.

Research on these differences is contradictory. Much of the contradiction is influenced by definitional inconsistency. For example, survey research indicates that the level of violence in African-American homes is greater than twice the level of violence in white American homes. African-American families are more likely to report violence and neglectful behaviors. Parents are more likely to use corporal punishment techniques. Thus, inappropriate and severe punishment practices may make up most of the greater level of violence in African-American homes. Depending on the definition, African-American families will either be considered to be physically abusive or to use corporal punishment.

More research is needed to understand the cultural differences and variables of maltreatment which have an impact on child maltreatment in the African-American community. Given the difficult economic situation of the African-American community overall, it is important to state that one major effective intervention strategy may be the general improvement of African-Americans' participation in the economic opportunity structure.

The paucity of knowledge on child maltreatment and ethnicity is due, at least in part, to the lack of attention to the racial composition of the targeted population (Cicchetti, 1989). However, the importance of such knowledge can lead directly to clearer, more reliable, comparable taxonomies of child maltreatment. For example, research that found ethnic contextual differences more precisely discussed the nuances of those differences (Spearly & Lauderdale, 1983; Zuravin & Starr, 1991). However, as Zuravin and Starr (1991) outlined, a body of knowledge about the effects of ethnicity is extremely important. In order to consolidate existing results, research on ethnicity and child maltreatment must begin by replicating previous studies on ethnic differences. The design of such studies should follow the criteria outlined by several researchers (Billingsley & Giovannoni, 1972; Korbin, 1987a; Zuravin & Starr, 1991), which include separate analysis of ethnic groups, analysis of specific forms of child maltreatment, and specific forms of child maltreatment by ethnic groups. Zuravin and Starr (1991) recommend investigating the contexts of the specific group, comparing maltreating and nonmaltreating families within each group, and distinguishing the various categories of maltreatment for each group. Until we know the effect ethnicity has on child maltreatment rates, our understanding of the phenomenon will continue to be limited. Such a limitation will undoubtedly continue to place children at further risk for maltreatment.

In the absence of conclusive research, we speculate that the familial network offered by the African-American family provides critical insulating factors. Korbin (1987b) suggest three ways in which familial networks serve a protective function. First, they give assistance to parents with childcare tasks and responsibilities. Second, they offer options for the temporary and/or permanent redistribution of children. Third, networks afford a context for collective standards and therefore scrutiny and enforcement of childcare practices. Embeddedness in kin and community acts against the social isolation that has been linked with child maltreatment.

Recognizing the complex interactions between the individual and the environment is the logical conclusion of the search for an ecological theoretical paradigm of child maltreatment. While the environment may place burdens on the individual that put him or her at risk for psychopathology, the individual may at the same time possess hereditary or experiential buffers that mitigate the effects of environment. Garmezy and his associates (1984) have demonstrated the importance of personal resources such as intelligence and achievement orientation in helping at-risk children cope. Similarly, the transactional risk threshold model offered by Cicchetti and Rizley (1981) and by Garbarino (1984) emphasizes the interactive aspect of the etiology of child maltreatment and accounts for why some families do not maltreat even in the face of great economic and personal adversity.

Clearly, then, the phenomenon of child maltreatment in the African-American family is the result of complex interactions between the environment and the individual. Although African Americans as a whole face greater levels of environmental and social stress, as attested by their disproportionate representation in the lower socioeconomic strata (Hacker, 1991; McAdoo, 1987; Fuchs, 1990), the evidence clearly indicates that the African-American family is highly adaptive in the face of adversity, showing greater resistance to certain types of child maltreatment due to its coping strategies. It is important to add that adaptability is not a feature unique to one race, but rather a feature that all people share. With that in mind, understanding how the environment and the individual interact in ways that promote or detract from adaptability will promote our efforts in child maltreatment prevention (McMurty, 1985).

Poor African-American families experiencing disruption are more likely to form an extended family and to be involved in co-residential sharing as a way of reducing the effects of low income than are other income or ethnic groups (Allen, 1979; Angel & Tienda, 1982; Cutright, 1971; Hofferth, 1984). Single-parent families, who have the highest likelihood of living below poverty level, are more likely to be involved in extended familial support systems than are dual-parent families. Furthermore, African-American middle- and working-class families are more likely to contribute financially to extended family support networks (Allen, 1979; Hofferth, 1984) and to have reduced consumable income because of additional adult and child household members (Cutright, 1978; Glick & Norton, 1979; Reid, 1982) than are other ethnic middle- and working-class families.

Children from poor mother-only families will fare better when the family is nested within an active extended familial support network than when the family is isolated (Kellam et al., 1977). Indeed, when extended family members are present in the home, the incidence of maltreatment may abate (Crockenberg, 1981; Egeland & Sroufe, 1981; Egeland, 1979; Egeland et al., 1987; Field & Ignotoff, 1981). The limited research on the direct effects of the extended family on child development has typically examined the effect of grandmother's presence on childrearing and child outcome. The presence of a responsive, sensitive grandmother seems to buffer the infant against the deleterious influence of an insensitive mother (Crittenden, 1988a; Crockenberg, 1981), to facilitate a secure mother–child attachment (Browne & Saqi, 1988; Crockenberg, 1981; Egeland & Sroufe, 1981), and to maintain adult–child contact and infant stimulation in working-mother situations (Field & Ignotoff, 1981).

The African-American extended family seems to act as an alternative to institutional interventions. In considering informal protective factors against child maltreatment, it is important to keep in mind the cooperative, interactive and affiliative nature of the African-American family which can be incorporated into child maltreatment intervention strategies. Specific family interventions include improving and facilitation the family's emotional climate, increasing parental knowledge, and facilitation the family's embeddedness in the extended family and community. Recognizing that, for many African Americans, the extended family is the family, and including it in preventive or treatment approaches as such, will enhance the natural coping abilities of the family, rather than work against it.

Changes in socioeconomic and sociocultural situations have been linked with an increase in child maltreatment. Even modest environmental changes can alter child care patterns. Most poor African-American families are greatly affected by changing social and economic structures that have strained the resources and ability of the family system to respond. These structural changes have altered the nature of American poverty, exposing the African-American community to an increased risk of child maltreatment (Korbin, 1979). Specifically, an increasing rate of persistent and concentrated poverty threatens the protective aspect of the African-American community. Concentrated and persistent poverty is associated with increased joblessness, diminished economic, social, and community resources and support systems, and abject isolation of families and communities. Increased economic distress and joblessness greatly threatens the familial network and leads to dissatisfaction with familial and personal networks (Dressler, 1985; Linn, Husaini, Whitten-Stovall, & Broomes, 1989). In any large urban areas, African-American communities are increasingly becoming enclaves of extreme isolation from the economic center of the city and are densely concentrated with families who are persistently impoverished over generations (Kasarda, 1989; Wacquant & Wilson, 1989).

Changes in the nature of work and technological advances also have influenced the ability of and opportunity for African Americans to find work. Indices of these dramatic changes include an increasing number of mother-only and adolescent families who are persistently dependent on social welfare programs, as well as the joblessness of African-American men, who then lack the desirable qualities of a marriageable partner (W. J. Wilson, 1987). The proportion of mother-only families living in such neighborhoods has dramatically increased in the last 25 years (McLanahan & Garfinkel, 1989). About 34% of African-American mother-only families live in socially isolated areas, whereas only 5% of white American mother-only families live in these neighborhoods. This fact becomes even more alarming when we consider that 56% of African-American births are to single mothers and that 28% of all African-American births are to adolescent women.

It is in part the unemployment and economic instability of African-American men that causes a considerable amount of family stress and a significant source of family isolation (Boone, 1985). Moreover, although divorce, desertion, separation, and extramarital births reflect typical reasons for father/husband absence and single-parent families, joblessness, incarceration, and mortality are significant correlates that influence the high disparity in the male/female ratio in the African-American community. Darity and Myers (1983, 1984) determined that the joblessness rate was a more significant predictor of familial and marital stability and economic well-being in the African-American community than either the family or individual demographic characteristics. Low income and joblessness often lead to the African-American family's inability to contribute to the well-being of its children and an increased likelihood that they will further diminish their resources and deepen their isolation (W. J. Wilson, 1987).

Clinical implications. Finally, professionals in the area of child maltreatment should be wary of making decisions based on the predominating ethnocentric universal literature. Because child maltreatment is not a homogeneous issue, its treatment should not be universal in nature. Workers in the field must be trained to offer culture-sensitive services. The responsiveness of the maltreating parent to the intervener may depend on the intervener's ability to understand the client's particular circumstance. It is important that the values, practices, and perspectives of ethnically different people be understood before intervention is offered (Thorton & Carter, 1986). Because of race-specific associations of socioeconomic factors, attitudes toward children, and childrearing practices, it is important to include culturally relevant factors in an intervention strategy. Only by abandoning traditional ethnocentric views and replacing them with a cross-cultural perspective will understanding be fostered and prevention of further maltreatment made possible.

Given current mandates for universal intervention strategies and research design, it is no wonder that our knowledge of ethnicity and child maltreatment is wanting. However, this review makes clear that it is equally if not more important to design research and intervention efforts that targeted populations. For example, Zuravin and Starr (1991) suggested that interventions focused on the entire population of lower socioeconomic white American population but only focused on a subpopulation of the lower socioeconomic African-American population. Interventions are particularly necessary for adolescent mothers who have given birth to a first child prior to their 18th birthday, have a history of adverse developmental experiences, are poorly attached to their families, lack close personal relationships, and are not in frequent contact with their families. It would be crucial to design a special package of services for adolescent mothers to convene at the time of the birth of their first born, including psychosocial support, and family assistance. Child protection advocates must not only adequately assess the needs of families regardless of race but also must apply services with race in mind. Child protection advocates must be alert to known characteristics of mothers that are correlated with maltreatment.

It follows then that services must occur within a culturally competent and sensitive context in which there is healthy respect for, and commitment to, policies that enhance services to diverse clientele. This includes equal distribution of resources among staff and clients served and monitoring staffing patterns and behaviors. However, multisystems approaches to maltreatment are more often an ideal situation than a reality.

Billingsley and Giovannoni (1972) observed that child welfare programs were never conceived to serve African American children. Such practices are marked by services that do not address the special concerns of African American children, services that do not treat African American children equitably in the system, and efforts to the situations that are fragmented and abortive.

One of the main difficulties in implementing intervention programs for child maltreatment is that ethnic minority issues are considered in terms of group differences and main effects whereas treatment is focused on the individual according to principles of individual differences (Green, Power, Steinbook, & Gaines, 1981). Standard practices have generally been developed with majority populations in mind, yet implementation with minority populations is expected without modification of clinical protocols. For example, although African-American and white American parents are similar in their child-rearing goals, African-American socialization cannot be adequately understood in terms of a comparison to white american standards (Boykin & Toms, 1985; Boyd-Franklin, 1987). Cicchetti (1989) has observed that maltreating parents do not exhibit a single set of personality traits or reflect a unique diagnostic category. However, the ways in which interventions address the broader perspective within and outside the family unit are often ignored in traditional intervention models.

Accordingly, R. L. Jones (1988) has suggested that the assessment of African Americans must include culturally specific definitions of *child maltreatment* and must demonstrate established ecologically reliable and valid procedures, appropriately planned intervention strategies, and follow-up assessment and observational opportunities. Anderson (1988) has argued for assessment and intervention procedures that reflect social significance as defined by the relevant situational necessity, social appropriateness of the assessment and evaluation, and the social importance of the treatment effects. These procedures suggest that, although the basic goals of childrearing may be similar, the specific parenting behaviors may differ in critical ways. Thus, a universal approach to the issue of child maltreatment in the African-American community will likely fall short of its goals (Samuda, 1975).

The difficulty of implementing prevention and intervention programs is that the etiology of the maltreatment is such that individual screening and treatment is not currently possible. Useful predictors of maltreatment often defy conceptually sound categories (Crittenden, 1988a,b; Starr, 1988). Research continues to reveal contradictory and conflicting results on predictor variables (Cicchetti, & Aber, 1980; Crittenden, 1988a). However, history of parental abuse as a child, parents' expectation of the child, familial stress and isolation, parent's marital status, and special characteristics of the child appear to be the most consistent variables that affect the African-American community.

Another concern that has not been adequately addressed involves the race–socioeconomic status confound. Often, intervention programs are designed according to specific characteristics of certain populations. Much of the research on prevalence is drawn from samples that overrepresent the lower socioeconomic strata of society. Moreover, the rate of maltreatment varies along population dimensions. Finally, definitional issues have not been resolved. Studies vary in what is considered *maltreatment*, including inadequate or incompetent parenting, failure to thrive, and low quality of care. To date, there still is no accurate screening device that permits sensitive and specific prediction of child maltreatment (cf. Cicchetti & Aber, 1980).

Although we do not dispute that child maltreatment exists in the African-American community, we argue that not only a culturally sensitive viewpoint, but also equally important, a viewpoint that accounts for the processes in the etiology of child maltreatment rather than simply observations of cause–effect relationships is necessary for an effective prevention strategy. Such a viewpoint would appreciate the inherent variability that exists in the African-American community. Child maltreatment reflects a critical social problem that possesses multiple influences occurring in broad environmental contexts. It is critical that research, clinical assessment, and social intervention avoid the ethnocentric misrepresentation that has existed in earlier efforts.

REFERENCES

Aber, J. L., Allen, J., Carlson, V., & Cicchetti. (1989). The effects of maltreatment on development during early childhood: Recent studies and their theoretical, clinical, and policy implications. In D. Cicchetti & V. Carlson (Eds.), *Child maltreatment: Theory and research on the causes and consequences of child abuse and neglect* (pp. 579–619). New York: Cambridge University Press.

Aber, J. L., III, & Zigler, E. (1981). Developmental considerations in the definition of child maltreatment. In R. Rizley & D. Cicchetti (Eds.), *Developmental perspectives on child maltreatment* (pp. 1–29). San Francisco: Jossey-Bass.

Adebimpe, V. (1981). Overview: White norms and psychiatric diagnosis of Black patients. *The American Journal of Psychiatry, 138*, 279–285.

Alfaro, J. D. (1981). Child neglect and cultural tradition. *Human Ecology Forum, 12*(1), 26–30.

Allen, W. R. (1979). Class, culture, and family organization: The effects of class and race on family structure in Urban America. *Journal of Comparative Family Studies, 10*, 301–313.

Angel, R., & Tienda, M. (1982). Headship and household composition among blacks, hispanics and other whites. *Social Forces, 61*, 508–531.

Altemeier, W. A., O'Connor, S., Sherrod, K. B., Tucker, D., & Vietze, P. (1986). Outcome of abuse during childhood among pregnant low income women. *Child Abuse and Neglect, 10*, 319–330.

American Humane Association. (1987). *Highlights of official child neglect and abuse reports, 1985.* Denver: American Humane Association.

Anderson, W. A. (1988). The behavioral assessment of conduct disorder in a Black child. In R. L. Jones (Ed.), *Psychoeducational assessment of minority group children* (pp. 193–224). Berkeley, CA: Cobb & Henry.

Aoyagi, K. (1978). Kinship and friendship in black Los Angeles: A study of migrants from Texas. In D. Shimkin, E. Shimkin, & D. Frate (Eds.), *The extended family in black societies* (pp. 277–355). Chicago: Aldine.

Arnold, E. (1982). The use of corporal punishment in childrearing in the West Indies. *Child Abuse and Neglect, 6,* 141–145.

Aschenbrenner, J. (1978). Continuities and variations in black family structure. In D. B. Shimkin, E. M. Shimkin, & D. A. Frate (Eds.), *The extended family in black societies* (pp. 181–200). Chicago: Aldine.

Barbarin, O. A. (1983). Coping with ecological transitions by Black families: A psychosocial model. *Journal of Community Psychology, 11,* 308–322.

Baumrind, D. (1971). Current patterns of parental authority. *Developmental Psychology Monographs, 4* (1, Part 2).

Baumrind, D. (1972). An exploratory study of socialization effects on black children: Some black-white comparisons. *Child Development, 43,* 261–267.

Beck, R. W., & Beck, S. H. (1989). The incidence of extended households among middle-aged Black and White women: Estimates from a 15-year panel study. *Journal of Family Issues, 10,* 147–168.

Beck, S. H., & Beck, R. W. (1984). The formation of extended households during middle age. *Journal of Marriage and the Family, 46,* 277–287.

Becker, W. (1964). Consequences of different kinds of parental discipline. In M. L. Hoffman & L. W. Hoffman (Eds.), *Review of child development research* (Vol. 1, pp. 169–209). New York: Sage.

Bell, C. C. (1991). Clinical care update: Preventive strategies for dealing with violence among Blacks. In R. L. Hampton (Ed.), *Black family violence* (pp. 164–174). Lexington, MA: Lexington Books.

Belle, D., Longfellow, C., & Makosky, V. P. (1982). Stress, depression and the mother-child relationship. *International Journal of Sociology of the Family, 12,* 251–263.

Belsky, J., Robins, E., & Gamble, W. (1984). The determinants of parental competence. In M. Lewis (Ed.), *Beyond the dyad* (pp. 257–280). New York: Plenum.

Berelson, B., & Steiner, G. A. (1984). *Human behavior: An inventory of scientific findings.* New York: Harcourt, Brace and World.

Besharov, D. (1981). Toward better research on child abuse and neglect: Making definitional issues on explicit methodological concern. *Child Abuse and Neglect, 5,* 383–390.

Billingsley, A. (1968). *Black families in white America.* Englewood, NJ: Prentice-Hall.

Billingsley, A., & Giovannoni, J. M. (1972). *Children of the storm: Black children and American child welfare.* New York: Harcourt Brace Javanovich.

Bloom, B. L., White, S. W., & Asher, S. J. (1979). Marital disruption as a stressful life event. In G. Levinger & D. C. Moles (Eds.), *Divorce and separation: Context, causes and consequences.* New York: Basic Books.

Bolton, F. G., Jr. (1978). Signals of family stress in high risk families. In M. L. Lauderdale, R. N. Anderson, & S. E. Cramer (Eds.), *Child abuse and neglect: Issues on innovations and implementation* (pp. 287–292). DHEW Publication No. (OHDS) 78-3014.

Bolton, F. G., & Laner, R. H. (1986). Child rearing children: A study of reportedly maltreating younger adolescents. *Journal of Family Violence, 1,* 181–196.

Bolton, F. G., & MacEachron, A. (1986). Assessing child maltreatment risk in recently divorced parent-child relationships. *Journal of Family Violence, 1,* 259–275.

Boone, M. S. (1985). Social and cultural factors in the etiology of low birthweight among disadvantaged Blacks. *Social Science and Medicine, 20,* 1001–1011.

Boyd-Franklin, N. (1987). The contribution of family therapy models to the treatment of black families. *Psychotherapy, 24,* 621–629.

Boykin, A. W., & Toms, F. D. (1985). Black child socialization. In H. P. McAdoo & J. L. McAdoo (Eds.), *Black Children* (pp. 33–52). Beverly Hills, CA: Sage Publications.

Brandewein, R. A., Brown, C. A., & Fox, E. M. (1974). Women and children last: The social situation of divorced mothers and their families. *Journal of Marriage and the Family, 36,* 498–451.

Bronfenbrenner, U. (1977). Toward an experimental ecology of human development. *American Psychologist, 32,* 513–531.

Bronfenbrenner, U., & Crouter, A. C. (1983). The evolution of environmental models in developmental research. In P. Mussen (Ed.), *Handbook of child psychology.* New York: Wiley.

Browne, K., & Saqi, S. (1988). Mother-infant interaction and attachment in physically abusing families. *Journal of Reproductive and Infant Psychology, 6,* 163–182.

Burgess, R. L., Anderson, E. S., Schellenbach, C. J., & Conger, R. D. (1981). A social interactional approach to the study of abusive families. In J. P. Vincent (Ed.), *Advances in family intervention: Assessment and theory: An annual compilation of research* (Vol. 2). Greenwich, CT: JAI Press.

Burgess, R. L., & Garbarino, J. (1983). Doing what comes naturally? An evolutionary perspective on child abuse. In G. Hotaling, M. Straus, R. Gelles, & D. Finkelhor (Eds.), *The dark side of families* (pp. 88–101). Beverly Hills, CA: Sage.

Carlson, V., Cicchetti, D., Barnett, D., & Braunwald, K. (1989). Disorganized/disoriented attachment relationships in maltreatment infants. *Developmental Psychology, 25,* 525–531.

Carter, E. A., & McGoldrick, M. (1980). Family life cycles and family therapy: An overview. In E. A. Carter & M. McGoldrick (Eds.), *The family life cycle.* New York: Gardner Press.

Cazenave, N. A., & Strauss, M. A. (1979). Race class network embeddedness and family violence: A search for potent support systems. *Journal of Comparative Family Studies, 10,* 280–299.

Cicchetti, D. (1989). How research on child maltreatment has informed the study of child development. In D. Cicchetti & V. Carlson (Eds.), *Child maltreatment: Theory and research on the causes and consequences of child abuse and neglect* (pp. 377–431). New York: Cambridge University Press.

Cicchetti, D. (1991) (Ed.). Defining psychological maltreatment [Special Issue]. *Development and Psychopathology, 3*(1).

Cicchetti, D., & Aber, J. L. (1980). Abused children—Abusive parents: An overstated case? *Harvard Educational Review, 50,* 244–255.

Cicchetti, D., & Barnett, D. (1991). Toward the development of a scientific nosology of child maltreatment. In W. Grove & D. Cicchetti (Eds.), *Thinking clearly about psychology: Essays in Honor of Paul E. Meehl, Volume 2: Personality and psychopathology* (pp. 341–377). Minneapolis, MN: University of Minnesota Press.

Cicchetti, D., Carlson, V., Braunwald, K. G., & Aber, J. L. (1987). The sequelae of child maltreatment. In R. J. Gelles & J. V. Lancaster (Eds.), *Child abuse and neglect* (pp. 277–298). Hawthorne, NY: Aldine DeGruyter.

Cicchetti, D., & Manly, J. T. (1990). A personal perspective on conducting research with maltreating families: Problems and solutions. In G. Brody & I. Sigel (Eds.), *Methods of family research, Vol. 2* (pp. 87–133). Hillsdale, NJ: Erlbaum.

Cicchetti, D., & Rizley, R. (1981). Developmental perspectives on the etiology, intergenerational transmission, and sequelae of child maltreatment. *New Directions for Child Development, 11,* 31–55.

Colletta, N. D. (1979). Support systems after divorce: incidence and impact. *Journal of Marriage and the Family, 41,* 837–846.

Colletta, N. D. (1981). Social support and risk of maternal rejection by adolescent mothers. *Journal of Psychology, 109,* 191–197.

Colletta, N. D. (1983). At risk for depression: A study of young mothers. *Journal of Genetic Psychology, 142,* pp. 301–310.

Coster, W. J., Gersten, M. S., Beeghly, M., & Cicchetti, D. (1989). Communicative functioning in maltreated toddlers. *Developmental Psychology, 25,* 1020–1029.

Crittenden, P. M. (1988a). Family and dyadic patterns of functioning in maltreating families. In

K. Browne, C. Davies, & P. Stratton (Eds.), *Early prediction and prevention of child abuse* (pp. 161–193). New York: John Wiley.

Crittenden, P. M. (1988b). Distorted patterns of relationship in maltreating families: The role of internal representational models. *Journal of Reproductive and Infant Psychology, 6,* 183–199.

Crnic, K., Greenberg, M. T., Ragonzin, A. S., Robinson, N. M., & Basham, R. B. (1983). Effect of stress and social support influence on mothers and premature and full-term infants. *Child Development, 54,* 209–217.

Crockenberg, S. B. (1981). Infant irritability, mother responsiveness and social support influences in the security of infant-mother attachment. *Child Development, 52,* 857–865.

Culp, R., Culp, A., Soulis, J., & Letts, D. (1989). Self-esteem and depression in abusive, neglecting, and nonmaltreating mothers. *Infant Mental Health Journal, 10,* 242–250.

Culp, R. E., Richardson, M. T., & Heide, J. S. (1987). Differential developmental progress of maltreated children in day treatment. *Social Work,* 497–499.

Cutright, P. (1971). Income and family events: Family income, family size and consumption. *Journal of Marriage and the Family, 33,* 161–173.

Daly, M., & Wilson, M. (1978). *Sex, evolution, and behavior.* Boston: Willard Grant.

Daniel, J. H., Hampton, R. L., & Newberger, E. H. (1983). Child abuse and accidents in black families: A controlled comparative study. *American Journal of Orthopsychiatry, 53,* 645–653.

Daniel, J. H., Hampton, R. L., & Newberger, E. H. (1987). Child abuse and accidents in Black families: A controlled comparative study. *Violence in the Black family: Correlates and consequences* (pp. 55–65). Lexington, MA: Lexington Books.

Darity, W., Jr., & Myers, S. L., Jr. (1983). Changes in Black family structure: Implications for welfare dependency. *American Economic Review Papers and Proceedings, 73,* 59–64.

Darity, W., Jr., & Myers, S. L., Jr. (1984). Does welfare dependency cause female headship? The case of the Black family. *Journal of Marriage and the Family, 46,* 765–779.

Dean, A. L., Malik, M. M., Richards, W., & Stringer, S. (1986). Effects of parental maltreatment on children's conceptions of interpersonal relationships. *Developmental Psychology, 22,* 617–626.

DeChesnay, M. (1986). Jamaican family structure: The paradox of normalcy. *Family Process, 25,* 293–300.

Dembo, R., Dertke, M., LaVoie, L., Borders, S., Washburn, M., & Schmeidler, J. (1987). Physical abuse, sexual victimization and illicit drug use: A structural analysis among high risk adolescents. *Journal of Adolescence, 10,* 13–33.

Dornbush, S. M., Carlsmith, J. M., Bushwall, S. J., Ritter, P. L., Leiderman, H., Hastorf, A. H., & Gross, R. T. (1985). Single parents, extended households, and the control of adolescence. *Child Development, 56,* 326–341.

Dressler, W. W. (1985). Extended family relationships, social support, and mental health in a southern black community. *Journal of Health and Social Behavior, 26,* 39–48.

Dubanoski, R. A. (1981). Child maltreatment in European-and-Hawaiian-Americans. *Child Abuse and Neglect, 5,* 457–466.

Dubanoski, R. A., & Snyder, K. (1980). Patterns of child abuse and neglect in Japanese and Samoan Americans. *Child Abuse and Neglect, 4,* 217–225.

Dubowitz, H., Hampton, R. L., Bithony, W. G., & Newberger, E. H. (1987). Inflicted and noninflicted injuries: Differences in child and family characteristics. *American Journal of Orthopsychiatry, 57,* 525–535.

Duncan, O. D. (1968). Inheritance of poverty or inheritance of race? In D. P. Moynihan (Ed.), *On understanding poverty* (pp. 116–149). New York: Basic Books.

Duvall, E. M. (1971). *Family development.* Philadelphia, PA: Lippincott.

Egeland, B. (1979). Preliminary results of a prospective study of the antecedents of child abuse. *Child Abuse and Neglect, 3,* 269–278.

Egeland, B., Jacobvitz, D., & Papatola, K. (1987). Intergenerational continuity of abuse. In R. J. Gelles & J. B. Lancaster (Eds.), *Child abuse and neglect* (pp. 255–276). Hawthorne, NY: Aldine DeGruyter.

Egeland, B., & Sroufe, L. A. (1981). Attachment and early maltreatment. *Child Development, 52,* 44–52.

Emery, R. E. (1982). Interparental conflict and the children of discord and divorce. *Psychological Bulletin, 92,* 310–330.

Emmerich, W. (1977). Structure and development of personal-social behaviors in economically disadvantaged preschool children. *Genetic Psychology Monographs, 95,* 191–245.

Fabrega, H. (1989). Cultural relations and psychiatric illness. *The Journal of Nervous and Mental Disease, 117,* 415–430.

Field, T. M., & Ignotoff, E. (1981). Videotaping effects on play and interaction behaviors of low income mothers and their infants. *Journal of Applied Developmental Psychology, 2,* 227–236.

Field, T. M., Widmayer, S. M., Stringer, S., & Ignatoff, E. (1980). Teenage, lower class, Black mothers and their preterm infants: An intervention and developmental follow-up. *Child Development, 51,* 426–436.

Finkelhor, D., & Baron, L. (1986). Risk factors of child sexual abuse. *Journal of Interpersonal Violence, 1,* 43–71.

Foster, H. J. (1983). African patterns in Afro-American family. *Journal of Black Studies, 14,* 201–232.

Fuchs, L. H. (1990). *The American kaleidoscope: Race, ethnicity, and the civic culture.* Hanover, NH: Wesleyan/New England Press.

Furstenberg, F. (1980). Burdens and benefits: The impact of early childbearing on the family. *Journal of Social Issues, 36,* 64–87.

Furstenberg, F., Brooks-Gunn, J., & Morgan, J. P. (1987). *Adolescent mothers in later life.* New York: Cambridge University Press.

Furstenberg, F., & Crawford, D. B. (1978). Family support: Helping teenagers to cope. *Family Planning Perspectives, 10,* 323–333.

Galambos, N. L., & Dixon, R. A. (1984). Adolescent abuse and the development of personal sense of control. *Child Abuse and Neglect, 8,* 285–293.

Garbarino, J., & Crouter, A. (1978). Defining the community context of parent-child relations: The correlates of child maltreatment. *Child Development, 49,* 604–616.

Garbarino, J., & Ebata, A. (1983). Ethnic and cultural differences in child maltreatment. *Journal of Marriage and Family, 51,* 721–736.

Garbarino, J., Guttman, E., & Seeley, J. W. (1986). *The psychologically battered child.* San Francisco, CA: Jossey-Bass.

Garbarino, J., Sebes, J., & Schellenbach, C. (1984). Families at risk for destructure parent-child relations in adolescence. *Child Development, 55,* 174–183.

Garbarino, J., & Sherman, D. (1980a). High-risk neighborhoods and high-risk families: The human ecology of child maltreatment. *Child Development, 51,* 188–198.

Garbarino, J., & Sherman, D. (1980b). Identifying high-risk neighborhoods. In J. Garbarino & H. Stocking (Eds.), *Protecting children from abuse and neglect: Developing and maintaining effective support systems for families.* San Francisco, CA: Jossey-Bass Publishers.

Garmezy, N., Masten, A. S., & Tellegen, A. (1984). The study of stress and competence in children: A building block for developmental psychopathology. *Child Development, 55,* 87–111.

Gaudin, J. M., & Polansky, N. A. (1986). Social distancing of the neglectful family. *Children and Youth Services Review, 8,* 1–12.

Gelles, R. J. (1978). Violence toward children in the United States. *American Journal of Orthopsychiatry, 57,* 525–536.

Gelles, R. J. (1987). What to learn from cross-cultural and historical research on child abuse and neglect: An overview. In R. J. Gelles & J. B. Lancaster (Eds.), *Child abuse and neglect* (pp. 15–30). Hawthorne, NY: Aldine DeGruyter.

Gephart, M. A., & Pearson, R. W. (1988). Contemporary research in the urban underclass. *Items: Newsletter of Social Science Research Council, 42*, 1–10.

Gil, D. G. (1970). *Violence against children*. Cambridge, MA: Harvard University Press.

Giovannoni, J. M. (1971). Parental mistreatment: Perpetrators and victims. *Journal of Marriage and the Family, 33*, 624–636.

Giovannoni, J. M., & Becerra, R. M. (1979). Child abuse and ethnicity. In J. M. Giovannoni (Ed.), *Defining child abuse* (pp. 73–85). New York: Free Press.

Giovannoni, J., & Billingsley, A. (1970). Child neglect among the poor: A study of parental adequacy in families of three ethnic groups. *Child Welfare, 49*, 196–204.

Glick, P. (1976). Living arrangements of children and young adults. *Journal of Comparative Family Studies, 7*, 321–333.

Glick, P. (1981). A demographic picture of black families. In H. P. McAdoo (Eds.), *Black families* (pp. 106–126). Beverly Hills, CA: Sage.

Glick, P., & Norton, A. J. (1979). Marrying, divorcing and living together in U.S. today. *Population Bulletin, 32*, 1–40.

Green, A. H., Power, E., Steinbook, B., & Gaines, R. (1981). Factors associated with successful and unsuccessful intervention with child abusive families. *Child Abuse and Neglect, 5*, 45–52.

Guttman, H. G. (1976). *The black family in slavery and freedom, 1750–1925*. New York: Vintage Press.

Hacker, A. (1991). *Two nations: Black and White, separate, hostile, and unequal*. New York: MacMillan.

Hale, J. (1982). *Black children: Their roots, culture and learning styles*. Provo, UT: Brigham Young University Press.

Halpenn, S. M. (1983). Family perspectives of abused children and their siblings. *Child Abuse and Neglect, 7*, 107–115.

Hampton, R. L. (1987a). Violence against black children: Current knowledge and future research needs. In R. L. Hampton (Ed.), *Violence in the Black family: Correlates and consequences* (pp. 1–15). Lexington, MA: Lexington Books.

Hampton, R. L. (1987b). Race, class, and child maltreatment. *Journal of Comparative Family Studies, 18*, 113–126.

Hampton, R. L., & Gelles, R. J. (1991). A profile of violence toward Black children. In R. L. Hampton (Ed.), *Black family violence* (pp. 21–34). Lexington, MA: Lexington Books.

Hampton, R. L., Gelles, R. J., & Harrop, J. (1991). Is violence in Black families increasing? A comparison of 1975 and 1985 national survey rates. In R. L. Hampton (Ed.), *Black family violence* (pp. 3–17). Lexington, MA: Lexington Books.

Heiss, J. (1977). *The case of the Black family: A sociological inquiry*. New York: Columbia University Press.

Hetherington, E. M. (1979). Divorce: A child's perspective. *American Psychologist, 34*, 851–858.

Hetherington, E. M., Cox, M., & Cox, R. (1977). The aftermath of divorce. In J. H. Stevens, Jr. & M. Matthews (Eds.), *Mother–child father–child relations*. Washington, DC: NAEYC.

Hill, R., & Schackleford, L. (1977). The black extended family revisited. *The Urban League Review, 1*, 18–24.

Hofferth, S. L. (1984). Kin network, race, and family structure. *Journal of Marriage and the Family, 46*, 791–806.

Jason, J., & Andereck, N. D. (1983). Fatal child abuse in Georgia: The epidemiology of severe physical child abuse. *Child Abuse and Neglect, 7*, 1–19.

Johnson, C. F., & Sowers, J. (1985). Injury variables in child abuse. *Child Abuse and Neglect, 9*, 207–216.

Jones, E. E. (1979). Personality characteristics of Black youth: A cross-cultural investigation. *Journal of Youth and Adolescence, 8*, 149–158.

Jones, R. L. (1988). Psychoeducational assessment of minority group children: Issues and perspectives. In R. L. Jones (Ed.), *Psychoeducational assessment of minority group children* (pp. 13–39). Berkeley, CA: Cobb & Henry.

Kasarda, J. (1989). Urban industrial transition and the urban underclass. *The Annals of American Academy of Political and Social Sciences, 501*, 26–47.

Kaufman, J., & Cicchetti, D. (1989). The effects of maltreatment on school-aged children's socioemotional development: Assessments in a day camp setting. *Developmental Psychology, 25*, 516–524.

Kazdin, A. E., Moser, J., Colbus, D., & Bell, R. (1985). Depressive symptoms among physically abused and psychiatrically disturbed children. *Journal of Abnormal Psychology, 94*, 298–307.

Kellam, S. G., Adams, R. G., Brown, C. H., & Ensminger, M. E. (1982). The long-term evolution of the family structure of teenage and older mothers. *Journal of Marriage and the Family, 44*, 539–554.

Kellam, S. G., Ensminger, M. E., & Turner, R. J. (1977). Family structure and the mental health of children: Concurrent and longitudinal community-wide studies. *Archives of General Psychiatry, 34*, 1012–1022.

Korbin, J. (1979). A cross-cultural perspective on the role of the community in child abuse and neglect. *Child Abuse and Neglect, 3*, 9–18.

Korbin, J. E. (1987a). Child abuse and neglect: The cultural context. In R. E. Helper & R. S. Kempe (Eds.), *The battered child* (pp. 3–41). Chicago: The University of Chicago Press.

Korbin, J. E. (1987b). Child maltreatment in cross-cultural perspectives: Vulnerable children and circumstances. In R. J. Gelles & J. B. Lancaster (Eds.), *Child abuse and neglect* (pp. 31–57). Hawthorne, NY: Aldine DeGruyter.

Ladner, J. A. (1972). *Tomorrow's tomorrow: The black woman.* New York: Anchor.

Landry, B., & Jendrek, M. S. (1978). The employment of wives in middle-class Black families. *Journal of Marriage and the Family, 42*, 787–797.

Langston, E. J. (1980). Kith and kin; natural support systems: Their implications for policies and program for the black aged. In E. P. Stanford (Ed.), *Minority aging policy issues for the '80's* (pp. 125–145). San Diego, CA: University Center on Aging, College of Human Services, San Diego State University.

Lassiter, R. F. (1987). Child rearing in black families: Child-abusing disciplines? In R. L. Hampton (Ed.), *Violence in the Black family: Correlates and consequences* (pp. 39–53). Lexington, MA: Lexington Books.

Lauderdale, M., Valiuna, A., & Anderson, R. (1980). Race, ethnicity, and child maltreatment: An empirical analysis. *Child Abuse and Neglect, 4*, 163–169.

Lee, G. R. (1977). *Family structure and interaction.* New York: Lippincott.

Leventhal, J. M. (1988). Can child maltreatment be predicted during perinatal period: Evidence from longitudinal cohort studies? *Journal of Reproductive and Infant Psychology, 6*, 139–161.

Lieberson, S. (1980). *A piece of pie.* Berkeley, CA: University of California Press.

Lieberson, S., & Carter, D. K. (1979). Making it in America: Differences between black and white ethnic groups. *American Sociological Review, 44*, 347–366.

Light, R. I. (1973). Abused and neglected children in America: A study of alternative policies. *Harvard Educational Review, 43*, 556–598.

Lindholm, K. H., & Willey, R. (1986). Ethnic differences in child abuse and sexual abuse. *Hispanic Journal of Behavioral Sciences, 8*, 111–125.

Linn, J. G., Husaini, B. A., Whitten-Stovall, R., & Broomes, L. R. (1989). Community satisfaction, life stress, social support, and mental health in rural and urban southern black communities. *Journal of Community Psychology, 17*, 78–88.

Longfellow, C. (1979). Divorce in context: Its impact on children. In G. Levinger & O. C. Moles (Eds.), *Divorce and separation: Context, causes and consequences* (pp. 287–306). New York: Basic Books.

Maccoby, E. E. (1980). *Social development: Psychological growth and the parent-child relationship.* New York: Harcourt Brace Jovanovich.

Maccoby, E. E., & Jacklin, C. N. (1980). Sex differences in aggression: A rejoinder and reprise. *Child Development, 51*, 964–980.

MacPhee, D., & Rattenborg, K. (1991, June). *Research and statutory definitions of child maltreatment: Comparison and policy implications.* Paper presented at the National Working Conference on Head Start in the Nineties, Washington, DC.

Martin, E. P. & Martin, D. (1978). *The black extended family.* Chicago: University of Chicago Press.

Martin, M. J., & Walters, J. (1982). Familial Correlates of selected types of child abuse and neglect. *Journal of Marriage and the Family, 44*, 267–276.

McAdoo, H. P. (1977a). A review of the literature related to family therapy in the Black community. *Journal of Contemporary Psychotherapy, 9*, 15–19.

McAdoo, H. P. (1977b, August). *The ecology of internal and external support systems of black families.* Paper presented at the Conference on Research Perspectives in the Ecology of Human Development, Cornell University, Ithaca, NY.

McAdoo, H. P. (1978). Factors related to stability in upwardly mobile black families. *Journal of Marriage and the Family, 40*, 761–776.

McAdoo, H. P. (1988). *Black families.* Beverly Hills, CA: Sage.

McLanahan, S. S., & Garfinkel, I. (1989). Single mothers, the underclass, and social policy. *The Annals of the American Academy of Political and Social Science, 501*, 92–105.

McLanahan, S. S., Wedmeyer, N. V., & Adelberg, T. (1981). Network structure, social support, and psychological well being in single-parent families. *Journal of Marriage and the Family, 43*, 601–612.

Miller, S. H. (1984). The relationship between adolescent childbearing and child maltreatment. *Child Welfare, 63*, 553–557.

McMurty, S. L. (1985). Secondary prevention of child maltreatment: A review. *Social Work*, 42–48.

Myers, H. F. (1982). Research on the Afro-American family: A critical review. In B. A. Bass, G. E. Wyatt, & G. J. Powell (Eds.), *The Afro-American family* (pp. 35–68). New York: Grune & Stratton.

Newberger, E. H. (1983). The helping hand strikes again: Unintended consequences of child abuse reporting. *Journal of Clinical Child Psychology, 12*, 307–311.

Newberger, C., & Cook, S. (1983). Parental awareness and child abuse: A cognitive-developmental analyses of urban and rural samples. *American Journal of Orthopsychiatry, 53*, 512–524.

Ogbu, J. U. (1981). Origins of human competence: A cultural-ecological perspective. *Child Development, 52*, 413–429.

Ogbu, J. U. (1988). Cultural diversity and human development in Black children and poverty: A developmental perspective. In D. T. Slaughter (Ed.), *New directions for child development* (No. 42). San Francisco: Jossey-Bass.

Olweus, D. (1980). Bullying among school boys. In R. Barnan (Ed.), *Children and violence.* Stockholm: Academic Literature.

Parcoe, J. M., & Eurp, J. A. (1984). The effect of mothers' social support and life changes on the stimulation of their children in the home. *American Journal of Public Health, 74*, 358–360.

Pearlin, L. I., & Johnson, J. S. (1977). Marital status, life strains, and depression. *American Sociological Review, 42*, 704–715.

Pelton, L. H. (1978). Child abuse and neglect: The myth of classlessness. *American Journal of Orthopsychiatry, 48*, 608–617.

Pelton, L. H. (1981). *The social context of child abuse and neglect.* New York: Human Sciences Press.

Perlmunn, J. (1988). *Ethnic differences.* Cambridge, MA: Cambridge University Press.

Peters, M., & deFord, C. (1978). The solo mother. In R. Staples (Ed.), *The Black family: Essays and studies* (pp. 192–201). Belmont, CA: Wadsworth.

Pianta, B. (1984). Antecedents of child abuse: Single and multiple factor models. *School Psychology International*, 5, 151–160.

Pierce, L. H., & Pierce, R. L. (1984). Race as a factor in the sexual abuse of children. *Social Work Research and Abstracts*, 20, 9–14.

Pierce, R. L., & Pierce, L. H. (1991). The need for cultural competencies in protective service work. In R. L. Hampton (Ed.), *Black family violence* (pp. 175–186). Lexington, MA: Lexington Books.

Pittman, K., & Adams, G. (1988). *Teenage pregnancy: An advocate's guide to the numbers.* Washington, DC: Children's Defense Fund.

Polansky, N. A. (1985). Determinants of loneliness among neglectful and other low-income mothers. *Journal of Social Service Research*, 8, 1–15.

Polansky, N. A., Ammons, P. W., & Gaudin, J. M., Jr. (1985). Loneliness and isolation in child neglect. *Social Casework: The Journal of Contemporary Social Work*, 66, 38–47.

Reid, J. (1982). Black America in the 1980's. *Population Bulletin*, 8, 1–15.

Reis, J., Barbera-Stein, L., Herz, E., Orne, J., & Bennett, S. (1986). A baseline evaluation of family support programs. *Journal of Community Health*, 11, 122–136.

Rubin, R. A. (1979). Measures of infant development and socioeconomic status as predictors of later intelligence and school achievement. *Developmental Psychology*, 15, 225–227.

Russell, D. E. H. (1983). The incidence and prevalence of intrafamilial and extrafamilial sexual abuse of female children. *Child Abuse and Neglect*, 7, 133–148.

Russell, D. E. H., Schurman, R. A., & Trocki, K. (1988). The long term effects of incestuous abuse. A comparison of Afro-American and White American victims. In G. E. Wyatt & G. J. Powell (Eds.), *Lasting effects of child sexual abuse* (pp. 119–134). Newbury Park, CA: Sage.

Samuda, R. J. (1975). *Psychological testing of American minorities: Issues and consequences.* New York: Harper & Row.

Sattin, D., & Miller, J. (1971). The ecology of child abuse within a military community. *American Journal of Orthopsychiatry*, 41, 675–678.

Savage, J. E., Adair, A. W., & Friedman, P. (1978). Community-social variables related to Black parent absent families. *Journal of Marriage and Families*, 40, 779–786.

Schilling, R. F., Schinke, S. P., Blythe, B. J., & Barth, R. P. (1982). Child maltreatment and mentally retarded patients: Is there a relationship? *Mental Retardation*, 20, 201–209.

Schneider-Rosen, Brawnwald, K., Carlson, V., & Cicchetti, D. (1985). Current perspectives in attachment theory: Illustration from the study of maltreated infants. In I. Bretherton & E. Waters (Eds.), *Monographs of the Society for Research in Child Development*, 50 (Serial No. 209), 194–210.

Seagull, E. A. (1987). Social support and child maltreatment: A review of the evidence. *Child Abuse and Neglect*, 11, 41–52.

Shimkin, D., Shimkin, E., & Frate, D. (Eds.). (1978). *The extended family in Black societies.* Chicago: Aldine.

Slade, B. B., Steward, M. S., Morrison, T. L., & Abramowitz, S. I. (1984). Locus of control, persistence, and use of contingency information in physically abused children. *Child Abuse and Neglect*, 8(4), 447–457.

Slaughter, D. T., & Dilworth-Anderson, P. (1988). Care of Black children with sickle cell disease: Fathers, maternal support, and esteem. *Family Relations*, 37, 281–287.

Slesinger, D. P. (1980). Rapid changes in household composition among low income mothers. *Family Relations*, 29, 221–228.

Smith, M. J. (1980). The social consequences of single parenthood: A longitudinal perspective. *Family Relations*, 29, 75–81.

Soldo, B., & Lauriat, P. (1976). Living arrangements among the elderly in the United States: A log-linear approach. *Journal of Comparative Family Studies*, 7, 351–366.

Spanier, G. (1989). Bequeathing family continuity. *Journal of Marriage and the Family*, 51(2), 3–14.

Spearly, J., & Lauderdale, M. (1982). Community characteristics and ethnicity in the prediction of child maltreatment rates. *Child Abuse and Neglect, 7,* 91–105.

Sroufe, L. A., & Fleeson, J. (1986). Attachment and the construction of relationships. In W. Hartup & Z. Rubin (Eds.), *Relationships and development* (pp. 51–71). Hillsdale, NJ: Erlbaum.

Stack, C. (1974). *All our kin: Strategies for survival in the black community.* New York: Harper & Row.

Starr, R. H. (1988). Pre- and perinatal risk and physical abuse. *Journal of Reproductive and Infant Psychology, 6,* 125–138.

Steinberg, L., Catalano, R., & Dooley, D. (1981). Economic antecedents of child abuse and neglect. *Child Development, 52,* 975–985.

Steinmetz, S. K. (1987). Family violence: Past, present, and future. In M. B. Sussman & S. K. Steinmetz (Eds.), *Handbook of marriage and the Family* (pp. 725–766). New York: Plenum.

Stevens, J. H. (1984). Black grandmothers' and Black adolescent mothers' knowledge about parenting. *Developmental Psychology, 20,* 1017–1025.

Stewart, C., Senger, M., Kallen, D., & Scheurer, S. (1987). Family violence in stable middle-class homes. *Social Work, 32,* 529–532.

Sweet, J. A. (1977, October). *Further indicators of family structure and process for racial and ethnic minorities.* Paper presented at the Conference on the Demography of Racial and Ethnic Groups, Austin, Texas.

Taylor, L., & Newberger, E. (1979). Child abuse in the international year of the child. *New England Journal of Medicine, 301,* 1205–1212.

Thorton, C. I., & Carter, J. H. (1986). Treatment considerations with black incestuous families. *Journal of the National Medical Association, 78,* 49–53.

Tienda, M., & Angel, R. (1982). Determinants of extended household structure: Cultural pattern or economic need? *American Journal of Sociology, 87,* 1360–1383.

Tinsley, B. R., & Parke, R. D. (1984). Grandparents as support and socialization agents. In M. Lewis (Ed.), *Beyond the dyad* (pp. 161–195). New York: Plenum Press.

Tolson, T. F. J., & Wilson, M. N. (1990). The impact of two- and three-generational Black family structure on perceived family climate. *Child Development, 61,* 416–428.

Toth, S. L., Manly, J. T., & Cicchetti, D. (1992). Child maltreatment and vulnerability to depression. *Development and Psychopathology, 4,* 97–112.

Trickett, P. K., & Susman, E. J. (1988). Parental perceptions of childrearing practices in physically abusive and nonabusive families. *Developmental Psychology, 24,* 270–276.

U.S. Bureau of the Census. (1991). *Household and family characteristics: March 1985.* (Current Population Report Series P-20, No. 447). Washington, DC: U.S. Government Printing Office.

U.S. Department of Health and Human Services. (1981). *Study findings: National Study of the Incidence and Prevalence of Child Abuse and Neglect.* Washington, DC: DHHS Publication No. (OHDS) 81-30325.

U.S. Department of Health and Human Services. (1988). *Study findings: National Study of the Incidence and Prevalence of Child Abuse and Neglect.* Washington, DC: DHHS Publication No. (OHDS) 20-01099.

van den Berghe, P. L. (1987). *The ethnic phenomenon.* New York: Praeger.

van den Berghe, P. L. (1988). The family and the biological bases of sociality. In E. E. Filsinger (Ed.), *Biosocial perspectives of the family* (pp. 39–60). Beverly Hills, CA: Sage.

Wacquant, L. J. D., & Wilson, W. J. (1989). Cost of racial and class exclusion in the inner-city. *The Annals of the American Academy of Political and Social Science, 501,* 8–25.

Weisheit, R. A. (1986). When mothers kill their children. *The Social Science Journal, 23,* 439–448.

White, R., Benedict, M. I., Wulff, L., & Kelley, M. (1987). Physical disabilities as risk for child maltreatment: A selected review. *American Journal of Orthopsychiatry, 57,* 93–101.

Wicker, A. W. (1979). *An introduction to ecological psychology.* Monterey, CA: Brooks/Cole Publishing Co.

Wilkinson, C. B. (1987). Introduction. In C. B. Wilkinson (Ed.), *Ethnic psychiatry* (pp. 1–11). New York: Plenum Press.

Wilson, M. N. (1984). Mothers' and grandmothers' perceptions of parental behavior in three-generational Black families. *Child Development, 55,* 1333–1339.

Wilson, M. N. (1986). The black extended family: An analytical review. *Developmental Psychology, 22,* 246–258.

Wilson, M. N. (1987). Classnotes on the Psychology of Oppression and Social Change. *Community Psychologist, 20,* 19–22. (Also in *Network: The Bulletin of the Australian Board of Community Psychologists of the Australian Psychological Society, 3,* 24–31.)

Wilson, M. N. (1989). Child development in the context of the Black extended family. *American Psychologist, 44,* 380–385.

Wilson, M. N., Hinton, I. D., Tolson, T. F. J., Simmons, F., Staples, W., Askew, T., & McKim, L. (1990, March). *An analysis of adult-child interaction patterns in diverse Black families.* Paper presented at the Human Development Conference, Richmond, VA.

Wilson, M. N., & Tolson, T. F. J. (1986). A social interaction analysis of two- and three-generational Black families. In P. Dail & R. Jewson (Eds.), *In praise of fifty years: Groves Conference on the Conservation of Marriage and the Family* (pp. 43–53). Lake Mills, IA: Graphic Publishing.

Wilson, M. N., Tolson, T. F. J., Hinton, I., & Kiernan, M. (1990). Flexibility and sharing of child care duties in Black families. *Sex Roles, 22,* 409–425.

Wilson, W. J. (1987). *The truly disadvantaged: The inner city, the underclass and public policy.* Chicago: University of Chicago Press.

Wortman, R. A. (1981). Depression, danger, dependency, denial: Work with poor Black single parents. *Journal of Orthopsychiatry, 51,* 662–671.

Wright, J. D., & Wright, S. R. (1976). Social class and parental values for children: A partial replication and extension of Kohn's thesis. *American Sociological Reviews, 41,* 527–537.

Wyatt, G. E. (1985). The sexual abuse of Afro-American and White-American women in childhood. *Child Abuse and Neglect, 9,* 507–519.

Wyatt, G. E. (1988). The relationship between child sexual abuse and adolescent sexual functioning in Afro-American and White American women. In R. A. Prentky & V. L. Quinsey (Eds.), *Human sexual aggression: Current perspectives. Annals of the New York Academy of Sciences* (pp. 111–122). New York: New York Academy of Sciences.

Wyatt, G. E. (1990). The aftermath of child sexual abuse of African American and White American women: the victim's experience. *Journal of Family Violence, 5,* 61–81.

Wyatt, G. E., & Peters, S. D. (1986). Issues in the definition of child sexual abuse in prevalence research. *Child Abuse and Neglect, 10,* 231–240.

Zuravin, S. J., & Starr, R. H. (1991). Psychological characteristics of mothers of physically abused and neglected children: Do they differ by race? In R. L. Hampton (Ed.), *Black family violence* (pp. 35–70). Lexington, MA: Lexington Books.

9

A Family/Relational Perspective on Maltreating Families: Parallel Processes Across Systems and Social Policy Implications*

Paul W. Howes
Dante Cicchetti

In this chapter, we review the theoretical, clinical, and empirical literature on child maltreatment from a family systems/relational perspective and highlight the social policy recommendations emanating from this work. Recent research conducted on normal families couched within a systems or a relational perspective has enhanced the theoretical (Belsky, 1981; Gottman, 1991; P. Minuchin, 1985; Sroufe & Fleeson, 1988) and empirical (Hinde & Stevenson-Hinde, 1988) foundations of family systems theory. These diverse contributions provide the opportunity to investigate child maltreatment from a family systems perspective. Additionally, the increasing knowledge of normal family processes that has occurred over the past several decades enables us to consider the functioning of nontypical families, thereby exemplifying one of the basic tenets of the discipline of developmental psychopathology—that the study of normal development informs, and is informed by, the study of abnormal development (Cicchetti, 1984; Rutter & Garmezy, 1983). Developmental psychopathology provides the theoretical framework within which our consideration of maltreating families takes place. This relatively new discipline integrates contributions from the broad areas of developmental psychology, clinical psychology, and psychiatry in its consideration of how maladaptive development unfolds (Cicchetti, 1990a, in press).

Our use of the term *child maltreatment* throughout this chapter refers to the physical abuse, sexual abuse, neglect, and emotional maltreatment of children, whether occurring singly or in various combinations. Although researchers have sought to identify different family dynamics associated with each specific form

* The authors thank the William T. Grant Foundation, the Kenworthy-Swift Foundation, Inc., the John D. and Catherine T. MacArthur Foundation Network on Early Childhood, the A. L. Mailman Family Foundation, Inc., the National Center on Child Abuse and Neglect (NCCAN), the National Institute of Mental Health (#RO3 MH48077-01), the Smith-Richardson Foundation, Inc., the Spencer Foundation, and the Spunk Fund, Inc. for their generous support of our work.

Moreover, we wish to acknowledge the clinical contributions of our colleagues at Mt. Hope Family Center, including, most notably, Michelle Carcione, Wendy Potenza D'Alfonso, Nancy Kratzert, Jody Manly, Barbara Mitchell, Fred Rogosch, and Sheree Toth.

of maltreatment, results remain largely inconclusive. Moreover, because our clinical work with maltreating families reveals that many forms of maltreatment are often present within a single family, we describe what we believe to be global dynamics characterizing maltreating families. In addition, even though child maltreatment occurs in all socioeconomic sectors, the stressors associated with living in adverse economic circumstances increase the likelihood of maltreatment occurring in families struggling with poverty (Gelles, 1992).

In this chapter, we address four goals. First, we describe our theoretical perspective integrating contributions from family systems/relational theory and developmental psychopathology. Second, we provide a comprehensive review of research on maltreating families and interpret this information within our theoretical framework. In accord with a developmental psychopathology perspective, we examine the developmental level of the family and explore how maltreating families may fail to progress adaptively from one level to the next. Third, at each level of family development we suggest directions for future research. Finally, the findings of our review are used to generate social policy recommendations.

Theoretical Foundations

The discipline of developmental psychopathology provides the theoretical structure or "macroparadigm" to integrate seemingly divergent scientific perspectives (Achenbach, 1990). A presentation of several important principles and issues that define the theoretical foundations for our discussion of existing research on child maltreatment from a family systems viewpoint follows. The integration of these perspectives also informs the social policy recommendations we ultimately make, which are derived from our discussion of the extant research literature.

In keeping with the history of the field of family therapy, we also draw upon the clinical observations of maltreating families by our colleagues and ourselves at Mt. Hope Family Center. The utility of clinical observations to inform research on psychopathological development is another central tenet of the discipline of developmental psychopathology (Cicchetti & Toth, 1991).

Transactional/Organizational model. Rather than relying on the historical emphasis on single etiological factors such as parental psychopathology, abject poverty, situational stress, or social isolation, theorists and researchers increasingly define the course of child maltreatment as being multifactorial in origin (Belsky, 1980; Cicchetti & Lynch, 1993; Cicchetti & Rizley, 1981; Garbarino, 1977). Similarly, children's and adult's developmental outcomes are viewed as having multiple, interrelated causal factors, rather than as being the direct outcomes of singular antecedents (Belsky & Vondra, 1989; Cicchetti & Rizley, 1981; Sameroff & Chandler, 1975). Consequently, an adequate model for conceptualizing the role of maltreatment phenomena on child and family functioning must be complex and developmental, allowing for multiple pathways to both adaptive and maladaptive outcomes.

Accordingly, the transactional/organizational model is probabilistic rather than mechanistic in its conceptualization of behavior. Potentiating vulnerability and challenger factors that make the development of psychopathology more likely, and compensatory protective and buffering factors that render the emergence of psychopathology less likely, are identified (Cicchetti & Lynch, 1993; Cicchetti & Rizley, 1981). This is in contrast to other models that are designed to determine the "cause" of discrete disorders or risk conditions. Throughout this chapter, our discussion of the maltreating family highlights the risk and protective factors for child maltreatment that exist at the level of the family.

We think that there are clear theoretical links between family systems theory and the transactional/organizational perspective (see also Minuchin, 1985, 1988). In particular, both family systems theorists (who examine multiple determinants of family interaction) and transactional/organizational thinkers (who investigate the multiple pathways underlying individual development) share the belief that developmental outcomes are complexly yet lawfully determined. Moreover, each perspective emphasizes that the whole of any phenomenon is greater than the sum of its component parts. In addition, both suggest that development (be it individual or family) is characterized by the progression from relatively diffuse and undifferentiated states to hierarchically organized and integrated, differentiated states (Cicchetti, 1990a; Werner, 1957). Progression from one level of organization to the next necessitates the development of certain competencies. As these competencies are attained, individuals and families address particular stage-salient issues at different developmental points (Cicchetti, 1990b).

A stage-salient issue is the defining developmental task that must be mastered for the individual or family to progress forward in their development and growth. As the demands for each point in development change, so, too, do the skills required to negotiate these stage-salient tasks. These issues also are important across the life-span of the individual, and must be coordinated and integrated with each successive stage-salient task. For example, we suggest that the formation of a secure attachment between child and parent facilitates the child's later movement toward autonomy from the parent. We stress, however, that a positive or negative outcome at one developmental period does not necessarily inoculate or doom the individual to success or failure at subsequent developmental periods. Due to the life span nature of each stage-salient issue, it is possible for an individual to diverge from a maladaptive (or adaptive) developmental pathway onto a more positive (or negative) course. However, because stage-salient issues are hierarchically organized, the longer an individual persists on deviant pathways, the more difficult change toward an adaptive pathways becomes.

Research stemming from this transactional/organizational model of child maltreatment suggests that maltreated children and their parents have difficulty initiating and maintaining intimate relationships (Cicchetti & Carlson, 1989; Cicchetti & Howes, 1991). Maltreating families are characterized by pervasive disturbances in relationships between family members in both parent–child

(Crittenden, 1981) and adult–adult (Egeland, Jacobvitz, & Sroufe, 1988) relationships. Specifically, members of maltreating families exhibit a higher frequency of negative feelings and appear to have difficulty regulating negative affect (Burgess & Conger, 1978). In fact, it has recently been suggested that it is the emotional, or relational, component of any maltreatment experience (physical or sexual abuse, neglect) that is most damaging to a child above and beyond the effect of any discrete incident (Garbarino, Guttman, & Seeley, 1988; Hart & Brassard, 1987). It is likely that relational disturbance is present in the family even before specific abusive acts occur (Alexander, 1992). In light of the importance of relationships, in the following section we examine in greater detail the existing research on intimate relationships and the regulation of affect, as well as how the gender of individuals may impact individual and dyadic patterns of affect regulation.

A relationships perspective: affect regulation and gender considerations. Recent theorists have highlighted the importance of social relationships in examining individual, dyadic, and family behaviors (Belsky & Pensky, 1988; Hinde, 1979; P. Minuchin, 1985; Sroufe & Fleeson, 1988). Drawing on this work, we focus on the qualitative and quantitative aspects of relationships in understanding the maltreating family system. Attention to what people do in relationships (the content) and how they do it (the process), as well as the characteristics of the relationship over time (consistency and coherence), is critical. Because we view maltreatment as one example of family relationships gone awry, a foundation in conceptualizing and understanding relationships is critical. We next describe contributions from several different sources that bear on our consideration of relationships, their function and malfunction.

Central to an understanding of relationships is the organization of behaviors designed to maintain a sense of security, or to regulate negative feelings (Kobak & Sceery, 1988). The regulation of affect, or how individuals manage the feelings they experience, has recently been addressed by a number of divergent empirical studies. For example, studies of physiological arousal in couples (e.g., Gottman & Levenson, 1988), studies of conduct-disordered children and coercive escalating cycles (Patterson, 1975), marital research on negative escalation in dysfunctional couples (e.g., Markman, 1981), and family research linking marital and parent–child relationships (Howes & Markman, 1989), all focus on how individuals, dyads, or families address emotional distress through a reliance on intrapsychic or relational resources.

To date, the most comprehensive theory on how individuals regulate affect in intimate relationships is attachment theory (Bowlby, 1969/1982). While attachment theory was first explored using infants and mothers (Ainsworth, Blehar, Waters, & Wall, 1978), the theory has since been extended to the study of preschoolers (e.g., Crittenden, 1992; Greenberg, Cicchetti, & Cummings, 1990), school-age children (e.g., Lynch & Cicchetti, 1991; Main, Kaplan, & Cassidy, 1985), adolescents (Kobak & Sceery, 1988), and on into adulthood (e.g., Ainsworth, 1989; Hazan & Shaver, 1987; Howes, Markman, & Lindahl, 1992; Parkes, Stevenson-Hinde, & Marris, 1991). The theory can therefore be conceptualized as a "cradle-to-grave" theory of intimate relationships (Cicchetti, Cummings, Greenberg, & Marvin, 1990).

Attachment theory is particularly relevant to the study of maltreatment because of the theory's focus on the emotional functioning of intimate relationships. Previous research has identified disruption in the attachments of maltreated infants (Carlson, Cicchetti, Barnett, & Braunwald, 1989) and young children (Cicchetti & Barnett, 1991; Crittenden, 1988; Crittenden & Ainsworth, 1989; Erickson, Egeland, & Pianta, 1989), and in dysfunctional families (Crittenden, Partridge, & Claussen, 1991). Moreover, attachment dysfunction is believed to be an important factor for the continuation of maltreatment across generations (Cicchetti, 1990b; Cicchetti & Lynch, 1993; Crittenden & Ainsworth, 1989; Egeland et al., 1988).

While a complete review of attachment theory is beyond the scope of this chapter, we highlight three important components of the theory that we integrate into our consideration of maltreating families. First, and very simply stated, the "security" of an attachment between individuals depends, in large part, on the degree to which they are able to soothe one another in times of the distress that all relationships face (i.e., the ability to regulate negative affect). Attachment theory suggests that individuals differ in their organizations of attachment behaviors, and in their relative abilities to maintain a sense of security in the face of distress. Individuals form specific strategies to maintain a sense of well being which become relatively stable over time (Bretherton, 1985). Second, the fashion in which this temporal stability in the pattern and organization of behavior in intimate relationships is achieved is through the operation of "internal representational models of attachment" (Bowlby, 1969/1982). Briefly, internal representational models are described by Bowlby as an individual's conscious and unconscious representations of oneself and other significant figures that guide subsequent behaviors in relationships. These models are constantly being revised and updated to take into account recent interactions that might guide an individual to a more productive interaction toward the end of maintaining one's sense of security. Third, a child's success in forming a secure attachment with a caregiver, and the resulting adaptive representational models of attachment relationships, have important developmental implications for future adaptation in intimate relationships (Sroufe & Fleeson, 1986, 1988).

Securely attached children have an internalized representation of a caregiver who is available and sensitive to their emotional needs and signals. Such children feel free to express their negative affects directly, and they expect to be soothed and reassured by their caregivers during times of stress. They thus are likely to spend less time distressed and more time engaged in positive interchanges. Through positive relationships with their caregivers, securely attached children experience emotion modulation. Consequently, regulation—as opposed to dysregulation—becomes familiar and anticipated. The internalization of this caregiving pattern, therefore, also includes the internalization of emotion regulation (Cicchetti, Ganiban, & Barnett, 1991). However, this is not the case in children with insecure attachment relationships, such as those who have been maltreated.

A number of studies have suggested that maltreated children have difficulties regulating negative affect. Findings ranging from an earlier emergence of facial expressions of negative affect in infancy (Gaensbauer, 1982), to a reluctance to discuss negative affects (Cicchetti & Beeghly, 1987), to difficulties modulating aggression in the context of peer relations (Main & George, 1985; Troy & Sroufe, 1987), to aggressive stimuli negatively impacting upon information processing and cognitive control functioning (Rieder & Cicchetti, 1989), coalesce to portray maltreated children as manifesting clear affect regulatory problems. Moreover, because maltreated youngsters often form Type D, disorganized/disoriented attachment relationships with their caregivers (Carlson et al., 1989), they are at heightened risk to develop "caregiver" attachment relationships with their parents during the preschool years and beyond (cf. Main et al., 1985).

Our focus on the regulation of affect, growing from an attachment theory perspective, also provides the opportunity for the integration of a seemingly unrelated field of inquiry. Parental substance abuse has been identified as a risk factor for child maltreatment by a number of authors (Junewicz, 1983; Kempe & Kempe, 1978; Murphy, Jellinek, Quinn, Smith, Poitrast, & Goshko, 1991; Newberger & Daniel, 1979). We suggest that the use of mind-altering substances can, in part, be understood as one strategy to establish and maintain the feelings of security and well-being that, for others, are fostered by intimacy and reciprocity in relationships. For those people poorly equipped to establish feelings of well-being with others due to a history of relationship dysfunction, the use of alcohol or other controlled substances may be the most reliable form of regulating negative affects and feeling secure. In our subsequent literature review, we examine how substance abuse may contribute to the development and maintenance of maltreating family systems.

As individuals in intimate relationships gain competence in regulating their own affect, the attachment or sense of relatedness stemming from a satisfying relationship, allows them to explore their own feelings separate from caregivers. Individuation and the development of autonomy over time increase the emotional distance between people in the context of connectedness. The process of individuation and differentiation in relationships has been addressed by theorists from the study of attachment (Bretherton, 1987) as well as by family systems theorists (Bowen, 1974). Ryan and Lynch (1989) describe the relationship between attachment and differentiation as supportive and complementary, with an adaptive attachment leading to emotional autonomy and differentiation in the relationship. While individuation is clearly a long-term task for the parent–child relationship, developmental theory highlights two stages of development that are particularly salient: toddlerhood (e.g., Mahler, Pine, & Bergman, 1975) and adolescence (Baumrind, 1987; Erikson, 1959). Our discussion of maltreating relationships across the family life cycle includes a consideration of the regulation of interpersonal distance in relationships. Our focus on individuation in relationships is consistent with family theorists such as Bowen (1974) and Salvador Minuchin (1974), who place a strong emphasis on the importance of regulating interpersonal space in relationships.

Researchers in the field of relationships and social interaction also highlight differences between vertical relationships and horizontal relationships (Hartup, 1986). *Vertical relationships* are those between individuals where one is primarily the caretaker, while the other is primarily the recipient of caretaking behaviors, such as parent–child relationships. *Horizontal relationships* are those between individuals where partners reciprocate in a more or less equivalent fashion towards the caretaking of one another, such as a marital relationship. We integrate Hartup's conceptualizations with some of the basic tenets of structural family therapy (S. Minuchin, 1974) in describing the structure of maltreating families.

Gender considerations. A relationship perspective, and specifically attachment theory, has made significant contributions to the understanding of individual's functioning in intimate relationships. However, one of the difficulties inherent in attachment theory growing from research on infancy is that little attention has been paid to gender differences in attachment quality for children or adults. This is unfortunate given the replicated observation that men and women behave in consistent and distinctly different ways in intimate relationships (Markman & Kraft, 1989). This research indicates that there are gender-specific differences in the ways marital partners deal with the negative feelings and conflict that all couples face. Specifically, women in distressed relationships are characterized by multiple attempts to discuss issues, while men in distressed relationships are characterized by trying to distance themselves from the conflict (Notarius & Pellegrini, 1987). The anticipation of conflict appears to be more arousing to men than to women, as evidenced by their higher skin conductance rates during marital problem discussions (Levenson & Gottman, 1985). In addition, previous researchers have suggested that stereotypic gender-based patterns of relating increase as the level of distress escalates in couples (Cowan, Cowan, Heming, & Miller, 1992; Gottman & Levenson, 1990; Markman & Kraft, 1989).

Similar research has not been conducted with maltreating couples; however, our experience at Mt. Hope Family Center indicates that couples in maltreating families are often short-lived, with multiple partnerships forming and breaking up over time, making this population a difficult one with which to conduct research from a family systems perspective. However, we argue that the developmental course of individuals growing up in maltreating families can be elucidated by considering possible deviation from the normative developmental paths of both attachment and gender identity. Our clinical observations suggest that exaggerated and rigidly defined gender roles may be an important component of the internalized representations of self and other employed in maltreating families that lead to familial structural risk factors (see below). We hypothesize that an emphasis on gender-specific behaviors may increase with the level of familial pathology, with our most disordered families showing the most primitive, rigid, and crystallized forms of gender roles.

Our theoretical consideration of gender development grows out of the developmental work of Chodorow (1978) and Gilligan (1982). Briefly, these theorists maintain that boys and girls face very different developmental tasks, stemming from the fact that the vast majority of children are initially raised by, and form primary attachments with, female caregivers. While young girls make a same-gender identification with their primary caregiver and adult model, boys must shift their identification as they differentiate from their mothers and identify with a male figure, typically their fathers. This difference leads girls to be more sensitive to affiliation with others and the attraction of emotional resources, while boys are led to be more sensitive to individuation from others and the pursuit of emotional resources. In terms of individuation and affiliation, the developmental needs of children to differentiate from their mothers may initially be salient, while with fathers the initial developmental task is to affiliate (Chodorow, 1978).

In addition to differences between boys and girls and husbands and wives, research indicates that parents are differentially reactive to marital discord in their interactions with their children on the basis of gender (Brody, Pelligrini, & Sigel, 1986). When marital discord is present in the family, men appear to distance from their children as well as their wives (Howes & Markman, 1989). Some studies indicate that the father–daughter relationship appears to be particularly negatively affected by marital discord (Amato, 1986; Belsky, Gilstrap, & Rovine, 1984; Goldberg & Easterbrooks, 1984), while the father–son relationship may be more robust in the face of family conflict (Burgess & Conger, 1978). An especially positive relationship between fathers and first-born sons appears to decrease the likelihood of divorce (Morgan, Lye, & Condran, 1988). Differences between boys' and girls' reactions to family discord appear to change when the fathers leave the home, since the detrimental effects of divorce appear to last longer for boys than girls (Hetherington, 1988).

While many questions remain unanswered, it can be said that issues of gender appear to become more salient as the level of stress and dysfunction increases for a family, that boys and girls face differing developmental tasks, and that family dysfunction is often signaled by the distancing or exit of the father/husband of the family. In our description of the maltreating family life cycle, we highlight how the exaggeration of these patterns may help to account for the types of family interaction and family configurations often observed due to relationship difficulties.

To summarize, our description of relationships across the family life cycle focuses on four components of family relationships: (a) the representation of affect regulation patterns stemming from attachment theory, with a particular focus on negative affect; (b) the regulation of interpersonal distance and the development of autonomy in intimate relationships; (c) the directionality of caregiving between partners; and (d) the impact of gender on the developmental course of individuals within maltreating families.

Family systems theory. Family systems theory can be conceptualized as a shift in focus from the intrapsychic functioning of individuals to the functioning of the entire family as the unit of study. In her 1985 review, Patricia Minuchin outlined six basic principles of family systems theory. First, families are an organized whole, with the elements which make up the system being interdependent. It follows from this principle that changes in one member of a family, brought on by individual development or outside pressures for adaptation, must be accompanied by changes in all other members of the family. For example, an infant learning to walk is a developmental milestone for the family as well as the child because caregivers and siblings must now deal with a much more mobile and potentially intrusive family member.

Second, the patterns of interaction that relate members of families together are circular rather than linear in nature. That is to say that interactions between members must always be considered as reactions as well as actions, and that no one member can accept the credit or blame for any given outcome. For example, a toddler's tantrum over going to bed is in part shaped by the parents reactivity to previous tantrums.

Third, family systems will work toward maintaining their current ways of relating, or system homeostasis, in the face of developmental or situational stressors. Families are resistant to change, and will do so only when their current ways of interacting significantly fail to meet the needs of their members. For example, a first-born adolescent's bids for independence may initially be met with firm resistance from parents only to ultimately give way when the child's competence and persistence break down the parents' resolve to keep the child close to the family.

Fourth, well-functioning families are never static or still, but are constantly evolving in response to the needs of their members. Family strategies that meet the needs of parents and children at one developmental level may not be effective in meeting the needs of that same family at the next developmental level. For example, a family's ability to connect and maintain closeness with a school-age child must give way to a family's ability to foster independence as that child reaches adolescence. However, while the observable behaviors will change over time, continuity may be maintained in the organization or patterns of behaviors for families (cf. Sroufe & Fleeson, 1988). For example, the family described here may change their behaviors to meet the needs of their adolescent, but the responsive and flexible organization of the family remains constant as new developmental challenges are encountered.

Fifth, families are organized by systems within systems, or subsystems.

Within a single family system, the functioning of the marital subsystem, parenting subsystem, and sibling subsystem is also important. For example, parents in the midst of a marital disagreement may have difficulty providing a united front as parents when faced with an angry, resistant adolescent.

Finally, Minuchin argued that individuals and family subsystems that comprise whole families are separated by boundaries, and that the ways family members interact across these boundaries are governed by rules and consistent patterns of interaction. For example, in most families it is understood that parents make decisions regarding day-to-day routines such as bedtimes, and that while discussion and some flexibility is possible the ultimate decision rests with the parent.

We, as well as other authors, have highlighted the natural conceptual bridge between family systems theory, attachment theory, and an organizational/transactional model (Alexander, 1992; Cicchetti & Howes, 1991; Marvin & Stewart, 1990; Sroufe & Fleeson, 1988; Stevenson-Hinde, 1990). While attachment theory and the organizational/transactional model have been applied primarily to individuals or dyadic (two-person) interactions, the same principles can be applied to the study of the family. For example, while affect regulation is a critical developmental issue for children and parent–child dyads, it also is an important adaptational task for the larger family system. Emotional dysregulation can be understood as a characteristic of the family system as well as of individuals and dyads (Coyne, Downey, & Boergers, 1992).

Similarly, if individuals create and maintain internal representational models of themselves and others, it follows that internal models of how the family operates must also be internalized. Such an argument is made by Reiss (1989), who draws the distinction between what he terms "the represented and practicing family." Briefly, the practicing family is the family that we as outside observers can examine in action. Families are characterized by consistencies in their practice of interactions, and these consistencies help to maintain the family as a predictable and constant organism. However, families are also represented in the minds of each of their members, who draw on internal representations of their family to help guide them in negotiating interactions. It is, therefore, possible that family members may think of their family operating in one way, while an outside observer who knew the family would describe its operation in a very different way.

Rigid and inflexible models of family interaction may be a risk factor for psychopathology and maltreatment. Crittenden (1988) provides evidence indicating that there is considerable continuity in the distortion of relationships across the familial spectrum in maltreating families, with parent–child difficulties being but one of many troubled subsystems for these families. She suggests that the concept of internal representational models provides a means for conceptualizing this continuity across relationships for these families. Such a continuity of relationships is believed to be found not only within families but also across generations in maltreating families (Kaufman & Zigler, 1989). Coherence in the patterns of relating in intimate relationships at the individual, dyadic, and family level may be passed on from generation to generation, fostering a continuation of maladaptive patterns over time. In addition, consistent patterns of relating in different family relationships may not merely be an outcome of interactions, but may reflect how individuals appear to search for similarities or coherence in selecting relationship partners (Coyne et al., 1992; Crittenden et al., 1991). In describing coherent relationships across the family life cycle in maltreating and healthy families, we integrate the work of others (Troy & Sroufe, 1987) indicating that different relationships for a given individual can be conceptualized as coherent if that individual adopts either role of the represented relationship in the subsequent relationship. For example, one who is victimized can be considered to be acting in congruence with this history if one later becomes the victimizer or the victim once again.

Despite the compelling evidence from a number of different areas suggesting that relationships are coherent within families, across a number of different relationships and across generations, it also is clear that relationships can change and individuals functioning in relationships can make decisions to alter their behaviors with intimate partners. We highlight points in the family life cycle where coherence or divergence from the inherited and family-based way of relating can be considered maladaptive or corrective.

In keeping with the perspective of family systems theory and the integrative focus of developmental psychopathology, we view a number of seemingly divergent problems as united by a pattern of relational dysfunction. We suggest that many of these problems are actually viewed as solutions by individuals designed to maintain some short-term feeling of security for participants at the expense of long-term adaptation. For example, we examine how issues such as substance abuse, delinquency, and teen pregnancy relate to the familial patterns that foster child maltreatment. Our aim is to provide a broad integrative framework stressing systemic links rather than to address these individual issues separately in great detail.

Finally, family therapists focus on the processes of change, and are careful to watch for dynamics at one level of a system that may also be operating in a similar fashion at other levels of the same system. In keeping with this model, we are especially vigilant to instances where the dynamics and processes of relationships within maltreating families parallel those dynamics and processes of relationships between the families and social agencies. In these instances when we observe consistent patterns of relating across divergent systems, we identify them as parallel processes. Our theoretical perspective suggests that strategies used to negotiate issues in one area of life (family relationships) may provide clues to understanding those strategies used by maltreating families to negotiate their interface with the social service system.

Family development: the family life cycle. In keeping with the viewpoint of previous developmentally oriented family thinkers (Carter & McGoldrick, 1980; Haley, 1971), we emphasize that families develop in a predictable sequence of developmental stages similar to that of individuals. The development of a family will inevitably and invariably include the negotiation of a sequence of critical stage-salient issues for the family and its members. A stage salient issue can be understood as a critical developmental task that must be at least partially mastered before further development can proceed unimpeded. Difficulties in gaining competence in any stage-salient issue increase the likelihood of negative consequences for subsequent development (Cicchetti, 1990b).

While all families must change in response to demands from inside and outside their boundaries, some are better equipped than others to accommodate these pressures. This dimension of variability is often referred to by family theorists as adaptability vs. rigidity (see Sroufe, 1989). Our discussion of maltreating family development across the family life cycle pays particular attention to the process of change from one developmental period to another. In examining these processes, we build on theoretical work describing differences between regulated change and chaotic change in families (Gottman, 1991). Regulated change is described as predictable and adaptive, while chaotic change is difficult to predict in terms of its onset and outcome.

The writings of Minuchin and his colleagues (Minuchin, Montalvo, Rosman, & Schumer, 1967) and Colon (1980), though focused on what they describe as "multiproblem poor families," are relevant to our discussion of the family life cycle of maltreating families. Families where child maltreatment is an issue can be conceptualized as a subset of the broader population described by these authors, and share many of the same issues. These authors describe an absence of growth over time for these families. Minuchin and his colleagues (1967) observe that the families lack specialization and differentiation, and are often characterized by "a peripheral male." A focus on specialization and differentiation is a clear theoretical link to the individual models of development described above. Minuchin and his associates, as well as Colon, suggest that the family life cycles of these families are truncated, with less time for family members to negotiate stage-salient issues that promote development. Drawing from his structuralist approach, Minuchin highlighted the family topologies of "enmeshed" and "disengaged" organizations in contrast to families described as "adaptive." Enmeshed families were poorly differentiated, without boundaries between family subsystems, and characterized by a predominance of chaos and conflict. Disengaged families were distanced and lacking in interaction, with little apparent affect holding the family unit together.

Through over a decade of work with maltreating families at the University of Rochester's Mt. Hope Family Center, our clinical observations and demographic data suggest that maltreating families often consist of clusters of multigenerational women and peripheral men who appear to cycle in and out of the family. Families may consist of a mother, grandmother, and children where father fig-

ures visit or stay for short periods of time. Lasting romantic heterosexual relationships are fairly rare, while impulsive couplings which sometimes produce
children prior to the dissolution of the relationship are more common. Consistent
with our observations and those of previous family researchers, we refer to this
familial organization as being characterized by a "rigid maternal axis with
peripheral males." Throughout the course of our developmental review, we
suggest a tentative model for how such family systems might develop over time,
and how such a structure increases the risk for child maltreatment.

The Family Life Cycle of Maltreating Families

Having discussed the theoretical underpinnings of our conceptualization of
maltreating families across the life cycle, we next describe six stage-salient
periods in the development of healthy and maltreating families: Mate Selection;
Transition to Parenthood and Early Attachment; Individuation at Toddlerhood;
School Age Affinity; Individuation at Adolescence; and Multigenerational Family Functioning. It is evident from our choice of labels, and consistent with the
thinking of previous family life cycle theorists noted above, that we have
selected the development of children as the basic framework upon which to build
our model of family development. However, it is important to remember that
each change in children necessitates changes in all other family members, and
that development does not end when individuals become adults. For each of the
six stages, where possible, we reference the existing literature on family interaction from studies of normative and at-risk populations. Some of the developmental stages we highlight have been more extensively researched than others from a
family perspective. In these instances, we draw upon research with children and
parents to supplement areas that have not been substantially addressed by a
family systems perspective.

Because family life is cyclic, we could begin our description at any point in
the course of the family's development. We begin with Mate Selection to provide
a chronological starting point for young families; however, the reader must be
cautioned that this "beginning" of the family is really a continuation of factors
that were, in large part, set in motion long before two young people meet.

As with individual development, developmental tasks that are most salient at
one family life cycle stage are ongoing in subsequent stages. The negotiation of
these issues must be coordinated and integrated with the negotiation of subsequent issues for the family. The ability of a family to negotiate one task is
predictive of success at gaining competence with the next task. Families who
experience problems with mastering one developmental task will likely experience problems with subsequent tasks, and the longer difficulties persist across
stages the more unlikely adaptive change becomes. In keeping with developmental and family life cycle conceptualizations, we hypothesize that maltreating
families have difficulty negotiating critical issues early in the life cycle which

place them at risk for subsequent dysfunction in the ensuing stages of family development. We discuss how incompetence in meeting normative structural/ developmental relationship tasks specifically hinders positive growth and makes maltreatment more likely. Moreover, we label the risk factors that decrease the probability of successfully resolving each salient family issue as "maltreating family structural risk factors." Furthermore, the compensatory factors that may protect or buffer the family and increase the likelihood of competent resolution of these family issues are called "maltreating family structural protective factors."

The discussion of each of the six family development stages contains five sections. First, stage salient structural tasks are outlined. We define these tasks as life-span challenges that are most important at discrete developmental periods for families. The tasks vary as to which members of the family will experience the greatest pressure for growth and adaptation, although we again stress that changes in any member of the system necessitate adaptation by all members. The tasks also vary in the form of relationships being negotiated (horizontal vs. vertical, same-gender vs. cross-gender), and the direction of growth in emotional distance that needs to take place (affiliation vs. individuation). We highlight the specific stage-salient tasks facing families defined by these dimensions, and describe structural features that characterize adaptation vs. maladaptation for families.

Second, relationship and gender considerations for each stage are discussed. We review theory, clinical work, and research on the relationships in maltreating families that characterize family development for the period, maintaining our focus on enduring patterns of behavior designed to address affect regulation. We frame our specific reviews on the dimensions of directionality (vertical vs. horizontal) and emotional distance (affiliation vs. individuation), and highlight how success in these relationships can be viewed as a protective factor against maltreatment, while failure can be viewed as a vulnerability factor for maltreatment. We also review existing research highlighting gender differences. In describing maltreating families, we are aware that the perpetrator of abuse may be the mother, father, sibling, or some other person. Our goal is to describe the family system in which abuse occurs. While we acknowledge that the perpetrator of abuse is an important factor in understanding its impact, our review is focused at the more global level of the family.

Third, maltreating family structural risk factors are outlined. Here we describe how difficulty or failure in forming lasting, flexible, and mutually satisfying relationships is a major risk factor for families. We suggest how such failure in dyadic relationships has implications for the development of the entire family structure, highlighting gender considerations. Specifically, we trace a possible developmental course that explains the "rigid maternal axis with peripheral males" structure of maltreating families noted earlier. We suggest that maltreating family members are both reactive to, and active in creating and perpetuating this family structure and developmental course.

Fourth, structural protective factors that may buffer a family against maltreatment issues are discussed. While families may experience some of the risk factors we discuss in their relationships and subsequent structure, some families do grow and function adaptively despite hardships, setbacks, and difficulties in earlier stages of the family life cycle. Attention to these protective factors is just as important as attention to risk factors in understanding the etiology and course of maltreating families (cf. Cicchetti & Lynch, 1993; Cicchetti & Rizley, 1981).

Finally, directions for future research are outlined following the review of existing research.

Stage 1: Mate selection. There is relatively little empirical research on mate selection in healthy or maltreating families (for an exception see Crittenden et al., 1991; for a discussion of an evolutionary hypothesis see Belsky, Steinberg, & Draper, 1991; Buss, 1989; Daly & Wilson, 1981). Our discussion originates primarily from a consideration of the profile of maltreating individuals, and from clinical and research observations on maltreating families.

Stage-salient structural tasks. The selection of an adult partner is often viewed as the beginning of a new family (Carter & McGoldrick, 1981). Therefore, the formation of a couple identity and the negotiation of a flexible, mutually satisfying horizontal relationship between adults is a critical first step on which subsequent levels of the family are built. The idea that the emotional characteristics of the adult romantic relationship "set the emotional tone" for subsequent child development has met with both theoretical (Satir, 1964) and empirical (Howes & Markman, 1989, 1991) support.

The importance of this developmental period is heightened by the knowledge that one's partner is the only major attachment in the family life cycle not determined by existing genetic or familial ties. While the relationships among family members such as parents and children, siblings, grandparents and children, and aunts and uncles are all defined at the time of their inception, in our society the choice of a romantic partner is determined only by the free choice of the two participants. Consequently, the mate selection period of development is a critical one for introducing diversity from both a genetic and relational perspective.

The successful negotiation of the mate selection stage in the family life cycle rests on the couple's ability to form a flexible and mutually supporting horizontal relationship. Such relationships are characterized by reciprocity in the partners' abilities to regulate each other's negative affect. Research from the marital literature suggests that the ability to handle conflict or negotiate the negative feelings that all couples encounter is the best predictor of relationship success as defined by staying together and reporting satisfaction (Markman, Duncan, Storaasli, & Howes, 1987). The success of a new couple is also dependent on each member's degree of differentiation from, or the successful regulation of interpersonal distance with, their family of origin (Carter & McGoldrick, 1980). Individuals who have grown up in families which provide support while fostering independence appear to be better equipped to form new relationships in comparison to those who prematurely leave the family (with unresolved issues) or continue to be enmeshed in family concerns and conflict.

Structurally, the adult romantic relationship is a critical horizontal support for family development. A strong adult partnership with clear boundaries allows for adaptive child development as parents look to one another for emotional resources rather than to their children. This minimizes the probability that a parent will reverse the directionality of caregiving in parent–child relationships.

Relationship and gender issues. The selection of a mate is heavily influenced by previous experiences in intimate relationships (Sroufe & Fleeson, 1988). In making this selection, men and women work from their representations of intimate relationships in forming expectations, selecting behaviors, and evaluating experiences (Hazan & Shaver, 1987). Strategies to regulate negative affect stemming from these representations of relationships are particularly important given the research reviewed earlier that highlights the importance of negative affect regulation for adaptive couple functioning.

Consistent with this conceptualization, recent research on normal couples from an attachment theory perspective suggests that an individual's attachment organization relates to observed patterns of marital interaction (Howes et al., 1991). Marital partners describing themselves as insecurely attached displayed more negative affect and less adaptive interactional skills during marital discussions. Difficulties in handling negative affect stemming from previous relationship experiences appear to act as a risk factor for couple conflict and dissolution.

We are aware of only one research project that directly examined the factors involved in mate selection for maltreating adults. Crittenden and her colleagues (1991) studied this issue in maltreating and nonmaltreating mothers and their husbands or boyfriends from an attachment theory perspective. Consistent with the idea that relationship history guides mate selection, these authors found that individuals reporting secure and adaptive relationships with their own mothers as children were very likely to select partners with similar recollections of adaptive childhoods. Similarly, individuals who reported feeling a great deal of ambivalence and conflict about their relationships with their mother, or those who could remember very little about their childhood relationships and may have been avoiding or blocking difficult memories, showed a strong tendency to seek out partners with parallel or complementary histories. Secure partners sought out one another, while insecure partners sought out partners with the same (what the authors call *matched*) or different (what the authors call *meshed*) insecure histories.

Conducting therapy with maltreating patients provides some hypotheses regarding the relationship patterns that eventually prove to be destructive for their adult intimate relationships. Maltreating parents often have difficulty fostering and maintaining a horizontal structure in their therapeutic relationships, but instead tend to pull clinically for a vertical organization. This might be mani-

fested by an unusually passive approach to the therapist with the client attempting to occupy a subordinate or "childish" position relative to the therapist. This
also is often manifested by an unusually controlling approach to the therapist
with the client attempting to occupy a superordinate or "parental" position
relative to the therapist. Many clients fluctuate between these two approaches,
alternating between passive and controlling behaviors with the therapist. In
interactions with their partners, extreme examples of this dynamic result in a
victim/victimizer structure that in some instances includes mutual spousal abuse.
In making the assumption, consistent with attachment theory, that maltreating
parents draw on related intimate relationship representations to negotiate their
interactions with their partners and their therapists, we are suggesting that this
horizontal/vertical confusion is an important risk factor for other adult relationships.

Our observations of maltreating parents indicate that their adult relationships
tend to be characterized by a high degree of instability and conflict. Multiple
partners over relatively brief periods of time are common. For example, one
mother at Mt. Hope Family Center reported living with five different men over 8
years, and conceiving and delivering children with three of them. Her decision to
stay with any of the men often was dictated by her becoming pregnant with one
of them. The extremes of her relational pattern were revealed by her description
of these men, who were initially and impulsively viewed in a highly roman-
ticized way, and then a short time later viewed as extremely negative. Once a
child was born, the mother's search for companionship shifted to her new child.
Her needs appeared to be met until the child began striving for autonomy from
the mother, at which time other male figures and new babies were again sought
after. Unfortunately, very little is known about the men who appear to travel
through these families.

In other instances, when a single partner remains with a mother over an extended period, the relationship is often characterized by multiple separations
and reunions with the male partner leaving and returning to the family system. A
second example from Mt. Hope Family Center illustrates this pattern. One
couple reported being married, divorced, and then reunited, with 15 in-and-out
of the house separations and reunions over a 7-year period. During periods of
separation the mother returned to her own mother's home, where a similar and
complementary pattern of reunion and separation was being played out between
mother and daughter. Once the mother's children began to be difficult to manage
and conflict erupted between the mother and her own mother, the father would
reappear, and the pattern would begin anew.

These case examples illustrate several important points. First, selecting a
mate and becoming a parent are often fused for these families. Impulsive decisions to connect with a partner, with pregnancy driving the decision to commit to
one another, make these pairings a high risk for conflict and dissolution.

Second, similar relationship issues of horizontal/vertical confusion appear to come up again and again with different partners, suggesting that relational difficulties are never processed but instead reenacted repeatedly, or "acted out." This consistency of destructive mate selections is an example of what we term *the maladaptive coherence of affect regulation strategies.* Partners appear to select each other based, in part, on a shared set of expectations of the structure of their relationship stemming from their histories in intimate relationships. In finding a partner that meets these expectations, maladaptive patterns of relating are crystallized and maintained across time and across subsequent relationships.

Third, issues of closeness and distance in relationships are often acted out physically rather than emotionally. While all couples experience periods of emotional closeness and distance, couples in maltreating families often move in and out of the home and/or the relationship in response to relational ebbs and flows.

Maltreating family structural risk factors. Maladaptive mate selection patterns can be considered as structural risk factors for maltreatment only to the degree that they set the stage for future parent–child difficulties. As we discussed earlier, for many at-risk families, mate selection and the transition to parenthood are one and the same. An early pregnancy fuses the first two stages of the family life cycle, leaving little room for development as a couple before facing the challenges of parenthood (Colon, 1980). While pregnancy may in some ways validate the couple and promote distancing from the family of origin, it can all too soon represent an impulsive and ill-informed choice that produces a living, needy reminder of the conflicted or failed partnership.

Single parenthood and/or step-family issues resulting from couple's formations and break-ups are clearly general risk factors for maltreatment. However, our discussion from a relationship perspective provides a sharper focus on why specific single parents might be at higher risk. A history of dysfunctional relationships, and resulting internal representational models of attachment with vertical/horizontal relationship confusion, not only makes the formation of a lasting adult partnership difficult, but also may lead the same needy adults ultimately to look to their children to meet their considerable emotional needs. Difficulties in the mate selection stage of family development can therefore be considered a structural risk factor for maltreatment, for, without a corrective emotional experience with a new mate, partners are likely to alter the directionality of caregiving in their subsequent relationships with their children. We elaborate upon this issue throughout the chapter in our discussions of the salient issues of family development.

Structural protective factors. While the mate selection period of the family life cycle affords the opportunity for the continuation of maladaptive patterns across generations in maltreating families, it also provides the chance for variation and movement toward more healthy forms of relating. Protective factors for such movement include exposure to relationships that model different ways of relating in intimate relationships. This experience may come from other family members, from new friends, from teachers, or from care providers in the social service system. Consistent with an evolutionary perspective on mate selection, Belsky, Youngblade, and Pensky (1989) suggest that physical attractiveness in women and economic viability in men also may be important protective factors in attracting higher functioning partners.

Directions for future research. The maltreating family life cycle stage of mate selection is an open area for the development and pursuit of new questions that need to be addressed by future research. We highlight some fundamental and preliminary questions that could help to begin the exploration of this family life-cycle stage.

First, more basic demographic information regarding the number of partners and the length of adult intimate relationships in maltreating families is necessary. While clinical observations clearly indicate the impulsive decisions and rapid changes in the romantic adult relationships of maltreating families, a careful epidemiological description of the phenomena would be an important next step in fostering a deeper understanding of this issue.

Second, much more research is needed on the processes that govern mate selections in nonmaltreating, healthy couples. We believe that attachment theory and a careful assessment of the representations of relationships are productive starting points to pursue such questions. Research on the processes that govern mate selections in maltreating couples could follow. As in other areas of research furthered by a developmental psychopathology perspective, advances in our understanding of normative development in the mate selection stage of the family life cycle could enhance our understanding of maladaptive processes at the same stage by highlighting developmental deviation.

Third, research on maltreating men in romantic relationships needs to be undertaken. While there is a growing literature on maltreating mothers as parents, there is more research on the absence of fathers on child development (e.g., Biller & Solomon, 1986) and on their peripheral or transient participation in many maltreating families. A family systems perspective urges the investigation of maltreatment beyond the child or the mother–child dyad to include fathers and their impact on the family system.

Finally, the mate selection stage of the family life cycle appears to be an excellent point of possible intervention in the transmission of relationship difficulties and maltreatment. Because, as we noted earlier, the selection of a mate is the only major attachment in the family life cycle not determined by biological relatedness, the diversity of possible mates provides an opportunity for intervention and change. Specifically, more adaptive patterns of relating might be fostered and maintained before a partnership is formed that would be based on maladaptive strategies for negotiating relationships.

Stage 2: Transition to parenthood and early attachment. While research from the child maltreatment literature has not focused specifically on the transition from couple to young family, ample research exists on the early interaction between maltreating mothers and their children as well as on the development of maltreated children from approximately age 12 months and beyond.

Stage-salient structural tasks. The arrival of a first child presents the new family with a number of difficult developmental tasks (Carter & McGoldrick, 1980). The new parents must meet the considerable and constant needs of the infant with sensitive, affectionate care while continuing to attend to the needs of one another. The ability to manage these competing demands depends on the success of each area independently. The formation of a secure attachment between parent and child has been the subject of a wealth of research. This task is the most prominent developmental issue of the infant's first year of life (Sroufe, 1979), and has a number of critical implications for the child's subsequent development (Cicchetti et al., 1990). The formation of a secure attachment is accomplished through sensitive and responsive interaction between caregiver and child designed to facilitate the infant's regulation of emotions and promote a sense of well-being (Sroufe, 1979). Parents who are carefully attuned to the feelings their children express are best able to respond to these signals and maintain this sense of security (Stern, 1985).

The birth of a child is nearly always accompanied by a decrease in the reported relationship satisfaction of the parents (e.g., Belsky, Spanier, & Rovine, 1983; Cowan et al., 1985). In effect, the arrival of the child "tests the mettle" of the young couple by placing a new and at times overwhelming number of demands on them (Satir, 1964). The ability of young parents to meet the demands of parenthood therefore depends, in part, on the strength and support of their adult intimate relationships. This stage provides an example of the hierarchical organization of family development—the success of the family in facing the developmental tasks of the previous stage (in this case mate selection) has a direct bearing on the success of the family in facing the developmental tasks of subsequent stages. This conceptualization is supported by longitudinal research indicating that premarital relationship satisfaction, conflict, and interaction patterns are predictive of later parent–child attachments (Howes & Markman, 1989, 1991).

The successful negotiation of the transition to parenthood and early attachment stage of the family life cycle is evidenced by the formation of clear and distinct parental and spousal roles. Adults in the family must interact not only as romantic partners but also as parents as well, necessitating a higher level of differentiation in their family roles. This, then, is an example of the regulation of interpersonal space that must occur in families if they are to grow in concert with similar developmental demands on individuals (Werner, 1957). Parents must look to their partner for emotional needs and assistance in affect regulation, which in turn allows them to provide the same for their child. Such a structural configuration allows for a clear and consistent directionality of caregiving, with parents maintaining a functional horizontal relationship while fostering the development of a new vertical relationship with their child.

In well-functioning families, the arrival of a new child and the formation of new vertical relationships allows family members to rethink and ultimately to rework their experiences in other vertical relationships. Through parenting, young adults are faced with the realization that their own parents faced many of the same hardships and dilemmas, providing the impetus to see their own relationships with their parents in new and different ways.

Relationship and gender issues. This stage of the family life cycle includes the negotiation of both parental and spousal/partner relationships. We, therefore, integrate a consideration of parent–child relationships in maltreating families with our earlier discussion of parent–parent or adult intimate relationships in maltreating couples.

A growing body of research has documented difficulties in the development of secure attachment relationships between maltreating parents and their young children (e.g., Carlson et al., 1989; Cicchetti & Barnett, 1991; Crittenden, 1988; Egeland & Sroufe, 1981; Schneider-Rosen & Cicchetti, 1984). In fact, estimates from these and other studies suggest that 70%–90% of maltreated infants form insecure attachments with their caregivers. While the developmental risks associated with any insecure attachment are considerable and well documented (e.g., Ainsworth et al., 1978; Bretherton & Waters, 1985; Sroufe, 1983), many maltreated infants show an unusual form of insecure attachment that falls outside the typical "avoidant" or "ambivalent" subtypes of insecure attachment relationships. Instead, as many as 82% of maltreated infants have been identified as exhibiting a "disorganized/disoriented" form of attachment relationship with their caregivers (Carlson et al., 1989). Rather than forming a consistent strategy for trying to maintain a sense of security with caregivers, maltreated infants often display a combination of approach and avoidance, "freezing" and other signs of apprehension, and unexplained aggressive outbursts in the presence of their maltreating caregiver. As these maltreated infants develop into young children, their attachment behaviors are often characterized as caretaking of the parent through nurturant behaviors, effecting a role reversal between parent and child.

In considering the manner of parenting that produces such an attachment organization, Main and Hesse (1990) hypothesize that parental frightened or frightening behavior could be a linking mechanism between caregiver behaviors and maltreated infant disorganized/disoriented attachment organization. These authors suggest that unresolved loss and histories of abuse may lead parents to react to internal frightening events (such as memories of abuse) that are not available to their child, making their behaviors very difficult for the infant to understand. This conceptualization is consistent with an attachment theory perspective that suggests that parents draw on their own experiences of being parented in selecting and evaluating behaviors to engage in with their child (Fonagy, Steele, & Steele, 1991).

The observation that maltreated children often develop caretaking, or role-reversal, relationships with their parents is conceptually congruent with the model we are describing. Specifically, if maltreating parents are experiencing failure in their adult intimate relationships as evidenced by vertical/horizontal relationship confusion, their representational models of attachment must also come into play during the transition to parenthood stage of family development. We suggest that maltreating parents look to their children for emotional caretaking in response to failed adult intimate relationships and representational models of attachment that confuse horizontal and vertical relationships.

Maltreating family structural risk factors. A new parent–child relationship with an emotionally needy parent looking to their child to meet their own intimacy needs is a structural risk factor for maltreating families. The directionality of caretaking in the parent–child relationship is reversed, and the relationship loses its vertical dimension and begins to resemble a horizontal relationship where the child cares for the parent as much as the parent cares for the child. While the organization of this relationship can be considered emotional abuse, specific instances of physical and/or sexual abuse and neglect could be understood as examples of failures on the child's part to meet their parents' needs that lead to anger, frustration, seduction, or abandonment of the child by the parent.

New children may also represent a serious threat to the adult intimate relationship of maltreating families. In a system with few emotional resources, the demands of the child on the mother can be viewed as direct competition for her affections by her partner. When a relationship fails with a child present, the normative stresses of parenting are compounded as a single parent tries to contend with the considerable demands of parenting without a supportive partner. If multiple partners and step-family configurations are present over time, adults without a biological relationship to the child may be put in the role of careproviders, further increasing the risk of maltreatment by the stepparent (see Daly & Wilson, 1981, and Trivers, 1974, for an explanation of these findings from an evolutionary/sociobiological perspective).

Structural protective factors. Just as the absence of a stable and mutually satisfying spousal relationship is a risk factor at this stage of family development, the presence of a supportive and nurturing partner is a powerful protective factor against child maltreatment. Parents who can rely on one another for emotional support and intimacy are less likely to look to their children for similar interactions. In keeping with our model of internal representations of relationships guiding the interactions and expectations of participants, it seems likely that those parents who are able to form lasting and satisfying relationships with partners may also be best prepared to address the relational needs of their children. It is not critical, however, that a parent have a mutually satisfying adult romantic relationship with the other parent of the child. Other relationships with family members (i.e., siblings, parents) or friends that meet the adult intimacy needs of the parent are protective factors as well.

Beyond the relational resources necessary to meet the demands of parenthood during the transition to this stage, the availability of occasional, reliable childcare is a protective factor for families. The changes parents must undergo in this transition are radical and difficult to prepare for. The use of other careproviders can give the new parent(s) the opportunities to pursue their individual interests without completely giving up the sense they had of themselves before they became parents.

Directions for future research. There is an extant literature on the transition to parenthood in normal families and the mother–child attachment in maltreating families. However, little attention has been paid to the transition to parenthood in maltreating families. Future research would benefit from a longitudinal consideration of the mother–child attachment in the context of the mother's adult relationships, allowing for an examination of possible compensations or reactions stemming from adult relationships that impact on the arrival of and early interaction with the child. Decisions to have children, or decisions not to take precautions to avoid pregnancy, may also be informed by an examination of the parents' relationships and internal representational models.

Stage 3: Individuation at toddlerhood. As children move from infancy to toddlerhood and initiate self-locomotion, the developmental needs of the child and demands on the family change considerably.

Stage-salient structural tasks. The transition from infancy to early childhood is characterized by the child's growing sense of himself or herself as a separate being with personal thoughts, feelings, and behaviors. Mahler and her colleagues (1975) characterized this developmental period as focused on the development of "separation–individuation." Similarly, previous developmental theorists such as Erikson (1950) conceptualized the central task for children in this stage to be the resolution of "autonomy vs. shame and doubt." Both, therefore, emphasize that the child's ability to physically move away from the caretaker raises issues around the emotional closeness or distance that is comfortable for the child.

Given the new developmental needs of the child, the family must develop and adjust to these needs. Parents, accustomed to the affectionate advances of their 15–18-month-old, are suddenly faced with a child who begins to assert his or her own needs in interactions. As children begin to assert their own needs and desires, the frequency and intensity of conflict between parents and children increases dramatically. As Lieberman and Pawl (1990) point out, the demands of the child striving for autonomy are considerable, placing a complementary stress on parents to modify their behaviors accordingly.

Relationship and gender issues. The relationship between parent and child changes dramatically during the preschool years as the child develops new capacities for verbal communication as well as locomotion. Attachment theorists have stressed that, in light of these developmental advances, the relationship between caregiver and child focuses on the development of a "goal-corrected partnership" (Bowlby, 1969/1982; Marvin, 1977). Simply stated, the parent–child relationship moves from a focus on the infant signalling needs to the parent to a focus on mutual communication between parent and child regarding their access to one another.

As with infancy, there is a wealth of research documenting disturbed parent–child relationships between parents and their toddlers in maltreating families (e.g., Cicchetti & Barnett, 1991; Crittenden, 1988). Previous research indicates that maltreated toddlers have difficulty regulating their emotions (Cicchetti & Howes, 1991), are delayed in their cognitive development (Aber & Cicchetti, 1984), and show language delays around describing their own internal states (Cicchetti & Beeghly, 1987). We view the failure of these children to develop competencies in these areas as manifestations of the relationship distortions present in the parent–child relationships.

In contrast to infancy, changes in the preschool age child's means of communication and cognitive sophistication include a new awareness of gender and gender-based behaviors. As toddlers gain an increased awareness of themselves as separate individuals, part of that awareness includes an identification of themselves as a boy or a girl (Lewis & Brooks-Gunn, 1979; Schneider-Rosen, 1990). Children in the preschool period are clearly sensitive to issues of gender in the ways they perceive and process information about themselves and others (Levy & Carter, 1989). Parents become more attuned to gender differences in this period of development as well, changing their expectations and interactions with their child based on the child's gender.

Because the toddler period shifts much of the focus of parent–child interaction to negotiation and the settling of differences, lasting impressions of the strategies used to solve problems may be made. For maltreating families, interpersonal distress may be completely ignored (i.e., neglected), or responded to with coercive and, at times, violent means. We suggest that maltreating families foster and maintain internal representations of intimate relationships organized around victimization and "rule by force." In a sample of preschool age children, Troy and Sroufe (1987) found that children with an avoidant attachment history were most likely to be victims as well as victimizers in their peer relationships depending on the characteristics of their partner. This study not only confirms that victimization can be an organizing principle of relationships for children, but also it illustrates that a representation of victimization can be acted out in relationships from both the giving (victimizer) and receiving (victim) role.

A child's gender also appears to play an important role in the understanding of maltreatment. For example, the risk of sexual abuse for girls appears to be at least five times greater than for boys (Conte, 1984). However, until adolescence the majority of maltreatment reports involve male children (Garbarino, 1989), and, in particular, males appear to outnumber females in physical abuse cases.

At least two studies exploring the relationships between mothers and their preschool children have uncovered a seductive pattern between some mothers and their sons (Sroufe, Jacobvitz, Mangelsdorf, DeAngelo, & Ward, 1985; Sroufe & Ward, 1980). These behaviors appear to fall short of sexual abuse but include some form of sensuality in the interaction. For example, mothers described as seductive during a problem-solving task used sensual physical contact, teasing, request for affection, and promises of affection to gain their son's compliance. Seductive mothers were found to be less able to foster autonomous behavior in their sons during this same problem-solving task. These mothers were rated as significantly different from other mothers, who were described as supportive, encouraging, or providing emotional support to their sons. For mothers who were labelled as seductive in the Sroufe and Ward (1980) study, nearly all reported a history of sexual abuse or incest in their families. The fact that seductive mothers were not seductive, but instead hostile and rejecting with their daughters, further demonstrates that parents form differential relationships with sons vs. daughters. As described above, these differences appear to be exaggerated and particularly salient for parents in distressed marriages (Brody, Pelligrini, & Sigel, 1986). The work of Sroufe and his colleagues suggests that parents growing up in especially dysfunctional families may also differentially relate to their children based on gender.

We are aware of some research that at least partially supports our hypothesis that the developmental path of boys and girls differs at this period, with boys focusing on individuation and girls on affiliation and relational factors as described earlier. Aber and Baker (1990) found that a measure of secure parent–child communication was negatively associated with later measures of autonomy for boys and positively associated with later measures of autonomy for girls in the preschool age range. They speculated that sensitive caretaking might have a differential impact on boys vs. girls in keeping with previous research on gender differences (Clarke-Stewart & Hevey, 1981). Aber and Baker (1990) also reported that girls appear to be more responsive to social stimuli than boys, a finding that is consistent with other studies (Haviland & Malatesta, 1981). Relating more directly to an autonomy dimension, Howes (1989) found that parental descriptions of high child dependency for toddlers appeared to operate as a negative indicator for boys but not for girls, again suggesting interesting but speculative differences between genders for children of this age. Finally, a study of physically abused children's responses to parental anger in this age range found that boys tended to respond to adult anger with their own anger, while girls responded to adult anger with fear (Hennessy, Rabideau, Cicchetti, & Cummings, in press).

While these studies examined different areas of functioning, it is interesting to note that the sex differences reported are consistent with our hypothesis. Boys, even at this early age, appear to be more focused on individuation (low dependency) and externalizing behaviors to cope with parental distress (i.e., their own anger), while girls appear to be focused on affiliation (higher dependency) and internalizing behaviors in response to parental distress (i.e., their own fear).

Maltreating family structural risk factors. The developmental changes inherent in this family life cycle stage place a strain on all parents. Caregivers who do not maltreat their children often find this period to be especially frustrating. However, the toddler or preschool period may be especially challenging for maltreating parent–child dyads, because the normative developmental issues of the child are at such odds with the particular demands of the maltreating dyad. Specifically, the move toward individuation and a focus on the child's needs central to this developmental period are especially challenging to parents looking to their children to meet their own adult intimacy needs. It is possible that parent and child could form what appears to be a relatively well-functioning attachment during the transition to parenthood and early attachment stage of the life cycle, only to experience a major reorganization with negative outcomes for the family when the child begins to strive for a greater degree of individuation.

Our clinical experience with families at Mt. Hope Family Center clearly illustrates this concept. In describing the developmental histories of their children, a large percentage of maltreating parents recall their children as "a really good baby who has no trouble at all." However, when asked to describe their children as toddlers, we are often told "that's when the problems began" and/or "my child seemed to turn into a different person then." These descriptions suggest that, in contrast to nonmaltreating parents, maltreating parents may misunderstand their child's normative developmental strivings toward individuation and autonomy as early signs of problematic oppositionality, and work to correct their children before problems persist and become crystallized. Therapy with parents during their child's transition from infancy to toddlerhood indicates that parents may personalize their child's noncompliance, leaving them feeling challenged to respond and maintain a sense of parental control and efficacy.

Developmental psychopathologists suggest that failure to negotiate the stage-salient issues of toddlerhood lead to disorders in the self-system (Cicchetti, 1991). Such a failure can be indicated clinically when a client appears to view the world "in black and white" or in "all or nothing" terms. People may be represented as all good or all bad, including the self. In more extreme circumstances, developmental failure at this stage of development may be manifested as a personality disorder (Cicchetti, 1991). Maltreating parents are often described as exhibiting extremes in their interactions with family members. The negotiation of this particular developmental milestone may be especially difficult for maltreating families.

The normative conflict between parents and children during this period also places considerable strain on the relationship between parents (if a parenting partner is present). Difficulties in negotiating the mate selection stage of family development will come into play once again here as partners who are in conflict face a new and stressful challenge to family harmony. The increased pressure placed on parents also is likely to expose and exaggerate differences in their own beliefs and styles about parenting. As limit setting and discipline become the central activities of parenting, and fathers and father figures begin to play a more active role, the differing developmental histories of the parents often lead to very different views on how discipline should be handled.

In addition, as children begin to play a more active and independent role in family interactions, the opportunities for drawing the child into marital and family disagreements increases dramatically. This process, referred to by family therapists as triangulation, places the child in the difficult position of being asked to "take sides" with one parent against the other. Such a family dynamic can interact strongly with the toddler's developmental disposition to view the world in a relatively discrete, all or nothing fashion. Previous research indicates that couples experiencing distress are more likely than happy couples to triangulate their child during marital discussions (Howes et al., 1992). Given the level of distress maltreating couples experience, and the likelihood that they may confide in their children as they search for emotional resources, we suggest that maltreating families are particularly at risk for triangulation in the face of conflict. Drawing children into adult conflicts may change the nature of parent–child interactions, negatively impacting the attachments (Howes et al., 1992).

Structural protective factors. The successful negotiation of the previous family life cycle stages is a clear protective factor against child maltreatment as children enter into the toddler stage of development and make new demands for autonomy from their caregivers. Parents who have formed a mutually satisfying romantic relationship (Stage 1), and who have negotiated the transition to parenthood and formed a secure attachment relationship with their child (Stage 2), will be better equipped to support one another during this stressful time. They also will be less likely to triangulate their child into marital discussions. Similarly, families who have successfully made the transition to parenthood and formed secure attachments with their children will be better able to foster and support the development of autonomy in their children during this developmental stage.

Directions for future research. The role of gender in the normative development of toddlers has only recently become of interest to researchers in the attachment and relational fields (e.g. Kerig, 1992). Because the time of individuation for the child is particularly stressful for maltreating families, this stage of the family life cycle is likely to be especially important. This developmental period may be critical to the formation of representational models of relationships in pairs and in threesomes, foursomes and beyond. Consequently, the role gender-based behaviors and expectations play at this developmental period need to be further explored. More research also should be conducted on how boys and girls differ in the forms of maltreatment they may be exposed to at this developmental period. An understanding of gender differences in patterns of maltreatment could further our knowledge of the causes and consequences of abuse and neglect, and ultimately inform interventions designed to prevent maltreatment.

Stage 4: School age affinity and exploration. As children begin to enter the school system in their community, a new phase of family development begins. Contact with the school system provides the opportunity for new relationships for children with peers and with teachers. For many families, sending a child off to school is also the first consistent and prolonged separation the child experiences with the parents, raising new issues in these relationships.

Stage-salient structural tasks. As children leave to enter school, the family system must make a number of adjustments to accommodate to this change. For well-functioning families, these changes might include new opportunities for parents (particularly the primary caregiver) to consider other personal pursuits. Families must feel comfortable that their children are ready to handle such a separation, and competent to face the challenges of more structured schooling. Such comfort is most likely with a successful negotiation of the separation/ individuation issues of toddlerhood.

The increased contact with new peers in school also provides a critical opportunity for the developing child to acquire new social skills (Dodge, 1983; Hartup, 1983). Again the relationship between parent and child must adjust to new cognitive sophistication in the child. Some developmental theorists have characterized this period for children as focused on "industry" (Erikson, 1950). The corresponding family developmental challenge is to provide a familial context within which the child can safely gain the competencies now available to them.

Relationship and gender issues. Developmental theory argues that the school-age child makes important same and cross-gender identifications during this family life cycle stage. In considering maltreating families in this stage of the family life cycle, we focus in particular on the careful descriptive analysis of maltreating and control families conducted by Burgess, Conger, and their colleagues (Burgess, Anderson, Schellenbach, & Conger, 1981; Burgess & Conger, 1978). The authors, drawing from a social interactional model, assessed both the frequencies and contingencies of behaviors by observing families interacting in their homes. For example, the investigators not only examined how frequently a child was negative, but also how likely a negative response from a child was if the parent initiated a negative response (and vice versa). If the child and parent responded to one another in a mutually negative way, the behavior was counted as *negative reciprocity*. This form of analysis allows for a more sophisticated examination of behaviors.

As expected, abusive and neglectful families interacted less frequently with one another, and when they did interact they were more negative than control families (Burgess & Conger, 1978). The negativity observed in the maltreating families is consistent with our hypothesis that relationships in these homes are negotiated and regulated through coercion as well as, for some, violence. We suggest, as we did earlier, that the negativity in maltreating families may reflect a representation of relationships that organizes around coercion and victimization. Beyond these broad and important findings, several gender-specific findings are of particular interest. In maltreating families, fathers and daughters were more likely to reciprocate negative behaviors than mothers and daughters. However, in control families the opposite pattern was found (Burgess et al., 1981).

How are we to understand these observations of the differential reciprocity in dyads of same vs. different gender pairings in light of the theoretical model we are proposing? We suggest that in the nonmaltreating families, mothers and daughters were actively engaged in negotiating differentiation and distancing (negative reciprocity) while fathers and daughters were engaged in cross-gender identification (positive reciprocity). Daughters can be conceptualized as increasing the interpersonal and emotional distance between themselves and their mothers while moving closer to their fathers in keeping with normative developmental expectations.

In contrast, for maltreating families mothers and daughters appear to be allied more closely (positive reciprocity) and may not be working toward differentiation. Fathers and daughters may not be making the cross-gender identification characterizing normative development, but instead appear to be maintaining a negative distance (negative reciprocity). We suggest, then, that the careful observational data from maltreating families indicate that daughters may be experiencing difficulties in differentiating from their mothers and moving closer to their fathers. The same-gender closeness observed between mothers and daughters in the maltreating families can be viewed as a protective strategy in the child's uncertain and frightening world.

It is interesting to note that much of the research by Burgess, Conger, and colleagues was conducted with a sample of maltreating families that included both a mother and father figure. Our clinical experience at Mt. Hope Family Center suggests that this population may be a more adaptive subset of maltreating families. We have found that the most troubled families are those where there are transient and temporary male partners, or no males present at all. Burgess, Conger, and their colleagues seem to have realized the importance of the number of caregivers in maltreating families, and studied a small sample of single-parent families to address this (Kimball, Stewart, Conger, & Burgess, 1980). They found that the rates of negative behavior for single-parent families were even higher than those observed in the two-parent maltreating families, and suggest that single-parenthood is a critical risk factor to consider in assessing child maltreatment.

In addition to intrafamilial relationships, families at this point in the family life cycle must address their children's growing relationships with teachers and with friends. Previous researchers have suggested that the way maltreated children interact with their family and their peers is closely related (Hartup, 1983). A focus on representational models allows a consideration of the question of whether there is coherence across the different domains of a child's relationship with parents, peers, and teachers (Cicchetti, Lynch, Shonk, & Manly, 1992).

The relationships of maltreated school-age children is one area of our review where a large, carefully matched sample of over 200 maltreated and nonmaltreated children have been studied. Lynch and Cicchetti (1991) found important similarities in the ways maltreated children relate to peers, parents, and teachers, and suggest that internal representational models could be the mechanism of continuity across these relationships. They found that maltreated children were more likely to show a "confused" pattern of relating to important others across these relational domains, also suggesting a developmental coherence over time from the disorganized attachment patterns in infancy described earlier.

Maltreating family structural risk factors. Ongoing relational difficulties place maltreating families at risk in this stage of the family life cycle. Because maltreated children have difficulties establishing a secure and autonomous relationship with their parent(s), they are poorly prepared to enter and maintain adaptive peer relationships as well.

A review of maltreating children's relationships with peers by Mueller and Silverman (1989) indicates two general findings. First, maltreated children show more physical and verbal aggression with peers than comparison children (George & Main, 1979; Troy & Sroufe, 1987). Moreover, they are likely to respond aggressively to both friendly approaches (Howes & Eldrege, 1985) and to signs of distress (Howes & Espinosa, 1985; Main & George, 1985) from other children. Second, Mueller and Silverman (1989) suggest that maltreated children exhibit avoidance and withdrawal in peer interactions compared to other children (George & Main, 1979; Jacobson & Straker, 1982). This was especially true of neglected children (Hoffman-Plotkin & Twentyman, 1984).

Given these difficulties, children from maltreating families are less likely to venture into the world of peer relationships to gain new competencies. This may limit their opportunities to experience other relationships which function to increase the interpersonal distance between themselves and their families. We suggest that delays in this normative developmental process contribute to a lack of vertical structure in maltreating families, keeping children close and incompetent at regulating interpersonal space as they face new challenges. We hypothesize that the forms of difficulties in regulating interpersonal space may vary between boys and girls; regardless, the impact of these difficulties is a family without clear generational hierarchies that structure and guide development.

Structural protective factors. While increased contact with peers and teachers can elucidate and exaggerate relational problems for children, the increased contact also affords the chance for maltreated children to experience relationships in new and different ways. Because representational models of relationships can be changed in response to new and different interactions, this stage in the family life cycle provides the maltreated child with increased opportunity to modify their relational styles (Egeland et al., 1988). A positive relational experience with a friend, teacher, or relative may buffer the child from some of the deleterious effects of maltreatment by showing the child there are alternatives to coercion in managing relationships (Lynch & Cicchetti, 1992).

Directions for future research. As we have discussed, this life stage for maltreating families has been more carefully studied than many. However, there are several questions that must be examined further. Because children at this developmental period are exposed to new relational experiences, more research is needed on how a child's representational model of the relationship with his or her parent impacts on the formation and maintenance of other relationships with peers and teachers. Critical questions include "What are the conditions of continuity and discontinuity," "What are the mechanisms of change for representational models at this age," and "How can maltreated children alter their models away from a victim/victimizer organization that may inhibit success in other relationships?"

There are also several issues related to the child's gender that deserve further attention. Given the higher negativity in maltreating families, how do boys and girls differentially react over time? If boys are responding aggressively out of anger and girls are responding warily out of fear, does this lead to different outcomes for them in relationships? Is the response to family dysfunction seen in maltreated children from multiproblem homes qualitatively different than the response of children from homes of divorce where boys are described as showing externalizing problems while girls are described as showing internalizing problems (Grych & Fincham, 1990)? Finally, because of the important same- and cross-gender identifications that children make during this stage in family development, more research is needed on the impact of fathers, father figures, and their absence for boys and girls. To study these men, researchers will need to devise new ways to conceptualize a couple that includes the approach/avoidant patterns of interaction impacting these families (see Cicchetti & Manly, 1990).

Stage 5: Individuation at adolescence. The onset of adolescence presents another major challenge and the need for reorganization to developing families. Changes in the biological and socioemotional functioning of males and females, with the onset of puberty and reproductive readiness, call for radical adjustments in behavior. At around the same time, developments in the cognitive and social-cognitive domains that occur with the advent of formal operational thinking allow adolescents to conceptualize, and therefore argue, their points on adult terms with their caregivers. Important developments in the representations of intimate relationships occur in concert with this leap in cognitive development which allow further individuation for the adolescent.

Stage-salient structural tasks. This stage in the family life cycle holds two important developmental tasks for children and the family. First, the family must adjust to the sudden physical and cognitive growth of their child during early adolescence. Most families experience some form of early "disequilibrium" as the family adjusts to the presence of a developing adolescent. For many healthy families this initial transitional period is met successfully as parent(s) and the adolescent learn ways of relating that establish a new equilibrium for the system.

Second, the family must prepare the adolescent to enter the world of adults and ultimately seek his or her own resources and social networks. Family theorists believe that transitions including the addition or loss of family members are the most stressful. Because the central developmental marker of this stage in the family cycle is the child's preparation for leaving and ultimate departure from the family, this stage requires one of the most radical adaptations for the family since the birth of the first child.

At the individual level, children's physical and cognitive maturation in early adolescence accompanies an important developmental milestone in their emotional functioning. Erikson (1950) suggested that this stage was focused on addressing the issue of "identity vs. identity confusion." He placed a special emphasis on adolescence as a key developmental period, arguing that it was here that the transition from child to adult is made. The establishment of a clear sense of identity on the individual level for an adolescent is manifest as a more completely differentiated relationship on the parent–child level. As adolescents gain a more carefully defined and integrated sense of themselves, they clarify their relationship with their parent.

As with all the stages we have described earlier, change for the adolescent child necessitates complementary changes by all other members of the family. Caregivers must not only respond to changes in their child, but also must begin to anticipate the new family structure after the adolescent leaves home. Consistent with other life stages, watching their child experience the pains of adolescence may awaken some parents' feelings about their past and the negotiation of this difficult transition. However, parental resonance to the feelings of their child may be even more intense at this life stage, since the memories of adolescence are newer and richer in cognitive complexity than memories of middle or early childhood.

Relationship and gender issues. The rapid developmental advances of adolescence necessitate changes in the form and quality of interactions within and beyond the family. The behavioral repertoire of the child also expands and diversifies, allowing the adolescent a much broader range of expressive outlets. This diversification is one important way that adolescents "try on" a number of different identities as they endeavor to integrate and consolidate their own.

The child's advanced biological, cognitive, and socioemotional development leading to increases in sexuality and the onset of reproductive readiness and fitness, signal the child's passage into adolescence. The biological capability to conceive and bear children at this age, and the normal developmental striving to seek and maintain romantic attachments, brings our discussion full circle to issues of mate selection once again. The socioemotional issues for adolescents include, not only the negotiation of relationships with friends, parents, siblings, and teachers, but also with romantic partners as their relational network expands (Garbarino, 1989). For well-functioning families, adolescence can be a time for the child to experiment and practice adult relationships without having to bear the full burden of such activities. Such practicing requires some span of time between reproductive readiness (the onset of adolescence) and the time when the child leaves home (the end of adolescence).

Differences between boys and girls clearly become more salient during adolescence with the onset of puberty and physical sexual maturity. Children may also become more aware of gender stereotypes at this time. While we are not aware of an existing literature on adolescent mate selection, we suggest that decisions about romantic partners are guided by the internal representational models of relationships formed over the course of the child's life. In keeping with our hypothesized divergent developmental paths for boys and girls, we suggest that normative differences between boys and girls become exaggerated during adolescence as children seek to integrate their own sexuality into their identities. We cannot site support for our model from the normative developmental literature on adolescents, but there are several pieces of evidence we discuss that suggest that differences between boys and girls increase as the level of pathology increases.

As parents of adolescents strive to form new relationships with their children, they draw on their own experiences of adolescence to guide their parenting. Their prior histories during this negotiation of interpersonal distance with their adolescents may be very important in understanding their parenting at this point in time.

Maltreating family structural risk factors. We suggest that, in response to their maltreatment experiences, abused adolescents may have formed internal representations of themselves and others that leave them poorly prepared to leave the family and function on their own as adults. The diversification of activities available to adolescents places them at much higher risk for exposure to controlled substances than are children at earlier age stages. Because the maltreated adolescent child must struggle with new relationships and subsequent feelings that are poorly regulated, they are at particular risk for turning to alcohol or drugs to obtain a sense of security. We suggest that alcohol and drug abuse during the teenage years can, in part, be viewed as an attempt by the child to manage feelings of anger and/or sadness that cannot be managed by their existing coping skills. In addition, because the use of these substances hinders performance and often functions as a means for avoiding vs. dealing with the difficult feelings, we believe that substance abuse plays a major role in perpetuating the maladaptive affect regulatory strategies of these children.

In maltreating families where the unwritten law of interacting has been that "might makes right," conflict between caregivers and children can escalate during adolescence as maltreated children are better able to fight back (Garbarino, 1989). If coercion has been the strategy used to regulate affect and provide structure in the family, then the changes in the adolescent's relative size and strength make this stage in the family life cycle a particularly dangerous one for the eruption of violence in maltreating families.

Some information on differences in the forms and frequency of maltreatment for boys compared to girls highlights gender differences at this stage. Garbarino

(1989) suggests that females are at higher risk for maltreatment than boys during adolescence more than at any other point in time. This may be due to an increase in reports of sexual abuse of adolescent girls, an increase in actual sexual abuse of girls, and the fact that maltreated boys may come to the attention of authorities through the judicial rather than the medical or social service systems. One way of conceptualizing these differences between adolescent girls' and boys' responses to maltreatment is that girls may pursue a more passive strategy to communicate their distress (i.e., teen pregnancy, sexual promiscuity and victimization) while boys may pursue a more active strategy (i.e., aggressive acting-out) that comes to the attention of the legal system. These different patterns of behavior between boys and girls at adolescence may also, in part, be related to a differential response to depression at this developmental stage. Recent research indicates that boys and girls both show increases in depressive symptomatology during adolescence (Angold & Rutter, 1992). However, by mid-adolescence girls are twice as likely as boys to manifest significant depressive symptomatology. We suggest that depression is a likely outcome of growing up in a maltreating family system, and may play an important role in understanding gender-based responses at adolescence (cf. Kaufman, 1991; Toth, Manly, & Cicchetti, 1992).

As these examples indicate, along with the diversification of behaviors and roles experienced in this life stage, adolescents also are much more directly impacted by systems in society beyond the family and/or school level. The economic situation of the family may be a much more salient issue for adolescents than for younger children since the care of adolescents is much more expensive (Garbarino, 1989) and adolescents are most likely more cognizant of their relative position in the social hierarchy.

Our clinical experience with maltreating families at Mt. Hope Family Center confirms that adolescent boys are more likely to leave the family and/or school at an early age in concert with their fathers or father figures who have also often left. There may be few avenues available to young males to establish a family identify other than by distinguishing themselves as fathers (Colon, 1980). In contrast, adolescent girls appear to be more likely to remain in the family. One of the strategies they may employ in efforts to better define their family role is to become a parent themselves. We have observed that these teen mothers may not only be striving to establish some clearer sense of identity when they become parents, but also that their transition to parenthood enables them to force the family system to accommodate the new generation. Many young mothers seize this opportunity to leave the family for the first time at this point, and appear to move toward their own individuation by leaving their child behind with their mother. However, these women often are ill prepared to live on their own and may soon return to the family.

In these examples, we see that for maltreated adolescents the length of time between the two developmental points of puberty and leaving the family may be compressed in time so as to be virtually indistinguishable. In maltreating families, the presence of an adolescent or young adult with needs and ideas all his or her own, as well as the physical and intellectual means to pursue them beyond the family, may be too much for these brittle and explosive systems to tolerate. Maltreating parents' own unresolved family of origin issues stemming from their own troubled histories surface once again as they view the same issues from the other side of the parent–adolescent relationship. Because the time available to practice adult activities and relationships is reduced for maltreating families, the transition to puberty and the move to leave home become fused and children from these families will not be as well prepared to face the challenges of young adulthood. They also may face stressors as a young adult (such as being a teen parent) that adolescents from the best functioning families would be unable to address successfully without support.

With the increased behavioral repertoire that is available to adolescents also comes a diversity of potential problems for them. As development branches out and becomes much more varied and complex during adolescence, maltreated children may experience a wide range of problems including teen pregnancy, substance abuse, delinquency, and criminal activities.

Structural protective factors. Just as the adolescent's explorations into the larger world of adults provide opportunities for a new and varied set of problems, they also provide opportunities for contact with a greater variety of people who may prove to exert positive influences on them. Because the role of peers is so important to adolescents, contact with a higher functioning peer group may allow the maltreated child to learn new ways of interacting which are more effective than those learned by him or her in the family. However, we again stress that adolescence is farther along in the developmental course and may, therefore, be a more difficult stage to intervene successfully in than earlier stages of life for these children.

Directions for future research. We believe that this period of the family life cycle is especially important to consider for maltreating families because the compression of adolescence and the birth of new children to young, poorly prepared parents is one of the central dynamics perpetuating these patterns across generations. More research is needed on the process of mate selection in adolescence, and on how issues from a child's family of origin impact on the selection of a romantic partner. How does the compression of time for this life stage impact boys and girls differentially, and what are the available alternatives for these children?

We also suggest that future research pursue the question of whether child maltreatment can be considered a unifying developmental dynamic integrating such divergent problems as teen pregnancy, delinquency, violence, depression, and substance abuse. We argue that the repertoire of behaviors may increase dramatically for adolescent children, but that the organization of behaviors communicating distress and the need for intervention remains constant.

Summary: Multigenerational families. Our review of the life cycle of maltreating families has stressed points of transition in the growing child's life that organize a family's development. We have described how relational delays and/or deviations across development may thwart the growth of families as a unit, and discussed how specific developmental difficulties around individuation and a secure sense of self can account for the collapsed structures of these families (Colon, 1980; S. Minuchin et al., 1967).

To describe a developmental model of family growth, we have divided the family life cycle into relatively discrete units. However, we acknowledge that family development is far more complex when we begin to consider that: (a) a single family may be struggling with several different stage salient issues at any one point in time, and (b) issues that are stage-salient continue to remain important across the life span for families. For example, a family with several children might be faced with the challenges of an adolescent striving for autonomy at the same time they face similar challenges with a younger sibling learning to walk or going off to school for the first time. The absence or inconsistent participation of a male partner may have differential impacts on levels of the same family, with young children blaming themselves while older children express their anger at the parent in the home. A father's absence may also mean different things to the family at different developmental points.

Our model of child maltreatment from a family/relational perspective stresses that optimal family growth is characterized by continuous development across the family life cycle. Such a model is consistent with Erikson's (1950) emphasis on adult development. The success of a young couple in forming the elusive stable adult romantic relationship is, in part, dependent on their own parents' success at fostering growth in a vertical relationship and their own abilities to address difficulties and maintain a sense of security as a couple. Delays in development for one generation impact all other generations of the family system. While our review focused on stages defined by the childrens' development, we stress that growth by children must be accompanied by positive advances in the preceding generations of the family if the child's development has the best chance to continue unimpeded.

In considering the impact of one generation on the next, we have utilized the concept of representational models of relationships that operate at the level of the family as well as at the level of the individual. We have reviewed extensive empirical work providing initial confirmation to what Sroufe and Fleeson (1988) have described as a coherence of family relationships in maltreating families. Not only do we find that maltreating families are characterized by relational difficulties across relationships in different domains (i.e., marital, parent–child, and peer problems), but also we suggest that the form and quality of these relationships are intimately related, or meshed (Crittenden et al., 1991), within families and may show a consistent and discrete pattern across generations.

We now highlight several dynamics that we suggest characterize maltreating families across the family life cycle. First, we view these families as characterized by a lack of vertical structure across generations. As successive generations experience difficulty in attaching, individuating, and developing a secure sense of self in relationships, the development of the family can become compressed. Colon (1980) describes this flattened structure as characterizing, not only the lack of vertical structure of the family, but also the temporal dimensions for the family. Stage salient issues must be faced more quickly and become intensified as the child is asked to face new tasks before the present ones are mastered.

Second, our focus on gender differences has examined evidence relating to the divergent developmental paths that boys and girls face in normal and maltreating families. Consistent with the empirical research presented above, we hypothesize that gender roles become more rigid and exaggerated in the most collapsed, dysfunctional families. An exaggeration of the normative developmental emphasis on closeness and social relating for girls might be the overly dependent, incompetent young girl who fails to develop far beyond childhood before she is suddenly and abruptly swept up in her new role as a young mother. Her failure to differentiate successfully from her own mother before a more adult identification takes place puts her at risk for repeating this pattern with her own children. We suggest that a multigenerational enmeshment of women is a natural outgrowth of delayed development and a lack of vertical growth for females, and describe this structure as the rigid maternal axis.

An exaggeration of the normative strivings for distance and a focus on mastery we have described for boys might be the angry, aggressive young boy who never grows out of bullying people to get his emotional needs met. The accelerated and compressed pace of development forces males in maltreating families to leave the family prematurely. If males are forced to differentiate emotionally from their mothers and families before security and trust is established, they may periodically return to their families and partners and coercively pursue emotional resources until distancing occurs again. We describe this structure as the peripheral male.

The rigid maternal axis and peripheral male patterns of family interaction do not, however, develop independently from one another. Rather, they are intimately linked and mesh into an integrated view of family functioning across time. Without the presence of consistent men in the home during childhood, little girls may have fewer opportunities to learn about relating to males. Without available and viable partners in young adulthood, women in struggling families may be less likely feel safe enough to venture out of the family. Similarly for males, difficulties in early development, perhaps aggravated by the absence of stable and reliable men, lead to early and incomplete individuation. Females as sources of emotional resources may be less available as they cling to one another, furthering the dynamic of distancing for young men. The relation between the rigidity of the maternal axis and the speed of cycle and level of coercion of the peripheral male is direct and reciprocal.

Finally, we have hypothesized that the concept of representational models of relationships and families provide a means of conceptualizing and communicating cross-generational influences (cf. Cicchetti & Lynch, 1993). We suggest that maltreating families may share representations of relationships that organize around coercion and victimization. Though family members may be the victim in one family relationship and the victimizer in another, the guiding relational principle is that the most powerful, coercive participant gains the most emotional resources. This depiction is consistent with our previous discussion of horizontal/vertical confusion in maltreating relationships, and also relates to the extremes of emotion often observed in maltreating families.

Despite the relational difficulties we have described, not all children from maltreating families exhibit the same levels of psychopathology, nor do they necessarily grow up to become maltreating parents themselves. Throughout our chapter we have described protective factors that make some children more resilient to the negative impact of maltreatment than others. These protective factors, while varying from one stage of the family life cycle to the next, all focus on altering the representational models of children from maltreating families through the provision of alternative relationships. We again wish to stress that representational models appear to be more flexible and receptive to change at younger ages, and that the longer maladaptive relational patterns persist, the more difficult the task of intervention at this level becomes. However, we believe that all individuals are capable of adaptive change in their representations of relationships if they are exposed to viable alternatives for relating that provide more consistent and positive experiences.

In summary, we have presented a model of maltreating families that has focused on: (a) the lack of individuation and hierarchical growth among family members, (b) the use of children as emotional resources, (c) the subsequent family system of the rigid maternal axis and the peripheral male, and (d) representational models lacking vertical skills and focusing on victim/victimizer principles of relating. We next suggest social policy implications stemming from these observations and the family life cycle model.

SOCIAL POLICY IMPLICATIONS

Any discussion of social policy must necessarily address issues that are political in nature. It is our intention, however, not to enter the political arena directly but to provide suggestions for policy makers about helping maltreating families that emerge directly from the research and clinical observations described. We wish to stress that we have sought to avoid advocating specific political positions, but rather have endeavored to base our thoughts and ideas on research and careful clinical documentation. However, we realize that some of our ideas will have echoes of a "liberal" approach, while others may approximate a more "conservative" approach.

Our recommendations are organized into five sections. The first area is broad, and addresses the importance of social service providers intervening at the level of the family with an appreciation for the family's developmental level. The last four recommendations are more specific, and address how the dynamics present within maltreating families that we have reviewed and discussed are repeated in parallel processes between maltreating families and social service agencies that may inadvertently support and maintain dysfunctional family structures. Our suggestions flow directly from the points we made regarding the relational characteristics of maltreating families. Although some of our prescriptions can be applied to all maltreating families, regardless of their socioeconomic circumstances, the greater prevalence of maltreatment within the poverty sector results in a number of recommendations specific to economically deprived families.

Family vs. individual interventions. Maltreating families often are involved with a variety of social service providers addressing different issues. For example, a family might interact with one department for basic needs such as financial assistance for child rearing, with a second department for help with parenting, and with a third department for employment counselling. In addition, within these diverse areas there may be multiple forms of assistance. For example, support in parenting could include a mandated protective worker, a volunteer or lay counselor, a substance abuse counselor, and a family therapist from one of the community children's agencies. Integrative meetings attended by Mt. Hope Family Center staff members have included as many as 12 helping professionals, outnumbering the family members by a large margin. The number of people working diligently to help these families can be overwhelming for service providers, and must certainly be experienced by our clients in a similar fashion.

In contrast, many families go without any services despite persistent and disturbing evidence that child maltreatment is present. The frequency and etiology of these oversights is beyond the scope of this chapter; however, epidemiological data suggest that there are many more families in need of help than those currently receiving it due to the lack of resources available to them (Barnett, Manly, & Cicchetti, this volume).

In utilizing a family systems perspective under the broad theoretical rubric of developmental psychopathology, it is both possible and important to view a number of seemingly divergent problems facing a family as intimately related and capable of benefitting from intervention at the family level. For example, many of the families we work with at Mt. Hope Family Center may be experiencing problems simultaneously in such diverse areas as substance abuse, teen pregnancy, delinquency, persistent poverty, and spousal abuse as well as child maltreatment. In trying to address each of these problems as distinct, it is easy to see how so many different agencies and workers could become involved with a single family.

We suggest that, when multiple care providers are all involved with the family to address different individual needs, the treatment of the family suffers without an integrated systemic perspective. A lack of coordinated services is clearly at odds with a cost-effective approach, and also may work against the therapeutic goals of helping these families by adding complexity and, in some instances, allowing "splitting," or the inadvertent working of one form of intervention against another, to maintain homeostasis. In keeping with our theoretical perspective, we further suggest that interventions directed at the level of the family, as opposed to targeting multiple individuals within the family, may best address the complex list of problem areas they face. A single family worker, or in extreme cases a small team of workers, might function more adaptively to integrate services and address the dynamics fostering incompetence and the lack of growth and differentiation described above. We believe that the coordination of services, as well as an appreciation of the family functioning as a unit, can lead to more effective and efficient intervention.

We are aware that this recommendation sounds a great deal like the "case manager model," which has largely failed to meet the growing needs of multi-problem families. We wish to stress that an integrated provision of services can best be accomplished by a professional who has a therapeutic relationship with the family beyond the traditional goal of simply coordinating concrete services. While the coordination of services is critical, we believe that a relational approach to treatment is the best form of intervention to address the interpersonal difficulties of maltreating families. Concrete services for maltreating families are an important part of any effective intervention, but we believe that change must take place in the representational models of maltreating family members to truly impact the family and minimize the risk of maltreatment.

We stated earlier that child maltreatment may be a unifying dynamic that can integrate the seemingly unrelated problem areas of teen pregnancy, delinquency, violence, depression, and substance abuse. For intervention to be most effective, changes in the representational models of maltreated children must begin to take hold before they reach adolescence and experience this "branching" of problems in response to their emotional neediness and distress. We suggest that interventions must take a preventive focus and attempt to modify the relational beliefs and expectations of children early in their development. The problem areas described above all can be linked to difficulty and/or failure in achieving and sustaining a sense of security for individuals. For example, teens may have children to fill their own emotional void; delinquency, violence, and depression may reflect the anger and sadness experienced by young people when emotional needs go unmet and no hope for change can be seen; substance abuse may be the only reliable way these children can find to achieve a temporary state of felt security so important to all of us. Each of these problem areas, therefore, can be viewed as a temporary "solution" to relational emptiness from the individual's perspective. However, each of these "solutions" clearly makes it more difficult for long-term, adaptive change to take place. We believe that social policies at the family level that provide a preventive/relational intervention have the best chance of altering the developmental course of maltreating families toward more adaptive functioning.

Parallel processes across systems. In keeping with a family systems' focus on fundamental issues being expressed at multiple levels of a system, we suggest that maltreating families approach the interface with social service agencies in much the same way that they approach relationships with important others. Such a conceptualization is in concert with attachment theory and the operation of internalized mental models of relationships (Bowlby, 1969/1982). It is reasonable to believe that maltreating parents will construct expectations of social service systems based on their representations of care providers who failed to meet their needs. We suggest that maltreating families may engage in parallel processes with the social service system, and that the current provision of social services may inadvertently foster and maintain structural family dysfunction in maltreating families.

Our review of the maltreating family life cycle ended with four summary points about relationship dynamics and structural characteristics we believe describe them. We now discuss how these four issues might reflect parallel processing and explore how changes in social policy could have important positive effects on these processes.

1. The lack of individuation and hierarchical growth. In our review, we have highlighted how maltreating families fail to foster competence and individuation in their children, instead promoting a dependency that is denied and avoided by the peripheral males and leads to the rigid maternal axis for females. The resulting structure lacks the hierarchical organization and differentiation that characterizes healthy family functioning. We suggest that the current form of providing social services to families may, in many ways, parallel the dynamics of the maltreating family by fostering dependency as opposed to competence and autonomy.

When parents only provide for the essential needs of their children without teaching their children over time how to meet these needs on their own, we suggest that parents have fostered their children's dependency and failed to provide the developmental scaffolding necessary for the children to gain competence. Similarly, when social service agencies provide for the basic necessities of food and shelter without also teaching skills and expecting an active contribution on the part of the family, a parallel dynamic of dependency is fostered that works against the development of competence. Because maltreating family members may have expectations at the relationship level that parallel their interactions with the social service system at the systemic level, the compound effect of these parallel processes is even more powerful and difficult to break.

In accord with many welfare reform programs around the country, we suggest that the provision of social services should include the clear expectation that recipients will either actively participate in a community service program or be involved in skill acquisition that will increase the likelihood of future autonomous functioning. Examples of such activities might be participation in caring for public parks, the creation of neighborhood watches to protect children travelling to and from school, or involvement in job training programs. While the specific forms of such community service clearly need to be further developed and delineated, we suggest that an expectation for participation will provide the opportunity for welfare recipients to gain competence and feel some mastery over a situation that currently appears to cycle through multiple generations of dependent families with no clear plan of how to break the cycle.

2. The use of children as emotional resources. We have described how children in maltreating families may be viewed as a potential emotional resource for needy parents who foster role-reversed relationships that are consistent with their internalized models of relationships. Children are viewed as emotional resources and try desperately to meet the adult intimacy needs of their parents at the expense of their own development.

We suggest that, for many families, children also come to be seen as resources for financial needs, as levels of aid increase with the number of children in the home. Clearly more aid is needed for families with more children. However, a parallel process appears to operate when increasing the number of children in the household is the only option available for parents seeking increases in emotional as well as financial resources. We are not suggesting that poor mothers are having children simply to increase their monetary recompense. Clearly, there are a number of psychological issues organized around the mother's own emotional neediness that provide more useful insight into this phenomena. However, we are stressing that the provision of financial assistance must not act in harmony with these dynamics. Perhaps mothers who are dependent on the government for support could be offered groups designed to explore their views on parenthood and encourage thoughtful family planning.

It also is important to find ways to intervene with adolescents before they become young parents dependent on social services for support. The prevention of early pregnancy through education and therapeutic intervention may provide adolescents with the emotional resources they desire without looking to a new child to meet those needs. Education and therapy should focus on how to negotiate intimate relationships with romantic partners in ways that provide a sense of security in adolescence. This work may be more important than focusing on parent–child relationships for adolescents, given the risk of early pregnancy in efforts to garner emotional resources. We therefore again wish to stress how important the mate selection period of family development is for maltreating families. The more time young adults have between the onset of physical maturity and reproduction, the better chance they have of providing for their children. Interventions are likely to be most successful if started before adolescence, however, when representational models of relationships may be more flexible and available to change.

3. The rigid maternal axis and the peripheral male. Our review has highlighted the absence of stable male figures in many maltreating families. We have presented a developmental model that suggests the origin of the family structure we see characterized by rigid maternal axes and peripheral males.

Throughout our review we have focused on developmental differences in gender development that may lead to this family configuration. Our policy recommendations focus on ways therapeutic and economic interventions can modify these gender-based patterns of relating.

In designing therapeutic interventions for maltreating families, policy makers and clinicians must consider the two very different reactions to unmet intimacy needs that men and women in these families may evidence. For women, therapy needs to address any lack of differentiation manifest by the construction of a multigenerational axis of women. Consequences of this structure can be explored, and alternative ways of relating discussed and modelled in the therapeutic relationship. For men, failed differentiation is manifested by their premature exodus from the family. This may be especially difficult given that males from maltreating families will view the development of any closeness and intimacy in the therapeutic dialogue as extremely threatening and incongruent with their representations of relationships. The lack of existing research on maltreating men is another example of the difficulties inherent in engaging them. To date, maltreatment research has grown from a focus on the maltreated child to a focus on the maltreating mother-child dyad. In extending research and subsequent understanding to the level of the family system, the inclusion of the men from these families is extremely important.

Economically, two factors that influence the form and level of financial assistance provided to families are very important to consider, given the relationship between finances and family structure that may inadvertently perpetuate this pattern (Rank, 1986). The individual earning or receiving funds to run the family has the greatest influence in how those funds are to be spent. First, AFDC funds are dispersed predominantly to mothers in families. This reflects the reality that, with the exception of single-parent father households and homes where grandparents are sole child-care providers, the vast majority of families include a maternal figure who cares for the children. Second, families with two adults must meet different criteria of income levels than families with one adult, reflecting the reality that a two-parent family provides some opportunity for one adult to work while the other parents. Our clinical and research experience with maltreating families at Mt. Hope Family Center indicate that many families maintain an illusion of single parenthood to maintain needed financial support. Fathers in these families often maintain a separate residence while visiting the family frequently.

We suggest that the provision of funds solely to mothers fosters a parallel process in these families that further minimizes the role of adult males. We also suggest that financially penalizing families with two parents works against the formation and maintenance of a functioning adult subsystem so critical to the operation of an adaptive family unit. If our social policies are designed to foster the stability of families, then we must find ways to include and empower the men who frequently are moving through these systems. Of course, as part of this process mechanisms for ensuring that funds are used for the support of children must be developed and implemented.

4. Representational models lacking vertical skills and the victim/ victimizer dynamic. As we have noted, the tendency to view others with suspicion and to expect victimization in relationships is a characteristic of maltreating families' representational models. We suggest that families view the provision of social services with similar negative expectations. Members of these families view themselves, and are viewed by others, to be victims of poverty, maltreatment, and extremely difficult histories. Victimization of these families at the systemic level is certainly inadvertent, and reflects an interaction among the families, the service provision system, and the larger society. If members of maltreating families are predisposed, by nature of their representational models, to expect victimization at the hands of the social service system, then they may behave in ways consistent with this expectation that make their ultimate victimization more likely.

Conclusion

In summary, in this chapter we have presented a developmental model of the family life cycle of maltreating families from a systemic perspective. We suggest that child maltreatment is but one problem embedded in a rigid, compressed family structure of troubled relationships. The very nature of maltreatment makes the continuation of this limited, compacted family structure more likely. We believe that the dynamics driving and reinforcing the family system from within are also important to consider in forming social policy recommendations designed to help maltreating families allow a more adaptive developmental pathway. Our policy recommendations maintain that, parallel to the care necessary for fostering development in children, our social service system must provide a balanced and caring approach that encourages growth and independence of these families. We must strive to meet more than the immediate needs of maltreating families by providing them with the relational and vocational tools necessary to succeed. Without this future oriented vision, the multitude of families trapped in a cycle of poverty, dependency, and victimization are likely to continue to foster this pattern in generations to come.

REFERENCES

Aber, J. L., & Baker, A. J. (1990). Security of attachment in toddlerhood: Modifying assessment procedures for joint clinical and research purposes. In M. Greenberg, D. Cicchetti, & E. M. Cummings (Eds.), *Attachment in the preschool years: Theory, research, and intervention* (pp. 427–460). Chicago: University of Chicago Press.

Aber, J. L., & Cicchetti, D. (1984). Socioemotional development in maltreated children: An empirical and theoretical analysis. In H. Fitzgerald, B. Lester & M. Yogman (Eds.), *Theory and research in behavioral pediatrics* (Vol. II, pp. 147–205). New York: Plenum Press.

Achenbach, T. (1990). What is "developmental" about developmental psychopathology? In J. Rolf, A. Masten, D. Cicchetti, K. Nuechterlein, & S. Weintraub (Eds.), *Risk and protective factors in the development of psychopathology* (pp. 29–48). New York: Cambridge University Press.

Ainsworth, M. S. (1989). Attachment beyond infancy. *American Psychologist, 44*, 709–716.

Ainsworth, M. S., Blehar, M. C., Waters, E., & Wall, S. (1978). *Patterns of attachment: A psychological study of the strange situation.* Hillsdale, NJ: Erlbaum.

Alexander, P. (1992). Application of attachment theory to the study of sexual abuse. *Journal of Consulting and Clinical Psychology, 60*, 185–195.

Amato, P. R. (1986). Marital conflict, the parent-child relationship and child self-esteem. *Family Relations, 35*, 403–410.

Angold, A., & Rutter, M. (1992). Effects of age and pubertal status on depression in a large clinical sample. *Development and Psychopathology, 4*, 5–28.

Baumrind, D. (1987). A developmental perspective on adolescent risk-taking in contemporary America. In C. Irwin (Ed.), *New directions for child development, 37*, 93–126. San Francisco: Jossey-Bass.

Belsky, J. (1980). Child maltreatment: An ecological integration. *American Psychologist, 35*, 320–335.

Belsky, J. (1981). Early human experience: A family perspective. *Child Development, 17*, 3–23.

Belsky, J., Gilstrap, B., & Rovine, M. (1984). The Pennsylvania infant and family development project. *Child Development, 55*, 692–705.

Belsky, J., & Pensky, E. (1988). Developmental history, personality, and family relationships: toward an emergent family system. In R. Hinde & J. Stevenson-Hinde (Eds.), *Relationships within families: Mutual influences* (pp. 193–217). Oxford: Oxford University Press.

Belsky, J., Spanier, G. B., & Rovine, M. (1983). Stability and change in marriage across the transition to parenthood. *Journal of Marriage and the Family, 45*, 567–577.

Belsky, J., Steinberg, L., & Draper, P. (1991). Childhood experience, interpersonal development, and reproductive strategy: An evolutionary theory of socialization. *Child Development, 62*, 647–670.

Belsky, J. & Vondara, J. (1989). Lessons from child abuse: The determinants of parenting. In D. Cicchetti & V. Carlson (Eds.), *Child maltreatment: Theory and research on the causes and consequences of child abuse and neglect* (pp. 153–202). New York: Cambridge University Press.

Belsky, J., Youngblade, L., & Pensky, E. (1989). Childrearing history, marital quality, and maternal affect: Intergenerational transmission in a low-risk sample. *Development and Psychopathology, 1*, 291–304.

Biller, H. B., & Solomon, R. S. (1986). *Child maltreatment and paternal deprivation.* Lexington, MA: Lexington Books.

Bowen, M. (1974). *Family therapy in clinical practice.* New York: Aronson.

Bowlby, J. (1982). *Attachment and loss, Vol. 1: Attachment.* New York: Basic Books. (Original work published 1969)

Bretherton, I. (1985). Attachment theory: Retrospect and prospect. In I. Bretherton & E. Waters (Eds.), Growing points of attachment theory and research. *Monographs of the Society for Research in Child Development, 50* (1-2, Serial No. 209), 3–35.

Bretherton, I. (1987). New perspectives on attachment relations: Security, communication, and internal working models. In J. Osofsky (Ed.), *Handbook of infant development* (pp. 1061–1100). New York: Wiley.

Bretherton, I., & Waters, E. (Eds.). (1985). *Growing points of attachment theory and research. Monographs of the Society for Research in Child Development, 50* (1-2, Serial No. 209).

Brody, G., Pelligrini, A., & Sigel, I. (1986). Marital quality and mother-child and father-child interactions with school-age children. *Developmental Psychology, 22*, 291–296.

Burgess, R. L., Anderson, E. A., Schellenbach, C. J., & Conger, R. D. (1981). A social interactional approach to the study of abusive families. In J. P. Vincent (Ed.), *Advances in family intervention, assessment and theory: An annual compilation of research* (Vol. 2, pp. 1–46). Greenwich, CT: JAI Press.

Burgess, R. L., & Conger, R. D. (1978). Family interaction in abusive, neglectful, and normal families. *Child Development, 49,* 1163–1173.

Buss, D. (1989). Sex differences in human mate preferences: Evolutionary hypotheses tested in 37 cultures. *Behavioral and Brain Sciences, 12,* 1–49.

Carlson, V., Cicchetti, D., Barnett, D., & Braunwald, K. (1989). Finding order in disorganization: Lessons from research on maltreated infant's attachments to their caregivers. In D. Cicchetti & V. Carlson (Eds.), *Child maltreatment: Theory and research on the causes and consequences of child abuse and neglect* (pp. 494–528). New York: Cambridge University Press.

Carter, E., & McGoldrick, M. (1980). *The family life cycle: A framework for family therapy.* New York: Gardner Press.

Chodorow, N. J. (1978). *The reproduction of mothering.* Berkeley, CA: University of California Press.

Cicchetti, D. (1984). The emergence of developmental psychopathology. *Child Development, 55,* 1–7.

Cicchetti, D. (1990a). A historical perspective on the discipline of developmental psychopathology. In J. Rolf, A. Masten, D. Cicchetti, K. Nuechterlein, & S. Weintraub (Eds.), *Risk and protective factors in the development of psychopathology* (pp. 2–28). New York: Cambridge University Press.

Cicchetti, D. (1990b). The organization and coherence of socioemotional, cognitive, and representational development: Illustrations through a developmental psychopathology perspective on Down Syndrome and child maltreatment. In R. A. Thompson (Ed.), *Socioemotional Development: Nebraska Symposium on Motivation, Vol. 36,* (pp. 259–366). Lincoln, NE: University of Nebraska Press.

Cicchetti, D. (1991). Fractures in the crystal: Developmental psychopathology and the emergence of the self. *Developmental Review, 11,* 271–287.

Cicchetti, D. (in press). What developmental psychopathology is about: Reactions, reflections, projections. *Developmental Review.*

Cicchetti, D., & Barnett, D. (1991). Attachment organization in maltreated preschoolers. *Development and Psychopathology, 3,* 397–412.

Cicchetti, D., & Beeghly, M. (1987). Symbolic development in maltreated youngsters: An organizational perspective. *New Directions for Child Development, 36,* 47–68.

Cicchetti, D., & Carlson, V. (Eds.). (1989). *Child maltreatment: Theory and research on the causes and consequences of child abuse and neglect.* New York: Cambridge University Press.

Cicchetti, D., Cummings, E. M., Greenberg, M., & Marvin, R. (1990). An organizational perspective on attachment beyond infancy: Implications for theory, measurement, and research. In M. Greenberg, D. Cicchetti, & E. M. Cummings (Eds.), *Attachment in the preschool years: Theory, research, and intervention* (pp. 3–49). Chicago: University of Chicago Press.

Cicchetti, D., Ganiban, J., & Barnett, D. (1991). Contributions from the study of high risk populations to understanding the development of emotion regulation. In J. Garber & K. Dodge (Eds.), *The development of emotion regulation and dysregulation* (pp. 15–48). New York: Cambridge University Press.

Cicchetti, D., & Howes, P. W. (1991). Developmental psychopathology in the context of the family: Illustrations from the study of child maltreatment. *Canadian Journal of the Behavioural Sciences, 23,* 257–281.

Cicchetti, D., & Lynch, M. (1993). Toward an ecological/transactional model of community violence and child maltreatment: Consequences for children's development. *Psychiatry, 56.*

Cicchetti, D., Lynch, M., Shonk, S., & Manly, J. T. (1992). An organizational perspective on peer relations in maltreated children. In R. D. Parke & G. W. Ladd (Eds.), *Family-peer relationships: Modes of linkage* (pp. 345–383). Hillsdale, NJ: Erlbaum.

Cicchetti, D., & Manly, J. T. (1990). A personal perspective on conducting research with maltreating families: Problems and solutions. In E. Brody & I. Sigel (Eds.), *Family research journeys: Vol. 2: Families at risk* (pp. 87–133). Hillsdale, NJ: Erlbaum.

Cicchetti, D., & Rizley, R. (1981). Developmental perspectives on the etiology, intergenerational transmission and sequelae of the child maltreatment. *New Directions for Child Development, 11,* 32–59.

Cicchetti, D., & Toth, S. L. (1991). The making of a developmental psychopathologist. In J. Cantor, C. Spiker, & L. Lipsitt (Eds.), *Child behavior and development: Training for diversity* (pp. 34–72). Norwood, NJ: Ablex Publishing Corp.

Clarke-Stewart, K. A., & Hevey, C. M. (1981). Longitudinal relations in repeated observations of mother-child interaction from 1 to 2 ½ years. *Developmental Psychology, 17,* 127–145.

Colon, F. (1980). The family life cycle of the multiproblem poor family. In E. Carter & M. McGoldrick (Eds.), *The family life cycle: A framework for family therapy* (pp. 343–382). New York: Gardner Press.

Conte, J. R. (1984). Progress in treating the sexual abuse of children. *Social Work,* pp. 258–263.

Cowan, C. P., Cowan, P. A., Heming, G., Garrett, E., Coysh, W., Curtis-Boles, H., & Boles, A. (1985). Transitions to parenthood: His, hers, and theirs. *Journal of Family Issues, 6,* 451–481.

Cowan, C. P., Cowan, P. A., Heming, G., & Miller, N. B. (1992). Becoming a family: Marriage, parenting, and child development. In P. Cowan & E. Hetherington (Eds.), *Family transitions* (pp. 79–104). Hillsdale, NJ: Erlbaum.

Coyne, J., Downey, G., & Boergers, J. (1992). Depression in families: A systems perspective. In D. Cicchetti & S. L. Toth (Eds.), *Rochester Symposium on Developmental Psychopathology, Vol. 4: Developmental perspectives on depression* (pp. 211–249). Rochester, NY: Erlbaum.

Crittenden, P. M. (1981). Abusing, neglecting, problematic, and adequate dyads: Differentiating by patterns of interaction. *Merrill-Palmer Quarterly, 27,* 201–208.

Crittenden, P. M. (1988). Distorted patterns of relationship in maltreating families: The role of internal representation models. *Journal of Reproductive and Infant Psychology, 6,* 183–199.

Crittenden, P. M. (1992). Quality of attachment in the preschool years. *Development and Psychopathology, 4,* 209–241.

Crittenden, P. M., & Ainsworth, M. S. (1989). Child maltreatment and attachment theory. In D. Cicchetti & V. Carlson (Eds.), *Child maltreatment: Theory and research on the causes and consequences of child abuse and neglect* (pp. 432–463). New York: Cambridge University Press.

Crittenden, P. M., Partridge, M. F., & Claussen, A. H. (1991). Family patterns of relationship in normative and dysfunctional families. *Development and Psychopathology, 3,* 491–512.

Daly, M., & Wilson, M. (1981). Child maltreatment from a sociobiological perspective. *New Directions for Child Development, 11,* 93–112.

Dodge, K. (1983). Behavioral antecedents of peer status. *Child Development, 54,* 1386–1399.

Egeland, B., Jacobvitz, D., & Sroufe, L. A. (1988). Breaking the cycle of abuse. *Child Development, 59,* 1080–1088.

Egeland, B., & Sroufe, A. (1981). Developmental sequelae of maltreatment in infancy. In R. Rizley & D. Cicchetti (Eds.), *Developmental perspectives in child maltreatment, 11* (pp. 77–92). San Francisco: Jossey-Bass.

Erickson, M. F., Egeland, B., & Pianta, R. (1989). The effects of maltreatment on the development of young children. In D. Cicchetti & V. Carlson (Eds.), *Child maltreatment: Theory and research on the causes and consequences of child abuse and neglect* (pp. 647–684). New York: Cambridge University Press.

Erikson, E. H. (1950). *Childhood and society.* New York: Norton.

Erikson, E. H. (1959). Identity and the life cycle: Selected papers. *Psychological Issues, 1*(1).

Fonagy, P., Steele, H., & Steele, M. (1991). Maternal representations of attachment during pregnancy predict the organization of infant-mother attachment at one year of age. *Child Development*, *62*, 891–905.

Gaensbauer, T. J. (1982). The differentiation of discrete affects. *The Psychoanalytic Study of the Child*, *37*, 29–66.

Garbarino, J. (1977). The human ecology of child maltreatment: A conceptual model for research. *Journal of Marriage and the Family*, *39*, 721–732.

Garbarino, J. (1989). Troubled youth, troubled families: the dynamics of adolescent maltreatment. In D. Cicchetti & V. Carlson (Eds.), *Child maltreatment: Theory and research on the causes and consequences of child abuse and neglect* (pp. 685–706). New York: Cambridge University Press.

Garbarino, J., Guttman, E., & Seeley, J. (1988). *The psychologically battered child*. San Francisco: Jossey-Bass.

Gelles, R. (1992). Poverty and violence toward children. *American Behavioral Scientist*, *35*, 258–274.

George, C., & Main, M. (1979). Social interactions of young abused children: Approach, avoidance, and aggression. *Child Development*, *50*, 306–318.

Gilligan, C. (1982). *In a different voice*. Cambridge, MA: Harvard University Press.

Goldberg, W. A., & Easterbrooks, M. A. (1984). The role of marital quality in toddler development. *Child Development*, *20*, 504–515.

Gottman, J. M. (1991). Chaos and regulated change in families: A metaphor for the study of transitions. In P. A. Cowan & E. M. Hetherington (Eds.), *Family transitions* (pp. 247–272). Hillsdale, NJ: Erlbaum.

Gottman, J. M. & Levenson, R. W. (1988). The social psychophysiology of marriage. In P. Noller & M. Fitzpatrick (Eds.), *Perspectives on marital interaction*. San Diego: College Hill.

Greenberg, M. T., Cicchetti, D., & Cummings, E. M. (Eds.). (1990). *Attachment in the preschool years: Theory, research, and intervention*. Chicago: University of Chicago Press.

Grych, J. H., & Fincham, F. D. (1990). Marital conflict and children's adjustment: A cognitive-contextual framework: *Psychological Bulletin*, *108*, 267–290.

Haley, (1971). *Changing families*. New York: Grune and Stratton.

Hart, S. N., & Brassard, M. R. (1987). A major threat to children's mental health: Psychological maltreatment. *American Psychologist*, *42*, 160–165.

Hartup, W. (1983). Peer relations. In P. Mussen (Ed.), *Handbook of child psychology* (pp. 103–196). New York: Wiley.

Hartup, W. (1986). On relationships and development. In W. Hartup & Z. Rubin (Eds.), *Relationships and development* (pp. 1–26). Hillsdale, NJ: Erlbaum.

Haviland, J. J., & Malatesta, C. Z. (1981). The development of sex differences in nonverbal signals: Fallacies, facts, and fantasies. In C. Mayo & N. M. Henley (Eds.), *Gender and non-verbal behavior* (pp. 183–208). New York: Springer-Verlag.

Hazan, C., & Shaver, P. (1987). Romantic love conceptualized as an attachment process. *Journal of Personality and Social Psychology*, *52*, 511–524.

Hennessy, K. D., Rabideau, G. J., Cicchetti, D., & Cummings, E. M. (in press). *Responses of physically abused children to different forms of interadult anger. Child Development*.

Hetherington, E. M. (1988). Parents, children, and siblings: Six years after divorce. In R. A. Hinde & J. Stevenson-Hinde (Eds.), *Relationships within families* (pp. 311–331). Oxford: Clarendon Press.

Hinde, R. A. (1979). *Towards understanding relationships*. Academic Press: London.

Hinde, R. A., & Stevenson-Hinde, J. (1988). *Relationships within families: Mutual influences*. Oxford: Clarendon Press.

Hoffman-Plotkin, D., & Twentyman, C. (1984). A multimodal assessment of behavioral and cognitive deficits in abused and neglected preschoolers. *Child Development*, *55*, 794–802.

Howes, C., & Eldredge, R. (1985). Responses to abused, neglected, and nonmaltreated children to the behaviors of their peers. *Journal of Applied Developmental Psychology*, *6*, 261–270.

Howes, C., & Espinosa, M. P. (1985). The consequences of child abuse for the formation of relationships with peers. *Child Abuse and Neglect*, *9*, 397–404.

Howes, P. W. (1989). *Family attachment: Interactional links between marriage and children.* Unpublished doctoral dissertation, University of Denver.

Howes, P. W., & Markman, H. J. (1989). Marital quality and child functioning: A longitudinal investigation. *Child Development*, *60*, 1044–1051.

Howes, P. W., & Markman, H. J. (April, 1991). *Longitudinal relations between premarital and prebirth adult interaction and subsequent parent-child attachment.* Paper presented at the Meetings of the Society for Research in Child Development, Seattle, Washington.

Howes, P. W., Markman, H. J., & Lindahl, K. (1992). *Managing conflict in the family: Family and marital correlates of parent–child attachment.* Manuscript submitted for publication.

Jacobson, R., & Straker, G. (1982). Peer group interaction of physically abused children. *Child Abuse and Neglect*, *6*, 321–327.

Junewicz, W. J. (1983). A protective posture toward emotional neglect and abuse. *Child Welfare*, *62*, 243–252.

Kaufman, J. (1991). Depressive disorders in maltreated children. *Journal of the American Academy of Child and Adolescent Psychiatry*, *30*, 257–265.

Kaufman, J., & Zigler, E. (1989). The intergenerational transmission of child abuse and the prospect of predicting future abusers. In D. Cicchetti & V. Carlson (Eds.), *Child maltreatment: Theory and research on the causes and consequences of child abuse and neglect* (pp. 129–152). New York: Cambridge University Press.

Kempe, R., & Kempe, C. H. (1978). *Child abuse.* Cambridge, MA: Harvard University Press.

Kerig, P. (1992). *Marital quality and gender differences in parent-child interaction.* Manuscript submitted for publication.

Kimball, W. H., Stewart, R. B., Conger, R. D., & Burgess, R. L. (1980). A comparison of family interaction in single versus two-parent abusive, neglectful, and control families. In T. Field, S. Goldberg, D. Stern, & A. Sostek (Eds.), *Interactions of high risk infants and children.* New York: Academic Press.

Kobak, R., & Sceery, A. (1988). Attachment in later adolescence: Working models, affect regulation, and perceptions of self and others. *Child Development*, *59*, 135–146.

Lewis, M., & Brooks-Gunn, J. (1979). *Social cognition and the acquisition of self.* New York: Plenum Press.

Levenson, R., & Gottman, J. (1985). Physiological affective predictors of change in relationship satisfaction. *Journal of Personality and Social Psychology*, *49*, 85–94.

Levy, G. D., & Carter, D. B. (1989). Gender schema, gender constancy, and gender-role knowledge: The roles of cognitive factors in preschoolers' gender-role stereotype attributions. *Developmental Psychology*, *25*, 444–449.

Lieberman, A. F., & Pawl, J. H. (1990). Disorders of attachment and secure base behavior in the second year of life. In M. Greenberg, D. Cicchetti, & E. M. Cummings (Eds.), *Attachment in the preschool years: Theory, research, and intervention* (pp. 375–397). Chicago: University of Chicago Press.

Lynch, M., & Cicchetti, D. (1991). Patterns of relatedness in maltreated and nonmaltreated children: Connections among multiple representational models. *Development and Psychopathology*, *3*, 206–277.

Lynch, M., & Cicchetti, D. (1992). Maltreated children's reports of relatedness to their teachers. *New Directions for Child Development*, *57*, 81–107.

Mahler, M., Pine, F., & Bergman, A. (1975). *The psychological birth of the human infant.* New York: Basic Books.

Main, M., & George, C. (1985). Response of abused and disadvantaged toddlers to distress in agemates: A study in the day care setting. *Developmental Psychology*, *21*, 407–412.

Main, M., & Hesse, E. (1990). Parents' unresolved traumatic experiences are related to infant disorganized attachment status: Is frightened and/or frightening parental behavior the linking mechanism? In M. Greenberg, D. Cicchetti, & E. M. Cummings (Eds.), *Attachment in the preschool years: Theory, research, and intervention* (pp. 161–184). Chicago: University of Chicago Press.

Main, M., Kaplan, N., & Cassidy, J. (1985). Security in infancy, childhood and adulthood: A move to the level of representation. In I. Bretherton & E. Waters (Eds.), *Growing points of attachment theory and research. Monographs of the Society for Research in Child Development*, 50 (1-2, Serial No. 209). 66–104.

Markman, H. J. (1981). The prediction of marital distress: A five-year follow up. *Journal of Consulting and Clinical Psychology*, 49, 760–762.

Markman, H. J., Duncan, S. W., Storaasli, R., & Howes, P. W. (1987). The prediction and prevention of marital distress: A longitudinal investigation. In K. Hahlweg & M. Goldstein (Eds.), *Understanding major mental disorders: The contribution of family interaction research* (pp. 266–289). New York: Family Process Press.

Markman, H. J., & Kraft, S. (1989). Men and women in marriage: Dealing with gender differences in marital therapy. *The Behavior Therapist*, 12, 51–56.

Marvin, R. M. (1977). An ethological-cognitive model for the attenuation of mother-child attachment and behavior. In T. M. Alloway, L. Krames, & P. Piner (Eds.), *Advances in the study of communication and affect, Vol. 3. The development of social attachments* (pp. 25–60). New York: Plenum.

Marvin, R. M., & Stewart, R. B. (1990). A family systems framework for the study of attachment. In M. Greenberg, D. Cicchetti, & E. M. Cummings (Eds.), *Attachment in the preschool years* (pp. 51–86). Chicago: University of Chicago Press.

Minuchin, P. (1985). Families and individual development: Provocations from the field of family therapy. *Child Development*, 56, 289–302.

Minuchin, P. (1988). Relationships within the systems perspective on development. In R. Hinde & J. Stevenson-Hinde (Eds.), *Relationships within families: Mutual influences* (pp. 7–26). Oxford: Clarendon Press.

Minuchin, S. (1974). *Families and family therapy.* Cambridge, MA: Harvard University Press.

Minuchin, S., Montalvo, B., Rosman, B. L., & Schumer, R. (1967). *Families of the slums.* New York: Basic Books.

Morgan, S., Lye, D., & Condran, G. (1988). Sons, daughters, and the risk of marital disruption. *American Journal of Sociology*, 94, 110–129.

Mueller, N., & Silverman, N. (1989). Peer relations in maltreated children. In D. Cicchetti & V. Carlson (Eds.), *Child maltreatment: Research and theory on the causes and consequences of child abuse and neglect* (pp. 529–578). New York: Cambridge University Press.

Murphy, M., Jellinek, M., Quinn, D., Smith, G., Poitrast, F. G., & Goshko, M. (1991). Substance abuse and serious child maltreatment: Prevalence, risk and outcome in a court sample. *Child Abuse and Neglect*, 15, 197–211.

Newberger, C. M., & Daniel, J. (1979). Knowledge and epidemiology of child abuse: A critical review of concepts. In R. Bourne & E. Newberger (Eds.), *Critical perspectives on child abuse* (pp. 19–25). Lexington, MA: Lexington Books.

Notarius, C., & Pellegrini, D. S. (1987). Differences between husbands and wives: Implications for understanding marital discord. In K. Hahlweg & M. Goldstein (Eds.), *Understanding major mental disorder: The contribution of family interaction research* (pp. 231–249). New York: Family Process Press.

Parkes, C. M., Stevenson-Hinde, J., & Marris, P. (Eds.). (1991). *Attachment across the lifecycle.* London: Routledge.

Patterson, G. (1975). *A social learning approach to family intervention.* Eugene, OR: Castalia Publishing Company.

Rank, M. R. (1986). Family structure and the process of exiting from welfare. *Journal of Marriage and the Family*, 48, 607–618.

Reiss, D. (1989). The represented and practicing family: Contrasting visions of family continuity. In A. Sameroff & R. Emde (Eds.), *Relationship disturbances in early childhood* (pp. 191–220). New York: Basic Books.

Rieder, C., & Cicchetti, D. (1989). Organizational perspective on cognitive control functioning and cognitive-affective balance in maltreated children. *Developmental Psychology, 25*, 382–393.

Rutter, M., & Garmezy, N. (1983). Developmental psychopathology. In P. Mussen (Ed.), *Handbook of child psychology* (Vol. IV, pp. 775–911). New York: Wiley.

Ryan, R., & Lynch, J. (1989). Emotional autonomy versus detachment: Revisiting the vicissitudes of adolescence and young adulthood. *Child Development, 60*, 340–356.

Sameroff, A. J., & Chandler, M. J. (1975). Reproductive risk and the continuum of caretaking casualty. In F. D. Horowitz (Ed.), *Review of child development research* (Vol. 4, pp. 187–244). Chicago: University of Chicago Press.

Satir, V. (1964). *Conjoint family therapy.* Palo Alto, CA: Science and Behavior Books.

Schneider-Rosen, K. (1990). The developmental reorganization of attachment relationships. In M. Greenberg, D. Cicchetti, & E. M. Cummings (Eds.), *Attachment in the preschool years: Theory, research, and intervention* (pp. 185–220). Chicago: University of Chicago Press.

Schneider-Rosen, K., & Cicchetti, D. (1984). The relationship between affect and cognition in maltreated infants: Quality of attachment and the development of visual self-recognition. *Child Development, 55*, 648–658.

Sroufe, L. A. (1979). Socioemotional development. In J. Osofsky (Ed.), *Handbook of infant development* (pp. 462–516). New York: Wiley.

Sroufe, L. A. (1983). Infant-caregiver attachment and patterns of adaptation in preschool: The roots of maladaptation and competence. In M. Perlmutter (Ed.), *Minnesota Symposium in Child Psychology* (Vol. 16, pp. 41–81). Hillsdale, NJ: Erlbaum.

Sroufe, L. A. (1989). Relationships and relationship disturbance. In A. Sameroff & R. Emde (Eds.), *Relationship disturbances in early childhood* (pp. 97–124). New York: Basic Books.

Sroufe, L. A., & Fleeson, J. (1986). Attachment and the construction of relationships. In W. Hartup & Z. Rubin (Eds.), *Relationships and development: Mutual Influences* (pp. 51–72). Hillsdale, NJ: Erlbaum.

Sroufe, L. A., & Fleeson, J. (1988). The coherence of family relationships. In R. A. Hinde & J. Stevenson-Hinde (Eds.), *Relationships within families: Mutual influences* (pp. 27–47). Oxford: Clarendon Press.

Sroufe, L. A., Jacobvitz, D., Mangelsdorf, S., DeAngelo, E., & Ward, M. J. (1985). Generational boundary dissolution between mothers and their preschool children: A relationship systems approach. *Child Development, 56*, 317–325.

Sroufe, L. A., & Ward, M. J. (1980). Seductive behavior of mothers of toddlers: Occurrence, correlates, and family origins. *Child Development, 51*, 122–1229.

Stern, D. (1985). *The interpersonal world of the infant.* New York: Basic Books.

Stevenson-Hinde, J. (1990). Attachment within family systems: An overview. *Infant Mental Health Journal, 11*, 218–227.

Toth, S. L., Manly, J. T., & Cicchetti, D. (1992). Child maltreatment and vulnerability to depression. *Development and Psychopathology, 4*, 97–112.

Trivers, R. L. (1974). Parent–offspring conflict. *American Zoologist, 14*, 249–264.

Troy, M., & Sroufe, L. A. (1987). Victimization among preschoolers: The role of attachment relationship history. *Journal of the American Academy of Child Psychiatry, 26*, 166–172.

Werner, H. (1957). The concept of development from a comparative and organismic point of view. In D. B. Harris (Ed.), *The concept of development* (pp. 125–148). Minneapolis: University of Minnesota Press.

10

Child Maltreatment and School Adaptation: Problems and Promises*

Dante Cicchetti
Sheree L. Toth
Kevin Hennessy

In recent times the educational system in our society has been subject to increased scrutiny due to perceived failures and shortcomings of its existing structures. Education has become a major sociopolitical issue. In particular, the concept of "school readiness" has captured the interest of child advocates, legislators, and state and national leaders in government (Crnic, Lamberty, & Burns, 1992; Kagan, 1990; NAEYC, 1990). The magnitude of the attention directed toward school readiness can be seen clearly in its prioritization as number one in the President's list of the top five goals for the field of education to achieve by the year 2000. Specifically, the goal states that, "by the year 2000, all children in America will start school ready to learn." While a laudable aim, its attainment clearly requires the implementation of broad-based efforts that support the family in its preparation of a child for the entrance into school. In this regard, an increasingly active interface between school and home must be initiated. In addition, the boundaries that exist between the family and the school must become more permeable, thereby allowing information to flow more smoothly and readily between these two levels of the ecology (cf. Cicchetti & Lynch, 1993).

Although many families are quite capable of providing their children with the cognitive and emotional resources that will stimulate their interest and enthusiasm for a forthcoming school experience, unfortunately the children most at risk for school failure are the very children whose families are less able to prepare them for an educational experience. In the absence of family support and the provision of early intervention services, children from impoverished, poorly

* We acknowledge the William T. Grant Foundation, the A.L. Mailman Family Foundation, Inc., the Smith Richardson Foundation, Inc., the Spencer Foundation, and the Spunk Fund, Inc. for their generous support of our work. Additionally, we appreciate the support of the Monroe County Department of Social Services and the New York State Department of Special Education. We also thank the educational staff of Mt. Hope Family Center for their insights and the efforts which they devote to promoting the well-being of maltreated children. Finally, we are grateful to Jennifer Boehles for typing this manuscript.

educated families are at heightened risk for perpetuating a cycle of school drop-out. Although an increase in early childhood educational programs has occurred in efforts to help ready children for school (Meisels & Shonkoff, 1990), the number of high risk children receiving services are substantially less than those being provided to children from nondisadvantaged backgrounds (see the report of the U.S. House of Representatives, Select Committee on Children, Youth, and Families, 1989). While the factors contributing to this distressing state of affairs can be debated, its existence underscores the importance of modifying the approach to early childhood education that has contributed to the failure to provide our most needy children and families with the resources necessary to help them, the children, succeed in school.

Based on a deep commitment to the belief that all children, including those from disadvantaged and minority backgrounds, warrant equality of educational opportunity, early childhood intervention programs have proliferated in our nation during the past several decades. The implementation of the Head Start program in 1965, and its subsequent success, can serve as a model for providing preventive services to high-risk children and families, some of whom undoubtedly are either at risk for or currently maltreating their children (Zigler & Valentine, 1979). According to Zigler, "in regard to economically disadvantaged children, a consensus now exists among behavioral scientists, policy makers, and even taxpayers that early intervention is a cost-effective method for combating the effects of poverty experienced early in life" (1990, p. ix). Due to growing evidence of the efficacy of early intervention for a multitude of high-risk groups, including developmentally disabled and maltreated children (see, for example, chapters in Meisels & Shonkoff, 1990, and Price, Cowen, Lorion, & Ramos-McKay, 1988), Zigler further contends that the importance of early intervention is widely embraced by "all elements of the political spectrum" (1990, p. ix).

In this chapter, we review legislative efforts that have been directed toward early educational services for children with special education needs. We also highlight legislation that has been proposed and implemented to protect abused and neglected children. Because research has shown that maltreated children share many difficulties with the more general population of special needs children for whom much of the educational legislation was developed, it is important to understand the broader context of educational policy efforts. We then summarize the research findings on the school functioning of maltreated children. We conclude by exploring policy-relevant implications for facilitating the educational success of children who have experienced maltreatment.

LEGISLATIVE OVERVIEW OF EARLY SPECIAL EDUCATIONAL SERVICES FOR CHILDREN

The 1960s marked the inception of the modern era in the early childhood intervention movement (Shonkoff & Meisels, 1990). Nineteen sixty-five witnessed the implementation of the most broad-reaching experiment of the decade, Project Head Start (Zigler & Valentine, 1979). From its more humble beginnings as an 8-week pilot program in the summer prior to school entrance, Head Start has evolved as a comprehensive system aimed at eradicating the harmful effects that poverty and disadvantage exert on child development and family life. Head Start Programs focused their intervention on the "whole child," not merely on facilitating cognitive development. Thus, these programs also expended a great amount of energy on children's socioemotional functioning and invested much energy on getting parent's involved with the intervention efforts. Consequently, parents participated both on a volunteer basis in program activities and in making decisions about the nature of services that would best help their family. This decision-making partnership between the parent and professional was revolutionary and continues to assume importance in the fields of education, sociology, and psychology.

While the 1960s focused on the problems of poverty and disadvantage, the decade of the 1970s underscored the needs of children with developmental disabilities. In 1972, a federal law (P.L. 92-424) was passed mandating all Head Start programs to reserve a minimum of 10% of their enrollment slots for children with identified disabilities. Two years later, monies for implementation grants to assist states in the planning and development of services for infants and preschoolers with disabilities were allocated by the federal government.

The year 1975 witnessed the passage of the Education for all Handicapped Children Act (P.L. 94-142). Though this law did not mandate states to provide services for all handicapped children, it did endorse the importance of doing so.

In 1986, over a decade later, the Education for Handicapped Act Amendment Acts (P.L. 99-457) was passed. Considered the most vital legislation ever enacted for children with developmental vulnerabilities, it called for "a statewide, comprehensive, coordinated, multidisciplinary, interagency program of early intervention services for all handicapped infants and their families" (P.L. 99-457, Sec. 671). Although P.L. 99-457 does not require services for all children less than age 6, it does provide incentives for states to offer intervention services to 3- to 6-year-olds, and it established a discretionary program to facilitate the enactment of comprehensive early intervention programs for children birth to 3 years. While these early intervention programs are not legally mandated, nonetheless all states have chosen to initiate planning activities for their implementation.

OVERVIEW OF CHILD ABUSE AND NEGLECT LEGISLATION

Although child abuse and neglect have occurred for centuries (Zigler & Hall, 1989), recent government legislation addressing the prevention and treatment of child maltreatment dates back to the 1960s. It was not until Kempe's work on the "battered child syndrome" (Kempe, Silverman, Steele, Droegemueller, & Silver, 1962) that child abuse and neglect became issues of growing national

concern. Increased awareness of the widespread incidence and possible deleterious effects of maltreatment led many states to adopt mandatory child abuse
and neglect reporting laws. By the late 1960s, all 50 states had some form of
legislation that required individuals to report suspected cases of child abuse or
neglect to state or local authorities (Nelson, 1984).

Federal laws designed to reduce the incidence of child abuse and neglect
quickly followed state efforts to address these problems. After a number of
attempts, Congress in 1974 enacted federal law P.L. 93-247, The Child Abuse
Prevention and Treatment Act (CAPTA). Through this legislation, the federal
government was authorized to provide financial assistance for identifying, preventing, and treating child abuse and neglect. One provision of the law called for
the creation of the National Center on Child Abuse and Neglect (NCCAN), to
provide research, data collection, information dissemination, and coordination
activities in the area of child maltreatment. In addition, NCCAN was authorized
to administer demonstration grant programs funded by the law, as well as to
provide technical assistance and support to innovative programs for preventing or
treating child abuse and neglect.

Due to CAPTA's initial success, the original legislation has been reauthorized
and expanded four times since 1974: (a) P.L. 95-266, the Child Abuse Prevention and Treatment and Adoption Reform Act of 1978; (b) P.L. 98-457, The
Child Abuse Amendments of 1984; (c) P.L. 100-294, The Child Abuse Prevention, Adoption, and Family Services Act of 1988; and (d) P.L. 102-295, The
Child Abuse, Domestic Violence, Adoption and Family Services Act of 1992.

Some of the more important changes in the earlier revisions of the Act were
efforts to strengthen eligibility requirements for states seeking grants for prevention and treatment activities. In order to obtain federal monies, states must have
implemented systems for both reporting child abuse and neglect and investigating such reports, as well as adopted laws providing immunity for persons
reporting incidents of abuse and neglect.

An important addition in the 1988 reauthorization of the law through the end
of 1991 was the creation of various discretionary grants available to public
agencies and nonprofit organizations for demonstration or service programs.
Included in the eligibility list are "programs which provide educational identification, prevention, and treatment services in cooperation with preschool and
elementary and secondary schools" (P.L. 100-294, Section 7:3). When considering the course of federal legislation in this area, then, it appears that educators
and other professionals are being called upon to become more active in efforts to
identify and treat victims of child abuse and neglect.

Moreover, P.L. 100-294 extended the responsibilities of NCCAN. It included
the establishment of a U.S. Inter-Agency Task Force on Child Abuse and
Neglect, comprised of individuals of other federal agencies with programs
related to child maltreatment and a U.S. Advisory Board on Child Abuse and
Neglect made up of a group of national experts appointed by the Secretary of the
Department of Health and Human Services (DHHS). The charge of the Task

Force was to provide ideas related to research, prevention, policy, and legislative issues (Willis, Holden, & Rosenberg, 1992). In addressing the importance of increased school involvement, one of the recommendations of this Advisory Board called for "a major initiative to establish and strengthen the role of every public and private school in the nation in the prevention, identification, and treatment of child abuse and neglect" (Department of Health and Human Services, U.S. Advisory Board on Child Abuse and Neglect, 1990, p. 142).

In an amendment to P.L. 102-295, it was noted that child abuse and neglect require a multidisciplinary, comprehensive, community services approach to treatment. Specifically, the reauthorized law states that abuse and neglect must be addressed via an integration of social service, legal, health, mental health, education, and substance abuse agencies. Moreover, it advocates the necessity of strengthening coordination among all levels of government with private agencies, civic, religious, and professional organizations.

Two additional pieces of child abuse legislation are noteworthy. In 1980, the Adoption Assistance and Child Welfare Act was implemented with the goal of preventing out-of-home placements and facilitating reunification in families where placement had occurred. Furthermore, in 1984 Congress expanded NCCAN's mission by implementing "Baby Doe" provisions, which required programs and procedures for responding to reports of medical neglect.

In addition to the provisions of federal legislation, the past two decades have witnessed profound changes at the state level. In fact, increased state legislative activity has emerged in response to the greater number of child maltreatment reports that have been filed. Between 1983 and 1988, the number of child abuse and neglect bills enacted by state legislators quadrupled, with most statutes striving to deal more effectively with the voluminous rise in the child abuse and neglect reports made to Child Protective Services (McDaniel, 1991). Contrary to the growing public awareness engendered by this legislation, an examination of federal expenditures under these laws for child abuse prevention and treatment activities is cause for concern. A recent report by the U.S. House of Representatives, Select Committee on Children, Youth and Families (1987) noted that, between 1981 and 1985, official reports of abuse and neglect cases rose approximately 55%. However, there was only a 2% increase in real funding during the same period to address these problems. Later assessments show continued decline in real resources to address the problems of child maltreatment. While the incidence of child abuse and neglect reports increased by 82% nationally between 1981 and 1989, federal expenditures under the Child Abuse Prevention and Treatment Act actually decreased by 20% during the same period, when measured in constant 1981 dollars (U.S. House of Representatives, Select Committee on Children, Youth and Families, 1989). Equally sobering is the level of United States Government expenditures in relation to military actions, foreign aid, and the protection of economic institutions. For example, $500 million dollars per day was spent on Desert Storm, and $90 million per day was directed toward the Savings and Loan bailout. For a mere $55 million dollars per day, every child in the United States could be moved out of the poverty level of existence (Children's Defense Fund, 1991).

Alarmed by the fact that child abuse had reached epidemic proportions in our nation, in June 1990 the U.S. Advisory Board on Child Abuse and Neglect labelled the first report it submitted to the Secretary of DHHS and the Congress *Child Abuse and Neglect: Critical First Steps in Response to a National Emergency*. The current scenario of increasing reports of abuse and neglect juxtaposed against declining federal expenditures for these problems suggests that educators and other professionals must assume an even larger role in advocating for expanded intervention and treatment services for maltreated children. There are a number of reasons why educators, in particular, should be involved in such issues. First, the magnitude and extent of child maltreatment in this country make it likely that an overwhelming majority of teachers and school administrators will personally encounter at least one child who has been, or is currently being, maltreated in some way. The opportunity that educators have for observation and extended daily contact with children places them in a unique position to identify and assist the maltreated child (Broadhurst, 1979; Crittenden, 1989; Lynch & Cicchetti, 1992). Such opportunities, coupled with training in recognizing the effects of maltreatment on child development and later adaptation, may help educators to promote appropriate and timely intervention and treatment services for these children and their families.

In addition, a number of legal issues encourage (and often compel) educators to become involved in matters of child maltreatment. For example, most states require educators to report suspected cases of child abuse and neglect (American Humane Association, 1987). In addition, many states provide penalties (i.e., fines and possible imprisonment) for persons who are mandated to report suspected abuse and neglect but fail to do so. Furthermore, the definition of *educator* in some of these laws extends beyond just principals, teachers, and guidance counselors, to include secretaries, bus drivers, health aides, and custodial staff. Given current statutes, it is thus imperative that educators strive even more actively to identify and advocate for maltreated children.

Furthermore, as our review of the recent research literature on maltreated children's adaptation to school in the next section suggests, child abuse and neglect may directly and indirectly impede children's learning processes. Insecure attachment relationships, low self-concept and self-esteem, problematic peer relationships, and impairments in motivational orientation to school, are all consequences of maltreatment that can adversely affect the capacity of these children to learn (Barnett, Manly, & Cicchetti; Howes & Cicchetti; Toth & Cicchetti; Wilson & Saft; all this volume). If educators are to teach maltreated children successfully, then it is essential to address the obstacles that restrict the learning process. Finally, issues of professional responsibility and personal commitment may provide the strongest reasons for educators to become involved in issues of child maltreatment. Clearly, maltreatment represents a threat to educators' investment in the health and welfare of children. From this perspective, educators' efforts to recognize and intervene in cases of maltreatment are a natural extension of their professional and personal commitments to protect and advance the best interests of children. For these reasons, we believe that it is critical for educators to be informed about the effects of maltreatment on school functioning so as to be well prepared to meet the needs of the children in their care.

SCHOOL FUNCTIONING OF MALTREATED CHILDREN

With just a few exceptions, most empirical studies of the developmental consequences of child maltreatment have been conducted in university-based research laboratories or in the children's homes (see, e.g., Cicchetti & Carlson, 1989; Cicchetti & Howes, 1991; Starr & Wolfe, 1991). Because the home is *the* major natural environment in the lives of infants and toddlers, and the laboratory can serve as a well-controlled environment for the detailed investigation of family interactional processes, these contexts may be the most appropriate settings for studying young maltreated children. However, as children grow older, the natural contexts of their lives rapidly expand beyond the confines of the home and the family and so their functioning can no longer be reasonably well approximated in the lab or home. If researchers wish to focus on stage-salient developmental tasks (Barnett, Manly, & Cicchetti, this volume; Cicchetti, 1989; Toth & Cicchetti, this volume), then future studies of maltreated children need to follow older maltreated children into the environments outside their homes that assume increased importance with development. As school is the focus for much of the peer and community life of children from the preschool years through adolescence, it is an especially important environment in which to examine the developmental processes and outcomes of maltreated children. In particular, these children's relationships with unfamiliar adults, especially new teachers and peers, become increasingly important. Additionally, teachers are important sources of information about children's social skills and social competence, because they observe them in the school setting. Teachers see a range of children's functioning, both academic and socioemotional, that often is not seen by parents. Furthermore, teacher reports are not affected by family dynamics, as so often is the case with parental reports.

Successful adaptation to school, including integration into the peer group, acceptable performance in the classroom, and the appropriate motivational orientation for achievement, is a stage-salient task for all children. The social and academic skills acquired in school are related to the development of later societal adjustment (Achenbach & Edelbrock, 1981). Moreover, social competence at school is a factor that has repeatedly been shown to predict later adjustment versus maladjustment in children ''at risk'' for psychopathology (Masten, Best, & Garmezy, 1990).

Based on theories postulating a hierarchical emergence of motives (Harter, 1981; Maslow, 1954), maltreated children would not be expected to achieve and do well in school (McClelland, 1988; Murray, 1938). Considering the home environment of these children, it is more likely that their physical needs, issues of safety, and quest for love and acceptance are more relevant and therefore more salient. Not surprisingly, the two major investigations of maltreated children's adaptation to school confirm these dire predictions.

As part of their prospective longitudinal study of the antecedents and consequences of child maltreatment, Erickson, Egeland, and Pianta (1989) assessed maltreated youngsters' adaptation to the social environment and the task demands of school entry. To examine how maltreated children were adapting to this new situation, information was obtained from teachers during the latter part of the school year.

Among the physically abused children studied, Erickson and her colleagues found that aggressive, noncompliant, acting-out behavior was very common. In addition, teachers reported that the maltreated children functioned more poorly on cognitive tasks and in the classroom. Quite strikingly, the conduct of these physically abused children in the school setting was so problematic that approximately half of them were referred either for special intervention services or were retained by the end of their first year of school.

Erickson et al. (1989) also found that the neglected children in their sample displayed the most severe and variable problems at school. These children performed more poorly on cognitive assessments than the physically and sexually abused youngsters. In the classroom, neglected children were described as anxious, inattentive, unable to understand their school work, lacking initiative, and heavily reliant upon the teacher for help, approval, and encouragement. In social situations, they manifested both aggressive and withdrawn behavior and were not well liked by their peers (cf. Cicchetti, Lynch, Shonk, & Manly, 1992; Mueller & Silverman, 1989). These neglected children were uncooperative with adults (i.e., teachers) and were insensitive and *unempathic* with their peers (cf. George & Main, 1979; Main & George, 1985). Moreover, they rarely expressed positive affect or a sense of humor. By the conclusion of their first year in school, 65% of the neglected children already had been referred for special intervention or were retained. One possible interpretation for the extremely poor functioning of the neglected children is that they have experienced a chronic and pervasive history of deprivation across all domains of development, cognitive, socioemotional, and linguistic (cf. Erickson et al., 1989).

Sexually abused children also exhibited a variety of problems adapting to the school environment. Their performance in school suffered because of their marked anxiety, inattentiveness, and inability to comprehend classroom expectations. These children also were not popular with their peers and were predominantly withdrawn or aggressive in social interactions. Most notably, Erickson and her colleagues (1989) highlighted the excessive dependency that sexually abused children displayed toward their teachers. Specifically, these youngsters' interactions with teachers were characterized by a strong need for approval and physical closeness in combination with a high incidence of seeking assistance in the classroom. The passive, dependent nature of these sexually abused children is congruent with the victim roles that they have experienced in their homes (cf. Sroufe & Fleeson, 1988; Troy & Sroufe, 1987).

In a large scale, well-controlled study, Eckenrode, Laird, and Doris (1993) examined the academic outcomes of 420 maltreated children (neglected, physically abused, or sexually abused) sampled from the total group of maltreated youngsters enrolled in regular (kindergarten–grade 12) classrooms (i.e., maltreated children not in a special education classroom). Eckenrode and his colleagues compared the school performance of these youngsters with a demographically well-matched group of nonmaltreated children. Utilizing school records as the primary source of measures of academic functioning, these investigators discovered a number of very interesting results. As we describe below, maltreatment was shown to affect girls and boys equally and its deleterious effects were evident throughout the entire range of grade levels.

Maltreated children scored significantly lower than the nonmaltreated children on math and reading standardized test scores (Iowa tests). Among the maltreated group and consistent with the results of Erickson et al. (1989), Eckenrode and his collaborators found that the neglected children performed most poorly on this standardized index of academic ability. Interestingly, the test scores of sexually abused children were not significantly different from that of controls (see Toth & Cicchetti, this volume for a discussion of delayed sequelae in sexually abused children).

With respect to other measures of school functioning, maltreated children received more Cs and Ds and fewer As and Bs than nonmaltreated comparison children. Similar to the results obtained from the standard test score performance measure, neglected children received the lowest grades, while the grades of sexually abused children were not statistically different from those of the comparison group. Additionally, as a group maltreated children were 2.5 times more likely to repeat a grade than were comparison children. Within the maltreated sample, the neglected and physically abused youngsters were those who were most likely to be retained in a grade.

Finally, Eckenrode et al. (1993) also found that maltreatment was associated with difficulties in the arena of social adjustment in the school setting. In particular, maltreated children were more likely to be referred to the principal, with physically abused youngsters receiving the highest number of referrals. In contrast, sexually abused children were no more likely to visit the principal than were the nonmaltreated youngsters. Furthermore, in junior and senior high, maltreated children were significantly more likely than nonmaltreated children to be suspended from school. An examination of maltreatment subtype differences revealed that physically abused children received the most suspensions, while neglected and sexually abused children were no different from the nonmaltreated youngsters in this regard.

We believe that a confluence of factors conspire to bring about the negative pattern of results documented in the studies of Erickson, Eckenrode, and their colleagues. As we alluded to earlier, the home environments of maltreated children do not foster the academic and interpersonal skills required for succeeding in school (Bradley, 1985; Rosario, Salzinger, Feldman, & Hammer, 1987; see also Barnett, Manly, & Cicchetti; Howes & Cicchetti; this volume). Trickett and her colleagues (Trickett, Aber, Carlson, & Cicchetti, 1991; Trickett & Susman, 1988) have found that maltreating parents, compared to nonmaltreating parents, are less satisfied with their children, perceive child rearing as more difficult and less enjoyable, provide less verbal reasoning, are less intellectually oriented, use more controlling disciplinary techniques, do not encourage the development of autonomy in their children even though they maintain high standards of achievement, and promote an isolate lifestyle for themselves and their children. In essence, maltreating parents have high expectations for their children without providing the corresponding supports for their children to achieve these goals. This pattern of caregiving is consistent with Baumrind's (1967, 1968) descriptions of "authoritarian" parenting, which is linked with less competence and lower school achievement among children.

The combination of a controlling environment and high performance demands also has been linked to an extrinsic motivational orientation toward task performance (Lepper, 1981), and is viewed as exerting a negative influence on children's classroom functioning (Harter, 1981). A significant body of empirical research has revealed that school performance, self-perceptions of competence, and motivational orientation all tend to be interrelated among school-age youngsters (Gottfried, 1990; Harter & Connell, 1984; Worland, Weeks, Janes, & Strock, 1984). Although the causal direction of these effects has yet to be clearly specified, a plausible hypothesis is that children who feel good about themselves tend to be intrinsically motivated and to perform competently on their school work (cf. Vondra, Barnett, & Cicchetti, 1989). Given a caregiving environment characterized by both family economic disadvantage *and* child maltreatment, one would expect to find consistent deficits in the motivational processes that contribute to children's engagement and performance in school. To compound this negative transaction, the behavior problems that maltreated children manifest in school, even if they are largely due to the experience of being maltreated, may necessitate the overcontrolling teaching styles that have been found to undermine an intrinsic motivational orientation in school.

If this finding is confirmed with maltreated children, then the risk that they will adopt an extrinsically motivated orientation towards their academic work will be exacerbated. Beginning support for these ideas comes from work conducted in the laboratory of the Harvard Child Maltreatment Project (Cicchetti &

Rizley, 1981). Aber and Allen (1987) concluded that maltreated children demonstrated less independent mastery motivation and a more extrinsically oriented motivation system than did a matched control group. Thus, it appears that maltreated children may indeed possess disturbances in their motivational orientation, which may explain some of the documented deficits in their school achievement.

Another important factor in resolving the task of adaptation to school may be secure readiness to learn. Aber and Allen (1987) proposed that *effectance motivation*, which is the intrinsic desire to deal competently with one's environment, and successful relations with novel adults (i.e., relations that are characterized neither by dependency nor wariness) are important components of children being able to adapt to their first major out-of-home environment and to the larger world that school represents. Zigler (1971), drawing upon Maslow's theory of a hierarchy of motives, has described effectance motivation as a "life-fulfilling" rather than "life-preserving" need and, consequently, as vulnerable to debilitating life experiences. Moreover, previous research by Zigler and his colleagues (Balla & Zigler, 1975; Yando, Seitz, & Zigler, 1978) indicates that social deprivation makes children both excessively dependent upon and wary of new adults.

Aber and Allen (1987) investigated whether maltreated preschool and early-school-age children were especially dependent upon or wary of novel adults as were other socially deprived children, and whether they, too, subordinated effectance motivation to the need to establish secure relationships with new adults. Aber and Allen found that maltreated children scored lower than non-maltreated children on a factor measuring secure readiness to learn in the company of novel adults.

The secure readiness to learn factor was composed of high effectance motivation and low dependency. Similar to the organizational construct of security of attachment (Toth & Cicchetti, this volume), secure readiness to learn can be conceptualized as an organizational construct of competence in early childhood. Like security of attachment, secure readiness to learn appears to represent a dynamic balance between establishing secure relationships with adults and feeling free to explore the environment in ways that will promote cognitive competence. The findings of Aber and Allen are particularly compelling because they are congruent with prior research on how maltreatment affects infants' and toddlers' development (Toth & Cicchetti, this volume). At both of these developmental stages, maltreatment interferes with the balance between the motivation to establish secure relationships with adults and the motivation to explore the world in competency-promoting ways.

In light of these results, many of the problems that maltreated children manifest in school appear to us to be derivative of a central problem—an over-concern with security issues reflecting an expectation of unresponsive, unavailable rejecting adults. The preoccupation with security-promoting operations over competence-promoting operations is a causal/mediating factor that links a history of maltreatment with delays in "school readiness" and with subsequent developmental difficulties in adapting to school.

Aber, Allen, Carlson, and Cicchetti (1989) examined the relation between parent-reported symptoms and the two constructs of secure readiness to learn and *outer-directedness*, which has been defined as an orientation to problem solving in which children rely on external cues rather than their own cognitive resources. Aber and his colleagues found no differences between maltreated and nonmaltreated comparison preschool children in levels of parent-reported symptoms. There were, however, clear associations between symptoms and the two developmental constructs. Low secure readiness to learn predicted social withdrawal, aggression, and depression in *maltreated* preschoolers, and high outer-directedness predicted social withdrawal and aggression in *nonmaltreated* comparison preschoolers.

The results of differential developmental correlates of symptomatology suggest that although maltreated and nonmaltreated children appear equally depressed, withdrawn, and aggressive, there may be different underlying developmental pathways that account for similar patterns in the overt expression of symptoms. Maltreated preschoolers may become symptomatic through a pathway of low secure readiness to learn, while nonmaltreated preschoolers may become symptomatic through a pathway of high outer-directedness (Aber et al., 1989).

In summary, it is apparent that the maltreated child is at multiple risk for poor school functioning. As Toth and Cicchetti (this volume) have noted, children's expectations about adult availability and responsivity are thought to develop in infancy and toddlerhood through interactions between children and their primary attachment figures. These expectations concerning the availability and predictability of adults are perpetuated through internal representational models of the self-in-relationships which, in turn, may influence both the construction of new relationships and the ability to explore and cope with the demands of unfamiliar and stressful situations such as adaptation to school. In essence, we believe that there is growing evidence for a causal chain extending from insecure attachment relationships to impaired self-perceptions to poor academic performance and social incompetence in school (cf. Vondra et al., 1989).

Now that research on the functioning of maltreated children in the school setting has been reviewed, it is important to explore the implications of these findings and to propose recommendations on how best to ensure that the school experience is a positive one for children who have been faced with so much adversity. Rather than continuing a negative developmental trajectory that originates in the maltreating home, we believe that school can buffer the emergence and/or continuation of the sequelae of maltreatment.

POLICY IMPLICATIONS OF RESEARCH ON THE ADAPTATION OF MALTREATED CHILDREN TO SCHOOL AND ON THE CONSEQUENCES OF CHILD ABUSE AND NEGLECT

As many contributors to this volume have demonstrated, researchers have made great progress in understanding the impact that maltreatment has upon child development. Every domain (e.g., cognitive, motivational, social, emotional, social-cognitive, linguistic, and representational development) and each stage-salient issue (e.g., secure attachment, good-quality representational models of the self and of the self in relation to others, effective peer relations, and adaptation to school) that have been investigated have revealed some significant areas of maladaptation in maltreated children that have serious implications for their functioning in classroom settings (Cicchetti, 1989, 1990; Cicchetti & Carlson, 1989; Starr & Wolfe, 1991; see also, Barnett, Manly, & Cicchetti; Howes & Cicchetti; and Toth & Cicchetti; all this volume). These difficulties place maltreated children at heightened risk for future behavior problems and psychopathology (Aber et al., 1989; Allen & Tarnowski, 1989; Cicchetti, 1990; Toth, Manly, & Cicchetti, 1992). While these findings must be both replicated and extended, including an enhanced emphasis on the processes and pathways by which these patterns of maladaptation eventuate, it is nonetheless quite clear that maltreated children encounter and experience a variety of difficulties in their adjustment to the school setting. The challenge to educators and interventionists lies in reaching these children early enough so as to foster in them the positive feelings of self-esteem and competence that they so desperately lack (Kaufman & Cicchetti, 1989; Toth et al., 1992; Vondra et al., 1989).

Before moving directly into our suggestions for modifications within the educational environment, it is important to pause and explore why any change is warranted. Certainly, few members of society would disagree about the importance of providing services designed to ameliorate the negative effects of child abuse and neglect. However, less consensus is likely to be forthcoming regarding what, if any, role the schools should play in this process. We believe the view of the responsibility of schools as being limited to the *education* of our children without consideration for their emotional well-being unless it directly impacts on *learning* to be short sighted and based on ill-informed logic. Clearly, there can be little doubt that maltreatment does adversely affect learning and academic achievement. Additionally, the disruptive influence that a maltreated child is likely to exert on the general educational milieu cannot be minimized. Over and above these effects, however, the long-term effects on the community of failing to provide remedial services to maltreated children are extensive. Issues such as school dropout, delinquency, and teen pregnancy all could be more adequately handled through the utilization of school-based preventive approaches. The goal of education cannot be the separation of cognitive capacities from the rest of the child. Only when schools recognize the child as an integrated being will learning be truly facilitated.

To illustrate this point, we draw upon some of our experiences encountered in seeking special services for maltreated children who were graduating from Mt. Hope Family Center, a therapeutic milieu setting for maltreated preschoolers. We have consistently found that educators are reluctant to approve special services for the children who have the highest intellectual abilities. In effect, these children were penalized because they were bright enough to be able to deal with academic demands. However, the issue of whether or not the child is able to realize his or her potential due to emotional concerns pales in comparison to having an intelligence quotient of over 100! Unfortunately, again, the most at risk children may fail to be provided with any preventively based services until their coping strategies become brittle and they begin to fail.

In order to avoid situations such as this, increased attention must be directed to the role of the schools in facilitating overall positive adaptation. In efforts to meet this challenge, the following policy recommendations must be considered and addressed.

1. Comprehensive, integrative assessments of the functioning of maltreated children must be conducted. As a result of the intensified national commitment to provide appropriate educational services for children considered to be "at risk" for the emergence of developmental difficulties, there has been a dramatic increase in educationally based programs of intervention. Unfortunately, evaluations of the effectiveness of these programs generally have not been conducted. In part, this state of omission may stem from the absence of assessment paradigms that are sufficiently sophisticated to provide a comprehensive portrayal of the developmental organization of atypical children. Because development may vary across domains of functioning, intervention goals must be broader than cognitive enrichment strategies (cf. Zigler & Valentine, 1979). Moreover, depending on the organization of strengths and weaknesses among domains of functioning, children with different needs may profit from different types of programs (see chapters in Meisels & Shonkoff, 1990).

Despite the obvious importance of comprehensively evaluating functioning in populations with special needs, until recently most studies utilized standardized normative tests, usually of academic achievement and intelligence, as outcome measures. Unfortunately, these conventional approaches often lack the power and specificity needed to inform intervention programs in ways that enable them to meet the individualized needs of a child. In order to elucidate the nature of maladaptation so that remedial services can be timed and guided most effectively, a developmentally based approach is needed (Cicchetti & Wagner, 1990).

Due to the complexity of functioning evidenced among children who have been maltreated, we believe that it is especially important to conduct assessments of multiple domains of development. Rather than focusing exclusively on cognitive development and functioning on academic tasks, we advocate for the utilization of an assessment approach incorporating cognitive, socioemotional, and linguistic/representational domains of development. By addressing a circumscribed area of functioning, an assessment may fail to uncover the full range of problems or to identify areas of strength. While we are not disputing that the primary objective of the school setting is education, we believe, and empirical research has documented, that the motivational and socioemotional sequelae related to the experiences of maltreatment also may impede academic progress. An example of the importance of assessing all domains of development can be found in the area of psycholinguistic research. In assessments of middle-SES populations, researchers have failed to identify relationships among caregiving, the quality of attachment relationships, and linguistic development (Bretherton, Bates, Benigni, Camaioni, & Volterra, 1979). However, in atypical populations, where the environment and ecology are more unsupportive, chaotic, disorganized, and stress laden (Bronfenbrenner, 1979; Garbarino & Gilliam, 1980) and stressors are more extreme, significant relations between linguistic and socioemotional factors are more likely to be evidenced. For example, empirical work has shown that maltreated children do evidence deficits in socioemotional development which may have an impact on the emergence of language skills. Specifically, maltreated toddlers manifest delays in expressive language, as well as limitations in their capacity to maintain sustained connected dialogues and to discuss and identify their own feelings (Cicchetti & Beeghly, 1987; Coster, Gersten, Beeghly, & Cicchetti, 1989). Additionally, disadvantaged children who were securely attached with their primary caregiver had more advanced language development than did insecurely attached children from similar backgrounds (Gersten, Coster, Schneider-Rosen, Carlson, & Cicchetti, 1986).

The importance of assessing the interrelations among developmental domains will become increasingly important to consider as the aforementioned laws pertaining to the birth–5 populations (e.g., P.L. 99-457) are enacted to include service provision for at risk children. Therefore, the use of assessment paradigms that allow for the exploration of a full range of child capabilities yields a much richer portrayal of functioning. In addition to enhancing our overall understanding of development, an approach such as this also facilitates the provision of necessary services. Perhaps most importantly, comprehensive assessments facilitate individualized planning within the educational setting. It is only through the accurate identification of problems that appropriate services can be provided. Because determination of emotional handicaps is difficult, especially in very young children, failure to apply comprehensive, multifaceted paradigms may result in the denial of services to children in need. It is much easier to identify handicaps due to cognitive deficits (e.g., mental retardation), or physical impairments (e.g., cerebral palsy), than those due to emotional difficulties. In fact, in the early years of life it is critical that "learning" not be viewed as independent from socioemotional development.

In particular, even though emotionally handicapped children are eligible to receive special education services under P.L. 94-142, few are designated to receive them (Morse, 1985). Instead, schools commonly view these children in terms of the disruptive behavior they display in the classroom, with suspension, expulsion, or dropout the likely outcome (Sandberg, 1987). Furthermore, older children designated as emotionally handicapped by the education system often are labelled as offenders. Sadly, these children virtually never get accurately classified as *abused* (Smith, Berkman, & Fraser, 1980; Smith, Black, & Campbell, 1980). Startlingly, to our knowledge there is no consistent policy in existence at either the federal or state level for how the juvenile justice system should handle cases of child abuse. Now that we know that maltreatment causes serious emotional damage and psychopathology in maltreated children (Cicchetti, 1989, 1990; Starr & Wolfe, 1991) and that emotional disturbances are common even in children below the age of 5 years (Institute of Medicine, 1989), more attention must be paid to children with emotional handicaps.

2. Intervention efforts must be targeted for the earliest possible period subsequent to the confirmation of maltreatment. Based on our understanding of the deleterious impact that maltreatment has on school functioning and later adjustment and competence, it is imperative that educational and therapeutic interventions for maltreated children commence as soon as possible after the identification of maltreatment has occurred. With such quick action on the part of educators and program specialists, the chances of lessening the damage instilled by early negative experiences of care are greatly enhanced. Moreover, the existing data on the developmental sequelae of maltreatment suggest that the earlier the intervention, the greater the likelihood of promoting competence and adaptation on subsequent developmental tasks. While the specific nature of these interventions will vary according to the child's developmental stage and type of maltreatment experienced, the importance of early intervention with maltreated children cannot be overemphasized. Because the educational setting may be the only channel available to these children, the role of the schools in this regard is essential.

3. Maltreated children should be provided the most appropriate and educationally beneficial environment possible. In view of the difficulties that maltreated children experience due to their poor quality attachment relationships and their negative sense of self, it is essential that these children be placed in a setting that will both support and encourage their efforts at individual mastery and achievement as well as enhance their perceptions of their own cognitive and social competence. In this type of environment, maltreated children may receive the special programs and services (e.g., individual and/or group therapy, speech/language therapy) that will enable them to begin to experience both themselves and others in a more positive and appropriate fashion.

At first glance, such a philosophy might appear incongruous with the current trend of "mainstreaming." However, given our present knowledge concerning the percentage of maltreated children requiring special educational and/or intervention services in the elementary grades (Christiansen, 1980; Eckenrode et al., 1993; Erickson et al., 1989; Vondra et al., 1989), any efforts to prevent such problems by assigning these children to specially designed preschool environments appears more than justified. Moreover, careful attention to the specific needs of maltreated children in such a setting might actually facilitate their later adaptation and success in more traditional classroom environments. Rather than considering nonspecialized settings as necessary prerequisites to more specialized placements, the provision of early intervention minimizes the likelihood of failure and the reinforcement of the child's already fragile self-esteem.

In addition to the most appropriate settings, aspects of the environment itself must be considered. Every effort should be made to create a classroom and school environment that is a positive alternative to that which maltreated children experience at home. Such an environment may make children feel safer and better able to engage in relationships with teachers and peers. Results from a study in our laboratory provide but one useful suggestion for the structure of the physical milieu of the classroom. On examining two groups of preschool and early school-age children, Rieder and Cicchetti (1989) found that aggressive stimuli impaired the cognitive control functioning of maltreated, but not of nonmaltreated children. These results suggest that a hypervigilance to aggressive stimuli may have emerged as a strategy for coping with a maltreating environment in order to alert a child to potential danger. Although this strategy may have been adaptive at one time, it is likely to present significant difficulties in the school environment. Because maltreated children readily assimilate aggressive stimuli, and because this assimilation disrupts the cognitive–affective balance, it may be important to minimize the presence of aggressive material in classroom settings.

Additionally, Crittenden (1989) suggests that maltreated children have special needs that leave them unprepared for school. As a result of unpredictable and uncontrollable home environments, maltreated children have very basic needs to experience predictability and socially appropriate control in their environments. For teachers to create this type of environment requires much more individualized attention than is available in most classrooms (Crittenden, 1989). Additionally, promoting the development of language and communication skills in maltreated children may increase their ability to relate effectively with others. Finally, teachers who can offer consistent affective experiences will help maltreated children to develop trust in others. Toward this end, it is important for teachers not to combine discipline and caring. Maltreated children have difficulty integrating the mixed message of firmness and caring; therefore, discipline should be carried out with neutral affect (Crittenden, 1989). Maltreated children can then learn to trust signs of positive regard from others. However, in order for improvements in children's interpersonal competence to generalize beyond the classroom, all of these steps need to be taken with an approach that will integrate parents and families into the therapeutic process. Without supportive counseling and education, maltreating parents may not be ready for, or approve of, changes in their children's ability to communicate their own needs and desires and or their attempts to achieve a more balanced, "goal-corrected" partnership (Cicchetti, Toth, & Bush, 1988).

4. As much as possible, educators and other service personnel should strive to involve parents in the intervention and treatment process. The transactional and ecological models of child maltreatment emphasize the importance of focusing on parent, child, and environmental factors and the manner in which they mutually influence one another to produce phenomena such as child abuse and neglect (Belsky, 1980; Cicchetti & Rizley, 1981; Howes & Cicchetti, this volume). Given this understanding, it is critical that intervention efforts incorporate each of these factors as part of a total treatment plan. Parents need to be educated regarding "normal" developmental processes so that they are better able to interact with their children in positive and growth-promoting ways. Moreover, the more knowledgeable parents are concerning their parenting abilities and the ways in which they interact with the development of their children, the more likely they are to be able to modify their interactional styles. This, in turn, can facilitate the emergence of positive self-esteem and competence in their children. The coordinated provision of therapeutic services to maltreating parents is equally important, as it is unlikely that sustained child gains can occur in the absence of a less detrimental caregiving environment.

Maltreating parents often have low self-esteem, feel like their fate is determined by external factors, and are disenfranchised members of society. Thus, empowering these parents to take some responsibility for and control over their lives may help them feel more competent to handle other vital aspects of their lives (cf. Howes & Cicchetti, this volume). By allowing parents to participate in choosing the supports they think will be most beneficial, and by integrating parents into treatment decisions made about their child, they will become more skillful at representing themselves and their child in other vital situations, such as lobbying for necessary special education services and connecting with their child's new teacher each year of school. By having parents interface with the educational system, it may be possible to decrease some of the threat that parents often associate with efforts spearheaded solely by mental health professionals. Throughout this empowerment process, respect must be shown for the parent's cultural embeddedness (see Sternberg, and Wilson & Saft, both this volume).

If the potential of educational environments to mitigate against the negative effects of maltreatment on child adaptation are to be realized, educators must be provided with sufficient resources to be able to assume these added responsibilities without becoming overburdened. Additionally, significant outreach efforts possibly including home visits, will be needed if the isolation which surrounds these families is to be penetrated. Though a plan such as this would require a significant investment of time and money, the benefits of such an approach in reaching disenfranchised families and facilitating the positive adaptation of children warrants the magnitude of the investment.

5. Educational curricula for maltreated children should be thoroughly grounded in developmental theory and focus on the "whole child," not merely on intellectual growth. Educational curricula for maltreated children must focus upon promoting age-appropriate developmental competencies across multiple domains of functioning. Because maltreated children experience impairments in a variety of developmental domains and because many of the cognitive deficits found in maltreated children may, in part, be due to disturbances in their motivational systems (Aber & Allen, 1987; Barahal, Waterman, & Martin, 1981), motivational and socioemotional goals should be an integral component of the overall educational approach (Grolnick, 1990). By devising developmentally appropriate curricula for maltreated children that are aimed at facilitating their growth and competence in *all* areas of functioning, educators may increase the likelihood that such efforts will lead to later adjustment and adaptation in these children.

6. Educators and specialists working with maltreated children should understand the developmental consequences of maltreatment. It is crucial that those individuals who work directly with maltreated children have extensive training in the processes of both "normal" and abnormal development and the ways in which teachers can facilitate healthy growth and adaptation in these children. Ideally, educators should be familiar with the individual history of each child with whom they deal so as to be aware and sensitive to the specific needs and requirements of that child. Depending on the extent of family dysfunction and the resulting child maladaptation, this may be best accomplished in a specialized preschool or school setting where therapists coordinate all parent-treatment efforts.

In the absence of a specialized setting with a coordinating therapist, awareness of child functioning as subject to the influence of occurrences at home is important. For example, those working with maltreated children must recognize that they often manifest extremes of behavior (from overly withdrawn or aggressive to overly dependent). As a result, these children typically pull for certain types of teacher interventions. In essence, they strive to re-create their prior experiences with attachment figures. Educators must be careful to provide specific interventions targeted to address these deficits in interpersonal functioning. Thus, being consistently controlling with a child who has already developed an external motivational orientation may further impair more intrinsically motivated strivings. Given the fact that these children often require special attention and care, further support for the provision of special preschool programs and services is justified as a means of promoting later adaptation to more conventional learning environments.

7. Teachers need to develop a "style" of relating with children that is congruent with what is known about the determinants of competence in school and the effects of maltreatment on children's functioning. In this regard, it is important that educators working with these children be adequately trained in techniques designed to enhance socioemotional development and competence rather than relying exclusively upon the utilization of cognitive enrichment and behavioral modification strategies with these youngsters. It is especially critical that teachers make sure that they do not engage in any physically or emotionally abusive interchanges with children.

For too long, our society has condoned the use of physical punishment as a means of disciplining children. Despite increased knowledge of the lack of effectiveness and detrimental consequences associated with the use of physical force as a means of control, many sectors of society continue to rely upon this strategy. Historically, the use of spanking in our schools was widely accepted. Although currently states vary with regard to their stance on this issue, corporal punishment continues to be relied on in many schools. We believe that resorting to physical punishment reflects a breakdown in more positive and appropriate methods of discipline and, as such, should be eliminated from all schools. The use of physical punishment with a child who has been maltreated is especially destructive and must not occur.

Despite the fact that the harmful effects of emotional maltreatment also have been well chronicled and documented (Brassard, Germain, & Hart, 1987; Hart & Brassard, 1991; Rosenberg, 1987), several leading scholars in the field have expressed concern over the occurrence of emotional abuse in the schools. As Broadhurst (1986) poignantly stated, "Educators . . . also include those who use verbal abuse . . . as a means of behavior control. Administrators who see only the result—subdued, fearful children (which they may interpret as a quiet classroom)—without examining the causes in effect become accomplices to the emotional abuse" (p. 20). Similarly, Garbarino and Gilliam posed the chilling question . . . "Where else may we find the legally and socially sanctioned abuse of children? We point to that social institution which, after the family, is the most important socializing agent in America, namely the school" (1980, p. 97).

Currently, personnel shortages plague the entire field of special education (Burke, McLaughlin, & Valdwieso, 1988). This paucity of trained professionals is even more acute in the area of early childhood and becomes further exacerbated when educators trained to address emotional handicaps are sought. Most special education teachers' training is behaviorally focused. This orientation may work against the very needs of the maltreated child as the use of external rewards may bring about an extrinsically based motivational orientation rather than an autonomous and intrinsically based system.

Clearly, funding must be allocated to provide incentives for prospective teachers to obtain expertise in these areas. Additionally, educational institutions must incorporate knowledge of abuse and neglect into their teacher preparation curricula. Just as importantly, educational settings which provide services to maltreated children must be awarded sufficient funding to ensure adequate monetary compensation to attract and retain qualified educators. Because working with children who have been maltreated is so difficult, it is imperative that resources be allocated to preparing professionals for this area. Often teachers who work in intensive day treatment settings for maltreated children work longer than teachers in other settings (e.g., 11 months vs. 9 months per year). The combination of the high stress associated with such positions due to the grim realities of these children's lives, and the lower salaries that these teachers receive, increases the likelihood of staff burnout and job termination.

8. Teachers should be sensitive to their role as potential alternate attachment figures who can ameliorate the negative developmental course of maltreated children. Teachers form an important component of the milieu in which school-aged children develop. School teachers constitute a group of nonfamilial adults with whom children have extensive involvement for at least nine months of the year beginning early in their lives. Moreover, teachers may assume a variety of roles including caretaker, mentor, disciplinarian, and companion. Negotiating relationships with teachers successfully is itself an important task for children, and it may promote the attainment of competence in other school-related developmental domains.

Children's relationships with their teachers may be important for another reason as well. It is possible that teachers function as alternative or secondary attachment figures. Making use of relationships with teachers in this way may be especially helpful for children coming from stressful family environments characterized by maltreatment. It is possible that maltreated children's relationships with their teachers can act as protective factors against the negative developmental outcomes associated with maltreatment (Lynch & Cicchetti, 1992). Positive and secure relationships with teachers may begin to compensate for some of the negative relationships histories that maltreated children have with their parents by providing new information for these children's representational models of themselves and others. As a result, relationships with teachers may function as enduring compensatory factors for maltreated children (Cicchetti & Rizley, 1981). One protective mechanism through which these relationships act is by influencing children's representational beliefs about themselves and others (Rutter, 1990). Attachment theory proposes that these organized mental representations are carried forward by the individual and used in subsequent interpersonal contexts.

Along these lines, Sroufe has demonstrated that the quality of preschool children's attachment histories with their primary caregivers influences their relationships with teachers (Sroufe, 1983; Sroufe & Fleeson, 1988). In the studies conducted by Sroufe and his colleagues, teacher contributions to these relationships were held constant by examining many children's relationships with the same teacher; as a result, it was possible to isolate the effects of children's attachment histories on teacher–child relationships. Coherent differences in teachers' behavior were found, depending on the children's attachment history. For children with histories of secure attachment, teachers had higher expectations for compliance and age-appropriate behavior, but they needed to exert less control over these children. Children with insecure avoidant attachment histories were subjected to more discipline and control by teachers, and teachers had lower expectations of compliance from them. Avoidant-history children also were the only children who elicited angry responses from teachers. Children with insecure resistant attachment histories also elicited higher levels of control from teachers. However, teachers also displayed more nurturance and tolerance toward these children. According to Sroufe, children's internalized representational models of relationships play an important role in eliciting behavior from social partners such as teachers. In many ways, preschool children's relationships with their teachers may replay their relationship history with their caregivers, thus confirming internal representational models that are based on that previous relationship history (Sroufe & Fleeson, 1988).

However, because teachers are a group of nonparental adults with whom maltreated children have frequent exposure, their role in altering negative relationship histories assumes significant importance. Supportive experiences with teachers may begin to impact negative models of self and others, and encourage maltreated children to become more engaged in school. The possibility of increased engagement in school is important because maltreated children are at risk for experiencing deficits in motivational orientation for achievement in school. To the extent that supportive relationships with teachers alter children's model of self and others, these relationships may encourage increased exploration and engagement in the environment. Additionally, if maltreated children are able to experience some success in school as the result of increased engagement, this experience could provide some positive feedback to their self models.

Supportive relationships with teachers, then, may lead to multiple pathways that help maltreated children end the pattern of abuse and relational incompetence; one pathway proposes that relationships with teachers alter representational models of the self and others, while another (but not mutually exclusive) pathway hypothesizes that relationships with teachers increase children's engagement in school. Both of these pathways may enhance the successful resolution of current and subsequent developmental issues, thereby promoting competence and preventing maladaptation. In recognition of the importance of attachment relationships, Barrett and Trevitt (1991) view teachers as educational attachment figures and advocate training teachers to become educational therapists. Likewise, teachers should prepare children in their classrooms for any upcoming leaves, vacations, and so on. Maltreated children are particularly sensitive to rejection, separation, and loss (Carlson, Cicchetti, Barnett, & Braunwald, 1989), thereby highlighting the need for teachers to function as positive attachment figures. Because maltreated children may have noxious child characteristics as a result of their personal experiences of abuse and neglect that affect teachers differently, it is desirable if there are at least two adult attachment figures in each classroom.

Unfortunately, maltreated children often have little opportunity to establish long-term, intimate relationships with their teachers. Maltreating families are very mobile, and children may change schools several times in one year. This kind of instability makes it difficult to form any kind of meaningful relationship with a teacher. Rather, the repeated moves may add to the experience of loss and unavailability of significant adults that becomes incorporated into maltreated children's representational models. Moreover, the way schooling is structured can make it difficult for children with self and interpersonal deficits to form intimate relationships with teachers. During the elementary school years, children change teachers every year, and once they advance to secondary school children no longer have one primary teacher with whom to relate. While children with healthier representational models likely are able to form important relationships with teachers (Howes & Hamilton, 1992a,b), children whose representational models of others are organized around fear and mistrust may have understandable difficulty in getting close to a novel adult during the course of one school year (Lynch & Cicchetti, 1992).

9. **An increased integration among the child welfare system, the special education system, the legal system, and child mental health must occur.** Historically, the provision of services to maltreated children has been hindered by splintering among the assumption of responsibility for various areas of functioning. Because the nature of the maltreatment experience cuts across the discrete areas traditionally associated with each of these agencies, an integrated system of intervention has not emerged. Consequently, rather than providing a comprehensive program of support to children who have experienced maltreatment, intervention efforts often work at cross purposes. This problematic situation is exacerbated by separate funding streams and difficulties in accessing services across these divisions. Parallel to approaches that treat various domains of development as separate entities (e.g., cognitive and emotion), these systems tend to focus on discrete needs, when an integrated approach is more likely to lead to positive change. To arrive at a truly integrated program of intervention, sweeping change in the structure of these systems is required. The role of the educational system in addressing the overall needs of maltreated children must not be minimized.

10. **Researchers must become increasingly invested in devising, conducting, and disseminating findings relevant to the school functioning of maltreated children.** Despite increasingly sophisticated findings on the effects of maltreatment on child development and school adaptation, results have been slow to be integrated into the main stream of educational planning. Although differences between maltreated children and demographically matched non-maltreated children have emerged consistently (see chapters in Cicchetti & Carlson, 1989, and Starr & Wolfe, 1991), the belief that the presence of poverty puts both groups of children at equal risk continues to prevail. In fact, this misperception has surfaced at committee meetings regarding the determination of special services needs. When trying to explain the magnitude of the deleterious effects of abuse on child functioning, advocates for the need for services have

been informed that "abused children are no worse off than poor children and the school district cannot provide services for the large numbers of children living in conditions of poverty." Clearly, this example elucidates the failure of research knowledge to reach those on the front lines of decision making.

If this breakdown in communication is to be rectified, it is important that researchers conceive their questions with the goal of having their results applied to areas involving the assessment and provision of educational services. Increased interactions among researchers and educators also could enhance the flow of information into applied arenas.

11. Efforts must be directed toward improving the identification of maltreatment within the schools. Because the school system may serve as the sole link between the child and the maltreating environment, school personnel are in a position where they may be the only group having access to a maltreated child. The lifestyles of maltreating families often preclude consistent involvement with other professionals in the community. For example, maltreating families often fail to provide medical care to their children. In extreme situations requiring emergency medical care, families often go from hospital to hospital, thereby avoiding any comprehensive assessment of the causes of injuries. In situations such as these, the maltreated child's teacher may be the only potential source for reports of frequent injuries or of the neglect of the child's needs.

In view of the extent of responsibility placed upon educators to detect and respond to cases involving maltreatment, it is imperative that these professionals be schooled on the signs of maltreatment and encouraged to feel comfortable enough to report their suspicions. Recent changes in professional certification laws requiring some educators to have completed a course on the identification of maltreatment is an important step forward in this area.

12. The interface between the schools and Child Protective Services must be strengthened if the educational arena is to be effective in treatment and advocacy for maltreated children. Currently no mechanisms are in place for exchanging information between the schools and child welfare agencies. Confidentiality laws developed to protect the privacy of families preclude open communication. However, this protective stance may reduce the ability of schools to respond to the special needs of maltreated children. Although confidentiality versus the dissemination of knowledge raises some difficult issues, current statutes need to be evaluated with regard to how best to promote the provision of needed services to maltreated children. Toward this end, confidentiality laws may need to be reconsidered. If educators are to be prepared on how to respond to maltreated children, then these professionals need to be granted access to which children have experienced maltreatment. While a major departure from current policies and practices, the noting of maltreatment in school records would allow educational institutions to provide appropriate levels of intervention to maltreated children. Additionally, updates on the status of service-related changes in the maltreated child's living situation (e.g., care provided by a relative, foster placement, residential treatment) also could result in increased sensitivity of teachers to children's needs.

SUMMARY

In this chapter we have described areas of concern for maltreated children in the school environment. Extant data clearly document that children who have experienced abuse or neglect are at risk for failure within the school setting due to the sequelae that are present at their entrance into school. Additionally these liabilities continue to be present throughout their schooling. Our recommendations for school modification and policy formation illustrate both the problems that permeate our current school system as well as the promises that revised educational policies can reap. We concur with Zigler's proposal for the School of the 21st Century, a system that would integrate formal schooling, child care, and family education and support (Zigler, 1989; Zigler & Ennis, 1989). Visionary approaches such as this are critical if help is to be provided for the children most at risk for difficulties in school.

Although the concept of "school readiness" has garnered much support, it is imperative that we move beyond rhetoric into concrete action plans that will enable this society to obtain the educational goals targeted to be achieved by the year 2000. As a society, we must all assume responsibility for assuring that maltreated children receive the necessary support to truly be "ready to learn." By focusing on the needs of the child, the necessary spirit of collaboration among all sectors of society is more likely to be facilitated.

We believe that the school environment must be an integral component of a system developed to meet the needs of vulnerable children and families more adequately. Because the school often may be the only community resource available to reach maltreating families, an increase in its ability to provide prevention and intervention services is imperative. The incorporation of knowledge into innovative educational programs will be essential in translating goals and recommendations into reality.

REFERENCES

Aber, J. L., & Allen, J. P. (1987). The effects of maltreatment on young children's socio-emotional development: An attachment theory perspective. *Developmental Psychology, 23,* 406–414.

Aber, J. L., Allen, J. P., Carlson, V., & Cicchetti, D. (1989). The effects of maltreatment on development during early childhood: Recent studies and their theoretical, clinical, and policy implications. In D. Cicchetti & V. Carlson (Eds.), *Child maltreatment: Theory and research on the causes and consequences of child abuse and neglect* (pp. 579–619). New York: Cambridge University Press.

Achenbach, T. M., & Edelbrock, C. S. (1981). Behavioral problems and competencies reported by parents of normal and disturbed children aged four through sixteen. *Monographs of the Society for Research in Child Development, 46* (188).

Allen, D., & Tarnowski, K. (1989). Depressive characteristics of physically abused children. *Journal of Abnormal Child Psychology, 17*, 1–11.

American Humane Association. (1987). *Child abuse reporting legislation in the 1980's.* Denver, CO: Author.

Balla, D., & Zigler, E. (1975). Preinstitutional social deprivation and responsiveness to social reinforcement in institutionalized retarded individuals: A six-year follow-up study. *American Journal of Mental Deficiency, 80*, 228–230.

Barahal, R., Waterman, J., & Martin, H. (1981). The social-cognitive development of abused children. *Journal of Consulting and Clinical Psychology, 49*, 508–516.

Barrett, M., & Trevitt, J. (1991). *Attachment behaviour and the schoolchild: An introduction to educational therapy.* London: Routledge.

Baumrind, D. (1967). Childcare practices anteceding three patterns of pre-school behavior. *Genetic Psychology Monographs, 75*, 43–88.

Baumrind, D. (1968). Authoritarian versus authoritative parental control. *Adolescence, 3*, 255–272.

Belsky, J. (1980). Child maltreatment: An ecological integration. *American Psychologist, 35*, 5–29.

Bradley, R. H. (1985). The HOME Inventory: Rationale and research. In J. E. Stevenson (Ed.), *Recent research in developmental psychopathology* (pp. 191–202). Elmsford, NY: Pergamon Press.

Brassard, M. R., Germain, R., & Hart, S. N. (Eds.). (1987). *Psychological maltreatment of children and youth.* New York: Pergamon Press.

Bretherton, I., Bates, E., Benigni, L., Camaioni, D., & Volterra, V. (1979). Relationships between cognition, communication, and quality of attachment. In E. Bates, L. Benigni, I. Bretherton, L. Camaioni, & V. Volterra (Eds.), *The emergence of symbols: Cognitions and communication in infancy.* New York: Academic Press.

Broadhurst, D. (1979). *The educator's role in the prevention and treatment of child abuse and neglect.* Washington, DC: U.S. Department of Health, Education, and Welfare.

Broadhurst, D. (1986). *Educators, schools, and child abuse.* Chicago: National Committee for the Prevention of Child Abuse.

Bronfenbrenner, U. (1979). *The ecology of human development: Experiments by nature and design.* Cambridge, MA: Harvard University Press.

Burke, P. J., McLaughlin, M. J., & Valdwieso, C. H. (1988). Young Children: Some policy implications. *Topics in Early Childhood Special Education, 8*(1), 73–80.

Carlson, V., Cicchetti, D., Barnett, D., & Braunwald, K. (1989). Finding order in disorganization: Lessons from research on maltreated infants' attachments to their caregivers. In D. Cicchetti & V. Carlson (Eds.), *Child maltreatment: Theory and research on the causes and consequences of child abuse and neglect* (pp. 494–528). New York: Cambridge University Press.

Children's Defense Fund. (1991). *The state of America's children 1991.* Washington, DC: Children's Defense Fund.

Christiansen, J. (1980). *Educational and psychological problems of abused children.* Saratoga, CA: Century Twenty-One Publishing.

Cicchetti, D. (1989). How research on child maltreatment has informed the study of child development: Perspectives from developmental psychopathology. In D. Cicchetti & V. Carlson (Eds.), *Child maltreatment: Theory and research on the causes and consequences of child abuse and neglect* (pp. 377–431). New York: Cambridge University Press.

Cicchetti, D. (1990). The organization and coherence of socioemotional, cognitive, and representational development: Illustrations through a developmental psychopathology perspective on Down syndrome and child maltreatment. In R. Thompson (Ed.), *Nebraska Symposium on Motivation, Vol. 36: Socioemotional development* (pp. 259–366). Lincoln: University of Nebraska Press.

Cicchetti, D., & Beeghly, M. (1987). Symbolic development in maltreated youngsters: An organizational perspective. *New Directions for Child Development, 36,* 5–29.

Cicchetti, D., & Carlson, V. (1989). (Eds.) *Child maltreatment: Theory and research on the causes and consequences of child abuse and neglect.* New York: Cambridge University Press.

Cicchetti, D., & Howes, P. (1991). Developmental psychopathology in the context of the family: Illustrations from the study of child maltreatment. *Canadian Journal of Behavioural Sciences, 23,* 257–281.

Cicchetti, D., & Lynch, M. (1993). Toward an ecological/transactional model of community violence and child maltreatment: Consequences for children's development. *Psychiatry.*

Cicchetti, D., Lynch, M., Shonk, S., & Manly, J. T. (1992). An organizational perspective on peer relations in maltreated children. In R. D. Parke & G. W. Ladd (Eds.), *Family-peer relationships: Modes of linkage* (pp. 345–383). Hillsdale, NJ: Erlbaum.

Cicchetti, D., & Rizley, R. (1981). Developmental perspectives on the etiology, intergenerational transmission and sequelae of child maltreatment. *New Directions for Child Development, 11,* 32–59.

Cicchetti, D., Toth, S., & Bush, M. (1988). Developmental psychopathology and incompetence in childhood: Suggestions for intervention. In B. Lahey & A. Kazdin (Eds.), *Advances in clinical child psychology* (Vol. 11, pp. 1–71). New York: Plenum.

Cicchetti, D., & Wagner, S. (1990). Alternative assessment strategies for the evaluation of infants and toddlers: An organizational perspective. In S. Meisels & J. Shonkoff (Eds.), *Handbook of early intervention* (pp. 245–277). New York: Cambridge University Press.

Coster, W. J., Gersten, M. S., Beeghly, M., & Cicchetti, D. (1989). Communicative Functioning in Maltreated Toddlers. *Developmental Psychology, 25,* 1020–1029.

Crittenden, P. (1989). Teaching maltreated children in the preschool. *Topics in Early Childhood Special Education, 9,* 16–32.

Crnic, K., Lamberty, G., & Burns, C. (1992, January). *Reconceptualizing school readiness: A historical perspective.* Paper presented at Bureau of Maternal and Child Health Conference entitled: School Readiness: Scientific Perspectives, Washington, DC.

Department of Health and Human Services, U.S. Advisory Board on Child Abuse and Neglect. (1990). *Child abuse and neglect: Critical first steps in response to a national emergency.* Washington, DC: U.S. Government Printing Office.

Eckenrode, J., Laird, M., & Doris, J. (1993). School performance and disciplinary problems among abused and neglected children. *Developmental Psychology, 29,* 53–62.

Erickson, M., Egeland, B., & Pianta, R. (1989). The effects of maltreatment on the development of young children. In D. Cicchetti & V. Carlson (Eds.), *Child maltreatment; Theory and research on the causes and consequences of child abuse and neglect* (pp. 647–684). New York: Cambridge University Press.

Garbarino, J., & Gilliam, G. (1980). *Understanding abusive families.* Lexington, MA: Lexington Books.

George, C., & Main, M. (1979). Social interactions of young abused children: Approach, avoidance, and aggression. *Child Development, 50,* 306–318.

Gersten, M., Coster, W., Schneider-Rosen, K., Carlson, V., & Cicchetti, D. (1986). The socioemotional bases of communicative functioning: Quality of attachment, language development, and early maltreatment. In M. E. Lamb, A. L. Brown, & B. Rogoff (Eds.), *Advances in developmental psychology* (Vol. 4, pp. 105–151). Hillsdale, NJ: Erlbaum.

Gottfried, A. E. (1990). Academic intrinsic motivation in young elementary school children. *Journal of Educational Psychology, 82,* 525–538.

Grolnick, W. (1990). Targeting children's motivational resources in early childhood education. *Educational Policy, 4,* 267–282.

Hart, S. & Brassard, M. (1991). Psychological maltreatment: Progress achieved. *Development and Psychopathology, 3,* 61–70.

Harter, S. (1981). A model of intrinsic mastery motivation in children: Individual differences and developmental change. In A. Collins (Ed.), *Minnesota symposia on child psychology* (Vol. 14, pp. 215–255). Hillsdale, NJ: Erlbaum.

Harter, S., & Connell, J. P. (1984). A model of children's achievement and related self-perceptions of competence, control, and motivational orientation. In J. G. Nicholls (Ed.), *Advances in motivation and achievement: The development of achievement motivation* (pp. 219–250). Greenwich, CT: JAI Press.

Howes, C., & Hamilton, C. (1992a). Children's relationships with caregivers: Mothers and childcare teachers. *Child Development, 63,* 859–866.

Howes, C., & Hamilton, C. (1992b). Children's relationships with child care teachers: Stability and concordance with parental attachments. *Child Development, 63,* 867–878.

Institute of Medicine. (1989). *Research on children and adolescents with mental, behavioral, and developmental disorders.* Washington, DC: National Academy Press.

Kagan, S. (1990). Readiness 2000: Rethinking rhetoric and responsibility. *Phi Delta Kappan, 72,* 272–279.

Kaufman, J., & Cicchetti, D. (1989). The effects of maltreatment on school-aged children's socioemotional development: Assessments in a day camp setting. *Developmental Psychology, 25,* 516–524.

Kempe, C. H., Silverman, F. N., Steele, B. B., Droegemueller, W., & Silver, H. K. (1962). The battered child syndrome. *Journal of the American Medical Association, 181,* 17–24.

Lepper, M. R. (1981). Intrinsic and extrinsic motivation in children: Detrimental effects of superfluous social controls. In W. A. Collins (Ed.), *Minnesota symposia on child psychology* (Vol. 14). Hillsdale, NJ: Erlbaum.

Lynch, M., & Cicchetti, D. (1992). Maltreated children's reports of relatedness to their teachers. *New Directions for Child Development, 57,* 81–107.

Main, M., & George, C. (1985). Response of abused and disadvantaged toddlers to distress in agemates: A study in the day care setting. *Developmental Psychology, 21,* 407–412.

Maslow, A. H. (1954). *Motivation and personality.* New York: Harper & Row.

Masten, A., Best, K., & Garmezy, N. (1990). Resilience and development: Contributions from the study of children who overcome adversity. *Development and Psychopathology, 2,* 425–444.

McClelland, D. (1988). *Human motivation.* New York: Cambridge University Press.

McDaniel, N. (1991). Improving services to abused and neglected children and their families. *Protecting Children, 8*(2), 10–12.

Meisels, S., & Shonkoff, J. (Eds.). (1990). *Handbook of early intervention.* New York: Cambridge University Press.

Morse, W. (1985). *The education and treatment of socioemotionally impaired youth.* Syracuse, NY: Syracuse University Press.

Mueller, N., & Silverman, N. (1989). Peer relations in maltreated children. In D. Cicchetti & V. Carlson (Eds.), *Child maltreatment: Theory and research on the causes and consequences of child abuse and neglect* (pp. 529–578). New York: Cambridge University Press.

Murray, H. A. (1938). *Explorations in personality.* New York: Oxford University Press.

NAEYC (1990). NAEYC Position Statement of School Readiness. *Young Children, 46,* 21–23.

Nelson, B. J. (1984). *Making an issue of child abuse.* Chicago: University of Chicago Press.

Price, R., Cowen, E., Lorion, R., & Ramos-McKay, J. (Eds.). (1988). *Fourteen ounces of prevention: A casebook for practitioners.* Washington, DC: American Psychological Association.

Rieder, C., & Cicchetti, D. (1989). Organizational Perspective on Cognitive Control Functioning and Cognitive-Affective Balance in Maltreated Children. *Developmental Psychology, 25,* 382–393.

Rosario, M., Salzinger, S., Feldman, R., & Hammer, M. (1987, April). *Home environments of physically abused and control school-age children.* Paper presented at the Biennial Meeting of the Society for Research in Child Development, Baltimore.

Rosenberg, M. S. (1987). New directions for research on the psychological maltreatment of children. *American Psychologist, 42,* 166–171.

Rutter, M. (1990). Psychosocial resilience and protective mechanisms. In J. Rolf, A. S. Masten, D. Cicchetti, K. H. Nuechterlein, & S. Weintraub (Eds.), *Risk and protective factors in the development of psychopathology* (pp. 181–214). New York: Cambridge University Press.

Sandberg, D. (1987). *Chronic acting out students and child abuse: A handbook for intervention.* Lexington, MA: Lexington Books.

Shonkoff, J., & Meisels, S. (1990). Early childhood intervention: The evolution of a concept, In S. Meisels & J. Shonkoff (Eds.), *Handbook of early intervention* (pp. 3–31). New York: Cambridge University Press.

Smith, C., Berkman, D., & Fraser, W. (1980). *A preliminary national assessment of child abuse and neglect and the juvenile justice system: The shadows of distress.* Washington, DC: U.S. Department of Justice, Office of Juvenile Justice and Delinquency Prevention.

Smith, C., Black, T., & Campbell, F. (1980). *A national assessment of case disposition and classification in the juvenile justice system: Inconsistent labeling: Vol. 1, Results of a Survey.* Washington, DC: U.S. Department of Justice, Office of Juvenile Justice and Delinquency Prevention.

Sroufe, L. A. (1983). Infant-caregiver attachment and patterns of adaptation in preschool: The roots of maladaptation and competence. In M. Perlmutter (Ed.), *Minnesota symposia in child psychology* (Vol. 16, pp. 41–83). Hillsdale, NJ: Erlbaum.

Sroufe, L. A., & Fleeson, J. (1988). The coherence of family relationships. In R. A. Hinde & J. Stevenson-Hinde (Eds.), *Relationships within families* (pp. 27–47). Oxford: Clarendon Press.

Starr, R., & Wolfe, D. (Eds.). (1991). *The effects of child abuse and neglect: Issues and research.* New York: Guilford.

Toth, S. L., Manly, J. T., & Cicchetti, D. (1992). Child maltreatment and vulnerability to depression. *Development and Psychopathology, 4,* 97–112.

Trickett, P. K., Aber, J. L., Carlson, V., & Cicchetti, D. (1991). The relationship of socioeconomic status to the etiology and developmental sequelae of physical child abuse. *Developmental Psychology, 27,* 148–158.

Trickett, P. K., & Susman, E. J. (1988). Parental perceptions of childrearing practices in physically abusive and nonabusive families. *Developmental Psychology, 24,* 270–276.

Troy, M., & Sroufe, L. A. (1987). Victimization among preschoolers: The role of attachment relationship history. *Journal of the American Academy of Child Psychiatry, 26,* 166–172.

U.S. Department of Health and Human Services. (1990). *Child abuse and neglect: Critical first steps in response to a national emergency.* Washington, DC: U.S. Government Printing Office.

U.S. House of Representatives, Select Committee on Children, Youth, and Families. (1987). *Abused children in America: Victims of official neglect.* Washington, DC: U.S. Government Printing Office.

U.S. House of Representatives, Select Committee on Children, Youth, and Families. (1989). *No place to call home: Discarded children in America.* Washington, DC: U.S. Government Printing Office.

Vondra, J., Barnett, D., & Cicchetti, D. (1989). Perceived and actual competence among maltreated and comparison school children. *Development and Psychopathology, 1,* 237–255.

Willis, D., Holden, E. W., & Rosenberg, M. (1992). Child maltreatment prevention: Introduction and historical overview. In D. Willis, E. W. Holden, & M. Rosenberg (Eds.), *Prevention of child maltreatment: Developmental and ecological perspectives* (pp. 1–14). New York: Wiley.

Worland, J., Weeks, D., Janes, C., & Strock, B. D. (1984). Intelligence, classroom behavior, and academic achievement in children at high and low risk for psychopathology: A structural equation analysis. *Journal of Abnormal Child Psychology, 12,* 437–454.

Yando, R., Seitz, V., & Zigler, E. (1978). *Imitation: A developmental perspective.* Hillsdale, NJ: Erlbaum.

Zigler, E. (1971). The retarded child as a whole person. In H. E. Adams & W. K. Boardmen (Eds.), *Advances in experimental clinical psychology* (Vol. 1). New York: Pergamon Press.

Zigler, E. (1989). Addressing the nation's child care crisis: The school of the twenty-first century. *American Journal of Orthopsychiatry, 59,* 484–491.

Zigler, E. (1990). Foreword, In S. Meisels & J. Shonkoff (Eds.), *Handbook of early intervention* (pp. ix–xiv). New York: Cambridge University Press.

Zigler, E., & Ennis, P. (1989). The school of the twenty-first century. *Division of Child, Youth, and Family Services Newsletter, 12,* 1 and 12–13.

Zigler, E. & Hall, N. (1989). Physical child abuse in America: Past, present and future. In D. Cicchetti & V. Carlson (Eds.), *Child maltreatment: Theory and research consequences of child abuse and neglect* (pp. 38–75). New York: Cambridge University Press.

Zigler, E., & Valentine, J. (Eds.). (1979). *Project Head Start: A legacy of the War on Poverty.* New York: The Free Press.

11

Child Maltreatment Research: Implications for Program Design

Deborah Daro

INTRODUCTION

The past 30 years have seen an exponential growth in the number of applied and basic research efforts on child abuse and neglect. A variety of disciplines and methodologies have been employed to help clarify the etiology of maltreatment as well as its impacts on child development, family well-being, and social stability. Of equal importance has been obtaining a greater understanding of how best to intervene at the clinical and systemic levels to both prevent maltreatment and to ameliorate its negative consequences.

Effectively applying existing research to program planning is a sensitive and difficult task, particularly with respect to child abuse. The literature is replete with examples of programs that have successfully mitigated the risk for or outcomes of maltreatment. These program models include:

- traditional methods of psychotherapy delivered either to the victim or perpetrator, in individual, group, or family settings (Briere, 1989; Kempe, 1987; McFarlane, Waterman, Conerly, Damon, Durfee, & Long, 1986; and Steele, 1987a);
- home visiting services, particularly those offered prior to or at birth and continuing for a 1- to 2-year period (Gray, Cutler, Dean & Kempe, 1979; Lutzker & Rice, 1984; Lutzker, 1987; Olds, Chamberlin & Tatlebaum, 1986);
- group-based educational and support programs targeting parents with children of various ages (Bavolek & Dillinger-Bavolek, 1985; 1988; Ellwood, 1988; Levine, 1988; Miller, 1988; Rodriguez & Cortez, 1988);
- self-help groups such as Parent's Anonymous (Cohn, 1979; Fritz, 1986; Junewicz, 1983; Moore, 1983);
- family resource centers that serve as clearinghouses for various educational and support services utilized by at-risk families (Kagan, Powell, Weissbourd, & Zigler, 1987);
- crisis intervention services and respite care nurseries (Cherry & Kirby, 1971; Green, 1976; Kempe & Helfer, 1976; Vaughan & Loadman, 1988); and
- child assault prevention programs aimed at educating children and their

caretakers in how to avoid maltreatment (Fryer, Kraizer, & Miyoski, 1987; Harvey, Forehand, Brown, & Holmes, 1988; Hazzard, 1990; Kolko, Moser, & Hughes, 1989; Wurtele, Saslawsky, Miller, Marrs, & Britcher, 1986).

Over and above these direct services lie broader efforts to alter the environmental conditions that contribute to elevated levels of maltreatment. Public and private efforts aimed at reducing poverty, enhancing access to quality medical care, improving the quality of early childhood education, and reducing societal violence are all believed by some to offer more efficient methods to confront child abuse than merely relying upon individualized strategies (Garbarino, 1988; Gil, 1981; Pelton, 1981; Wolock & Horowitz, 1979).

In many instances, child abuse intervention strategies have been used interchangeably as primary, secondary, and tertiary prevention. Program caseloads frequently include abusive or neglectful families as well as families classified as being at-risk for future maltreatment. Similarly, a given strategy, such as home visitor programs, is being utilized in one community as a prevention service for teen parents and in another community as a court-mandated alternative to foster care placement for cases involving serious physical abuse. Unfortunately, very few evaluations of these efforts have been sensitive to this specific client difference. Programs serving both active abusers and families at-risk rarely disaggregate their impact findings along this dimension. Further, primary and tertiary prevention programs generally utilize different outcome measures (e.g., changes in knowledge levels versus changes in personal functioning), making the direct comparison of impacts across programs difficult if not impossible. Consequently, the available program evaluation data is not well suited to addressing the specific question of what strategies work best as primary prevention versus secondary or tertiary prevention. In fact, one might argue that this particular distinction may not be the most relevant for those interested in establishing more effective interventions. Far more important may be how service impacts differ in terms of such key client variables as parenting experience, parenting problems, personal function, and social integration. As discussed below, both the causal research and program evaluation data on abusive populations are well suited to addressing these types of questions.

The purpose of this chapter is to cull from the pool of child abuse research those findings that offer concrete guidelines to those designing child abuse interventions. Because no single program has been identified as a panacea for all forms of maltreatment or all populations, particular attention is paid to the range of individuals best served by a given service delivery system or staffing pattern. Given the breadth and multidisciplinary nature of these efforts and the variety of populations being served, two specific areas will be addressed in this chapter:

- the specific contribution basis research on the causes of maltreatment make to the overall program planning process; and

• the specific program components (e.g., service content, provider characteristics, duration, and intensity) found to be most effective in altering abusive or potentially abusive parenting behavior.

Given these limitations, a wide range of research will not be covered under this effort. Most notable is the absence of interventions targeted directly to maltreatment victims. While such efforts have been effective in buffering both the immediate and long-term consequences of abuse, a careful assessment of their most effective features lies beyond the scope of this effort. Similarly, limited attention is paid to the actual or potential aggregate impacts of social reforms such as expanded welfare policies or new health care delivery systems.

The chapter begins with a discussion of the various causal theories of maltreatment and the specific lessons they provide regarding program design. The chapter then explores the program evaluation literature and its contributions to developing more effective program structures. Specifically, questions of maltreatment subpopulations, service location, provider characteristics and service duration and intensity are explored. The chapter concludes with a discussion of the aggregate accomplishments of the current child abuse service systems and the implications of these accomplishments on future program planning and research.

CAUSAL THEORIES OF ABUSE AND THEIR PROGRAM IMPLICATIONS

A number of factors go into determining an individual's parenting style. Efforts to model this process generally include some combination of developmental history, personality factors, social interactions or social networks, familial relationships, and child characteristics (Belsky & Vondra, 1990; Sameroff & Chandler, 1975; Sandler, 1979). Broad causal theories have been used to explain the general relationship between specific individual or environmental conditions and child abuse. The theories most commonly found in the literature range from interpersonal functioning theories, such as psychodynamic and learning theories, to systemic and social explanations for maltreatment, as suggested by theories of stress and poverty (Newberger & Newberger, 1982). For purposes of identifying the program design implications of this body of work, the theories can be classified into four general groups:

psychodynamic theory: suggests that parents would be less abusive if they better understood themselves and their role as parents;
learning theory: suggests that parents would be less abusive if they knew, more specifically, how best to care for their children;
environmental theory: suggests that parents would be less abusive if they had greater resources available to them in terms of material support or social support for a given set of actions; and

ecological theory: suggests that parents would be less abusive if a network of services or supports existed to compensate for individual, situational, and environmental shortcomings.

Each of these theoretical frameworks is intuitively appealing in its capacity to explain the phenomenon of child abuse and to offer creative ways to address its incidence.

Psychodynamic Theory: Reparenting the Parent

Psychodynamic theory places a heavy emphasis on the parent's level of functioning in explaining abusive behavior (Bolton & Bolton, 1987). Individuals with diminished capacity due to developmental disabilities or substance dependency or abuse are less able, all things being equal, to adequately care for their children than individuals without these functional limitations. Individuals who have difficulty managing their personal choices and emotions often find it difficult, if not impossible, to manage and care for children, particularly if the children are unusually demanding or needy. While these individuals may have an adequate understanding of appropriate parenting skills, they lack the personal capacity to implement these skills in a consistent and effective manner. Similarly, individuals suffering from severe or even relatively moderate psychological disorders may be less able to cope with the unpredictable nature of children or the routine demands of child care.

Initial work with abusive families placed a heavy emphasis on the provision of therapeutic services to maltreating adults for purposes of changing parental personalities or behaviors (Steele & Pollack, 1971; Helfer, 1975). Although originally developed for the physical abuser, the use of individual and group therapy has been incorporated over time into treatment programs serving adults demonstrating a wide range of abusive behavior. The early and continued use of formal psychotherapy has a good deal of theoretical appeal. Many of the problems reported by maltreating adults are issues which have historically been addressed through psychiatric services (Steele, 1987a). These characteristics include notions that the child's responsibility is to care for the parent, difficulty in managing anger or aggressive impulses, rigidity, low self-esteem, and a history of maltreatment. While the causes of maltreatment rarely lie in a single disorder, the poor personal functioning of many abusive and neglectful adults have supported continued attempts to apply therapeutic methods to this problem.

In justifying his emphasis on therapeutic interventions, Steele (1987b) has noted that parenting skills are acquired through two basic avenues: (a) culture and advice from family and friends, and (b) patterns acquired in infancy and early childhood as a result of one's own experiences of being parented. Dealing with inappropriate patterns gleaned from the first of these avenues can be addressed through such methods as crisis therapy or educational programs.

However, those with a history of maltreatment will need, in Steele's words, to be "re-parented" or provided the basic tools of emphatic awareness and understanding that were never given them in their childhood.

The devastating impacts of maltreatment on one's ability to parent are clear. Looking across a number of retrospective studies, Kaufman and Zigler (1990) estimate that an abused child is six times more likely than his or her nonabused counterpart to be an abusive parent. In the most significant prospective study on the intergenerational cycle of maltreatment, the Minnesota Mother-Child Project reported dramatic maltreatment rates for those mothers who had been abused as children. Of the 47 mothers in this category, 34% were identified as abusing their children, 6% exhibited other problematic behaviors, and 30% were classified as borderline caretakers. In contrast, of the 35 mothers in the sample judged to have been raised in an emotionally supportive family, only one mother was currently maltreating her child (Egeland, 1988).

When faced with parents who have experienced maltreatment as a child, Steele argues that no significant long lasting change will occur unless deeper issues are addressed. "The clear recognition and treatment of the underlying needs of the perpetrator are essential in order to change and improve his or her child caring abilities" (Steele, 1987b, p. 384). Indeed, in examining the reasons behind why some individuals in their sample were able to break the abuse cycle, Egeland and his colleagues noted the ability of the "survivor" mothers to successfully engage in long-term therapy, allowing them to integrate their early experiences of abuse (Egeland, Jacobvitz, & Sroufe, 1988).

Despite the theoretical appeal and success of psychiatric treatment, formidable barriers exist to its uniform implementation. The characteristics of the clients themselves suggest limited utility for these methods. Kempe and Kempe (1978) noted that physically abusive or neglectful families are often too dysfunctional and chaotic to benefit from formal therapy. Others have noted that the problems presented by maltreating parents are the very issues for which therapeutic interventions have the least success, particularly when the clients have very limited intellectual capacity or psychological maturity (Dumas, 1984; Lorian, 1978; Wahler, 1980; Wells, 1981). Further, fixed appointments, center-based services, and techniques void of immediate and obvious application to current, everyday problems hold little interest for this population (Holmes, 1978).

Even if clients were capable of successfully engaging in a therapeutic relationship, the number of maltreating families and the limited resources available for psychiatric services suggest practical limits to their consistent and unique application. For example, Bourne (1979) has noted several reasons why insight therapy is not useful with maltreating populations. Over and above the cost and duration of these services lies what Bourne considers to be unreasonable demands on emotionally fragile clients—the ability to rapidly establish a trusting relationship and the ability to be personally introspective. He also notes that use of this method elevates the importance of individual psychopathology in the violent family, thereby minimizing the role of social and environmental factors.

Certainly, individuals who are unable to establish emotional attachments to their children or who exhibit serious psychological problems face tremendous difficulties as parents. Such individuals are unlikely to recognize their own difficulties, not to mention the impacts of their behaviors on their children. While a difficult population to reach through therapeutic efforts, problem-focused, goal-oriented therapies have been successful (Egeland & Erickson, 1990; Feshback, 1980; Rivara, 1985; Wolfe, Sandler, & Kaufman, 1981). While personal variables such as poor comprehension, slow learning, the absence of social support, and intrafamilial disagreements continue to limit a client's ability to successfully engage in any service, goal-oriented approaches can better accommodate these and similar difficulties (Goldstein, 1973).

Howing and her colleagues (Howing, Wodarski, Gaudin, & Kurtz, 1989; Howing, Wodarski, Kurtz, & Gaudin, 1989) cite numerous studies which suggest that the use of behavioral-based therapy techniques offer more promise than traditional individual therapy. They suggest this method is useful with neglectful and particularly physically abusive parents. Techniques cited include verbal instruction, modeling, behavior rehearsal, and use of parent training manuals. When consistently applied in an ongoing program, these techniques improve self-control and control of anger, two of the most frequently cited preconditions for physical abuse.

Learning Theory: Knowledge and Skill Building

While still focusing on the parent, learning theory emphasizes the individual's lack of skills and knowledge rather than poor psychological functioning. Under this theoretical framework, abuse occurs because parents simply do not know how to care for their children or have a limited repertoire of discipline or child care techniques that are either harmful or ineffective. Further, these adults may have a history of maltreatment and poor parenting, or they may be too young or too inexperienced to comprehend what is expected of them as parents. The intuitive appeal of this theory is that the solution to the maltreatment problem may lie less in the realm of expensive and intensive psychotherapy and more in the realm of education. If parents can be trained or taught how to parent, the cycle of abuse could be broken through consistent intervention, for example, with all first-time parents. Parenting education programs are well suited to filling this type of informational gap either through written material, group presentations, or individual home instruction. In many respects, conveying this type of basic knowledge to parents may be the easiest task to improving parenting potential.

Beyond providing parents with general information, however, lies the more difficult task of helping parents translate knowledge into behavior. For some parents, this transition will be a natural extension of having received the information or of having observed appropriate caregiving. For other parents, the transition will be significantly more difficult. Parents who experienced healthy care as children, or who observed or perhaps assisted their parents in the care of younger siblings, will have less difficulty making use of the knowledge parenting education resources offer than will parents who lack concrete, positive experiences. For this latter group, identifying and addressing the barriers parents face in meeting their child's needs can be a complex and time consuming task. Service providers may need to spend several sessions simply modeling the implementation of basic parenting information or assisting parents in securing necessary support services such as medical care or day care.

In addition to modeling parenting behavior, providers need to integrate these behaviors into a client's overall home environment. Olds and Henderson (1990), for example, found that offering parent education, without equal emphasis on conditions in the home environment, is unlikely to have sustained impact. Similarly, merely focusing on the enhancement of social and material conditions in the home, without a focused and individualized educational program, is insufficient to affecting change. They conclude, as others have, that "the simultaneous provision of education and social support are essential" (Olds & Henderson, 1990, p. 755).

In working with the most dysfunctional families, one successful approach has been to combine parenting instruction with a therapeutic approach (Gambrill, 1983). Testing this notion, Wolfe, Edwards, Manion, and Koverola (1988) achieved notable success by combining agency-abused family support services with training in child management. Their sample included 30 women, drawn from the caseload of a child protective service agency, who were randomly assigned to receive either both individual and group services or group services alone.

Individual training sessions with the parent and child were scheduled weekly for 90 minutes, shifting to biweekly once gains were evident. The content was based on a social learning approach and aimed at emergent problems in child management and child development. Training was competency based whereby the therapist progressed to more advanced skills once basic skills were achieved. In addition to receiving feedback from the therapist, participants viewed videotaped sessions and critiqued their own behavior.

In contrast to this intense individual service, informational sessions were held twice a week for 2 hours each in groups of 8–10 participants. These sessions included social activities and informal discussion on a variety of parenting and personal topics such as the mother's personal growth and maturity, improved self-esteem and development of adequate social support. Children attended day care during the sessions.

At 3-month follow-up for both groups, mothers who received individual parent training in addition to group services for an average of 20 weeks reported fewer and less intense child behavior problems and indicated fewer adjustment problems associated with the risk of maltreatment than did the controls who attended only the group services for an average of 18 weeks. The treatment group fell within the normal range on the Child Abuse Potential Inventory (Milner, 1980) at follow-up, while the controls, although improving, remained at-risk. This pattern was supported by caseworker ratings at 1 year follow-up, which showed greater improvement and a lowered risk of maltreatment among clients who received both forms of intervention combined.

Wolfe and his colleagues concluded that a certain amount of discontentment is needed to motivate clients to participate in these types of services. Anecdotally, they noted that parents with very young children (less than 15 months of age) often were less committed than parents with preschoolers and toddlers, presumably due to the fewer problems shown during this preambulatory stage of child development. Engaging and retaining clients hinged, in their opinion, on the degree to which participants viewed the topics being presented as having direct relevance to their lives and the problems they faced in rearing their children.

Environmental Theory: Altering the Culture or Society

The third theoretical approach listed above moves the discussion away from a focus on individual characteristics and toward the broader structural and cultural environment. Rather than viewing maltreatment as emanating from a lack of motivation or skill on the parent's part, this casual theory focuses on the potentially dominant role of certain societal conditions and values. Poverty, with its corresponding limits on personal choice, and societal values that condone violence, racism, and sexism, are forces that often overwhelm the limited resistance of families who find themselves trapped in a cycle of distress (Pelton, 1981). Depending on the type of abuse in question, the social features that contribute to the problem differ, but the direction and intensity of the impacts remain. Attitudes that condone, even promote, corporal punishment, and the importance placed on individualism, competition, and the "private family," contribute to a generally violent environment (Garbarino, 1988; Gelles & Straus, 1988).

As one might expect, the interventions suggested by this theory seek changes within communities and value systems. Attacking the underlying causes of abuse under this theoretical assumption requires changes in social attitudes and practices. In addition to broad-scale public awareness campaigns to clarify the relationship between certain societal norms and potential maltreatment, proponents of this approach support policy changes to reduce the level of stress families face due to poverty or the shortage of necessary support services. Improvements in housing, health care systems, and educational services, as well as increased access to job training and employment opportunities, are among the strategies frequently promoted within the context of an environmental explanation for maltreatment (Wolock & Horowitz, 1979). Further, prevention advocates have called for universal or significantly expanded educational and support services to all families (Cohn, 1983; Helfer, 1982) or to those at risk of a wide range of health and caregiving disorders (Olds & Henderson, 1990).

Ecological Theory: Developing an Integrated Response

None of these three theoretical approaches is incorrect in its explanation of maltreatment. However, none can adequately, on its own, explain the abuse riddle. The final theoretical framework cited above, the ecological model, integrates the interpersonal characteristics of a family with its surrounding environmental and cultural realities (Belsky, 1980; Brofenbrenner, 1979; Garbarino, 1977). This theory focuses, not merely on the functioning of individuals and the functioning of the various spheres in which they operate (e.g., the family, the community, and the broader social/political environment) but rather on the interaction of these spheres. Some have classified these interactions in terms of a hierarchical structure, differentiating between sufficient causes and necessary causes (Garbarino, 1977). Framing the interactions in a different way, Cicchetti and Rizley (1981) allocate risk factors into one or two broad categories: *potentiating factors*, which increase the probability of the occurrence of maltreatment; and *compensatory factors*, which decrease the risk of maltreatment. The risk factors attributed to each of these categories are further divided into those which are transient *state* factors and those which are more permanent *trait* factors. According to Cicchetti and Rizley abuse occurs only in those situations where the potentiating factors exceed the compensatory or buffering conditions.

The implications of the ecological theory for program planning is twofold. First, the theory underscores the need to simultaneously address the problem on a number of levels, including changes in the individual, the manner in which that individual relates to other family members, and the manner in which the family unit interacts with its immediate community as well as with broader social and cultural norms. No single prevention approach will address the multiple causes of maltreatment nor the way these causal factors influence the actions of an individual parent. Second, the transactional risk model highlights the fact that emphasis must be placed, not only on minimizing the characteristics of individuals or communities viewed as contributing to an elevated risk of maltreatment, but also on maximizing the characteristics of individuals or communities which buffer families against abuse. For example, it is not sufficient to merely suggest parents not use physical force in disciplining their children. An effective intervention system must also offer alternative discipline methods and address the conditions that lead a parent to consider the use of physical discipline not only appropriate but necessary.

Summary

Collectively, the causal research on maltreatment highlight two broad issues that shape the overall design of child abuse intervention systems: the need to provide a diversity of interventions, and the need to be sensitive to different cultural and racial values affecting family life and parenting practices.

First, successfully treating and preventing child maltreatment involves simultaneously altering the potential perpetrator, the potential victim, and the environment in which both exist. To accomplish this task, child abuse treatment and prevention services are housed in a variety of institutional and community-based settings and incorporate a wide range of services. Individual, family and group-based services have been established to address the therapeutic and supportive needs for families involved in all forms of maltreatment (Ammerman & Hersen, 1990; Bolton & Bolton, 1987; Daro, 1988). Crisis hot lines, respite care centers, and self-help groups have emerged throughout the country to provide those families at imminent risk of harming their child a method to access immediate assistance (Daro, 1988; Levine, 1988; Weiss & Jacobs, 1988). Child abuse prevention services ranging from public awareness efforts, to parenting enhancement services, to child assault prevention classes in the school are found in communities throughout this country (Daro, Casey, & Abrahams, 1990). Political efforts to improve the social service safety net for families with the fewest material resources, and to combat the environmental hazards children face, while rarely implemented as fully as necessary, are viewed as vital and necessary components in any comprehensive child abuse response system (Garbarino, 1988; Gil, 1981; Pelton, 1981).

This diversity of interventions is needed, not only at the systems level, but also at the individual client level. In other words, not only do communities need to support a variety of interventions, but individual families must have access to a range of therapeutic, educational, and supportive services in order to effectively combat the multiple causes of maltreatment. In some instances, this diversity of services can be found under the rubric of a single intervention. In other cases, families will need to simultaneously or sequentially access services from multiple agencies.

A number of researchers have noted that clinical success is based, not merely on the successful provision of a single service, but also on the successful provision of a diverse service package. For example, Herrenkohl and Herrenkohl (1978) found that casework services plus supplemental individual or group therapy produced more promising outcomes than the sole provision of casework services. Similarly, Green, Power, Steinbrook and Gaines (1981) found that a combination of home visits, service-oriented telephone advocacy, and outpatient psychotherapy resulted in a reduced likelihood for maltreatment. More recently, Miller and Whittaker (1988) reported on the importance of explicitly incorporating methods to enhance social support into programs targeting abusive and neglectful populations. The authors note that the wide range of needs presented by maltreating families make it unrealistic to assume that a specific intervention can address them. Consequently, parents need help in identifying the social supports available to them and the skills needed to access these supports in time of crisis.

Second, research on the causal patterns of maltreatment underscore the importance of recognizing cultural differences in parenting patterns and social organization. The battle for culturally competent social services is long-standing in this country. Debate has been particularly sharp in the area of family interventions and child welfare services. The many and diverse cultures found among families in the United States speak against adopting too rigid a standard of family well-being and "correct" methods of parent–child interactions. Despite the longevity of this debate, many have noted the absence of adequate information as to the cultural and ethnic factors that may influence the occurrence of child maltreatment and the delivery of effective interventions (Cross, Bazron, Dennis, & Isaacs, 1989; Garbarino, Cohn, & Ebota, 1982; Mann, 1990).

Achieving a culturally competent service system requires service providers and agency administrators to acknowledge that cultural differences as well as similarities exist within the population and that such differences are value free. The process requires practitioners to be aware of the cultures represented among their caseload, understand the basic parameters of these cultures, and recognize that cultural diversity will affect a family's participation in service delivery (Anderson & Fenichel, 1989).

Of particular importance is the need for service providers to understand how the concept of *family* is defined in a given culture, and to recognize that individuals and families make different choices based upon cultural forces. If service providers deny these choices or mislabel them, interventions can compound rather than resolve parenting dilemmas. Based on her assessment of the African-American family, Slaughter (1988) noted three implications for service planners: to recognize, and incorporate into the treatment plan, the importance of the extended and/or augmented family; to establish program goals in light of the cultural-ecological realities of racial and ethnic minority family life; and to recognize the diversity within racial and ethnic minority communities. Looking across the range of responses different cultural groups might exhibit to certain risk factors for maltreatment, Derezotes and Snowden (1990) concurred with Slaughter that interventions must be selected in light of the family's cultural orientation and preferences. For example, when faced with an African American or Hispanic adult presenting problems of distress or personal dissatisfaction, they recommend drawing upon the coping strategies most common in these cultures (e.g., religious institutions) rather than referring the client to psychotherapy. Similarly, the use of extended family members to combat social isolation may be far more appropriate with families from these cultures than relying upon formal support systems.

The absence of significant empirical research on service impacts for families from different racial and cultural backgrounds limits the discussion of best practice standards with these populations. While theoretically practitioners may well need to be cognizant of the differences in family life and parenting responsibilities among people of color, it remains unclear if such differences demand unique intervention systems. Indeed the requisite differences may be more a matter of the manner, rather than the form, in which services are delivered. Further, in certain cases, the stronger predictors of success may lie in other key demographic characteristics. For example, a recent evaluation of child abuse prevention services targeting adolescent parents found no significant differences in outcomes by the client's race. African American and White teens responded equally well (and equally poorly) to the various interventions tested. Age (i.e., 16 years of age or under and over 16) and the initial point of service delivery (i.e., pregnant or postbirth) were far more accurate than race in predicting client outcomes (Center on Child Abuse Prevention Research, 1990). Such findings are far from conclusive. They merely suggest that the relationship between cultural competency and program outcomes require a great deal of further study.

EVALUATIVE DATA REGARDING PROGRAM STRUCTURE

The scholarly and popular literature on child maltreatment is, to say the least, abundant. As the number of treatment and prevention services have increased so have the number of evaluation studies and summaries of these studies. Individuals concerned with more effectively incorporating the results of this literature into the program planning process have utilized both qualitative and, more recently, quantitative summary methods. By far the most common strategy is a written description of various program evaluations and a selective summary of their findings. These efforts have focused broadly on programs working with violent families (Bolton & Bolton, 1987) as well as more narrowly on child abuse and neglect (Daro, 1988; Howing, Wodarski, Gaudin, & Kurtz, 1989). More recently, attempts have been made to utilize metaanalysis to summarize the results of early parenting interventions to prevent child abuse (Gray & Halpern, 1989) and to understand the impacts of family programs (Hauser-Cram, 1988).

This research base is not without its problems or its critics. Howing, Wodarski, Kurtz, and Gaudin (1989) note that child maltreatment research has yet to adequately address a number of basic questions, such as the effects of maltreatment and the behavioral, affective, and cognitive antecedents of abuse. As a result, interventions which may or may not make sense have proliferated. Major problems with existing evaluative efforts cited by these authors include poor operational definitions for various maltreatment types, the absence of clear, theoretical considerations, and overemphasis on the importance of group rather than individual differences, the absence of longitudinal or posttermination studies, potential sampling bias, the absence of adequate controls, and the lack of reliable and valid outcome measures.

Further, Azar (1988) suggests that public attention and concern with maltreatment may lead to the rapid development of programs which cannot be justified, given the field's rudimentary knowledge base. Poor or incomplete basic research may lead to the development of programs targeting behaviors or attitudes that are only tangential to child abuse or neglect. Rather than moving forward with program development, she calls for a more detailed understanding of what separates maltreating from nonmaltreating populations.

Such concerns over the utility of evaluative research are well placed and are common among the program evaluations cited in this effort. However, limiting the pool of useful program evaluations to only those efforts which meet strict standards of scientific purity may be impractical and unrealistic. The multicausal nature of maltreatment, and the diversity of the at-risk population, bode against the identification of universal behaviors or attitudes which interventions might address. While the present pool of evaluative research most certainly has its problems and limitations, it does offer at least preliminary guidelines for shaping intervention programs and systems.

Effectively utilizing research to enhance child abuse program planning is more than replicating a promising intervention. The process involves careful attention to the context in which the program will be placed, the proposed target population it will serve, and the broader social service environment in which it will operate. Program evaluations which document changes in specific outcome measures provide only one important standard for determining whether a given program is a promising candidate for replication. Far more important is understanding whether the program's organizational auspice, client characteristics, and community service system mirror the conditions in the community or client population in need of a new intervention. Rather then offering clear models for replication, research on child abuse programs more often provides service planners with numerous building blocks to utilize in constructing the most relevant service system for their particular situation.

Not all evaluative research in the area of child maltreatment present a uniform picture. The diversity of disciplines engaged in this field, the various levels of need among the at-risk population, and the range of public support for what may be perceived as intrusive interventions into the private family suggest that agreement would not be reached on all issues. This section reviews the evaluative data from four major service dimensions in which conflicting findings have been identified. These include:

- questions of maltreatment subpopulations or client targeting;
- questions of service location;
- questions of staff qualifications; and
- questions of service intensity and duration.

Subpopulations of Maltreatment

Child maltreatment has long been studied as a series of unique behaviors or subpopulations. While all maltreating families are technically in violation of the same statute, substantive differences exist among a mother who leaves her infant unattended, a stepfather who sexually abuses his daughter, and a parent who physically injures a child in the course of administering ''normal'' discipline. Expectations that different abusive or neglectful behaviors have different causal explanations has been supported by both theoretical and clinical research (AAPC, 1988; Daro, 1988; Giovannoni & Becerra, 1979; Milner & Robertson, 1980; Westat Associates, 1988). Further, different types of maltreatment have been found to have differential impacts on the cognitive and emotional development of children (Egeland, Sroufe, & Erickson, 1983).

Recognition of these differences has led to the proliferations of strategies which target specific aspects of the maltreatment problem. While the most notable of these efforts have been services directed toward the perpetrators and victims of child sexual abuse, specialized services also have emerged for families involved in physical abuse, neglect, and emotional maltreatment. The implications of this type of service targeting was extensively tested by Daro (1988).

In a study of 19 federally funded clinical demonstration programs, she found that various interventions had differential impacts depending upon the family's primary type of maltreatment as identified by the family's caseworker. The criteria used in making this determination included the duration of the maltreatment, its impacts on the children, and the family's perception of their major difficulty. Of the 829 adults for whom a specific form of maltreatment was identified as primary, 33% were classified as primarily involved in neglect, 28% primarily involved in emotional maltreatment, 17% primarily involved in sexual abuse, and 15% primarily involved in physical abuse. Seven percent of the sample was classified as high risk, having not yet abused or neglected their children.

The three outcome measures utilized in this federal evaluation were: the clinician's assessment of the client's overall progress, reincidence during treatment, and the clinician's assessment of the client's likelihood for future maltreatment. Across the three outcome variables, specific services explained a greater degree of variance with respect to a client's overall progress, with client characteristics and the type and severity of the initial maltreatment accounting for a larger proportion of the variance on the other two outcome measures. Of particular note was the strength of the client's attitude toward services. This particular variable was a very strong predictor in determining success with respect to child sexual abuse. This measure explained 30% of the variance on overall progress for sexual abuse, and 17% of the propensity for future maltreatment. In contrast, this variable explained less than 6% of the variance for families involved in emotional maltreatment and 8% of the variance for families involved in child neglect.

With respect to specific services, Daro (1988) found that a combination of therapeutic care, including individual, family, and group service, was particularly successful with families involved in child sexual abuse. Psychological assessment and diagnostic services and the gradual introduction of different service components, moving from individual therapy, to family therapy to group therapy, realized the greatest success in reducing a family's propensity for future maltreatment and in enhancing overall adult functioning. The initial success with families involved in sexual abuse achieved by the demonstration projects paralleled the findings of others (Anderson & Schafer, 1979; Bander, Fein, & Bishop, 1982; Giarretto, 1976; Sgroi, 1982). In generalizing these findings to all cases of sexual abuse, it is important to bear in mind that the vast majority of these cases involved father–daughter or stepfather–daughter incest. Further, a sizable number of perpetrators in these samples admitted their guilt and accepted responsibility for their actions.

Families involved in child neglect responded best to programs incorporating family therapy approaches, augmented by case management services and in-home visits which allowed for practitioners to model a variety of parenting skills. While this group of families did not reposed well to formalized parenting education or material on child development, they did benefit from the ongoing provision of services and concrete assistance in resolving specific child care problems such as discipline, toilet training, and household management.

Finally, families involved primarily in emotional maltreatment were best served by programs offering formal classes on parenting, child development, and personal management. Such classes, when followed by an open discussion or support group meeting, provided parents an opportunity to explore the application of the theoretical concepts presented in the class to real life situations.

While Daro was unable to directly address the relative effectiveness of different services with families primarily involved in physical abuse due to sample size limitations, the unique needs of this subpopulation have been studied by others. While family therapy has shown some gains with neglectful families and sexual abuse, it may be problematic with physically abusive families based on the tendency of these parents to be self-centered and to have destructive relationships with their children (Malone, 1979) and to have their own need to be nurtured (Mann & McDermott, 1983). It has been suggested that the treatment of physical abuse should focus on improving parent–child interactions and on increasing parental flexibility in responding to child behavior. In contrast, treatment with neglectful parents should center on the provision of supportive services and the development of increased family cohesion and parental responsiveness (Brunk, Henggeler, & Whelan, 1987; Herrenkohl, Herrenkohl, & Egolf, 1983).

While these and other studies have begun the process of identifying useful interventions for those experiencing different forms of maltreatment, the utility of this research avenue has clear limitations for at least two reasons. First, a number of client factors may be equally critical to consider in developing effective interventions. It is unclear, as with the issue of cultural identification, if an individual's primary form of maltreatment is the most important or universal client targeting factor. Segmenting families might better be done in terms of the targeted child's age, the age of the primary caretaker or the presence of a substance abuse problem. In all likelihood, the most salient client feature will differ across families and across circumstances. Rather than holding rigid ideas as to how to best organize service systems, program planners may be best served by remaining open to a range of client typologies.

Second, attempts to rigorously compare the characteristics, service needs and service outcomes of different subpopulations of maltreatment is confounded by multiple patterns of maltreatment. In Daro's sample, for example, only one-third of the clients presented a single form of maltreatment. Most were involved in at least two of the four major categories of maltreatment she identified, with 4% of the sample presenting all four types. While the implementation of strict criteria for determining the primary type of maltreatment in such families can vastly improve the reliability of the ranking, any scheme will involve rater subjectivity and therefore potential bias in how families are classified. On the other hand, if such studies are limited only to those families exhibiting a single form of maltreatment, the research may be based on unrepresentative, and potentially very limited, samples.

These limitations notwithstanding, the conceptualization of child maltreatment in terms of recognizable subpopulations is useful in a number of ways. While overlapping membership most certainly exists, the paradigm protects practitioners from identifying a single causal correlate or single intervention as a singular solution to all maltreatment. If program planners have learned only one thing over the past three decades, it should be that allowing one type of maltreatment to dominate our thinking leaves us with a response system and practice standards inappropriate for the full range of relevant concerns.

Service Location

An historical tension has existed regarding the most appropriate location for delivering services aimed at improving one's parenting abilities. While wide variation exists in the content, structure and flexibility of both home-based and center-based service models, it is the location of service that has engendered the most debate. Home-based interventions have been seen as an opportunity to deliver individualized health and social services to families and to provide practitioners with an opportunity to influence the quality of the family's living environment. In contrast, group-based interventions are viewed as a less intrusive and more efficient method of reaching large numbers of families in need. While the majority of research on these methods requires a leap of faith regarding the unique contribution service location (as opposed to service content or duration for example) has made to the observed outcomes, the empirical evidence does support the efficacy of both models.

With respect to home visitors, a variety of programs utilizing different types of providers (e.g., nurses, graduate students, paraprofessionals) and emphasizing different topics (e.g., health education, child development, social supports) have proven successful in reducing the likelihood for maltreatment. One of the strongest cases for this service model has been made by David Olds and his colleagues (1986) at the University of Rochester. The 400 participants in this study, all of whom were first-time mothers, were randomly assigned to one of four conditions in which the most intensive level of services involved regular pre- and postnatal home visits by a nurse practitioner. The nurse home visitor carried out three major activities: parent education regarding fetal and infant development, the involvement of family members and friends in child care and support of the mother, and the linkage of family members with other health and human services.

Those who received the most intensive intervention had a significantly lower incidence of reported child abuse over the 2-year postbirth study period. While 19% of the comparison group at greatest risk for maltreatment (i.e., poor, unmarried teens) were reported for abuse or neglect, only 4% of their nurse-visited counterparts were reported. Of these cases, 50% involved reports of neglect only and 50% involved reports of neglect and physical abuse. In addition to having a lower reported rate of child abuse, those infants whose mothers received ongoing nurse home visits had fewer accidents and were less likely to require emergency room care. The mothers also reported less frequent need to punish or restrict their children.

Reduction in child abuse rates also has been observed in repeated evaluations of Project 12-Ways, a multifaceted home-based service program in central Illinois. In this instance, services are provided in the client's home by advanced graduate students and cover such topics as parenting skills, stress management, self-control, assertiveness training, health maintenance, job placement, and marital counseling. In assessing the program, Lutzker and Rice (1984, 1987) have documented significantly fewer repeated abuse and neglect incidents among program recipients than among similar families not receiving this intervention. While enrolled in the program, only 2% of a randomly selected number of Project 12-Ways's clients were reported for maltreatment, compared to 11% of the control group. In the year following termination of services, 10% of the treatment families and 21% of the nontreatment families were reported for maltreatment.

Larson (1980) noted similar gains in an assessment of the Prenatal Intervention Project in Montreal, but only in cases in which such visits began prior to the child's birth. In this case, the home visitors were women with undergraduate degrees in child psychology who had received special training in preventive health care. The home visits were designed to provide information about general caretaking topics and the need for regular well-child care. Participants were also encouraged to talk to their infants and to respond to their vocalizations. Child development counseling involved reviewing with the mother her child's developmental competence and suggesting types of activities she could engage in to promote the child's skills. Children whose mothers began receiving services in the seventh month of pregnancy had a lower accident rate and exhibited fewer feeding problems. In addition, the mothers scored higher on assessments of maternal behavior and in providing appropriate and stimulating home environments.

The use of trained, lay volunteers as home visitors also has been found effective in reducing the risk of abuse. The C. Henry Kempe National Center for the Treatment and Prevention of Child Abuse and Neglect pioneered the use of lay home visitors with at-risk mothers. Gray et al.'s (1979) evaluations of this effort found it reduced child abuse potential and enhanced mother–infant relationships. While not measuring a reduction in child abuse and neglect directly, the Ford Foundation's Child Survival/Fair Start Initiative suggests that well trained community volunteers can provide effective services to families at-risk. The six programs that participated in this effort were housed in community health clinics, child care and social service agencies, and small, independent organizations, all of which adopted a multidisciplinary approach in tackling problems of maternal and infant health and infant development. Parents participating in these programs demonstrated an increased ability to secure routine and preventive health care for their infants and a greater openness in discussing family problems and utilizing community resources (Larner, 1990).

These and similar studies have suggested that providing clients with solid, long-lasting gains require the provision of services in the home. Frankel (1988) noted, in a review of placement prevention services, that design features such as being home based, flexible working hours, provision of practical help, small caseloads, and intensive services were more critical to positive outcomes than specific techniques such as teaching communication skills, helping with expressing feelings, or altering behavior. Further, at least one study has suggested that group-based knowledge may not be transferred to the home unless home instruction is also provided (Goldstein, Keller, & Erne, 1985).

Finally, Olds and his colleagues offer strong support for the home visitor concept. They have noted that the method offers a unique opportunity to engage those individuals too dysfunctional to participate in group-based services. Unless a program has a major home visitation component, Olds and Henderson (1990) have argued that a significant portion of the families who need the service the most will not receive it. This point also has been emphasized by Powell (1986), who noted that center-based services successfully engage primarily those mothers who feel confident in their lives prior to enrolling in the program.

Despite concerns over potential client selectivity, center-based service delivery methods have produced positive gains in overall parenting skills and in the use of community resources (Levine, 1988). Many of these programs are school-based or utilize community-based organizations, thereby increasing their availability to high-risk populations. For example, Avancé Educational Programs for Parents and Teens serves a predominantly low income Mexican-American community in San Antonio through the provision of comprehensive parenting education. The 9-month service period includes center-based weekly bilingual discussions on child growth and development, toy-making classes, day care practicum, field trips, library use, transportation, information and referral, and communal holiday celebrations. Evaluations of these efforts have found participants more hopeful about the future, more willing to assume the role of educator with their children, holding less severe conceptions of punishment, and more willing to utilize social supports to gain help (Rodriguez & Cortez, 1988).

One of the most widely disseminated group based models is the Minnesota Early Learning Demonstration (MELD), an intensive 2-year parenting education and support program. MELD's mission is to get families off to a good start and to eliminate the potential for maltreatment by never letting abusive or neglectful patterns begin. The MELD staff believe that there is no one right way to parent and participants are encouraged to make the childrearing choices that are appropriate for them and their children. The program adopts an individualized and empowerment model in which clients are exposed to solid parenting information and provided alternative methods to address different child-rearing issues. They are then encouraged to make their own choices in light of this new information base.

Although the program has never been evaluated in terms of child abuse prevention, the immediate outcomes demonstrated by program participants are encouraging (Ellwood, 1988; Miller, 1988). An evaluation of the MELD Young Moms program conducted by the Child Welfare League of America noted that 80% of the participants had finished or were completing high school compared to an overall school completion rate of only 20% for the general adolescent parent population. Also, while 25% of all teenage mothers experience a repeat pregnancy within a year of their first birth, MELD Young Mom participants have a repeat pregnancy rate of only 10%–15%. Changes also were noted in the parents' use of discipline, where the percentage of parents who spanked their children decreased from 56% at the start of the program to only 12% at the conclusion of services.

The collective results outlined above underscore the difficulty in addressing the myriad of issues associated with an increased risk for maltreatment under the rubric of a single service framework. Offering services in a client's home has a number of distinct advantages. Such services offer the provider an excellent opportunity to assess the safety of the child's living environment and to work with the mother in very concrete ways to improve parent–child interactions. The method also affords the client a degree of privacy and the practitioner a degree of flexibility difficult to achieve in center-based programs. Individuals who may be reluctant to attend weekly sessions at a community-based service center or local hospital either because they are uncomfortable about sharing their experiences with other parents or because they find it difficult to travel to the center find home-based services a welcomed alternative.

The method, however, is not without drawbacks. The costs of these programs can be quite significant, particularly if the home visitors are professionals. Even if trained paraprofessionals or volunteers are used, the strategy is highly labor intensive and involves considerable transportation costs. Further, the home setting makes it potentially more difficult to focus on parent–child relationships or on a given set of parenting skills. A clinician may need to spend considerable time focusing the mother on the issues or tasks to be addressed during the visit and away from the normal, daily distractions found in home settings. Finally, the method itself does not afford the practitioner the opportunity to draw on the benefits of a group service model, nor the client to work through his or her difficulties with others in similar conditions.

In contrast, parenting services offered through a community-based family service center or health care facility provide participants with an opportunity to share childrearing and personal problems with other parents in similar situations. This exchange serves an important validation function for parents, allowing them to acknowledge their difficulties and stresses while accepting peer suggestions on how best to cope with the demands of young children. Strategies such as the MELD program establish an ongoing support of parents to draw upon during and outside the actual service delivery process, further reducing the level of isolation. Often the physical location of the group meetings can become identified as a general support center for all parents to utilize in addressing a wide range of issues or, as in the case of the Fair Start Initiative, facilitate parents utilizing health care services (Larner, 1990). Also, videotaping parent–child interactions, and developing personalized work plans, can individualize group services such that each parent feels his or her unique needs and strengths are being identified (Crittenden, 1990; Egeland & Erickson, 1990).

The major difficulty these programs face is the organizational demands they place on group participants. Regular attendance at weekly group meetings requires a good deal of motivation and structure on the part of a young mother. Evaluations of these efforts suggest that only a fraction of the participants are able to demonstrate this level of control. Drop-out rates of as high as 40 to 50% have been noted by several evaluators (Johnson & Breckenridge, 1982; and Lochman & Brown 1980). Unlike the home-based models, continued participation in a center-based program is contingent upon a parent's willingness to cope with the transportation and child care demands inherent in attending any event outside one's home. It is logical to assume that parents exhibiting this motivational level will be predisposed to taking full advantage of the support and educational benefits offered by center-based services. However, parents lacking this motivation and who may be among those at greatest risk for maltreatment will be unlikely to sustain involvement with these programs long enough to achieve the most positive outcomes.

Reaching the full spectrum of the "at risk" population requires some combination of both home-based and center-based programs. Center-based services, particularly if they are associated with local junior high and senior high school programs for adolescent parents, offer excellent opportunities for a highly motivated teenage mother not only to improve her parenting skills but also to continue her education and to establish a stable life for herself and her infant. Home-based programs, with their more individualized and flexible service delivery system, will be particularly useful with a more isolated population and with those mothers lacking the interest or motivation to participate in a group program.

Staff Characteristics

A combination of factors go into establishing competent and effective social service providers. At the most basic level, these factors can be divided into technical skills and interpersonal skills. A number of academic programs exists to transfer the technical skills necessary to effectively provide educational and support services to parents abusing or at-risk of maltreating their children. The most common disciplines noted among those professional staff working in child abuse treatment and prevention programs include social work, nursing, education, special education, psychology, and child development.

While such professionals are assumed to be technically competent, it is less clear that formal training provides the interpersonal skills necessary to successfully engage and retain at-risk families. Research on the interpersonal skills most successful in fostering positive and sustained client–provider relationships include an active interest in new ideas, an active interest in people and an ability to engage people socially, an ability to accept people's life situations without prejudging them, an ability to relate to a family's experiences without becoming enmeshed in the family's problem cycles, and relative stability in his or her own personal life (Halpern & Larner, 1987). These characteristics have been found to be particularly essential in working with teenage parents where the provider's value system may suggest that having children at a very young age does a disservice to both the youth and the infant. An analysis of provider attitudes in at least one teen parent program found that a staff member's expectations play a significant role in the extent to which material was accurately presented to the teen and the extent to which the teen responded in a positive manner (Musick, Bernstein, Percansky, & Scott, 1987).

To create the structure of social support central in the treatment and prevention of child abuse, many programs employ the services of individuals who come from within the same community and share many of the same values and experiences as program participants. The rational for the use of paraprofessional service providers results, at least in part, from the belief that they are more likely than trained professionals to possess the interpersonal skills desired for effective service provision. Paraprofessionals also are utilized to ameliorate program efficiency and effectiveness (Austin, 1978). Underlying this rationale is the notion that paraprofessionals are thought to provide more cost-effective services as well as relieve professionals from doing the work that can be done by those with less training and skills (Carkhuff, 1968).

The incorporation of paraprofessionals in the provision of child abuse and neglect treatment services has a long history. Both the initial work of the C. Henry Kempe Center for the Treatment and Prevention of Child Abuse and Neglect and the Ford Foundation Child Survival/Fair Start Initiative found strong support for the use of lay counselors. In a final review of the Fair Start program, Larner (1990) noted that program supervisors felt that program participants were "more open, relaxed and responsive with the lay workers than they would have been with professionals" (Larner, 1990, p. 9). The first major evaluation of federally funded child abuse and neglect treatment programs concluded that, relative to any other discrete services or combination of services, lay services—lay counseling and Parents Anonymous—resulted in the most positive treatment outcomes, although this finding was more frequently true for adults who were at risk of maltreatment than active abusers. With respect to the physical abuse population, the study found that the use of supplemental services such as group therapy and parent education classes further enhanced outcomes (Cohn, 1979).

The continued growth of Parents Anonymous (PA) chapters and the positive responses reported by program participants further support the effectiveness of the lay therapy model (Fritz, 1986; Junewicz, 1983; Moore, 1983). These groups provide participants with an opportunity to validate their sense of frustration in being unable to effectively cope with the many and varied demands of parenting. The weekly meetings offer participants, not only support and friendship, but also knowledge regarding child development and positive parenting practices. Although directed by the participants themselves and a lay volunteer leader, the group has ongoing access to a clinical professional. This professional volunteer coordinates service referrals for those group participants needing more structured counseling or formal therapy.

The use of paraprofessionals, however, has its problems. Despite the strong support for this staffing concept among those involved in the Ford Foundation's Child Survival/Fair Start Initiative, Halpern and Larner (1987) noted that paraprofessionals had difficulty providing all of the assistance clients needed in the areas of health care, child care and mental health services. Further, Parents Anonymous, while a very useful intervention, has had difficulty sustaining its groups. Over one-quarter of the PA groups operating in the state of Washington between 1980 and 1982 ceased functioning because of the loss of their volunteer professional sponsors (Blitzinsky, 1982). In the majority of these cases, the volunteers simply felt overwhelmed by the demands of the group, noting that a greater percentage of the group than they had anticipated required some form of counseling or service referrals. This high demand for therapeutic services among group participants have led others to conclude that the self-help method offers families only limited support and should never be construed as an adequate substitute for professional intervention (Powell, 1979).

Over and above these skill and organizational issues are the personal problems paraprofessionals may experience. At times the indigenous qualities of paraprofessionals may prove counterproductive. These include over identification with the client, excessive dependency on the client, projecting one's own situation onto the client, or low expectations (Austin, 1978). Others have noted that the advantages of paraprofessionals may be overstated adding that class and cultural barriers between provider and client can be overcome by carefully selecting providers who are compassionate and sensitive to differences in life style and childrearing methods. Olds and Henderson (1990) report that others have observed that parents are sometimes reluctant to reveal personal matters to indigenous workers from the neighborhood because they fear a loss of privacy, a problem that is reduced when parents communicate with professionals. Further, professionals may be more successful in helping a family communicate with local health care, welfare and educational systems.

As with the case of service location, the appropriate staffing pattern for a given program will require careful attention to the needs of the target population, the flexibility of staff, the availability of resources, and the availability of other services. Activities need to be carefully assessed to determine if all or a portion of them can be undertaken by trained, lay volunteers or employees. Further, the attitudes of clients as well as their functioning levels need to be considered. If the population is skeptical of professionals and unwilling to engage in "professional" services, the use of paraprofessionals may be unavoidable. While severely dysfunctional parents or clients might best be served by professional personnel, such individuals might also benefit from the personal appeal of an individual facing circumstances similar to their own. It is on this very personal problem-solving level that the paraprofessional offers the strongest resource for program managers (Carkhuff, 1968). Further, as demand for services increase, cost factors cannot be ignored and may require creative problem solving to secure competent staff with fixed or reduced resources.

Concerns over the inappropriate identification with clients and the potential clash of values between provider and client are critical. Regardless of the decision to use professionals or paraprofessionals, certain principles are key:

- rigorous review of the underlying values of staff with respect to the target population, particularly when the target population is engaged in an activity some may view as inappropriate (e.g., teen parents, substance abusing parents, etc.);
- initial and ongoing training of staff with respect to program goals and objectives;
- ongoing staff supervision and support, allowing staff multiple opportunities to raise issues surrounding the delivery of service; and
- continuous reassessment to insure that the staffing pattern selected for a given program represents the most viable solution given personnel skills and client needs.

Service Duration and Intensity

The final debate currently facing the field is the question of service duration and intensity. The continuum of child abuse treatment and prevention services have long included both short-term and extensive interventions. Brief, crisis-intervention services, such as respite care centers and telephone hotlines or warmlines, have consistently been viewed as cost effective methods for conveying knowledge and providing support to parents under stress (Cherry & Kirby, 1971; Green, 1976; Kempe & Helfer, 1976). In an evaluation of a crisis respite center with a 90-day follow-up period, Vaughan and Loadman (1987) noted that 72% of the participants reported a reduction of stress, 100% expressed less isolation, and no children served by the center were hospitalized for an abuse or neglect related incident for at least 90 days following program participation.

Beyond these immediate interventions, however, it had been widely thought that the complexity of abusive families require extended interventions. While there is some evidence of a high correlation between length of time in treatment and low reincidence (Silver, Dublin, & Lourie, 1971), the interpretation of this relationship is not clear-cut. Prior to the passage of the Adoption Assistance and Child Welfare Act of 1980 (PL 96-272), child welfare cases tended to remain open for at least 2 years, with the specific treatment being a function of the number and severity of problems in the family, the client's motivation or willingness to remain in treatment, and the structure and content of the given service package (Daro, 1988). Questioning the maxim "longer is better," at least one study has noted the importance of client preference and openness to treatment in determining a family's length of stay (Johnson & L'Esperance, 1984).

The emergence of family-based interventions which target those families at risk of foster care placement and provide services for a relatively brief period of time has directly challenged the need for multiyear services. Dramatic reductions in the need for placement have been recorded by short-term, family-based programs operating in the state of Washington (Kinney, Madsen, Fleming, & Haapala, 1977), Florida (Paschal & Schwahn, 1986), Wisconsin (Landsman, 1985), and Nebraska (Leeds, 1984), as well as Maryland, Massachusetts, and Minnesota (Kamerman & Kahn, 1990).

In an effort to look across these and similar programs for common factors of success, Nelson and her colleagues (Nelson, Landsman, & Deutelbaum, 1990) reviewed a number of studies conducted on the effectiveness of family preservation services. All of the services they reviewed appeared generally successful in avoiding the need for placement for 70%–90% of their caseload. While differing in service focus and location, the treatment periods were relatively brief in all of the models assessed (i.e., 30 days to 7 months).

Satisfaction with these types of interventions, however, is far from universal. Frankel (1988) suggests that many of the programs fail to take families actively involved in child abuse and neglect and may be screening out those most in need. His review of the evidence suggest that the programs are best in improving parental issues, family relationships, and the use of community resources, and least successful in dealing with social issues, child performance, and household adequacy. Similarly, in assessing the effectiveness of these efforts, Magura (1981) questioned the efficiency of attempting to prevent an event as seemingly unpredictable as placement. "Devoting disproportionate amounts of time and effort to the uncertain prevention of some placements may inevitably short-change the majority of children referred to protective services who lack adequate nurturing and could benefit from additional casework" (Magura, 1981, p. 208).

The issue of duration is equally unclear with respect to prevention. A number of the most promising home-based as well as center-based programs provided services for 1 to 2 years (Ellwood, 1988; Lutzker & Rice, 1984, 1987; Olds et al., 1986). Further, at least two longitudinal studies suggest that comprehensive parenting services provided over 2 years not only produce initial gains, but that these gains are strengthened over time (Seitz, Rosenbaum, & Apfel, 1985; Wiedner, Poisson, Lourie, & Greenspan, 1988). Areas showing improvement include parenting skills, parent–child relationships, educational achievement, employment rates, and economic well-being.

Positive findings also have been noted among prevention programs providing parenting services for a relatively short period of time (Rodriguez & Cortez, 1988; Wolfe et al., 1988). Taylor and Beauchamp (1988) report notable differences in parenting knowledge, skills, and attitudes among participants receiving only four visits by a student nurse volunteer compared to a no-service control group. Program participants received one visit while in the hospital and three subsequent home visits 1, 2 and 3 months postpartum. Those who received the visits scored significantly higher on tests of child development, expressed more democratic ideas regarding child rearing, demonstrated more positive parent–infant interactions, and demonstrated greater problem-solving abilities.

In a review of 20 outcome studies conducted on home-visiting programs, Heinicke, Beckwith, and Thompson (1988) determined that a certain number of sessions are required in order to develop a trusting relationship between a family and program worker. Interestingly, the minimum number of sessions and program length they suggest is relatively short term. Their analysis indicated that more pervasive and sustained effects on child and parent were likely to be realized when the intervention included 11 or more contacts over at least a 3-month period.

The appropriate duration of a given service will vary depending upon its overall goal and the initial functioning of its target population. Those programs seeking to convey knowledge or to alter a very limited range of behaviors may well be able to accomplish their mission in relatively brief periods of time, particularly if they are providing service to a highly motivated client population. In contrast, those seeking to address a wide range of personal and situational disorders or intervening with an extremely dysfunctional population should be prepared to offer their services for an extended period of time.

While the tendency may be to expand the intervention period in direct proportion to the number of service goals or the complexity of a program's caseload, longer service periods are not necessarily better nor likely to produce the most positive outcomes. Programs which require a lengthy involvement on the part of the client might experience high dropout rates, thereby failing to meet the needs of those at greatest risk. Further, Daro (1988) found that, independent of the number or types of services a client received, the length of time a client is involved with a program proved a significant contributor to positive outcomes. Adult clients included in her study of 19 clinical child abuse and neglect treatment programs who received services for less than 6 months and longer than 18 months were less likely than clients served for 6 to 18 months to be viewed by their clinician as making overall progress in treatment and demonstrating a reduced propensity for future maltreatment. While the predictive strength of this measure varied across different subpopulations of maltreatment, the direction was consistent. These patterns, while not always statistically significant, suggest that simply retaining a client in a program for an extended period of time may not produce more positive outcomes. The potential for any intervention strategy may diminish after 18 months. For clients not making any significant progress after a year and a half of services, clinicians might be wiser to refer the client to another type of intervention than to continue offering more of the same service.

IMPLICATIONS FOR FUTURE PROGRAM PLANNING AND RESEARCH

While universal success among services is nonexistent, several service features or components have been identified as increasing the probability of success with diverse populations. The program evaluation literature reviewed above suggest the following promising design features:

- supporting parents in their childrearing responsibilities is best done by initiating services prior to or as close to the birth of the first child as possible.
- parenting enhancement services need to be tied to a child's specific developmental level and recognize the unique challenges involved in caring for and disciplining children of various ages.
- regardless of service location, it is important to provide opportunities for parents to model the interactions or discipline methods being promoted through the intervention.
- while child development knowledge can be transferred to parents in a relatively brief period of time (i.e., 6 to 12 weeks), changing attitudes and strengthening parenting and personnel skills often requires a longer time commitment (i.e., over 6 months).
- self-help groups, such as Parents Anonymous, offer a strong complement to other educational and therapeutic efforts.
- an emphasis on social supports and the ability to access needed assistance

from sources is a critical element of programs seeking to insure the safety of children beyond the immediate intervention period.

- a balance of home-based and group-based alternatives for parents are needed in order to address those isolated and uncomfortable in group settings as well as those who appreciate opportunities to share problems with other parents.
- parents need to be provided with multiple opportunities to engage in services through both institutional and community-based agencies.

Collectively, child abuse treatment and prevention efforts have met with mixed results. Not all families have equal access to or benefit from the current pool of child abuse interventions. Families in need of these services can be thought of as falling into one of three distinct groups: consumer families, dependent families, and broken families. The following sections highlight the relative success of treatment and prevention efforts in altering abusive and neglectful behaviors with respect to these three populations and the program and research challenges each present.

Consumer Families

Consumer Families are those parents who recognize their limitations with respect to child development knowledge, parenting skills, and the use of formal and informal supports. While they may not be able to articulate their specific shortcomings or needs, they are aware that they need to secure additional help from some source to met their parenting responsibilities. These individuals will sign up for parenting education classes at the local community center or hospital will join parent-support groups and will seek out various written material. When under stress or when having lashed out at their child, they may call hot lines or ask a friend for assistance. On balance, it appears the current child abuse intervention system is very responsive to this segment of the population.

A tremendous growth has occurred over the past few years in the number of voluntary parent assistance programs, particularly within hospitals and local school districts. Since 1985, the National Committee for Prevention of Child Abuse (NCPCA) has monitored the availability of key child abuse prevention services in 29 randomly selected counties across the United States, utilizing the sample drawn for the most recent federally funded National Study on the Incidence of Child Abuse and Neglect (Westat Associates, 1988). Comparisons of the services available in the hospitals, schools and community-based agencies located within these counties between 1985 and 1988 indicate a sharp increase in certain areas. As of 1988, over 90% of hospitals with maternity wards provided parenting education to those who delivered at their facilities. Fourteen percent more hospitals provided parenting classes prior to birth, and 10% more provided postbirth parenting classes, in 1988 than in 1986. In terms of social services, almost one third of the hospitals, 10% more than in 1986, offered parent support groups. Further, parenting education and life skills training is close to a universal requirement in the nation's high schools, with over 97% of the districts indicating that these services are not only available but mandatory for graduation. Finally, virtually all of the community-based agencies in the sample counties providing services to families and children consider parent enhancement a major function. The most common services sponsored by these agencies include parent self-help groups (40%), in-home parent aid services (33%), parenting education classes (65%), and crisis intervention services (67%) (Daro et al., 1990).

These data suggest that the present child abuse intervention system is well suited to creating an environment in which parents are encouraged to seek assistance with their childrearing questions. The program challenge this population presents to the field is providing these services in accessible locations and with sufficient frequency to effectively meet the growing demand for information and support. Continued involvement of primary service institutions such as hospitals and schools are key to sustaining current momentum.

While theoretically appealing, the empirical evidence regarding the efficacy of voluntary parenting services remains incomplete. Improving the quality of these services requires additional research efforts. Specifically, enhancing services to those parents able and willing to access them will require better and more consistent data on the quality and content of the programs being developed across different institutional settings, comparable and reliable data on the number and characteristics of the families being served through these efforts, and evaluative data both on the impacts these efforts are having on parent–child interactions and on how these impacts differ across various client targeting strategies, service locations, staffing patterns, and service duration.

Dependent Families

The second group of interest, *dependent families*, pose a more complex task for program planners. These individuals may not know they need assistance or if they do know they need assistance they may not know how to access it (Norton, 1990). The problem here is developing universal services in which a more careful determination of need can be made. Also, services need to be integrated, to allow parents to move from one service to the next as their child develops. Families in this subpopulation, particularly those involved in child neglect, generally are not good at applying a theoretical concept to their own child's behavior or adjusting a technique to suit their child's development (Daro, 1988).

On balance, treatment and prevention services have failed to keep pace with the number and types of families needing more extensive assistance in meeting their parenting responsibilities. Many existing services are group-based, educational services best suited for those parents willing and able to access these options. Far fewer services exist for the more isolated, less educated or more poorly functioning parent. For example, only one quarter of the hospitals with maternity wards provide any type of home visitor services following the birth of a child and only 3% of the hospitals provide any type of crisis hot line or drop in services. Further, only 9% of the nation's high schools provide on-site day care for parenting teens. And, since 1986, there are fewer community-based resources in several critical areas—crisis intervention services and therapeutic services for abused children, particularly young children (Daro et al., 1990).

While, as discussed above, some notable gains have been made with this population, continued success with these families require greater expansion of the more intensive efforts. For example, new parents within this population will require more than merely access to written material or parenting education classes. Follow-up, home-based services will be needed to allow for a more careful assessment of the family's needs and environment and greater opportunities to observe parent–child interactions. The program challenge this population presents to the field is making prevention services attractive and nonstigmatizing. Parent education and support services need to be packaged not as child abuse prevention but as more general efforts to assist parents in meeting their childrearing responsibilities. Greater sensitivity is needed to different cultural interpretations of family responsibility, parenting practices and attitudes toward formal support systems. To the extent that service provision can be expanded within particular high-risk communities and provided through existing community-based organizations or voluntary agencies, much of the stigma associated with present child welfare intervention might be minimized.

Beyond expanding the number of services, further research is needed to identify those service components best suited to engaging and retaining dependent families. Once identified, different methods on child targeting, outreach, service location, and staff configuration need to be systematically compared in terms of their ability to have measurable impacts of parenting behaviors and the use of social supports. Equally important is obtaining a greater understanding of how cultural values influence parent–child interactions, methods of coping with personal as well as family difficulties, and interactions with formal service systems. Once identified and validated across different populations, these issues can then be integrated into expanded professional and volunteer training programs. Finally, assessments of programs targeting at-risk communities versus at-risk families are needed to determine if aggregate changes in a community's service delivery system or parenting norms results in a measurable reduction in maltreatment rates.

Broken Families

The final group, the *broken families*, are those families whose members have failed to integrate the social, emotional, and cognitive competencies needed for healthy development. Often, the parents in these families exhibit serious functional problems such as extreme disorganization, substance abuse and violent behavior. To date, these individuals have been very poor candidates for prevention and have not responded well to treatment services (Cohn & Daro, 1988).

Historically, experts have suggested that a relatively small percentage of families fall into this category. For example, the Kempes reported that roughly 10% of the physically abusive parents with whom they worked failed to respond to treatment. The characteristics common in these families included sadistic parents; some mentally handicapped parents, psychotic and borderline parents, and alcohol and substance abusers; violent and aggressive psychopaths; and those families where there had been prior violent deaths due to child abuse (Kempe & Kempe, 1978). In recent years, however, concern has been raised that the number of parents falling into these categories is increasing, as evidenced by the high number of child abuse fatalities and drug-related abuse cases. Since 1986, over three children a day have been reported as fatal victims of maltreatment, with an estimated 6,900 of these cases identified between 1985 and 1990 (Daro & McCurdy, 1990). While, historically, approximately 30%–40% of child abuse reports have involved substance abuse, current estimates place this range at 40%–90%. A DSS study of child abuse and neglect investigations in Boston reported by Kowal (1990) found that nearly two-thirds of supported reports of child abuse over a two week period in December involved "illicit drug or excessive alcohol use." And even more alarming, for children under 1 year of age, nearly all (89%) of the supported reports involved families with substance abuse problems. According to one study, as many as 1 in 10 babies born in the United States, or 375,000 infants annually, are exposed to illegal drugs in the womb (Chasnoff, 1989).

On balance, public service systems have not met the needs of this population. For example, the capacity of child protective services to meet the therapeutic needs of abused and neglected children and their parents has been severely compromised. Between 1976 and 1988, Federal support for child abuse and neglect declined 35% while the number of reports rose 229%. A recent assessment of the child welfare system conducted by Kamerman and Kahn found "no state providing enough family services to meet generally accepted standards of community responsibility. Most agencies focus almost exclusively on child and family crises" (Kamerman & Kahn, 1990). Finally, the American Association for Protecting Children estimate that states are spending only one-fourth of what is actually needed to properly provide protective services.

There are at least two reasons for the continued high levels of serious child abuse. On the one hand, services, while increasingly widespread, may not be accessible to those families most in need of assistance. Home visitor programs, early parenting education and child development instruction and ongoing support services may not be sufficiently available or effectively disseminated. As a result, large numbers of families are not receiving the services they need to avoid various forms of maltreatment. If this explanation is correct, then achieving a reduction in the most severe levels of violence against children will hinge on the expansion and better targeting of key services.

However, it is possible that the problem is not merely one of inadequate supply or poor dissemination. Families involved in the most violent and serious forms of maltreatment may not be responsive to the current arsenal of services. If this explanation is correct, a simple expansion of existing treatment and prevention service models may not realize significant reduction in the most violent cases of maltreatment. Working with this segment of the at-risk population may require new ways of delivering treatment and prevention services.

Identifying these more effective service delivery systems will require an "open door" policy between researchers and practitioners. New research will be needed to better articulate the barriers these parents face in making positive life choices for themselves as well as their children. Research efforts such as the Infant Development Project in Chicago, which is endeavoring to understand what observed patterns of interaction mean to high-risk families and how these patterns relate to the developmental outcomes for children (Norton, 1990), need to be encouraged and expanded. Limited resources and increasing demands suggest the need for a more efficient allocation of resources. To this end, a greater understanding is needed regarding how high-risk individuals and families view formal support systems and how elements of these systems can best work together to provide a consistent and comprehensive network of services. Finally, expanded research is needed on those high-risk individuals and families who successfully engage in services. More descriptive information is needed to determine the staff characteristics, outreach efforts and service delivery methods most successful in reaching families at high risk for maltreatment. Once these factors are identified, their impacts on client retention and client outcomes need to be formally tested through well designed program evaluations.

CONCLUSIONS

Selecting a prevention program for replication is more than simply identifying the program with the most promising outcomes. Program structure, staffing, and content must always be arrayed against the characteristics of the client population being assisted and the community in which the services are delivered. In reviewing model programs for possible replication, the following questions should be addressed:

- does the program address the risk factors you want to address (i.e., parenting knowledge, parenting skills, education for children, etc.)?
- can the intensity and duration of the intervention be sustained with the resources you have available?
- does your staff need additional training or skill building in order to adequately provide the service?

- has the program been successful with the types of families or individuals you anticipate serving with your intervention (i.e., share the same race, culture, or family structure)?
- is the program's success dependent upon the availability of other services in the community?

Successful interventions require careful planning both prior to and after their implementation. While program evaluation findings can provide a useful framework for structuring this planning activity, they cannot replace it. Preventing child abuse remains largely a community-specific activity that requires continuous attention to shifting population, agency, and community service characteristics.

REFERENCES

American Association for Protecting Children (AAPC). (1988). *Highlights of official child neglect and abuse reporting, 1986*. Denver: American Human Association.

Ammerman, R., & Hersen, M. (1990). *Treatment of family violence*. New York: Wiley.

Anderson, L., & Shafter, G. (1979). The character-disordered family: a community treament model for family. *American Journal of Orthopsychiatry, 49*, 436–445.

Anderson, P., & Fenichel, E. (1989). *Serving culturally diverse families of infants and toddlers with disabilities*. Washington DC: National Center for Clinical Infant Programs.

Austin, M. J. (1978). *Professionals and paraprofessionals*. New York: Human Science Press.

Azar, S. (1988). Methodological considerations in treatment outcome research in child maltreatment. In G. Hotaling, D. Finkelhor, J. Kirkpatrick, & M. Straus (Eds.), *Coping with family violence: Research and policy perspectives (pp. 288–289)*. Beverly Hills, CA: Sage.

Bander, K., Fein, E., & Bishop, G. (1982). Evaluation of child sexual abuse programs. In S. Sgroi (Ed.), *Handbook of clinical interventions in child sexual abuse*. Lexington, MA: Lexington Books.

Bavolek, S., & Dellinger-Bavolek, J. (1985). *Nurturing program for parents and children birth to five years*. Eau Claire, WI: Family Development Resources.

Bavolek, S., & Dellinger-Bavolek, J. (1988). *Nurturing program for teenage parents and their families*. Eau Claire, WI: Family Development Resources.

Belsky, J. (1980). Child maltreatment: An ecological integration. *American Psychologist, 35*, 320–335.

Belsky, J., & Vondra, J. (1990). Lessons for child abuse: The determinants of parenting. In D. Cicchetti & V. Carlson (Eds.), *Child maltreatment: Theory and research on the causes and consequences of child abuse and neglect (pp. 153–202)*. Cambridge, UK: Cambridge University Press.

Blizinsky, M. (1982). Parents Anonymous and the private agency: Administrative cooperation. *Child Welfare, 61*(5), 305–311.

Bolton, F., & Bolton, S. (1987). *Working with violent families*. Beverly Hills, CA: Sage.

Borman, L., & Lieber, L. (1984). *Self-help and the treatment of child abuse*. Chicago: National Committee for Prevention of Child Abuse.

Bourne, R. (1979). Child abuse and neglect: An overview. In Bourne, R. & Newberger, E. (Eds.), *Critical perspectives on child abuse (pp. 1–14)*. Lexington, MA: Lexington Books.

Briere, J. (1989). *Therapy for adults molested as children: Beyond survival*. New York: Springer.

Brofenbrenner, U. (1979). *The ecology of human development*. Cambridge, MA: Harvard University Press.

Brunk, M., Henggeler, S., & Whelan, J. (1987). Comparison of multisystemic therapy and parent training in the brief treatment of child abuse and neglect. *Journal of Consulting and Clinical Psychology, 55*(2), 171–178.

Carkhuff, R. (1968). Differential functioning of lay and professional helpers. *Journal of Counseling Psychology, 15*(2), 117–126.

Center on Child Abuse Prevention Research. (1990). *Adolescent parent services evaluation: Final report* (Prepared for the William T. Grant Foundation under grant no. 725.1162). Chicago: National Committee for Prevention of Child Abuse.

Chasnoff, I. (1989). Drug use and women: establishing a standard of care. *Annals of the New York Academy of Sciences, 562*, 208–210.

Cherry B., & Kirby, A. (1971). Obstacles to the delivery of medical care to children of neglecting parents. *American Journal of Public Health, 61*, 568–573.

Cicchetti, D., & Rizley, R. (1981). Developmental perspectives on the etiology, intergenerational transmission, and sequence of child maltreatment. *New Directions for Child Development, 11*, 31–55.

Cohn, A. (1979). Effective treatment of child abuse and neglect. *Social Work, 24*(6), 513–519.

Cohn, A. (1983). *An approach to preventing child abuse.* Chicago: National Committee for Prevention of Child Abuse.

Cohn, A., & Daro, D. (1988). Is treatment too late: What ten years of evaluative research tell us. *Child Abuse and Neglect. 11*(3), 433–442.

Crittenden, P. (1990). Strategies for changing parental behavior. *The Advisor, 4*(2), 9.

Cross, T., Bazron, B., Dennis, K., & Isaacs, M. (1989). *Toward a culturally competent system of care.* Washington, DC: Child and Adolescent Service System Program Technical Assistance Center, Georgetown University Child Development Center.

Daro, D. (1988). *Confronting child abuse.* New York: Free Press.

Daro, D., Casey, K., & Abrahams, N. (1990). *Reducing child abuse 20% by 1990: Preliminary assessment.* Chicago: National Committee for Prevention of Child Abuse.

Daro, D., & McCurdy, K. (1991). *Current trends in child abuse reporting and fatalities: The results of the 1990 Annual 50-State Survey.* Chicago: National Committee for Prevention of Child Abuse.

Derezotes, D., & Snowden, L. (1990). Cultural factors in the intervention of child maltreatment. *Child and Adolescent Social Work Journal, 7*(2), 161–175.

Dumas, J. (1984). Child, adult interactional and socioeconomic setting events as predictors of parent training outcome. *Education and Treatment of Children, 7*, 351–364.

Egeland, B. (1988). Breaking the cycle of abuse: Implications for prediction and intervention. In K. Browne, C. Davies, & P. Stratton (Eds.), *Early prediction and prevention of child abuse.* New York: Wiley.

Egeland, B. & Erickson, M. (1990). Rising above the past: Strategies for helping new mothers break the cycle of abuse and neglect. *Zero to Three, 11*(2), 20–25.

Egeland, B., Jacobvitz, D., & Sroufe, L. (1988). Breaking the cycle of abuse. *Child Development, 59*(4), 1080–1088.

Egeland, B., Sroufe, A., & Erickson, M. (1983). The developmental consequences of different patterns of maltreatment. *Child Abuse and Neglect, 7*(4), 459–469.

Ellwood, A. (1988). Prove to me that MELD makes a difference. In H. Weiss & F. Jacobs (Eds.), *Evaluating family programs (pp. 303–314).* New York: Aldine.

Feshback, S. (1980). Child abuse and the dynamics of human aggression and violence. In G. Gerber, C. Ross, & E. Zigler (Eds.), *Child abuse: An agenda for action.* New York: Oxford University Press.

Frankel, H. (1988). Family-centered home-based services in children's protection: A review of the services. *Social Service Review, 62*, 137–157.

Fritz, M. (1986). Parents Anonymous: Helping clients to accept professional services, a personal opinion. *Child Abuse and Neglect, 10*, 121–123.

Fryer, G., Kraizer, S., & Miyoski, T. (1987). Measuring actual reduction of risk to child abuse: A new approach. *Child Abuse and Neglect, 11*, 173–179.

Gambrill, E. (1983). Behavioral interventions with child abuse and neglect. *Progress in Behavior Modification, 15*, 1–56.

Garbarino, J. (1977). The human ecology of child maltreatment: A conceptual model for research. *Journal of Marriage and the Family, 39*, 721–735.

Garbarino, J. (1988). *The future as if it really mattered.* Longmount, CO: Bookmakers Guild.

Garbarino, J., Cohn, A., & Ebota, A. (1982). *The significance of cultural and ethnic factors in preventing child abuse: An exploration of research findings.* Chicago: National Committee for Prevention of Child Abuse.

Gelles, R., & Straus, M. (1988). *Intimate violence: The causes and consequences of abuse in the American family.* New York: Simon and Schuster.

Giarretto, H. (1976). The treatment of father–daughter incest: a psychological approach. *Children Today, 5*, 2–5, 34–35.

Gil, D. (1981). The United States versus child abuse. In L. Pelton (Ed.), *Social context of child abuse and neglect.* New York: Human Service Press.

Giovannoni, J. M. & Becerra, R. (1979). *Defining child abuse.* New York: Free Press.

Goldstein, A. (1973). *Structured learning therapy: Toward a psychotherapy for the poor.* New York: Academic Press.

Goldstein, A., Keller, H., & Erne, D. (1985). *Changing the abusive parent.* Campaign, IL: Research.

Gray, E., & Halpren, R. (1989). *Early parenting intervention to prevent child abuse: A meta-analysis* (Final report to the National Center on Child Abuse and Neglect, U.S. Department of Health and Human Services. Grant No. 90-CA-1333).

Gray, J., Cutler, C. A., Dean, J. G., & Kempe, C. H. (1979). Prediction and prevention of child abuse and neglect. *Journal of Social Issues, 35*(2), 127–139.

Green, A. (1976). A psychodynamic approach to the study and treatment of child abusing parents. *Journal of the American Academy of Child Psychology, 15*, 414–442.

Green, A., Power, E., Steinbrook, B., & Gaines, R. W. (1981). Factors associated with successful and unsuccessful intervention with child abusing families. *Child Abuse and Neglect, 5*, 45–52.

Halpern, R., & Larner, M. (1987). Lay family support during pregnancy and infancy: The Child Survival/Fair Start Initiative. *Infant Mental Health Journal, 8*(2), 130–143.

Harvey, P., Forehand, R., Brown, C., & Holmes, T. (1988). The prevention of sexual abuse: Examination of the effectiveness of a program with kindergarten-age children. *Behavior Therapy. 19*, 429–435.

Hauser-Cram, P. (1988). The possibilities and limitations of meta-analysis in understanding family program impact. In H. Weiss & F. Jacobs (Eds.), *Evaluating family programs* (pp. 445–460). New York: Aldine.

Hazzard, A. (1990). Prevention of child sexual abuse. In R. Ammerman & M. Hersen (Eds.), *Treatment of family violence (pp. 354–384).* New York: Wiley.

Heinicke, C., Beckwith, L., & Thompson, A. (1988). Early intervention in the family system: A framework and review. *Infant Mental Health Journal, 9*, 111–141.

Helfer, R. (1975). *The diagnostic process and treatment programs.* Washington, DC: U.S. Department of Health, Education and Welfare.

Helfer, R. (1982). A review of the literature on the prevention of child abuse and neglect. *Child Abuse and Neglect, 6*, 251–261.

Herrenkohl, R., & Herrenkohl, E. (1978). *An investigation of the effects of a multi-dimensional service program on recidivism/discontinuation of child abuse and neglect.* Washington, DC: U.S. Department of Health, Education and Welfare. (Grant #90-C-428.)

Herrenkohl, R., Herrenkohl, E., & Egolf, B. (1983). Circumstances surrounding the occurrence of child maltreatment. *Journal of Consulting and Clinical Psychology, 51*, 424–431.

Holmes, M. (1978). *Child abuse and neglect programs: Practice and theory*. Washington, DC: National Institute of Mental Health.

Howing, P., Wodarski, J., Gaudin, J., & Kurtz, P. (1989). Effective interventions to ameliorate the incidence of child maltreatment: Empirical base. *Social Work, 34*(4), 330–338.

Howing, P., Wodarski, J., Kurtz, P., & Gaudin, J. (1989). Methodological issues in child maltreatment research. *Social Work Research and Abstracts, 25*, (3), 3–7.

Johnson, D., & Breckenridge, J. (1982). The Houston Parent-Child Development Center and the primary prevention of behavior problems in young children. *American Journal of Community Psychology, 10*, 305–316.

Johnson, W., & L'Esperance, J. (1984). Predicting the recurrence of child abuse. *Social Work Research and Abstracts, 20*(2), 21–26.

Joyce, T. (1990). The dramatic increase in the rate of low birth weight in New York City: An aggregate time-series analysis. *American Journal of Public Health, 80*(6), 682–684.

Junewicz, W. (1983). A protective posture toward emotional neglect and abuse. *Child Welfare, 62*(3), 243–253.

Kagan, S., Powell, D., Weissbourd, B., & Zigler, E. (Eds.). (1987). *America's family support programs*. New Haven, CT: Yale University Press.

Kamerman, S., & Kahn, A. (1990). Social services for children, youth and families in the United States. *Children and Youth Services Review*. Special Issue. 12(1/2).

Kaufman, J., & Zigler, E. (1989). The intergenerational transmission of child abuse. In D. Cicchetti & V. Carlson (Eds.), *Child maltreatment: Theory and research on the causes and consequences of child abuse & neglect (pp. 129–150)*. Cambridge, UK: Cambridge University Press.

Kempe, R. (1987). A developmental approach to the treatment of the abused child. In R. Helfer & R. Kempe (Eds.), *The battered child (4th ed., pp. 360–381)*. Chicago: University of Chicago Press.

Kempe, R., & Kempe, C. H. (1978). *Child abuse*. Cambridge, MA: Harvard University Press.

Kempe, H., & Helfer, R. (1976). *Child abuse and neglect: The family and community*. Cambridge, MA.: Ballinger.

Kempe, C. H., Silverman, F., Steele, B., Droegemueller, W., & Silver, H. (1962). The battered child syndrome. *Journal of the American Medical Association, 181*(17), 17–24.

Kinney, J., Madsen, B., Fleming, T., & Haapala, D. (1977). Homebuilders: Keeping families together. *Journal of Consulting and Clinical Psychology, 45*(4), 667–673.

Kolko, D., Moser, J., & Hughes, J. (1989). Classroom training in sexual victimization awareness and prevention skills: An extension of the Red Flag/Green Flag people program. *Journal of Family Violence, 4*(1), 25–45.

Kowal, L. (1990). Project protect in Massachusetts: Visualizing help for children living with family violence and substance abuse. *Protecting Children, 6*(4), 9–11.

Landsman, M. (1985). *Evaluation of fourteen child placement projects in Wisconsin*. Iowa City, IA: The National Resource Center on Family Based Services, University of Iowa.

Larner, M. (1990). A 'Fair Start' for parents and infants. *High Scope Review, 9*(1), 5–6, 8–10.

Larson, C. (1980). Efficacy of prenatal and postpartum home visits on child health and development. *Pediatrics, 66*, 191–197.

Leeds, S. (1984). *Evaluation of Nebraska's Intensive Services Project*. Iowa City, IA: The National Resource Center on Family Based Services, University of Iowa.

Levine, C. (Ed.). (1988). *Programs to strengthen families*. Chicago: Family Resource Coalition.

Lochman, J., & Brown, M. (1980). Evaluation of dropout clients and of perceived usefulness of a parent education program. *Journal of Community Psychology, 8*, 132–139.

Lorian, R. (1978). Research on psychotherapy and behavior change with the disadvantaged. In S. Garfield & A. Bergin (Eds.), *Handbook of psychotherapy and behavior change: An empirical analysis (pp. 903–938)*. New York: Wiley.

Lutzker, J. & Rice, J. (1984). Project 12-Ways: Measuring outcome of a large in-home service for treatment and prevention of child abuse and neglect. *Child Abuse and Neglect, 8*, 519–524.

Lutzker, J., & Rice, J. (1987). Using recidivism data to evaluate Project 12-Ways: An ecobehavioral approach to the treatment and prevention of child abuse and neglect. *Journal of Family Violence, 2*(4), 283–290.

MacFarlane, K., Waterman, J., Conerly, S., Damon, L., Durfee, M., & Long, S. (1986). *Sexual abuse of young children.* New York: The Guilford Press.

Magura, S. (1981). Are services to prevent foster care effective? *Children and Youth Services Review, 3*, 193–212.

Malone, C. (1979). Child psychiatry and family therapy: an overview. *Journal of the American Academy of Child Psychiatry. 18*, 4–21.

Mann, E., & McDermott, J. (1983). Play therapy for victims of child abuse and neglect. In C. Schaefer & K. O'Connor (Eds.) *Handbook of play therapy.* New York: Wiley, 283–307.

Mann, J. (1990). Drawing on cultural strengths to empower families. *Protecting Children, 7*(3), 3–5.

Miller, J., & Whittaker, J. (1988). Social services and social support: Blended programs for families at risk of child maltreatment. *Child Welfare, 67*(2), 161–174.

Miller, S. (1988). The child welfare league of America's adolescent parents projects. In H. Weiss & F. Jacobs (Eds.), *Evaluating family programs (pp. 371–388).* New York: Aldine.

Milner, J. (1980). *The child abuse potential inventory manual.* Webster, NC: Psytec Corporation.

Milner, J., & Robertson, K. (1990). Comparison of physical child abusers, intrafamilial sexual child abusers, and child neglecters. *Journal of Interpersonal Violence, 5*(1), 37–48.

Moore, J. (1983). The experience of sponsoring a Parents Anonymous group. *Social Casework, 64*, 585–592.

Musick, J., Bernstein, B., Percansky, C., & Scott, F. (1987). A chain of enablement: Using community-based programs to strengthen relationships between teen parents and their infants. *Zero to Three, 8*(2), 1–6.

Nelson, B. (1984). *Making an issue of child abuse.* Chicago: University of Chicago.

Nelson, K., Landsman, M., & Deutelbaum, W. (1990). Three models of family-centered placement prevention services. *Child Welfare, 69*(1), 3–21.

Newberger, C., & Newberger, E. (1982). Prevention of child abuse: theory, myth and practice. *Journal of Prevention Psychiatry, 1*(4), 443–451.

Norton, D. (1990). Understanding the early experience of black children in high risk environments: Culturally and ecologically relevant research as a guide to support for families. *Zero to Three, 10*(4), 1–7.

Olds, D., Chamberlin, R., & Tatlebaum, R. (1986). Preventing child abuse and neglect: A randomized trial of nurse home visitation. *Pediatrics, 78*, 65–78.

Olds, D., & Henderson, C., Jr. (1990). The prevention of maltreatment. In D. Cicchetti & V. Carlson (Eds.), *Child maltreatment (pp. 722–763).* New York: Cambridge University Press.

Paschal, J., & Schwahn, L. (1986). Intensive crisis counseling in Florida. *Children Today, 15*(6), 12–16.

Pelton, L. (1981). *Social context of child abuse and neglect.* New York: Human Service Press.

Powell, T. (1979). Comparison between self-help groups and professional services. *Social Casework, 60*, 561–565.

Rivara, F. (1985). Physical abuse in children under two: A study of therapeutic outcomes. *Child Abuse and Neglect, 9*(1), 85–88.

Rodriguez, G., & Cortez, C. (1988). The evaluation experience of the Avancé Parent-Child Education Program. In H. Weiss & F. Jacobs (Eds.), *Evaluating family programs (pp. 287–302).* New York: Aldine.

Sameroff, A., & Chandler, M. (1975). Reproductive risk and the continuum of caretaking casualty. In F. Horowitz (Ed.), *Review of child development research: Vol. 4.* Chicago: University of Chicago Press.

Sandler, J. (1979). *Effects of adolescent pregnancy on mother–infant relations. A transactional model of reports to the Center for Population Research.* Bethesda, MD: National Institutes of Health.

Seitz, V., Rosenbaum, L., & Apfel, N. (1985). Effects of family support intervention: A ten-year follow-up. *Child Development, 56*, 376–391.

Sgroi, S. (1982). *Handbook of clinical interventions in child sexual abuse.* Lexington, MA: Lexington Books.

Silver, L., Dublin, C., & Lourie, R. (1971). Does violence breed violence? Contributions from a study of the child-abuse syndrome. *American Journal of Psychiatry, 126*, 404–407.

Slaughter, D. (1988). Programs for racially and ethnically diverse American families: Some critical issues. In H. Weiss & F. Jacobs (Eds.), *Evaluating family programs (pp. 461–476).* New York: Aldine.

Steele, B. (1987a). Psychodynamic factors in child abuse. In R. Helfer & Kempe, R. (Eds.), *The battered child (4th ed., pp. 81–114).* Chicago: University of Chicago Press.

Steele, B. (1987b). Reflections on the therapy of those who maltreat children. In R. Helfer & R. Kempe (Eds.), *The battered child (4th ed., pp. 382–391).* Chicago: University of Chicago Press.

Steele, B., & Pollack, C. (1971). The battered child's parents. In A. Skolnick & J. Skolnick (Eds.), *Family in transition.* Boston: Little, Brown.

Taylor, D., & Beauchamp, C. (1988). Hospital-based primary prevention strategy in child abuse: A multi-level needs assessment. *Child Abuse and Neglect, 12* (3), 343–354.

Vaughan, M., & Loadman, W. (1988, September). *Evaluating the effectiveness of a crisis nursery: turning point's experiences to date.* Paper presented at the VII International Congress on Child Abuse and Neglect, Rio de Janeiro, Brazil.

Wahler, R. (1980). The insular mother: Her problems in parent-child treatment. *Journal of Applied Behavior Analysis, 13*, 207–219.

Weiss, H., & Jacobs, F. (Eds.). (1988). *Evaluating family programs.* New York: Aldine.

Wells, S. (1981). A model of therapy with abusive and neglectful families. *Social Work, 26*(2), 113–116.

Westat Associates. (1988). *Study findings: Study of national incidence and prevalence of child abuse and neglect.* Washington, DC: U.S. Department of Health and Human Services, National Center on Child Abuse and Neglect.

Wieder, S., Poisson, S., Lourie, R., & Greenspan, S. (1988). Enduring gains: A five-year follow-up report on the Clinical Infant Development Program. *Zero to Three, 8*(4), 6–11.

Wolfe, D., Edwards, B., Manion, I., & Koverola, C. (1988). Early intervention for parents at risk of child abuse and neglect: A preliminary investigation. *Journal of Consulting and Clinical Psychology, 56*(1), 40–47.

Wolfe, D., Sandler, J., & Kaufman, K. (1981). A competency-based parent training program for child abusers. *Journal of Consulting and Clinical Psychology, 49*, 633–640.

Wolock, I., & Horowitz, B. (1979). Child maltreatment and material deprivation among AFDC-recipient families. *Social Service Review, 53*, 175–194.

Wurtele, S., Saslawsky, D., Miller, C., Marrs, S., & Britcher, J. (1986). Teaching personal safety skills for potential prevention of sexual abuse: A comparison of treatments. *Journal of Consulting and Clinical Psychology, 54*, 688–692.

12

Child Abuse Intervention Research: Implications for Policy*

David A. Wolfe

Attempts to prevent the abuse of children began soon after attention was drawn to this problem in the early 1960s, and researchers and practitioners have been trying ever since to determine what methods are most effective in this regard. The "treatment" of child abuse is understandably plagued by poor definitions of what (or who) exactly is being treated, what constitutes "success," and how services can be delivered in such a way as to minimize the harm to the child (and his or her family constellation). The complexity of what we have come to consider physical abuse of children poses terrific challenges to our understanding of this phenomenon and our choices to intervene and/or prevent its occurrence. It stands to reason, therefore, that little consensus exists as to the formation of policy directions for this problem (e.g., Gerbner, Ross, & Zigler, 1980).

From a naive viewpoint (the only one that existed for several years), the treatment of physical abuse has been synonymous with the cessation of physical injuries to the child. It has long been reasoned that physical abuse is harmful because the child is at-risk of serious physical injuries. Throughout the first decade of child abuse research the effects of abuse on the child were described in terms of physical injuries and little more. Because the problem landed in the laps of primary medical care facilities, the focus was directed to the physical injuries of the children as well as the presumed underlying psychopathology of the parents. This focus gave the problem visibility, and led to a number of positive steps to outline detection and protection services (see Daro, 1990, for discussion).

However, recognition of the more hidden manner in which child abuse affects the development of children has emerged very slowly (Aber & Cicchetti, 1984). Rather than focusing on physical injuries alone, social scientists have been attempting to document the much more subtle and pervasive psychological injuries that may arise from prolonged maltreatment by caregivers (Garbarino, Guttman, & Seeley, 1986; Shirk, 1988). As well, more attention has been drawn to the factors that often accompany child abusive incidents, with the intention of offsetting the probability of abuse through the reduction of stressful circum-

* The preparation of this chapter was supported in part by a grant from the Medical Research Council of Canada.

stances impinging on families (Belsky & Vondra, 1989; Cicchetti & Rizley, 1981).

This chapter will address several of the most significant concerns that have shaped our intervention efforts with physically abusive families to date. Beginning with definitional and theoretical considerations, a number of issues are raised that impact on our rationale and choices of intervention strategies. Current forms of intervention with abusive families are reviewed, beginning with the mandated approach operated by the state. Although such services are pervasive and have been in operation for many years, little evaluation has been conducted as to their short- and long-range impact on the child and his or her family. In contrast, a growing number of psychologically based intervention studies have been reported in the last decade, which offer promise for improving the delivery of services to this divergent population.

Although an improvement over the informal evaluations of mandated interventions, these recent studies still contain methodological inadequacies common to the field of child maltreatment that must be taken into account in interpreting their findings (Mash & Wolfe, 1991). For example, research designs are often inadequate to draw firm conclusions, because most studies are naturalistic correlational field research that does not permit true experimentation. Many studies involve subject samples that in all likelihood contain mixed forms of maltreatment (e.g., physical, sexual, psychological abuse), which confounds the findings that may relate to physical abuse alone. In addition, child abuse researchers face a major challenge in attempting to control for related factors that may have direct or indirect effects on children's adjustment, such as marital discord, socioeconomic disadvantage, poor social supports, etc.

More specifically, intervention studies often pose a number of restrictions that make interpretation difficult. Fink and McCloskey (1990), for example, reviewed 13 major evaluations of child abuse and neglect prevention programs published between 1978 and 1988 (i.e., those types of programs that have the greatest likelihood of influencing policy decisions). They found that only half of these evaluations used control groups, and virtually all of the researchers failed to define *abuse* more specifically, beyond simple report information. This finding is reflected in the wider range of intervention studies as well. In a recent review of child abuse prevention programs, Wekerle and Wolfe (in press) found that interpretation of findings is commonly hampered by lack of adequate sample size, limited follow-up evaluation, insufficient measurement of behavior change, lack of random assignment, and failure to involve a no-treatment control group. These limitations clearly pose major obstacles to formulating unambiguous social policy recommendations.

Despite the limitations inherent in evaluating prevention and treatment programs for abusive families, a number of interesting suggestions emerge from these developments that can have a profound effect on social policy in the years to come. These suggestions are used to formulate prevention-oriented social policy recommendations in the concluding section of the chapter.

As an overview and introduction to this topic, it should be noted that intervention with physically abusive families differs on a number of levels from more traditional intervention practices. First, a higher proportion of these clients are intellectually low functioning (Schilling & Schinke, 1984), which limits the utility of insight-oriented treatment approaches. In addition to such cognitive limitations, abusive parents often have quite different expectations of what takes place in therapy, which are important for involvement in the therapeutic process. They often approach psychological treatment in much the same way as medical treatment, expecting the treatment to eliminate the "pain" they are reporting (Azar & Wolfe, 1989). Finally, we can contrast traditional problems faced in psychotherapy with those of abusive parents by noting the fact that many of the latter are not voluntarily seeking assistance. Thus, from the outset abusive parents may be resistant to the goals of therapy, unfamiliar with the course and nature of psychological treatments, and confused by the explanations and information being provided on their behalf. The result can often lead to less than a desirable outcome on the part of both the client and the therapist. Consequently, our approach to providing useful services to such families may require a different angle—one in which the special needs of this population receive principle consideration.

Definitional Considerations

To sort out directions for policy in this area, it is necessary to establish a consensus as to the definition of *child abuse*. Practically speaking, such a definition implies the establishment of parameters that define the minimum and maximum interpretations of this phenomenon, rather than a set of precise criteria. Although straightforward in its purpose, this task is still far from producing an adequate and consistent definition (Giovannoni, 1989). If the priorities of policy makers and practitioners are to identify causes, to predict the occurrence, to find methods of prevention, and to develop effective interventions for this problem, then greater agreement must be reached as to the criteria for determining what is child abuse (Mash & Wolfe, 1991).

For almost three decades, the most common definition of *physical abuse* has taken the form of a discrete category that divides those who are abusive from those who are not. Thus, early definitions of *abuse* focused on intentional acts of omission or commission that placed the child in jeopardy of physical harm (Kempe & Helfer, 1972), which followed from a medical/psychiatric explanation. This working definition persists, despite tremendous criticism of its shortcomings (e.g., Giovannoni, 1989; Parke, 1977). In a recent criticism of this lack of consensus and its impact on child abuse research, Mash and Wolfe (1991) note that *abuse* subsumes many different actions and is clearly not a uniform, homogeneous phenomenon. Any particular action could be labeled as *abusive* on the basis of considerable discretion. Such decisions may take into account the age of the child, severity, chronicity, circumstances of the acts, cultural norms, intentions and characteristics of the abuser, and many other factors before considering to label the act as abusive. Unfortunately, most definitions rely heavily on the presence of physical harm (i.e., the "consequences" of the act) rather than on the overt behaviors of the parent or their psychological impact (McGee & Wolfe, 1991).

This definitional conundrum has been bypassed in many different ways by the various theoretical proponents, yet it remains a considerable roadblock to much of our treatment and prevention efforts. It can be argued that no single correct definition of *abuse* will meet all of the diverse functions that are required of definitions in this area (Zuravin, 1991). For this reason, we must accept that *child abuse* will differ according to the goals associated with a legal, case management, treatment, or research context (Aber & Zigler, 1981; Mash & Wolfe, 1991).

In the present context of intervention research and policy formation, it is perhaps wisest to formulate our definition in conjunction with the goals of childrearing, rather than strictly legal, cultural, or medical criteria. For purposes of intervention, therefore, *child abuse* can be defined in terms of the degree to which a parent uses aversive or inappropriate control strategies with his or her child and/or fails to provide minimal standards of caregiving and nurturance (Wolfe, 1987, 1991). This viewpoint intends to draw attention to those aspects of abuse that resemble "typical" childrearing methods except in terms of their severity. As well, such a definition highlights, not only the physically harmful methods a parent may use, but those methods as well that may be inadequate to meet the child's psychological development. It is clearly recognized that such a definition rests more heavily on the psychological literature that seeks to define appropriate parenting style and child developmental outcomes, rather than on the determination of wrongdoing or the violation of some arbitrary standard. Yet such styles can be observed and measured more readily than can acts of physical abuse (e.g., Crittenden, 1988; Egeland, 1991; Oldershaw, Walters, & Hall, 1989), and, most importantly, they lead more directly to intervention or prevention objectives that fit with parental needs and expectations (Azar & Wolfe, 1989).

Conceptual Theories of Etiology and Intervention

The manner in which *child abuse* is conceptualized sets the parameters for its definition and subsequent intervention goals. In this regard, the field has been a fertile ground for producing theories and definitions that approach this complex problem from quite diverse perspectives. These are reviewed briefly herein to establish the background for critiquing the major forms of intervention with abusive families that follows. Readers who would like more detail and history of these developments are referred to synopses by Daro (1990), Kelly (1983), Parke and Collmer (1975), and Wolfe (1987).

Broadly speaking, psychological intervention with reported child abusers has developed gradually from an individually based pathology model to an all-encompassing ecological model, with an evolving emphasis on the importance of the parent–child relationship and its context. Simultaneously, the orientation toward the treatment issue, that is, how the abusive act is viewed, has shifted gradually away from a parent-focused, deviance viewpoint and more toward one that accounts for the vast number of stress factors that impinge on the developing parent–child relationship (see also Daro, this volume). As we shall see, this shift has resulted in encouraging gains in treatment outcomes, yet the field remains split between the promising research findings, on the one hand, and the realities of child protection and welfare on the other hand. Unfortunately, the dominant theme in most services to abusive families remains that of protection, not treatment (Azar & Wolfe, 1989). To assess any gains made over the past two decades in treatment outcome, it is necessary to separate what is truly "treatment" from what is actually delivered to identified families in practice (Wolfe, 1984).

Intervention with child abusive parents began in the mid-1960s following early descriptions of this problem and its severity (e.g., Kempe, Silverman, Steele, Droegemueller, & Silver, 1962). Based largely on the view that the abusive parent was psychiatrically disturbed, treatment modalities were established that were aimed at the personality characteristics that underlie such deviant behavior. This framework was built on the assumption that parents would be less abusive if they understood themselves better and their role as parents, and it required individually based psychotherapy (see Steele & Pollock, 1968). Many of the treatment objectives were congruous with those identified with other personality-disordered populations: recognition of the unresolved conflicts from one's past and the associated defense mechanisms, insight into how one deals with family-related problems on the basis of these previously unconscious conflicts, and resolution of the problem through identification of appropriate coping resources.

The influence of social learning theorists at first posed a challenge to this view, arguing instead that parents would be less abusive if they learned more specifically how best to care for their children and to control anger and aggressive behavior (Burgess, 1979; Reid, Taplin, & Lorber, 1981). Insight into the cause of their problems with their child, it was argued, was a circuitous and often unsuccessful approach due to the parent's low intellectual functioning and motivation, the pressures on the parent to learn to manage their behavior with their child quickly, and the important role that the child plays in the development of the caregiver's abusive behavior. Both viewpoints maintained the significance of the individual adult's behavior, but differed in terms of its etiology and, consequently, its treatment. Moreover, the social learning perspective placed greater emphasis on the dynamics of the emerging parent–child relationship, wherein the behavior of both parties (the parent and the child) was the result of the reciprocal influence of one individual on the other.

Treatment directions that emanated from the social learning perspective were more narrow and specific in scope than were those based on parental psychopathology. This fact contributed to the increase in the number of treatment evaluation studies to emerge from the child abuse literature in the 1980s (see Azar & Wolfe, 1989; Daro, this volume; Isaacs, 1982; Smith, 1984), in that the intervention objectives were more readily described, measured, and evaluated relative to a control condition. However, the very same emphasis that improved the evaluative capability of this approach led to criticisms that the focus was too narrow and often overlooked other important aspects of the abusive situation. In particular, few studies directed attention to the behavior of the abused child or to the contextual factors that imposed considerable stress on the family, any of which could infringe on the likelihood of a successful outcome over time (Smith, 1984). Social learning-based interventions, in the main, advanced our knowledge of the reciprocal influence of the parent and child in abusive families and established the important ground work for specific techniques that could be used to modify undesirable interactions. However, these methods require considerable effort and tailoring to the needs and circumstances of each family, especially if such assistance is made available only after abusive patterns have emerged (Wolfe, 1991).

During the 1970s and 1980s sociological research findings began to yield a number of major environmental variables associated with the occurrence of abuse, and encouraged the growth of ecologically based explanations of this phenomenon (for a review of these findings, see Garbarino, 1977; Gil, 1970; Light, 1973). The ecological viewpoint posited that parents would be less abusive if a network of services or supports existed to compensate for the individual, situational, and environmental contributors to abusive parental behavior (Daro, 1990). According to this view, child abuse occurs as a function of the person–environment interaction, and the casualties of this interchange are inevitable in the absence of compensatory supports and services (Cicchetti & Rizley, 1981). The intervention objectives that flowed from this model included competency-enhancing services such as the provision of prenatal and postnatal education and guidance, family planning and management skills, and related family support services, as well as objectives directed at reducing the environmental demands on the family, such as provision of proper daycare, housing, employment skills, and so on. To date these interventions remain promising, especially when considered in conjunction with empirical findings from the previous two approaches noted above, yet their ultimate impact depends to a large extent on *a shift in policy towards maximizing early assistance to families,* rather than detection and services after the fact.

What emerges from the preceding overview of the three main psychosocial treatment approaches to child abuse is the recognition that theoretical formulations have become less contradictory. This may reflect the fact that they share important commonalities and do not necessarily represent radically opposed viewpoints of child abuse. The major distinction that can be inferred from these approaches is the amount of significance each places on the parent as the principle cause of abuse, as contrasted with situational circumstances and the larger sociocultural milieu (Wolfe, 1987). The existing models all represent attempts to understand, and intervene with, individual characteristics of abusive parents in relation to prior experience and current demands.

As summarized by Azar and Wolfe (1989), three tenets can be extracted from these models that form the basis for an intervention strategy for this population. The first of these tenets relates to the importance of recognizing and studying the context of child maltreatment, which is typically one of social and economic family deprivation. Accordingly, abuse is seen not as an isolated social phenomenon or a personality defect of the parent per se; rather, it is viewed as the product of individual parent and child vulnerabilities and the negative cultural, community, and familial influences affecting daily life, such as unemployment, restricted educational and occupational opportunities, poor housing, and so on.

The second tenet drawn from these theories relates to the social-interactional process that occurs on a daily basis between parent and child, as well as other family and community members. The emphasis in this regard is primarily upon the processes (i.e., reciprocation of aversive behavior, reinforcement of inappropriate behavior, conditioned emotional arousal, etc.) that define the relationship between the parent and the child. Thus, the importance of how the parent and child learn to relate to one another within the context of the family and the larger social structure is underscored in these theories, and relates directly to intervention and prevention planning.

Finally, Azar and Wolfe (1989) point out the significance of learning-based explanations for aggressive behavior that cut across these major theories. They point out that the person's level of arousal, and his or her beliefs about the *source* of the arousal, can play a critical role in the development of aggression in the family. Regardless of the original contributing sources to anger and arousal (e.g., daily hassles, stressful interpersonal encounters, etc.), this tenet maintains that the child's availability and lower status position makes him or her a likely target for blame, particularly among adults who are predisposed to poor problem solving and self-control. The resulting anger and arousal interferes with rational problem solving, and the parent may engage in attempts to eliminate the perceived sources of stress (i.e., the child's behavior) through harsh punishment. In such a state, the individual is less aware of his or her actions, and the act of physical punishment itself can become invigorating or cathartic (Zillman, 1979).

CURRENT METHODS OF LEGAL AND PSYCHOSOCIAL INTERVENTION

State Intervention: Its Role and Its Shortcomings

Legal and social precedents for intervention on behalf of maltreated children have slowly become established over the 20th century. The first of these precedents, and the one that remains most prominent today, was established by the passage of the Social Security Act in the U.S. in the 1930s (and subsequently by the Child Abuse and Neglect Act of 1974). This law made child protection a public responsibility, thereby diminishing the need for voluntary agencies. As a result, the most common form of intervention for abused children has been removal from their homes (either into a foster home or a daycare placement) or court-ordered supervision and/or treatment. Before reviewing the research findings on psychosocial intervention with abusive families, therefore, the nature and results of interventions by the State will be discussed.

The "State" in this case refers to the governments of individual states and provinces in North America that set their own statutes for complying with federal child abuse and neglect legislation (in the U.S., this child welfare legislation is the Child Abuse and Neglect Act of 1974; in Canada, punitive sanctions are established by the Criminal Code of Canada, and child welfare legislation is set provincially). These statutes become the vehicles by which policy is made and enforced, and they have established what has become the most widely mandated form of intervention in North America. The social policy upon which state intervention was developed lies at the roots of our current and future efforts to prevent child abuse, yet unfortunately there appears to be little interchange between what the empirical literature has discovered about this and other intervention forms and the pragmatic realities of current practice.

State intervention was predicated on the assumption that alternative care by the state (i.e., removing children from abusive or dangerous family environments) was a benevolent intervention when families had failed or violated standards of care. Alternative care was assumed to remove the child from harm and provide a stable and therapeutic environment, as well as to provide a brief period for family rehabilitation (Azar & Wolfe, 1989). This view has been challenged more recently by the realization that not all interventions are beneficial and, in fact, can do more harm than good in some cases by introducing further victimization and disruption into the child's life (Melton, 1990; Wolfe & Jaffe, 1990). Thus, much confusion presently exists between the needs and rights of children and families.

This awareness of potential harm to the child has led to the development of an increasing focus on children's rights and some fundamental safeguards regarding their entry into the care of the state and ongoing review of the state's intervention. However, this shift in focus has lost its initial attractiveness because of the awareness that procedural complications may create delays or that a sequence of failed "least intrusive" measures may not be in the child's best interests. The policy issues emanating from this realization point to the need to strike a balance between the two related concerns of children's developmental needs and the state's responsibility to provide them with the least intrusive intervention.

The costs of operating the current North American system of mandated State intervention (without any formal treatment services) are the first issue one faces when describing this approach. Unquestionably, child maltreatment costs the public enormously in terms of alternative placements and protective services. Daro (1990) estimates that *serious* abuse cases (which constitute only 3% of all reports!) cost the U.S. annually at least $20 million in hospital costs and $7 million in rehabilitation costs for the victims. Based on 1983 figures, she notes that the total reported cases cost society a minimum of $460 million in administration and foster care placements. Intensive treatment, if available, can run from between $2860 per family per year (for lay therapy and support services) to over $28,000 per family per year for comprehensive services (including child treatment). Daro points out that, if only the severely abused in 1983 received any of these treatment services for 1 year, the costs would have exceeded $662 million. Clearly, many of these dollars are necessary to mount *any* type of widespread attack on abuse and thus costs will always be high. The question that warrants greater consideration, however, is whether these dollars are being spent on the appropriate *type* of service.

Two recent studies of alternatives to foster care and protective services shed some light on this issue of who benefits from state intervention, and what changes can be made to improve these efforts. Wald, Carlsmith, and Leiderman (1988) reported on a comprehensive study that addressed the issue of whether maltreated children benefit more from foster care or from improved home care. By enlisting the cooperation of state and county protective service agencies, these researchers were able to compare children in two jurisdictions who had been placed in either home care of foster care. Children in one jurisdiction who qualified for foster care placement were matched with a comparable group of children at-risk in another jurisdiction who received home care services. The researchers assessed the children's development on a wide variety of measures, including physical development and health status, cognitive development, academic performance, emotional problems, social behavior, parent–child relations, and the child's satisfaction with self, peers, and school.

They found that improved services to families (i.e., counseling, healthcare, parent education and support) can help to keep abused and neglected children in their home residences, but not without significant costs. That is, children in both settings showed signs of emotional stress and adjustment difficulties that related to the dilemmas in their respective environments. At home, they had to deal with ongoing family disorganization and conflict, and in foster care settings children had to confront disruption and adapt to a new family system. Therefore, the impact of either placement must be evaluated not only in terms of the children's personal safety, but also in reference to their social, emotional, and intellectual development. In either home care or foster care these children require a high level of services for many years to cope with the trauma that they have experienced. In their conclusions, Wald et al. (1988) state, "The services cannot be short-term or inexpensive. In many instances, both the children and the family may require several years of assistance. Although we cannot be certain that new services will alleviate their problems, current efforts are not adequate" (p. 200).

Rather than comparing home services to foster care services for children, Jones (1987) conducted an early intervention effort in which 142 families with 243 at-risk children were provided with multiple services, including counseling, financial assistance, medical services, and help with housing problems. The purpose of this study was to determine whether such services, offered in the context of a protective service agency, could have an impact on children's entry into alternative care (and, thereby, reduce costs and potential harm).

Children's entry into care could be significantly predicted among this sample on the basis of seven family background and family problem factors, such as mother or father's functioning, income and housing, and child health. The researcher further discovered that predisposing factors (i.e., those that increase the statistical risk of entering foster care) tend to consist of family background characteristics (e.g., income, housing, etc.), whereas it was the family problem characteristics that precipitated the actual entry into care. The four major areas comprising these predisposing and precipitating factors included: (a) the unavailability of the mother, (b) limited backup resources, (c) problems in the child's functioning, and (d) lateness of intervention. It would appear from these results that each of these factors signifies vulnerability for entry into care, and provides valuable clues to enhancing service effectiveness. Because the mere presence of the parents (particularly the mother), and not the quality of their functioning per se, was the key to children remaining in the home, Jones (1987) argues that just "being on the job," and not necessarily being very good at it, is an important resource for the child. Added to this factor is the importance of backup resources, such as social support, relatives, mother's education, and financial adequacy, that provide indirect assistance to the developing parent/ child relationship.

Although both the Wald et al. (1988) and the Jones (1987) studies can be criticized on methodological grounds (see previous discussion of major issues), they demonstrate that alternatives to foster care and related state interventions are feasible, especially for those children who possess key family resources. Ways of further improving the chances of such alternative measures are suggested by the discussion of prevention and early intervention strategies later on in this chapter.

Critique of the Legal and Social Context of Intervention Services

Mandated social intervention with abused children as discussed above is recognized as the oldest and most universal response to this problem. Consequently, this strategy has amassed the most criticism and derision in the child welfare field, deservedly or not. In discussing some of these criticisms, therefore, it is important to keep in mind that other approaches are relative newcomers and as yet largely untested, as well as the fact that such criticism is valuable given the immense significance such decisions have on the lives of the children.

The following discussion addresses three themes that have been raised by critics: (a) the possibility that the interface between child welfare and legal interventions can be harmful to children in important ways or, at a minimum, are unhelpful to the family; (b) concerns that there are major injustices in the service delivery system; and (c) that the system has been lax in ensuring continuity of care in line with a child's developmental level. Conclusions regarding the policy concerns raised by mandated state intervention in its present form follow from this discussion.

The interface between child welfare and legal interventions may be harmful or unhelpful. One of the major criticisms levied against mandated intervention that involves, in particular, the removal of children from their families is the adversarial, rather than supportive, atmosphere of this approach (Besharov, 1988; Wald et al., 1988; Melton, 1990). Legal statutes, by their very nature and design, "outlaw" certain parental behaviors, an intent that is largely justified and guided by our social values. However, such statutes are not capable of guiding communities in directing appropriate *services* for families, especially services that might prevent or reduce the need for more intrusive forms of intervention. Thus, in the process of providing mandated services for families and children, the most visible violators will receive the brunt of the resources, and little will remain for those who may benefit from psychosocial interventions (e.g., family counseling, job training, etc.).

This argument is bolstered by the apparent paradox of some forms of state intervention. The legal system that developed the means for providing a "safety net" for abused children arose from the belief that it is in children's best interest to protect them from abuse and neglect. Paradoxically, such protection carries with it certain risks to the child's ongoing development and family relationship. Critics argue that these risks have been largely overlooked or underplayed until recently.

Melton (1990), an outspoken critic of the foster care system, refers to it as being "in crisis." He believes this crisis is due to the fact that it is not child-centered and, consequently, provides very minimal services to involved children. He describes the foster care system as having poor integration of services that are rarely individualized for a child, a perception that is shared by some of the professionals working within the system (e.g., The Future of Foster Care, 1988). From a psychological perspective, he notes that what children think of as being stressful (e.g., changing residences or being away from friends and family) often differs from what adults may think is stressful (e.g., living with parents who are sometimes abusive). This viewpoint on children's reality and coping reactions to stressful events is consistent with the findings in reference to children of battered women (Jaffe, Wolfe, & Wilson, 1990) and children undergoing parental divorce and other major life changes (Felner, 1984; Grych & Fincham, 1990), who often report considerable stress in relation to the day-to-day changes that are ongoing even *after* the identified "stressful events" are over.

It is accepted that the foster care system and its overseer, protective services, are operating well beyond their capacity in the U.S. and Canada (Besharov, 1988; The Future of Foster Care, 1988). Unfortunately, as Melton (1990) points out, when the net was widened by legal statutes to catch more abusers, the system became unable to monitor the more serious cases (largely because additional resources or organization were not provided). Melton further argues that the failure of this system has been created in part by conceptual flaws—that is, both the right and the left have attempted to reconceptualize broad social problems in terms of child maltreatment. As a result of its conception and its existence, therefore, children receive very little treatment services. In parallel, services to the parents rarely focus on interactions with their children (which is, of course, primarily the original concern; Mash, 1991).

Injustices in the service delivery system. A second criticism of the current manner of officially responding to child abuse and neglect concerns what factors may (unintentionally) influence the decision-making process of determining who should be placed in care of the state. That is, are children placed in care on the basis of a rational, consistent decision-making process, or on a more arbitrary basis according to circumstances that are unrelated to the level of need of their families?

Gil (1987) has argued that child abuse is a symptom of fundamental inequalities, such as poverty, social disadvantage, and discrimination. Because individuals have no choice in their social conditions, those parents who are most disadvantaged are the most likely to receive more "intrusive" forms of intervention, rather than proper resources and assistance. Thus, according to Gil, abusive parents are, to a certain extent, "scapegoats" for societal ills that exist at much broader levels. Others have used similar reason to argue that the current system nets only the "violators" and does little to assist families *until* they become violators (Besharov, 1988). Although unproven, some investigators contend that more coercive forms of intervention are imposed on more socially disadvantaged clients, whereas greater tolerance and assistance may be afforded to the cultural and economic majority (Gil, 1987; Melton, 1990).

These questions about what social factors may be influencing the child welfare system remain problematic also because case finders and decision makers (including judges) may vary quite significantly from one community to another. Despite the lack of careful record keeping, some general trends relating to who is admitted to care seem consistent from the literature. Based on recent reports of the experiences of children's services in Ontario, which seem somewhat representative of other North American states and provinces, the data suggest that several major injustices do exist in the delivery of services to at-risk families (from Wolfe & Jaffe, 1990):

1. A great deal of variation in admitting to care appears to be related to the discrepancy amongst clinicians and other "gatekeepers" in terms of their perceived needs of children and their individual decision-making tendencies (MCSS, 1988).
2. Alternatives to care are most likely to be considered when the resources are available to make such alternatives a meaningful choice.
3. There are consistent risk factors that, by themselves and in combination with other stressors, seem to predict which children will enter the care of the state. These factors include poverty (i.e., being from a family on welfare), living in public housing, and children of single mothers (MCSS, 1988).

One glaring finding that emerges from these available data is that the choice of who is admitted to the care of the state is significantly driven by the resources possessed by each individual family in comparison to those resources that may be alternatively available in the community. Not surprisingly, children from families who lack the most in fundamental resources are those that are most likely to be seen as in need of placement. Furthermore, children and youth from poor families are twice as likely to return to care after being returned home on a trial basis and, thus, end up spending longer periods of time in care than do children from adequate-income families (Loo, cited in Raychaba, 1988). Yet, we have very little information at present as to whether the *children* in care (as opposed to their families of origin) demonstrate distinct needs and symptoms from the children who remain with their families. Decisions to place children into the care of the state often appear to be based on individual interpretations and predictions of each family's future direction and present resources, rather than on the basis of a more uniform, unbiased policy derived from empirical validation and equal opportunity (Giovannoni, 1988; MCSS, 1988).

Ensuring that continuity of services are provided in line with each child's developmental level. The belief that early life experiences strongly influence subsequent adult functioning and vulnerability to psychopathology has been widely supported by empirical findings confirming the importance of early childhood attachment (for review, see Cicchetti, 1989; Paterson & Moran, 1988). One of the major tenets of attachment theory is that once an attachment is established, the infant uses the parent as a secure base from which to explore and learn from the environment. The attachment system is inactive during low stress periods, but can become reactivated at any time—causing the infant to attempt to reestablish contact with the secure attachment figure. Considerable research has demonstrated the importance of this attachment process in the development of the child's cognitive and social competence. Early attachment is most clearly disrupted when no primary attachment figure is available or when the attachment figure becomes physically or psychologically unavailable.

In light of this important developmental process, our current policy of foster care needs to consider how its operation may be counterproductive in terms of ensuring the continuity of attachment figures for the child. Although children can have more than one attachment figure, they usually cannot thrive in an environment where such figures are inconsistently available or frequently changed. In view of this need, social policy should be more in tune with the developmental needs of children at various ages. Similarly, such policy must acknowledge the long-term impact of placing a child with a foster parent without constant contact with the primary attachment figure (even if that attachment is less than ideal).

Foster care is designed to be a temporary placement, yet researchers note that children too often remain in foster care until the age of majority (Tuma, 1989). This growing tendency for children to remain beyond the intended six month period has been described as "foster care drift," in which temporary placements become permanent, without the benefit of suitable planning. This phenomenon has led to the promotion of permanency planning, which refers to the policy of taking prompt, decisive action that is aimed at either placing the children with a permanent foster family or maintaining him or her in the family with the provision of adequate services. With the growing acceptance of permanency planning, policy planners will need to design suitable evaluation studies to determine the long-range impact of this shift in foster care utilization.

In conclusion, it would be naive to consider interventions by the state simply as beneficial or damaging. State intervention to remove children from their families is generally accepted in North America as an essential last resort for aiding children in families with major difficulties. Major readjustments to the present system are not impossible, yet such changes will most likely need to be preceded by major revisions of the purpose and intent of state intervention. In keeping with some of the emerging findings on what services work best for disadvantaged families (some of which are reviewed in later sections), child protection agencies may have to be prepared to provide opportunities for the type of training or therapy that this population may require. More and more, courts are indicating that parental rights cannot be terminated when it is shown that agencies did not make appropriate efforts to ensure the provision of therapeutic or remedial services. Unfortunately, in many cases the only "intervention" is the passage of time, so the requisite skills and modifications needed to return the child to the family are incomplete. Striking a balance between parental rights and children's rights remains a critical challenge for future research and policy development.

EDUCATIONAL AND THERAPEUTIC INTERVENTIONS

In the past two decades, a number of educational and therapeutic strategies for assisting abusive families have been reported. In the main, these strategies have focused on the remediation of behavioral skills, providing basic knowledge of child development and childrearing, and therapies aimed at anger control and the management of major stressors on the family. Unfortunately, these treatment approaches have usually developed separately from, rather than in association with, the much larger role of the state. In only rare circumstances have mandated services included empirically derived treatment opportunities developed for this population (Daro, 1990, this volume).

Several highlights of the findings from the limited number of studies in this area are presented, followed by a critique and policy implications. Because space does not permit the detailed coverage of this topic, discussion is limited to an overview of studies that have attempted to modify the behavior of physically parents, their children, and/or their family circumstances and stress factors. For more details as to the clinical procedures evaluated in these and related approaches, the reader is referred to Azar and Wolfe (1989), Kelly (1983), and Wolfe (1991).

Treatment of Abusive Parents and Their Children in the Family Context

Experimental treatment methods for abusive parents were first reported in the mid-1970s. These treatments consisted primarily of small-N research designs aimed at modifying identified problematic behaviors of the parent, such as their negative cognitions (Denicola & Sandler, 1980), low rate of reinforcement (Sandler, VanDercar, & Milhoan, 1978), and their use of inappropriate forms of punishment (Wolfe & Sandler, 1981). These early studies followed closely in the footsteps of the highly successful social-learning-based research on the treatment of conduct problem children and their families (e.g., Patterson, Reid, Jones, & Conger, 1975) and the treatment of noncompliance in children (e.g., Forehand &

McMahon, 1981). The primary therapeutic modality was based on social learning theory, that is, structured to allow parents to acquire and rehearse new, more appropriate childrearing techniques or skills to replace their reliance on power-assertive methods.

The strategy used to achieve this aim was relatively straightforward and had been well tested with other (nonabusive) parenting populations. Therapists/researchers addressed the most salient and recognized problems that, in most cases, were identified *by the parents*, in order to interest them in learning new methods of child management (ostensibly to "cure" the child's behavior problems, but more specifically to modify the parents' inappropriate childrearing methods). By focusing on problems that were meaningful to the parent (in contrast to asking the parents to submit to treatment of their "personality"), behavioral strategies were able to demonstrate changes in specific identified parenting problems that were closely related to abusive episodes.

Most of the treatment services that evolved from this behavioral framework involved some form of skills training (Azar & Wolfe, 1989). Such training has been utilized with abusive parents primarily in the three general areas of parent training, anger control, and stress management. Parent training, by far the most widely explored application of skills training, is based on a practical application of learning principles: educating parents about very basic contingency management principles (e.g., reinforcement, punishment, consistency, etc.); modeling for the parents (via films or live demonstrations) new ways of problem solving and increasing child compliance; rehearsing the desired skills in nonthreatening situations, with increasingly more and more realistic applications (i.e., practicing in the home with the therapist); and providing feedback (verbal or, in some instances, videotaped) to the parents regarding their performance of these behaviors.

As the application of these principles grew, additional therapeutic techniques (in particular, cognitive restructuring) were added to deal with some of the residual beliefs or emotional responses underlying to some extent the expression of abusive behavior. Self-control and anger-control techniques, again derived from studies of nonabusive populations, have been used to reduce abusive parents' heightened arousal level and poorer ability to cope with stress (e.g., Azar & Twentyman, 1984; Nomellini & Katz, 1983; Wolfe, Sandler, & Kaufman, 1981). These techniques most commonly involve several components, including the use of early detection of anger-arousal cues (e.g., physiological and/or cognitive cues), replacing anger-producing thoughts with more appropriate ones, and teaching self-control skills that would lessen the likelihood of emotional outbursts and rage. These latter skills are developed through training in stress reduction (often done in conjunction with child management training). Stress reduction generally involves instructing parents in relaxation techniques and cognitive-behavioral methods of reducing stress, followed by rehearsal of new coping strategies during imagined and live interactions with their child (e.g., Egan, 1983; Wolfe et al., 1981).

Due to the intertwined causes of child abuse (i.e., the interaction of individual, family, marital, community, and sociocultural factors; Belsky & Vondra, 1989; Garbarino, 1977), some treatment efforts have also been directed at levels other than (or in addition to) the parent's immediate behavior. Outcome studies in this regard have tailored their methods to the specific needs of the families they are serving, such as marital, financial, personal, or even employment-related problems. For example, clinical studies have reported some success with abusive and/or neglectful parents by focusing on symptoms of depression (Conger, Lahey, & Smith, 1981), migraine headaches (Campbell, O'Brien, Bickett, & Lutzker, 1983), home safety skills (Lutzker, 1984), and recognition of health-related symptoms in their children (Delgado & Lutzker, 1985). By and large these studies, while reporting positive findings, can be considered only preliminary due to the challenge of overcoming methodological limitations with this population (e.g., no control group, small-N designs that limit external validity; weak measures; see Mash & Wolfe, 1991).

Critique of Educational and Therapeutic Interventions

The above-mentioned literature on treatment of physically abusive parents stands out as the only empirically supported intervention for this population. Despite important gains in this respect, considerable confusion still exists over the effectiveness of *any* form of intervention with parents once they have been identified as physically abusive (Wolfe & Wekerle, in press). Following a discussion of a recent metaanalysis of physical abuse intervention studies, some recent trends towards early intervention and prevention are examined in an attempt to highlight some promising developments in this area.

Videka-Sherman (1989) recently conducted a metaanalysis of child abuse intervention and prevention programs, which points out the common features of these programs and the extent of their effectiveness. From 124 studies involving treatment of child maltreatment, 23% were identified as focusing on physical abuse, 4% neglect, and 23% sexual abuse (the remaining 48% involved mixed samples of maltreatment). After noting that the vast majority of these studies used uncontrolled designs (e.g., 47% were pre-post or one-group ex post facto designs, and 29% were single-subject), she restricted her analysis to the 25 experimental or quasiexperimental studies that would permit more valid overall conclusions.

The most frequently occurring treatment modality in these 25 studies was some form of individual treatment of the parent (48%) or the family (35%). The specific strategies included a wide range of (overlapping) approaches, including role modeling and rehearsal (31%), referrals to other social services (35%), child management skills training (31%), teaching about child development (31%), some form of environmental modification or services (34%), shaping new behaviors (28%), use of books or didactic methods (28%), and home visits (48%).

Videka-Sherman (1989) reports that the largest effect sizes were associated with methods based on social learning (average effect size = 1.14, based on six studies) and related educational approaches (average effect size = 1.04, based on five studies). The relatively few (N = 4) psychodynamically based treatment studies produced the lowest average effect size (.47). It is interesting to note that certain intervention components were associated with greater effectiveness across these studies. Preparing the client in some fashion for the treatment process was associated with higher effect sizes, as were programs that offered specific guidelines to follow. As well, those programs that focused on interpersonal skill enhancement of the parent resulted in better outcomes than did those involved strictly with an intrapersonal or social system emphasis.

This metaanalysis of 25 studies with abusive parents is suggestive, on the one hand, of important gains that have been made with this population. On the other hand, it points to the caution one must use in drawing conclusions, based on the relative paucity of research. Very few studies followed up the participants long enough to ensure a low reincidence rate of abuse or its high-risk indicators (e.g., harsh, power-assertive child-rearing, or use of physical punishment). In view of the concerns noted over a decade ago based on early, uncontrolled clinical trials with abusive families (i.e., 30% of parents seriously reabused their children *during treatment*; Cohn, 1979), we still have a considerable way to go toward determining the most effective form of intervention in the long run.

Some of the prominent factors contributing to this lackluster success with tertiary treatment of child abusers have to do with the nature of the target population and our general tendency to miss the mark in servicing their needs. First of all, there is a marked tendency for parents to be unwilling to seek help until it is forced upon them or the problem becomes major. Their avoidance of services makes sense, however, in light of our current strategy for combating child abuse. Currently, our child welfare system functions on the basis of reaction to crises and conflicts, and consequently little effort is directed toward the "front-end" of the child welfare system. Those families who are most in need often receive very little support and assistance until they commit a major violation of childcare practices.

By and large child abuse policy has been primarily one of detection and labeling of offenders. Such identification is intended to be followed by "treatment," yet the inadequate services in this regard are surpassed only by the criminal justice system. Ironically, this approach serves to identify *some* of the major offenders, but in so doing it reduces our chances significantly for assisting the much larger majority of potentially abusive or inadequate parents. When treatment services are offered in this manner, i.e., the person must commit an offense and be identified and labeled, it is understandable that many adults will perceive them as threatening and undesirable.

Unfortunately, by the time official attention is drawn to the problem (due to parents' reluctance to seek help, failure of parents and professionals to identify a burgeoning problem, offenses that are below the threshold for official response, etc.), it may be too late to reverse some of the patterns that have formed. To combat this avoidance of services, policy planners need to study ways to make the available services more attractive to potential clients. As well, a need exists to look more closely at the fact that family support services are usually offered by the same agency that is mandated to apprehend the child if deemed in need of protection.

This conflict between supportive assistance and intrusive intervention is unavoidable under our current policy for child abuse intervention. To this end, serious consideration should be given to the possibility of building in a "two-tiered" system for aiding families. The first tier would consist of prevention activities and services for families aimed at assistance and education in child care issues, which would be expected to have a positive effect on the incidence of admitting children into care. The second tier would consist of the more familiar child welfare/protection efforts that are designed to insure that community standards are upheld and children's needs are adequately met (Wolfe & Jaffe, 1990).

Emerging Trends in Early Intervention and Prevention

Despite the knowledge that treatment of abusive families is limited in success, there are certain accepted principles that form the basis for innovative assistance. For example, it is accepted that rearing children is adversely affected by bearing them at an early age, having a child with developmental impairments or special needs, lacking support of friends or neighbors when under stress, worrying about job and income, and not knowing what to expect developmentally from a child (Maccoby & Martin, 1983). These basic principles suggest that a more productive approach to child abuse may be to prevent its occurrence through proper education and support, with less reliance on a "safety net" to catch those who fail.

Recent investigators have approached the prevention of child abuse from the point of view of maximizing the child's developmental strengths through a focus on child-centered stimulation activities involving the parent. This strategy is derived from research on abused children indicating that the effects of abuse are cumulative over time, creating something of a domino effect on subsequent development (Aber & Cicchetti, 1984; Shirk, 1988). According to this argument, children's development may be delayed or disrupted not only by the isolated episodes of violence or rejection, but also by the everyday actions taken by parents who are not sensitive to children's needs and abilities. Because of its relevance to prevention and treatment, this distinction between transient and enduring effects of maltreatment remains an important issue for longitudinal research (Cicchetti, 1989; Cicchetti & Rizley, 1981).

The impact that a developmental orientation has on treatment and prevention directions holds considerable promise. Although relatively simple in concept, this theme takes a somewhat radical departure from most current efforts to treat child victims of maltreatment and to prevent its recurrence (Wolfe, Wekerle, & McGee, 1992). First, a child's symptoms would be seen as an understandable result of his or her efforts to learn social behaviors without the benefit of sensitive parenting or careful guidance. The identified *referral concern*, there-fore, shifts from one that assesses current problematic behavior alone toward one that identifies the developmental concerns that underlie such expressions. This premise directs intervention to the strengthening of developmentally relevant tasks or skills, in addition to specific presenting complaints (Cicchetti, 1989).

Second, prevention and intervention efforts can be planned from an earlier point in time in such a way that undesirable (and potentially problematic) developmental deficits can be minimized. Rather than relying on aversive contin-gencies (i.e., detecting abuse and neglect and imposing changes on the family), a developmentally guided intervention/prevention strategy works on the principle of providing the least intrusive, earliest assistance possible. The focus is shifted away from identifying misdeeds of the parent, and more toward promoting an optimal balance between the needs of the child and the abilities of the parent.

The major goals of prevention-focused programs include, for example: in-creasing parents' knowledge of child development and the demands of parenting; enhancing parents' skill in coping with stress related to caring for small children, enhancing parent/child attachment and communication, increasing parents' knowledge of home management, reducing/sharing the burden of childcare, and increasing access to social and health services for all family members. As summarized by Halpern (1990), beyond the basic needs for protection from harm and provision of adequate nourishment, infants need a parent who "mediates" the degree of environmental stimulation, who is sensitive to their needs, and who is consistent and available. Toddlers, in addition, need more play activities, a stimulating physical and social environment, firm, consistent, yet flexible con-trol, and the absence of restrictiveness. Several recent studies exemplify some of the progress being made in achieving these prevention goals, as reviewed below.

Studies involving high-risk parents. Reasoning that child abuse can be prevented by voluntarily assisting families who show high-risk indicators, sever-al investigators have made strides in expanding the role of professional services. A controlled test of the specific effectiveness of behavioral parenting training with at-risk parents was reported by Wolfe, Edwards, Manion, and Koverola (1988). Participants were selected on the basis of maternal age (under 25), child age (9 months to 5 years), involvement of child protective services, and scores in the at-risk range on the Child Abuse Potential Inventory (Milner, 1986). Overall, parent training was associated with positive maternal, child, and environmental gains on self-report measures relative to controls receiving traditional services only. Furthermore, the authors found that children in both conditions showed significant gains (over preintervention) in adaptive abilities, a finding they link to the fact that all children were involved in structured daycare activities twice per week throughout the 20-week program.

Seitz (1985) reports on a longitudinal study in which it was demonstrated that comprehensive parenting services not only produced initial gains but that these gains were strengthened over time. Their target sample received a coordinated set of medical and social services, such as well baby visits, home visits by a psychologist, social worker, or nurse, and day-care services. Relative to controls, the 10-year follow-up of these families indicated that mothers in the experimental condition achieved greater educational levels, better employment history of the primary wage earner, and better school performance by the children.

The strongest support to date for the efficacy of preventative pre- and postnatal programs originates from the ongoing work of Olds and his colleagues (Olds & Henderson, 1989; Olds, Henderson, Chamberlin, & Tatelbaum, 1986). These researchers targeted first-time parents who also possessed one or more specific risk factors (i.e., 47% were teen parents, 62% single parents, 61% low SES). While any first-time mothers were eligible, subjects were recruited from a semirural community that had New York State's highest rates of reported and confirmed child abuse. In addition, 85% of subjects met at least one risk criterion, and 23% possessed all three.

These researchers offered varying degrees of childcare services to participants that ranged from minimal (i.e., screening only of child sensory and developmental problems) to quite intensive (i.e., screening, plus regular prenatal and well-child care, plus pre- and postnatal nurse home visits providing resource linkages and developmental education). Significant gains were noted for the two nurse-visited groups as a whole, relative to the two non-visited groups. Within the nurse-visited groups, the most gains were found for those mothers who were deemed at highest risk (i.e., poor, single, teen parents), although some of these gains attained significance levels associated with trends only. These results offer the strongest evidence supporting prenatally initiated home visits as a strategy for improving child cognitive development, maternal perceptions of child behavior, mother–child interactions, child medical care, and the incidence of child abuse, at least during the time of intervention (see also Cicchetti, Toth, & Bush, 1988; Lyons-Ruth, Connell, & Zoll, 1989).

While acknowledging the major limitations of these representative, preliminary studies (see Fink & McCloskey, 1990), in general the findings support the short-term efficacy of family support with specific "at-risk" parents. These gains are somewhat modest, however, in view of the fairly intensive efforts expended. Most critical is the need for an appreciable follow-up period so that maintenance of gains and "sleeper" effects (i.e., those emerging after program completion) may be assessed (Wekerle & Wolfe, in press).

In sum, family support studies ranging in definition of at-risk parents have found short-term positive outcomes, particularly for those mothers deemed at greatest risk (e.g., young, relatively poor mothers; Daro, 1990). While many positive gains have been found in terms of parenting knowledge and attitudes, some studies have also found improvements in observed parent–child interactions, disciplinary behavior, and official reports of maltreatment following intervention (see Daro, this volume; Wekerle & Wolfe, in press, for reviews). There is some evidence to suggest that multi-leveled programs (i.e., offering additional services as parents require them over a longer period of time) are worth the additional effort and expense, when compared to less intensive services. Overall, those programs that span from one to three years and provide a personalized approach (e.g., home visits) stand out as most successful in achieving the desired outcomes. Those services deemed most promising in this regard include those that focus on providing opportunities for attachment and relationship formation, opportunities for learning about available services for families prior to a crisis, and opportunities for positive experiences in childrearing. By and large, these evolving programs have made strong efforts to "fit" their services to the existing family values and have respected each family's need for privacy and autonomy.

FORMULATING A PREVENTION-ORIENTED SOCIAL POLICY

In deciding where to direct our resources to reduce physical child abuse and neglect, we are faced immediately with the question of whether our efforts should be directed at stopping something bad, or at increasing something good (Helfer, 1982). These two choices are more than just semantic distinctions—they represent the crucial choice between a protective (i.e., interception) vs. a preventative (i.e., enhancement) stance. Clearly, the most dysfunctional families will continue to maltreat children, requiring service availability for intervention as well as prevention. Yet the significance of directing our resources more toward proper family assistance and support is made clear when child abuse is considered less in terms of physical injuries and more in terms of its impact on children's psychological development (e.g., cognitive, social, emotional, and behavioral adaptation; Cicchetti et al., 1988; Wolfe, 1987).

Most forms of family violence toward children (i.e., physical abuse, exposure to wife assault, and psychological abuse), as well as childrearing inadequacies (e.g., emotional and physical neglect) entail many of the actions and circumstances that are indicative of socialization failure. Therefore, a critical need exists to discover and implement different ways of preventing such failure well in advance of the establishment of abusive and rejecting patterns of childrearing. This prevention task is now a distinct possibility in view of our acquired knowledge of the social and psychological causes of maltreatment, and thus a top priority exists to formulate, implement, and evaluate the effectiveness of prevention-oriented, family support programs. Such a strategy is a recognized move away from our existing approach—rather than setting up a system that necessitates a serious breach in legally acceptable childcare before intervention is applied, our efforts should be responsive and proactive towards family development and unique cultural distinctions. We have entered a time in which there is a reemphasis on family integrity, as opposed to out-of-home placements (Reid, 1985), and in conjunction with this movement social service and mental health agencies are looking for ways to offer assistance to families (whether intact, single-parent, reconstituted, etc.) that eliminates or reduces the need for protective supervision.

How should policy guide our use of resources? Child maltreatment seems to arise most often during periods of stressful role transition for parents, such as the postnatal period of attachment, the early childhood period of increasing socialization pressures, times of family instability and disruption (e.g., divorce, single parenthood, change in caregivers), or following chronic detachment from social supports and services. Fortunately, we now recognize many of the precursory patterns that accompany a gradual transition toward abusive socialization patterns, yet our current system is impotent to apply this knowledge to assist families unless a "crisis" brings them to our attention. This approach is unacceptable for several reasons, not the least of which is its "reactive" emphasis and limited utility once problems have emerged. Our existing child welfare system needs to be modified and strengthened such that it permits individuals to seek assistance routinely and with minimal risk to the family unit—to make family support as universally acceptable as health care (Garbarino, 1987). This model requires a retooling of our current child welfare system, away from a reactive, protective stance and closer to the ideal of preventative mental health: suitable services to all individuals that are based on promotion of healthy family relationships.

The overriding goal of child abuse prevention from the perspective of healthy child development, therefore, is the establishment of positive socialization practices that are responsive to situational and developmental changes. Such healthy practices serve to buffer the child against other socialization pressures that can be stressful or negative, and reduce the need for the parent to rely on power-assertive methods to control the child. To this advantage, the research findings reviewed above generally point to successful ways of teaching such strategies to parents, especially if offered early on in the development of the parent–child relationship. Regrettably, very few such programs are implemented on a wide scale or tailored to the needs of different communities, families, or problems. The purpose of child abuse prevention should involve much more than forestalling events that are harmful to a child; prevention can also involve activities that enhance something positive for the child, the most important of which is a positive parent–child relationship.

Key Factors for Prevention Services

The need of all families for support and education. Adequate supports, both instrumental and emotional, are important for the healthy functioning of families. Accordingly, a needs assessment should be conducted to determine what is available to all families, and what is needed. Such supportive services should include, at a minimum, formal, agency-based services, quasiformal supports (e.g., self-help groups), and informal supports that are accessible to individual families.

Family support programs (e.g., Garbarino, 1987) offer a range of concrete, social, and psychological services to address the needs of low-income families with small children. The challenge remains to expand these services to more at-risk families who have poor histories of childcare and a poor record of successful responsibilities (e.g., employment). The value of a family support (i.e., enhancement) strategy, in contrast to an interception approach, is that it provides a "flexible mix of concrete, clinical, and supportive services in a nonbureaucratic, family-like context (Halpern, 1990, p. 15). Needless to say, such a model requires a different allocation of resources and professional commitment.

Clarifying our community values and our prevention orientation. Some policy planners have been advocating for the establishment of "minimum standards of care" for each community. Such standards would be a negotiation between professional expertise and knowledge, on the one hand, and community standards, values, and culture on the other hand (e.g., Garbarino, 1987). Proponents of such an endeavor believe this information would provide a more well-defined guideline for establishing what the minimum standards of care should be, and when state intervention is viewed by the community as a necessary step.

Similarly, policy planners need to look at the community's willingness to implement family support programs at a broad and more comprehensive level. Such programs are aimed at preventing the breakdown of families who require alternative care, and evidence is emerging as to their efficacy and impact on positive child and family development (e.g., Olds et al., 1986). Social scientists emphasize that social support systems are the mechanisms by which corrective measures for families are naturally provided, yet such systems may require our deliberate planning and implementation to insure that families receive adequate nurturance and feedback on their childrearing (Wolfe, 1987).

Looking Ahead at Research Needs

Prevention efforts, especially those targeted at younger children and their parents, are showing the beginning signs of fulfilling some of the promise that proponents have argued. Recent reviews of the more methodologically sound studies have concluded that such efforts as home visitors and family support services (e.g., parent training, household safety and organization) are associated with more positive parenting knowledge, attitudes, skills, and behavior, as well as fewer child injuries, emergency room visits, and reports to protective agencies (Fink & McCloskey, 1990; Wekerle & Wolfe, in press). Moreover, those programs that appear to be having the greatest impact have multiple components (e.g., home visits, parent support groups, day-care or nursery school) and longer duration of involvement (i.e., 2 to 5 years).

Based on our learning to date, what suggestions can we offer to researchers and policy planners to improve on our state of knowledge? In terms of program design, several issues stand out as being worthy of further research and development (Ministry of Community and Social Services, 1989): Programs should focus on geographical areas that contain a number of high-risk indicators, be accessible to a wide range of clientele in a manner that avoids stigmatization, appeal to those at highest risk (e.g., poor; teen parents), involve the community in all phases of development and implementation, embody a developmental approach that recognizes the stages of the family life cycle and child development, provide temporal continuity over several years, be flexible and adaptable to the needs of families, and be delivered in a manner that is sensitive to the cultural and social diversity of families.

Moreover, research designs for evaluating such programs need to be of the highest quality possible, within the constraints of community-based research (i.e., the difficulty in conducting a true experimental design, and the dilemma of adhering to a careful intervention procedure given the changing needs of family and community). Despite these limitations, it is essential that future research designs carefully involve some type of comparison group (either randomly assigned controls, or children from other communities, etc.); pre- and postprogram measures of children, parents, and community factors that are deemed crucial to long-term abuse prevention; experimental or quasiexperimental designs; and a cohort of program children and nonprogram children that can be followed over a long time frame. Finally, the definition and selection of the sample merits careful consideration. Greater attention must be paid to the importance of selecting subjects from nonbiased sources, such as protective services, hospitals, etc., and greater detail provided as to the sociodemographic makeup of the participants. The promise of such prevention efforts warrants such a rigorous scientific commitment to evaluation and design, which in turn will lead to important changes in social policy.

REFERENCES

Aber, J. L., & Cicchetti, D. (1984). The socio-emotional development of maltreated children: An empirical and theoretical analysis. In H. Fitzgerald, B. Lester, & M. Yogman (Eds.), *Theory and research in behavioral pediatrics* (Vol. 2, pp. 147–205). New York: Plenum.

Aber, J. L., & Zigler, E. (1981). Developmental considerations in the definition of child maltreatment. In R. Rizley & D. Cicchetti (Eds.), *Developmental perspectives on child maltreatment* (pp. 1–29). San Francisco: Jossey-Bass.

Azar, S. T., & Twentyman, C. T. (1984, November). *An evaluation of the effectiveness of behaviorally versus insight oriented treatments with maltreating mothers.* Paper presented at the annual meeting of the Association for the Advancement of Behavior Therapy, Philadelphia.

Azar, S. T., & Wolfe, D. A. (1989). Child abuse and neglect. In E. J. Mash & R. A. Barkley (Eds.), *Behavioral treatment of childhood disorders* (pp. 451–489). New York: Guilford.

Belsky, J., & Vondra, J. (1989). Lessons from child abuse: The determinants of parenting. In D. Cicchetti & V. Carlson (Eds.), *Child maltreatment: Theory and research on the causes and consequences of child abuse and neglect* (pp. 153–202). New York: Cambridge University Press.

Besharov, D. J. (1988). *Protecting children from abuse and neglect: Policy and practice.* Springfield, IL: Charles Thomas.

Burgess, R. L. (1979). Child abuse: A social interactional analysis. In B. B. Lahey & A. Kazdin (Eds.), *Advances in clinical child psychology* (Vol. 2, pp. 142–172). New York: Plenum.

Campbell, R. V., O'Brien, S., Bickett, A. D., & Lutzker, J. R. (1983). In-home parent training of migraine headaches and marital counseling as an ecobehavioral approach to prevent child abuse. *Journal of Behavior Therapy and Experimental Psychiatry, 14,* 147–154.

Cicchetti, D. (1989). How research on child maltreatment has informed the study of child development: Perspectives from developmental psychopathology. In D. Cicchetti & V. Carlson (Eds.), *Child maltreatment: Theory and research on the causes and consequences of child abuse and neglect* (pp. 377–431). New York: Cambridge University Press.

Cicchetti, D., & Rizley, R. (1981). Developmental perspectives on the etiology, intergenerational transmission, and sequelae of child maltreatment. In D. Cicchetti & R. Rizley (Eds.), *New directions for child development: Developmental perspectives on child maltreatment* (pp. 31–55). San Francisco: Jossey-Bass.

Cicchetti, D., Toth, S., & Bush, M. (1988). Developmental psychopathology and incompetence in childhood: Suggestions for intervention. In B. B. Lahey & A. E. Kazdin (Eds.), *Advances in clinical child psychology* (Vol. 11, pp. 1–70). New York: Plenum.

Cohn, A. H. (1979). Essential elements of successful child abuse and neglect treatment. *Child Abuse & Neglect, 3,* 491–496.

Conger, R. D., Lahey, B. B., & Smith, S. S. (1981, July). *An intervention program for child abuse: Modifying maternal depression and behavior.* Paper presented at the Family Violence Research Conference, University of New Hampshire, Durham.

Crittenden, P. M. (1988). Relationships at risk. In J. Belsky & T. Nezworski (Eds.), *Clinical implications of attachment* (pp. 136–174). Hillsdale, NJ: Erlbaum.

Daro, D. (1990). *Confronting child abuse: Research for effective program design.* New York: Free Press.

Delgado, A. E., & Lutzker, J. R. (1985, November). *Training parents to identify and report their children's illness.* Paper presented at the annual convention of the Association for the Advancement of Behavior Therapy, Houston.

Denicola, J., & Sandler, J. (1980). Training abusive parents in cognitive behavioral techniques. *Behavior Therapy, 11,* 263–270.

Egan, K. (1983). Stress management and child management with abusive parents. *Journal of Clinical Child Psychology, 12,* 292–299.

Egeland, B. (1991). A longitudinal study of high risk families: Issues and findings. In R. Starr & D. Wolfe (Eds.), *The effects of child abuse and neglect: Issues and findings.* (pp. 31–56). New York: Guilford.

Felner, R. D. (1984). Vulnerability in childhood. In M. C. Roberts & L. Peterson (Eds.), *Prevention of problems in childhood* (pp. 133–169). New York: Wiley.

Fink, A., & McCloskey, L. (1990). Moving child abuse and neglect prevention programs forward: Improving program evaluations. *Child Abuse & Neglect, 14,* 187–206.

Forehand, R. L., & McMahon, R. J. (1981). *Helping the noncompliant child: A clinician's guide to parent training.* New York: Guilford.

Garbarino, J. (1977). The human ecology of child maltreatment: A conceptual model for research. *Journal of Marriage and the Family, 39,* 721–735.

Garbarino, J. (1987). Family support and the prevention of child maltreatment. In S. L. Kagan, D. R. Powell, B. Weissbourd, & E. F. Zigler (Eds.), *America's Family Support Programs* (pp. 99–114). New Haven, CT: Yale University Press.

Garbarino, J., Guttman, E., & Seeley, J., (1986). *The psychologically battered child.* San Francisco: Jossey-Bass.

Gerbner, G., Ross, C. J., & Zigler, E. (Eds.). (1980). *Child abuse: An agenda for action.* New York: Oxford.

Gil, D. G. (1970). *Violence against children: Physical child abuse in the United States.* Cambridge, MA: Harvard University Press.

Gil, D. G. (1987). Maltreatment as a function of the structure of the social systems. In M. R. Brassard, R. Germain, & S. N. Hart (Eds.), *Psychological maltreatment of children and youth* (pp. 159–170). Elsford, NY: Pergamon.

Giovannoni, J. (1989). Definitional issues in child maltreatment. In D. Cicchetti & V. Carlson (Eds.), *Child maltreatment: Theory and research on the causes and consequences of child abuse and neglect* (pp. 3–37). New York: Cambridge University Press.

Grych, J. H., & Fincham, F. D. (1990). Marital conflict and children's adjustment: A cognitive-contextual framework. *Psychological Bulletin, 108,* 267–290.

Halpern, R. (1990). Poverty and early childhood parenting: Toward a framework for intervention. *American Journal of Orthopsychiatry, 60,* 6–17.

Helfer, R. (1982). A review of the literature on the prevention of child abuse and neglect. *Child Abuse & Neglect, 6,* 251–261.

Isaacs, C. D. (1982). Treatment of child abuse: A review of the behavioral interventions. *Journal of Applied Behavior Analysis, 15,* 273–294.

Jaffe, P., Wolfe, D. A., & Wilson, S. (1990). *Children of battered women.* Newbury Park, CA: Sage.

Jones, M. A. (1987). *A second chance for families: Five years later—Follow-up of a program to prevent foster care.* New York: Child Welfare League of America.

Kelly, J. A. (1983). *Treating abusive families: Intervention based on skills training principles.* New York: Plenum.

Kempe, C. H., & Helfer, R. E. (1972). *Helping the battered child and his family.* Philadelphia: Lippincott.

Kempe, C. H., Silverman, F. N., Steele, B. F., Droegemueller, W., & Silver, H. K. (1962). The battered child syndrome. *Journal of the American Medical Association, 181,* 17–24.

Light, R. (1973). Abused and neglected children in America: A study of alternative policies. *Harvard Educational Review, 43,* 556–598.

Lutzker, J. R. (1984). Project 12-Ways: Treating child abuse and neglect from an ecobehavioral perspective. In R. F. Dangel & R. A. Polster (Eds.), *Parent training: Foundations of research and practice.* New York: Guilford.

Lyons-Ruth, K., Connell, D. B., & Zoll, D. (1989). Maternal relations and infant attachment behavior at 12 months. In D. Cicchetti & V. Carlson (Eds.), *Child maltreatment: Theory and research on the causes and consequences of child abuse and neglect* (pp. 464–493). New York: Cambridge University Press.

Maccoby, E. E., & Martin, J. A. (1983). Socialization in the context of the family: Parent-child interaction. In P. H. Mussen (Ed.), *Handbook of child psychology* (4th Ed.). New York: J. Wiley & Sons.

Mash, E. J. (1991). Measurement of parent–child interaction in studies of child maltreatment. In R. Starr & D. Wolfe (Eds.), *The effects of child abuse and neglect: Issues & Research* (pp. 203–256). New York: Guilford.

Mash, E. J., & Wolfe, D. A. (1991). Methodological issues in research on child abuse. *Criminal Justice and Behavior, 18,* 8–30.

McGee, R., & Wolfe, D. A. (1991). Psychological maltreatment: Towards an operational definition. *Development and Psychopathology, 3,* 3–18.

Melton, G. B. (1990). Child protection: Making a bad situation worse? *Contemporary Psychology, 35,* 213–214.

Milner, J. S. (1986). *The Child Abuse Potential Inventory: Manual* (2nd Ed.). Webster, NC: Psytec Corp.

Ministry of Community and Social Services (MCSS). (1988). *Investing in children: New directions in child treatment and child and family intervention.* Queen's Park, Toronto: Queen's Printer for Ontario.

Ministry of Community and Social Services (MCSS). (1989). *Better beginnings, better futures: An integrated model of primary prevention of emotional and behavioral problem.* Queen's Park, Toronto: Queen's Printer for Ontario.

Nomellini, S., & Katz, R. C. (1983). Effects of anger control training on abusive parents. *Cognitive Therapy and Research, 7,* 57–68.

Oldershaw, L., Walters, G. C., & Hall, D. K. (1989). A behavorial approach to the classification of different types of physically abusive mothers. *Merrill-Palmer Quarterly, 35,* 255–279.

Olds, D. L., & Henderson, C. R., Jr. (1989). The prevention of maltreatment. In D. Cicchetti & V. Carlson (Eds.), *Child maltreatment: Theory and research on the causes and consequences of child abuse and neglect* (pp. 722–763). New York: Cambridge University Press.

Olds, D. L., Henderson, Jr., C. R., Chamberlin, R., & Tatelbaum, R. (1986). Preventing child abuse and neglect: A randomized trial of nurse home visitation. *Pediatrics, 78,* 65–78.

Parke, R. D. (1977). Socialization into child abuse: A social interactional perspective. In J. L. Tapp & F. J. Levine (Eds.), *Law, justice, and the individual in society: Psychological and legal issues* (pp. 183–199). New York: Holt, Rinehart & Winston.

Parke, R. D., & Collmer, C. W. (1975). Child abuse: An interdisciplinary analysis. In E. M. Hetherington (Ed.), *Review of child development research* (Vol. 5, pp. 509–590). Chicago: University of Chicago Press.

Paterson, R. J., & Moran, G. (1988). Attachment theory, personality development, and psychotherapy. *Clinical Psychology Review, 8,* 611–636.

Patterson, G. R., Reid, J. B., Jones, R. R., & Conger, R. E. (1975). *A social learning approach to family intervention* (Vol. I: *Families with aggressive children*). Champaign, IL: Research Press.

Raychaba, B. (1988). *To be on our own with no direction from home. A report on the special needs of youth leaving the care of the child welfare system.* Ottawa: National Youth in Care Network.

Reid, J. B. (1985). Behavioral approaches to intervention and assessment with child abusive families. In P. H. Bornstein & A. E. Kazdin (Eds.), *Handbook of clinical behavior therapy with children* (pp. 772–802). Homewood, IL: Dorsey Press.

Reid, J. B., Taplin, P., & Lorber, R. (1981). A social interactional approach to the treatment of abusive families. In R. B. Stuart (Ed.), *Violent behavior: Social learning approaches to prediction, management, and treatment* (pp. 83–101). New York: Brunner/Mazel.

Sandler, J., VanDercar, C., & Milhoan, M. (1978). Training child abusers in the use of positive reinforcement practices. *Behavior Research and Therapy, 16,* 169–175.

Schilling, R. F., & Schinke, S. P. (1984). Maltreatment and mental retardation. *Prospectives and Progress in Mental Retardation, 1,* 11–22.

Seitz, V. (1985). Effects of family support intervention: A ten-year follow-up. *Child Development, 56,* 376–391.

Shirk, S. R. (1988). The interpersonal legacy of physical abuse of children. In M. Straus (Ed.), *Abuse and victimization across the lifespan.* Baltimore: Johns Hopkins Press.

Smith, J. E. (1984). Non-accidental injury to children—I: A review of behavioral interventions. *Behavior Research and Therapy, 22,* 331–347.

Steele, B. J., & Pollock, C. (1968). A psychiatric study of parents who abuse infants and small children. In R. Helfer & C. H. Kempe (Eds.), *The battered child* (pp. 89–133). Chicago: The University of Chicago Press.

The future of foster care. (1988). *The Journal of the Ontario Association of Children's Aid Societies*, pp. 3–20.

Tuma, J. M. (1989). Mental health services for children: The state of the art. *American Psychologist, 44,* 188–199.

Videka-Sherman, L. (1989, October). *Therapeutic issues for physical and emotional child abuse and neglect: Implications for longitudinal research.* Paper presented at a research forum entitled "Issues in the longitudinal study of child maltreatment." The Institute for the Prevention of Child Abuse, Toronto.

Wald, M. S., Carlsmith, J. M., & Leiderman, P. H. (1988). *Protecting abused and neglected children.* Palo Alto, CA: Stanford University Press.

Wekerle, C., & Wolfe, D. A. (in press). Prevention of child physical abuse and neglect: Promising new directions. *Clinical Psychology Review.*

Wolfe, D. A. (1984). Treatment of abusive parents: A reply to the special issue. *Journal of Clinical Child Psychology, 13,* 192–194.

Wolfe, D. A. (1987). *Child Abuse: Implications for child development and psychopathology.* Newbury Park, CA: Sage.

Wolfe, D. A. (1991). *Preventing physical and emotional abuse of children.* New York: Guilford Press.

Wolfe, D., Edwards, B., Manion, I., & Koverola, C. (1988). Early intervention for parents at risk of child abuse and neglect: A preliminary investigation. *Journal of Consulting and Clinical Psychology, 56,* 40–47.

Wolfe, D. A., & Jaffe, P. (1990). The psychosocial needs of children in care. In L. C. Johnson & D. Barnhorst (Eds.), *Children, families, and public policy in the 1990's* (pp. 231–246). Toronto: Thompson Educational Publishing.

Wolfe, D. A., & Sandler, J. (1981). Training abusive parents in effective child management. *Behavior Modification, 5,* 320–335.

Wolfe, D. A., Sandler, J., & Kaufman, K. (1981). A competency-based parent training program for abusive parents. *Journal of Consulting and Clinical Psychology, 49,* 633–640.

Wolfe, D. A., & Wekerle, C. (in press). Treatment strategies for child physical abuse and neglect: A critical progress report. *Clinical Psychology Review.*

Wolfe, D. A., Wekerle, C., & McGee, R. (1992). Developmental disparities among abused children: Directions for prevention. In R. DeV. Peters & R. McMahon (Eds.), *Aggression and violence throughout the lifespan.* Newbury Park, CA: Sage.

Zillman, D. (1979). *Hostility and aggression.* Hillsdale, NJ: Erlbaum.

Zuravin, S. J. (1991). Research definitions of child physical abuse and neglect: Current problems. In R. Starr & D. Wolfe (Eds.), *Effects of child abuse and neglect: Issues and research* (pp. 100–128). New York: Guilford Press.

13

Child Maltreatment: Where Do We Go from Here in Our Treatment of Victims?*

Sheree L. Toth and Dante Cicchetti

We are guilty of many errors and many faults, but our worst crime is abandoning the children, neglecting the fountain of life. Many of the things we need can wait. The child cannot. Right now is the time his bones are being formed, his blood is being made, and his senses being developed—to him we cannot answer tomorrow. His name is today.

—Gabriela Mistral

While efforts to prevent the occurrence of child abuse are critical (Daro, this volume; Wolfe, this volume), the stark reality that confronts us is that, in the last decade, the numbers of children who have experienced some form of maltreatment have escalated. According to NIS-II, the National Incidence Study completed in 1986 (Unites States Department of Health and Human Services, 1988), approximately 16.3 children per 1,000 were victims of abuse or neglect, a figure suggesting that over 1 million children were maltreated in that year. When the definition of *maltreatment* was expanded to include children at risk for maltreatment who may not yet have suffered harm, estimates rose to over 1½ million cases nationwide. Even if the more conservative definition of *maltreatment* that requires demonstrable harm to the child is adhered to, the 1986 study reflects a 67% increase over the incidence rate obtained in NIS-I, which was completed in 1980 (United States Department of Health and Human Services, 1981). Additionally, a review of official nationwide statistics on child protective service reports reveals a preponderance of child victims in the 0 to 5-year age group, especially with regard to severe forms of physical abuse (American Humane

* First and foremost, we thank the children and families with whom we have worked and who have contributed to our thinking in this area. We also appreciate the input of our colleagues at Mt. Hope Family Center over the years, including Debra Bartenstein, Paul Howes, Nancy Kratzert, Michael Lynch, Jody Todd Manly, Barb Mitchell, Wendy Potenza-D'Alfonso, Fred Rogosch, and Debra Smarsh. The support and cooperation of the Monroe County Department of Social Services, especially Diane Larter and Katherine Sosin, also have been instrumental in facilitating the provision of services to maltreated children. We also acknowledge the support of the Smith Richardson Richardson Foundation, Inc. Finally, our thanks to Fred Rogosch and Jody Todd Manly for their comments on an earlier draft of this chapter and to Jennifer Boehles for her help with manuscript preparation.

Associations, 1988). In fact, according to these statistics the average age of child victims was 2.8 and 5.5 years, respectively, for fatalities and major physical injury.

Thus, as a society we are faced with an increasing number of children who are suffering the effects of having been maltreated. Since Kempe's identification of the *battered child syndrome* (Kempe, Silverman, Steele, Droegemueller, & Silver, 1962), research directed toward assessing the consequences of child maltreatment on the course of development has burgeoned (Cicchetti & Carlson, 1989). Unfortunately, to date efforts to provide and evaluate treatment directed toward the amelioration of the sequelae of maltreatment have lagged behind.

In this chapter, we review research findings on the effects of maltreatment on adaptation. We also discuss intervention approaches which have been devised to treat child victims of maltreatment. Finally, we explore the systemic difficulties that we see as hindering the availability of services to maltreated children and provide suggestions relevant to policy development and implementation that are likely to facilitate the provision of theoretically based interventions for maltreated children.

THE SEQUELAE OF MALTREATMENT

We bring an organizational perspective on development (Cicchetti & Sroufe, 1978; Sroufe & Waters, 1976; Werner, 1948) to bear on our consideration of the effects of child maltreatment. According to this conceptual framework, development involves a process that encompasses reorganizations among and within behavioral and biological systems (Cicchetti & Schneider-Rosen, 1986). This lifelong process occurs through the emergence of increasing differentiation and hierarchic integration and explains continuity in developmental adaptation despite constitutional, biological, and environmental changes (Sroufe, 1979b).

Normal development proceeds through the emergence and successful resolution of a series of socioemotional, cognitive, social-cognitive, and representational competencies. Conversely, pathological development may be seen as a lack of integration among competencies or as an integration of pathological structures (Cicchetti & Schnieder-Rosen 1986; Kaplan, 1966; Sroufe, 1979b). Because early structures form the foundation for the support of later competencies, future adaptation or maladaptation is linked closely with success or failure on prior developmental tasks. Therefore, the early effects of maltreatment (e.g., insecure attachment relationships) may be incorporated into the developmental process in such a way as to affect future adaptation adversely with regard, for example, to peer relationships (Cicchetti, Lynch, Shonk, & Manly, 1992).

The process of ontogenesis consists of a series of stage-salient issues that, while differing in relative importance at various ages, remain critical to adaptation across the life span. As new issues emerge, prior issues may decrease in importance. However, due to the ongoing and hierarchical nature of development, all issues exert a significant role on the child's current and future adaptation. Because stage-salient developmental issues continue to undergo differentiation and must be integrated and coordinated with subsequent developmental tasks throughout the life course, no one is ever completely inoculated against the unfolding of later problems or doomed to maladaptation by early failures. Thus, there is room for optimism concerning the ability for interventions to ameliorate the harmful consequences of maltreatment.

In our review of the sequelae of maltreatment, we focus on the stage-salient issues of attachment, the self-system, and peer relations. While by no means reflecting a comprehensive review of the sequelae of maltreatment literature, these issues encompass areas that are likely to lead to maladaptation unless intervention is provided. Additionally, in keeping with our life-span approach we explore the sequelae associated with each issue, not just at its period of ascendance or apogee, but over the course of development.

Due to their central importance in early and future adaptation, we consider the attachment relations of maltreated children as an organizing construct that can be useful in obtaining a better understanding of the processes that affect their development across the lifespan. Increasingly, researchers and theoreticians are emphasizing the role of representational models as a mechanism whereby attachment is transmitted across generations and diverse relationships (Bretherton, 1985; Cicchetti & Lynch, 1993; Main, Kaplan, & Cassidy, 1985; Rutter, 1988; Sroufe & Fleeson, 1986, 1988). It is the early parent-child relationship that contributes to the child's sense of self, as well as to attitudes and expectations about current and future relationships. Although models specific to a given relationship are generated, the early internal representation of the parent-child relationship also may result in more generalized expectations about the self and the self in relation to others. In situations involving child maltreatment, caregiving experiences involving unavailability, inconsistency, and fear are likely to contribute to the expectation that other social partners will behave similarly. Even when faced with individuals who seemingly do not fit this negative expectation, children with a history of insecure attachment may behave so as to distance others or repeat the maladaptive interactional patterns that they have previously experienced (Lynch & Cicchetti, 1992).

Because attachment theorists believe that relationships are internally represented with respect both to self and other (Ainsworth, 1989; Bowlby, 1969/1982), each model of some "other" relationship figure is thought to have a corollary representation of the self. Thus, if a maltreated child views a caregiver as rejecting and punitive, the child may similarly have developed a self model that is permeated by feelings of unworthiness. The negative self view, in turn, may impact upon the child's interactions with others adversely. In our presentation of the effect of maltreatment on stage-salient issues, the role of the child's early caregiving environment and the child's resulting representational models of self and other will serve to unify our discussion.

Attachment

One of the most robust findings on the effects of maltreatment on development stems from the area of attachment theory (Cicchetti, 1990). The formation of a secure attachment relationship with the primary caregiver is an early stage-salient issue that not surprisingly has been found to be disrupted in infants who have been maltreated. Early relationship histories result in the formation of representational models of attachment figures, of the self, and of the self in relation to others. In turn, these representational models serve to organize affects, cognitions, and expectations about future interactions.

A number of studies have shown that maltreated infants form insecure attachments with their primary caregivers (Cicchetti, 1989; Crittenden, 1988; Egeland & Sroufe, 1981; Schneider-Rosen, Braunwald, Carlson, & Cicchetti, 1985). In fact, unlike the preponderance of secure attachments found in nonmaltreated children, estimates of insecurity in maltreated children have ranged form 70% to 100% across studies (Cicchetti, 1989; Crittenden & Ainsworth 1989). Initially, researchers were largely unable to identify any consistently predominant category of insecurity among maltreated toddlers. However, over time the presence of unusual patterns involving moderate to high levels of both resistance and avoidance were observed in maltreated children (Crittenden, 1988; Main & Solomon, 1986, 1990). Unlike the more traditional attachment classifications of secure (Type B), anxious avoidant (Type A), and anxious resistant (Type C), the maltreated children who could not be classified consistently lacked an organized strategy for dealing with stressful separations from and reunions with their caregivers. This disorganized/disoriented (Type D) pattern has subsequently been found to be quite prevalent in maltreated children. In fact Carlson, Cicchetti, Barnett, and Braunwald (1989) identified over 80% of their sample of maltreated infants as Type D, as compared with 20% in an economically disadvantaged comparison group of infants. Similar findings of high rates of atypical attachments in maltreated children have been obtained by other investigators as well (Lyons-Ruth, Repacholi, McLeod, & Silva, 1991).

Several explanations have been proposed to account for the preponderance of atypical attachment relations in maltreated infants. Because inconsistent care is a hallmark of maltreating families, combinations of insensitive overstimulation, which has been linked to avoidant attachment, and insensitive understimulation, which has been associated with resistant attachment, are likely to be present (Belsky, Rovine, & Taylor, 1984; Crittenden, 1985; Lyons-Ruth, Connell, Zoll, & Stahl, 1987). The combination of these caregiving styles could lead to the contradictory features associated with Type D attachments. The fear that pervades maltreating families also has been viewed as central to the emergence of the disorganized/disoriented attachment (Main & Hesse, 1990). Finally the common pattern of child parentification in maltreating families, where role reversal results in the child caring for the parent, may reflect an underlying disorganized attachment relationship (Carlson et al., 1989; Cicchetti & Barnett, 1991; Main et al., 1985).

In view of the prevalence of insecure attachment in maltreated infants, specifically of a disorganized/disoriented nature, questions arise as to the continuity of insecurity into later years of life. Findings of substantial stability in Type D attachment across the first two years of live are beginning to emerge. For example, Barnett, Ganiban, and Cicchetti (1992) report that approximately 60% of infants who were classified at type D at 12 months of age had the same classification at 24 months of age. Moreover, 90% of the infants classified as Type D at 24 months of age had previously received the Type D classification.

Although historically attachment has been viewed as most salient during infancy and early toddlerhood, investigators have begun to explore attachment relationships, as well as behavioral concomitants of certain attachment classification, throughout the lifecourse (Ainsworth, 1985, 1989; Bretherton, 1985; Main et al. 1985). Although the role of attachment in the preschool years and beyond remains a largely empirical issue (Cicchetti, Cummings, Greenberg, & Marvin 1990), the viability of the attachment construct beyond infancy is receiving support (see Greenberg, Cicchetti, & Cummings, 1990; Parkes, Stevenson-Hinde, & Marris, 1991).

Because the developmental capacities that emerge during the preschool period allow the attachment relationship to become more interpersonally connected while the child simultaneously evidences increased autonomy, this period of transition is especially important (Cicchetti & Barnett, 1991). In a cross-sectional study of attachment relationships of maltreated youngsters that contained children as old as 48 months, Crittenden (1988) found that maltreated 25- through 48-month-old children evidenced more insecurity than did nonmaltreated children. Additionally, Crittenden found that an atypical classification (A/C) was more prevalent in older and more seriously maltreated preschoolers. Evidence that 48-month-old maltreated children failed to demonstrate a goal-corrected partnership with their mothers also was obtained. Because the ability to negotiate with the caregiver to reach agreement is generally expected in preschoolers of this developmental level, the lack of a goal-corrected partnership was noteworthy.

In a cross-sectional/longitudinal investigation of 125 maltreated and non-maltreated children from the lower socioeconomic strata, Cicchetti and Barnett (1991) found that 30-, 36-, and 48-month-old maltreated preschoolers were significantly more likely to evidence insecure attachment relations with their mothers then were the nonmaltreated comparison children. The proportion of children evidencing each type of insecurity varied at each of the age levels assessed and the percentage of maltreated children classified as having an atypical attachment ranged from 36.4% at 30 months to 27.8% at 48 months. Interestingly for our purposes, Cicchetti and Barnett (1991) also found that the high percentage of nonmaltreated children who were classified as securely attached were likely to remain so, whereas the small number of maltreated children who exhibited secure attachments were unlikely to remain secure over the course of the longitudinal period they were assessed.

Thus, similar to research with maltreated infants and toddlers, findings are emerging to support the presence of insecure attachment relationships in pre-schoolers. Although few longitudinal investigations of the stability of attachment from infancy into and beyond the preschool years in maltreated youngsters have be conducted (Cicchetti & Barnett, 1991), the apparent stability of attachment in short-term longitudinal assessments, in conjunction with cross-sectional findings of greater insecurity of attachment relations in maltreated youngsters at various ages, lends support to the hypothesis of continuity of maladaptation on this stage-salient issue.

In addition to standard assessments of child-caregiver relationships, attachment theory predicts that primary attachment relationships affect the development of future relationships (Bowlby, 1969/1982; Sroufe & Fleeson, 1988). Therefore, because research has show that maltreated children evidence a preponderance of insecure attachment relationships during infancy and into the preschool years, these youngsters might be expected to experience patterns of maladaptive relationships into the school years and beyond. In an effort to explore the patterns of relatedness of maltreated children, Lynch and Cicchetti (1991) obtained assessments from 7- to 12-year-old children within a summer camp setting. Using a modified version of a self-report measure developed by Wellborn and Connell (1987), Lynch and Cicchetti (1991) assessed the extent to which the children's need for relatedness, one of three primary needs for the self according to Connell (1990), were being met. By assessing relationship quality along two continuous dimensions of *emotional quality* and *psychological proximity seeking*, Lynch and Cicchetti believe that a portrayal of internal representational models of relationship figures can be obtained, and that the resulting configurations are consistent with predictions made by attachment theory. In reporting their feelings of relatedness, comprised of feeling connected with the social surround and the experience of oneself as worthy and capable of love, maltreated children were significantly more likely to evidence confused patterns of relatedness than nonmaltreated children. In contrast, nonmaltreated youngsters were more likely to report optimal patterns of relatedness. Children who have optimal patterns of relatedness report higher than average levels of emotional quality and lower than average amounts of psychological proximity seeking. On the other hand, children with a confused pattern of relatedness report high levels of emotional quality as well as extremely high amounts of psychological proximity seeking. Substantial concordance was found among the children's reports of relatedness with all relationship figures, including mother, teachers, and peers (Lynch & Cicchetti, 1991).

Evidence that early insecure attachment relationships continue to exert an effect even into adulthood also has been obtained. Investigators have found that a mother's unresolved distress regarding her own childhood relationship experiences adversely affects her ability to form a secure attachment with her child (Main & Goldwyn, 1984; Main et al., 1985). Findings that, as adults, previously maltreated women tend to perpetuate their early histories of maladaptive relationships also have emerged (Burgess, Anderson, Schellenbach, & Conger, 1981; Crittenden, Partridge, & Claussen, 1991; Hunter & Kilstrom, 1979). In addition to providing support for the long-term detrimental effects of maltreatment, these data also provide evidence for the intergenerational transmission of maltreatment (Main & Goldwyn, 1984). Mothers who were abused as children but did not go on to perpetuate the cycle of abuse against their own offspring have been shown to be more likely to have experienced a supportive relationship during childhood, to have participated in therapy at some point in their lives, to have a supportive stable relationship with a mate, to be able to express open and appropriately angry feelings about their childhoods, and to have evidenced an active processing of their early experiences (Egeland, Jacobvitz, & Sroufe, 1988; Hunter & Kilstrom, 1979).

Taken together, the lifelong significance of disturbed attachment relations in individuals who experienced maltreatment during childhood highlights the importance of considering and attempting to modify the effects of maltreatment on the development of intimate relationships. In addition, because attachment exerts a powerful effect on adaptation in other areas of development, including the emergence of self and relationships with others, its role is especially critical.

The Development of Self

A sense of self as separate from the caregiver and as capable of autonomous functioning emerges as a stage-salient issue during the latter part of the second year of life (Emde, Gaensbauer, & Harmon, 1976; Lewis & Brooks-Gunn, 1979) and marks the transition from largely sensorimotor to representational capabilities. Between 24 and 30 months, toddlers become able to construct increasingly differentiated and sophisticated representations of the self in relation to others (Greenspan & Porges, 1984). These changes allow for the examination of the emerging self through an assessment of symbolic capacities. Because the child is more able to utilize symbolic channels for the communication of needs and feelings, advances in the ability to regulate affect also emerge (Cicchetti, Cummings, Greenberg, & Marvin, 1990).

At this time the representational models of self and other formed as a function of the primary attachment relationship also become more clearly manifested. Because emotions give meaning to the self, their regulation must be achieved if adaptive functioning is to occur (Cicchetti, Beeghly, Carlson, & Toth, 1990; Emde, 1980; Stern, 1985). Thus, the examination of the increased representational capacities and the regulation of emotion inherent in the emergence of the self reveals important implications for understanding the effects of child maltreatment on development.

Difficulties with emotion regulation have been observed as early as the first few months of life, where maltreated babies have been described as evidencing four variant patterns of affect differentiation including: retarded, depressed, labile, and angry (Gaensbauer, Mrazek, & Harmon, 1980). In a case report, Gaensbauer and Hiatt (1984) found that two severely physically abused 3-month-old infants expressed a high degree of negative affect (e.g., fear, anger, sadness) and a paucity of positive emotion, while a third infant who had suffered severe emotional neglect evidenced a generally blunted affect profile. Additionally, because negative affects such as anger, sadness, and fear reactions normally are not thought to develop until after approximately 6 months of age (Campos, Barett, Lamb, Goldsmith, & Stenberg, 1983; Sroufe, 1979a), the presence of fear reactions in 3-month-old maltreated infants suggests the presence of hypervigilance based on their early caregiving experiences. The apparent differentiation of emotion expression based on the type of negative caregiving history raises interesting possibilities for future investigations on how maltreatment experiences may accelerate the development of fear in infancy. This observation also provides useful explanatory power for understanding the preponderance of atypical disorganized-disoriented Type ''D'' attachments in maltreated children, a classification considered to be closely linked with the introjection of fear into the caregiving relationship.

Similar findings of an increase in negative affectivity in conjunction with a paucity of positive expression have been found with older infants and toddlers between the ages of 18 and 30 months (Egeland & Sroufe, 1981; Schneider-Rosen & Cicchetti, 1984, 1991). Additionally, maltreated children have been found to evidence more anger, increased frustration with mother, noncompliance, and aggression. Although some differences between physically abused and neglected children have been described, both groups of children reveal less positive and more negative affect.

Because socialization plays a significant role on a child's expression of affect, caregivers can influence the types of emotion that a child is able to express, as well as the range, variation, intensity, and duration of emotion expression (Cicchetti & Schneider-Rosen, 1984; Malatesta & Wilson, 1988). In this regard, parents who talk about their own feelings and who use emotion words during their interactions with their children, may teach them to do so as well, thereby providing the child with a means of controlling nonverbal emotional expressions through fostering the ability to more competently access their emotion experiences (Cicchetti, Ganiban, & Barnett, 1991). Conversely, caregivers who do not discuss their feelings, and who attempt to avoid or defend against emotionally arousing experiences, may foster an overcontrolled coping style in their children (Cicchetti et al., 1991). Thus, the denial and avoidance so often seen in maltreating parents during their normal discourse with their children may well be transmitted to the children, thereby adversely affecting the child's ability to cope with negative affective states once they are encountered. A similar state of affairs is seen in maltreating adults who have difficulty dealing with negative affect yet who have problems managing their aggressive impulses once they do occur (Wolfe, 1985). This, in turn, may lead to the internalizing and externalizing disorders so often present in victims of child maltreatment (Cicchetti & Carlson, 1989; Toth, Manly, & Cicchetti, 1992).

In efforts to explore the role of socialization on emotion language, Beeghly and Cicchetti (1987) examined the impact of early child maltreatment and quality of mother–child attachment on the emergence of internal state language. These investigators found that insecurely attached children at all ages (i.e., 24, 30, and 36 months) and maltreated children at 30 and 36 months evidenced less mature internal state language than did the nonmaltreated, securely attached comparison children. Securely attached children, regardless of maltreatment status, talked more about internal states, possessed a more extensive internal state vocabulary, were increasingly likely to talk about the internal states of self and of other, and were less bound to their surrounds in their language use than were the insecurely attached children. Additionally, main effects of maltreatment emerged, with maltreated youngsters using fewer internal state words, attributing internal states to fewer social agents, and being more context dependent in their language usage. The finding that maltreated toddlers spoke less about physiological states such as hunger and thirst, and less about negative affects such as hate, anger, and sadness, is of special relevance to the area of emotion regulation. These results suggest that the socialization histories of maltreated children prevent them from being in touch with their feelings and thereby contribute to difficulties with emotion regulation (Cicchetti & Beeghly, 1987). In fact, the responses of caregivers to the use of negative emotion words, and to references to the self and one's desires, may lead to anxiety in children who, in efforts to allay the anxiety, may modify their discourse and/or their actual cognitive processing. This possibility becomes even more likely when viewed in relation to the early fear reactions and negative emotion expressions of maltreated infants. Corroboration of the hypothesis regarding maltreating parents' avoidance or denial of negative affect and socialization of a similar style in their children has been obtained in a study that found that maltreating mothers spoke less about the emotional states of their infants and used more behavioral directives than did nonmaltreating mothers (Cicchetti, 1990).

Differences in the interactional styles of maltreating and nonmaltreating mothers also have been observed, with maltreating mother–child dyads evidencing low levels of reciprocity, low rates of verbal interaction, limited positive exchanges, and disharmony (Burgess & Conger, 1978; Crittenden, 1981; Howes & Cicchetti, this volume). Maltreating parents also have shown less positive behavior and less positive affect in their interactions with their children (Bousha & Twentyman, 1984; Lahey, Conger, Atkeson, & Treiber, 1984). In an examination of play behavior in mother–child dyads (Alessandri, 1992), maltreating mothers were found to use significantly fewer prompts to help focus their children's attention, were less mutually interactive with and less responsive to their children, and made more negative comments to their children. The children exposed to low maternal involvement and frequent criticism also were less likely to evidence highly developed forms of symbolic play, but rather engaged in more functional or sensorimotor play. Additionally, these children were more likely to exhibit problems with self-regulation and to experience peer difficulties. Thus, in addition to findings of less symbolically rich language usage among maltreated children, data are emerging to suggest that maltreated children also suffer impairments in their capacities to represent symbolically sophisticated content in their play (Alessandri, 1991, 1992).

Findings such as these on the limited symbolic capacities and constricted affective styles of maltreated children are consistent with the work of Crittenden (1988; Crittenden & DiLalla, 1988), who proposes that during the second year of life maltreated children learn not only to inhibit the expression of negative affect, but also to exhibit false positive affect during interactions with their parents but not with strangers. This positive affective presentation is not considered to be a true representation of the child's feelings, but rather to reflect a "false self" developed to please the parent (Main & Solomon, 1990). This overt presentation also is commensurate with the compulsive compliance to the caregiver evidenced by maltreated children (Crittenden & DiLalla, 1988). It may be that, in their quest to avoid parental disapproval and to gain acceptance from a rejecting, punitive caregiver, the self system of maltreated children veers away from a normal developmental pathway (cf. Cicchetti, 1991).

In moving beyond infancy and toddlerhood, atypicalities in the self systems of maltreated children continue to be documented. Results have increasingly shown that maltreated children evidence deficits in self-concept and self-esteem (Allen & Tarnowski, 1989; Kazdin, Moser, Colbus, & Bell, 1985; Toth et al., 1992). In general, maltreated children have been shown to be less self-accepting and to possess greater feelings of inadequacy and lower self-esteem than their non-maltreated peers. In some cases, these feelings of low self-worth have contributed to the presence of clinically significant depressive symptomatology (Allen & Tarnowski, 1989; Kazdin et al., 1985; Kaufman, 1991; Toth et al., 1992). In trying to understand the greater prevalence of depression among maltreated children, investigators have begun to discuss possible linkages among insecure attachment, impaired self systems, and depression (Rose & Abramson, 1992; Toth et al., 1992).

Because clinical reports have suggested that maltreated children sometimes defend against low self-esteem by portraying unrealistic and exaggerated competencies (Yates, 1981), it also is important to assess the relation between perceived and actual competence in maltreated children. In fact, when comparing self-reports of maltreated children with those of teachers, maltreated pre-schoolers were found to rate themselves higher on peer acceptance and to evidence exaggerated perceptions of physical competence when compared with their nonmaltreated age-mates (Vondra, Barnett, & Cicchetti, 1990). An extension of this study to the school-age years revealed that younger maltreated children (1st–3rd grade) continue to overinflate their competence, while older maltreated children (4th–6th grade) rated themselves more negatively and consistent with teacher ratings (Vondra, Barnett, & Cicchetti, 1989).

The finding that younger maltreated children overrate their abilities is remarkably consistent with the denial of negative affect and "overbright" presentation noted among maltreated infants and toddlers. If taken at face value, findings such as these could lead to erroneous conclusions that children who have been maltreated are relatively unaffected by the experience as long as the maltreatment stops. Rather, we maintain that the positive presentations of many maltreated youngsters reflect the roots of an impaired self system, the magnitude of which will emerge over time.

The veracity of this interpretation derives support from retrospective studies of adults who were abused as children. In addition to the relationship difficulties and tendency to perpetuate maltreatment with their own children discussed with respect to attachment relations, clinical case reports and research investigations cohere to reveal a greater likelihood that maltreated children develop severe psychopathology in their adult years (Bemporad & Romano, 1992; Cole & Putnam, 1992), and that disturbances of self may serve as a common link with the emergence of psychopathology in adulthood.

In their review of studies attempting to explore the childhood histories of adults with depressive disorders, Bemporad and Romano (1992) found that, in 16 of the 17 studies reviewed, reflecting a cohort of nearly four thousand individuals, depressed persons evidenced a significantly more frequent history of childhood maltreatment than did nondisordered controls or individuals evidencing other diagnoses. Moreover, these authors concluded that overt loss in childhood was less important than was the individual's perceptions regarding their relationship with their primary caregiver during childhood. In interpreting these findings, Bemporad and Romano (1992) posited a developmental link from childhood maltreatment to later depression through the creation of a self-schema involving negative conceptualizations of the self and of the self in relation to others.

Victims of childhood sexual abuse also have been found to exceed expected prevalence rates on a number of psychiatric diagnoses, including borderline personality disorder, multiple personality disorder, somataform disorders, eating disorders, and substance abuse disorders (Cole & Putnam, 1992). In their explication of these diverse disorders as reflecting an underlying disruption in self-development, Cole and Putnam (1992) discuss deviations in intrapsychic processes involved in defining, regulating, and integrating aspects of the self and deviations in the capacity to experience trust and confidence in the stability of relationships.

Thus, a range of adult psychopathology in childhood victims of various types of maltreatment can be understood as emanating from disturbances in the self-system. While diverse developmental pathways may lead to different overt manifestations of psychopathology, the disturbed self-system, with its origins in the dysfunctional parent–child attachment relationship, may well serve as the fundamental link among these clinical disorders.

Peer Relationships

Peer relationships serve as an important issue of the school-age years, and the successful resolution of this task signifies important implications for future development. Because family and peer relationships have been described as interacting "synergistically" (Hartup, 1983), maltreated children, with their histories of insecure attachment relations and impaired self system development, are at risk for experiencing peer difficulties. Additionally, because poor peer relationships have been associated with a range of behavioral disorders (Hartup, 1983; Kohlberg, LaCrosse, & Ricks, 1972; Robins, 1966), incompetence with peers bodes poorly for overall functioning (Asher & Coie, 1990; Rubin, Hymel, Mills, & Rose-Krasnor, 1991). The potential role of positive peer relationships also has been documented, with one study finding that the best predictor of adolescent mental health was peer ratings from 11 years prior (Cowen, Pederson, Babigian, Izzo, & Trost, 1973). In children who have experienced maltreatment, the presence of positive peer relations could be especially important in promoting positive adaptation. Unfortunately, the representational models of the self and other that characterize maltreated children are likely to lead them to approach peers with skepticism and mistrust.

One of the first published empirical studies of peer interactions in maltreated children found elevated levels of aggression and avoidance among physically abused toddlers (George & Main, 1979). In a subsequent investigation, these investigators also noted that abused toddlers responded to peer distress with fearful, threatening, angry behavior that was intermingled with comforting gestures. Nonabused toddlers, conversely, responded to the distress of peers with prosocial behavior (Main & George, 1985). In a series of studies, it also was concluded that the effects of maltreatment on peer interaction are not universal, but rather that certain behaviors, such as peer distress, and situational factors, such as the presence of a known versus an unknown peer and the type of activity occurring, either stimulated or inhibited aggression toward peers in maltreated children (Howes, 1983; Howes & Eldridge, 1985; Howes & Espinosa, 1985).

In bringing an organizational perspective to bear on peer relationships in school-age maltreated children, Cicchetti and his colleagues conducted a comprehensive assessment of 5- through 12-year-old maltreated and nonmaltreated comparison children in naturalistic school and day camp settings (Cicchetti et al., 1992). Data collected in two separate camp settings revealed that maltreated children were viewed by both peers and adults as less socially competent. Assessments of social competence, including areas such as social behaviors, social efficacy, quality of peer relations, and personality and behavioral profiles revealed that camp counselors rated maltreated children as significantly less competent socially, lower in self-esteem, and more anxious than their nonmaltreated agemates.

An assessment of the children's representations of peer relationships also yielded some interesting findings. Using the relatedness measure previously described (Wellborn & Connell, 1987), Cicchetti, Lynch, and their associates (1992) explored three categories of peer relationships, including: (a) classmates from the recently completed school year, (b) a best friend, and (c) children in the child's camp group. Assessments obtained from 215 maltreated and demographically matched nonmaltreated children between the ages of 7 and 11 confirmed prior normative findings on children's peer relatedness. For all children, regardless of maltreatment status, reports of higher emotional quality were correlated with reports of a lower need for psychological proximity seeking. Additionally, all children possessed models of peer relationships that were specific to a particular relationship, but that also evidenced some shared variance. This finding, which is consistent with the attachment literature regarding the discordance of children's attachments with different caregivers (Bretherton, 1985), supports the formation of global *and* specific internal representational models of relationships.

Although differences between maltreated and nonmaltreated youngsters on either dimension of relatedness for the three sets of peer relationships were not obtained, an examination of specific patterns of children's relatedness to their mothers showed some interesting effects on peer relationships. For example, children with optimal patterns of relatedness to their mothers, characterized by high levels of positive emotion and low levels of psychological proximity seeking, similarly tended to have optimal patterns of relatedness to their peers. As predicted by attachment theory, it may be that the children's patterns of relating with a primary caregiving figure are influencing their relationships with peers. With respect to maltreatment status, maltreated children desired to be closer to both their best friend and their camp peers significantly more than the nonmaltreated youngsters. This yearning for closeness was especially true for maltreated children with the most negative patterns of relatedness to their mothers. Thus, these findings suggest that maltreated children are motivated to obtain the closeness that they lack with caregivers through the formation of connectedness with peers. Because the peer relations of maltreated children are largely unsuccessful, they are likely to be thwarted in this quest.

In a comprehensive review of the literature on peer relations in maltreated children, Mueller and Silverman (1989) described two major themes emerging across studies, with maltreated children evidencing either heightened aggression toward or withdrawal from peers. A number of investigators have hypothesized that physically abused children tend to evidence heightened levels of physical and verbal aggression toward peers (George & Main, 1979; Hoffman-Plotkin & Twentyman, 1984). This interpretation is consistent with Crittenden's work on relationships in maltreating and adequate families and her subsequent discussions of representational models (Crittenden, 1988; Crittenden & Ainsworth, 1989). According to Crittenden, physical abuse leads to the emergence of models characterized by distrust and may cause inappropriately defensive or aggressive behavior. Experiences of neglect, conversely, may lead to a lack of a sense of personal efficacy and withdrawal from interactions. A combination of abuse and neglect could lead to the presence of acting out behaviors in combination with withdrawal (Crittenden, 1988). Because results of interactional differences based on type of maltreatment experience have not emerged consistently (Jacobson & Straker, 1982; Straker & Jacobson, 1981), further work is necessary before firm conclusions can be drawn regarding subtype-specific peer difficulties.

An exploration of the "peer relations" of adults who were maltreated as children provides support for a continuation of early histories of maladaptive relationships (Crittenden et al., 1991; Hunter & Kilstrom, 1979). Clinically, this pattern is striking, with currently maltreating mothers evidencing a high likelihood of having experienced abuse during their own childhood, and a resulting pattern involving ongoing victimization as manifested in their mate selection (cf. Howes & Cicchetti, this volume). Consistent with formulations from attachment theory, these women seem to have represented themselves as unworthy of love and respect and repeatedly attend to those aspects of their environments that reinforce these views of self and of self in relation to others.

The work of Crittenden and her colleagues (Crittenden et al., 1991) on family patterns of relationships sheds some further light on this phenomenon. In a study of 53 maltreating and adequate families, the quality of attachment of mothers and male partners was compared with each other as well as with the quality of attachment with their child. Interestingly, securely attached individuals were highly likely to be coupled with a similarly secure partner, while insecurely attached individuals either "matched" their partner on insecurity or "meshed" their mate by possessing a different but still insecure attachment pattern. Meshed couples exhibited the highest incidence of spouse abuse, and secure couples evidenced the lowest rates of spousal abuse. Additionally, in all but one couple in which both members were "good enough" parents, adequate childrearing histories also were reported. Positive relations between maternal attitude toward attachment and attachment classifications in the Strange Situation also were revealed. Thus, although procedural caveats are made by these authors (Crittenden et al., 1991), the finding that securely attached individuals tended to choose securely attached partners, while insecure individuals evidenced involvement with insecure mates, suggests a propensity of victims of maltreatment to continue to form maladaptive relationships into adulthood.

TREATMENT FOR VICTIMS OF MALTREATMENT

The literature on the sequelae of maltreatment clearly conveys the adverse and often lifelong effects of childhood abuse and neglect. In the absence of intervention, victims of maltreatment evidence maladaptation on a range of stage-salient issues and are at risk for the emergence of psychopathology both during childhood and into the adult years. Moreover, their inadequate caregiving histories place maltreated children in jeopardy of perpetuating maladaptive relationships throughout the life course. In view of the significant difficulties associated with childhood maltreatment, the interventions available to these children become of paramount importance.

Historically, it has been assumed that the "treatment" of choice in cases involving child maltreatment involves direct intervention with the perpetrator in efforts to stop the abuse (Azar, Barnes, & Twentyman, 1988; Mann & McDermott, 1983). According to this approach, the elimination of abuse, whether through parental improvement or through removal of the child from the abusive situation, reflects a successful and finite intervention. While certainly serving a necessary function, this attitude has resulted in a failure to address the child's needs. Of the intervention programs initially proposed by the National Center for the Prevention of Child Abuse, all six were parent-focused (Parke & Collmer, 1975). Moreover, in a national survey of child abuse treatment programs between 1974 and 1981, very few children were found to receive any direct treatment services (Solnit, 1980). This concentration on parental interventions has culminated in a dearth of theoretically grounded and proven interventions for children who are suffering the ill effects of having been maltreated. In fact in a review of over 1,500 articles on child abuse and neglect, Fantuzzo (1990) identified only two articles that evaluated the effectiveness of child-focused interventions and that met minimal methodological standards. This state of affairs can be better understood within the historical context of child protective efforts.

Since the identification of child maltreatment as a significant social problem, professionals have focused their efforts on the protection of the child. This zeitgeist resulted in two phases of activity (Fantuzzo, 1990). The first phase, designed to detect and take corrective action in cases of child maltreatment, was initiated by physicians, legislators, and law enforcement personnel. The primary outcome of this movement was the removal of child victims from their homes and their placement in alternate caregiving environments. In reaction to factors such as parental advocacy and earlier detection of maltreatment and risk for maltreatment, the second phase of professional activity was initiated. Mental health professionals led this movement, with its focus on treating the problem. Because the "problem" was narrowly defined as addressing parental roles in abuse, interventions focused on parents, and child-specific needs, were largely ignored. Fortunately, during this phase research investigations on the effects of child maltreatment on adaptation also were initiated and their results began to underscore the necessity of directing interventions toward child-specific needs. Therefore, it is critical that child therapy with maltreated children be provided, and that, where possible, the effectiveness of these interventions be evaluated. While mental health providers largely have come to acknowledge the importance of providing child-focused therapeutic interventions for maltreatment, this stance has not been fully accepted by the child welfare system. We will return to this issue more fully in our discussion of policy-relevant considerations.

Approaches to Therapy

Despite advocation for the utilization of intervention approaches for maltreated children based on our knowledge regarding the consequences of maltreatment (Cicchetti, Taraldson, & Egeland, 1978; Cicchetti & Toth, 1987; Friedrich & Einbenter, 1983), a theoretically derived approach to therapy for this population has been slow to emerge. Although the last decade has witnessed a proliferation of writings on considerations in the conduct of child therapy with maltreated children (Gil, 1991; James, 1989; Justice & Justice, 1990; Mann & McDermott, 1983), a developmentally based, empirically validated therapeutic approach to addressing the sequelae of maltreatment has not yet evolved. Certainly, theoreticians and clinicians have proposed various approaches to treating the maltreated child. However, the field is far from a consensus regarding how best to provide therapy for a maltreated child. In essence, suggested techniques range from nondirective play therapy to behavior modification. Interestingly, the range of suggested treatments may reflect the very real heterogeneity of functioning manifested by maltreated children. Because diversity exists with regard to etiological factors that contribute to the occurrence and perpetuation of maltreatment, as well as to the type of maltreatment experienced and the child's response to the abusive act, so, too, is treatment effectiveness likely to vary. Just as it is impossible to describe the "typical" maltreated child, it is unlikely that a treatment paradigm will be available to meet the needs of all maltreated children. Rather, in the application of therapeutic strategies to the amelioration of the trauma of abuse, clinicians must first conduct a comprehensive assessment of the effects of the abuse and plan a treatment strategy targeted at the identified problem areas. Rather than reviewing various treatment approaches, many of which have been derived from the general armamentarium of child interventions, we believe a core set of issues must be considered when providing therapy to a maltreated child, regardless of the actual technique that is utilized. Although we do not intend to provide specific recommendations for the provision of therapy to maltreated children in this chapter, we believe that research on the sequelae of maltreatment needs to be considered regardless of the therapeutic orientation that is being brought to treatment.

A primary issue to consider when providing therapy to a maltreated child involves the need to address the ecology of the maltreatment experience. Even when a therapist is providing individual child psychotherapy, it is important to remember that the child does not exist in isolation, but continues to be affected by the home, school, and broader community. This basic fact that is present in all child therapy becomes intensified when treating a maltreated child. The current environment, whether the child remains in the care of a maltreating family or has been removed to an alternate placement, must be considered during the course of treatment and is likely to affect the child's response to treatment. Additionally, issues such as the availability of positive relationships in the child's life, whether with a grandparent, teacher, or peer, must be evaluated and may emerge as an important issue in the child's treatment. The child therapist also can be extremely helpful in communicating with the child's teacher and helping to promote a positive school environment. Because a teacher may not have knowledge about the life experiences that may be contributing to the child's behavioral problems, this interface is extremely important (Cicchetti, Toth, & Hennessy, this volume). Whether or not the child ever has experienced a positive relationship also will serve as a marker of the likelihood of the child being receptive to forming a therapeutic alliance. Knowledge regarding the child's history of relationships, in turn, may guide the therapist in determining whether to utilize a relationship-based form of therapy or to pursue more behaviorally oriented techniques.

In addition to the immediate environmental context of the maltreated child, the broader systemic forces that exert powerful influences on the child also must be addressed. A child therapist can, and should, play an integral role in making recommendations regarding decisions such as continued foster placement or reunification, as well as serve a major supportive function to the child during these difficult transitions. Because the maltreated child may be reticent regarding impending changes or may be unaware of changes until they occur, it is the responsibility of the therapist to remain apprised of alterations in areas such as living placement, parental visitation, and court appearances. Additionally, as a stable person who often has the most in-depth and consistent knowledge of the child, the therapist can become an advocate for the child and an anchor in a system that all too frequently sacrifices the well-being of the child due to staff and placement shortages, staff turnover, and legalistic policies and procedures that, once set in motion, are difficult to channel effectively. Therapy with a maltreated child cannot be limited to the confines of the playroom, but must transcend the safety of the office to confront and impact upon the factors that may continue to assault the child in his or her daily life.

When providing psychotherapy to a child who has been maltreated, the status of the maltreatment also must be ascertained. Although a child who has become known to the system ideally should have the cessation of maltreatment assured, anyone familiar with child abuse and neglect realizes that a continuum of risk frequently continues to be present. The likelihood of the child's future maltreatment must be assessed and this knowledge must be integrated into treatment. Efforts to facilitate trust and security certainly are doomed to failure if the therapist cannot be reasonably certain that the risk of maltreatment is low. In cases where the therapist questions the safety of the child's environment, it is important that the therapist help the child develop a resource network to insure better security and a plan on how to proceed should the child experience further maltreatment. Additionally, during the course of therapy the child who has experienced maltreatment may become better able to express anger. Unless an ongoing interface with the child's caregivers is maintained to help them handle their child's negative affect appropriately, the risk of maltreatment may increase (Cicchetti, Toth, & Bush, 1988). If the child does not feel that the therapist understands his or her fears and can be depended upon during times of crisis, little real progress is likely to occur over the course of treatment.

The provision of therapy to a maltreated child also poses a challenge to therapists to remain objective enough so as not to diminish their effectiveness as credible advocates or as individuals able to listen with acceptance to the unfolding of stories of maltreatment involving pain and suffering. Despite their traumatic histories, many maltreated children continue to cling to their parents. Even children who are able to condemn an abusive act often try to make excuses for their parents' behavior or to portray their caregivers in a positive light. If therapists are too zealous in their encouragement of a child's negative side of the ambivalence toward caregivers, the child may become less willing to express pain and more likely to try to portray a positive family life. Because research has provided evidence for the emergence of a "false self" in maltreated children, supporting the unveiling of a history that the child has sought to avoid is a gradual process that cannot be rushed. Although the therapist may view open acknowledgement of anger as a therapeutic goal, it is the child's ability to process multiple feelings and to arrive at a personal resolution that must be encouraged. While the therapist may personally feel angered and repulsed by maltreatment scenarios, an acceptance of the total child is necessary for therapeutic progress to occur. Additionally, although the therapist certainly may need to express the inappropriateness of abusive behaviors, this need not be linked with a rejection of the child's caregivers. To be effective in work with maltreated children, the child therapist must be able to listen empathically, encourage problem solving when necessary, and remain accepting of the child's rate of disclosure and capacity to process difficult material cognitively and affectively.

Attention to developmental considerations also is of paramount importance when devising and implementing treatment for a maltreated child. To begin, it is important to recognize that developmental level is not necessarily synonymous with chronological age (Rutter, 1989; Wohlwill, 1973). Thus, depending on their developmental level, two 7-year-old children might, for example, present very differently and require a psychotherapeutic approach that is commensurate with each of their unique needs and capacities. In this regard, the meaning of a maltreatment experience for a child will vary as a function of the period during which the maltreatment occurred. This basic fact helps to explain, at least in part, why the effects of a similar event differ with respect to the sequelae that emerge. In an initial assessment of treatment goals, the clinician needs to evaluate how maltreatment affects individual domains of development, including cognitive, linguistic, representational, social-cognitive, and socioemotional and interpersonal functioning. When exploring these developmental domains, within subject variability is likely to emerge. For example, a child may present as advanced cognitively, but with lags in social-cognitive and socioemotional development. The effects of the combination of these advances and delays and the resulting interrelations among domains need to be thoroughly understood and can affect the child's ability to respond to various therapeutic approaches.

The effect of maltreatment on the overall organization of development also needs to be kept in mind. As we discussed earlier, stage-salient issues such as attachment continue to evolve across the life span, and new strengths and/or vulnerabilities can emerge at any time. In exploring treatment with traumatized children, James (1989) emphasizes the importance of providing developmentally sequenced treatment. Such "sequenced treatment is necessary because past traumatic events will have different or additional meaning to the child as he matures, which can impair the progress of development" (p. 5). A similar point is made by Berliner in her description of the delayed sequelae evidenced in sexually abused children. According to Berliner (1991), the developmental process may explain some delayed effects of abuse and overt sequelae may not emerge until certain stages of development or critical life events occur. This scenario also may explain the prevalence of psychopathology in the adult years in previously maltreated children. Thus, in working with abused children, the impact of the unfolding developmental process on the emergence of sequelae needs to be considered. A child who appears to be asymptomatic immediately after the identification of abuse may manifest symptomatology over time with the emergence of increasing sophistication in certain domains of development. In addition to a careful assessment of all domains of functioning and of their interrelations at the point of entrance into treatment (see, for example, Cicchetti, Toth, & Hennessy, this volume, and Cicchetti & Wagner, 1990), the effects of development on functioning underscore the importance of the availability of therapy at periods well beyond the occurrence of the maltreatment experience. For example, a preschooler who has completed a successful course of therapy as measured by a decrease in aggressive behavior may need to reenter therapy when impaired self-esteem emerges in later years. Additionally, if seeking to prevent the emergence of future psychopathology, the provision of preventive therapeutic services to maltreated children who are not manifesting difficulties should be considered.

In building upon an organizational developmental approach to therapy, special consideration also needs to be directed to the role of those stage salient issues that have been shown to be adversely affected by experiences of maltreatment. An especially important issue in this regard involves the attachment relationship histories of maltreated children and the effects of insecure attachments on the negotiation of subsequent tasks, such as self-development and the formation of peer relations. Although certain symptom manifestations can be treated beneficially through the provision of more circumscribed techniques, we advocate for a comprehensive approach to therapy in which the role of the child's negotiation of early issues of development is considered in relation to symptom manifestation at the time of referral for treatment.

Finally, issues related to termination require special consideration when providing psychotherapy to a child who has been maltreated. Because the maltreated child is likely to be mistrustful and reluctant to engage with a therapist, once the child comes to view the therapist as an important person the relationship is likely to possess great significance for the child. This is especially true of children who have experienced multiple out-of-home placements or instability among caregivers. Once trust has been established, the process of termination holds the risk of undoing much progress that has occurred during therapy. The maltreated child must be given sufficient time to accept the end of therapy. Additionally, during termination a presentation of concrete reasons why the child will no longer see the therapist are important. Open-ended terminations with maltreated children are likely to give rise to self-blaming and efforts to "be good enough" to have the therapist want to stay. A well-conducted process of termination may enable the child to process prior losses and the associated anger and sadness within the context of a supportive relationship.

Treatment Outcome Studies

In reviewing the literature on the effectiveness of treatment for child victims, one is left with a consistent and nagging concern regarding the dearth of studies in this area. Despite the presence of an increasing number of articles and books on the provision of therapy to child victims, single case studies and methodologically flawed studies continue to dominate the outcome literature. However, data on the effectiveness of child therapy have emerged and are relevant to our consideration of treatment for victims of maltreatment.

The first meta-analytic effort to assess the effectiveness of child psychotherapy, conducted by Casey and Berman (1985), concluded that the positive outcome of child therapy is commensurate with that of adult therapy, and that treated children evidenced better outcomes than did nontreated children. Similar findings were obtained by Weisz and his colleagues in their meta-analytic review of therapy outcome studies for children and adolescents (Weisz, Weiss, Alicke, & Klotz, 1987). These investigators found that children who had received therapy were functioning better than children not receiving treatment, and that children evidenced more improvement than did adolescents. Thus, the effectiveness of therapy for child mental health needs has received support.

However, similar support has not yet been obtained with respect to therapy for maltreated children. In reviewing those studies that have sought to evaluate the effectiveness of treatment for maltreated children, three types of evaluations emerge. These include: (a) program evaluations of demonstration projects, (b) evaluation of day treatment programs, and (c) evaluation of specific types of therapeutic interventions.

In one of the first attempts to evaluate the effect of treatment on victims of abuse, 70 abused children between 2 and 7 years of age were evaluated in three different centers (Cohn, 1979). The provision of various and unclearly specified forms of treatment and the use of subjective clinician ratings of outcome clouded the usefulness of this national demonstration project. However, this study was important in its findings of gains in areas such as interacting with adults and increased self-image among maltreated children and in its effort to convey that victims of maltreatment could benefit from treatment. Overall, 50% to 70% of children who received treatment evidenced improvements in functioning (Cohn & Daro, 1987).

Benefits accrued to maltreated children as a result of involvement in day treatment programs also have been documented. Howes and Espinosa (1985) found that maltreated preschoolers in well-established peer groups were similar to nonmaltreated children and evidenced more positive social skills than did maltreated children in newly formed peer groups. Similarly, Parish, Myers, Brandner, and Templin (1985) reported developmental gains in maltreated children attending a therapeutic preschool. In a more methodologically rigorous evaluation study that utilized a control group, Heide and Richardson (1987) found that maltreated children receiving day treatment services exhibited gains in various developmental domains, including perceptual-motor, cognitive, gross motor, socioemotional, and language skills.

While laudable in their efforts, these studies are consistently hindered by the lack of specification of treatment and the provision of multiple therapeutic strategies that preclude isolation of treatment effects. In efforts to address shortcomings such as these, investigators have increasingly sought to utilize random assignment of maltreated children to intervention groups with clearly specified approaches.

In one such study, Nicol, Smith, Kay, Hall, Barlow, and Williams (1988) compared a focused casework approach that employed behavioral techniques to modify family interactions with a structured program of individual play therapy. Abusive families were randomly assigned to treatment conditions and pre- and posttreatment home observations were conducted to assess parent–child interactions. These investigators concluded that the focused casework approach was significantly more effective than was the play therapy. Despite methodological improvements, the results of this study also must be viewed with caution. The lack of detailed information on the nature of the treatment provided and the absence of data on whether or not treatments were implemented accurately are problematic. Additionally, the play therapy did not reflect any particular theoretical orientation and served more as a no treatment control than as a viable therapeutic strategy. The failure to utilize any outcome measures that would be theoretically expected to be associated with positive child therapy outcome also raises concern. The significant age span of children (birth to 14), and the lack of discussion of the relation of development to outcome, as well as the absence of social validity data to evaluate the significance of the reported behavioral changes, further compromise the utility of this study. Finally, the inclusion of caregivers in only one intervention approach further confuses exactly which intervention strategy is being evaluated.

We wish to emphasize that in efforts to conduct methodologically rigorous therapy outcome studies, investigators must not lose track of the unique challenges posed by child maltreatment. Many of the comprehensive programs of intervention have arisen out of the very real acknowledgement of the multifaceted and complex needs of maltreated children and their families. Clearly, then, we are not proposing that child-focused approaches be provided in isolation of the child's caregiving and broader ecological environment. To assume that child therapy can be effective in the absence of interventions provided to eliminate the continuation of abuse is naive at best and potentially extremely detrimental. Rather, we are focusing on child therapy as a necessary and historically underutilized component of a multifaceted program of treatment for children who have experienced maltreatment. Just as hindsight allows us to question the utility of intervention provided solely to parents, so too might it warn us against overzealously embracing child-focused strategies in lieu of directing attention to the needs of maltreating families (see, for example, Cicchetti et al., 1978; Howes & Cicchetti, this volume). In effect, we argue that, once a child has been maltreated, the cessation of the trauma and an improved caregiving environment are necessary but not sufficient conditions to insure positive child adaptation. Rather, we propose that professionals concerned with child welfare must work together to design, provide, and evaluate theoretically grounded therapy for victims of child maltreatment. In this regard, knowledge of the effects of maltreatment on development and the incorporation of this into a focused approach to child therapy are critical.

Fantuzzo and his associates have taken some important steps in this direction with their development and evaluation of an intervention paradigm designed to increase positive social interactions among maltreated children who evidenced social dysfunction. In a series of studies, these investigators found that withdrawn maltreated preschoolers evidenced significant increases in positive social behavior in response to peer-mediated, but not adult-mediated interventions (Davis & Fantuzzo, 1989; Fantuzzo, Jurecic, Stovall, Hightower, Goins, & Schactel, 1988). Although extraneous factors such as maltreatment history and family functioning were identified as confounds that might have affected treatment outcome, these studies are noteworthy for their efforts to incorporate theoretical and methodological standards into the evaluation of interventions designed for maltreated children.

Research Prescriptions

Before moving into our discussion of the implications of work on the sequelae of child maltreatment and therapy outcome studies for policy decision making, we direct our attention to suggestions for necessary research directions in this area. Because it is critical that those in the policy arena have access to research data that can help them to address the needs of maltreated children, efforts must be directed toward the design and conduct of studies that will provide this information. Toward this goal, we recommend the following:

1. *Research on the sequelae of child maltreatment must be expanded, and these investigations must become increasingly theoretically guided and longitudinal in nature.*

In our conceptualization of the sequelae of child maltreatment within a lifespan perspective, the sophisticated reader cannot help being struck by the absence of data that traces development from infancy or childhood into adolescence and adulthood. Although we have sought to integrate an array of data on development across the lifespan, these data are largely cross-sectional or short-term longitudinal in nature and preclude a delineation of developmental pathways. Moreover, because much of the information on relationship disturbance and psychopathology in adulthood is derived from retrospective recollections of childhood, clear causal linkages cannot be made.

Efforts to strengthen the literature on the effects of child maltreatment on adaptation throughout the lifecourse require researchers to initiate longitudinal investigations. Though fraught with difficulties, the potential value to be derived from this time intensive work warrants its conduct.

2. *Efforts to specify the experience of maltreatment and to operationalize all associated variables must be expanded.*

In reaction to early research investigations that largely failed to provide any information on the maltreatment variable, investigators have become increasingly sophisticated in their attempts to specify exactly what the nature of the maltreatment experience has been. As an outgrowth of this effort, an assumption that children experience discrete subtypes of maltreatment has reached ascendance. However, because research and clinical experience suggest that pure subtypes of maltreatment are rare, investigators must be cautioned against making erroneous assumptions about their sample composition. We have found that although the Department of Social Services may indicate a case as founded on a specific charge, such as neglect, a comprehensive review of caregiving history frequently reveals the presence of additional types of maltreatment. The "pure" subtype approach to classification also is antithetical to the conceptualizations of researchers investigating emotional maltreatment, who argue that this form of maltreatment accompanies all others and may result in the most severe sequelae (Garbarino, Guttman, & Seeley, 1986). Although we concur with the importance of operationalizing the maltreatment variable, we caution investigators to be certain that their subtype classification truly reflects the history of maltreatment. Progress being made toward developing classification systems is critical and must continue (Barnett, Manly, & Cicchetti, this volume). However, in a quest for a methodologically rigorous design, investigators must be certain not to fail to identify multiple subtypes of maltreatment.

In addition to attention to subtype of maltreatment, efforts to articulate variables such as severity, chronicity, and the developmental period during which maltreatment occurred also must be continued (Barnett et al., this volume). Because these factors may be intimately related to response to treatment, their elucidation is especially important in the design and evaluation of child therapy outcome investigations.

3. *Creative efforts to evaluate child therapy within the very real context of a maltreating home environment must be developed.*

Our review of outcome studies for maltreated children has highlighted the difficulties confronting investigators in this area. Because child maltreatment results in the culling together of an array of service delivery systems, it is all but impossible to offer child therapy in isolation of the provision of a more comprehensive array of interventions. Moreover, even if this were possible, the effectiveness of treating the child victim without intervening with the parental perpetrator would be doomed to failure if the child remained in the home. Even in cases of foster care placement, the utility of providing therapy that does not address the issues that arise for the child within the context of a "substitute" family or that does not interface with the biological family system is highly questionable. Because children in foster care frequently are returned to their families of origin, the failure to incorporate this possibility into a program of therapy might prove to be detrimental to the child's future adaptation. Although we focus on child therapy in this chapter, the provision of family treatment also is an important therapeutic approach to consider (Cicchetti, Taraldson, & Egeland, 1978; Howes & Cicchetti, this volume).

Creativity in the design and evaluation of outcome studies is needed in order to deal with the provision of multiple types of treatment and the inability of investigators to control the involvement of the child and/or family in services that may be mandated. Ethical difficulties associated with failing to provide services to children who have been identified as maltreated also pose significant challenges to researchers in this area. Even the use of a waiting list control group of children is unacceptable if services could otherwise be made available. The use of quasiexperimental designs has been discussed with regard to situations encountered in the provision of early intervention services that preclude the utilization of randomized treatment (Hauser-Cram, 1990). Similarly, the application of quasiexperimental designs to the evaluation of services for maltreated children holds considerable promise.

4. *The importance of incorporating developmental considerations into the design and evaluation of treatment programs for maltreated children must be emphasized.*

Just as the consequences of a potentially maltreating act may vary as a function of the period in development during which the event occurred, so too may the effectiveness of therapy depend upon the appropriateness of the approach to the developmental period. The atheoretical provision of therapy without consideration either for the developmental impact of the maltreatment or for the child's capacity to utilize therapy to process the maltreatment is likely to be ineffective. In practice, child therapists must attend to the process of development. Thus, the therapeutic stance with respect to a child who sustained physical abuse during toddlerhood and may have minimal overt recollections of the experience is necessarily very different from the approach employed with an adolescent who continues to be at risk for abuse. It is critical that any effort to evaluate therapeutic outcome take issues such as these into account. Moreover, because research is increasingly revealing varied consequences of maltreatment sustained at different periods of development, the design and targeting of intervention toward the sequelae associated with specific developmental issues is a promising avenue to pursue (Cicchetti, Toth, & Bush, 1988).

5. *Investigators of child therapy outcome in the area of child abuse and neglect must clearly define their criteria for success.*

Historically, the early intervention literature has relied on cognitive gain as a measure of program effectiveness (Meisels & Shonkoff, 1990). Investigators of the effectiveness of services for maltreated children must be careful not to fall into a similar conundrum involving reliance on outcome measures that are not theoretically linked with areas of difficulty or developmentally meaningful constructs. Applying interventions targeted at specific deficits and employing measures appropriate for assessing change in the variable of interest are especially important in the evaluation of child therapy. For example, if social withdrawal is of concern and an intervention model directed toward facilitating positive peer interactions is provided, the outcome measures must be able to assess social interaction and peer relationships adequately. In order to gain a comprehensive evaluation of child functioning, multiple domains of development and relevant stage-salient issues must be assessed.

> 6. *Despite the difficulties inherent in implementing and evaluating therapy for child victims of maltreatment, it is of the utmost importance that work be conducted in this area.*

Even basic researchers are confronted with the difficulties inherent in conducting investigations in the area of maltreatment (Cicchetti & Manly, 1990). The mistrust of families for any representatives of a ''system'' that they feel has victimized them, high mobility rates, and the challenges of modifying assessment scales and paradigms developed and formed on nonrisk samples for maltreating families are but a few of the challenges that accompany efforts to conduct work in the area of maltreatment. When these obstacles are coupled with additional roadblocks associated with convincing funding bodies that maltreatment does not take place in a laboratory environment and that research therefore cannot easily adhere to the same degree of methodological rigor associated with more readily controlled independent variables, even the most dedicated investigators may throw their hands up in despair. To extend an already difficult line of research into the arena of therapy outcome requires truly Herculean effort. However, unless funding institutions recognize the realities of this research and encourage investigators to venture into this territory, generations of maltreated children will most certainly fail to be provided with the best available services. The costs of this omission to these children, as well as to society, are staggering and must be avoided.

SOCIAL POLICY CONSIDERATIONS

An exploration of the role of mental health providers in the provision of services for maltreated children raises some serious questions as to the impact that has been made. Conversely, when attempting to assess the quality of intervention provided to victims of maltreatment within the child welfare system, similar shortcomings are revealed. Why has it been so difficult to make mental health services available to maltreated children, and, extending this train of thought, why has so little research been done on the effectiveness of various therapeutic approaches for maltreated children? To begin to understand part of this unfortunate situation, one has only to picture an assemblage of a group of child welfare advocates and child mental health providers. Although both groups of individuals are extremely invested in assuring the well-being of children, significant differences between the two camps quickly emerge. For example, if asked to address the "treatment" needs of maltreated children, a rather straightforward question, little consensus can be found. While mental health providers quickly launch into discussions of diagnostic evaluations and individual versus family therapy, child welfare personnel are more apt to explore the availability of protective services personnel and the relative merits of home based support services versus out of home placement. As each faction vehemently argues the importance of their respective positions and the associated resources required to provide "treatment" to maltreated children, tempers rise, frustration builds, and little agreement is forthcoming. Add to this conundrum a researcher who discusses the need to operationalize the variable of interest and the importance of utilizing random assignment in conjunction with control groups to assess treatment effectiveness, and even the most dedicated efforts to develop a unified plan for action are doomed to failure. While somewhat of an exaggeration to make a point, the historically separate professional pathways taken by child welfare advocates, mental health providers, and researchers make communication challenging. Because few avenues for cross-communication have been available, typically each group has proceeded in efforts to provide for maltreated children in a way that is consistent with their own conceptualizations of the problem of child abuse and neglect. Unfortunately, scenarios such as this have led to a fragmentation among services and a failure in the very goal shared by all—the well-being of our children.

In order to address the schism that has hampered the provision of therapeutic services to maltreated children, all professionals will need broadened vision and a commitment to integrating all relevant knowledge to better meet the needs of maltreated children. Unless the gatekeepers of the system, specifically the child protective assessment and intake teams, recognize the importance of treating the child as well as providing concrete services and addressing family support needs, multitudes of maltreated children will fail to receive the services that could help them to achieve more adaptive functioning. Historically, the "services" provided by many child protective agencies have consisted almost solely of investigative activities, with little effort directed toward the amelioration of the effects of maltreatment (McDaniel, 1991). Unfortunately, in addition to a possible lack of knowledge regarding treatment needs, limited child protective resources have required a focus on the identification of maltreatment. With increasingly limited resources many states are unable even to fulfill legislative mandates. In fact, according to the American Humane Association (1988), there has been a national trend to screen maltreatment reports and to prioritize investigative activities as a function of the severity of the report. Not surprisingly, a reduction in services provided also has occurred. Rather than moving forward toward more comprehensive services for maltreated children, we appear to be falling farther behind in our efforts to address what has been termed "a national crisis."

The fragmentation among professionals and, consequently, among services has been spawned, in part, by the absence of a comprehensive national policy regarding how best to address the needs of troubled children and families. This state of affairs is summarized by Kammerman and Kahn (1989), who emphasize the impossibility of providing a comprehensive system of services when programs are administered by scattered divisions and governed by an array of large and small pieces of legislation.

Thus, our first, and perhaps foremost recommendation for insuring adequate treatment services for maltreated children pertains to *the development of a federally mandated, integrated policy for the identification, assessment, and provision of follow-up services to children and families where maltreatment has occurred.* This is a crucial step in increasing communication among all professionals concerned with the needs of maltreated children. In arriving at this policy, input from *all* professionals will be essential. Although this will pose a challenge, hopefully it will allow us to move beyond the conflicts and disagreements that currently plague efforts to provide for the mental health needs of maltreated children. Although the 1992 reauthorization of the Child Abuse and Prevention Act (P. L. 102-295) takes some important steps in this direction, a great deal of work at the state and local level, as well as increased financial resources, will be necessary to begin to approximate these goals. In order to truly work together in our efforts to ameliorate the occurrence, recurrence, and sequelae of maltreatment, some significant organizational changes among providers of mental health, education, legal, health care, and social services will be necessary (Cicchetti & Toth, this volume). The development of an overarching organizational structure with a commitment to increasing communication among all divisions that currently seek to address the needs of at risk and maltreated children is an essential step in this direction.

If we are to arrive at an adequate national policy, we consider the following considerations to be important. As will be seen, their attainment requires integrated efforts among everyone involved with the area of maltreatment.

1. *Our educational efforts in preparing professionals to meet the needs of maltreated children must be improved.*

We must not delay in our efforts to improve the training of those grappling with issues of child abuse and neglect. Training certainly must be provided to the child protective worker who repeatedly is confronted with decisions that affect the course of a child's life. In addition to investigative skills and support service provision, we urge that these individuals be provided with information regarding how to recognize a child who is in need of mental health services. The reality of difficulties associated with delayed stress reactions and sequelae that emerge only in adulthood suggests that therapy should be provided to any child who has experienced maltreatment. Minimally, we suggest that protective service workers be apprised of the immediate and long-term effects of maltreatment and make efforts to refer children for treatment evaluations.

Similarly, the training of therapists must include a consideration of broader systemic issues that accompany work with children in the welfare system. Rather than harshly judging the inadequacy of services offered by child protective workers, an increased understanding of the limitations in person-power and financial resources is necessary. Mental health consultation provided from a base of knowledge about the realities of the welfare system could be one avenue for improving communication among professionals. Cooperative rather than adversarial relationships between the welfare and mental health systems are needed to adequately benefit the child who has experienced maltreatment.

The training of therapists in order to prepare them to deal effectively with multiproblem maltreating families also needs to be revolutionized. Because these families typically have limited resources and are skeptical about the potential benefits of mental health services, traditional models of therapy fail to meet their needs. Rather than expecting compliance with regularly scheduled office visits, a model of therapy involving extensive outreach and utilization of more innovative approaches needs to be incorporated into the preparation of clinicians (cf. Cicchetti, Taraldson, & Egeland, 1978).

2. *The integration of developmental principles into the training of researchers and clinicians interested in maltreated children is needed.*

Because the sequelae of maltreatment may vary as a function of the developmental period during which the trauma was experienced, researchers need to utilize developmentally sensitive measurement strategies when assessing adaptation or maladaptation. Issues such as resiliency, described as adaptive functioning despite significant adversity, also need to be studied over a long enough period of time so that developmental changes can be explored. Therapists also need to be knowledgeable about the effects of maltreatment on development and must incorporate this knowledge into therapy. In order to achieve these goals, many educational institutions will need to expand their curriculums to better address the integration of developmental theory and knowledge into coursework on psychopathology (Cicchetti & Toth, 1991).

3. *Mechanisms to allow for the continuity of services to maltreated children must be developed.*

With increased insurance limits on mental health services, therapy is being governed by the imposition of external time limits. Although this trend is of concern to all areas of mental health, it threatens to be especially damaging to maltreated children. Because the effects of maltreatment may insidiously undermine the child's sense of self (Toth et al., 1992), symptomatology may not consolidate into a diagnosable behavioral disorder, despite detrimental effects on the course of development. In these cases, treatment may not be viewed as necessary. Additionally, because the formation and maintenance of a relationship are likely to be necessary in treating a maltreated child, arbitrary session limits are likely to impede or preclude therapeutic progress. Finally, because the sequelae of maltreatment will vary over time, continued courses of therapy may be necessary into adulthood. If therapy is to be effective, funding bodies must make provisions for multiple, and at times lengthy, involvement in therapy.

4. *Data on the effectiveness of therapy for maltreated children is essential.*

If expectations for policy modification and increased resource allocation are to be realized, we must be able to present concrete data regarding the effectiveness of therapy for maltreated children. Overall, a dearth of data on the effectiveness of services for maltreated children has impeded policy initiatives (Department of Health and Human Services, U.S. Advisory Board on Child Abuse and Neglect, 1990). In the area of psychotherapy for maltreated children, the absence of outcome data is even more striking. Before we can convince others to focus on the provision of therapy for victims of abuse and to provide increased funding to support these services, we must arm ourselves with data on the effectiveness of these services and on the repercussions of failing to provide them.

5. *In the provision of therapy to maltreated children, sensitivity toward the ethnic, racial, and cultural milieu of the child must be maintained.*

Because much maltreatment occurs among the lower socioeconomic strata of our society, and because minority populations are overrepresented among the poor, the therapist who works with maltreated children is likely to have a significant number of clients who are members of a distinct cultural group. It is critical that the therapist not impose his or her value structure on the therapeutic context, and that he or she be knowledgeable about societal norms and expectations of the individuals for whom intervention is being provided (Wilson & Saft, this volume). To have a well-prepared cohort of therapists who are qualified to deal with culturally significant issues, increased training regarding racial, ethnic, and cultural differences and the recruitment of greater numbers of minorities into the area of maltreatment is necessary.

6. *Tertiary prevention efforts directed at decreasing the emergence of psychopathology in maltreated children must be intensified.*

Although in the area of child maltreatment, prevention generally is associated with the need to provide services directed toward stopping the occurrence or recurrence of maltreatment (i.e., primary and secondary prevention), we believe that resources also must be directed toward the prevention of the adverse consequences of maltreatment in children who have been abused or neglected. Because statistics show that a large number of children suffer severe maltreatment prior to the age of 5, it is especially important that services be made available for this group of youngsters. In the area of mental health, there often is a perception that, prior to school age, children do not need to be involved in therapy unless they are evidencing significant developmental delays. Because a developmental psychopathology approach argues that early insults may exert much more severe and deleterious consequences over time due to the hierarchical integration of developmental capacities (Cicchetti, 1990), young maltreated children are at extreme risk for future emotional disorders. Additionally, findings of the delayed appearance of sequelae in some maltreated children further argue for the importance of early intervention for maltreated children. Although we concur that more traditional preventive efforts are necessary, until the rate of the occurrence of maltreatment is zero, we believe that the provision of therapeutic services to the maltreated child is an area that cannot be disregarded. In achieving this goal, it will be important that increases in treatment funding not occur at the expense of funding for prevention programs. Rather, we want to emphasize the importance of providing adequate support for both of these areas.

7. *We must become increasingly sophisticated at providing legislators and policy advocates with information gained from research investigations.*

Currently, the flow of information from the academic research arena into forums that are formulating policy is a trickle at best. Although a great deal of research in the area of maltreatment possesses policy implications, too little of it ever reaches the desks or chambers of those in positions to implement change. This failure is by no means a unidirectional occurrence. Researchers often conceive their questions and conduct their investigations without giving sufficient consideration to the "real world" questions that child advocates and service providers are grappling with. Once concluded, the findings from many informative projects are relegated to publication in research journals. While certainly necessary for scientific progress, researchers need to become increasingly skilled and interested in framing and disseminating their findings so that they can be consumed by those working in the policy arena. Similarly, efforts must be increased by child advocates to seek out information that may be beyond the bounds of standard journals and publications. Put simply, both researchers and child advocates must become increasingly invested in seeking out input and knowledge from each other. This interchange is likely to result in increasingly rich investigative efforts that can have a real impact on the world in which maltreated children live. Moreover, clinicians and researchers who are knowledgeable about the issues facing maltreated children must take a more active role in seeing that their input is heard by those in the legislative and policy arenas.

SUMMARY

In this chapter we have summarized findings on the effects of child maltreatment on adaptation across the lifespan. We believe that these findings support the importance of providing therapy to children who have been maltreated, with the goal of preventing the emergence of emotional maladaptation and future psychopathology. Despite the importance of psychotherapeutic interventions for these children, we also have discussed the relative absence of outcome data on the effectiveness of therapy. Recommendations for research, therapy, and for the incorporation of both of these areas into policy formulation on the needs of maltreated children have been presented.

Certainly, the recommendations put forth in this chapter will require increased financial resources. Toward this goal, it is critical that the negative impact on society of failing to provide for these children be elucidated. As funding for a myriad of social ills becomes increasingly competitive, allocation of limited resources is likely to be directed toward those concerns that have the most solid base of popular support. Additionally, funding bodies are more likely to invest in intervention services that have been documented to be effective. In this regard, researchers in the area of maltreatment carry an onerous responsibility. Investigations into the sequelae of maltreatment across the life course, as well as data on therapy outcome will prove to be invaluable in positioning the realm of maltreatment as a social problem warranting additional resources. To meet this challenge, researchers, clinicians, social welfare personnel, legal professionals, and policy formulators must unite to advocate for the welfare of our children. Separately, professionals in each of these areas possess substantial expertise. Together, their voices cannot be ignored.

REFERENCES

Ainsworth, M. (1985). Attachments across the life span. *Bulletin of the New York Academy of Medicine, 61*, 792–812.

Ainsworth, M. (1989). Attachments beyond infancy. *American Psychologist, 44*, 709–716.

Allen, D., & Tarnowski, K. (1989). Depressive characteristics of physically abused children. *Journal of Abnormal Child Psychology, 71*, 1–11.

Alessandri, S. M. (1991). Play and social behaviors in maltreated preschoolers. *Development and Psychopathology, 3*, 191–206.

Alessandri, S. M. (1992). Mother–child interactional correlates of maltreated and nonmaltreated children's play behavior. *Development and Psychopathology, 4*, 257–270.

American Humane Association. (1988). *Highlights of official child neglect and abuse reporting, 1986*. Denver, CO: The American Humane Association.

Asher, S., & Coie, J. (Eds.) (1990). *Peer rejection in childhood*. New York: Cambridge University Press.

Azar, S. T., Barnes, K. T., & Twentyman, C. T. (1988). Developmental outcomes in physically abused children: Consequences of parental abuse or the effects of a more general breakdown in caregiving behaviors? *The Behavior Therapist, 11*, 27–32.

Barnett, D., Ganiban, J., & Cicchetti, D. (1992, April). *Temperament and behavior of youngsters with disorganized attachments: A longitudinal study.* Paper presented at the International Conference on Infant Studies, Miami.

Beeghly, M., & Cicchetti, D. (1987). An Organizational Approach to Symbolic Development in Children with Down Syndrome. *New Directions for Child Development, 36,* 5–29.

Belsky, J., Rovine, M., & Taylor, D. G. (1984). The Pennsylvania Infant and Family Development Project, 3: The origins of individual differences in infant–mother attachment: Maternal and infant contributions. *Child Development, 55,* 718–728.

Bemporad, J. R., & Romano, S. J. (1992). Childhood Maltreatment and Adult Depression: A review of research. In D. Cicchetti & S. L. Toth (Eds.), *Rochester Symposium on Developmental Psychopathology, Vol. 4: Developmental perspectives on depression.* (pp. 351–375). Rochester, NY: University of Rochester Press.

Berliner, L. (1991). Clinical work with sexually abused children. In C. R. Hollin & K. Howells (Eds.), *Clinical approaches to sex offenders and their victims* (pp. 209–228). New York: Wiley and Sons.

Bousha, D. M., & Twentyman, C. T. (1984). Mother–child interactional style in abuse, neglect, and control groups: Naturalistic observations in the home. *Journal of Abnormal Psychology, 93,* 106–114.

Bowlby, J. (1982). *Attachment and loss* (Vol. 1). New York: Basic Books. (Original work published 1969).

Bretherton, I. (1985). Attachment theory: Retrospect and prospect. In I. Bretherton & E. Waters (Eds.), *Growing points of attachment theory and research. Monographs of the Society for Research in Child Development, 50,* 3–38.

Burgess, R. L., Anderson, E. A., Schellenbach, C. J., & Conger, R. D. (1981). A social interactional approach to the study of abusive families. In J. P. Vincent (Ed.), *Advances in family intervention, assessment and theory: An annual compilation of research* (Vol. 2, pp.1–46). Greenwich, CT: JAI Press Inc.

Burgess, R. L., & Conger, R. D. (1978). Family interaction in abusive, neglectful, and normal families. *Child Development, 49,* 1163–1173.

Campos, J., Barnett, L., Lamb, M., Goldsmith, H. L., & Stenberg, C. (1983). Socioemotional development. In M. Haith & J. Campos (Eds.), *Handbook of child psychology: Vol. 2. Infancy and Developmental Psychology* (pp. 783–915). New York: Wiley.

Carlson, V., Cicchetti, D., Barnett, D. & Braunwald, K. (1989). Finding order in disorganization: Lessons from research on maltreated infants' attachments to their caregivers. In D. Cicchetti & V. Carlson (Eds.), *Child maltreatment: Theory and research on the causes and consequences of child abuse and neglect* (pp. 494–528). New York: Cambridge University Press.

Casey, R. J., & Berman, J. S. (1985). The outcome of psychotherapy with children. *Psychological Bulletin, 98,* 388–400.

Cicchetti, D. (1989). How research on child maltreatment has informed the study of child development: Perspectives from developmental psychopathology. In D. Cicchetti & V. Carlson (Eds.), *Child maltreatment: Theory and research on the causes and consequences of child abuse and neglect* (pp. 377–431). New York: Cambridge University Press.

Cicchetti, D. (1990). The organization and coherence of socioemotional, cognitive, and representational development: Illustrations through a developmental psychopathology perspective on Down syndrome and child maltreatment. In R. Thompson (Ed.), *Nebraska Symposium on Motivation, Vol. 36: Socioemotional development* (pp. 259–366). Lincoln: University of Nebraska Press.

Cicchetti, D. (1991). Fractures in the crystal: Developmental psychopathology and the emergence of the self. *Developmental Review, 11,* 271–287.

Cicchetti, D., & Barnett, D. (1991). Attachment organization in preschool aged maltreated children. *Development and Psychopathology, 3,* 397–411.

Cicchetti, D., & Beeghly, M. (1987). Symbolic development in maltreated youngsters: An organizational perspective. *New Directions for Child Development, 36,* 5–29.

Cicchetti, D., Beeghly, M., Carlson, V., & Toth, S. L. (1990). The emergence of the self in atypical populations. In D. Cicchetti & M. Beeghly (Eds.), *The self in transition: Infancy to childhood* (pp. 309–344). Chicago: University of Chicago Press.

Cicchetti, D., & Carlson, V. (Eds.) (1989). *Child maltreatment: Theory and research on the causes and consequences of child abuse and neglect.* New York: Cambridge University Press.

Cicchetti, D., Cummings, E. M., Greenberg, M., & Marvin, R. (1990). An organizational perspective on attachment beyond infancy: Implications for theory, measurement, and research. In M. Greenberg, D. Cicchetti, & M. Cummings (Eds.), *Attachment in the preschool years: Theory, research and intervention* (pp. 3–49). Chicago: University of Chicago Press.

Cicchetti, D., Ganiban, J., & Barnett, D. (1991). Contributions from the study of high risk populations to understanding the development of emotion regulation. In K. Dodge & J. Garber (Eds.), *The development of emotion regulation* (pp. 15–48). New York: Cambridge University Press.

Cicchetti, D., & Lynch, M. (1993). Toward an ecological/transactional model of community violence and child maltreatment: Consequences for children's development. *Psychiatry. 56.*

Cicchetti, D., Lynch, M., Shonk, S., & Manly, J. T. (1992). An organizational perspective on peer relations in maltreated children. In R. D. Parke & G. W. Ladd (Eds.), *Family-peer relationships: Modes of linkage.* (pp. 345–383). Hillsdale, NJ: Erlbaum.

Cicchetti, D., & Manly, J. T. (1990). A personal perspective on conducting research with maltreating families: Problems and solutions. In E. Brody & I. Sigel (Eds.), *Family research: Volume 2: Families at risk* (pp. 87–133). Hillsdale, NJ: Erlbaum.

Cicchetti, D., & Schneider-Rosen, L. (1984). Theoretical and empirical considerations in the investigation of the relationship between affect and cognition in atypical populations of infants: Contributions to the formulation of an integrative theory of development. In C. Izard, J. Kagan, & R. Zajonc (Eds.), *Emotions, cognition and behavior* (pp. 366–406). New York: Cambridge University Press.

Cicchetti, D., & Schneider-Rosen, K. (1986). An organizational approach to childhood depression. In M. Rutter, C. Izard, & P. Read (Eds.), *Depression in young people, clinical and developmental perspectives* (pp. 71–134). New York: Guilford.

Cicchetti, D., & Sroufe, L. A. (1978). An organizational view of affect: Illustration from the study of Down's syndrome infants. In M. Lewis & L. Rosenblum (Eds.), *The development of affect* (pp. 309–350). New York: Plenum Press.

Cicchetti, D., Taraldson, B., & Egeland, B. (1978). Perspectives in the treatment and understanding of child abuse. In A. Goldstein (Ed.), *Prescriptions for child mental health and education* (pp. 301–391). New York: Pergamon Press.

Cicchetti, D., & Toth, S. L. (1987). The application of a transactional risk model to intervention with multi-risk maltreating families. *Zero to Three,* pp. 1–8.

Cicchetti, D., & Toth, S. L. (1991). The making of a developmental psychopathologist. In J. Cantor, C. Spiker, & L. Lipsitt (Eds.), *Child Behavior and development: Training for diversity* (pp. 34–72). Norwood, NJ: Ablex.

Cicchetti, D., Toth, S., & Bush, M. (1988). Developmental psychopathology and incompetence in childhood: Suggestions for intervention. In B. Lahey & A. Kazdin (Eds.), *Advances in clinical child psychology* (Vol. 11, pp. 1–71). New York: Plenum.

Cicchetti, D., & Wagner, S. (1990). Alternative assessment strategies for the evaluation of infants and toddlers: An organizational perspective. In S. Meisels & J. Shonkoff (Eds.), *Handbook of early intervention* (pp. 246–277). New York: Cambridge University Press.

Cohn, A. H. (1979). An evaluation of three demonstration child abuse and neglect treatment programs. *Journal of the American Academy of Child Psychiatry, 18,* 283–291.

Cohn, A., & Daro, D. (1987). Is treatment too late: What ten years of evaluative research tells us. *Child Abuse and Neglect, 11,* 433–442.

Cole, P., & Putnam, F. (1992). Effect of incest on self and social functioning: A developmental psychopathology perspective. *Journal of Clinical and Consulting Psychology, 60,* 174–184.

Connell, J. P. (1990). Context, self, and action: A motivational analysis of self-system processes across the life span. In D. Cicchetti & M. Beeghly (Eds.), *The self in transition: Infancy to childhood* (pp. 61–98). Chicago: The University of Chicago Press.

Cowen, E., Pederson, A., Babigian, H., Izzo, L., & Trost, M. (1973). Long-term follow-up of early detected vulnerable children. *Journal of Consulting and Clinical Psychology, 41,* 438–446.

Crittenden, P. M. (1981). Abusing, neglecting, problematic, and adequate dyads: Differentiating by patterns of interaction. *Merrill-Palmer Quarterly, 27,* 201–208.

Crittenden, P. M. (1985). Maltreated infants: Vulnerability and resilience. *Journal of Child Psychology and Psychiatry and Allied Disciplines, 26,* 85–96.

Crittenden, P. M. (1988). Relationships at risk. In J. Belsky & T. Nezworski (Eds.), *Clinical implications of attachment theory* (pp. 136–174). Hillsdale, NJ: Erlbaum.

Crittenden, P. M., & Ainsworth, M. (1989). Attachment and child abuse. In D. Cicchetti & V. Carlson (Eds.), *Child maltreatment: Research and theory on the consequences of child abuse and neglect* (pp. 432–463). New York: Cambridge University Press.

Crittenden, P. M., & DiLalla, D. L. (1988). Compulsive compliance: The development of an inhibitory coping strategy in infancy. *Journal of Abnormal Child Psychology, 16,* 585–599.

Crittenden, P. M., Partridge, M. F., & Claussen, A. H. (1991). Family patterns of relationship in normative and dysfunctional families. *Development and Psychopathology, 3,* 491–512.

Davis, S. & Fantuzzo, J. W. (1989). The effects of adult and peer social initiations on social behavior of withdrawn and aggressive maltreated preschool children. *Journal of Family Violence, 4,* 227–248.

Department of Health and Human Services, United States Advisory Board on Child Abuse and Neglect. (1990). *Child abuse and neglect: Critical first steps in response to a national emergency.* Washington, DC: Department of Health and Human Services, U.S. Advisory Board on Child Abuse and Neglect.

Egeland, B., Jacobvitz, D., & Sroufe, L. A. (1988). Breaking the cycle of abuse. *Child Development, 59,* 1080–1088.

Egeland, B., & Sroufe, L. A. (1981). Developmental sequelae of maltreatment in infancy. *New Directions for Child Development, 11,* 77–92.

Emde, R. (1980). Levels of meaning for infant emotions: A biosocial view. In W. A. Collins (Ed.), *Minnesota symposia on child psychology* (Vol. 13, pp. 1–37). Hillsdale, NJ: Erlbaum.

Emde, R., Gaensbauer, T., & Harmon, R. (1976). *Emotional expression in infancy: A biobehavioral study.* New York: International Universities Press.

Fantuzzo, J. W. (1990). Behavioral treatment of the victims of abuse and neglect. *Behavior Modification, 14,* 316–339.

Fantuzzo, J. W., Jurecic, L., Stovall, A., Hightower, A. D., Goins, C., & Schactel, D. (1988). Effects of adult and peer social initiations on the social behavior of withdrawn, maltreated preschool children. *Journal of Consulting and Clinical Psychology, 56,* 34–39.

Friedrich, W. N., & Einbender, A. J. (1983). The abused child: A psychological review. *Journal of Clinical and Consulting Psychology, 12,* 244–256.

Gaensbauer, T., & Hiatt, S. (1984). Facial communication of emotion in early infancy. In N. A. Fox & R. J. Davidson (Eds.), *The psychobiology of affective development* (pp. 207–230). Hillsdale, NJ: Erlbaum.

Gaensbauer, T., Mrazek, D., & Harmon, R. (1980). Affective behavior patterns in abused and/or neglected infants. In N. Freud (Ed.), *The understanding and prevention of child abuse: Psychological approaches.* London: Concord Press.

Garbarino, J., Guttmann, E., & Seeley, J. W. (1986). *The psychologically battered child: Strategies for identification, assessment, and intervention.* San Francisco: Jossey Bass.

George, C. & Main, M. (1979). Social interactions of young abused children: Approach, avoidance, and aggression. *Child Development, 50,* 306–318.

Gil, E. (1991). *The healing power of play: Working with abused children*. New York: Guilford Press.

Greenberg, M., Cicchetti, D., & Cummings, E. M. (Eds). (1990). *Attachment in the preschool years*. Chicago: University of Chicago Press.

Greenspan, S. I., & Porges, S. W. (1984). Psychopathology in infancy and early childhood: Clinical perspectives on the organization of sensory and affective-thematic experience. *Child Development*, *55*, 49–70.

Hartup, W. (1983). Peer relations. In P. Mussen (Ed.), *Handbook of child psychology* (Vol. 4, pp. 103–196). New York: Wiley.

Hauser-Cram, P. (1990). Designing meaningful evaluations of early intervention services. In S. J. Meisels & J. P. Shonkoff (Eds.), *Handbook of early intervention* (pp. 583–602). New York: Cambridge University Press.

Heide, J., & Richardson, M. T. (1987). Maltreated children's developmental scores: Treatment versus no treatment. *Child Abuse and Neglect*, *11*, 29–34.

Hoffman-Plotkin, D., & Twentyman, C. T. (1984). A multimodal assessment of behavioral and cognitive deficits in abused and neglected preschoolers. *Child Development*, *55*, 794–802.

Howes, C. (1983). Patterns of friendship. *Child Development*, *54*, 1041–1053.

Howes, C., & Eldredge, R. (1985). Responses to abused, neglected, and nonmaltreated children to the behaviors of their peers. *Journal of Applied Developmental Psychology*, *6*, 261–270.

Howes, C., & Espinosa, M. P. (1985). The consequences of child abuse for the formation of relationships with peers. *Child Abuse and Neglect*, *9*, 397–404.

Hunter, R. S., & Kilstrom, N. (1979). Breaking the cycle in abusive families. *American Journal of Psychiatry*, *136*, 1320–1322.

Jacobson, E., & Straker, G. (1982). Peer group interaction of physically abused children. *Child Abuse and Neglect*, *6*, 321–327.

James, B. (1989). *Treating traumatized children: New insights and creative interventions*. Lexington, MA: Lexington Books.

Justice, B., & Justice, R. (1990). *The abusing family*. New York: Plenum Press.

Kammerman, S. B., & Kahn, A. J. (1989). *Social services for children, youth and families in the United States*. New York: The Annie E. Casey Foundation.

Kaplan, B. (1966). The study of language in psychiatry: The comparative developmental approach and its application to symbolization and language in psychopathology. In S. Arieti (Ed.), *American handbook of psychiatry*. New York: Basic Books.

Kaufman, J. (1991). Depressive disorders in maltreated children. *American Journal of Child and Adolescent Psychiatry*, *30*, 257–265.

Kazdin, A. E., Moser, J., Colbus, D., & Bell, R. (1985). Depressive symptoms among physically abused and psychiatrically disturbed children. *Journal of Abnormal Psychology*, *94*, 298–307.

Kempe, C. H., Silverman, F. N., Steele, B. B., Droegemueller, W., & Silver, H. K. (1962). The battered child syndrome. *Journal of the American Medical Association*, *181* 17–24.

Kohlberg, L., LaCrosse, J., & Ricks, D. (1972). The predictability of adult mental health from child behavior. In B. Wolman (Ed.), *Manual of child psychopathology* (pp. 1217–1284). New York: Wiley.

Lahey, B., Conger, R. D., Atkeson, B. M., & Treiber, F. A. (1984). Parenting behavior and emotional status of physically abusive mothers. *Journal of Consulting and Clinical Psychology*, *52*, 1062–1071.

Lewis, M., & Brooks-Gunn, J. (1979). *Social cognition and the acquisition of self*. New York: Plenum Press.

Lynch, M., & Cicchetti, D. (1991). Patterns of relatedness in maltreated and nonmaltreated children: Connections among multiple representational models. *Development and Psychopathology*, *3*, 207–226.

Lynch, M., & Cicchetti, D. (1992). Maltreated children's reports of relatedness to their teachers. *New Directions in Child Development*, *57*, 81–107.

Lyons-Ruth, K., Connell, D., Zoll, D., & Stahl, J. (1987). Infants at social risk: Relationships among infant maltreatment, maternal behavior, and infant attachment behavior. *Developmental Psychology, 23*, 223–232.

Lyons-Ruth, K., Repacholi, B., McLeod, S., & Silva, E. (1991). Disorganized attachment behavior in infancy: Short-term stability, maternal and infant correlates. *Development and Psychopathology, 3*, 207–226.

Main, M., & George, C. (1985). Response of abused and disadvantaged toddlers to distress in agemates: A study in the day care setting. *Developmental Psychology, 21*, 407–412.

Main, M., & Goldwyn, R. (1984). Predicting rejecting of her infant from mother's representation of her own experience: Implications for the abused-abusing intergenerational cycle. *Child Abuse and Neglect, 8*, 203–217.

Main, M., & Hesse, P. (1990). Lack of resolution of mourning in adulthood and its relationship to infant disorganization: some speculations regarding causal mechanisms. In M. Greenberg, D. Cicchetti, & E. M. Cummings (Eds.), *Attachment during the preschool years* (pp. 161–182). Chicago: University of Chicago Press.

Main, M., Kaplan, N., & Cassidy, J. C. (1985). Security in infancy, childhood and adulthood: A move to the level of representation. In I. Bretherton & E. Waters (Eds.), *Growing points of attachment theory and research: Monographs of the Society for Research in Child Development, 50*, (Serial No. 209, 66–104).

Main, M., & Solomon, J. (1986). Discovery of a disorganized/disoriented attachment pattern. In T. B. Brazelton & M. W. Yogman (Eds.), *Affective development in infancy* (pp. 95–124). Norwood, NJ: Ablex Publishing Corp.

Main, M., & Solomon J. (1990). Procedures for identifying infants as disorganized/disoriented during the Ainsworth Strange Situation. In M. Greenberg, D. Cicchetti & E. M. Cummings (Eds.), *Attachment during the preschool years* (pp. 121–160). Chicago: University of Chicago Press.

Malatesta, C. Z., & Wilson, A. (1988). Emotion, cognition, interaction in personality development: A discrete emotions, functionalist analysis. *British Journal of Social Psychology, 27*, 91–112.

Mann, E. & McDermott, J. (1983). Play therapy for victims of child abuse and neglect. In C. Shaefer & K. O'Connor (Eds.), *Handbook of play therapy* (pp. 283–307). New York: Wiley.

McDaniel, N. (1991). Improving services to abused and neglected children and their families. *Protecting children, 8*, 10–12.

Meisels, S., & Shonkoff, J. (Eds.). (1990). *Handbook of early intervention*. New York: Cambridge University Press.

Mueller, N., & Silverman, N. (1989). Peer relations in maltreated children. In D. Cicchetti & V. Carlson (Eds.), *Child maltreatment: Theory and research on the causes and consequences of child abuse and neglect* (pp. 529–578). New York: Cambridge University Press.

Nicol, A. R., Smith, J., Kay, B., Hall, D., Barlow, J., & Williams, B. (1988). A focused casework approach to the treatment of child abuse: A controlled comparison. *Journal of Child Psychology and Psychiatry, 29*, 703–711.

Parish, R. A., Myers, P. A., Brandner, A., & Templin, K. H. (1985). Developmental milestones in abused children, and their improvement with a family-oriented approach to the treatment of child abuse. *Child Abuse and Neglect, 9*, 245–250.

Parke, R. D., & Collmer, C. W. (1975). Child abuse: An interdisciplinary analysis. In E. Mavis Hetherington (Ed.), *Review of child development research* (Vol. 5, pp. 509–590). Chicago: University of Chicago Press.

Parkes, M., Stevenson-Hinde, J., & Marris, P. (Eds.). (1991). *Attachment across the life cycle*. London: Routledge.

Robins, L. (1966). *Deviant children grown up*. Baltimore, MD: Williams & Williams.

Rose, D., & Abramson, L. (1992). Developmental predictors of depressive cognitive style: Research and theory. In D. Cicchetti & S. L. Toth (Eds.), *Rochester Symposium on Developmental*

Psychopathology, Vol. 4: Developmental perspectives on depression (pp. 323–349). Rochester, NY: University of Rochester Press.

Rubin, K., Hymel, S., Mills, R., & Rose-Krasnor, L. (1991). Conceptualizing different developmental pathways to and from social isolation in childhood. In D. Cicchetti & S. L. Toth (Eds.), *Rochester Symposium on Developmental Psychopathology, Vol. 2: Internalizing and externalizing expressions of dysfunction* (pp. 91–122). Hillsdale, NJ: Erlbaum.

Rutter, M. (1988). Epidemiological approaches to developmental psychopathology. *Archives of General Psychiatry, 45,* 486–495.

Rutter, M. (1989). Age as an ambiguous variable in developmental research. *International Journal of Behavioral Development, 12,* 1–34.

Schneider-Rosen, K., Braunwald, K., Carlson, V., & Cicchetti, D. (1985). Current perspectives in attachment theory: Illustration from the Study of Maltreated Infants. In I. Bretherton & E. Waters (Eds.), *Growing points in attachment theory and research. Monographs of the Society for Research in Child Development, 50* (Serial No. 209), 194–210.

Schneider-Rosen, K., & Cicchetti, D. (1984). The relationship between affect and cognition in maltreated infants: Quality of attachment and the development of visual self-recognition. *Child Development, 55,* 648–658.

Schneider-Rosen, K., & Cicchetti, D. (1991). Early self-knowledge and emotional development: Visual self-recognition and affective reactions to mirror self-image in maltreated and non-maltreated toddlers. *Developmental Psychology, 27,* 481–488.

Solnit, A. (1980). Too much reporting, too little service: Roots and prevention of child abuse. In G. Gerbner, C. Ross, & E. Zigler (Eds.), *Child abuse: An agenda for action* (pp. 135–146). New York: Oxford University Press.

Sroufe, L. A. (1979a). Socioemotional development. In J. Osofsky (Ed.), *Handbook of infant development* (pp. 462–516). New York: Wiley.

Sroufe, L. A. (1979b). The coherence of individual development. *American Psychologist, 34,* 834–841.

Sroufe, L. A., & Fleeson, J. (1986). Attachment and the construction of relationships. In W. Hartup & Z. Rubin (Eds.), *Relationships and development* (pp. 51–71). Hillsdale, NJ: Erlbaum.

Sroufe, L. A., & Fleeson, J. (1988). The coherence of family relationships. In R. A. Hinde & J. Stevenson-Hinde (Eds.), *Relationships within families* (pp. 27–47). Oxford: Clarendon Press.

Sroufe, L. A., & Waters, E. (1976). The ontogenesis of smiling and laughter: A perspective on the organization of development in infancy. *Psychological Review, 83,* 173–189.

Stern, D. (1985). *The interpersonal world of the infant.* New York: Basic Books.

Straker, G., & Jacobson, R. S. (1981). Aggression, emotional maladjustment, and empathy in the abused child. *Developmental Psychology, 17,* 762–765.

Toth, S. L., Manly, J. T., & Cicchetti, D. (1992). Child maltreatment and vulnerability to depression. *Development and Psychopathology, 4,* 97–112.

United States Department of Health and Human Services. (1981). *Study findings: National Study of incidence and severity of child abuse and neglect.* DHHS Publication No. (OHDS) 81-30325, Washington, DC.

United States Department of Health and Human Services. (1988). *Study findings: National Study of incidence and prevalence of child abuse and neglect.* DHHS Publication No. (OHDS) 20-01099, Washington, DC.

Vondra, J., Barnett, D., & Cicchetti, D. (1989). Perceived and actual competence among maltreated and comparison school children. *Development and Psychopathology, 1,* 237–255.

Vondra, J., Barnett, D., & Cicchetti, D. (1990). Self-concept, motivation, and competence among preschoolers from maltreating and comparison families. *Child Abuse and Neglect, 14,* 525–540.

Weisz, J. R., Weiss, B., Alicke, M. D., & Klotz, M. L. (1987). Effectiveness of psychotherapy with children and adolescents: A meta-analysis for clinicians. *Journal of Consulting and Clinical Psychology, 55*(4), 542–549.

Wellborn, J., & Connell, J. (1987). *Manual for the Rochester Assessment Package for Schools.* Unpublished Manuscript, University of Rochester.

Werner, H. (1948). *Comparative psychology of mental development.* New York: International Universities Press.

Wohlwill, J. (1973). *The study of behavioral development.* New York: Academic Press.

Wolfe, D. (1985). Child abusive parents: An empirical review and analysis. *Psychological Bulletin, 97*, 462–482.

Yates, A. (1981). Narcissistic traits in certain abused children. *American Journal of Orthopsychiatry, 51*, 55–62.

Author Index

Subject Index